Lecture Notes in Computer Science 2289

Edited by G. Goos, J. Hartmanis, and J. van Leeuwen

T0241813

Springer
Berlin
Heidelberg
New York
Barcelona
Hong Kong
London
Milan
Paris
Tokyo

Claire J. Tomlin   Mark R. Greenstreet (Eds.)

Hybrid Systems: Computation and Control

5th International Workshop, HSCC 2002
Stanford, CA, USA, March 25-27, 2002
Proceedings

 Springer

Series Editors

Gerhard Goos, Karlsruhe University, Germany
Juris Hartmanis, Cornell University, NY, USA
Jan van Leeuwen, Utrecht University, The Netherlands

Volume Editors

Claire J. Tomlin
Stanford University, Department of Aeronautics and Astronautics
250 Durand Building MC4035, Stanford, CA 94305-4035, USA
E-mail: tomlin@stanford.edu

Mark R. Greenstreet
University of British Columbia, Department of Computer Science
201-2366 Main Mall, Vancouver BC, V6T 1Z4, Canada
E-mail: mrg@cs.ubc.ca

Cataloging-in-Publication Data applied for

Die Deutsche Bibliothek - CIP-Einheitsaufnahme

Hybrid systems : computation and control ; 5th international workshop ;
proceedings / HSCC 2002, Stanford, CA, USA, March 25 - 27, 2002. Claire
J. Tomlin ; Mark R. Greenstreet (ed.). - Berlin ; Heidelberg ; New York ;
Barcelona ; Hong Kong ; London ; Milan ; Paris ; Tokyo : Springer, 2002
   (Lecture notes in computer science ; Vol. 2289)
   ISBN 3-540-43321-X

CR Subject Classification (1998): C.3, C.1.m, F.3, D.2, F.1.2, J.2, I.6

ISSN 0302-9743
ISBN 3-540-43321-X Springer-Verlag Berlin Heidelberg New York

Springer-Verlag Berlin Heidelberg New York
a member of BertelsmannSpringer Science+Business Media GmbH

http://www.springer.de

© Springer-Verlag Berlin Heidelberg 2002
Printed in Germany

Typesetting: Camera-ready by author, data conversion by Boller Mediendesign
Printed on acid-free paper   SPIN: 10846351   06/3142   5 4 3 2 1 0

Preface

This volume contains the proceedings of the *Fifth Workshop on Hybrid Systems: Computation and Control* (HSCC 2002), which was held in Stanford, California during March 25-27, 2002. The Hybrid Systems Workshops attract researchers interested in the modeling, analysis, control, and implementation of systems which involve the interaction of both discrete and continuous state dynamics. The newest results and latest developments in hybrid system models, formal methods for analysis and control, computational tools, as well as new applications and examples are presented at these annual meetings.

The Fifth Workshop continues the series of workshops held in Grenoble, France (HART'97), Berkeley, California, USA (HSCC'98), Nijmegen, The Netherlands (HSCC'99), Pittsburgh, Pennsylvania, USA (HSCC 2000), and Rome, Italy (HSCC 2001). Proceedings of these workshops have been published by Springer-Verlag, in the Lecture Notes for Computer Science (LNCS) series.

This year, we assembled a technical program committee with a broad expertise in formal methods in computer science, control theory, software engineering, numerical analysis and artificial intelligence; as well as experts in science and industry who are working in the application of hybrid system methods to problems in their domains. In response to our Call for Papers, 73 high quality manuscripts were submitted. After detailed review and discussion of these papers by the program committee, 33 papers were accepted for presentation at the workshop, and the final versions of these papers appear in this volume.

As is the tradition established by previous workshops, the accepted papers span an exciting range of topics, from formal methods of model abstraction, refinement and reduction, to fault diagnosis and recovery, to new methods for synthesizing and analyzing control for hybrid systems. As the theory of hybrid systems starts to mature, we are aware of the importance of good application of this theory: we are happy to include a strong set of application papers, including the hybrid analysis of engine control and power systems, robotic assemblies and smart actuators. Also, now that computational problems in hybrid systems are coming to the fore, we are pleased to note the growing interest in the development of sound numerical techniques for hybrid systems analysis, and to include several numerical papers in this volume.

We are pleased to acknowledge the National Science Foundation and Stanford University for financial support of this workshop. We thank our Program Committee for their technical support in reviewing the papers. Finally, our great thanks goes to our Organizing Committee, including Ian Mitchell, who installed and managed the automatic software for paper submission and review, Ronojoy

Ghosh, who designed the conference web site and managed the computer server, and to Sherann Ellsworth and Dana Parga, who organized and handled all of the local arrangements of venues, catering, hotels, and registration.

March 2002

Claire J. Tomlin
Mark R. Greenstreet
Workshop Co-Chairs
Stanford University, Stanford CA

Organization

Steering Committee

Panos Antsaklis (University of Notre Dame)
Maria Domenica Di Benedetto (University of L'Aquila, Italy)
Mark Greenstreet (University of British Columbia)
Thomas A. Henzinger (University of California, Berkeley)
Bruce H. Krogh (Carnegie Mellon University)
Nancy Lynch (Massachusetts Institute of Technology)
Oded Maler (VERIMAG, France)
Manfred Morari (Swiss Federal Institute of Technology, ETH, Zürich)
Amir Pnueli (Weizmann Institute, Israel)
Anders Ravn (Aalborg University, Denmark)
Alberto Sangiovanni–Vincentelli (PARADES; University of California, Berkeley)
Claire J. Tomlin (Stanford University)
Jan H. van Schuppen (CWI, Amsterdam, The Netherlands)
Frits Vaandrager (University of Nijmegen, The Netherlands)

Program Committee

Rajeev Alur (University of Pennsylvania)
Eugene Asarin (VERIMAG, France)
Uri Ascher (University of British Columbia)
Panos Antsaklis (University of Notre Dame)
Gautam Biswas (Vanderbilt University)
Michael Branicky (Case Western Reserve University)
Ken Butts (Ford Research Laboratory)
Christos G. Cassandras (Boston University)
David Dill (Stanford University)
Maria Domenica Di Benedetto (University of L'Aquila, Italy)
Datta Godbole (Honeywell Labs)
Mark Greenstreet (University of British Columbia)
João Hespanha (University of California, Santa Barbara)
Thomas A. Henzinger (University of California, Berkeley)
Bruce H. Krogh (Carnegie Mellon University)
Alexander B. Kurzhanski (Moscow State University)
Stefan Kowalewski (Bosch, Germany)
Michael Lemmon (University of Notre Dame)
Nancy Leveson (Massachusetts Institute of Technology)
Nancy Lynch (Massachusetts Institute of Technology)
John Lygeros (University of Cambridge, UK)
Oded Maler (VERIMAG, France)

Sheila McIlraith (Stanford University)
Manfred Morari (Swiss Federal Institute of Technology, ETH, Zürich)
Pieter Mosterman (Institute of Robotics and Mechatronics, DLR, Germany)
George Pappas (University of Pennsylvania)
Linda Petzold (University of California, Santa Barbara)
Maria Prandini (University of Brescia, Italy)
Anders Rantzer (Lund Institute of Technology, Sweden)
Anders Ravn (Aalborg University, Denmark)
Harvey Rubin (University of Pennsylvania)
Patrick Saint-Pierre (University of Paris-Dauphine, France)
Alberto Sangiovanni–Vincentelli (PARADES; University of California, Berkeley)
Shankar Sastry (University of California, Berkeley)
Janos Sztipanovits (Vanderbilt University)
Claire J. Tomlin (Stanford University)
Frits Vaandrager (University of Nijmegen, The Netherlands)
Arjan van der Schaft (University of Twente, Enschede, The Netherlands)
Jan H. van Schuppen (CWI, Amsterdam, The Netherlands)
Brian Williams (Massachusetts Institute of Technology)

Additional Referees

Sherif Abdelwahed	Emilio Frazzoli	C. G. Panayiotou
Palle Andersen	Goran Frehse	Giordano Pola
Andrea Balluchi	Robert Goldman	Shawn Schaffert
Alexandre Bayen	J.W. Goodwine	Henrik Schiøler
Calin Belta	Ronojoy Ghosh	Ying Shang
Alberto Bemporad	Maurice Heemels	Oleg Sokolsky
Antonio Bicchi	M. Iordache	Thomas Steffen
Francesco Borrelli	R. Izadi-Zamanabadi	Olaf Stursberg
Paul Caspi	T. John Koo	Ye Sun
Cenk Çavuşoğlu	X. Koutsoukos	Paulo Tabuada
Eva Crück	Salvatore La Torre	Fabio Torrisi
Thao Dang	Daniel Liberzon	Herbert Tanner
Elena De Santis	Hai Lin	Lothar Thiele
Stefano Di Gennaro	Qiang Ling	René Vidal
Sebastian Engell	Domenico Mignone	Rafael Wiesnewski
Lei Fang	Ian Mitchell	Sergio Yovine
Ansgar Fehnker	Supratik Mukhopadhyay	Jun Zhang
G. Ferrari-Trecate	Luigi Palopoli	Wenyi Zhang

Organizing Committee

Sherann Ellsworth
Ronojoy Ghosh
Mark Greenstreet

Ian Mitchell
Dana Parga
Claire Tomlin

Sponsoring Institutions

National Science Foundation
Stanford University

Table of Contents

Abstracts of Invited Presentations

Papers

Hybrid and Embedded Software Technologies for Production Large-Scale Systems

David Sharp

Technical Fellow
The Boeing Company
PO Box 516
St. Louis, MO 63166
Phone: (314) 233-5628
Fax: (314) 233-8323
david.sharp@boeing.com

In 1995, an initiative was launched at Boeing (then McDonnell Douglas) to assess the potential for reuse of operational flight program (OFP) software across multiple fighter aircraft platforms, and to define and demonstrate a supporting system architecture based upon open commercial hardware, software, standards and practices. The following year, this became a key element of the Bold Stroke Open System Architecture avionics affordability initiative which applied these techniques to the broader tactical aircraft mission processing domain. The Bold Stroke architecture, application components, middleware framework, and development processes have been leveraged for an increasing number of aircraft avionics systems.

Our experiences on this effort have demonstrated the dramatic increases in software development productivity possible through use of cross-platform reuse and highly portable and standardized run-time subsystems. They have also highlighted weaknesses in several areas which (1) significantly impact overall system cost, quality, and timeliness, many of which are unique to large-scale distributed real-time embedded (DRE) systems; and (2) limit their application within a wider range of domains, including those associated with control.

Embedded system product lines depend on suitable domain specific architectures, run-time frameworks, application component libraries, and component development and integration tools and processes, and stress these capabilities beyond what would be sufficient for single system development approaches. In weapon systems, key remaining technology hurdles include (1) integration of thousands of periodic and aperiodic software components with hard and soft real-time deadlines; (2) enlargement in scope of quality of service resource management services from single processors to widely networked systems; (3) establishment of safety critical and mixed criticality run-time frameworks; (4) interoperability with closed legacy systems; (5) retention of high security levels while opening up strike assets to greater and greater levels of tactical network connectivity; and (6) infusing new technologies into fielded systems. In addition to these "design-centric" challenges, additional critical challenges are contained at the front and back ends (i.e. requirements definition and verification) of the embedded system development process.

C.J. Tomlin and M.R. Greenstreet (Eds.): HSCC 2002, LNCS 2289, pp. 1–2, 2002.
© Springer-Verlag Berlin Heidelberg 2002

Boeing is engaged in a number of DARPA and Air Force Research Laboratory programs to begin addressing these challenges. Of particular relevance to this workshop is the DARPA Software Enabled Control program. As part of our Open Control Platform project therein, we have collaborated with leading Hybrid Systems researchers and have created initial Application Programming Interfaces (APIs) and implementations to support hybrid systems development.

This talk will discuss Boeing's experiences in these endeavors and real-world challenges which could benefit from advances in hybrid systems technology. It is hoped that this discussion will foster a context for hybrid systems research which is transitionable to production system development use.

Numerical Methods for Differential Systems with Algebraic Equality and Inequality Constraints

Uri M. Ascher

Professor
Department of Computer Science
University of British Columbia
CS/CICSR 223, 2366 Main Mall
Vancouver, B.C.
V6T 1Z4 CANADA
Phone: (604) 822-4907
Fax: (604) 822-5485
ascher@cs.ubc.ca
http://www.cs.ubc.ca/~ascher/

Differential equations with algebraic constraints arise naturally in robotics simulations (especially constrained multibody systems), optimal control problems, electric circuit design, and other seemingly unrelated applications such as adaptive gridding for partial differential equations with moving fronts.

Ordinary differential equations (ODE) with equality constraints (DAE) have been well researched. Of paramount importance is the index - roughly, the number of differentiations it takes to transform a given DAE into an ODE. The higher the index the tougher it is to solve the DAE directly. Multibody systems with holonomic constraints have index 3, whereas nonholonomic constraints yield index 2. Since the latter are more complex and harder to work with, this leads to an apparent paradox, which I'll explain away. Hybrid systems arise when the index changes at switching points, a special case of which is the question of consistent initialization.

ODEs with inequality algebraic constraints (DAI) have been much less researched. Think of the standard form of an optimal control problem, but without the optimization functional: this gives rise to a viability problem. Now, how can the resulting freedom be used to yield a fast algorithm that efficiently produces a "good" solution? I will describe an approach we developed with Ray Spiteri and Dinesh Pai involving delay-free discretization, local control and local planning, and I'll give a cold blooded assessment of its advantages and disadvantages.

C.J. Tomlin and M.R. Greenstreet (Eds.): HSCC 2002, LNCS 2289, pp. 3–3, 2002.
© Springer-Verlag Berlin Heidelberg 2002

From Models to Code: The Missing Link in Embedded Software

Thomas A. Henzinger

Professor
Electrical Engineering and Computer Sciences
University of California at Berkeley
Berkeley, CA 94720-1770
Phone: (510) 643-2430
Fax: (510) 643-5052
tah@eecs.berkeley.edu
http://www-cad.eecs.berkeley.edu/~tah/

Much of hybrid systems design and validation happens at the level of mathematical models. While some tools offer automatic code generation from mathematical models, manual code optimization and integration is often necessary to achieve non-functional aspects such as concurrency, resource management, and timing. In the process, the tight correspondence between model and code is lost, raising the issue of implementation correctness and causing difficulties for code reuse.

We submit that these problems can be alleviated by using an intermediate layer, which we call *software model*. A software model is closer to code than a mathematical model. While the entities of a mathematical model are, typically, matrices, equations, and perhaps state diagrams, the entities of a software model are data structures and procedures. For example, a software model may specify the representation for storing a matrix, the algorithm and precision for evaluating an equation, and the mechanism and time for communicating the result.

However, a software model is more abstract than code. While code is executed by a particular OS and hardware platform, a software model is executed by a virtual machine [2]. Common software models are high-level programming language, but for embedded software, the model needs to include constructs for expressing concurrency and timing. A software model specifies the logical concurrency and interaction of processes, not the physical process distribution and communication protocol. Similarly, an embedded software model specifies the timing of process interactions with the environment, not the process schedules on a specific platform. For example, a software model may specify when a sensor is read, which sensor reading is used for computing an actuator value, and when the actuator is set, without specifying a CPU and priority for the computation.

In short, a software model separates the platform-independent from the platform-dependent issues in embedded software development. The explicit use of a software model provides a great deal of flexibility in the optimization, integration, and reuse of embedded components. By orthogonalizing concerns, it also facilitates improved code generation and formal verification. We illustrate these advantages with the software model *Giotto* [1], which is designed for high-

C.J. Tomlin and M.R. Greenstreet (Eds.): HSCC 2002, LNCS 2289, pp. 5–6, 2002.

performance control applications, and also discuss design decisions that lead to software models with different characteristics.

This talk is based on joint work with Ben Horowitz and Christoph Kirsch.

References

1. T.A. Henzinger, B. Horowitz, and C.M. Kirsch. Giotto: A time-triggered language for embedded programming. In *Proc. Embedded Software* (EMSOFT), LNCS 2211, pp. 166–184. Springer-Verlag, 2001.
2. T.A. Henzinger and C.M. Kirsch. The Embedded Machine: Predictable, portable real-time code. In *Proc. Programming Language Design and Implementation* (PLDI). ACM Press, 2002.

Hybrid System Models of Navigation Strategies for Games and Animations

Eric Aaron, Franjo Ivančić, and Dimitris Metaxas

Department of Computer and Information Science
University Of Pennsylvania
200 South 33rd Street
Philadelphia, PA USA 19104-6389
eaaron@graphics.cis.upenn.edu, ivancic@saul.cis.upenn.edu,
dnm@graphics.cis.upenn.edu

Abstract. The virtual worlds of computer games and similar animated simulations may be populated by autonomous characters that intelligently navigate in virtual cities. We concretely apply hybrid system theory and tools to model navigation strategies for virtual characters. In particular, we present hybrid systems for both *low-level* (local) and *high-level* (global) navigation strategies, and we describe how we modeled these systems using the hybrid system specification tool CHARON. Further, we directly employed our hybrid system models to generate animations that demonstrate these navigation strategies. Overall, our results suggest that hybrid systems may be a natural framework for modeling aspects of intelligent virtual actors. We also present a small verification example for a simple navigation strategy, and we briefly discuss obstacles to widespread practical applicability of verification in this problem domain.

1 Introduction

The sophisticated virtual worlds in computer games and other animations are often inhabited by a variety of characters. Some characters are directly controlled by game players; decisions are generally made for them by humans. Other characters, however —such as background characters with which protagonists interact in virtual cities— are not externally controlled. They autonomously move through their virtual world and intelligently make their own decisions.

Consider such a background character in an animated game world, navigating from the southwest corner of its virtual city to the northeast corner. While in continuous motion, it must choose what streets to take to get across its city. Aspects of the city may vary in real time; the strategies that the character uses for making navigation decisions may also vary in real time, reflecting its dynamic environment. This kind of global, *high-level* decision making —on the order of street selection— may be naturally modeled as a hybrid system. Its discrete dynamics describe instantaneous transitions between modes of decision-making strategy or locomotion. In each mode, continuous dynamics may describe both

C.J. Tomlin and M.R. Greenstreet (Eds.): HSCC 2002, LNCS 2289, pp. 7–20, 2002.
© Springer-Verlag Berlin Heidelberg 2002

the character's continuous navigation and the evolution of its priorities for real-time decision making.

Realistic navigation behavior also requires *low-level* decision making —on the order of local perception— to intelligently guide a character in immediate concerns such as local obstacle avoidance. Relatedly, a character must also dynamically decide what strategy to use to for low-level behavior: If it does not perceive obstacles in its local environment, for example, it might opt against slow, non-linear, collision-avoidant motion in favor of a simple, linear local path. Like the high-level case described above, such a low-level decision-making system may also be naturally described as a hybrid system. The conceptual structure is similar: Discrete dynamics describe instantaneous transitions between modes of locomotion or strategy; continuous dynamics describe trajectories of a character's navigation and values for local decision making.

A typical animation approach to such modeling would not be grounded in any particular system-theoretical foundation; formal methods for specification or verification could not apply. In contrast, we have implemented models of both low-level and high-level navigation strategies in the general-purpose hybrid system specification tool CHARON [4, 5], thus providing theoretical foundations for the models. We begin our paper by describing the strategies and their CHARON models, then describing how CHARON was used to generate animated simulations of agent navigation. We also consider verification for hybrid models of navigation strategies for virtual characters. We present a small example verification in which HyTech[1] [18] mechanically checked a collision-avoidance result about a simple race-like game, and we discuss obstacles to widespread application of verification to this problem domain.

We demonstrate our hybrid system models through a series of applications and experiments, presenting simple animated simulations of virtual worlds with multiple actors, targets, and obstacles [1].

2   Modeling Navigation Strategies in CHARON

We model navigation systems using the hybrid system specification tool CHARON [4, 5]. The architecture of a hybrid system in CHARON is expressed as *hierarchical agents*, a model conceptually similar to hybrid automata. The key features of CHARON are:

Hierarchy. The building block for describing the system architecture is an *agent* that communicates with its environment via shared variables. The building block for describing flow of control inside an atomic agent is a *mode*. A mode is basically a hierarchical state machine, i.e., it may have submodes and transitions connecting them. CHARON allows *sharing* of modes so that the same mode definition can be instantiated in multiple contexts.

---

[1] We used HyTech for verification because, as of this writing, the model checking facilities for CHARON are still under development.

Discrete updates. Discrete updates are specified by *guarded actions* labeling transitions connecting the modes. Actions may call externally defined Java functions to perform complex data manipulations.

Continuous updates. Some of the variables in CHARON can be declared *analog*, and they flow continuously during continuous updates that model passage of time. The evolution of analog variables can be constrained in three ways: *differential* constraints (e.g., by equations such as $\dot{x} = f(x, u)$), *algebraic* constraints (e.g., by equations such as $y = g(x, u)$), and *invariants* (e.g., $|x - y| \leq \varepsilon$) that limit the allowed durations of flows. Such constraints can be declared at different levels of the mode hierarchy.

Modular features of CHARON allow succinct and structured description of complex systems. (Similar features are supported by the languages SHIFT [13] and STATEFLOW (see `www.mathworks.com`).) Among other benefits, this modularity provides a natural-seeming structure for modeling navigation systems with multiple levels of behavior. We model both low-level and high-level navigation strategies in CHARON, and we then use the CHARON simulator to create animations of navigation in virtual worlds.

3 Dynamical Navigation Systems for Virtual Worlds

3.1 Overview

There have been many approaches to guiding the navigation of intelligent virtual characters. Artificial intelligence-based techniques have been successfully used for cognitively empowered agents [22] and animated actors [14]; perception and dynamics-based techniques [8, 25] are often more readily able to adapt to dynamic environments. Our particular approach to low-level agent navigation is based on the method in [15], a scalable, adaptive approach to modeling autonomous agents in dynamic virtual environments. Our approach to high-level navigation is a new application (and significant extension) of ideas in [2]. Like treatments of similar issues in the field of behavioral robotics [7, 20, 21, 23], we consider only two-dimensional motion, although the mathematical foundations for three-dimensional navigation already exist [15].

For purposes of modeling navigation strategies, our virtual worlds consist of three kinds of agents: *actors*, *targets* that represent actors' goals, and *obstacles* that actors attempt to avoid. All are represented as spheres; we can represent an agent by its size, location, heading angle, and velocity.[2] There may be multiple actors, obstacles, and targets in a navigation system. Further, obstacles and targets may be static and/or moving. These components provide a general conceptual palette that can be used to express a broad range of behaviors; in this paper, we restrict ourselves to navigation.

For simplicity of presentation, we exclude extraneous concerns from our high-level modeling, considering only phenomena relevant on that higher level. In

---

[2] The mathematical treatment in [15] admits a more complex representation of agents.

particular, we do not consider low-level, local navigation in our demonstrations of high-level navigation strategy. This does not, however, suggest that the two levels could not be conjoined. Our high-level and low-level navigation strategies are modeled as hierarchical hybrid systems; integrating the lower level into the higher-level model (or vice versa) is a straightforward addition of new layers of hierarchy, which is readily supported by CHARON.

3.2   Low-Level Navigation Strategy

We model low-level navigation using non-linear *angular attractor* and *repeller* functions that represent the targets and obstacles (respectively) in the virtual world. Another non-linear system combines their weighted contributions in calculating an actor's angular velocity, dynamically adapting to real-time changes in the environment. Together, these systems generate natural-appearing motion on a local scale, avoiding collisions and other undesirable behaviors. The agent heading angle ϕ is computed by a non-linear dynamical system of the form:

$$\dot{\phi} = f(\phi, \mathbf{env}) = |w_{tar}|f_{tar} + |w_{obs}|f_{obs} + n, \qquad (1)$$

where f_{tar} and f_{obs} are the attractor and repeller functions for the system, and w_{tar} and w_{obs} are their respective weights on the agent. (n is a noise term, which helps prevent the system from becoming trapped at critical points.)

The weights themselves are determined by computing the fixed points of the following non-linear system:

$$\begin{cases} \dot{w}_{tar} = \alpha_1 w_{tar}(1 - w_{tar}^2) - \gamma_{12} w_{tar} w_{obs}^2 + n \\ \dot{w}_{obs} = \alpha_2 w_{obs}(1 - w_{obs}^2) - \gamma_{21} w_{obs} w_{tar}^2 + n \end{cases}, \qquad (2)$$

where the α and γ parameters are designed to reflect conditions for the stability of the system. Many other parameters are also concealed in the terms presented above. For instance, a repeller function f_{obs} depends on parameters that determine how much influence obstacles will have on an actor.

This is only an overview of one significant part of the agent steering system. There is considerably more detail to the system, including applications to three-dimensional environments, dynamic control of forward velocity, and modeling of low-level personality attributes such as aggression and agility. The above presentation, however, gives a feel for the kind of mathematics involved, suggesting the complexity involved in implementing it.

The only other low-level strategy we consider is the trivial one: moving straight to a target without any kind of complex obstacle avoidance or world representation. The continuous dynamics of our hybrid model follow directly from the above descriptions. With only two significant modes of continuous movement, the discrete dynamics are also conceptually simple.

Figure 1 is a schematic representation of the agent architecture behind our model of a virtual character performing low-level navigation. Agents are represented as rectangles. Note the hierarchy: The navigating character agent (outermost) has five component sub-agents, including Position to determine its

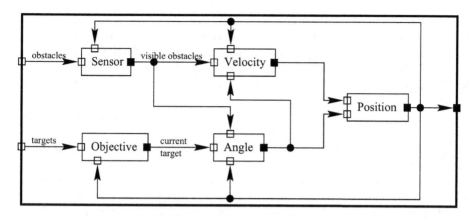

Fig. 1. The agent-level architecture of a character performing low-level navigation.

current position in a virtual world, Sensor to manage perception, Objective to determine its next target, and Angle, the dynamics of which we have described in this section. We do not represent component submodes within agents (e.g., the complex and simple angle computation modes within Angle); the discrete dynamics of mode transitions are not especially interesting for this model. The agent architecture level is much more significant. With the interplay among its components, a sufficiently perceptive animated character can decide whether complex, time-consuming obstacle-avoidant behavior is required in its environment and act appropriately, as demonstrated by examples in section 4.

3.3   High-Level Navigation Strategy

In contrast to the local focus of low-level navigation strategies, the high-level model presented in this section describes how virtual characters might make more global decisions. More precisely, our high-level model describes how characters decide which streets and intersections to visit when moving about a grid city (i.e., a city consisting only of parallel north/south streets and parallel east/west streets, intersecting in a grid pattern). Unlike traditional, artificial intelligence-based approaches that utilize planners or search methods to create such behavior, we express our high-level decision making system in a dynamical system.

A typical high-level navigation task for a character would be to travel from an initial intersection to a goal intersection under time constraints, e.g., from the southwestern-most intersection to the northeastern-most intersection within 20 seconds. A character dynamically decides its path one *path-component* (i.e., a "city block") at a time; as it arrives at an intersection, it decides which path-component to take next, without pre-planning of any kind. In our actor/target modeling framework (see section 3.1), each intersection in the city is modeled as a target. An actor selects and reaches successive targets until it gets to its eventual goal. Note that an actor does not necessarily take the shortest or fastest path. Its goal is realistic behavior — there is no other criterion for optimality. This echoes a larger, primary distinction between animation and related methods in behavioral robotics: Robotics approaches are typically not concerned with high-level, character-oriented features such as realistic, individualized behavior for actors.

For decision making, characters analyze their virtual world based on a pre-specified set $\mathcal{I}$ of attributes, e.g., distance between intersections, or attractiveness of path-components. (In our model, characters typically base decisions on three or four attributes. It would be straightforward, however, to implement a larger set $\mathcal{I}$ within this framework.) The decisions that a character makes depend on both internal and external factors: the values of attributes $i{:}\mathcal{I}$ in the external world immediately around it; and the internal, autonomously determined weights w_i it gives to each of those attributes.

To represent the dynamic influence of the world on a character, each w_i evolves in real time, as described by differential equations of the form

$$\dot{w}_i = c_{i,m} \cdot t_{i,m} + env_{i,m}(PC, time). \tag{3}$$

(This differential form is a simplification of the actual CHARON model, but it conveys the general feel of the continuous dynamics.) For a given character in a *behavioral mode* m (as defined below), $c_{i,m}{:}\mathbb{R}$ is a scaling factor, $t_{i,m}{:}\mathbb{R}$ represents the intended trend of evolution for w_i, and the continuous piecewise linear function $env_{i,m}(PC, time)$ encodes reactions to environmental factors such as attributes of the path-component PC on which the character currently travels. In addition, *time* is an argument to *env*, which allows the character to react to real-time conditions, e.g., running late for its deadline.

Our general approach is influenced by the philosophy of behavioral robotics (e.g., [7, 9, 23]): Decision making is a behavior in which characters react to the world around them; patterns and tendencies in decision-making may be grouped and modeled as higher-order behavior. We refer to these higher-order behaviors as *behavioral modes*, and we model them as CHARON modes, each corresponding to a different general navigation strategy. Instantaneous changes in strategy — i.e., a character's deciding that it can no longer take time for sightseeing and must instead hurry on to its eventual goal— comprise the discrete dynamics of our hybrid model. Differential equations of the form in (3) describe the continuous dynamics of decision making in each mode.

At any time, a character is in one of three behavioral modes:

Eager *Eager mode* encodes the idea that a character may act rushed, making decisions to get close to its eventual goal as soon as possible. When navigating between distant points, such as the southwest and northeast corners of the city, this strategy leads characters to take paths with many turns, approximating the diagonal line between those opposite corners.

Simple-path *Simple-path mode* encodes the idea that a realistic virtual character might decide on a path to its goal that requires as few turns as possible.

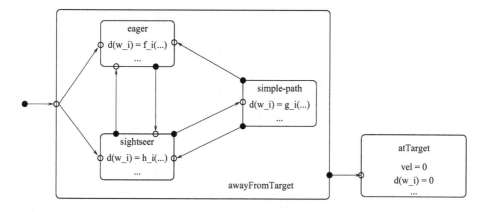

Fig. 2. A schematic representation of our model of high-level navigation strategy.

Characters using this strategy are assumed to be in less of a hurry than those in eager mode, and they move at a slightly slower velocity.

Sightseer *Sightseer mode* encodes the idea that a realistic virtual character might decide to see the sights while moving toward its goal. Such a character would still tend to decide to go toward its goal, not away from it, but it would also decide to go on attractive path-components along the way. This may lead to circuitous, but realistic, paths. Characters using this strategy also move even more slowly than those in simple-path mode.

Transitions between these three behavioral modes are triggered primarily by conditions on the weights w_i that characters use in decision making. Notably, transitions are not directly dependent upon character position in time and space. In particular, they are not constrained to occur only when a character is at an intersection, nor are they triggered by arrival at an intersection.

These three behavioral modes are intended to encode reasonable behaviors that virtual characters walking around a grid city might exhibit. The strategies contain numerous arguable assumptions, e.g., that a character in eager mode should have greater velocity than one in simple-path mode. Designers of games or animations might rightly make other choices for their characters, perhaps creating more sophisticated strategies, and implement them in the same flexible fundamental framework. We have not, however, mentioned all the details relevant for such extensions. The overview here is intended only to convey the overall feel of the system and permit readers to understand how decision-making modes change during the simulations described in section 4.3.

Figure 2 is a schematic representation of the dynamics of our high-level model. The rounded-off boxes are modes; lines between them indicate directed transitions. In this model, a virtual character is in one of two top-level modes: `awayFromTarget`, in which its navigation is as previously described in this section; and the far less interesting `atTarget`, representing it having reached its goal and stopped. We graphically represent only the top layer of hierarchy in `awayFromTarget`; its component submodes may be further hierarchical.[3] The experiment presented in section 4.3 demonstrates that even these relatively simple dynamics can yield interesting navigation behavior.

4   Navigation Applications and Experiments

4.1   Creating Animations from Hybrid System Models

Our navigation systems are implemented in CHARON using the key concepts noted in section 2. Modes are created to represent continuous behaviors; particular continuous dynamics (e.g., the non-linear system described in section 3.2) are represented as differential or algebraic constraints of a form such as `diff { d(angle) = AngleFunction(angle,...) }`. If constraints are necessary to limit the time in a particular mode, they are represented as invariants such as `inv {Cond && !Cond2 && distance(x,y)<=distance(x,z) }`. Guarded transitions between modes are presented in a straightforward `trans from Mode1 to Mode2 when Cond do Effect` syntax; when the guard `Cond` is true, the transition is enabled, and if it is taken, statement `Effect` is executed along with the system's jump from `Mode1` to `Mode2`. The behavior of agents follows from the systems described by modes. Each atomic agent is declared to begin in some mode, and it follows the behavior described there. The behavior of a hierarchical agent is, of course, determined by the behavior of its sub-agents. In this way, the underlying continuous mathematics and relations between modes of behavior are explicitly represented in a CHARON program. Further, the modularity of CHARON code makes it easy to change one aspect of a system while leaving others intact. For example, it is straightforward to add new modes to our high-level navigation system without unduly interfering with existing ones.

CHARON also generates numerical simulations of hybrid systems, which we exploited in creating animations from CHARON system specifications. We simply simulated our navigation systems in CHARON, then used a small translation routine (like a Perl script) to format the output of those simulations so that a previously developed application (developed for research outside of the context of hybrid systems) could create graphical displays.

Figures 3–5 contain images from our animations. In this paper, actors are the lightest objects, obstacles are the darkest objects, and targets are an intermediate gray. In the actual animations, actors, obstacles, and targets are distinguished by color. (CHARON-generated animations, including those from which these Figures were taken, may be seen at [1].)

4.2   Low-Level Navigation Simulations

Figures 3 and 4 show frames from an animation that demonstrates the low-level navigation strategy described in section 3.2. An actor, moving from the lower

---

[3] For brevity, we omit discussion of mode invariants and transition conditions, both of which are among the factors that designers might change to effect different behavior for their characters.

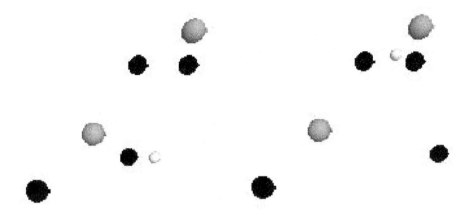

Fig. 3. An actor (lightest object) has already swerved around a stationary obstacle (darkest) and is now reacting to avoid a moving obstacle.

Fig. 4. The same actor as in Figure 3, later in the same animation, having switched to simpler behavior and passing between two obstacles.

left to the upper right, performs a simple three-segment task: reach target one; then reach target two; then wait for some pre-specified span of time, move off of target two, and celebrate — puff up with pride, perhaps at a job well done. In the first segment (Figure 3), the actor avoids a static obstacle and a moving obstacle on the way to a first target. It need not engage in complex evasive behavior in the second segment (Figure 4); it will reach the second target by simply traveling in a straight line, so it may intelligently switch to a simpler system for navigation. Animations at [1] also demonstrate that if the actor did not switch to a simpler behavior for segment two, it would perform unnecessary obstacle avoidance. (See [3] for further discussion.)

4.3   High-Level Navigation Simulations

We present a single demonstration of our high-level navigation model: an animation in which eight characters (actors) simultaneously navigate through a virtual grid city. (We used eight actors because it resulted in a variety of intelligent, individualized decision making without an excessively cluttered display. No limitation of our model dictated that choice.) In the animation, the grid city is represented by its intersections (targets). Characters intelligently navigate from intersection to intersection using the trivial low-level strategy: linear, non-obstacle-avoidant motion. Figure 5 shows a frame from the animation. The supplementary website [1] contains the full animation as well as CHARON output indicating the behavioral mode changes made by each character.

Each character embodies an instantiation of the general strategy for high-level navigation; differences in characters' initial weights on attributes of the

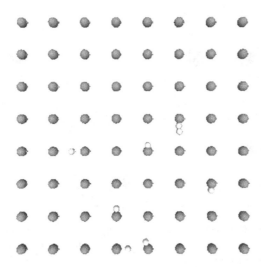

Fig. 5. A demonstration of high-level navigation strategy: Eight autonomous actors (lighter spheres) navigate from the lower left of a grid city to the upper right. They display individualized, intelligent behavior as they navigate from intersection (darker sphere) to intersection. This is a frame from one-third through the animation.

world (as described in section 3.3) are sufficient to generate distinct intelligent behaviors. Although all characters go from the same starting point to the same eventual goal using the same general navigation strategy, the animation [1] shows each character taking its own individual path, each one a sensible simulation of intelligent human behavior. This is the essence of our demonstration: Our hybrid model captures a strategy that, with only simple modifications, can reflect a range of intelligent navigation behaviors. This is precisely what is needed for characters in the virtual worlds of computer games.

4.4 Experiences with CHARON Specification and Simulation

The CHARON language proved to be a natural framework for specifying our animation systems, explicitly representing characters' dynamic behaviors —and transitions among them— in a formal and intuitive structure. There were, however, some capabilities not yet implemented in the CHARON language that would have conceptually simplified our modeling, such as array structures and the dynamic creation of agents. These restrictions prevented us from using some straightforward modeling approaches that animators might favor. For instance, we needed to create all possible obstacles and targets in a virtual world before any characters encountered them, unavoidably creating many agents that turned out to be irrelevant (i.e., no actor ever encountered them).

When we tested CHARON on large-scale applications (an order of magnitude larger than any demo presented in this paper), these language restrictions had significant consequences for our simulations. Because we could not dynamically declare agents or group individual variables together in array structures, extremely large numbers of parameters were explicitly declared at the onset. This overload was severe enough so that, in some cases, the Java compiler was unable to compile the results of the CHARON simulator generator. Even when compilation succeeded, the large number of variables and parameters slowed data generation: With CHARON simulation, the value of each variable is written to a file at every time step; thus, an unnecessarily large number of variables results in unnecessarily slow data-file creation.

Indeed, for very large applications, we found data generation to be troublingly slow. More efficient methods, perhaps with some domain-specific routines, would be needed for wide acceptance among animators. We have not yet explored simulation approaches from the animation community to see if any animation-oriented techniques might be applicable to the specific purposes of this paper, or perhaps even adaptable to improve hybrid system simulation in general.

5   Considering Verification: A Small Example

Despite significant undecidability barriers for general hybrid systems, property verification is decidable in restricted cases [6, 19]. Consider, for example, systems in which modes constrain every variable to constant velocity; changes require transitions between modes. Simple navigation systems (far simpler than those detailed in sections 3.2 and 3.3) can be specified in this restricted framework, and many properties are decidable for such systems.

To demonstrate this, we specified the rudiments of a race-like game in the model checker HyTech [18] and mechanically checked collision-avoidance. Our game system contains three agents, two racing actors and one obstacle, each moving at constant speed around a square, two-lane track. The rules of the race encode that each actor race on the inside lane whenever possible. Racers may move to the outside lane to pass slower agents, but they move promptly back when they are done passing. An animation of this scenario can be found at [1].

In an infinite race, would the two racers ever collide? Although we thought we had specified collision-avoidant behavior, we were mistaken. HyTech discovered a scenario in which a collision would occur: when the faster racer is changing lanes in front of the slower racer *at the corner of the track*, as represented in Figure 6. (Note that Figure 6 is not a frame from an actual animation; HyTech output, which is too lengthy to include here, may be found at [1].)

Our small example illustrates the potential for mechanical verification to detect errors that human designers miss. It also, however, illustrates limitations that prevent verification from being of practical interest in the near future. The system we verified was constrained in two ways: It had extremely simple navigation behavior and low dimensionality. Practical game designers could not be thus

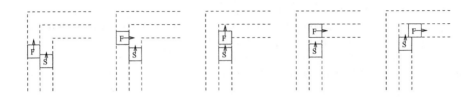

Fig. 6. A block diagram of unexpected collision behavior in a simple race game, as detected by HyTech. The faster racer (marked with "F") has passed the slower one (marked with "S"), but the slower one catches up on a corner.

constrained, which creates significant obstacles. In section 6, we briefly discuss possibilities for practical application of verification to this problem domain.

6   Conclusions

The presence of mixed continuous/discrete dynamics is not uncommon in computer game applications, but such hybrid dynamical systems are generally designed and presented without regard for underlying hybrid system theory. In contrast, we concretely applied hybrid system theory and tools, using CHARON [4, 5] to implement models of both low-level and high-level navigation strategies for virtual characters. Further, we directly utilized our CHARON models to generate animations that demonstrated the navigation strategies.

We did not create a single model that integrates the two levels, but the fundamental support for hierarchy in CHARON makes it a straightforward exercise to do so. Indeed, because theoretical hybrid system models can simultaneously integrate and distinguish high-level and low-level behavior, they may also be a natural framework for modeling other aspects of intelligent virtual actors.

We also presented a small verification result, a simple, mechanically checked property about collisions in a race-like game animation. This suggests another possible application of hybrid system modeling: reasoning about games and animation systems. (The animation-oriented [3] contains a brief discussion about expressing animation system properties in modal logics for hybrid systems.) Because of the complex mathematics (hence robust undecidability [6]) and high dimensionality of systems in practical game applications, however, we do not expect that current verification tools will be immediately useful in this domain. It would be a significant theoretical advance merely to render reachability problems decidable for game-oriented systems, perhaps by using techniques of *approximation* [11, 17, 24] or *abstraction* [10, 12, 16] to effectively reduce complexity. Practical tractability is also a major concern; verifying systems of high dimensionality demands significant computational resources. Improved processing technology might help, as might distributed or compositional algorithms for piecewise verification. Without escaping undecidability, however, even major advances in those areas might not be applicable. Furthermore, without at least prototype practical tools to concretely demonstrate the fruits of rigor in this domain, many animators and game designers may well not see reasons to alter their current looser, non-system-theoretic methods.

Although animation and computer game development literature generally fails to acknowledge it, there is a relationship between hybrid system theory and navigation strategies for intelligent virtual actors. Our paper has demonstrated several ways in which hybrid systems may be applied; advances in the theoretical power of hybrid system logics or the practical power of verification tools may well extend our current presentation, leading to further application and, perhaps, acceptance in the animation community. We cannot yet know whether formal specification or verification will strongly influence the development of games and animations. The current results, however, suffice to demonstrate how hybrid systems theory can extend animators' vocabulary and perspective on character navigation in virtual worlds.

Acknowledgments

We thank: Rajeev Alur for advice and support; Oleg Sokolsky for assistance with the verification example; and Siome Goldenstein, Thao Dang, Jan Allbeck, and Norm Badler for helpful discussions. We also appreciate the many thoughtful comments made by reviewers of this paper. This research was supported in part by NSF grant NSF-SBR 8920230.

References

[1] E. Aaron, F. Ivančić, and S. Goldenstein. Supplementary material, demonstrations, and CHARON-generated animations. Available at
http://www.cis.upenn.edu/~eaaron/hscc02_supplement.html.

[2] E. Aaron and D. Metaxas. Considering hierarchical hybrid systems for intelligent animated agents. In *Proceedings of the First Workshop on Radical Agent Concepts.* Springer Verlag, 2002.

[3] E. Aaron, D. Metaxas, F. Ivančić, and O. Sokolsky. A framework for reasoning about animation systems. In *Proceedings of the Third International Workshop on Intelligent Virtual Agents*, volume 2190 of *Lecture Notes in Artificial Intelligence*, pages 47–60. Springer Verlag, 2001.

[4] R. Alur, R. Grosu, Y. Hur, V. Kumar, and I. Lee. Modular specification of hybrid systems in CHARON. In N. Lynch and B. H. Krogh, editors, *Hybrid Systems : Computation and Control*, volume 1790 of *Lecture Notes in Computer Science*. Springer Verlag, 2000.

[5] R. Alur, R. Grosu, I. Lee, and O. Sokolsky. Compositional refinement for hierarchical hybrid systems. In *Hybrid Systems : Computation and Control*, volume 2034 of *Lecture Notes in Computer Science*, pages 33–48. Springer Verlag, 2001.

[6] R. Alur, T. Henzinger, G. Lafferriere, and G. Pappas. Discrete abstractions of hybrid systems. *Proceedings of the IEEE*, 88:971–984, July 2000.

[7] R. C. Arkin. Integrating behavioral, perceptual, and world knowledge in reactive navigation. *Robotics and Autonomous Systems*, 6:105–122, 1990.

20   Eric Aaron, Franjo Ivančić, and Dimitris Metaxas

[8] D. Brogan, R. Metoyer, and J. Hodgins. Dynamically simulated characters in virtual environments. *IEEE Computer Graphics and Applications*, 18(5):59–69, Sep/Oct 1998.

[9] Rodney A. Brooks. A robust layered control system for a mobile robot. *IEEE Journal of Robotics and Automation*, RA-2(1):14–23, 1986.

[10] P. Cousot and R. Cousot. Static analysis of embedded software: Problems and perspectives, invited paper. In T.A. Henzinger and C.M. Kirsch, editors, *Proc. First Int. Workshop on Embedded Software, EMSOFT 2001*, volume 2211 of *Lecture Notes in Computer Science*, pages 97–113. Springer Verlag, 2001.

[11] T. Dang and O. Maler. Reachability analysis via face lifting. In T. Henzinger and S. Sastry, editors, *Hybrid Systems : Computation and Control*, volume 1386 of *Lecture Notes in Computer Science*, pages 96–109. Springer Verlag, Berlin, 1998.

[12] S. Das, D. L. Dill, and S. Park. Experience with predicate abstraction. In *Computer Aided Verification*, volume 1633 of *Lecture Notes in Computer Science*, pages 160–171. Springer Verlag, 1999.

[13] A. Deshpande, A. Göllu, and L. Semenzato. Shift programming language and run-time systems for dynamic networks of hybrid automata. Technical report, University of California at Berkeley, 1997.

[14] J. Funge. *AI for Games and Animation*. A K Peters, 1999.

[15] S. Goldenstein, M. Karavelas, D. Metaxas, L. Guibas, E. Aaron, and A. Goswami. Scalable nonlinear dynamical systems for agent steering and crowd simulation. *Computers And Graphics*, 25(6):983–998, 2001.

[16] S. Graf and H. Saidi. Construction of abstract state graphs with PVS. In O. Grumberg, editor, *Proc. 9th International Conference on Computer Aided Verification (CAV'97)*, volume 1254, pages 72–83. Springer Verlag, 1997.

[17] T.A. Henzinger and P.-H. Ho. A note on abstract-interpretation strategies for hybrid automata. In P. Antsaklis, A. Nerode, W. Kohn, and S. Sastry, editors, *Hybrid Systems II*, Lecture Notes in Computer Science 999, pages 252–264. Springer-Verlag, 1995.

[18] T.A. Henzinger, P.-H. Ho, and H. Wong-Toi. A user guide to HYTECH. In E. Brinksma, W.R. Cleaveland, K.G. Larsen, T. Margaria, and B. Steffen, editors, *TACAS 95: Tools and Algorithms for the Construction and Analysis of Systems*, Lecture Notes in Computer Science 1019, pages 41–71. Springer-Verlag, 1995.

[19] T.A. Henzinger, P.W. Kopke, A. Puri, and P. Varaiya. What's decidable about hybrid automata? *Journal of Computer and System Sciences*, 57:94–124, 1998.

[20] E. Large, H. Christensen, and R. Bajcsy. Scaling the dynamic approach to path planning and control: Competition among behavioral constraints. *International Journal of Robotics Research*, 18(1):37–58, 1999.

[21] J.C. Latombe. *Robot Motion Planning*. Kluwer Academic Publishers, 1991.

[22] H. Levesque and F. Pirri, editors. *Logical Foundations for Cognitive Agents: Contributions in Honor of Ray Reiter*. Springer, 1999.

[23] M. J. Matarić. Integration of representation into goal-driven behaviour based robots. *IEEE Trans on Robotics & Automation, June 1992*, 8(3):304–312, 1992.

[24] G. J. Pappas and S. Sastry. Towards continuous abstractions of dynamical and control systems. In P. Antsaklis, W. Kohn, A. Nerode, and S. Sastry, editors, *Hybrid Systems IV*, volume 1273 of *Lecture Notes in Computer Science*, pages 329–341. Springer Verlag, Berlin, Germany, 1997.

[25] X. Tu and D. Terzopoulos. Artificial fishes: Physics, locomotion, perception, behavior. In *Proc. of SIGGRAPH '94*, pages 43–50, 1994.

Hybrid Control of a Truck and Trailer Vehicle[*]

Claudio Altafini[1], Alberto Speranzon[2][**], and Karl Henrik Johansson[2]

[1] SISSA-ISAS International School for Advanced Studies,
via Beirut 4, 34014 Trieste, Italy,
altafini@ma.sissa.it
[2] Department of Signals, Sensors and Systems, Royal Institute of Technology,
SE-10044 Stockholm, Sweden,
albspe@s3.kth.se, kallej@s3.kth.se

Abstract. A hybrid control scheme is proposed for the stabilization of backward driving along simple paths for a miniature vehicle composed of a truck and a two-axle trailer. When reversing, the truck and trailer can be modelled as an unstable nonlinear system with state and input saturations. Due to these constraints the system is impossible to globally stabilize with standard smooth control techniques, since some initial states necessarily lead to that the so called jack-knife locks between the truck and the trailer. The proposed hybrid control method, which combines backward and forward motions, provide a global attractor to the desired reference trajectory. The scheme has been implemented and successfully evaluated on a radio-controlled vehicle. Results from experimental trials are reported.

1 Introduction

Control of kinematic vehicles is an intensive research area with problems such as trajectory tracking, motion planning, obstacle avoidance etc. For a recent survey see [6, 5, 16]. The current paper discusses the problem of automatically reversing the truck and trailer system shown in Figure 1. The miniaturized vehicle is a 1:16 scale of a commercial vehicle and reproduces in detail its geometry. The vehicle is radio-controlled, has four axles, an actuated front steering, and an actuated second axle. According to the theory of vehicle control, our system is a general 3-trailer, because of the kingpin hitching between the second axle and the dolly. The off-axle connection is important, since it indicates that the system is neither differentially flat [19] nor feedback linearizable [20]. Hence, motion planning techniques, like those based on algebraic tools [10, 25] cannot be applied. Like a full-scale truck and trailer, our vehicle presents saturations on the steering angle and on the two relative angles between the bodies. These constraints, which are often overlooked in the literature, are of major concern here. The control task is to drive the vehicle backward along a preassigned path.

---

[*] This work was supported by the Swedish Foundation for Strategic Research through its Center for Autonomous Systems at the Royal Institute of Technology.
[**] Corresponding author.

C.J. Tomlin and M.R. Greenstreet (Eds.): HSCC 2002, LNCS 2289, pp. 21–34, 2002.
© Springer-Verlag Berlin Heidelberg 2002

Fig. 1. Radio-controlled truck and trailer used in the experiments.

This problem is quite challenging, due to the unstable nonlinear dynamics and the state and input constraints.

The main contribution of the paper is a new hybrid feedback control scheme to stabilize the backward motion of the truck and trailer. It is argued that backward driving along a given line is impossible from a generic initial condition with a single controller. Instead we suggest a hybrid control strategy, where three different low-level controls are applied: one for backward driving along a line, one for backward driving along an arc of a circle, and one for forward driving. By switching between these control strategies, it is possible to solve the problem. The control design can be viewed as an exercise in hierarchical control design [26] , where the control problem is divided into tasks which individually can be solved using standard control techniques.

A hybrid control scheme for stabilizing Dubins vehicle [9] is proposed in [3]. Backward steering control for other vehicle configurations are considered in [8, 13, 15, 17, 18, 23]. For further discussion on the particular vehicle in this paper, see [2, 1]. The outline of the paper is as follows. The model of the system is presented in Section 2. In Section 3 the switching control scheme is presented together with the design of the low-level controls. Analysis of the switching controller is presented in Section 4. Experimental results are shown in Section 5.

2   Modeling

A nonlinear dynamic model for the truck and trailer vehicle is presented in this section. Linearized versions, which will be used in the control design, are given, and state constraints are discussed.

2.1   Nonlinear Model

A schematic picture of the truck and trailer system is shown in Figure 2. The system consists of three links indexed 1, 2, and 3. Let (x_3, y_3) be the cartesian

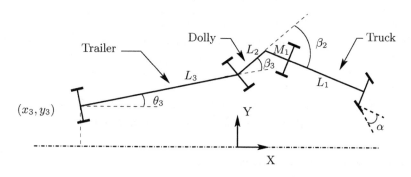

Fig. 2. Schematic picture of the system.

coordinates of the midpoint of the rearmost axle, θ_3 the absolute orientation angle of that axle, β_2 the relative orientation angle between the dolly and the truck body, β_3 the relative orientation angle between the rearmost trailer body and the dolly, and α the steering angle. The lengths of the body parts are denoted L_1, L_2, L_3, and M_1, as indicated in the figure. For the miniature vehicle, we have $L_1 = 0.35$ m, $L_2 = 0.22$ m, $L_3 = 0.53$ m, and $M_1 = 0.12$ m. The kinematics are described by the following equations:

$$\dot{x}_3 = v \cos \beta_3 \cos \beta_2 \left(1 + \frac{M_1}{L_1} \tan \beta_2 \tan \alpha \right) \cos \theta_3 \tag{1a}$$

$$\dot{y}_3 = v \cos \beta_3 \cos \beta_2 \left(1 + \frac{M_1}{L_1} \tan \beta_2 \tan \alpha \right) \sin \theta_3 \tag{1b}$$

$$\dot{\theta}_3 = v \frac{\sin \beta_3 \cos \beta_2}{L_3} \left(1 + \frac{M_1}{L_1} \tan \beta_2 \tan \alpha \right) \tag{1c}$$

$$\dot{\beta}_3 = v \cos \beta_2 \left(\frac{1}{L_2} \left(\tan \beta_2 - \frac{M_1}{L_1} \tan \alpha \right) - \frac{\sin \beta_3}{L_3} \left(1 + \frac{M_1}{L_1} \tan \beta_2 \tan \alpha \right) \right) \tag{1d}$$

$$\dot{\beta}_2 = v \left(\frac{\tan \alpha}{L_1} - \frac{\sin \beta_2}{L_2} + \frac{M_1}{L_1 L_2} \cos \beta_2 \tan \alpha \right) \tag{1e}$$

where the control inputs are the steering angle (α) and the longitudinal velocity at the second axle (v). The sign of v gives the direction of motion: $v > 0$ corresponds to forward motion and $v < 0$ to backward motion. All the variables are measurable using the sensors mounted on the system. We are interested in stabilizing the system along simple paths such as straight lines and arcs of circles. In most cases, the position variable x_3 will be neglected. Therefore, define the configuration state $\mathbf{p} = [y_3, \ \theta_3, \ \beta_3, \ \beta_2]^T$. The state equations can then be written as

$$\dot{\mathbf{p}} = v\big(\mathcal{A}(\mathbf{p}) + \mathcal{B}(\mathbf{p}, \ \alpha)\big) \tag{2}$$

Note that the drift is linear in the longitudinal velocity v. Since we are interested in stabilization around paths, we may introduce the arclength $ds \overset{\triangle}{=} v\,dt$ and consider

$$\frac{d\mathbf{p}}{ds} = \frac{v}{|v|}\left(\mathcal{A}(\mathbf{p}) + \mathcal{B}(\mathbf{p}, \alpha)\right)$$

From this expression, we see that only the sign of v matters. In the following, we therefore assume that v takes value in the index set $\mathcal{I} \overset{\triangle}{=} \{\pm 1\}$.

2.2   Linearization along Trajectories

The steering angle α can be controlled such that the system (1) is asymptotically stabilized along a given trajectory. The stabilizing controller in each discrete mode of the hybrid controller will be based on LQ control. For the purpose of deriving these controllers, we linearize the system along straight lines and circular arcs.

Straight Line A straight line trajectory of (1) corresponds to an equilibrium point $(\mathbf{p}, \alpha) = (\mathbf{p}_e, \alpha_e)$ of (2) with $\mathbf{p}_e = \mathbf{0}$ and the steering input $\alpha_e = 0$. Linearizing the system (2) around this equilibrium point yields

$$\dot{\mathbf{p}} = v\left(\left(\left.\frac{\partial \mathcal{A}(\mathbf{p})}{\partial \mathbf{p}}\right|_{(\mathbf{p}_e)} + \left.\frac{\partial \mathcal{B}(\mathbf{p}, \alpha)}{\partial \mathbf{p}}\right|_{(\mathbf{p}_e, \alpha_e)}\right)(\mathbf{p} - \mathbf{p}_e) + \left.\frac{\partial \mathcal{B}(\mathbf{p}, \alpha)}{\partial \alpha}\right|_{(\mathbf{p}_e, \alpha_e)}(\alpha - \alpha_e)\right)$$

$$= v\,(A\,\mathbf{p} + B\,\alpha) \tag{3}$$

where

$$A = \left.\frac{\partial \mathcal{A}(\mathbf{p})}{\partial \mathbf{p}}\right|_{(0)} = \begin{bmatrix} 0 & 1 & 0 & 0 \\ 0 & 0 & 1/L_3 & 0 \\ 0 & 0 & -1/L_3 & 1/L_2 \\ 0 & 0 & 0 & -1/L_2 \end{bmatrix}, \quad B = \left.\frac{\partial \mathcal{B}(\mathbf{p}, \alpha)}{\partial \mathbf{p}}\right|_{(0, 0)} = \begin{bmatrix} 0 \\ 0 \\ -M_1/(L_1 L_2) \\ (L_2 + M_1)/(L_1 L_2) \end{bmatrix} \tag{4}$$

The characteristic polynomial is

$$\det\left(sI - vA\right) = s^2 \left(s + \frac{v}{L_2}\right)\left(s + \frac{v}{L_3}\right) \tag{5}$$

Hence the system is stable in forward motion ($v > 0$), but unstable in backward motion ($v < 0$). The presence of *kingpin hitching* (i.e. $M_1 \neq 0$) makes the system not differentially flat (see [19]) and not feedback equivalent to chained form. What this implies can be seen considering the linearization (3) and the transfer function from α to y_3:

$$C\left(sI - vA\right)^{-1} v\,B = v^3\,M_1 \frac{(v/M_1 - s)}{L_1 L_2 L_3 \det\left(sI - vA\right)} \tag{6}$$

The presence of the kingpin hitching introduces zero dynamics in the system. The zero dynamics is unstable if $v > 0$ and stable otherwise. When $M_1 = 0$ the system can be transformed into a chain of integrators by applying suitable feedback [21, 24].

Circular Arc Consider the subsystem of (1) corresponding to the state $\bar{\mathbf{p}} = [\beta_3, \beta_2]^T$ and denote it as

$$\dot{\bar{\mathbf{p}}} = v\big(\bar{A}(\bar{\mathbf{p}}) + \bar{B}(\bar{\mathbf{p}}, \alpha)\big) \tag{7}$$

A circular arc trajectory of (1) is then an equilibrium point $(\bar{\mathbf{p}}_e, \alpha_e)$ of (7), with α_e being a fixed steering angle and $\bar{\mathbf{p}}_e = [\beta_{3e}, \beta_{2e}]^T$ being given by

$$\beta_{2e} = \arctan\left(\frac{M_1}{r_1}\right) + \arctan\left(\frac{L_2}{r_2}\right), \qquad \beta_{3e} = \arctan\left(\frac{r_3}{L_3}\right) \tag{8}$$

where $r_1 = L_1/\tan\alpha_e$, $r_2 = \sqrt{r_1^2 + M_1^2 - L_2^2}$, and $r_3 = \sqrt{r_2^2 - L_3^2}$ are the radii of the circular trajectories of the three rear axles. Linearization of (7) around $(\bar{\mathbf{p}}_e, \alpha_e)$ gives

$$\dot{\bar{\mathbf{p}}} = v\big(\bar{A}(\bar{\mathbf{p}} - \bar{\mathbf{p}}_e) + \bar{B}(\alpha - \alpha_e)\big) \tag{9}$$

where

$$\bar{A} = \begin{bmatrix} \dfrac{\cos\beta_{2e}\cos\beta_{3e}}{L_3} + \dfrac{\cos\beta_{2e}}{L_2} + \dfrac{\sin\beta_{2e}\sin\beta_{3e}}{L_3} + \dfrac{M_1}{L_1}\left(\dfrac{\sin\beta_{2e}}{L_2} - \dfrac{\cos\beta_{2e}\sin\beta_{3e}}{L_3}\right)\tan\alpha_e \\ 0 \qquad\qquad -\dfrac{\cos\beta_{2e}}{L_2}\left(1 + \dfrac{M_1}{L_1}\tan\beta_{2e}\tan\alpha_e\right) \end{bmatrix}$$

$$\bar{B} = \begin{bmatrix} -\dfrac{M_1}{L_1}\left(\dfrac{\cos\beta_{2e}}{L_2} + \dfrac{\sin\beta_{2e}\sin\beta_{3e}}{L_3}\right)(1 + \tan^2\alpha_e) \\ \dfrac{1}{L_1}\left(1 + \dfrac{M_1}{L_2}\cos\beta_{2e}\right)(1 + \tan^2\alpha_e) \end{bmatrix}$$

2.3   State and Input Constraints

An important feature of the truck and trailer vehicle is its input and the state constraints. In particular, for the considered miniature vehicle we have the following limit for the steering angle

$$|\alpha| \leq \alpha_s = 0.43 \text{ rad} \tag{10}$$

and for the relative angles

$$|\beta_2| \leq \beta_{2s} = 0.6 \text{ rad}, \qquad |\beta_3| \leq \beta_{3s} = 1.3 \text{ rad} \tag{11}$$

A consequence of the latter two constraints is the appearing of the so called jack-knife configurations, which correspond to at least one of the relative angles β_2 and β_3 reaching its saturation value. When the truck and trailer is this configuration, it is not able to push anymore the trailer backwards. The states y_3 and θ_3 do not present saturations. Due to limited space when maneuvering, however, it is convenient to impose the constraints

$$|y_3| \leq y_{3s} = 0.75 \text{ m}, \qquad |\theta_3| \leq \theta_{3s} = \pi/2 \text{ rad} \tag{12}$$

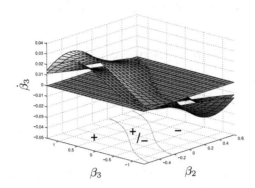

Fig. 3. The right-hand side of equation (1d) as a function of β_2 and β_3 for $\alpha = \pm\alpha_s$. For certain choices of (β_2, β_3), the input constraint on α leads to the jack-knife configuration since for these values both $\dot\beta_3$ and β_3 are positive. The plus and minus signs indicate the (β_2, β_3) regions where $\dot\beta_3$ is necessarily positive and negative, respectively, regardless of α.

The domain of definition of **p** is thus given by

$$D = (-y_{3s},\ y_{3s}) \times (-\theta_{3s},\ \theta_{3s}) \times (-\beta_{3s},\ \beta_{3s}) \times (-\beta_{2s},\ \beta_{2s}) \qquad (13)$$

Note that the since the steering driver of the miniature vehicle tolerates very quick variations, we do not assume any slew rate limitations on α.

3   Switching Control

The switched control strategy is presented in this section together with the low-level controls, but first some motivation for investigating switching controls are discussed.

3.1   Why Switching Control?

It is easy to show that due to the saturations of the input and the state, it is not possible to globally stabilize the truck and trailer along a straight line using only backward motion. Consider the right-hand side of equation (1d) for $v = -1$, and note that $\dot\beta_3$ depends on β_2, β_3, and α. The two surfaces in Figure 3 show how $\dot\beta_3$ depends on β_2 and β_3 for the two extreme cases of the steering angle α, i.e., $\alpha = -\alpha_s$ and $\alpha = \alpha_s$, respectively. It follows that there are initial states such that both β_3 and $\dot\beta_3$ are positive, regardless of the choice of α (for example, $\beta_2 = -\beta_{2s}$ and $\beta_3 = \beta_{3s}$). Starting in such a state leads necessarily to that the truck and trailer vehicle ends up in the jack-knife configuration, when driving backwards. Naturally, this leads to the idea of switching the control between backward and forward motion (as a manual driver would do). Before

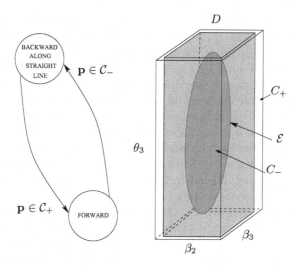

Fig. 4. Two states switching control and a picture of the sets $\mathcal{C}_-$ and $\mathcal{C}_+$ with respect to $\mathcal{E}$.

we present how this switching can be done, note that even without input and state constraints it is not possible to use the same state feedback controller in forward and backward motion. This follows simply from that if the system (2) with $v = 1$ is asymptotically stable for a smooth control law $\alpha = -K(\mathbf{p})$, then the corresponding system with $v = -1$ is unstable.

3.2   Switching Control Strategy

A simplified version of the proposed hybrid control is shown to the left in Figure 4. The hybrid automaton consists of two discrete modes: backward driving along a straight line and forward driving. The switchings between the modes occur when the continuous state reach certain manifolds. The control design consists now of two steps: choosing these manifolds and determining local controllers that stabilize the system in each discrete mode. Suppose a stabilizing control law $\alpha = -K_B(\mathbf{p})$ has been derived for the backward motion ($v = -1$) of the system (2). Let $\mathcal{E} \subset D$ denote the largest ellipsoid contained in the region of attraction for the closed-loop system. From the discussion in previous section, we know that $\mathcal{E}$ is not the whole space D. If the initial state $\mathbf{p}(0) \in D$ is outside $\mathcal{E}$, then K_B will not drive the state to the origin. As proposed by the hybrid controller in Figure 4, we switch in that case to forward mode ($v = 1$) and the control law $\alpha = -K_F(\mathbf{p})$. The forward control K_F is chosen such that the trajectory is driven into $\mathcal{E}$. When the trajectory reaches $\mathcal{E}$, we switch to backward motion. The sets $\mathcal{C}_- \subset D$ and $\mathcal{C}_+ \subset D$ on the edges of the hybrid automaton in Figure 4 define the switching surfaces. To avoid chattering due to measurement noise and to add robustness to the scheme, the switching does not take place exactly on the surface of $\mathcal{E}$. Instead $\mathcal{C}_-$ is slightly smaller than $\mathcal{E}$, and $\mathcal{C}_+$ is larger than $\mathcal{E}$, see the sketch to the right in Figure 4. It is reasonable to choose $\mathcal{C}_-$ (the set defining the switch from forward to backward mode) of the same shape as $\mathcal{E}$, but scaled with a factor $\rho \in (0,1)$. There is a trade-off in choosing ρ: if ρ is close to one, then the system will be sensitive to disturbances; and if ρ is small, then the convergence will be slow since the forward motion will be very long. In the implementations we chose ρ in the interval $(0.7, 0.8)$. The set $\mathcal{C}_+$ (defining the switch from backward to forward mode) is chosen as a rescaling of D. In the implementation, the factors were selected as unity in the y_3 and the θ_3 component, but 0.8 and 0.7 in the β_2 and β_3 component, respectively. The choice is rather arbitrary. The critical point is that β_2 and β_3 should not get too close to the jack-knife configuration ($|\beta_2| = \beta_{2s}$ and $|\beta_3| = \beta_{3s}$). Experiments on the miniature vehicle with the hybrid controller in Figure 4 implemented show that time spent in the forward mode is unacceptably long. The reason is that the time constant of θ_3 is large. To speed up convergence, we introduce an intermediate discrete mode which forces θ_3 to recover faster. This alignment control mode corresponds, for example, to reversing along an arc of circle. The complete switching controller is shown in Figure 5. Thus, the hybrid automaton consists of three discrete modes: backward driving along a straight line, backward driving along an arc of a circle, and forward driving. The switchings between the discrete modes are defined by the following sets:

$$\Omega = \{\mathbf{p} = [y_3, \theta_3, \beta_3, \beta_2]^T \in D : |\theta_3| < \tilde{\theta}_3 \text{ or } y_3\theta_3 < 0\}$$
$$\Psi = \{\mathbf{p} = [y_3, \theta_3, \beta_3, \beta_2]^T \in D : |\theta_3| < \tilde{\theta}_3/2, |y_3| < \tilde{y}_3\}$$
$$\Phi = \{\mathbf{p} = [y_3, \theta_3, \beta_3, \beta_2]^T \in D : [0,0,\beta_3,\beta_2]^T \in \mathcal{C}_-\}$$

where $\tilde{\theta}_3$ and $\tilde{y}_3$ are positive design parameters. In the implementation we choose $\tilde{\theta}_3 = 0.70$ rad and $\tilde{y}_3 = 0.02$ m. In the figure, recall that Ω^c denotes the complement of Ω. The interpretation of the switching conditions in Figure 5 are as follows. Suppose the initial state $\mathbf{p}(0)$ is in $\mathcal{C}_+$ (thus outside the region of attraction for the backward motion system) and that the hybrid controller starts in the forward mode. The system stays in this mode until β_2 and β_3 are small enough, i.e., until (β_2, β_3) belongs to the ellipse defined by Φ. Then a switch to the alignment control mode for backward motion along an arc of a circle occurs. The system stays in this mode until $|y_3|$ is sufficiently small, when a switch is taken to the mode for backward motion along a straight line. The other discrete transitions in Figure 5 may be taken either due to that the alignment originally is good enough or due to disturbances or measurement noise.

3.3 Low-Level Controls

In this section we briefly describe how the three individual state-feedback controllers $\alpha = -K(\mathbf{p})$, applied in each of the discrete modes of the hybrid controller, were derived and what heuristics that had to be incorporated.

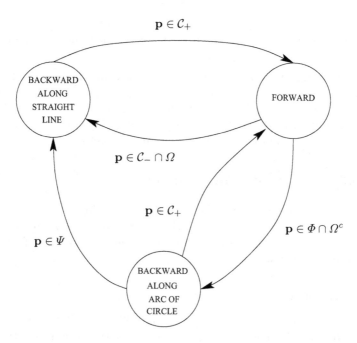

Fig. 5. Three states switching control.

Backward along Straight Line For the discrete mode for the backward motion along a straight line, we design a LQ controller $\alpha = -K_B\mathbf{p}$ based on the linearized model (3) with $v = -1$. The choice of cost criterion is

$$J_B = \int_0^\infty \left(\mathbf{p}^T Q_B \mathbf{p} + \alpha^2\right) dt \qquad Q_B = Q_B^T > 0 \tag{14}$$

The heuristic we have adopted let us choose Q_B as a diagonal matrix, where the y_3 weight is the smallest, the θ_3 weight one order of magnitude larger, and the β_3 and β_2 weights another two orders of magnitude larger. The reason for having large weights on β_3 and β_2 is to avoid saturations. In general, the intuition behind this way of assigning weights reflects the desire of having decreasing closed-loop bandwidths when moving from the inner loop to the outer one. For example, the relative displacement y_3 is related to β_3 and β_2 through a cascade of two integrators, as can be seen from the linearization (4). It turns out that such a heuristic reasoning is very important in the practical implementation in order to avoid saturations.

Forward The state-feedback control in the forward mode is designed based on pole placement. Since closed-loop time constant of y_3 is of several orders of magnitude larger than for the other three states of $\mathbf{p}$, the measurement y_3 is not used in the forward controller. Instead consider the state $\hat{\mathbf{p}} = [\theta_3, \beta_3, \beta_2]^T$ and the corresponding linearized system. We choose a controller gain K_F such that the linearized system has three closed-loop poles of the same order of magnitude.

Backward along Arc of Circle For the backward motion mode, we consider the stabilization of the relative angles $\bar{\mathbf{p}} = [\beta_3, \beta_2]^T$ of the corresponding linearized subsystem (9). The state-feedback controller $\alpha = -K_A\bar{\mathbf{p}}$ is derived based on LQ control. Recall that stabilizing the origin for (9) corresponds to stabilizing the truck and trailer along a circular trajectory.

4 Analysis of Switching Control

In this section, the closed-loop system with the switching controller is analyzed. First, a discussion on how to estimate the region of attraction for the reversing truck and trailer is presented, then a result on asymptotic stability for the hybrid control system is reviewed.

4.1 Region of Attraction

The switching conditions in the hybrid control scheme discussed in previous section were partially based on an estimate $\mathcal{E}$ of the region of attraction for the closed-loop system in backward motion. It is in general difficult to obtain an accurate approximation for the region of attraction, particularly for systems with state and input constraints [11]. In this paper we rely on the numerical simulation of the closed-loop behavior. Hence, considering the nonlinear system (2) with $v = -1$ and closed-loop control $\alpha = -K_B\mathbf{p}$:

$$\dot{\mathbf{p}} = -\big(\mathcal{A}(\mathbf{p}) + \mathcal{B}(\mathbf{p}, -K_B\mathbf{p})\big) \tag{15}$$

In order to obtain a graphical representation of the results, we disregard y_3. This is reasonable as long as the initial condition $y_3(0)$ satisfies the artificial constraint $y_3(0) \leq y_{3s}$ introduced in Section 2. Note that this constraint does not influence the analysis of the other states, since y_3 does not enter the differential equations (1c)–(1e). The black region in Figure 6 shows states $\hat{\mathbf{p}} = [\theta_3, \beta_3, \beta_2]^T$ that belong to the region of attraction. We notice that this cloud of initial conditions closely resembles an ellipsoid. The figure also shows an ellipsoid strictly contained in the region of attraction, which has simply been fitted by hand. Note that the considered problem is related to finding the reachability set for a hybrid system with nonlinear continuous dynamics. For our purposes, we used numerical simulations validated by practical experiments, in order to have a mathematical description of $\mathcal{E}$. It would be interesting to apply recent reachability tools [7, 4, 12, 14] on this highly nonlinear problem.

4.2 Stability Analysis

Consider system (2)

$$\dot{\mathbf{p}} = v\big(\mathcal{A}(\mathbf{p}) + \mathcal{B}(\mathbf{p}, \alpha)\big)$$

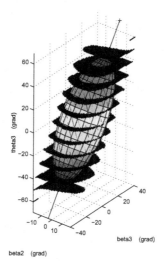

Fig. 6. Region of attraction (in black) for the backward motion obtained through simulation of the nonlinear closed-loop system. An approximating ellipsoid is fitted inside.

under the switching control defined in Figure 4. It is straightforward to show that there exists a stabilizing controller if full state-feedback is applied in both the backward and the forward mode, see [2]. Note, however, that the low-level control for the forward motion discussed in previous section did not use feedback from y_3. Hence, we need a result on the boundedness of y_3. Such a bound can be derived and then under rather mild assumptions it can be proved that the closed-loop system with the two-state hybrid controller is asymptotically stable in a region only slightly smaller than D (see [2] for details).

5   Implementation and Experimental Results

The controller for the truck and trailer shown in Figure 1 was implemented using a commercial version of PC/104 with an AMD586 processor and with an acquisition board for the sensor readings. The signals from the potentiometers for the relative angles β_2 and β_3 were measured via the AD converter provided with the acquisition board, while the position of the trailer was measured using two encoders, placed on the wheels of the rearmost axle. The sampling frequency was about 10 Hz, which was sufficient since the velocity was very low. Figures 7 and 8 show an experiment that starts with a forward motion for the realignment of the trailer and truck, followed by a backward motion along an arc of circle. (The backward motion along a line is not shown, since the truck reached the wall before ending the manoeuvre). The entire motion of the system is depicted in the left of Figure 7 with the configurations at two instances for the forward

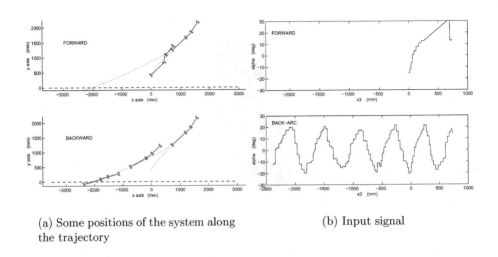

(a) Some positions of the system along
the trajectory

(b) Input signal

Fig. 7. Experiment: sketch of the motion of the vehicle. Notice that the all the measures along x_3 are respect the center of the last axle of the trailer. The input signal is divided in two subplots one for the forward and the other backward (along an arc) motion.

motion and three for the backward. The input signal is shown in the right side of Figure 7. The left graphs of Figure 8 show the state variable y_3 and θ_3 relative to the manoeuvre of Figure 7, but with another scaling. The initial condition is $\beta_2(0) = -40$ deg and $\beta_3(0) = 40$ deg with $\theta_3(0) = 42$ deg. This means that the initial condition is outside the ellipsoid $\mathcal{E}$, hence the hybrid controller starts in the forward motion mode. After a while, the two relative angles β_3 and β_2 are small (and thus the truck and trailer is realigned). This is illustrated to the right in Figure 8, which shows β_3 and β_2 as a function of x_3. Since $y_3 \cdot \theta_3 > 0$, the controller now switches to the mode for backward along an arc of a circle. In total the system travels a distance of 2.5 m in the backward mode and 0.7 m in the forward mode. Some videos showing the motion of the system can be downloaded from [22].

References

[1] C. Altafini. Controllability and singularities in the n-trailer system with kingpin hitching. In *Proceedings of the 14th IFAC World Congress*, volume Q, pages 139–145, Beijing, China, 1999.

[2] C. Altafini, A. Speranzon, and B. Wahlberg. A feedback control scheme for reversing a truck and trailer vehicle. *Accepted for publication in IEEE Transaction on Robotics and Automation*, 2001.

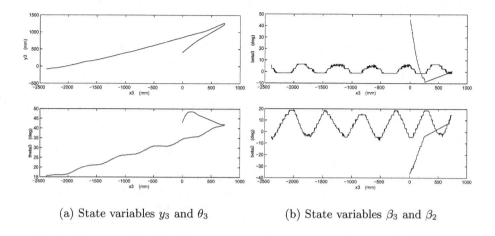

(a) State variables y_3 and θ_3 (b) State variables β_3 and β_2

Fig. 8. Experiment: state variables $[y_3, \theta_3, \beta_3, \beta_2]$ relative to the maneuver shown in the previous picture.

[3] A. Balluchi, P. Soueres, and A. Bicchi. Hybrid feedback control for path tracking by a bounded-curvature vehicle. In *Proceedings of the 4th International Workshop, Hybrid System: Computation and Control*, pages 133–146, Rome, Italy, 2001.

[4] O. Bournez, O. Maler, and A. Pnueli. Orthogonal polyhedra: Representation and computation. In F. Vaandrager and J. van Schuppen, editors, *Hybrid systems: Computation and Control*, volume 1569 of *LNCS*, 1999.

[5] C. Canudas de Wit. *Trends in mobile robot and vehicle control.* Lecture notes in control and information sciences. Springer-Verlag, 1998. In K.P. Valavanis and B. Siciliano (eds), Control problems in robotics.

[6] C. Canudas de Wit, B. Siciliano, and B. Bastin. *Theory of robot control.* Springer-Verlag, 1997.

[7] T. Dang and O. Maler. Reachability analysis via face lifting. In T.A. Henzinger and S. Sastry, editors, *Hybrid Systems: Computation and Control*, volume 1006 of *LNCS*, pages 96–109. Springer, 1998.

[8] A.W. Divelbiss and J. Wen. Nonholonomic path planning with inequality constraints. In *Proceedings of IEEE Int. Conf. on Robotics and Automation*, pages 52–57, 1994.

[9] L.E. Dubins. On curves of minimal length with a constraint on average curvature an with prescribed initial and terminal position and tangents. *American Journal of Mathematics*, 79:497–516, 1957.

[10] M. Fliess, J. Levine, P. Martin, and P. Rouchon. Flatness and defect of nonlinear systems: introductory theory and examples. *Int. Journal of Control*, 61(6):1327–1361, 1995.

[11] K.T. Gilbert, E.G.and Tan. Linear systems with state and control constraints: the theory and application of maximal output admissible set. *IEEE Transactions on Automatic Control*, 36:1008–1020, 1991.

[12] M.R. Greenstreet and M. Mitchell. Reachability analysis using polygonal projection. In *In [VS99]*, pages 76–90, 1999.

[13] D.H. Kim and J.H. Oh. Experiments of backward tracking control for trailer systems. In *Proceedings IEEE Int. Conf. on Robotics and Automation*, pages 19–22, Detroit, MI, 1999.

[14] A.B. Kurzhanski and P. Varaiya. Ellipsoidal techniques for reachability analysis. In N. In Lynch and B. Krogh, editors, *Hybrd Systems: Computation and Control*, volume 1790 of *Lecture Notes in Computer Sciences*, pages 203–213. Springer-Verlag, 2000.

[15] F. Lamiraux and J.P. Laumond. A practical approach to feedback control for a mobile robot with trailer. In 3291-3296, editor, *Proc. IEEE Int. Conf. on Robotics and Automation*, Leuven, Belgium, 1998.

[16] J.P. Laumond. *Robot Motion Planning and Control*. Lecture notes in control and information sciences. Springer-Verlag, 1998.

[17] W. Li, T. Tsubouchi, and S. Yuta. On a manipulative difficulty of a mobile robot with multiple trailers for pushing and towing. In *Proceedings IEEE Int. Conf. on Robotics and Automation*, pages 13–18, Detroit, Mi, 1999.

[18] Y. Nakamura, H. Ezaki, Y. Tan, and W. Chung. Design of steering mechanism and control of nonholonomic trailer systems. In *Proceeding of IEEE Int. Conf. on Robotics and Automation*, pages 247–254, San Francisco, CA, 2000.

[19] P. Rouchon, M. Fliess, J. Levine, and P. Martin. Flatness, motion planning and trailer systems. In *Proc. 32nd IEEE Conf. on Decision and Control*, pages 2700–2075, San Antonio, Texas, 1993.

[20] M. Sampei, T. Tamura, T. Kobayashi, and N. Shibui. Arbitrary path tracking control of articulated vehicles using nonlinear control theory. *IEEE Transaction on Control Systems Technology*, 3:125–131, 1995.

[21] O.J. Sørdalen. Conversion of the kinematics of a car with n trailers into chained form. In *Proc. IEEE Int. Conf. on Robotics and Automation*, pages 382–387, Atlanta, Georgia, 1993.

[22] A. Speranzon. Reversing a truck and trailer vehicle.
http://www.s3.kth.se/~albspe/truck/.

[23] K. Tanaka, T. Taniguchi, and H.O. Wang. Trajectory control of an articulated vehicle with triple trailers. In *Proc. IEEE International Conference on Control Applications*, pages 1673–1678, 1999.

[24] D. Tilbury, R. Murray, and S. Sastry. Trajectory generation for the n-trailer problem using Goursat normal form. *IEEE Trans. on Automatic Control*, 40:802–819, 1995.

[25] M. van Nieuwstadt and R. Murray. Real time trajectory generation for differentially flat systems. *International Journal of Robust and Nonlinear Control*, 8(38):995–1020, 1998.

[26] P. Varaiya. Smart cars on smart roads: Problems of control. *IEEE Transactions on Automatic Control*, 38(2):195–207, February 1993.

Reachability Analysis of Hybrid Systems via Predicate Abstraction

Rajeev Alur, Thao Dang, and Franjo Ivančić

Department of Computer and Information Science
University of Pennsylvania
http://www.seas.upenn.edu/hybrid/

Abstract. Predicate abstraction has emerged to be a powerful technique for extracting finite-state models from infinite-state discrete programs. This paper presents algorithms and tools for reachability analysis of hybrid systems by combining the notion of predicate abstraction with recent techniques for approximating the set of reachable states of linear systems using polyhedra. Given a hybrid system and a set of user-defined boolean predicates, we consider the finite discrete quotient whose states correspond to all possible truth assignments to the input predicates. The tool performs an on-the-fly exploration of the abstract system. We demonstrate the feasibility of the proposed technique by analyzing a parametric timing-based mutual exclusion protocol and safety of a simple controller for vehicle coordination.

1 Introduction

Inspired by the success of model checking in hardware verification and protocol analysis [8,17], there has been increasing research on developing techniques for automated verification of hybrid (mixed discrete-continuous) models of embedded controllers [1,3,15]. The state-of-the-art computational tools for model checking of hybrid systems are of two kinds. Tools such as KRONOS [11], UP-PAAL [20], and HYTECH [16] limit the continuous dynamics to simple abstractions such as rectangular inclusions (e.g. $\dot{x} \in [1,2]$), and compute the set of reachable states exactly and effectively by symbolic manipulation of linear inequalities. On the other hand, emerging tools such as CHECKMATE [7], d/dt [5], and level-sets method [14,21], approximate the set of reachable states by polyhedra or ellipsoids [19] by optimization techniques. Even though these tools have been applied to interesting real-world examples after appropriate abstractions, scalability remains a challenge.

In the world of program analysis, predicate abstraction has emerged to be a powerful and popular technique for extracting finite-state models from complex, potentially infinite state, discrete systems [10,13]. A verifier based on this scheme requires three inputs, the (concrete) system to be analyzed, the property to be verified, and a finite set of boolean predicates over system variables to be used for abstraction. An abstract state is a valid combination of truth values to the boolean predicates, and thus, corresponds to a set of concrete states.

C.J. Tomlin and M.R. Greenstreet (Eds.): HSCC 2002, LNCS 2289, pp. 35–48, 2002.
© Springer-Verlag Berlin Heidelberg 2002

There is an abstract transition from an abstract state A to an abstract state B, if there is a concrete transition from some state corresponding to A to some state corresponding to B. The job of the verifier is to compute the abstract transitions, and to search in the abstract graph for a violation of the property. If the abstract system satisfies the property, then so does the concrete system. If a violation is found in the abstract system, then the resulting counter-example can be analyzed to test if it is a feasible execution of the concrete system. This approach, of course, does not solve the verification problem by itself. The success crucially depends on the ability to identify the "interesting" predicates, and on the ability of the verifier to compute abstract transitions efficiently. Nevertheless, it has led to opportunities to bridge the gap between code and models and to combine automated search with user's intuition about interesting predicates. Tools such as Bandera [9], SLAM [6], and Feaver [18] have successfully applied predicate abstraction for analysis of C or Java programs.

Inspired by these two trends, we develop algorithms for invariant verification of hybrid systems using discrete approximations based on predicate abstractions. Consider a hybrid automaton with n continuous variables and a set L of locations. Then the continuous state-space is $L \times \mathbb{R}^n$. For the sake of efficiency, we restrict our attention where all invariants, switching guards, and discrete updates of the hybrid automaton are specified by linear expressions, and the continuous dynamics is linear, possibly with bounded input. For the purpose of abstraction, the user supplies initial predicates $p_1 \ldots p_k$, where each predicate is a polyhedral subset of $\mathbb{R}^n$. In the abstract program, the n continuous variables are replaced by k discrete boolean variables. A combination of values to these k boolean variables represents an abstract state, and the abstract state space is $L \times \mathbb{B}^k$. Our verifier performs an on-the-fly search of the abstract system by symbolic manipulation of polyhedra.

The core of the verifier is the computation of the transitions between abstract states that capture both discrete and continuous dynamics of the original system. Computing discrete successors is relatively straightforward, and involves computing weakest preconditions, and checking non-emptiness of an intersection of polyhedral sets. For computing continuous successors of an abstract state A, we use a strategy inspired by the techniques used in CHECKMATE and d/dt. The basic strategy computes the polyhedral slices of states reachable from A at fixed times $r, 2r, 3r, \ldots$ for a suitably chosen r, and then, takes the convex-hull of all these polyhedra to over-approximate the set of all states reachable from A. However, while tools such as CHECKMATE and d/dt are designed to compute a "good" approximation of the continuous successors of A, we are interested in testing if this set intersects with a new abstract state. Consequently, our implementation differs in many ways. For instance, it checks for nonempty intersection with other abstract states of each of the polyhedral slices, and omits steps involving approximations using orthogonal polyhedra and termination tests.

Postulating the verification problem for hybrid systems as a search problem in the abstract system has many benefits compared to the traditional approach of computing approximations of reachable sets of hybrid systems. First, the expensive operation of computing continuous successors is applied only to abstract states, and not to intermediate polyhedra of unpredictable shapes and complexities. Second, we can prematurely terminate the computation of continuous successors whenever new abstract transitions are discovered. Finally, we can explore with different search strategies aimed at making progress in the abstract graph. For instance, our implementation always prefers computing discrete transitions over continuous ones. Our early experiments indicate that improvements in time and space requirements are significant compared to a tool such as d/dt.

We demonstrate the feasibility of our approach using two case studies. The first one involves verification of a parametric version of Fischer's protocol for timing-based mutual exclusion. The correctness of the protocol depends on two parameters δ and Δ. Traditional tools can analyze such problems very efficiently for fixed values of these parameters. Recently, there have been some results for parametric versions of the problem [4]. In our analysis, $b = (\delta > \Delta)$ is used as one of the initial predicates. The abstract search nicely reveals that the bad states are reachable precisely from those initial states in which the predicate b is false. The second example involves verification of a longitudinal controller for the leader car of a platoon from the IVHS projects [12]. Our concrete model consists of 4 continuous variables, linear dynamics with one bounded input, and 17 initial predicates. The verifier could establish absence of collisions without using any significant computational resources.

2 Hybrid Automata

2.1 Syntax

We denote the set of all n-dimensional linear expressions $l : \mathbb{R}^n \to \mathbb{R}$ with Σ_n and the set of all n-dimensional linear predicates $\pi : \mathbb{R}^n \to \mathbb{B}$, where $\mathbb{B} := \{0, 1\}$, with $\mathcal{L}_n$. A linear predicate is of the form $\pi(x) := \sum_{i=1}^{n} a_i x_i + a_{n+1} \sim 0$, where $\sim \in \{\geq, >\}$ and $\forall i \in \{1, \ldots, n+1\} : a_i \in \mathbb{R}$. Additionally, we denote the set of finite conjunctions of n-dimensional linear predicates by $\mathcal{C}_n$.

Definition 1 (Hybrid Automata). *A n-dimensional **hybrid automaton** is a tuple $H = (\mathcal{X}, L, X_0, I, f, T)$ with the following components:*

- *$\mathcal{X} \subseteq \mathbb{R}^n$ is a **continuous state space**.*
- *L is a finite set of **locations**. The **state space** of H is $X = L \times \mathcal{X}$. Each state thus has the form (l, x), where $l \in L$ is the discrete part of the state, and $x \in \mathcal{X}$ is the continuous part.*
- *$X_0 \subseteq \mathcal{X}$ is the set of **initial states**.*
- *$I : L \to \mathcal{C}_n$ assigns to each location $l \in L$ a finite conjunction of linear predicates $I(l)$ defining the **invariant** conditions that constrain the value of the continuous part of the state while the discrete part is l. The hybrid automaton can only stay in location l as long as the continuous variable x satisfies $I(l)$, i.e. $\forall i \in I(l) : i(x) = 1$. We will write $\mathcal{I}_l$ for the invariant set of location l, that is the set of all points x satisfying all predicates in $I(l)$. In other words, $\mathcal{I}_l := \{x \in \mathcal{X} \mid \forall i \in I(l) : i(x) = 1\}$.*

- $f : L \to (\mathbb{R}^n \to \mathbb{R}^n)$ *assigns to each location* $l \in V$ *a* **continuous vector field** $f(l)$ *on* x. *While staying at location* l *the evolution of the continuous variable is governed by the differential equation* $\dot{x} = f(l)(x)$.
- $T : L \to 2^{\mathcal{C}_n \times L \times (\Sigma_n)^n}$ *is a function capturing discrete transition jumps between two discrete locations. A transition* $(g, l', r) \in T(l)$ *consists of an initial location* l, *a destination location* l', *a set of* **guard** *constraints* g *and a* **reset** *mapping* r. *From a state* (l, x) *where all predicates in* g *are satisfied the hybrid automaton can jump to location* l' *at which the continuous variable* x *is reset to a new value* $r(x)$. *We will write* $\mathcal{G}_{ll'}$ *for the guard set of a transition* $(g, l', r) \in T(l)$ *which is the set of points satisfying all linear predicates of* g, *that is,* $\mathcal{G}_{ll'} := \{x \in \mathcal{X} \mid \forall e \in g : e(x) = 1\}$.

We restrict our attention to hybrid automata with linear continuous dynamics, that is, for every location $l \in L$, the vector field $f(l)$ is linear, i.e. $f(l)(x) = A_l x$ where A_l is an $n \times n$ matrix. As we shall see later in Section 4.2, our reachability analysis can also be applied to hybrid systems having linear continuous dynamics with uncertain, bounded input of the form: $\dot{x} = A_l x + B_l u$.

2.2   Semantics

We will explain the semantics of a hybrid automaton by defining its underlying transition system. Let $\Phi_l(x, t) = e^{A_l t} x$ denote the flow of the system $\dot{x} = A_l x$.

The underlying transition system of H is $T_H = \{X, \to, X_0\}$. The state space of the transition system is the state space of H, i.e. $X = L \times \mathcal{X}$. The transition relation $\to \subseteq X \times X$ between states of the transition system is defined as the union of two relations $\to_C, \to_D \subseteq X \times X$. The relation $\to_C$ describes transitions due to continuous flow, whereas $\to_D$ describes the transitions due to discrete jumps.

$$(l, x) \to_C (l, y) :\Leftrightarrow \exists t \in \mathbb{R}_{\geq 0} : \Phi_l(x, t) = y \wedge \forall t' \in [0, t] : \Phi_l(x, t') \in \mathcal{I}_l. \quad (1)$$

$$(l, x) \to_D (l', y) :\Leftrightarrow \exists (g, l', r) \in T(l) : x \in \mathcal{G}_{ll'} \wedge y = r(x). \quad (2)$$

We introduce now some basic reachability notation. We define the set of *continuous successors* of a set of states (l, P) where $l \in L$ and $P \subseteq \mathcal{X}$, denoted by $\text{Post}_C(l, P)$ as: $\text{Post}_C(l, P) := \{(l, y) \in X \mid \exists x \in P \ (l, x) \to_C (l, y)\}$. Similarly, we define the set of *discrete successors* of (l, P), denoted by $\text{Post}_D(l, P)$, as: $\text{Post}_D(l, P) := \{(l', y) \in X \mid \exists x \in P \ (l, x) \to_D (l', y)\}$.

2.3   Discrete Abstraction

Let us now define a discrete abstraction of the hybrid system H with respect to a given k-dimensional vector of linear predicates $\Pi = (\pi_1, \pi_2, \ldots, \pi_k)$. We can partition the continuous state space $\mathcal{X}$ into at most 2^k states, corresponding to the 2^k possible boolean evaluations of Π; hence, the infinite state space X of H is reduced to $|L| 2^k$ states in the abstract system. From now on, we will refer to the hybrid system H as the *concrete system* and its state space X as the *concrete state space*.

Definition 2 (Abstract state space). *Given a n-dimensional hybrid system* $H = (\mathcal{X}, L, X_0, f, I, T)$ *and a k-dimensional vector* $\Pi \in (\mathcal{L}_n)^k$ *of n-dimensional linear predicates we can define an* **abstract state** *as a tuple* $(l, \boldsymbol{b})$, *where* $l \in L$ *and* $\boldsymbol{b} \in \mathbb{B}^k$. *The abstract state space for a k-dimensional vector of linear predicates hence is* $Q := L \times \mathbb{B}^k$.

Definition 3 (Concretization function). *We define a* **concretization function** $C_\Pi : \mathbb{B}^k \to 2^{\mathcal{X}}$ *for a vector of linear predicates* $\Pi = (\pi_1, \dots, \pi_k) \in (\mathcal{L}_n)^k$ *as follows:* $C_\Pi(\boldsymbol{b}) := \{x \in \mathcal{X} \mid \forall i \in \{1, \dots, k\} : \pi_i(x) = b_i\}$. *Denote a vector* $\boldsymbol{b} \in \mathbb{B}^k$ *as* **consistent** *with respect to a vector of linear predicates* $\Pi \in (\mathcal{L}_n)^k$, *if* $C_\Pi(\boldsymbol{b}) \neq \emptyset$. *We say that an abstract state* $(l, \boldsymbol{b}) \in Q$ *is* **consistent** *with respect to a vector of linear predicates* Π, *if* $\boldsymbol{b}$ *is consistent with respect to* Π.

If all predicates in Π are indeed linear predicates, it can be shown that $C_\Pi(\boldsymbol{b})$ is a convex polyhedron for any $\boldsymbol{b} \in \mathbb{B}^k$.

Definition 4 (Discrete Abstraction). *Given a hybrid system* $H = (\mathcal{X}, L, X_0, f, I, T)$, *we define its abstract system with respect to a vector of linear predicates* Π *as the transition system* $H_\Pi = (Q, \xrightarrow{\Pi}, Q_0)$ *where*

- *the abstract transition relation* $\xrightarrow{\Pi} \subseteq Q \times Q$ *is defined as follows:*

$$(l, \boldsymbol{b}) \xrightarrow{\Pi} (l', \boldsymbol{b}') :\Leftrightarrow \exists x \in C_\Pi(\boldsymbol{b}), y \in C_\Pi(\boldsymbol{b}') : (l, x) \to (l', y);$$

- *the set of initial states is* $Q_0 = \{(l, \boldsymbol{b}) \in Q \mid \exists x \in C_\Pi(\boldsymbol{b}) : (l, x) \in X_0\}$.

To be able to distinguish transitions in the abstract state space due to a discrete jump in the concrete state space from those transitions that are due to continuous flows, we introduce the following two relations $\xrightarrow{\Pi}_D, \xrightarrow{\Pi}_C \subseteq Q \times Q$:

$$(l, \boldsymbol{b}) \xrightarrow{\Pi}_D (l', \boldsymbol{b}') :\Leftrightarrow \exists (g, l', r) \in T(l), x \in C_\Pi(\boldsymbol{b}) \cap \mathcal{G}_{ll'} :$$
$$(l, x) \to_D (l', r(x)) \wedge r(x) \in C_\Pi(\boldsymbol{b}'), \qquad (3)$$

$$(l, \boldsymbol{b}) \xrightarrow{\Pi}_C (l', \boldsymbol{b}') :\Leftrightarrow \exists x \in C_\Pi(\boldsymbol{b}), t \in \mathbb{R}_{\geq 0} : \Phi_l(x, t) \in C_\Pi(\boldsymbol{b}') \wedge$$
$$\forall t' \in [0, t] : \Phi_l(x, t') \in \mathcal{I}_l. \qquad (4)$$

We can now define the successors of an abstract state $(l, \boldsymbol{b})$ by discrete jumps and by continuous flows, denoted respectively by $\text{Post}_D^\Pi(l, \boldsymbol{b})$ and $\text{Post}_C^\Pi(l, \boldsymbol{b})$, as: $\text{Post}_D^\Pi(l, \boldsymbol{b}) := \{(l', \boldsymbol{b}') \in Q \mid (l, \boldsymbol{b}) \xrightarrow{\Pi}_D (l', \boldsymbol{b}')\}$, and $\text{Post}_C^\Pi(l, \boldsymbol{b}) := \{(l', \boldsymbol{b}') \in Q \mid (l, \boldsymbol{b}) \xrightarrow{\Pi}_C (l, \boldsymbol{b}')\}$.

3   Reachability Analysis

For the reachability analysis, it could be assumed that all guards and invariants of a hybrid automaton H are included in the vector of linear predicates Π which will be used for our abstract state space reachability exploration. On the other hand, one may reduce the state space of the abstract system by not including all guards and invariants, but rather only include linear predicates that are important for the verification of the given property.

3.1 Computing Discrete Successors of the Abstract System

Given an abstract state $(l, \boldsymbol{b}) \in Q$ and a particular transition $(g, l', r) \in T(l)$ we want to compute all abstract states that are reachable. A transition $(g, l', r) \in T(l)$ is *enabled* in an abstract state $(l, \boldsymbol{b})$ with respect to Π, if $C_\Pi(\boldsymbol{b}) \cap \mathcal{G}_{ll'} \neq \emptyset$.

We define a tri-valued logic using the symbols $\mathcal{T} := \{0, 1, *\}$. 0 denotes that a particular linear predicate is always false for a given abstract state, 1 that it is always true, whereas $*$ denotes the case that a linear predicate is true for part of the abstract state, and false for the rest. We can define a function $t : \mathbb{B}^k \times (\mathcal{L}_n)^k \times \mathcal{L}_n \to \mathcal{T}$ formally as:

$$t(\boldsymbol{b}, \Pi, e) = \begin{cases} 1 \;, & \text{if } C_\Pi(\boldsymbol{b}) \neq \emptyset \wedge \forall x \in C_\Pi(\boldsymbol{b}) : e(x) = 1; \\ 0 \;, & \text{if } C_\Pi(\boldsymbol{b}) \neq \emptyset \wedge \forall x \in C_\Pi(\boldsymbol{b}) : e(x) = 0; \\ * \;, & \text{otherwise.} \end{cases}$$

As will be described shortly, we can use this tri-valued logic to reduce the size of the set of feasible abstract successor states. For later use, let us define the number of positions in a k-dimensional vector $\boldsymbol{t} \in \mathcal{T}^k$ with element $*$ as $||\boldsymbol{t}||_*$.

Given a particular transition $(g, l', r) \in T(l)$ and a given linear predicate $e : \mathbb{R}^n \to \mathbb{B}$, we need to compute the boolean value of a linear predicate e after the reset r, which is $e(r(x))$. It can be seen that $e \circ r : \mathbb{R}^n \to \mathbb{B}$ is another linear predicate. It should be noted that given e and r we can easily compute $e \circ r$. If we generalize this for a vector of predicates $\Pi = (\pi_1, \dots, \pi_k)^T \in (\mathcal{L}_n)^k$ by $\Pi \circ r := (\pi_1 \circ r, \dots, \pi_k \circ r)^T$, the following lemma immediately follows.

Lemma 1. *Given a k-dimensional vector $\boldsymbol{b} \in \mathbb{B}^k$, a vector of n-dimensional linear predicates $\Pi \in (\mathcal{L}_n)^k$, and a reset mapping $r \in (\Sigma_n)^n$, we have:*

$$x \in C_{\Pi \circ r}(\boldsymbol{b}) \Leftrightarrow r(x) \in C_\Pi(\boldsymbol{b}).$$

We can now compute the possible successor states of an enabled transition $(g, l', r) \in T(l)$ from a consistent abstract state $(l, \boldsymbol{b})$ with respect to a vector of linear predicates $\Pi = (\pi_1, \dots, \pi_k)$ as $(l', \boldsymbol{b}')$, where $\boldsymbol{b}' \in \mathcal{T}^n$ and each component b'_i is given by: $b'_i = t(\boldsymbol{b}, \Pi, \pi_i \circ r)$. If $b'_i = 1$, then we know that the corresponding linear predicate $\pi_i \circ r$ is true for all points $x \in C_\Pi(\boldsymbol{b})$. This means that all states in $C_\Pi(\boldsymbol{b})$ after the reset r will make π_i true. Similarly, if $b'_i = 0$ we know that the linear predicate will always be false. Otherwise, if $b'_i = *$, then there exist concrete continuous states in $C_\Pi(\boldsymbol{b})$ that after the reset r force π_i to become true, as well as other concrete continuous states that make π_i to become false. Hence, the tri-valued vector $\boldsymbol{b}' \in \mathcal{T}^n$ represents $2^{||\boldsymbol{b}'||_*}$ many possibilities, which combined with location l' make up at most $2^{||\boldsymbol{b}'||_*}$ many abstract states. We define $c : \mathcal{T}^k \to 2^{\mathbb{B}^k}$ as: $c(\boldsymbol{t}) := \{\boldsymbol{b} \in \mathbb{B}^k \mid \forall i \in \{1, \dots, k\} : t_i \neq * \Rightarrow t_i = b_i\}$.

An abstract state $(l', e) \in Q$ is a discrete successor of $(l, \boldsymbol{b})$, if $e \in c(\boldsymbol{b}')$ and $C_{\Pi \circ r}(e)$ intersects with $C_\Pi(\boldsymbol{b})$ and the guard of the corresponding transition, which is formulated in the following theorem.

Theorem 1. *Given an abstract state* $(l, \boldsymbol{b}) \in Q$ *with respect to a k-dimensional vector of n-dimensional linear predicates* Π, *a transition* $(g, l', r) \in T(l)$ *and the corresponding guard set* $\mathcal{G}_{ll'}$, *we have* $\forall \boldsymbol{v} \in \mathbb{B}^k$:

$$C_{\Pi or}(\boldsymbol{v}) \cap C_\Pi(\boldsymbol{b}) \cap \mathcal{G}_{ll'} \neq \emptyset \Leftrightarrow (l, \boldsymbol{b}) \xrightarrow{\Pi}_D (l', \boldsymbol{v}).$$

Proof: If $C_{\Pi or}(\boldsymbol{v}) \cap C_\Pi(\boldsymbol{b}) \cap \mathcal{G}_{ll'}$ is not empty, we can pick a point $x \in C_{\Pi or}(\boldsymbol{v}) \cap C_\Pi(\boldsymbol{b}) \cap \mathcal{G}_{ll'}$. As $x \in \mathcal{G}_{ll'}$, we found a discrete transition in the concrete state space $(l, x) \rightarrow_D (l', r(x))$. We know that $x \in C_\Pi(\boldsymbol{b})$. Additionally we know that $x \in C_{\Pi or}(\boldsymbol{v})$ and by using Lemma 1 we have $r(x) \in C_\Pi(\boldsymbol{v})$. Hence, this corresponds to a transition in the abstract state space $(l, \boldsymbol{b}) \xrightarrow{\Pi}_D (l', \boldsymbol{v})$.

If, on the other hand, we have $(l, \boldsymbol{b}) \xrightarrow{\Pi}_D (l', \boldsymbol{v})$ for a discrete transition $(g, l', r) \in T(l)$, we must have: $\exists x \in C_\Pi(\boldsymbol{b}) : x \in \mathcal{G}_{ll'} \wedge r(x) \in C_\Pi(\boldsymbol{v})$. Using Lemma 1, this means that $\exists x \in C_\Pi(\boldsymbol{b}) : x \in \mathcal{G}_{ll'} \wedge x \in C_{\Pi or}(\boldsymbol{v})$. Hence we found that $C_{\Pi or}(\boldsymbol{v}) \cap C_\Pi(\boldsymbol{b}) \cap \mathcal{G}_{ll'} \neq \emptyset$. ∎

Note, that if we assume that all the linear predicates of the guard $g \in \mathcal{C}_n$ are part of the k-dimensional vector of linear predicates Π, then we can skip the additional check, whether $C_{\Pi or}(\boldsymbol{v}) \cap C_\Pi(\boldsymbol{b})$ intersects with the guard set $\mathcal{G}_{ll'}$. In addition, we can restrict the search for non-empty intersections to $\boldsymbol{v} \in c(\boldsymbol{b}')$ instead of the full space $\mathbb{B}^k$ due to the aforementioned observations.

3.2 Computing Continuous Successors of the Abstract System

Our procedure for computing continuous successors of the abstract system A_Π is based on the following observation. By definition, the abstract states $(l, \boldsymbol{b}')$ is reachable from $(l, \boldsymbol{b})$ if the following condition is satisfied

$$PostC(l, C_\Pi(\boldsymbol{b})) \cap C_\Pi(\boldsymbol{b}') \neq \emptyset, \tag{5}$$

where $\mathtt{Post}_c$ is the successor operator of the concrete system H. Intuitively, the above condition means that while staying at location l the concrete system admits at least one trajectory from a point $x \in C_\Pi(\boldsymbol{b})$ to a point $y \in C_\Pi(\boldsymbol{b}')$. Therefore, the set of continuous successors of an abstract state $(l, \boldsymbol{b})$ can be written as follows: $\mathtt{Post}_C^\Pi(l, \boldsymbol{b}) = \{(l, \boldsymbol{b}') \mid \mathtt{Post}_c(l, C_\Pi(\boldsymbol{b})) \cap C_\Pi(\boldsymbol{b}') \neq \emptyset\}$. The test of the condition (5) requires the computation of continuous successors of the concrete system, and for this purpose we will make use of a modified version of the reachability algorithm implemented in the verification tool $\mathtt{d/dt}$ [5]. For a clear understanding, let us first recap this algorithm.

The approach used by $\mathtt{d/dt}$ works directly on the continuous state space of the hybrid system and uses orthogonal polyhedra to represent reachable sets, which allows to perform all operations, such as boolean operations and equivalence checking, required by the verification task. Basically, the computation of reachable sets is done on a step-by-step basis, that is each iteration k computes an over-approximation of the reachable set for the time interval $[kr, (k+1)r]$ where r is the time step. Suppose P is the initial convex polyhedron. The set P_r of successors at time r of P is the convex hull of the successors at time r

of its vertices. To over-approximate the successors during the interval $[0, r]$, the convex hull $C = conv(P \cup P_r)$ is computed and then enlarged by an appropriate amount. Finally, the enlarged convex hull is over-approximated by an orthogonal polyhedron. To deal with invariant conditions that constrain the continuous evolution at each location, the algorithm intersects P_r with the invariant set and starts the next iteration from the resulting polyhedron.

It is worth emphasizing that the goal of the orthogonal approximation step in the reachability algorithm of d/dt is to represent the reachable set after successive iterations as a unique orthogonal polyhedron, which facilitates termination checking and the computation of discrete successors. However, in our predicate abstraction approach, to compute continuous successors of the abstract system we will exclude the orthogonal approximation step for the following reasons. First, checking condition (5) does not require accumulating concrete continuous successors. Moreover, although operations on orthogonal polyhedra can be done in any dimension, they become expensive as the dimension grows. This simplification allows us to reduce computation cost in the continuous phase and thus be able to perform different search strategies so that the violation of the property can be detected as fast as possible. In the sequel, for simplicity, we will use an informal notation $\mathtt{APost}_C^\Pi(l, P, [0, r])$ to denote the above described computation of an over-approximation of concrete continuous successors of (l, P) during the time interval $[0, r]$ and the outcome of $\mathtt{APost}_C^\Pi$ is indeed the enlarged convex hull mentioned earlier. The algorithm for over-approximating continuous successors of the abstract system is given below. It terminates if the reachable set of the current iteration is included in that of the precedent iteration. This termination condition is easy to check but obviously not sufficient, and hence in some cases the algorithm is not guaranteed to terminate. An illustration of Algorithm 1 is shown in Figure 1.

Algorithm 1 Over-Approximating the Abstract Continuous-Successors of $(l, \boldsymbol{b})$

$R_c \leftarrow \emptyset; \quad P^0 \leftarrow C_\Pi(\boldsymbol{b}); \quad k \leftarrow 0 ;$
repeat
$\quad P^{k+1} \leftarrow \mathtt{APost}_C^\Pi(l, P^k, [0, r]);$
$\quad$ **for all** $(l, \boldsymbol{b}') \in Q \setminus R_c$ **do**
$\quad\quad P' \leftarrow C_\Pi(\boldsymbol{b}');$
$\quad\quad$ **if** $P^{k+1} \cap P' \neq \emptyset$ **then**
$\quad\quad\quad R_c := R_c \cup (l, \boldsymbol{b}') ;$
$\quad k \leftarrow k + 1 ;$
until $P^{k+1} \subseteq P^k$
return R_c ;

In each iteration k, to avoid testing all unvisited abstract states $(l, \boldsymbol{b}')$, we will use a similar idea to the one described in the computation of discrete successors. We can determine the tri-valued result of the intersection of the time slice P^k with the half-space corresponding to each predicate in Π, allowing us to eliminate the abstract states which do not intersect with P^k.

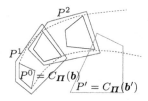

Fig. 1. Illustration of the computation of continuous successors. After two iterations new abstract state (l, b') is reachable.

3.3   Search Strategy

The search in the abstract state space can be performed in a variety of ways. Our goal is to make the discovery of counter-examples in the abstract state space given a reachability property as fast as possible. In the case that the property is true we need to search the entire reachable abstract sub-space.

We perform a DFS, which usually does not find a shortest counter-example possible. On the other hand, it only stores the current trace of abstract states from an initial abstract state on a stack. In case we find an abstract state that violates the property, the stack contents represent the counter-example. This is generally much more memory efficient than BFS.

We give a priority to computing discrete successors rather than continuous successors. This decision is based on the fact that computing a discrete successor is generally much faster than computing a continuous one.

During the computation of continuous successors we abort or interrupt the computation when a new abstract state is found. Not running the fixpoint computation of continuous successors to completion may result in a substantial speed-up when discovering a counter-example, if one exists. A simplified sketch of the algorithm is given as Algorithm 2.

Algorithm 2 Abstract State Space Reachability Analysis via DFS
  stack ← new Stack () ;
  push initial state onto stack ; {for simplicity assume, there is only one such state}
  repeat
    if stack.top().violatesProperty() **then**
      return stack ;
    if $\text{Post}_D^{\Pi}(\text{stack.top}()) \neq \emptyset$ **then**
      push one state in $\text{Post}_D^{\Pi}(\text{stack.top}())$ onto the stack ;
    else if $\text{Post}_C^{\Pi}(\text{stack.top}()) \neq \emptyset$ **then**
      push one state in $\text{Post}_C^{\Pi}(\text{stack.top}())$ onto the stack ;
    else
      stack.pop() ;
  until stack.isEmpty()
  return "Property is guaranteed!" ;

Using the aforementioned approach we can prove the following theorem which states the soundness of Algorithm 2.

Theorem 2. *If Algorithm 2 terminates and reports that the abstract system is safe, then the corresponding concrete system is also safe.*

We additionally include an optimization technique in the search strategy. Consider a real counter-example in the concrete hybrid system. There exists an equivalent counter-example that has the additional constraint that there are no two consecutive transitions due to continuous flow in the equivalent counter-example. This is due to the so-called semi-group property of hybrid systems, namely: $(l, x) \rightarrow_C (l, x') \land (l, x') \rightarrow_C (l, x'') \Rightarrow (l, x) \rightarrow_C (l, x'')$. We are hence searching only for counter-examples in the abstract system that do not have two consecutive transitions due to continuous flow. By enforcing this additional constraint we eliminate some fake counter-examples that could have been found otherwise in the abstract transition system. The fake counter-examples that are eliminated are due to the fact that $(l, \boldsymbol{b}) \xrightarrow{\Pi}_C (l, \boldsymbol{b'})$ and $(l, \boldsymbol{b'}) \xrightarrow{\Pi}_C (l, \boldsymbol{b''})$ does *not* imply that $(l, \boldsymbol{b}) \xrightarrow{\Pi}_C (l, \boldsymbol{b''})$. Hence, we are in fact not computing the whole relation $\xrightarrow{\Pi}_C$ as it was defined above, but only a part of it without compromising the conservativeness of our approach. We illustrate this optimization technique in Figure 2.

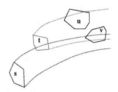

Fig. 2. An optimization technique in the search strategy: If the abstract state t can only be reached by continuous transitions, we will not explore its continuous successors by the same continuous dynamics. Hence, in the above example the abstract state u will not be regarded as reachable. On the other hand, v will be reached by continuous flow from s.

Also, in order to force termination of the continuous search routine, we can limit the number of iterations k to some value $K_{\max}$. This way we can bound the computation of $\text{Post}_C^{\Pi}(l, \boldsymbol{b})$ for an abstract state $(l, \boldsymbol{b})$.

4   Implementation and Experimentation

4.1   Mutual Exclusion with Time-Based Synchronization

We will first look at an example of mutual exclusion which uses time-based synchronization in a multi-process system. The state machines for the two processes are shown in Figure 3. We will use this example for two reasons. The first reason is that it is small enough to be used effectively for an illustration of our approach. A second reason is that it is similar to examples that have been used as case-studies in other verification tools as well. Tools like KRONOS [11] and UPPAAL[20] for example have solved this example for specific values for the positive parameters δ and Δ. We want to solve the parametric version of the problem, that is using parameters without specifying values for δ and Δ, which has not been done previously.

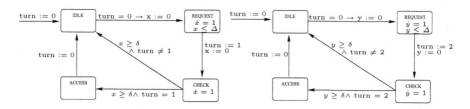

Fig. 3. The two processes for the mutual exclusion example

The possible execution traces depend on the two positive parameters Δ and δ. If the parameters are such that $\Delta \geq \delta$ is true, we can find a counter-example that proves the two processes may access the shared resource at the same time. The trace of abstract states that represents a valid counter-example in the original system is given in Figure 4.

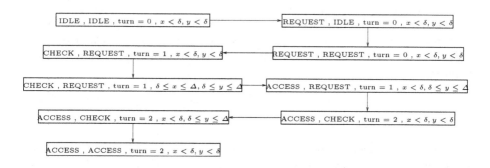

Fig. 4. A counter-example trace for the mutual exclusion problem for the parameter setting $\Delta \geq \delta$. The predicates that were used to find this counter-example are the predicates given by the guards and invariants of the composed hybrid system. These are: $x \geq \delta, y \geq \delta, x \leq \Delta$ and $y \leq \Delta$. The states do not show the constantly true linear predicates over the parameters $\Delta \geq \delta$, $\Delta > 0$ and $\delta > 0$.

On the other hand, if $\delta > \Delta$, then the system preserves mutual exclusive use of the shared resource. In order to prove this using our predicate abstraction algorithm, we needed to include the intuitive predicates $x \geq y$ and $y \geq x$ in addition to the predicates already mentioned in the caption of Figure 4. The reachability analysis finds 54 reachable abstract states, which all maintain the mutual exclusion property. The computation of this result takes a few seconds, and the memory requirements are negligible.

4.2   Vehicle Coordination

We have also successfully applied our predicate abstraction technique to verify a longitudinal controller for the leader car of a platoon moving in an Intelligent Vehicle Highway System (IVHS). Let us first briefly describe this system. Details on the design process can be found in [12]. In the leader mode all the vehicles inside a platoon follow the leader. We consider a platoon i and its preceding platoon $(i-1)$. Let v_i and a_i denote respectively the velocity and acceleration of platoon i, and d_i is its distance to platoon $(i-1)$. The most important task of a controller for the leader car of each platoon i is to maintain the distance d_i equal to a safety distance $D_i = \lambda_a a_i + \lambda_v v_i + \lambda_p$ (in the nominal operation $\lambda_a = 0$, $\lambda_v = 1sec$, and $\lambda_p = 10m$). Other tasks the controller should perform are to track an optimal velocity and trajectories for certain maneuvers. The dynamics of the system are as follows: $\dot{d_i} = v_{i-1} - v_i$, $\dot{v}_{i-1} = a_{i-1}$, $\dot{v}_i = a_i$, and $\dot{a}_i = u$, where u is the control. Without going into details, the controller for the leader car of platoon i proposed in [12] consists of 4 control laws u which are used in different regions of the state space. These regions are defined based on the values of the relative velocity $v_i^e = 100(v_{i-1} - v_i)/v_i$ and the error between the actual and the safe inter-platoon distances $e_i = d_i - D_i$. When the system changes from one region to another, the control law should change accordingly. The property we want to verify is that a collision between platoons never happens, that is, $d_i \geq 0$. Here, we focus only on two regions which are critical from a safety point of view: "track optimal velocity" ($v_i^e < 0$ and $e_i > 0$) and "track velocity of previous car" ($v_i^e < 0$ and $e_i < 0$). The respective control laws u_1 and u_2 are as follows:

$$u_1 = -d_i - 3v_{i-1} + (-3 - \lambda_v)v_i + -3a_i, \tag{6}$$
$$u_2 = 0.125d_i + 0.75v_{i-1} + (-0.75 + -0.125\lambda_v)v_i - 1.5a_i. \tag{7}$$

Note that these regions correspond to situations where the platoon in front moves slower and, moreover, the second region is particularly safety critical because the inter-platoon distance is smaller than desired.

We model this system by a hybrid automaton with 4 continuous variables (d_i, v_{i-1}, v_i, a_i) and two locations corresponding to the two regions. The continuous dynamics of each location is linear as specified above, with u specified by (6) and (7). To prove that the controller of the leader car of platoon i can guarantee that no collision happens regardless of the behavior of platoon $(i-1)$, a_{i-1} is treated as *uncertain input* with values in the interval $[a_{min}, a_{max}]$ where a_{min} and a_{max}

are the maximal deceleration and acceleration. The invariants of the locations are defined by the constraints on e_i and v_i^e and the bounds on the velocity and acceleration. The guards of the transitions between locations are the boundary of the invariants, i.e. $e_i = 0$ (for computational reasons the guards are "thickened", more precisely, the transitions are enabled when e_i is in some small interval $[-\varepsilon, \varepsilon]$). The bad set is specified as $d_i < 0$. To construct the discrete abstract system, in addition to the predicates of the invariants and guards we use two predicates $d_i \leq 0$ and $d_i \geq 2$ which allow to separate safe and unsafe states, and the total number of initial predicates are 17. For the initial set specified as $5 \leq d_i \leq 1000 \ \wedge \ 5 \leq v_{i-1} \leq 15 \ \wedge \ 18 \leq v_i \leq 30$, the tool found 16 reachable abstract states and reported that the system is safe. The computation took 4 minutes on a Pentium 2. For *individual continuous modes* this property has been proven in [22] using optimal control techniques.

5   Conclusions

We have presented foundations and an initial prototype implementation for automated verification of safety properties of hybrid systems by combining ideas from predicate abstraction and polyhedral approximation of reachable sets of linear continuous systems. We are excited about the promise of this approach, but additional research and experiments are needed to fully understand the scope of the method. Two research directions are of immediate importance. First, the number of abstract states grows exponentially with the number of linear predicates used for abstraction. We have presented a couple of heuristics that avoid examination of all abstract states while computing the successors of a given abstract state. However, more sophisticated methods that exploit the structure of abstract states are needed. Also, heuristics for guiding the search can be useful to avoid the expensive computation of successors. Second, we have solely relied on the intuition of the designer to obtain the initial set of predicates. If the predicate abstraction verification algorithm returns a counter-example, we cannot be sure that the found counter-example corresponds to a real counter-example in the concrete system. It may be a fake counter-example instead, due to missing predicates important for the verification of the property at hand. We are working on a second module that will check the validity of a counter-example, and analyze it to introduce additional predicates, if needed. We are also incorporating the verifier with the tool CHARON, a modeling and analysis environment for hierarchical hybrid systems [2].

Acknowledgments. This research was supported in part by DARPA ITO Mobies award F33615-00-C-1707 and by NSF ITR award. We thank the members of Penn's hybrid systems group for discussions and feedback.

References

1. R. Alur, C. Courcoubetis, N. Halbwachs, T.A. Henzinger, P. Ho, X. Nicollin, A. Olivero, J. Sifakis, and S. Yovine. The algorithmic analysis of hybrid systems. *Theoretical Computer Science*, 138:3–34, 1995.

2. R. Alur, T. Dang, J. Esposito, R. Fierro, Y. Hur, F. Ivančić, V. Kumar, I. Lee, P. Mishra, G. Pappas, and O. Sokolsky. Hierarchical hybrid modeling of embedded systems. In *Embedded Software, First Intern. Workshop*, LNCS 2211. 2001.
3. R. Alur, T. Henzinger, G. Lafferriere, and G. Pappas. Discrete abstractions of hybrid systems. *Proceedings of the IEEE*, 2000.
4. A. Annichini, E. Asarin, and A. Bouajjani. Symbolic techniques for parametric reasoning about counter and clock systems. In *Comp. Aided Verification*, 2000.
5. E. Asarin, O. Bournez, T. Dang, and O. Maler. Approximate reachability analysis of piecewise-linear dynamical systems. In *Hybrid Systems: Computation and Control, Third International Workshop*, LNCS 1790, pages 21–31. 2000.
6. T. Ball and S. Rajamani. Bebop: A symbolic model checker for boolean programs. In *SPIN 2000 Workshop on Model Checking of Software*, LNCS 1885. 2000.
7. A. Chutinan and B.K. Krogh. Verification of polyhedral-invariant hybrid automata using polygonal flow pipe approximations. In *Hybrid Systems: Computation and Control, Second International Workshop*, LNCS 1569, pages 76–90. 1999.
8. E.M. Clarke and R.P. Kurshan. Computer-aided verification. *IEEE Spectrum*, 33(6):61–67, 1996.
9. J.C. Corbett, M.B. Dwyer, J. Hatcliff, S. Laubach, C.S. Pasareanu, Robby, and H. Zheng. Bandera: Extracting finite-state models from Java source code. In *Proceedings of 22nd Intern. Conf. on Software Engineering*. 2000.
10. S. Das, D. Dill, and S. Park. Experience with predicate abstraction. In *Computer Aided Verification, 11th International Conference*, LNCS 1633, 1999.
11. C. Daws, A. Olivero, S. Tripakis, and S. Yovine. The tool KRONOS. In *Hybrid Systems III: Verification and Control*, LNCS 1066, 1996.
12. D. Godbole and J. Lygeros. Longitudinal control of a lead card of a platoon. *IEEE Transactions on Vehicular Technology*, 43(4):1125–1135, 1994.
13. S. Graf and H. Saidi. Construction of abstract state graphs with PVS. In *Proc. 9th Conference on Computer Aided Verification*, volume 1254, 1997.
14. M. Greenstreet and I. Mitchell. Reachability analysis using polygonal projections. In *Hybrid Systems: Computation and Control, Second Intern. Workshop*, LNCS 1569. 1999.
15. N. Halbwachs, Y. Proy, and P. Raymond. Verification of linear hybrid systems by means of convex approximations. In *Intern. Symposium on Static Analysis*, LNCS 864. 1994.
16. T.A. Henzinger, P. Ho, and H. Wong-Toi. HyTech: the next generation. In *Proceedings of the 16th IEEE Real-Time Systems Symposium*, pages 56–65, 1995.
17. G.J. Holzmann. The model checker SPIN. *IEEE Transactions on Software Engineering*, 23(5):279–295, 1997.
18. G.J. Holzmann and M.H. Smith. Automating software feature verification. *Bell Labs Technical Journal*, 5(2):72–87, 2000.
19. A. Kurzhanski and P. Varaiya. Ellipsoidal techniques for reachability analysis. In *Hybrid Systems:Computation and Control, Third Intern. Workshop*, LNCS 1790. 2000.
20. K. Larsen, P. Pettersson, and W. Yi. UPPAAL in a nutshell. *Springer International Journal of Software Tools for Technology Transfer*, 1, 1997.
21. I. Mitchell and C. Tomlin. Level set methods for computation in hybrid systems. In *Hybrid Systems:Computation and Control, Third Intern. Workshop*, volume LNCS 1790. 2000.
22. A. Puri and P. Varaiya. Driving safely in smart cars. Technical Report UBC-ITS-PRR-95-24, California PATH, University of California in Berkeley, July 1995.

Towards Computing Phase Portraits of Polygonal Differential Inclusions*

Eugene Asarin, Gerardo Schneider, and Sergio Yovine

VERIMAG
2 Av. Vignate, 38610 Gières, France
{asarin,gerardo,yovine}@imag.fr

Abstract. Polygonal hybrid systems are a subclass of planar hybrid automata which can be represented by piecewise constant differential inclusions. Here, we study the problem of defining and constructing the phase portrait of such systems. We identify various important elements of it, such as viability and controllability kernels, and propose an algorithm for computing them all. The algorithm is based on a geometric analysis of trajectories.

1 Introduction

Given a (hybrid) dynamical system one can ask whether a point (or set) is reachable from another, or one can ask for a full qualitative picture of the system (say, its phase portrait). An answer to the second question provides very useful information about the behavior of the system such as "every trajectory except the equilibrium point in the origin converges to a limit cycle which is the unit circle". The reachability question has been an important and extensively studied research problem in the hybrid systems community. However, there have been very few results on the qualitative properties of trajectories of hybrid systems [1,3,5,7,8,9,10]. In particular, the question of defining and constructing phase portraits of hybrid systems has not been directly addressed except in [9], where phase portraits of deterministic systems with piecewise constant derivatives are explored.

In this paper we study phase portraits of polygonal hybrid systems (or, SPDIs), a class of nondeterministic systems that correspond to piecewise constant differential inclusions on the plane (Fig. 1). It is not a priori clear what the phase portraits of such systems exactly are. To begin with, we concentrate on studying the qualitative behavior of sets of trajectories having the same cyclic pattern. In [1], we have given a classification of cyclic behaviors. Here, we rely on this information to more deeply study the qualitative behavior of the system. In particular, we are able to compute the *viability* kernel [2,4] of the cycle, that is, the set of points which can keep rotating in the cycle forever. We show that this kernel is a non-convex polygon (often with a hole in the middle) and give a

---

* Partially supported by Projet IMAG MASH "Modélisation et Analyse de Systèmes Hybrides".

C.J. Tomlin and M.R. Greenstreet (Eds.): HSCC 2002, LNCS 2289, pp. 49–61, 2002.
© Springer-Verlag Berlin Heidelberg 2002

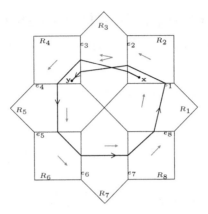

Fig. 1. An SPDI and its trajectory segment.

non-iterative algorithm for computing the coordinates of its vertices and edges. Clearly, the viability kernel provides useful insight about the behavior of the SPDI around the cycle. Furthermore, we are also (and even more) interested in the limit behaviors. We introduce a notion of *controllability* kernel, a cyclic polygonal stripe within which a trajectory can reach any point from any point. We show how to compute it and argue that this is a good analog of the notion of limit cycle. Indeed, we prove that the distance between any infinite trajectory performing forever the same cyclic pattern and the controllability kernel always converges to zero.

In section 4 we show that any simple (without self-crossings) infinite trajectory converges to one of those "limit cycles" (controllability kernels). We conclude that controllability kernels are important elements of the phase portrait of an SPDI yielding an analog of Poincaré-Bendixson theorem for simple trajectories. We apply all these results to compute (elements of) the phase portrait by enumerating all the feasible cyclic patterns and computing its viability and controllability kernels. We also discuss difficulties related to self-crossing trajectories, which can, for example, randomly walk in two adjacent controllability kernels.

2   Preliminaries

2.1   Truncated Affine Multivalued Functions

A (positive) *affine* function $f : \mathbb{R} \to \mathbb{R}$ is such that $f(x) = ax + b$ with $a > 0$. An *affine multivalued* function $F : \mathbb{R} \to 2^{\mathbb{R}}$, denoted $F = \langle f_l, f_u \rangle$, is defined by $F(x) = \langle f_l(x), f_u(x) \rangle$ where f_l and f_u are affine and $\langle \cdot, \cdot \rangle$ denotes an interval. For notational convenience, we do not make explicit whether intervals are open, closed, left-open or right-open, unless required for comprehension. For an interval $I = \langle l, u \rangle$ we have that $F(\langle l, u \rangle) = \langle f_l(l), f_u(u) \rangle$. The inverse of F is defined by

$F^{-1}(x) = \{y \mid x \in F(y)\}$. It is not difficult to show that $F^{-1} = \langle f_u^{-1}, f_l^{-1} \rangle$. These classes of functions are closed under composition.

A *truncated affine multivalued* function (TAMF) $\mathcal{F} : \mathbb{R} \rightarrow 2^{\mathbb{R}}$ is defined by an affine multivalued function F and intervals $S \subseteq \mathbb{R}^+$ and $J \subseteq \mathbb{R}^+$ as follows: $\mathcal{F}(x) = F(x) \cap J$ if $x \in S$, otherwise $\mathcal{F}(x) = \emptyset$. For convenience we write $\mathcal{F}(x) = F(\{x\} \cap S) \cap J$. For an interval I, $\mathcal{F}(I) = F(I \cap S) \cap J$ and $\mathcal{F}^{-1}(I) = F^{-1}(I \cap J) \cap S$. We say that $\mathcal{F}$ is *normalized* if $S = \mathsf{Dom}\mathcal{F} = \{x \mid F(x) \cap J \neq \emptyset\}$ (thus, $S \subseteq F^{-1}(J)$) and $J = \mathsf{Im}\mathcal{F} = \mathcal{F}(S)$.

The following theorem states that TAMFs are closed under composition [1].

Theorem 1. The composition of two TAMFs $\mathcal{F}_1(I) = F_1(I \cap S_1) \cap J_1$ and $\mathcal{F}_2(I) = F_2(I \cap S_2) \cap J_2$, is the TAMF $(\mathcal{F}_2 \circ \mathcal{F}_1)(I) = \mathcal{F}(I) = F(I \cap S) \cap J$, where $F = F_2 \circ F_1$, $S = S_1 \cap F_1^{-1}(J_1 \cap S_2)$ and $J = J_2 \cap F_2(J_1 \cap S_2)$.

2.2 SPDI

An *angle* $\angle_{\mathbf{a}}^{\mathbf{b}}$ on the plane, defined by two non-zero vectors $\mathbf{a}, \mathbf{b}$ is the set of all positive linear combinations $\mathbf{x} = \alpha \, \mathbf{a} + \beta \, \mathbf{b}$, with $\alpha, \beta \geq 0$, and $\alpha + \beta > 0$. We can always assume that $\mathbf{b}$ is situated in the counter-clockwise direction from $\mathbf{a}$.

A *simple planar differential inclusion* (SPDI) is defined by giving a finite partition $\mathbb{P}$ of the plane into convex polygonal sets, and associating with each $P \in \mathbb{P}$ a couple of vectors $\mathbf{a}_P$ and $\mathbf{b}_P$. Let $\phi(P) = \angle_{\mathbf{a}_P}^{\mathbf{b}_P}$. The SPDI is $\dot{\mathbf{x}} \in \phi(P)$ for $\mathbf{x} \in P$.

Let $E(P)$ be the set of edges of P. We say that e is an *entry* of P if for all $\mathbf{x} \in e$ and for all $\mathbf{c} \in \phi(P)$, $\mathbf{x} + \mathbf{c}\epsilon \in P$ for some $\epsilon > 0$. We say that e is an *exit* of P if the same condition holds for some $\epsilon < 0$. We denote by $in(P) \subseteq E(P)$ the set of all entries of P and by $out(P) \subseteq E(P)$ the set of all exits of P.

Assumption 1 *All the edges in $E(P)$ are either entries or exits, that is, $E(P) = in(P) \cup out(P)$.*

Example 1. Consider the SPDI illustrated in Fig. 1. For each region R_i, $1 \leq i \leq 8$, there is a pair of vectors $(\mathbf{a}_i, \mathbf{b}_i)$, where: $\mathbf{a}_1 = \mathbf{b}_1 = (1, 5)$, $\mathbf{a}_2 = \mathbf{b}_2 = (-1, \frac{1}{2})$, $\mathbf{a}_3 = (-1, \frac{11}{60})$ and $\mathbf{b}_3 = (-1, -\frac{1}{4})$, $\mathbf{a}_4 = \mathbf{b}_4 = (-1, -1)$, $\mathbf{a}_5 = \mathbf{b}_5 = (0, -1)$, $\mathbf{a}_6 = \mathbf{b}_6 = (1, -1)$, $\mathbf{a}_7 = \mathbf{b}_7 = (1, 0)$, $\mathbf{a}_8 = \mathbf{b}_8 = (1, 1)$. ∎

A *trajectory segment* of an SPDI is a continuous function $\xi : [0, T] \rightarrow \mathbb{R}^2$ which is smooth everywhere except in a discrete set of points, and such that for all $t \in [0, T]$, if $\xi(t) \in P$ and $\dot{\xi}(t)$ is defined then $\dot{\xi}(t) \in \phi(P)$. The *signature*, denoted $\mathsf{Sig}(\xi)$, is the ordered sequence of edges traversed by the trajectory segment, that is, $e_1, e_2, \ldots$, where $\xi(t_i) \in e_i$ and $t_i < t_{i+1}$. If $T = \infty$, a trajectory segment is called a *trajectory*.

Assumption 2 *We will only consider trajectories with infinite signatures.*

2.3   Successors and Predecessors

Given an SPDI, we fix a one-dimensional coordinate system on each edge to represent points laying on edges [1]. For notational convenience, we indistinctly use letter e to denote the edge or its one-dimensional representation. Accordingly, we write $\mathbf{x} \in e$ or $x \in e$, to mean "point $\mathbf{x}$ in edge e with coordinate x in the one-dimensional coordinate system of e". The same convention is applied to sets of points of e represented as intervals (e.g., $\mathbf{x} \in I$ or $x \in I$, where $I \subseteq e$) and to trajectories (e.g., "ξ starting in x" or "ξ starting in $\mathbf{x}$").

Now, let $P \in \mathbb{P}$, $e \in in(P)$ and $e' \in out(P)$. For $I \subseteq e$, $\mathsf{Succ}_{e,e'}(I)$ is the set of all points in e' reachable from some point in I by a trajectory segment $\xi : [0,t] \to \mathbb{R}^2$ in P (i.e., $\xi(0) \in I \wedge \xi(t) \in e' \wedge \mathsf{Sig}(\xi) = ee'$). We have shown in [1] that $\mathsf{Succ}_{e,e'}$ is a TAMF[1].

Example 2. Let $e_1, \ldots, e_8$ be as in Fig. 1 and $I = [l, u]$. We assume a one-dimensional coordinate system such that $e_i = S_i = J_i = (0, 1)$. We have that:

$$F_{e_1 e_2}(I) = \left[\frac{l}{2}, \frac{u}{2}\right] \quad F_{e_2 e_3}(I) = \left[l - \frac{1}{4}, u + \frac{11}{60}\right]$$

$$F_{e_i e_{i+1}}(I) = I \quad 3 \leq i \leq 7 \quad F_{e_8 e_1}(I) = \left[l + \frac{1}{5}, u + \frac{1}{5}\right]$$

with $\mathsf{Succ}_{e_i e_{i+1}}(I) = F_{e_i e_{i+1}}(I \cap S_i) \cap J_{i+1}$, for $1 \leq i \leq 7$, and $\mathsf{Succ}_{e_8 e_1}(I) = F_{e_8 e_1}(I \cap S_8) \cap J_1$. ∎

Given a sequence $w = e_1, e_2, \ldots, e_n$, Theorem 1 implies that the successor of I along w defined as $\mathsf{Succ}_w(I) = \mathsf{Succ}_{e_{n-1}, e_n} \circ \ldots \circ \mathsf{Succ}_{e_1, e_2}(I)$ is a TAMF.

Example 3. Let $\sigma = e_1 \cdots e_8 e_1$. We have that $\mathsf{Succ}_\sigma(I) = F(I \cap S) \cap J$, where:

$$F(I) = \left[\frac{l}{2} - \frac{1}{20}, \frac{u}{2} + \frac{23}{60}\right] \tag{1}$$

$S = (0, 1)$ and $J = (\frac{1}{5}, 1)$ are computed using Theorem 1. ∎

For $I \subseteq e'$, $\mathsf{Pre}_{e,e'}(I)$ is the set of points in e that can reach a point in I by a trajectory segment in P. We have that[1]: $\mathsf{Pre}_{e,e'} = \mathsf{Succ}_{e,e'}^{-1}$ and $\mathsf{Pre}_\sigma = \mathsf{Succ}_\sigma^{-1}$.

Example 4. Let $\sigma = e_1 \ldots e_8 e_1$ be as in Fig. 1 and $I = [l, u]$. We have that $\mathsf{Pre}_{e_i e_{i+1}}(I) = F_{e_i e_{i+1}}^{-1}(I \cap J_{i+1}) \cap S_i$, for $1 \leq i \leq 7$, and $\mathsf{Pre}_{e_8 e_1}(I) = F_{e_8 e_1}^{-1}(I \cap J_1) \cap S_8$, where:

$$F_{e_1 e_2}^{-1}(I) = [2l, 2u] \quad F_{e_2 e_3}^{-1}(I) = \left[l - \frac{11}{60}, u + \frac{1}{4}\right]$$

$$F_{e_i e_{i+1}}^{-1}(I) = I \quad 3 \leq i \leq 7 \quad F_{e_8 e_1}^{-1}(I) = \left[l - \frac{1}{5}, u - \frac{1}{5}\right]$$

Besides, $\mathsf{Pre}_\sigma(I) = F^{-1}(I \cap J) \cap S$, where $F^{-1}(I) = [2l - \frac{23}{30}, 2u + \frac{1}{10}]$. ∎

---

[1] In [1] we explain how to choose the positive direction on every edge in order to guarantee positive coefficients in the TAMF.

3   Qualitative Analysis of Simple Edge-Cycles

Let $\sigma = e_1 \cdots e_k e_1$ be a simple edge-cycle, i.e., $e_i \neq e_j$ for all $1 \leq i \neq j \leq k$. Let $\mathsf{Succ}_\sigma(I) = F(I \cap S) \cap J$ with $F = \langle f_l, f_u \rangle$ (we suppose that this representation is normalized). We denote by $\mathcal{D}_\sigma$ the one-dimensional discrete-time dynamical system defined by Succ_σ, that is $x_{n+1} \in \mathsf{Succ}_\sigma(x_n)$.

Assumption 3 *None of the two functions f_l, f_u is the identity.*

Let l^* and u^* be the fixpoints[2] of f_l and f_u, respectively, and $S \cap J = \langle L, U \rangle$. We have shown in [1] that a simple cycle is of one of the following types:

STAY. The cycle is not abandoned neither by the leftmost nor the rightmost trajectory, that is, $L \leq l^* \leq u^* \leq U$.

DIE. The rightmost trajectory exits the cycle through the left (consequently the leftmost one also exits) or the leftmost trajectory exits the cycle through the right (consequently the rightmost one also exits), that is, $u^* < L \vee l^* > U$.

EXIT-BOTH. The leftmost trajectory exits the cycle through the left and the rightmost one through the right, that is, $l^* < L \wedge u^* > U$.

EXIT-LEFT. The leftmost trajectory exits the cycle (through the left) but the rightmost one stays inside, that is, $l^* < L \leq u^* \leq U$.

EXIT-RIGHT. The rightmost trajectory exits the cycle (through the right) but the leftmost one stays inside, that is, $L \leq l^* \leq U < u^*$.

Example 5. Let $\sigma = e_1 \cdots e_8 e_1$. We have that $S \cap J = \langle L, U \rangle = (\frac{1}{5}, 1)$. The fixpoints of Eq. (1) are such that $l^* = -\frac{1}{10} < \frac{1}{5} < u^* = \frac{23}{30} < 1$. Thus, σ is EXIT-LEFT.   ∎

The classification above gives us some information about the qualitative behavior of trajectories. Any trajectory that enters a cycle of type DIE will eventually quit it after a finite number of turns. If the cycle is of type STAY, all trajectories that happen to enter it will keep turning inside it forever. In all other cases, some trajectories will turn for a while and then exit, and others will continue turning forever. This information is very useful for solving the reachability problem [1].

Example 6. Consider again the cycle $\sigma = e_1 \cdots e_8 e_1$. Fig. 2 shows part of the reach set of the interval $[0.6, 0.65] \subset e_1$. Notice that the leftmost trajectory exits the cycle in the third turn while the rightmost one shifts to the right and "converges to" the limit $u^* = \frac{23}{30}$. Clearly, no point in $[0.6, 0.65]$ will ever reach a point of e_1 smaller than $L = \frac{1}{5}$ or bigger than u^*. Fig. 2 has been automatically generated by the SPeeDi toolbox we have developed for reachability analysis of SPDIs based on the results of [1].   ∎

The above result does not allow us to directly answer other questions about the behavior of the SPDI such as determine for a given point (or set of points)

---

[2] Obviously, the fixpoint x^* is computed by solving a linear equation $f(x^*) = x^*$.

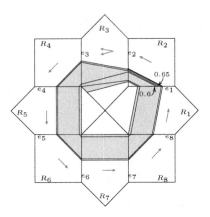

Fig. 2. Reachability analysis.

whether: (a) there exists (at least) one trajectory that remains in the cycle, and (b) it is possible to control the system to reach any other point. In order to do this, we need to further study the properties of the system around simple edge-cycles.

3.1   Viability Kernel

Let $K \subset \mathbb{R}^2$. A trajectory ξ is *viable* in K if $\xi(t) \in K$ for all $t \geq 0$. K is a *viability domain* if for every $\mathbf{x} \in K$, there exists at least one trajectory ξ, with $\xi(0) = \mathbf{x}$, which is viable in K. The *viability kernel* of K, denoted $\mathsf{Viab}(K)$, is the largest viability domain contained in K^3. The same concepts can be defined for $\mathcal{D}_\sigma$, by setting that a trajectory $x_0 x_1 \ldots$ of $\mathcal{D}_\sigma$ is viable in an interval $I \subseteq \mathbb{R}$, if $x_i \in I$ for all $i \geq 0$.

Theorem 2. *For $\mathcal{D}_\sigma$, if σ is not DIE then $\mathsf{Viab}(e_1) = S$, else $\mathsf{Viab}(e_1) = \emptyset$.*[4]

The viability kernel for the continuous-time system can be now found by propagating S from e_1 using the following operator.

For $I \subseteq e_1$ let us define $\overline{\mathsf{Pre}}_\sigma(I)$ as the set of all $\mathbf{x} \in \mathbb{R}^2$ for which there exists a trajectory segment ξ starting in $\mathbf{x}$, that reaches some point in I, such that $\mathsf{Sig}(\xi)$ is a suffix of $e_2 \ldots e_k e_1$. It is easy to see that $\overline{\mathsf{Pre}}_\sigma(I)$ is a polygonal subset of the plane which can be calculated using the following procedure. First define

$$\overline{\mathsf{Pre}}_e(I) = \{\mathbf{x} \mid \exists \xi : [0, t] \to \mathbb{R}^2, t > 0 \,.\, \xi(0) = \mathbf{x} \wedge \xi(t) \in I \wedge \mathsf{Sig}(\xi) = e\}$$

and apply this operation k times: $\overline{\mathsf{Pre}}_\sigma(I) = \bigcup_{i=1}^{k} \overline{\mathsf{Pre}}_{e_i}(I_i)$ with $I_1 = I$, $I_k = \mathsf{Pre}_{e_k, e_1}(I_1)$ and $I_i = \mathsf{Pre}_{e_i, e_{i+1}}(I_{i+1})$, for $2 \leq i \leq k - 1$.

---

[3] We do not define the viability kernel to be closed as in [2].
[4] Notice that this theorem can be used to compute $\mathsf{Viab}(I)$ for any $I \subseteq e_1$.

Now, let

$$K_\sigma = \bigcup_{i=1}^{k} (int(P_i) \cup e_i) \qquad (2)$$

where P_i is such that $e_{i-1} \in in(P_i)$, $e_i \in out(P_i)$ and $int(P_i)$ is the interior of P_i.

Theorem 3. *If σ is not DIE,* $\mathsf{Viab}(K_\sigma) = \overline{\mathsf{Pre}}_\sigma(S)$, *otherwise* $\mathsf{Viab}(K_\sigma) = \emptyset$.

This result provides a non-iterative algorithmic procedure for computing the viability kernel of K_σ.

Example 7. Let $\sigma = e_1 \ldots e_8 e_1$. Fig. 3 depicts: (a) K_σ, and (b) $\overline{\mathsf{Pre}}_\sigma(S)$ ∎

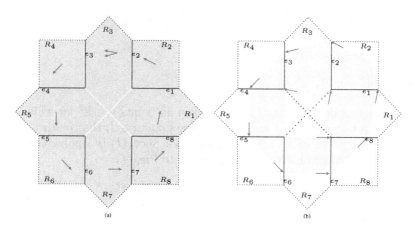

Fig. 3. Viability kernel.

3.2   Controllability Kernel

We say $K \subset \mathbb{R}^2$ is *controllable* if for any two points $\mathbf{x}$ and $\mathbf{y}$ in K there exists a trajectory segment ξ starting in $\mathbf{x}$ that reaches an arbitrarily small neighborhood of $\mathbf{y}$ without leaving K. More formally, K is controllable iff $\forall \mathbf{x}, \mathbf{y} \in K, \forall \delta > 0, \exists \xi : [0,t] \to \mathbb{R}^2, t > 0 . (\xi(0) = \mathbf{x} \wedge |\xi(t) - \mathbf{y}| < \delta \wedge \forall t' \in [0,t] . \xi(t') \in K)$. The *controllability kernel* of K, denoted $\mathsf{Cntr}(K)$, is the largest controllable subset of K. The same notions can be defined for the discrete dynamical system $\mathcal{D}_\sigma$.

Define

$$\mathcal{C}_\mathcal{D}(\sigma) = \begin{cases} \langle L, U \rangle & \text{if } \sigma \text{ is EXIT-BOTH} \\ \langle L, u^* \rangle & \text{if } \sigma \text{ is EXIT-LEFT} \\ \langle l^*, U \rangle & \text{if } \sigma \text{ is EXIT-RIGHT} \\ \langle l^*, u^* \rangle & \text{if } \sigma \text{ is STAY} \\ \emptyset & \text{if } \sigma \text{ is DIE} \end{cases} \qquad (3)$$

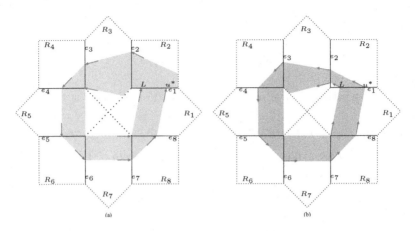

Fig. 4. Predecessors and successors of a simple cycle.

Theorem 4. *For $\mathcal{D}_\sigma$, $\mathcal{C}_\mathcal{D}(\sigma) = \mathsf{Cntr}(S)$.*

For $I \subseteq e_1$ let us define $\overline{\mathsf{Succ}}_\sigma(I)$ as the set of all points $\mathbf{y} \in \mathbb{R}^2$ for which there exists a trajectory segment ξ starting in some point $x \in I$, that reaches $\mathbf{y}$, such that $\mathsf{Sig}(\xi)$ is a prefix of $e_1 \ldots e_k$. The successor $\overline{\mathsf{Succ}}_\sigma(I)$ is a polygonal subset of the plane which can be computed similarly to $\overline{\mathsf{Pre}}_\sigma(I)$.

Example 8. Let $\sigma = e_1 \cdots e_8 e_1$. Fig. 4 depicts: (a) $\overline{\mathsf{Pre}}_\sigma(L, u^*)$, (b) $\overline{\mathsf{Succ}}_\sigma(L, u^*)$, with $L = \frac{1}{5} < u^* = \frac{23}{30}$. ∎

Define

$$\mathcal{C}(\sigma) = (\overline{\mathsf{Succ}}_\sigma \cap \overline{\mathsf{Pre}}_\sigma)(\mathcal{C}_\mathcal{D}(\sigma)) \tag{4}$$

Theorem 5. $\mathcal{C}(\sigma) = \mathsf{Cntr}(K_\sigma)$.

This result provides a non-iterative algorithmic procedure for computing the controllability kernel of K_σ.

Example 9. Let $\sigma = e_1 \cdots e_8 e_1$. Recall that σ is EXIT-LEFT with $L = \frac{1}{5} < u^* = \frac{23}{30}$. Fig. 5(a) depicts $\mathsf{Cntr}(K_\sigma)$. ∎

Convergence. A trajectory ξ *converges* to a set $K \subset \mathbb{R}^2$ if $\lim_{t \to \infty} dist(\xi(t), K) = 0$. For $\mathcal{D}_\sigma$, convergence is defined as $\lim_{n \to \infty} dist(\xi_n, I) = 0$. The following result says that the controllability kernel $\mathcal{C}_\mathcal{D}(\sigma)$ can be considered to be a kind of (weak) limit cycle of $\mathcal{D}_\sigma$.

Theorem 6. *For $\mathcal{D}_\sigma$, any viable trajectory in S converges to $\mathcal{C}_\mathcal{D}(\sigma)$.*

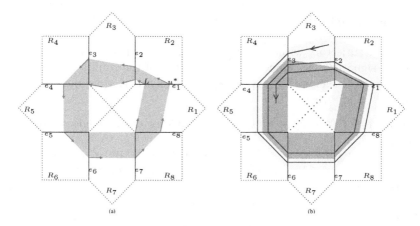

Fig. 5. Controllability kernel of a simple cycle.

Furthermore, $\mathcal{C}(\sigma)$ can be regarded as a (weak) limit cycle of the SPDI. The following result is a direct consequence of Theorem 3 and Theorem 6.

Theorem 7. *Any viable trajectory in K_σ converges to $\mathcal{C}(\sigma)$.*

Example 10. Fig. 5(b) shows a trajectory with signature $\sigma = e_1 \cdots e_8 e_1$ which is viable in K_σ and converges to $\mathcal{C}(\sigma)$. ∎

STAY cycles. The controllability kernels of STAY-cycles have stronger limit cycle properties. We say that K is *invariant* if for any $x \in K$, every trajectory starting in x is viable in K. The following result is a corollary of the previous theorems.

Corollary 1. *Let σ be STAY. Then,*
(1) $\mathcal{C}(\sigma)$ is invariant.
(2) There exists a neighborhood K of $\mathcal{C}(\sigma)$ such that any viable trajectory starting in K converges to $\mathcal{C}(\sigma)$.

Fixpoints. Here we give an alternative characterization of the controllability kernel of a cycle in SPDI. As in [7], let us call a point x in e_1 a *fixpoint* iff $x \in \mathsf{Succ}_\sigma(x)$. We call a point $\mathbf{x} \in K_\sigma$ a *periodic point* iff there exists a trajectory segment ξ starting and ending in $\mathbf{x}$, such that $\mathsf{Sig}(\xi)$ is a cyclic shift of σ (hence, there exists also an infinite periodic trajectory passing through x). The following result is a corollary of the previous theorems and definitions.

Corollary 2. *For SPDIs,*
(1) $\mathcal{C}_\mathcal{D}(\sigma)$ is the set of all the fixpoints in e_1.
(2) $\mathcal{C}(\sigma)$ is the set of all the periodic points in K_σ.

4   Phase Portrait

Let ξ be any trajectory without self-crossings. Recall that ξ is assumed to have an infinite signature. An immediate consequence of the results proven in [1] is that $\mathsf{Sig}(\xi)$ can be canonically expressed as a sequence of edges and cycles of the form $r_1 s_1^* \ldots r_n s_n^\omega$, where

1. For all $1 \leq i \leq n$, r_i is a sequence of pairwise different edges, and s_i is a simple cycle.
2. For all $1 \leq i \neq j \leq n$, r_i and r_j are disjoint, and s_i and s_j are different.
3. For all $1 \leq i \leq n-1$, s_i is repeated a finite number of times.
4. s_n is repeated forever.

Hence,

Theorem 8. *Every trajectory with infinite signature which does not have self-crossings converges to the controllability kernel of some simple edge-cycle.*

Corollary 3.   *1. Any trajectory ξ with infinite signature without self-crossings is such that its limit set $\mathrm{limit}(\xi)$ is a subset of the controllability kernel $\mathcal{C}(\sigma)$ of a simple edge-cycle σ.*
2. Any point in $\mathcal{C}(\sigma)$ is a limit point of a trajectory ξ with infinite signature without self-crossings

We conclude that controllability kernels are important elements of the phase portrait of an SPDI yielding an analog of Poincaré-Bendixson theorem for simple trajectories. Moreover, all such components of the phase portrait can be algorithmically constructed. Indeed, since there are finitely many simple cycles, the following algorithm computes all the limit sets and their attraction basins for such kind of trajectories:

for each simple cycle σ **compute** $\mathcal{C}(\sigma)$, $\overline{\mathsf{Pre}}_\sigma(S)$

Example 11. Fig. 6 shows an SPDI with two edge cycles $\sigma_1 = e_1, \cdots, e_8, e_1$ and $\sigma_2 = e_{10}, \cdots, e_{15}, e_{10}$, and their respective controllability kernels. Every simple trajectory eventually arrives (or converges) to one of the two limit sets and rotates therein forever.   ∎

Self-crossing trajectories. Actually, the previous example illustrates the difficulties that arise when exploring the limit behavior of self-crossing trajectories of an SPDI. The figure shows that there exist infinite self-crossing (and even periodic) trajectories that keep switching between the two cycles forever. In this particular case, it can be shown that all trajectories converge to the "joint controllability kernel" $\mathsf{Cntr}(K_{\sigma_1} \cup K_{\sigma_2})$ which turns out to be $\mathcal{C}(\sigma_1) \cup \mathcal{C}(\sigma_2)$[5]. However, the analysis of limit behaviors of self-cutting trajectories in the general case is considerably more difficult and challenging.

---

[5] The cross-shaped region is the bridge between the two cycles.

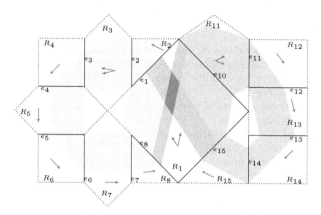

Fig. 6. Another SPDI and its "phase-portrait".

5   Concluding Remarks

The contribution of this paper is an automatic procedure to analyze the qualitative behavior of non-deterministic planar hybrid systems. Our algorithm enumerates all the "limit cycles" (i.e., controllability kernels) and their local basins of attraction (i.e., viability kernels).

Our analysis technique for a single cycle is very similar to the one used in [7] for n-dimensional systems. However, for polygonal systems, we are able to prove further properties such as controllability of and convergence to the set of fixpoints, and that there are only a finite number of them. These results are the analog of Poincaré-Bendixson for polygonal differential inclusions. The difference with [9] is that our results hold for non-deterministic systems.

This work is a first step in the direction of finding an algorithm for automatically constructing the complete phase portrait of an SPDI. This would require identifying and analyzing other useful structures such as stable and unstable manifolds, orbits (generated by identity Poincaré maps), bifurcation points (resulting of the non-deterministic qualitative behavior at the vertices of the polygons), limit behaviors of self-intersecting trajectories, etc.

We are currently developing a tool for qualitative analysis of SPDIs. The tool already implements the reachability algorithm published in [1] as well as most of the basic functionalities required for constructing the phase portrait. We have used it to analyze (though not completely automatically) all the examples of this paper.

Acknowledgments. We are thankful to S. Bornot, J. Della Dora, P. Varaiya for the valuable discussions. We thank G. Pace for his contribution to the development of the tool.

References

1. E. Asarin, G. Schneider and S. Yovine On the decidability of the reachability problem for planar differential inclusions. In *HSCC'01*. LNCS 2034, 2001. Springer.
2. J-P. Aubin. A survey on viability theory. SIAM J. Control and Optimization vol. **28**, 4 (1990) 749–789.
3. J-P. Aubin. The substratum of impulse and hybrid control systems. In *HSCC'01*. LNCS 2034, 2001. Springer.
4. J-P. Aubin and A. Cellina. Differential Inclusions. A Series of Comprehensive Studies in Mathematics **264** (1984). Springer.
5. A. Deshpande and P. Varaiya. Viable control of hybrid systems. In Hybrid Systems II, 128–147, LNCS 999, 1995. Springer.
6. M. W. Hirsch and S. Smale. Differential Equations, Dynamical Systems and Linear Algebra. (1974) Academic Press Inc.
7. M. Kourjanski and P. Varaiya. Stability of Hybrid Systems. In Hybrid Systems III, 413–423, LNCS 1066, 1995. Springer.
8. P. Kowalczyk and M. di Bernardo. On a novel class of bifurcations in hybrid dynamical systems. In *HSCC'01*. LNCS 2034, 2001. Springer.
9. A. Matveev and A. Savkin. Qualitative theory of hybrid dynamical systems. (2000) Birkhäuser Boston.
10. S. Simić, K. Johansson, S. Sastry and J. Lygeros. Towards a geometric theory of hybrid systems. In *HSCC'00*. LNCS 1790, 2000. Springer.

A   Appendix

Let $\sigma = e_1 \cdots e_k e_1$ be a simple edge-cycle, i.e., $e_i \neq e_j$ for all $1 \leq i \neq j \leq k$. Let $\mathsf{Succ}_\sigma(I) = F(I \cap S) \cap J$ with $F = \langle f_l, f_u \rangle$ (we suppose that this representation is normalized). We denote by $\mathcal{D}_\sigma$ the one-dimensional discrete-time dynamical system defined by Succ_σ, that is $x_{n+1} \in \mathsf{Succ}_\sigma(x_n)$. For $x \in \mathbb{R}$ and $I \subset \mathbb{R}$, $x < I$ means that $x < y$ for all $y \in I$.

Theorem 2 *For $\mathcal{D}_\sigma$, if σ is not DIE then $\mathsf{Viab}(e_1) = S$, otherwise $\mathsf{Viab}(e_1) = \emptyset$.*
Proof. If σ is DIE, $\mathcal{D}_\sigma$ has no trajectories. Therefore, $\mathsf{Viab}(e_1) = \emptyset$.
Let σ be not DIE. We first prove that any viability domain is a subset of S: Let I be a viability domain. Then, for all $x \in I$, there exists a trajectory starting in x which is viable in I. Then, $x \in \mathsf{DomSucc}_\sigma = S$. Thus, $I \subseteq S$.
Now, let us prove that S is a viability domain: It suffices to show that for all $x \in S$, $\mathsf{Succ}_\sigma(x) \cap S \neq \emptyset$.
Let $x \in S$.
If σ is STAY, we have that both l^* and u^* belong to $S \cap J$. It follows that both $f_l(x)$ and $f_u(x)$ are in S.
If σ is EXIT-LEFT, we have that $l^* < S \cap J$ and $u^* \in S \cap J$. Then, $f_u(x) \in S$.
If σ is EXIT-RIGHT, we have that $l^* \in S \cap J$ and $u^* > S \cap J$. Then, $f_l(x) \in S$.
If σ is EXIT-BOTH, we have that $l^* < S \cap J$ and $u^* > S \cap J$. If $x \in J$: then $x \in F(x)$. If $x < J$: then $f_l(x) < x < S \cap J$, and either $f_u(x) \in S \cap J$ or $f_u(x) > S \cap J$ (the other case yields a contradiction). If $x > J$: similar to the previous case.
Thus, for all $x \in S$, $\mathsf{Succ}_\sigma(x) \cap S \neq \emptyset$.
Hence, $\mathsf{Viab}(e_1) = S$. $\qquad\qquad\qquad\qquad\qquad\qquad\qquad\qquad\qquad\qquad\qquad\quad$ □

Theorem 3 *If σ is not DIE,* $\text{Viab}(K_\sigma) = \overline{\text{Pre}}_\sigma(S)$, *otherwise* $\text{Viab}(K_\sigma) = \emptyset$.
Proof: If σ is DIE, trivially $\text{Viab}(K_\sigma) = \emptyset$.
Let σ be not DIE. We first prove that any viability domain K, with $K \subseteq K_\sigma$, is a subset of $\overline{\text{Pre}}_\sigma(S)$: Let $\mathbf{x} \in K$. Then, there exists a trajectory ξ such that $\xi(0) = \mathbf{x}$ and for all $t \geq 0$, $\xi(t) \in K$. Clearly, the sequence $x_1 x_2 \ldots$ of the intersections of ξ with e_1 is a trajectory of $\mathcal{D}_\sigma$. Then, by Theorem 2, $x_i \in S$ for all $i \geq 1$. Thus, $\mathbf{x} \in \overline{\text{Pre}}_\sigma(S)$.
It remains to prove that $\overline{\text{Pre}}_\sigma(S)$ is a viability domain. Let $\mathbf{x} \in \overline{\text{Pre}}_\sigma(S)$. Then, there exists a trajectory segment $\bar{\xi} : [0, T] \to \mathbb{R}^2$ such that $\bar{\xi}(T) \in S$ and $\text{Sig}(\bar{\xi})$ is a suffix of σ. Theorem 2 implies that $\bar{\xi}(T)$ is the initial state of some trajectory ξ with $\text{Sig}(\xi) = \sigma^\omega$. It is straightforward to show that for all $t \geq 0$, $\xi(t) \in \overline{\text{Pre}}_\sigma(S)$. Concatenating $\bar{\xi}$ and ξ, we obtain a viable trajectory starting in $\mathbf{x}$.
Hence, $\text{Viab}(K_\sigma) = \overline{\text{Pre}}_\sigma(S)$. □

Theorem 4 *For $\mathcal{D}_\sigma$,* $\mathcal{C}_\mathcal{D}(\sigma) = \text{Cntr}(S)$.
Proof. Controllability of $\mathcal{C}_\mathcal{D}(\sigma)$ follows from the reachability result in [1]. To prove that $\mathcal{C}_\mathcal{D}(\sigma)$ is maximal we reason by contradiction. Suppose it is not. Then, there should exist a controllable set $C \supset \mathcal{C}_\mathcal{D}(\sigma)$. Since $C \subseteq S \cap J$, there should exist $y \in C$ such that either $y < l^*$, or $y > u^*$. In any case, controllability implies that for all $l^* < x < u^*$, there exists a trajectory segment starting in x that reaches an arbitrarily small neighborhood of y. From [1] we know that $Reach(x) \subset (l^*, u^*)$, which yields a contradiction. Hence, $\mathcal{C}_\mathcal{D}(\sigma)$ is the controllability kernel of S. □

Theorem 5 $\mathcal{C}(\sigma) = \text{Cntr}(K_\sigma)$.
Proof. Let $\mathbf{x}, \mathbf{y} \in \mathcal{C}(\sigma)$. Since $\mathbf{y} \in \overline{\text{Succ}}_\sigma(\mathcal{C}_\mathcal{D}(\sigma))$, there exists a trajectory segment starting in some point $w \in \mathcal{C}_\mathcal{D}(\sigma)$ and ending in $\mathbf{y}$. Let ϵ be an arbitrarily small number and $B_\epsilon(\mathbf{y})$ be the set of all points $\mathbf{y}'$ such that $|\mathbf{y} - \mathbf{y}'| < \epsilon$. Clearly, $w \in \overline{\text{Pre}}_\sigma(B_\epsilon(\mathbf{y})) \cap \mathcal{C}_\mathcal{D}(\sigma)$. Now, since $\mathbf{x} \in \overline{\text{Pre}}_\sigma(\mathcal{C}_\mathcal{D}(\sigma))$, there exists a trajectory segment starting in $\mathbf{x}$ and ending in some point $z \in \mathcal{C}_\mathcal{D}(\sigma)$. Since $\mathcal{C}_\mathcal{D}(\sigma)$ is controllable, there exists a trajectory segment starting in z that reaches a point in $\overline{\text{Pre}}_\sigma(B_\epsilon(\mathbf{y})) \cap \mathcal{C}_\mathcal{D}(\sigma)$. Thus, there is a trajectory segment that starts in $\mathbf{x}$ and ends in $B_\epsilon(\mathbf{y})$. Therefore, $\mathcal{C}(\sigma)$ is controllable. Maximality follows from the maximality of $\mathcal{C}_\mathcal{D}(\sigma)$ and the definition of $\overline{\text{Succ}}_\sigma$ and $\overline{\text{Pre}}_\sigma$. Hence, $\mathcal{C}(\sigma)$ is the controllability kernel of K_σ. □

Theorem 6 *For $\mathcal{D}_\sigma$, any viable trajectory in S converges to $\mathcal{C}_\mathcal{D}(\sigma)$.*
Proof. Let $x_1 x_2 \ldots$ a viable trajectory. Clearly, $x_i \in S \cap J$ for all $i \geq 2$. Recall that $\mathcal{C}_\mathcal{D}(\sigma) \subseteq S \cap J$. There are three cases: (1) There exists $N \geq 2$ such that $x_N \in \mathcal{C}_\mathcal{D}(\sigma)$. Then, for all $n \geq N$, $x_n \in \mathcal{C}_\mathcal{D}(\sigma)$. (2) For all n, $x_n < \mathcal{C}_\mathcal{D}(\sigma)$. Therefore, $x_n < l^*$. Let $\hat{x}_n$ be such that $\hat{x}_1 = x_1$ and for all $n \geq 1$, $\hat{x}_{n+1} = f_l(\hat{x}_n)$. Clearly, for all n, $\hat{x}_n \leq x_n < l^*$, and $\lim_{n \to \infty} \hat{x}_n = l^*$, which implies $\lim_{n \to \infty} x_n = l^*$. (3) For all n, $x_n > \mathcal{C}_\mathcal{D}(\sigma)$. Therefore, $u^* < x_n$. Let $\hat{x}_n$ be such that $\hat{x}_1 = x_1$ and for all $n \geq 1$, $\hat{x}_{n+1} = f_u(\hat{x}_n)$. Clearly, for all n, $u^* < x_n \leq \hat{x}_n$, and $\lim_{n \to \infty} \hat{x}_n = u^*$, which implies $\lim_{n \to \infty} x_n = u^*$. Hence, $x_1 x_2 \ldots$ converges to $\mathcal{C}(\sigma)$. □

Dynamical Qualitative Analysis of Evolutionary Systems

Jean-Pierre Aubin[1] and Olivier Dordan[2]

[1] Centre de Recherche Viabilité, Jeux, Contrôle, Université de Paris-Dauphine
[2] M.A.B Université Victor Segalen

Abstract. Kuipers' QSIM algorithm for tracking the monotonicity properties of solutions to differential equations has been revisited by Dordan by placing it in a rigorous mathematical framework. The Dordan QSIM algorithm provides the transition laws from one qualitative cell to the others.
We take up this idea and revisit it at the light of recent advances in the field of "hybrid systems" and, more generally, "impulse differential equations and inclusions".
Let us consider a family of "qualitative cells $Q(a)$" indexed by a parameter $a \in \mathcal{A}$: We introduce a dynamical system on the discrete set of qualitative states prescribing an order of visit of the qualitative cells and an evolutionary system govening the "continuous" evolution of a system, such as a control system. The question arises to study and characterize the set of any pairs of qualitative and quantitative initial states from which start at least one order of visit of the qualitative cells and an continuous evolution visiting the qualitative cells in the prescribed order. This paper is devoted to the issues regarding this question using tools of set-valued analysis and viability theory.

Introduction

For many problems, we have an imperfect knowledge of the model and we may be interested by few features (often of a qualitative nature) of the solution, so that we see at once that the concept of partial knowledge involves two types of ideas:

1. require less precision in the results (for instance, signs of the components of vectors instead of their numerical values),
2. take into account a broader universality or robustness of these results with respect to uncertainty, disturbances and lack of precisions.

Qualitative physics takes up this issue by exploring the use of qualitative representations in controlling engineering problems. Those qualitative representations are, for instance, used for representing experimental and/or observational data. This is always the case when captors or sensors can only collect very shallow information like signs of the variables. In this particular case the number of

C.J. Tomlin and M.R. Greenstreet (Eds.): HSCC 2002, LNCS 2289, pp. 62–75, 2002.

qualitative values is finite. Those qualitative values will be labeled and the set of labels is denoted $\mathcal{A}$. The connection with quantitative values is obtain with qualitative cells defined by a finite family $\mathbf{Q} := \{Q_a\}_{a \in \mathcal{A}}$ where $\{Q_a\}_{a \in \mathcal{A}}$ is the a subset of a quantitative space denoted X. Variables take on different qualitative values at different times as they evolve under an "evolutionary system" $\mathcal{S} : X \rightsquigarrow \mathbf{C}(0, \infty; X)$ where $\mathcal{S}$ is set valued map associating with any initial state $x \in X$ a (possibly empty) set $\mathcal{S}(x)$ of evolutions $x(\cdot) : t \in \mathbf{R}_+ \mapsto x(t) \in X$. This covers ordinary differential equations, differential inclusions, controlled systems or parameterized systems, that may even be path-dependent.

In the first section we shall give all definitions relative to qualitative cells, in the second one we shall introduce qualitative viability domain and capture basins, characterize them in terms of minimax problems in the third section and in terms of capture basins in the forth section. The "Qualitative Viability Kernel Algorithm" is proposed to compute those kernels. We proceed by providing a geometric characterization of qualitative viability in terms of contingent cones in the sixth section. We use it in the seventh section to revisit the basic example of "monotonic cells", that are the sets $K(a)$ defined by

$$K(a) := \{x \in K \mid f(x) \in a\mathbf{R}_+^n\}$$

where $a \in \mathcal{A} := \{-, +\}^n$ K is a closed viability domain under $\mathcal{S}$ which is generated by an ordinary differential equation $x'(t) = f(x(t))$. The eight section relates the above study with the chaos à la Saari, a situation in which whatever a prescribing order of visits is given, there exists at least one evolution visiting it.

1   Definitions

Definition 1. *Let us consider a finite family* $\mathbf{Q} := \{Q(a)\}_{a \in \mathcal{A}}$ *of "qualitative cells"* $Q(a) \subset X$ *of a subset* X. *A set-valued map* $\Phi : \mathcal{A} \rightsquigarrow \mathcal{A}$ *is* consistent *with a family* $\mathbf{Q} := \{Q(a)\}_{a \in \mathcal{A}}$ *of qualitative cells if*

$$\forall \, a \in \mathcal{A}, \ \forall \, b \in \Phi(a), \ Q(a) \cap Q(b) \neq \emptyset$$

We shall say that a family $\mathbf{C}$ *of qualitative cells* $C(a)$ *is contained in the family* $\mathbf{Q}$ *if for every* $a \in \mathcal{A}$, $C(a) \subset Q(a)$. *A family* $\mathbf{Q}$ *is closed if all the qualitative cells* $Q(a)$ *are closed.*

We shall say that $K \subset X$ *is* covered *by a finite family* $\mathbf{Q} := \{Q(a)\}_{a \in \mathcal{A}}$ *of qualitative cells* $Q(a) \subset K$ *if*

$$K = \bigcup_{a \in \mathcal{A}} Q(a)$$

We can always associate with a family $\mathbf{Q}$ of qualitative cells the largest consistent map $\widehat{\Phi}_{\mathbf{Q}}$ defined by

$$\forall \, a \in \mathcal{A}, \ \widehat{\Phi}_{\mathbf{Q}}(a) := \{b \mid Q(a) \cap Q(b) \neq \emptyset\}$$

Hence, Φ is consistent with $\mathbf{Q}$ if and only if $\Phi \subset \widehat{\Phi}_{\mathbf{Q}}$.

The set-valued map $\Phi : \mathcal{A} \leadsto \mathcal{A}$ defines the discrete dynamic process $\mathcal{S}_\Phi :$ $\mathcal{A} \leadsto \mathcal{A}^{\mathbf{N}}$ associating with any $a \in \mathcal{A}$ the family of discrete evolutions $\boldsymbol{a} :=$ $\{a_n\}_{n \geq 0} \in \mathcal{S}_\Phi(a)$ starting at a and satisfying

$$\forall\, n \geq 0, \;\; a_{n+1} \;\in\; \Phi(a_n)$$

on the set of indexes (qualitative states).

It induces the corresponding order of visit of cells $Q(a_n)$ of continuous evolutions $t \mapsto x(t)$ in the following sense:

Definition 2. *We shall say that a continuous evolution $t \mapsto x(t)$ visits the cells $Q(a) \in \mathbf{Q}$ in the order prescribed by a discrete system Φ consistent with $\mathbf{Q}$ if there exist a qualitative state $a \in \mathcal{A}$, a sequence $\boldsymbol{a} \in \mathcal{S}_\Phi(a)$ and a nondecreasing sequence $\mathcal{T}(x(\cdot)) := \{t_n\}_{n \geq 0}$ of impulse times $t_n \geq 0$ such that*

$$\forall\, t \in [t_n, t_{n+1}], \;\; x(t) \in Q(a_n) \;\&\; x(t_{n+1}) \;\in\; Q(a_{n+1})$$

for all $n \geq 0$ or until an impulse time t_N when

$$\forall\, t \in [t_N, +\infty[, \;\; x(t) \;\in\; Q(a_N)$$

Let $f : X \times Y \mapsto X$ be a single-valued map describing the dynamics of a control system and $P : X \leadsto Y$ the set-valued map describing the state-dependent constraints on the controls.

First, any solution to a control system with state-dependent constraints on the controls

$$\begin{cases} i) \;\; x'(t) \;=\; f(x(t), u(t)) \\ ii) \;\; u(t) \;\in\; P(x(t)) \end{cases}$$

can be regarded as a solution to the differential inclusion $x'(t) \in F(x(t))$ where the right hand side is defined by $F(x) := f(x, P(x)) := \{f(x, u)\}_{u \in P(x)}$.

Therefore, from now on, as long as we do not need to implicate explicitly the controls in our study, we shall replace control problems by differential inclusions.

We denote by

$$\mathrm{Graph}(F) := \{(x, y) \in X \in Y \mid y \in F(x)\}$$

the graph of a set-valued map $F : X \leadsto Y$ and $\mathrm{Dom}(F) := \{x \in X \mid F(x) \neq \emptyset\}$ its domain.

We denote by $\mathcal{S}(x) \subset \mathcal{C}(0, \infty; X)$ the set of absolutely continuous functions $t \mapsto x(t) \in X$ satisfying

$$\text{for almost all } t \geq 0, \;\; x'(t) \;\in\; F(x(t))$$

starting at time 0 at x: $x(0) = x$. The set-valued map $\mathcal{S} : X \leadsto \mathcal{C}(0, \infty; X)$ is called the solution map associated with F.

Most of the results of viability theory are true whenever we assume that the dynamics is Marchaud:

Definition 3 (Marchaud Map). *We shall say that F is a* Marchaud map *if*

$$\begin{cases} i) & \text{the graph of } F \text{ is closed} \\ ii) & \text{the values } F(x) \text{ of } F \text{ are convex and compact} \\ iii) & \text{the growth of } F \text{ is linear: } \exists\, c > 0 \mid \forall\, x \in X, \\ & \|F(x)\| := \sup_{v \in F(x)} \|v\| \;\leq\; c(\|x\| + 1) \end{cases}$$

This covers the case of Marchaud control systems where $(x, u) \mapsto f(x, u)$ is continuous, affine with respect to the controls u and with linear growth and when P is Marchaud.

We recall the following version of the important Theorem 3.5.2 of **Viability Theory**, [1, Aubin]:

Theorem 1. *Assume that $F : X \rightsquigarrow X$ is Marchaud. Then the solution map $\mathcal{S}$ is upper semicompact with nonempty values: This means that whenever $x_n \in X$ converge to x in X and $x_n(\cdot) \in \mathcal{S}(x_n)$ is a solution to the differential inclusion $x' \in F(x)$ starting at x_n, there exists a subsequence (again denoted by) $x_n(\cdot)$ converging to a solution $x(\cdot) \in \mathcal{S}(x)$ uniformly on compact intervals.*

Actually, the basic results that we shall use only few properties of the solution map $\mathcal{S}$: Its upper semicompactness mentioned above, and the translation and concatenation properties that we now define:

Definition 4. *An evolutionary system is a set-valued map $\mathcal{S} : X \rightsquigarrow \mathcal{C}(0, \infty; X)$ satisfying*

1. *the* translation property*: Let $x(\cdot) \in \mathcal{S}(x)$. Then for all $T \geq 0$, the function $y(\cdot)$ defined by $y(t) := x(t + T)$ is a solution $y(\cdot) \in \mathcal{S}(x(T))$ starting at $x(T)$,*
2. *the* concatenation property*: Let $x(\cdot) \in \mathcal{S}(x)$ and $T \geq 0$. Then for every $y(\cdot) \in \mathcal{S}(x(T))$, the function $z(\cdot)$ defined by*

$$z(t) := \begin{cases} x(t) & \text{if } t \in [0, T] \\ y(t - T) & \text{if } t \geq T \end{cases}$$

belongs to $\mathcal{S}(x)$.

The solution maps of differential inclusions, of differential inclusions with memory ([15, Haddad]), of partial differential inclusions (see [17, Shi Shuzhong]), of mutational equation $\overset{\circ}{x} \ni f(x)$ on metric spaces (see [7, Aubin]), of impulse differential equations (see [9,10, Aubin & Haddad]), etc. share these two properties and are examples of evolutionary systems.

We shall present our study for any evolutionary system $\mathcal{S} : X \rightsquigarrow \mathbf{C}(0, \infty; X)$ governing the evolution $x(\cdot) : t \mapsto x(t)$ of the state.

2   Qualitative Viability Kernels and Capture Basins

2.1   Definitions

Definition 5. *Let us consider an evolutionary system $S : X \rightsquigarrow \mathbf{C}(0, \infty; X)$, a set-valued map $\Phi : \mathcal{A} \rightsquigarrow \mathcal{A}$ and two families $\mathbf{Q}$ and $\mathbf{C} \subset \mathbf{Q}$.*

We shall denote by $\mathrm{QualViab}_{(S,\Phi)}(\mathbf{Q}, \mathbf{C})$ the set of pairs (a, x) where $x \in Q(a)$ from which start a sequence $\boldsymbol{a} := \{a_n\}_{n \geq 0} \in S_{\Phi}(a)$ and an evolution $x(\cdot) \in S(x)$ visiting the cells $Q(a_n)$ in the prescribed order until it possibly reach a target $C(a_N)$ at a finite step a_N. We shall say that it is the qualitative viability kernel *of the family $\mathbf{Q}$ with family $\mathbf{C}$ of targets under the qualitative evolutionary system (S, Φ).*

If the subsets $C(a)$ are empty, we set

$$\mathrm{QualViab}_{(S,\Phi)}(\mathbf{Q}) := \mathrm{QualViab}_{(S,\Phi)}(\mathbf{Q}, \emptyset)$$

and we say that $\mathrm{QualViab}_{(S,\Phi)}(\mathbf{Q})$ is the qualitative viability kernel *of the family $\mathbf{Q}$.*

We shall denote by $\mathrm{QualCapt}_{(S,\Phi)}(\mathbf{Q}, \mathbf{C})$ the set of pairs (a, x) where $x \in Q(a)$ from which start an evolution $x(\cdot) \in S(x)$ and $\boldsymbol{a} := \{a_n\}_{n \geq 0} \in S_{\Phi}(a)$ visiting the cells $Q(a_n)$ in the prescribed order $\{a_n\}$ until it reaches a target $C(a_N)$ at a finite step a_N. We shall say that it is the qualitative capture basin *of the family $\mathbf{C}$ qualitative viable in the family $\mathbf{Q}$ under the qualitative evolutionary system (S, Φ).*

We shall say that

1. *$\mathbf{Q}$ is* qualitatively viable outside $\mathbf{C}$ *under the pair (S, Φ) if*

$$\mathbf{Q} \subset \mathrm{QualViab}_{(S,\Phi)}(\mathbf{Q}, \mathbf{C})$$

2. *$\mathbf{Q}$* qualitatively captures $\mathbf{C}$ *under the pair (S, Φ) if*

$$\mathbf{Q} \subset \mathrm{QualCapt}_{(S,\Phi)}(\mathbf{Q}, \mathbf{C})$$

3. *$\mathbf{C} \subset \mathbf{Q}$ is* qualitatively isolated *in $\mathbf{Q}$ if*

$$\mathrm{QualViab}_{(S,\Phi)}(\mathbf{Q}, \mathbf{C}) \subset \mathbf{C}$$

We observe at once:

Lemma 1. *The map $(\mathbf{Q}, \mathbf{C}) \mapsto \mathrm{QualViab}_{(S,\Phi)}(\mathbf{Q}, \mathbf{C})$ satisfies*

$$\mathbf{C} \subset \mathrm{QualViab}_{(S,\Phi)}(\mathbf{Q}, \mathbf{C}) \subset \mathbf{Q}$$

and is increasing in the sense that

If $\mathbf{C}_1 \subset \mathbf{C}_2$ & $\mathbf{Q}_1 \subset \mathbf{Q}_2$, then $\mathrm{QualViab}_{(S,\Phi)}(\mathbf{Q}_1, \mathbf{C}_1) \subset \mathrm{QualViab}_{(S,\Phi)}(\mathbf{Q}_2, \mathbf{C}_2)$

Furthermore, the map $\mathbf{C} \mapsto \mathrm{QualViab}_{(S,\Phi)}(\mathbf{Q}, \mathbf{C})$ satisfies

$$\mathrm{QualViab}_{(S,\Phi)}\left(\mathbf{Q}, \bigcup_{i \in I} \mathbf{C}_i\right) = \bigcup_{i \in I} \mathrm{QualViab}_{(S,\Phi)}(\mathbf{Q}, \mathbf{C}_i)$$

Example : Fluctuations For instance, in the case when $K := Q(a_1) \cup Q(a_2)$ and $Q(a_1) \cap Q(a_2) \neq \emptyset$, and when $\Phi(a_1) = a_2$ and $\Phi(a_2) = a_1$ and when $C(a_1) := C(a_2) := \emptyset$, the qualitative viability of $\mathbf{Q}$ under $(\mathcal{S}, \Phi)$ describes a property of fluctuation when starting from any $x \in K$, there exists at least one evolution $x(\cdot)$ visiting the two qualitative cells $Q(a_1)$ and $Q(a_2)$ alternatively. $\square$

Example: Qualitative Oscillators and equilibria   Assume that a family $\mathbf{Q}$ of qualitative cells is qualitatively viable under the qualitative evolutionary system $(\mathcal{S}, \Phi)$. Any periodic solution $a := \{a_0, \ldots, a_{N-1}\}$ of period N of the discrete system $x_{n+1} \in \Phi(x_n)$ gives rise to a qualitative oscillator: ¿From any initial state $x_0 \in Q(a_0)$ starts at least one evolution that visits the cells $Q(a_0), \ldots, Q(a_{N-1}), Q(a_0), \ldots$ periodically.

In particular, a cell associated with a fixed point $\bar{a} \in \Phi(\bar{a})$ of the discrete map Φ is viable under the evolutionary system $\mathcal{S}$, and thus, can be regarded as a qualitative equilibrium.

3   Minimax Characterization

We denote by $\mathcal{D}(\mathbf{Q}, \mathbf{C})$ the set of families $\mathbf{P}$ of qualitative cells $P(a)$ contained in $\mathbf{Q}$ and containing $\mathbf{C}$.

Theorem 2. *The qualitative viability kernel* $\mathrm{QualViab}_{(\mathcal{S}, \Phi)}(\mathbf{Q}, \mathbf{C})$ *of a family* $\mathbf{Q}$ *of qualitative cells with family* $\mathbf{C} \subset \mathbf{Q}$ *of targets is*

1. *the largest family* $\mathbf{P} \in \mathcal{D}(\mathbf{Q}, \mathbf{C})$ *viable outside the family* $\mathbf{C}$ *under the qualitative evolutionary system* $(\mathcal{S}, \Phi)$,
2. *the smallest subset* $\mathbf{P} \in \mathcal{D}(\mathbf{Q}, \mathbf{C})$ *isolated in* $\mathbf{Q}$ *under the qualitative evolutionary system* $(\mathcal{S}, \Phi)$,
3. *the unique minimax* $\mathbf{P} \in \mathcal{D}(\mathbf{Q}, \mathbf{C})$ *in the sense that*

$$\mathbf{P} = \mathrm{QualViab}_{(\mathcal{S}, \Phi)}(\mathbf{Q}, \mathbf{P}) = \mathrm{QualViab}_{(\mathcal{S}, \Phi)}(\mathbf{P}, \mathbf{C})$$

The same properties hold true for the qualitative viable-capture map $\mathrm{QualCapt}_{(\mathcal{S}, \Phi)}(\mathbf{Q}, \mathbf{C})$ *of a target* $\mathbf{C}$ *viable in* $\mathbf{Q}$.

4   A Representation Theorem

If $Q(a) \cap Q(b) \neq \emptyset$, we shall set

$$\begin{cases} \mathrm{Viab}_{\mathcal{S}}(Q(a), Q_b) := \mathrm{Viab}_{\mathcal{S}}(Q(a), Q_b \cap Q(a)) \\ \mathrm{Capt}_{\mathcal{S}}(Q(a), Q_b) := \mathrm{Capt}_{\mathcal{S}}(Q(a), Q_b \cap Q(a)) \end{cases}$$

Theorem 3. *A family* $\mathbf{Q}$ *is qualitatively viable outside a qualitative family* $\mathbf{C} \subset \mathbf{Q}$ *under* $(\mathcal{S}, F)$ *if and only if*

$$\forall\, a \in \mathcal{A}, \quad Q(a) \subset \mathcal{B}(\mathbf{Q}, \mathbf{C})(a) := C(a) \cup \bigcup_{b \in \Phi(a)} \mathrm{Capt}_{\mathcal{S}}(Q(a), Q(b))$$

Consequently, the qualitative viability kernel of the family **Q** *with target* **C** *under the qualitative evolutionary system* $(\mathcal{S}, \Phi)$ *is the largest family* **P** *between the families* **C** *and* **Q** *satisfying the above property.*

4.1 Prerequisite from Viability Theory

We shall need the following definitions and results from Viability Theory:

Definition 6. *Let* $C \subset K \subset X$ *be two subsets, C being regarded as a target, K as a constrained set.*

1. *The subset* $\mathrm{Viab}(K, C)$ *of initial states $x_0 \in K$ such that at least one solution $x(\cdot) \in \mathcal{S}(x_0)$ starting at x_0 is viable in K for all $t \geq 0$ or viable in K until it reaches C in finite time is called the* viability kernel of K with target C under $\mathcal{S}$.
   A subset $C \subset K$ *is said to be* isolated *in K by $\mathcal{S}$ if it coincides with its viability kernel:*
   $$\mathrm{Viab}(K, C) = C$$

2. *The subset* $\mathrm{Capt}^K(C)$ *of initial states $x_0 \in K$ such that C is reached in finite time before possibly leaving K by at least one solution $x(\cdot) \in \mathcal{S}(x_0)$ starting at x_0 is called the* viable-capture basin *of C in K and*
   $$\mathrm{Capt}(C) := \mathrm{Capt}^X(C)$$
   is said to be the capture basin *of C.*

3. *When the target $C = \emptyset$ is the empty set, we set*
   $$\mathrm{Viab}(K) := \mathrm{Viab}(K, \emptyset) \; \& \; \mathrm{Capt}^K(\emptyset) = \emptyset$$
   and we say that $\mathrm{Viab}(K)$ *is the viability kernel of K.*
   A subset K is a repeller *under $\mathcal{S}$ if its viability kernel is empty, or, equivalently, if the empty set is isolated in K.*

In other words, the viability kernel $\mathrm{Viab}(K)$ is the subset of initial states $x_0 \in K$ such that at least one solution $x(\cdot) \in \mathcal{S}(x_0)$ starting at x_0 is viable in K for all $t \geq 0$. Furthermore, we observe that

$$\mathrm{Viab}(K, C) = \mathrm{Viab}(K \backslash C) \cup \mathrm{Capt}^K(\emptyset) \tag{1}$$

Consequently, the viability kernel $\mathrm{Viab}(K, C)$ of K with target C coincides with the capture basin $\mathrm{Capt}^K(C)$ of C viable in K whenever the viability kernel $\mathrm{Viab}(K \backslash C)$ is empty, i.e., whenever $K \backslash C$ is a repeller:

$$\mathrm{Viab}(K \backslash C) = \emptyset \Rightarrow \mathrm{Viab}(K, C) = \mathrm{Capt}^K(C) \tag{2}$$

This happens in particular when K is a repeller, or when the viability kernel $\mathrm{Viab}(K)$ of K is contained in the target C.

It will also be useful to handle hitting and exit functions and Theorem 4 below:

Definition 7. *Let $C \subset K \subset X$ be two subsets. The functional $\tau_K : \mathcal{C}(0, \infty; X) \mapsto \mathbf{R}_+ \cup \{+\infty\}$ associating with $x(\cdot)$ its* exit time $\tau_K(x(\cdot))$ *defined by*

$$\tau_K(x(\cdot)) := \inf\{t \in [0, \infty[\mid x(t) \notin K\}$$

is called the exit functional.

The (constrained) hitting (or minimal time) functional $\varpi_{(K,C)}$ defined by

$$\varpi_{(K,C)}(x(\cdot)) := \inf\{t \geq 0 \mid x(t) \in C \ \& \ \forall s \in [0,t], \ x(s) \in K \}$$

has been introduced in [11, Cardaliaguet, Quincampoix & Saint-Pierre]). We set

$$\varpi_C(x(\cdot)) := \varpi_{(X,C)}(x(\cdot))$$

If $\mathcal{S}$ is the solution map associated with the map F, the function $\tau_K^{\#} : K \mapsto \mathbf{R}_+ \cup \{+\infty\}$ defined by

$$\tau_K^{\#}(x) := \sup_{x(\cdot) \in \mathcal{S}(x)} \tau_K(x(\cdot))$$

the upper exit function and the function $\varpi_{(K,C)}^{\flat} : K \mapsto \mathbf{R}_+ \cup \{+\infty\}$ defined by

$$\varpi_{(K,C)}^{\flat}(x) := \inf_{x(\cdot) \in \mathcal{S}(x)} \varpi_{(K,C)}(x(\cdot))$$

is called the lower (constrained) hitting function

We shall need the following:

Theorem 4. Let $F : X \rightsquigarrow X$ be a strict Marchaud map and C and K be two closed subsets such that $C \subset K$. Then the hitting function $\varpi_{(K,C)}^{\flat}$ is lower semicontinuous and the exit function $\tau_K^{\#}$ is upper semicontinuous. Furthermore, for any $x \in \mathrm{Dom}(\varpi_{(K,C)}^{\flat})$, there exists one solution $x^{\flat}(\cdot) \in \mathcal{S}(x)$ which hits C as soon as possible before possibly leaving K

$$\varpi_{(K,C)}^{\flat}(x) = \varpi_{(K,C)}(x^{\flat}(\cdot))$$

and for any $x \in \mathrm{Dom}(\tau_K^{\#})$, there exists one solution $x^{\#}(\cdot) \in \mathcal{S}(x)$ which remains viable in K as long as possible:

$$\tau_K^{\#}(x) = \tau_K(x^{\#}(\cdot))$$

(see Proposition 4.2.4 of [1,3, Aubin], for instance)

5   The Qualitative Viability Kernel Algorithm

Since the qualitative viability kernel map is the largest fixed point of the map $\mathbf{Q} \mapsto \mathcal{B}(\mathbf{Q}, \mathbf{C})$, we can use the Qualitative Viability Kernel Algorithm defined in the following way :

Starting with $\mathbf{Q}_0 := \mathbf{Q}$, we define recursively the families $\mathbf{Q}_n$ by

$$\forall a \in \mathcal{A}, \ \forall n \geq 0, \ Q_{n+1}(a) := C(a) \cup \bigcup_{b \in \Phi(a)} \mathrm{Capt}_{\mathcal{S}}(Q_n(a), Q_n(b))$$

Theorem 5. *Let us assume that the families* $\mathbf{Q}$ *and* $\mathbf{C} \subset \mathbf{Q}$ *are closed and that the evolutionary system* $\mathcal{S}$ *is upper semi-compact. Then the family* $\mathbf{Q}_n$ *are closed and*

$$\text{QualViab}_{(\mathcal{S},\Phi)}(\mathbf{Q}, \mathbf{C}) = \bigcap_{n \geq 0} \mathbf{Q}_n$$

6   Characterization of Qualitative Viability

We now provide another characterization of the qualitative viability kernel of a family of qualitative cells:

Theorem 6. *Let us assume that the evolutionary system* $\mathcal{S}$ *is upper semicompact, that the family* $\mathbf{Q}$ *is closed (i.e., the subsets* $Q(a)$ *are closed), that for every* $b \in \Phi(a)$, $Q(a)\backslash C(b)$ *is a repeller and that* Φ *is consistent with* $\mathbf{Q}$.

Then the family $\mathbf{Q}$ *is qualitatively viable under* $(\mathcal{S}, \Phi)$ *outside* $\mathbf{C}$ *if and only if for every* $a \in \mathcal{A}$, *the subsets* $Q(a)\backslash \left(C(a) \cup \bigcup_{b \in \Phi(a)} Q(a) \right)$ *are locally viable.*

Proof. We have to prove that from any $x \in Q(a)$, there exists $b \in \Phi(a)$ and an evolution $x(\cdot) \in \mathcal{S}(x)$ viable in $Q(a)$ until it reaches some $C(a)$ in finite time or until it reaches some $Q(b)$ where $b \in \Phi(a)$ in finite time. There exists an evolution $x^\sharp(\cdot) \in \mathcal{S}(x)$ that maximizes the exit time $t^\sharp := \tau_{Q(a)}^\sharp(x) := \tau_{Q(a)}(x^\sharp(\cdot))$ on $\mathcal{S}(x)$. We deduce that $x^\sharp(t^\sharp)$ belongs to $M(a) := C(a) \cup \bigcup_{b \in \Phi(a)} \Phi(b)$. Otherwise, $x^\sharp(t^\sharp)$ would belong to $Q(a)\backslash M(a)$. Since this set is locally viable by assumption, there exists at least one evolution $y(\cdot) \in \mathcal{S}(x^\sharp(t^\sharp))$ viable in $Q(a)\backslash M(a) \subset Q(a)$ on a nonempty interval $[0, T]$. Concatenating $y(\cdot)$ with $x(\cdot)$, we would obtain an evolution $\widetilde{x}(\cdot) \in \mathcal{S}(x)$ viable in $Q(a)$ on an interval $[0, t^\sharp + T]$, a contradiction.

When the evolutionary system $\mathcal{S} := \mathcal{S}_F$ comes from a differential inclusion $x' \in F(x)$, we can characterize the local viability thanks to the Viability Theorem[1]. We recall that the contingent cone $T_L(x)$ to $L \subset X$ at $x \in L$ is the set of directions $v \in X$ such that there exist sequences $h_n > 0$ converging to 0 and v_n converging to v satisfying $x + h_n v_n \in K$ for every n (see for instance [8, Aubin & Frankowska]) or [16, Rockafellar & Wets] for more details).

Theorem 7. *Let us assume that the set-valued map* $F : X \rightsquigarrow X$ *is Marchaud, that the family* $\mathbf{Q}$ *is closed, that for every* $b \in \Phi(a)$, $Q(a)\backslash C(b)$ *is a repeller and that* Φ *is consistent with* $\mathbf{Q}$.

Then the family $\mathbf{Q}$ *is qualitatively viable under* (F, Φ) *outside* $\mathbf{C}$ *if and only if for every* $a \in \mathcal{A}$,

$$\forall\, a \in \mathcal{A},\ \forall\, x \in Q(a)\backslash \left(C(a) \cup \bigcup_{b \in \Phi(a)} Q(b) \right),\quad F(x) \cap T_{Q(a)}(x) \neq \emptyset$$

---

[1] See for instance Theorems 3.2.4, 3.3.2 and 3.5.2 of [1, Aubin].

7   Applications to Monotonic Cells

We posit the assumptions of the Viability Theorem for differential equations (called the Nagumo Theorem):

$$\begin{cases} i) & f \text{ is continuous with linear growth} \\ ii) & K \text{ is a closed viability domain} \end{cases} \tag{3}$$

Therefore, from every initial state $x_0 \in K$ stars a solution to the differential equation

$$x'(t) \;=\; f(x(t)) \tag{4}$$

viable (remaining) in K.

For studying the qualitative behavior of the differential equation (4), i.e., the evolution of the functions $t \mapsto \text{sign}(x'(t))$ associated with solutions $x(\cdot)$ of the differential equation, we split the viability domain K of the differential equation into 2^n "monotonic cells" $K(a)$ defined by

$$K(a) \;:=\; \{x \in K \mid f(x) \in a\mathbf{R}^n\}$$

where $a \in \mathcal{A} := \{-,+\}^n$

Indeed, the quantitative states $x(\cdot)$ evolving in a given monotonic cell $K(a)$ share the same monotonicity properties because, as long as $x(t)$ remains in $K(a)$,

$$\forall\, i = 1,\ldots,n, \;\; \text{sign of } \frac{dx_i(t)}{dt} \;=\; a_i$$

These monotonic cells are examples of qualitative cells

7.1   Monotonic Behavior of Observations of the State

But before proceeding further, we shall generalize our problem — free of any mathematical cost — to take care of physical considerations.

Instead of studying the monotonicity properties of each component $x_i(\cdot)$ of the state of the system under investigation, which can be too numerous, we shall only study the monotonicity properties of m functionals $V_j(x(\cdot))$ on the state (for instance, energy or entropy functionals in physics, observations in control theory, various economic indexes in economics) which do matter.

The previous case is the particular case when we take the n functionals V_i defined by $V_i(x) := x_i$.

We shall assume for simplicity that these functionals V_j are continuously differentiable around the viability domain K.

We denote by $\mathbf{V}$ the map from X to $Y := \mathbf{R}^m$ defined by

$$\mathbf{V}(x) \;:=\; (V_1(x),\ldots,V_m(x))$$

Lemma 2. *Let us assume that f is continuously differentiable and that the m functions V_j are twice continuously differentiable around the viability domain K. If v belongs to the contingent cone to the $\overline{K}_a$ at x, then condition*

$$v \in T_K(x) \quad \& \quad \forall\, i \in I_0(x), \ \text{sign of } (g'(x)v)_i = a_i \ \text{ or } \ 0$$

is satisfied.

The converse is true if we posit the transversality assumption[2]:

$$\forall\, x \in \overline{K}_a, \ g'(x)C_K(x) - a\mathbf{R}_+^{I_0(x)} = \mathbf{R}^m$$

Proof. Since the large qualitative cell $\overline{K}_a$ is the intersection of K with the inverse image by g of the convex cone $a\mathbf{R}_+^m$, we know that the contingent cone to $\overline{K}_a$ at some $x \in \overline{K}_a$ is contained in

$$T_K(x) \cap g'(x)^{-1}T_{a\mathbf{R}_+^m}(g(x))$$

and is equal to this intersection provided that the "transversality assumption"

$$g'(x)C_K(x) - C_{a\mathbf{R}_+^m}(g(x)) = \mathbf{R}^m$$

is satisfied. On the other hand, we know that $a\mathbf{R}_+^m$ being convex,

$$C_{a\mathbf{R}_+^m}(y) = T_{a\mathbf{R}_+^m}(y) = aT_{\mathbf{R}_+^m(ay)} \supset a\mathbf{R}_+^m$$

and that $v \in T_{\mathbf{R}_+^m}(z)$ if and only if

$$\text{whenever } z_j = 0, \text{ then } v_j \geq 0$$

Consequently, $v \in T_{a\mathbf{R}_+^m}(g(x))$ if and only if

$$\text{whenever } g(x)_j = 0, \text{ then sign of } v_j = a_j \ \text{ or } \ 0$$

i.e., $T_{a\mathbf{R}_+^m}(g(x)) = a\mathbf{R}_+^{I_0(x)}$.

Hence v belongs to the contingent cone to $\overline{K}_a$ at x if and only if v belongs to $T_K(x)$ and $g'(x)v$ belongs to $T_{a\mathbf{R}_+^m}(g(x))$, i.e., the sign of $(g'(x)v)_j$ is equal to a_j or 0 whenever j belongs to $I_0(x)$.

We denote by $I(a,b)$ the set of indexes $i \in \{1,\ldots,m\}$ such that $b_i = -a_i$ and by $I_\Phi(a) := \bigcup_{b \in \Phi(a)} I(a,b)$. Hence, to say that x belongs to $K(a) \setminus \left(\bigcup_{b \in \Phi(a)} K(b) \right)$ means that the sign of $g_i(x)$ is equal to a_i for all $i \notin I_\Phi(a)$.

We introduce the notation

$$\overline{K}_a^i := \{ x \in \overline{K}_a \mid g(x)_i = 0 \}$$

[2] The cone $C_K(x)$ denotes the Clarke tangent cone to K at x. See for instance [8, Aubin & Frankowska]

Theorem 8. *Let us assume that f is continuously differentiable and that the m functions V_j are twice continuously differentiable around the viability domain K.*

We posit the transversality assumption:

$$\forall\, x \in \overline{K}_a, \ \ g'(x)C_K(x) - a\mathbf{R}_+^{I_0(x)} \ = \ \mathbf{R}^m$$

Let Φ be a set-valued map consistent with $\mathbf{Q}$.

Then $\mathbf{Q}$ is qualitative viable under $(\mathcal{S}_f, \Phi)$ if and only if for any $a \in \{-,+\}^m$, for any $i \notin I_\Phi(a)$, for any $x \in K(a)^i$, the sign of $h_i(x)$ is equal to a_i.

Proof. This is a consequence of Theorem 7 and Lemma 2.

We shall denote by Γ the set-valued map from $\mathcal{R}^m$ to itself defined by

$$\forall\, a \in \mathcal{R}^m, \ (\Gamma(a))_i \text{ is the set of signs of } h_i(x) \text{ when } x \in \overline{K}_a^i$$

Hence the necessary and sufficient condition for the qualitative viability of monotonic cells can be written in the symbolic form:

$$\forall\, a \in \{-,+\}^n, \ \ \Gamma(a)|_{I_\Phi(a)} \subset a|_{I_\Phi(a)}$$

Hence, the knowledge of the map Ψ allows us to characterize the qualitative viability of a monotonic cells under a differential equation.

8   Chaos à la Saari

We associate with the sequence $a_0, a_1, \ldots$ the subsets $\mathbf{C}_{a_0 a_1 \cdots a_n}$ defined by induction by $\mathbf{C}_{a_n} := Q(a_n)$,

$$\mathbf{C}_{a_{n-1} a_n} := \mathrm{Capt}(Q(a_{n-1}), Q(a_n))$$

which is the subset of $x \in Q(a_{n-1})$ such that there exists $x(\cdot) \in \mathcal{S}(x)$ viable in $Q(a_{n-1})$ until it reaches $Q(a_n)$ in finite time. For $j = n - 2, \ldots, 0$, we define recursively the cells:

$$\mathbf{C}_{a_j a_{j+1} \cdots a_n} := \mathrm{Capt}(Q(a_j), \mathbf{C}_{a_{j+1} \cdots a_n})$$

Lemma 3. *Let us assume that $\mathcal{S}$ is upper semicompact and that the cells $Q(a)$ $(a \in \mathcal{A})$ of the family Q are closed repellers. Given a sequence of qualitative indexes $a_0, \ldots, a_n, \ldots$, such that $Q(a_n) \cap Q(a_{n+1}) \neq \emptyset$, the set $\mathbf{C}_{a_0 a_1 \cdots a_n \cdots}$ is the set of initial states $x_0 \in Q(a_0)$ from which at least one evolution visits the cells $Q(a_j)$ is the prescribed order $a_0, \ldots, a_n, \ldots,$.*

Proof. Let us consider an element x in the intersection $\mathbf{C}_{a_0 a_1 \cdots a_n \cdots} := \bigcap_{n=0}^{\infty}$ $\mathbf{C}_{a_0 a_1 \cdots a_n}$ is nonempty.

Let $T := \sup_{a \in \mathcal{A}} \sup_{x \in Q(a)} \tau^{\sharp}_{Q(a)}(x)$, which is finite since the cells $Q(a)$ are repellers.

Let us take an initial state x in Q_{∞} and fix n. Hence there exists $x_n(\cdot) \in \mathcal{S}(x)$ and a sequence of $t_n^j \in [0, jT]$ such that

$$\forall \, j = 1, \ldots, n, \quad x_n(t_n^j) \in \mathbf{C}_{a_j \cdots a_n} \subset Q(a_j)$$

Indeed, there exist $y_1(\cdot) \in \mathcal{S}(x)$ and $\varpi^{\flat}_{\mathbf{C}_{a_1 \cdots a_n}}(y_1(\cdot)) \in [0, T]$ such that $y_1(\varpi^{\flat}_{\mathbf{C}_{a_1 \cdots a_n}}(y_1(\cdot)))$ belongs to $\mathbf{C}_{a_1 \cdots a_n}$. We set $t_n^1 := \varpi^{\flat}_{\mathbf{C}_{a_1 \cdots a_n}}(y_1(\cdot))$, $x_n^1 = y_1(t_n^1)$ and $x_n(t) := y_1(t)$ on $[0, t_n^1]$.

Assume that we have built $x_n(\cdot)$ on the interval $[0, t_n^k]$ such that $x_n(t_n^j) \in \mathbf{C}_{a_j \cdots a_n} \subset Q(a_j)$ for $j = 1, \ldots, k$. Since $x_n(t_n^k)$ belongs to $\mathbf{C}_{a_k \cdots a_n}$, there exist $y_{k+1}(\cdot) \in \mathcal{S}(x_n(t_n^k))$ and $\varpi^{\flat}_{\mathbf{C}_{a_{k+1} \cdots a_n}}(y_{k+1}(\cdot)) \in [0, T]$ such that

$$y_{k+1}(\varpi^{\flat}_{\mathbf{C}_{a_{k+1} \cdots a_n}}(y_{k+1}(\cdot))) \in \mathbf{C}_{a_{k+1} \cdots a_n}$$

We set

$$t_n^{k+1} := t_n^k + \varpi^{\flat}_{\mathbf{C}_{a_{k+1} \cdots a_n}}(y_{k+1}(\cdot)) \quad \& \quad x_n(t) := y_{k+1}(t + \varpi^{\flat}_{\mathbf{C}_{a_{k+1} \cdots a_n}}(y_{k+1}(\cdot)))$$

on $[t_n^k, t_n^{k+1}]$. When $k = n$, we extend $x_n(\cdot)$ to $[t_n^n, \infty[$ by any solution to the evolutionary system starting at $x_n(t_n^n)$ at time t_n^n.

Since the sequence $x_n(\cdot) \in \mathcal{S}(x)$ is compact in the space $\mathbf{C}(0, \infty; X)$, a subsequence (again denoted $x_n(\cdot)$) converges to some solution $x(\cdot) \in \mathcal{S}(x)$ to the evolutionary system. By extracting successive converging subsequences of $t_{n_1}^1, \ldots, t_{n_j}^j, \ldots$, we infer the existence of t_j's in $[0, jT]$ such that $x_{n_j}(t_{n_j}^j)$ converges to $\bar{x}(t_j) \in Q(a_j)$, because the functions $x_n(\cdot)$ remain in an equicontinuous subset.

A situation in which all the subsets $\mathbf{C}_{a_0 a_1 \cdots a_n}$ are nonempty should generate a kind of chaos, which was introduced by Donald Saari:

Definition 8. *We shall say that the covering of K by a family of closed subsets $Q(a)$ ($a \in \mathcal{A}$) is chaotic à la Saari under $\mathcal{S}$ if for any sequence $a_0, a_1, \ldots$, there exists at least one solution $x(\cdot) \in \mathcal{S}(x)$ to the evolutionary system is viable $Q(a_{j-1})$ on $[t_{j-1}, t_j]$ and and a sequence of elements $t_j \geq 0$ such that $x(t_j) \in Q(a_j)$ for all $j \geq 0$.*

Theorem 9 (Chaotic Behavior). *Let us assume that a compact viability domain K of the upper semicompact map $\mathcal{S}$ is covered by a family of closed repellers $Q(a)$ ($a \in \mathcal{A}$) satisfying the following controllability assumption:*

$$K \subset \bigcap_{a \in \mathcal{A}} \bigcup_{t \geq 0} \vartheta_{\mathcal{S}}(t, Q(a))$$

Then, for any sequence $a_0, a_1, \ldots, a_n, \ldots$, there exists at least one evolution $x(\cdot) \in \mathcal{S}(x)$ to and a sequence of elements $t_j \geq 0$ such that $x(\cdot)$ is viable $Q(a_{j-1})$ on $[t_{j-1}, t_j]$ and $x(t_j) \in Q(a_j)$ for all $j \geq 0$.

Proof. The controllability assumption implies that subsets $\mathbf{C}_{a_0 a_1 \cdots a_n}$ are nonempty. They are closed since the evolutionary system is assume to be upper semicompact. Therefore the intersection $\mathbf{C}_{a_0 a_1 \cdots a_n \cdots} := \bigcap_{n=0}^{\infty} \mathbf{C}_{a_0 a_1 \cdots a_n}$ is nonempty.

References

1. AUBIN J.-P. (1991) **Viability Theory**
2. AUBIN J.-P. (1996) **Neural Networks and Qualitative Physics: A Viability Approach**, Cambridge University Press Birkhäuser, Boston, Basel, Berlin
3. AUBIN J.-P. (1999) **Impulse Differential Inclusions and Hybrid Systems: A Viability Approach**, Lecture Notes, University of California at Berkeley
4. AUBIN J.-P. (2000) *Optimal Impulse Control Problems and Quasi-Variational Inequalities Thirty Years Later: a Viability Approach*, in **Contrôle optimal et EDP: Innovations et Applications**, IOS Press
5. AUBIN J.-P. (2001) *Viability Kernels and Capture Basins of Sets under Differential Inclusions*, SIAM J. Control, 40, 853-881
6. AUBIN J.-P. & CATTE F. (2001) *Fixed-Point and Algebraic Properties of Viability Kernels and Capture Basins of Sets,*
7. AUBIN J.-P. (1999) **Mutational and morphological analysis: tools for shape regulation and morphogenesis**, Birkhäuser
8. AUBIN J.-P. & FRANKOWSKA H. (1990) **Set-Valued Analysis**, Birkhäuser, Boston, Basel, Berlin
9. AUBIN J.-P. & HADDAD G. (2001) *Cadenced runs of impulse and hybrid control systems*, International Journal Robust and Nonlinear Control
10. AUBIN J.-P. & HADDAD G. (2001) *Path-Dependent Impulse and Hybrid Systems*, in **Hybrid Systems: Computation and Control**, 119-132, Di Benedetto & Sangiovanni-Vincentelli Eds, Proceedings of the HSCC 2001 Conference, LNCS 2034, Springer-Verlag
11. CARDALIAGUET P., QUINCAMPOIX M. & SAINT-PIERRE P. (1994) *Temps optimaux pour des problèmes avec contraintes et sans contrôlabilité locale* Comptes-Rendus de l'Académie des Sciences, Série 1, Paris, 318, 607-612
12. CRUCK E. (2001) *Target problems under state constraints for nonlinear controlled impulsive systems*, UBO # 01-2001
13. DORDAN O. (1992) *Mathematival problems arising in qualitative simulation of a differential equation*, Artificial Intelligence, 55, 61-86
14. DORDAN O. (1995) **Analyse qualitative**, Masson
15. HADDAD G. (1981) *Topological properties of the set of solutions for functional differential differential inclusions*, Nonlinear Anal. Theory, Meth. Appl., 5, 1349-1366
16. ROCKAFELLAR R.T. & WETS R. (1997) **Variational Analysis**, Springer-Verlag
17. SHI SHUZHONG (1988) *Nagumo type condition for partial differential inclusions*, Nonlinear Analysis, T.M.A., 12, 951-967

Design of Observers for Hybrid Systems*

Andrea Balluchi[1], Luca Benvenuti[2], Maria D. Di Benedetto[3], and
Alberto L. Sangiovanni–Vincentelli[1,4]

[1] PARADES, Via di S. Pantaleo, 66, 00186 Roma, Italy.
`balluchi,alberto@parades.rm.cnr.it`
[2] DIS, Università di Roma "La Sapienza", Via Eudossiana 18, 00184 Roma, Italy.
`luca.benvenuti@uniroma1.it`
[3] DIE, Università dell'Aquila, Poggio di Roio, 67040 L'Aquila, Italy.
`dibenede@ing.univaq.it`
[4] EECS, University of California at Berkeley, CA 94720, USA.

Abstract. A methodology for the design of dynamical observers for hybrid plants is proposed. The hybrid observer consists of two parts: a *location observer* and a *continuous observer*. The former identifies the current location of the hybrid plant, while the latter produces an estimate of the evolution of the continuous state of the hybrid plant. A synthesis procedure is offered when a set of properties on the hybrid plant is satisfied. The synthesized hybrid observer identifies the current location of the plant after a finite number of steps and converges exponentially to the continuous state.

1 Introduction

The state estimation problem has been the subject of intensive study by both the computer science community in the discrete domain (see [14,6,12]), and the control community in the continuous domain (see the pioneering work of Luenberger [10]), but has been scantly investigated in the hybrid system domain.

The authors investigated for years the use of a hybrid formalism to solve control problems in automotive applications (see [3]). The hybrid control algorithms developed are based on full state feedback, while only partial information about the state of the hybrid plant is often available. This motivates this work on the design of observers for hybrid systems. Some partial results are given in [4], where an application to a power-train control problem is considered. In this paper, the authors present a general procedure to synthesize hybrid observers.

The literature on observers design in the discrete and the continuous domain is rich. Here we briefly summarize some of the results that are relevant for our presentation. In the control literature, Ackerson first introduced in [1] the state estimation problem for switching systems, represented as continuous systems

---

* The work has been conducted with partial support of PARADES, a Cadence, Magneti-Marelli and ST-microelectronics E.E.I.G, by the European Community Projects IST-2001-33520 CC (Control and Computation) and IST-2001-32460 HYBRIDGE, and by CNR PF–MADESSII SP3.1.2.

C.J. Tomlin and M.R. Greenstreet (Eds.): HSCC 2002, LNCS 2289, pp. 76–89, 2002.
© Springer-Verlag Berlin Heidelberg 2002

subject to a known dynamics taken from a set of given ones and with no state resets. Subsequently, state estimation was considered by several authors in a probabilistic framework (see e.g. [17]). Gain switching observers for nonlinear systems were studied in [8].

In the discrete systems literature, Ramadge gave in [14] the definition of current–location observability for discrete event dynamic systems, as the property of being able to estimate the current location of the system, after a finite number of steps from the evolution of the input and output signals. A well-known approach for the estimation of the current location of an automaton is the computation of the so-called *current-location tree*, described in [6], that gives the subset of locations the system can be in at the current time. Interesting results on location estimation for discrete systems are also presented in [12], where a slightly different definition of observability is used.

In [2], Alessandri and Coletta considered the problem of observers design for hybrid systems, whose continuous evolution is subject to linear dynamics assuming knowledge of the discrete state at each time.

In this paper, the assumption on discrete state knowledge is removed and the more general case where only some hybrid inputs and outputs (both either discrete or continuous) of the hybrid plant are measurable is addressed. The objective is to devise a hybrid observer that reconstructs the complete state from the knowledge of the hybrid plant inputs and outputs, achieving generation of the plant location sequence and exponential convergence of the continuous state estimation error.

As described in Section 2, the proposed hybrid observer consists of two parts: a *location observer* and a *continuous observer*. The former identifies the current location of the hybrid plant, while the latter produces an estimate of the evolution of the continuous state of the hybrid plant. In Section 3, it is first tackled the case where the current location of the given hybrid plant can be reconstructed *using the discrete input/output information only*, without the need of additional information from the evolution of the continuous part of the plant. When the evolutions of the discrete inputs and outputs of the hybrid plant are not sufficient to estimate the current location, the continuous plant inputs and outputs can be used to obtain some additional information that may be useful for the identification of the plant current location. This case is treated in Section 4. Due to space limitation, some proofs are not reported. They can be found in the extended version of the paper available at the PARADES' web page *http://www.parades.rm.cnr.it*.

2   Structure of the Hybrid Observer

Let H_p denote the model of a given hybrid plant with N locations and let (q, x), (σ, u) and (ψ, y) stand, respectively, for the hybrid state, inputs and outputs of the plant. Our aim is to design a hybrid observer for the plant that provides an estimate $\tilde{q}$ and an estimate $\tilde{x}$ for its current location q and continuous state x, respectively. We assume that the discrete evolution of q is described as follows:

$$q(k+1) \in \varphi\left(q(k), \sigma(k+1)\right) \tag{1}$$

$$\sigma(k+1) \in \phi\left(q(k), x(t_{k+1}), u(t_{k+1})\right) \tag{2}$$

$$\psi(k+1) = \eta\left(q(k), \sigma(k+1)\right) \tag{3}$$

where $q(k) \in Q$ and $\psi(k) \in \Psi$ are, respectively, the location and the discrete output after the k-th input event $\sigma(k) \in \Sigma \bigcup \{\epsilon\}$, and t_k denotes the unknown time at which this event takes place. $Q = \{q_1, \cdots, q_N\}$ is the finite set of locations with $N = |Q|$, Ψ is the finite set of discrete outputs, Σ is the finite set of input events and internal events depending on the continuous state x and input u, and ϵ is the *silent event*[1]. $\varphi : Q \times \Sigma \to 2^Q$ is the transition function, $\eta : Q \times \Sigma \to \Psi$ is the output function and $\phi : Q \times X \times U \to 2^\Sigma$ is the function specifying the possible events where $X \subseteq \mathbb{R}^n$, $U \subseteq \mathbb{R}^m$ are the continuous state and control values domains. Moreover, we assume that the continuous evolution of x is described by a linear time–invariant system

$$\dot{x}(t) = A_i\, x(t) + B_i\, u(t) \tag{4}$$

$$y(t) = C_i\, x(t) \tag{5}$$

with $y(t) \in \mathbb{R}^p$ and $A_i \in \mathbb{R}^{n \times n}$, $B_i \in \mathbb{R}^{n \times m}$, $C_i \in \mathbb{R}^{p \times n}$ depending on the current plant location q_i. Note that the plant hybrid model does not allow continuous state resets.

In this paper we present a methodology for the design of exponentially convergent hybrid observers defined as follows

Definition 1. *Given the model of a hybrid plant H_p as in (1–5) and given a maximum convergence error $M_0 \geq 0$ and a rate of convergence μ, a hybrid observer is said to be* exponentially convergent *if its discrete state $\tilde{q}$ exhibits correct identification of the plant location sequence after some steps and the continuous observation error $\zeta = \tilde{x} - x$ converges exponentially to the set $\|\zeta\| \leq M_0$ with rate of convergence greater than or equal to μ, that is*

$$\tilde{q}(k) = q(k) \qquad\qquad \forall k > K, \text{ for some } K \in \mathbb{N}^+ \tag{6}$$

$$\|\zeta(t)\| \leq e^{-\mu t}\|\zeta(t_K)\| + M_0 \qquad \forall t > t_K. \tag{7}$$

The structure of the proposed hybrid observer is illustrated in Figure 1. It is composed of two blocks: a *location observer*, and a *continuous observer*.

The *location observer* receives as input the plant inputs (σ, u) and outputs (ψ, y). Its task is to provide the estimate $\tilde{q}$ of the discrete location q of the hybrid plant at the current time. This information is used by the *continuous observer* to construct an estimate $\tilde{x}$ of the plant continuous state that converges exponentially to x. The continuous plant input u and output y are used by the continuous observer to this purpose.

---

[1] This event is introduced to model different possible situations for the discrete dynamics. For example, if $\phi(q, x, u) = \{\epsilon\}$, then there is no discrete transition enabled while if $\phi(q, x, u) = \{\sigma_1, \epsilon\}$, then it is possible either to let time pass or to take the discrete transition associated to σ_1. Moreover, if $\phi(q, x, u) = \{\sigma_1\}$, then the discrete transition associated to σ_1 is forced to occur. This is useful for example to model internal transitions due to the continuous state hitting a guard.

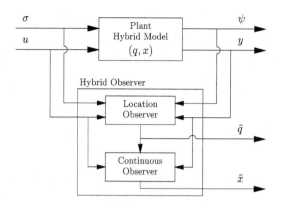

Fig. 1. Observer structure: location observer H_l and continuous observer H_c.

3   Location and Continuous Observers Decoupled Synthesis

In this section, necessary and sufficient conditions for a decoupled design of a location observer and a continuous observer achieving exponential convergence according to Definition 1 are given.

3.1   Location-Observer Design

Definition 2. *Let us denote by $\mathcal{M}$ the FSM associated to the hybrid plant H_p defined by (1),*

$$\sigma(k+1) \in \widehat{\phi}\,(q(k)) = \bigcup_{x \in X, u \in U} \phi\,(q(k), x, u)$$

and (3). The FSM $\mathcal{M}$ is said to be current–location observable if there exists an integer K such that for any unknown initial location $q_0 \in Q$ and for every input sequence $\sigma(k)$ the location $q(i)$ can be determined for every $i > K$ from the observation sequence $\psi(k)$ up to i.

An observer $\mathcal{O}$ that gives estimates of the location $q(k)$ of $\mathcal{M}$ after each observation $\psi(k)$ is the FSM

$$\tilde{q}(k+1) \in \varphi_O\,(\tilde{q}(k), \psi(k+1)) \tag{8}$$
$$\psi_O(k+1) = \tilde{q}(k) \tag{9}$$

with $Q_O \in 2^Q$, $\Sigma_O = \Psi$, $\Psi_O = Q_O$. The input of the observer is the output $\psi(k)$ of $\mathcal{M}$ and the output produced by $\mathcal{O}$ is an estimate $\tilde{q}(k)$ of the location $q(k)$, representing the subset of Q of possible locations into which $\mathcal{M}$ could have been transitioned after the k-th event. The observer transition function φ_O is constructed by inspection of the given FSM following the algorithm for

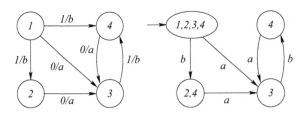

Fig. 2. A simple FSM $\mathcal{M}$ (left) and its observer $\mathcal{O}$ (right).

the computation of the *current–location observation tree* as described in [6]. The construction starts from the initial location $\tilde{q}(0)$ of $\mathcal{O}$: since the initial location of $\mathcal{M}$ is unknown, then $\tilde{q}(0) = Q$. When the first input event $\psi(1)$ is received, then the observer makes a transition to the location $\tilde{q}$ corresponding to the set

$$\{q \mid \exists s \in Q : q \in \varphi(s,\sigma), \text{ with } \sigma \in \widehat{\phi}(s) \text{ such that } \psi(1) = \eta(s,\sigma)\}$$

that depends on the value of $\psi(1)$. In fact, the number of observer locations at the second level depends on the number of possible events $\psi(1)$. By iterating this step, one can easily construct the third level of the tree whose nodes correspond to the sets of possible locations into which $\mathcal{M}$ transitioned after the second event. Since this procedure produces at most $2^N - 1$ observer locations, then the construction of the observer necessarily ends.

Consider for example the FSM $\mathcal{M}$ in figure 2 for which $Q = \{1,2,3,4\}$, $\Sigma = \{0,1\}$ and $\Psi = \{a,b\}$. The observer $\mathcal{O}$ of this FSM has four locations, i.e. $Q_O = \{\{1,2,3,4\},\{2,4\},3,4\}$ (see figure 2).

The following theorem gives necessary and sufficient conditions for an FSM to be current–location observable. The theorem has its origins in a result of [12], where a different definition of observability was considered.

Theorem 1. *An FSM $\mathcal{M}$ is current–location observable iff for the corresponding observer $\mathcal{O}$ defined as in (8–9):*

(i) the set $Q \cap Q_O$ is nonempty;
(ii) every primary cycle $Q^i_c \subset Q_O$ includes at least one location in Q, i.e. the set $Q^i_c \cap Q$ is nonempty[2];
(iii) the subset $Q \cap Q_O$ is φ_O-invariant[3].

Hence, if conditions *(i)*, *(ii)* and *(iii)* of Theorem 1 are satisfied by the FSM associated to the hybrid plant H_p, then the hybrid observer can be obtained by a decoupled synthesis of the location observer and the continuous observer. The location observer H_l coincides with the observer $\mathcal{O}$ described above and fulfils condition (6) of Definition 1 with location observer transitions synchronous with hybrid plant transitions.

---

[2] This condition corresponds to that of prestability of $\mathcal{O}$ with respect to the set $Q \cap Q_O$, as introduced in [13].

[3] Following [13], a subset S is said to be φ-invariant if $\bigcup_{q \in S} \varphi(q, \phi(q)) \subset S$.

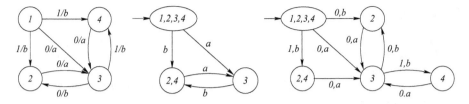

Fig. 3. FSM $\widetilde{\mathcal{M}}$ (left) and its observers without (center) and with (right) inputs measurements.

The following examples illustrate how Theorem 1 works. For the FSM $\mathcal{M}$ and the corresponding observer $\mathcal{O}$ in figure 2: $Q \cap Q_O = \{3, 4\}$ and the only cycle Q_c^1 of $\mathcal{O}$ is composed of locations in Q, i.e. $Q_c^1 = \{3, 4\}$. Moreover it is easy to verify that the set $Q \cap Q_O$ is invariant. Then, $\mathcal{M}$ is current–location observable. Consider next the FSM $\widetilde{\mathcal{M}}$ and its observer $\widetilde{\mathcal{O}}$ in Figure 3. The observer has three locations: $Q_O = \{\{1, 2, 3, 4\}, \{2, 4\}, 3\}$, $Q \cap Q_O = \{3\}$ and the only cycle Q_c^1 of $\widetilde{\mathcal{O}}$ includes location 3, i.e. $Q_c^1 = \{\{2, 4\}, 3\}$. However, since location 3 is not invariant, then $\widetilde{\mathcal{M}}$ is not current–location observable. Note that while it is easy to check whether conditions *(i)* and *(ii)* of Theorem 1 are satisfied, verifiying condition *(iii)* is more involved. An algorithm of complexity $O(N)$ to check φ-invariance can be found in [13].

Assuming measurability of the input sequence $\sigma(k)$, current–location observability can be redefined by replacing in Definition 2 the sequence $\psi(k)$ with the sequence $(\sigma(k), \psi(k))$. The knowledgement of the input sequence may help in the estimation process. For instance, the FSM $\widetilde{\mathcal{M}}$ becomes current–location observable when both input and output sequences are considered as shown in figure 3.

3.2 Continuous Observer Design

The continuous observer H_C is a switching system whose dynamics depend on the current estimate $\tilde{q}$ of the hybrid plant location q provided by the location observer. The scheme of the continuous observer is readily obtained using the classical Luenberger's approach [10]:

$$\dot{\tilde{x}}(t) = F_i \tilde{x}(t) + B_i u(t) + G_i y(t) \quad \text{if } \tilde{q} = q_i. \tag{10}$$

where $F_i = (A_i - G_i C_i)$. If $q = q_i$, the corresponding dynamics of the observation error $\zeta = \tilde{x} - x$ is $\dot{\zeta}(t) = F_i \zeta(t)$. The gain matrix G_i is the design parameter used to set the velocity of convergence in each location. As pointed out in [2], the stabilization of this continuous observer is more complex than the stabilization of a single dynamics in (10) and can be achieved using the results on hybrid systems stabilization presented in [5] and [16]. In particular, exponential convergence of the hybrid observer is guaranteed by the following lemma:

Lemma 1. *Assume that*

- **H1**: *for* $i = 1 : N$, *all couples* (A_i, C_i) *in (4–5) are observable;*
- **H2**: *the hybrid system* H_p *exhibits transitions with time separation greater than or equal to some* $D > 0$;
- **H3**: *the location observer* H_l *identifies instantaneously changes in the hybrid system location.*

The proposed hybrid observer H_l–H_c *is exponentially convergent, with a given rate* μ *and convergence error* $M_0 = 0$, *if gains* G_i *in (10) are chosen such that*

$$\alpha(A_i - G_i C_i) + \frac{\log[nk(A_i - G_i C_i)]}{D} \leq -\mu \tag{11}$$

where $\alpha(A)$ *is the spectral abscissa of the matrix* A *and* $k(A) = \|T\| \|T^{-1}\|$ *with* T *such that* $T^{-1}AT$ *is in the Jordan canonical form.*

The proof of this lemma can be obtained as a simplification of that of Theorem 4 reported in Section 4.2. Notice that condition **H3** is guaranteed by the current–location observability of the FSM associated to H_p assumed in this section.

Remark 1. A solution to the problem of exponentially stabilizing switching systems can be obtained from Lemma 1, with regard to the class of systems satisfying: controllability of all couples (A_i, B_i) (in place of **H1**), the transition separation property **H2** and with either known or observable current location q_i. For such systems, the problem of exponential stabilization reduces to the existence of state feedback gains K_i satisfying $\alpha(A_i - B_i K_i) + \log[nk(A_i - B_i K_i)]/D \leq -\mu$.

4　Location and Continuous Observers Interacting Synthesis

When the evolutions of the discrete inputs and outputs of the hybrid plant are not sufficient to estimate the current location, the continuous plant inputs and outputs can be used to obtain some additional information that may be useful for the identification of the plant current location. In Section 4.1, a methodology for selecting where the continuous information should be supplied and how it should be processed is described. The processing of the continuous signals of the plant gives reliable discrete information only after some delay with respect to plant location switchings. This results in a coupling between the location observer parameters and the continuous observer parameters as described in Section 4.2.

4.1　Location-Observer Design

When the FSM describing the discrete evolution of the hybrid plant is not current–location observable from the available input/output discrete sequences, then, in order to estimate the current–location, it is natural to turn to the information available from the continuous evolution of the plant. In particular,

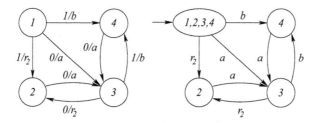

Fig. 4. The system $\widehat{\mathcal{M}}$ (left) and its observer $\widehat{\mathcal{O}}$ (right).

residual signals can be used to detect a change in the continuous dynamics of the plant and the resulting signatures can be used as additional inputs to the current–location observer described in Section 3.1.

Introduction of signatures. Consider for example the system $\widetilde{\mathcal{M}}$ in Figure 3 and assume that only the discrete plant output ψ is available. Assume also that a signature r_2 can be produced for detecting the continuous dynamics associated to state 2. Then, when the system enters state 2, signal r_2 is available and can be used as an input for the discrete observer. A representation of the FSM associated to the hybrid plant plus the generator of the signature r_2 can be obtained by adding an output r_2 to each arc entering location 2. By doing this the FSM $\widehat{\mathcal{M}}$ shown in Figure 4 is obtained from $\widetilde{\mathcal{M}}$. By the introduction of signature r_2, $\widehat{\mathcal{M}}$ is now current–location observable. Figure 4 shows the observer of $\widehat{\mathcal{M}}$, obtained applying the synthesis described in Section 3.1. In the general case, if the discrete representation of a given hybrid plant H_p is not current–location observable, then one may introduce a number of signatures detecting some of the different continuous dynamics of the plant to achieve current–location observability for the combination of the hybrid plant and the signature generator. Necessary and sufficient conditions for current–location observability of the composition hybrid plant and the signature generator are given in Theorem 1. If dynamics parameters in (4–5) are different in each location, then current–location observability can always be achieved in this way. The complete scheme of the location observer is shown in Figure 5. The *signatures generator* is described in the following Section. The *location identification logic* is a discrete observer synthesized as described in Section 3.1.

Signatures generator. The task of the signature generator is similar to that of a fault detection and identification algorithm (see [11] for a tutorial). Indeed, the signatures generator has to decide whether or not the continuous system is obeying to a particular dynamics in a set of known ones. Assuming that the location observer has properly recognized that the hybrid plant H_p is in location q_i, i.e. $\tilde{q} = q_i$, then the location observer should detect a fault from the evolution of $u(t)$ and $y(t)$ when the plant H_p changes the location to some $q_j \neq q_i$ and should identify the new location q_j. The time delay in the location change detection and identification is critical to the convergence of the overall hybrid observer. We denote by Δ an upper bound for such delay.

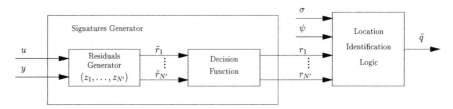

Fig. 5. Location observer structure.

Since, when a change of location occurs, the continuous dynamics of the plant suddenly change, then the fault detection algorithms of interest are those designed for abrupt faults [7]. The general scheme is composed of three cascade blocks: the *residuals generator*, the *decision function*, and the fault decision logic, renamed here *location identification logic*, see Figure 5. The *signature generator* is the pair residuals generator–decision function. Assume that, in order to achieve current–location observability for the discrete evolution of the hybrid plant H_p, the signature generator has to detect N' different continuous dynamics (4–5) associated to a subset of states $\mathcal{R} \subseteq Q$. The simplest and most reliable approach for our application is to use a bank of N' Luenberger observers (see [7]), one for each plant dynamics in $\mathcal{R}$, as residual generators:

$$\dot{z}_j(t) = H_j z_j(t) + B_j u(t) + L_j y(t) \tag{12}$$

$$\tilde{r}_j(t) = C_j z_j(t) - y(t) \tag{13}$$

where $H_j = A_j - L_j C_j$ and L_j are design parameters. The N' residual signals $\tilde{r}_j$ are used to identify the continuous dynamics the plant is obeying to. Indeed, no–vanishing residuals $\tilde{r}_j(t)$ correspond to $j \neq i$. The decision function outputs N' binary signals as follows:

$$r_j(t) = \begin{cases} true & \text{if } \|\tilde{r}_j(t)\| \leq \varepsilon \\ false & \text{if } \|\tilde{r}_j(t)\| > \varepsilon \end{cases} \qquad \text{for } j = 1, \ldots, N' \tag{14}$$

where the threshold ε is a design parameter. In the following theorem, a sufficient condition for ensuring $r_i = true$ in a time Δ after a transition of the hybrid plant H_p to a dynamics (A_i, B_i, C_i) is presented.

Theorem 2. *For a given $\Delta > 0$, $\varepsilon > 0$ and a given upper bound Z_0 on $\|x - z_i\|$, if the estimator gains L_i in (12) are chosen such that*

$$\alpha(H_i) \leq -\frac{1}{\Delta} \log \frac{n \|C_i\| k(H_i) Z_0}{\varepsilon} \tag{15}$$

then r_i becomes true before a time Δ elapses after a change in the plant dynamics parameters to the values (A_i, B_i, C_i).

Consider the j–th residual generator and assume that there is a transition from location q_j to location q_i, so that the continuous state x of H_p is governed by dynamics defined by parameters $(A_i, B_i, C_i) \neq (A_j, B_j, C_j)$. Unfortunately, as shown for example by the following theorem, there are cases where we cannot prevent the signal r_j from remaining *true* for an unbounded time:

Theorem 3. *If the matrix $(C_j - C_i)B_i + C_j(B_i - B_j)$ is invertible, with $i \neq j$, then for any hybrid plant initial condition, the class of plant inputs $u(t)$ that achieves $r_j(t) = true$ for all $t > \Delta$ after a change in the plant dynamics parameters to (A_i, B_i, C_i) is not empty.*

In the general case, the set of configurations and the class of plant inputs for which the signatures (14) fail to properly identify the continuous dynamics can be obtained by computing the maximal safe set and the maximal controller for dynamics (4–5) and (12-13) with respect to a safety specification defined in an extended state space that contains an extra variable τ representing the elapsed time after a plant transition. More precisely, the set of configurations for which a wrong signature may be produced up to a time $t' > \Delta$ after a plant location change, is given by those configurations $(0, x^0, z_j^0)$ from which there exists a plant continuous input $u(t)$ able to keep the trajectory inside the set $[0, t'] \times \{(x, z_j) \in \mathbb{R}^{2n} | \, \| C_j z_j - C_i x \| \leq \varepsilon \}$. However, since in pratical applications the resulting maximal controller is very small, the case of non proper identification is unlikely to occur.

4.2   Continuous Observer Design

The continuous observer[4] is designed as in the previous case (see Section 3.2). Exponential convergence of the continuous observer is analyzed considering the complete hybrid system obtained by composing the hybrid model H_p and the observer hybrid model H_l and H_c. The overall hybrid system has $N \times N$ locations of type $(q_i, \tilde{q}_j)$, the former corresponding to plant locations and the latter corresponding to observer locations. To each location $(q_i, \tilde{q}_j)$, the continuous dynamics

$$\dot{x}(t) = A_i x(t) + B_i u(t) \tag{16}$$
$$\dot{\zeta}(t) = F_j \zeta(t) + [(A_i - A_j) - G_j(C_i - C_j)]\, x(t) + (B_i - B_j)u(t) \tag{17}$$

is associated. By integrating (17) we have

$$\zeta(t) = e^{F_j t}\zeta(0) + e^{F_j t} \star v(t) \tag{18}$$

where $\star$ denotes the convolution operator and $v(t) = [(A_i - A_j) - K(C_i - C_j)]\, x(t) + (B_i - B_j)u(t)$. The following notation will be used in the sequel ([15]):

$\|m(t)\|_\infty = \max\limits_{k=1,q} \sup\limits_{t \geq 0} |m_k(t)|$, the L^∞–norm of q–dimensional signals $m : \mathbb{R} \to \mathbb{R}^q$;

$\|M\|_\infty$ and $\|M\|_1$ the L^∞ and the L^1–norm of a matrix M, respectively.

---

[4] The Luenberger observers (12) contained in the residual generators, which are designed to converge to the same state variable x, do not provide a satisfactory estimate of the evolution of x since they are tuning according to (15) in order to meet the specification of producing a residual with a transient time less than Δ. Hence, they exhibit a large overshoot which is undesirable for feedback purpose.

Theorem 4. *Assume that*

- **H1**: *for $i = 1 : N$, all couples (A_i, C_i) in (4–5) are observable;*
- **H2**: *there exist $X > 0$ and $U > 0$, such that $\|x(t)\|_\infty \leq X$ and $\|u(t)\|_\infty \leq U$, so that*

$$\|v(t)\|_\infty \leq V = \max_{q_i, q_j \in \mathcal{R}} \| [(A_i - A_j) - G_j(C_i - C_j)] \|_1 X + \|B_i - B_j\|_1 U \tag{19}$$

- **H3**: *the hybrid system H_p exhibits transitions with time separation greater than or equal to some $D > 0$.*

Given a $\mu > 0$ and an $M_0 > 0$, if the observer gains G_i are chosen such that

$$\alpha(A_i - G_i C_i) + \frac{\log[nk(A_i - G_i C_i)]}{\beta} \leq -\mu \tag{20}$$

for some $\beta \in (0, D)$, and if

- **H4**: *the location observer H_l identifies a change in the hybrid system location within time*

$$\Delta \leq \min \left\{ \min_{q_i \in \mathcal{R}} \frac{1 - e^{-\mu\beta}}{n\sqrt{n}\,k(A_i - G_i C_i)V} M_0, \; D - \beta \right\} \tag{21}$$

then the proposed hybrid observer H_l–H_c is exponentially convergent with rate μ and convergence error M_0.

Proof. Consider two subsequent transitions of the hybrid plant H_p, occurring at times t_k and t_{k+1} respectively. By hypothesis **H1**, $t_{k+1} - t_k \geq D$. Since by **H4**, $\Delta \leq D - \beta$, the location observer H_l identifies the k-th and $k + 1$-th state transitions at some times t'_k and t'_{k+1}, respectively, with $t'_k - t_k \leq \Delta$ and $t'_{k+1} - t_{k+1} \leq \Delta$. Furthermore, notice that, by **H3** and **H4**, $t'_{k+1} - t'_k \geq t_{k+1} - t'_k \geq D - \Delta \geq \beta > 0$. Since $\tilde{q} = q$ in the time interval $[t'_k, t_{k+1}]$, then, by condition **H1** on observability of dynamics (4–5), convergence to zero of $\zeta(t)$ at any desired velocity can be obtained by proper choice of gains G_j. In particular, observer gains G_j satisfying inequality (20), for some $\beta \in (0, D)$, can be selected. However, since $\tilde{q} \neq q$ when $t \in [t_{k+1}, t'_{k+1}]$, $\zeta(t)$ may fail to converge later. Hence, the convergent behavior for $t \in [t'_k, t_{k+1}]$ has to compensate the divergent behavior for $t \in [t_{k+1}, t'_{k+1}]$. By (18), we have

$$\zeta(t) = e^{F_j(t - t'_k)}\zeta(t'_k) + \int_0^{t - t'_k} e^{F_j(t - t'_k - \tau)} v(\tau + t'_k)\, d\tau \quad \forall t \in (t'_k, t'_{k+1}] \tag{22}$$

where $v(t) = 0$ for $t \in (t'_k, t_{k+1}]$. By the Lemma 2 reported in appendix, the evolution of the transient term can be bounded as follows

$$\|e^{F_j(t - t'_k)}\zeta(t'_k)\| \leq nk(F_j)e^{\alpha(F_j)(t - t'_k)}\|\zeta(t'_k)\| \tag{23}$$

Furthermore, for the forced term, since by **H4** $t - t_{k+1} \leq \Delta$, we have

$$\left\| \int_0^{t-t'_k} e^{F_j(t-t'_k-\tau)} v(\tau + t'_k) \, d\tau \right\| \leq nk(F_j) \int_0^{t-t_{k+1}} e^{\alpha(F_j)(t-t_{k+1}-\tau)} \|v(\tau + t_{k+1})\| \, d\tau$$

$$\leq nk(F_j) \sup_{t \geq 0} \|v(t)\| \int_0^{t-t_{k+1}} e^{\alpha(F_j)\tau} \, d\tau \leq n\sqrt{n}k(F_j)\|v(t)\|_\infty \frac{e^{\alpha(F_j)(t-t_{k+1})} - 1}{\alpha(F_j)}$$

$$\leq n\sqrt{n}k(F_j)V(t - t_{k+1}) \leq n\sqrt{n}k(F_j)V\Delta \qquad \forall t \in [t_{k+1}, t'_{k+1}] \quad (24)$$

Then, using (21), by (23) and (24), equation (22) can be upper bounded as follows

$$\|\zeta(t)\| \leq nk(F_j)e^{\alpha(F_j)(t-t'_k)}\|\zeta(t'_k)\| + \left(1 - e^{-\mu\beta}\right)M_0 \qquad \forall t \in (t'_k, t'_{k+1}] \quad (25)$$

Hence, the evolution of the norm of the observation error $\|\zeta(t)\|$ is upper bounded by the evolution of a hybrid system as described in Lemma 3 reported in appendix, with $\gamma = \alpha(F_j)$, $a = nk(F_j)$, $b = \left(1 - e^{-\mu\beta}\right)M_0$, and continuous state resets separation greater than or equal to β.

Then, by Lemma 3, if the observer gains are chosen according to (20), the observation error converges exponentially to the set

$$\|x - \tilde{x}\| = \|\zeta(t)\| \leq \frac{b}{(1 - e^{-\mu\beta})} = M_0$$

with velocity of convergence greater than or equal to $-\mu$. **Q.E.D.**

5   Using Guards to Improve Continuous State Estimation

In some cases the detection of a discrete transition in the hybrid plant can be used to improve the convergence of the observer continuous state $\tilde{x}$ to the plant continuous state x. Indeed, as represented in (2), plant discrete transitions may depend on the value of plant continuous state x through the guards modelled by functions $\phi(\cdot)$.

A simple case is when complete information on the plant continuous state x can be obtained at some time from the detection of a plant discrete transition. This allows the continuous observer to jump to the current value of the plant continuous state, zeroing instantaneously the observation error. Suppose that the plant is in location q_i and that, at some time t_k, the event σ_j that produces a forced transition corresponding to the state x hitting a guard is identified. Instantaneous detection of the plant continuous state can be achieved if the following system of equation admits a unique solution for x:

$$\begin{aligned} C_i\, x &= y(t_k^-) \\ \sigma_j &\in \phi\left(q_i, x, u(t_k^-)\right) \end{aligned} \qquad (26)$$

A similar condition can be used to obtain open loop observers for the components of the continuous plant state that lie on the unobservable subspace, when condition **H1** in either Lemma 1 or in Theorem 4 is not fullfilled. Instantaneous detection of the not observable components of the continuous plant state can be achieved if equations (26) admit a unique solution for them.

Conclusions

A methodology for the design of exponentially convergent dynamical observers for hybrid plants has been presented. In the proposed hybrid dynamical observer, a location observer and a continuous observer provide, respectively, estimates of the plant current location and continuous state. Both the case where the current plant location can be reconstructed by using discrete input/output information only, and the more complex case where some additional information from the continuous evolution of the plant is needed to this purpose have been considered.

References

1. G. A. Ackerson and K. S. Fu. On state estimation in switching environments. *IEEE Trans. on Automatic Control*, 15(1):10–17, 1970.
2. A. Alessandri and P. Coletta. Design of luenberger observers for a class of hybrid linear systems. In *Hybrid Systems: Computation and Control*, volume 2034 of *LNCS*, pages 7–18. Springer–Verlag, Berlin Heidelberg, 2001.
3. A. Balluchi, L. Benvenuti, M. D. Di Benedetto, C. Pinello, and A. L. Sangiovanni-Vincentelli. Automotive engine control and hybrid systems: Challenges and opportunities. *Proceedings of the IEEE*, 88, "Special Issue on Hybrid Systems" (invited paper)(7):888–912, July 2000.
4. A. Balluchi, L. Benvenuti, M. D. Di Benedetto, and A. L. Sangiovanni Vincentelli. A hybrid observer for the driveline dynamics. In *Proc. of the European Control Conference 2001*, pages 618–623, Porto, P, 2001.
5. M. Branicky. Multiple lyapunov functions and other analysis tools for switched and hybrid systems. *IEEE Trans. on Aut. Contr.*, 43(4):475–482, 1998.
6. P. E. Caines, R. Greiner, and S. Wang. Dynamical logic observers for finite automata. In *Proceedings of 27th Conference on Decision and Control*, pages 226–233, Austin, TX, 1988.
7. P. M. Frank. Fault diagnosis in dynamic systems using analytical and knowledge–based redundancy — a survey and some new results. *Automatica*, 26(3):459–474, 1990.
8. Y. Liu. Switching observer design for uncertain nonlinear systems. *IEEE Trans. on Automatic Control*, 42(1):1699–1703, 1997.
9. C. Van Loan. The sensitivity of the matrix exponential. *SIAM Journal of Number Analysis*, 14(6):971–981, December 1977.
10. D.G. Luenberger. An introduction to observers. *IEEE Transactions on Automatic Control*, 16(6):596–602, Dec 1971.
11. M.-A. Massoumnia, G.C., Verghese, and A.S. Willsky. Failure detection and identification. *IEEE Transactions on Automatic Control*, 34(3):316–21, March 1989.
12. C. M. Özveren and A. S. Willsky. Observability of discrete event dynamic systems. *IEEE Trans. on Automatic Control*, 35:797–806, 1990.
13. C. M. Özveren, A. S. Willsky, and P. J. Antsaklis. Stability and stabilizability of discrete event dynamic systems. *Journal of the Association for Computing Machinery*, 38:730–752, 1991.
14. P. J. Ramadge. Observability of discrete event–systems. In *Proceedings of 25th Conference on Decision and Control*, pages 1108–1112, Athens, Greece, 1986.
15. M. Vidyasagar. *Nonlinear Systems Analysis*. Prentice–Hall, Inc, Englewood Cliffs, N.J., 1978.

16. H. Ye, A. N. Michel, and L. Hou. Stability theory for hybrid dynamical systems for switched and hybrid systems. *IEEE Trans. on Automatic Control*, 43(4):461–474, 1998.

17. Q. Zhang. Hybrid filtering for linear systems with non-baussian disturbances. *IEEE Trans. on Automatic Control*, 45(1):50–61, 1999.

Appendix

Lemma 2 ([9]). *Let A be a matrix in $\mathbb{R}^{n \times n}$. Then*

$$\|e^{A\tau}\| \leq n\,k(A)\,e^{\alpha(A)\tau} \qquad \forall \tau \geq 0 \qquad (27)$$

where $\alpha(A)$ is the spectral abscissa (i.e. the maximal real part of the eigenvalues) of matrix A and $k(A) = \|T\|\,\|T^{-1}\|$ with T such that $T^{-1}AT$ is in the Jordan canonical form.

Lemma 3. *Consider a single–location hybrid system with a scalar continuous variable x. Let x be subject to the dynamics $\dot{x} = \gamma x$, with $\gamma < 0$, and to the resets $x(t_k) := ax(t_k^-) + b$ occuring at some unspecified sequence of times $\{t_k\}$, with $a \geq 1$ and $b \geq 0$. The evolution of $x(t)$ can be described as follows*

$$x(t) = e^{\gamma(t-t_{k-1})}x(t_{k-1}) \qquad\qquad \text{for } t \in [t_{k-1}, t_k) \quad (28)$$
$$x(t_k) = ax(t_k^-) + b = ae^{\gamma(t_k-t_{k-1})}x(t_{k-1}) + b \qquad\qquad (29)$$

Assume that there exists a lower bound β on reset events separation, i.e. $t_k - t_{k-1} \geq \beta > 0$ for all $k > 1$.

If $x(t_0) > 0$ and $\gamma + \frac{\log a}{\beta} = -\mu < 0$, then $x(t)$ converges exponentially to the set $[0, \frac{b}{1-e^{-\mu\beta}}]$ with rate of convergence equal to or greater than μ.

Proof. By (29), since $e^{-\mu(t_k-t_{k-i})} \leq e^{-i\mu\beta}$ then

$$x(t_k) \leq e^{\frac{\log a}{\beta}(t_k-t_{k-1})}\,e^{\gamma(t_k-t_{k-1})}x(t_{k-1}) + b = e^{-\mu(t_k-t_{k-1})}x(t_{k-1}) + b$$
$$\leq e^{-\mu(t_k-t_0)}x(t_0) + b\sum_{i=0}^{k-1}e^{-i\mu\beta} < e^{-\mu(t_k-t_0)}x(t_0) + \frac{b}{1-e^{-\mu\beta}}$$

This proves that, after each reset the value $x(t_k)$ of the state is upper bounded by an exponential with rate $-\mu$ that converges to the point $\frac{b}{1-e^{-\mu\beta}}$. This shows exponential convergence to the set $[0, \frac{b}{1-e^{-\mu\beta}}]$ at resets times t_k. Readily, the same results can be extended to the open intervals between resets times by noting that during the continuous evolution the rate of convergence $-\gamma$ is lower than $-\mu$.   **Q.E.D.**

Guaranteed Overapproximations of Unsafe Sets for Continuous and Hybrid Systems: Solving the Hamilton-Jacobi Equation Using Viability Techniques[*]

Alexandre M. Bayen[1], Eva Crück[2], and Claire J. Tomlin[1]

[1] Hybrid Systems Laboratory, Stanford University, Stanford, CA
bayen@stanford.edu, tomlin@stanford.edu
[2] Laboratoire de Recherches Balistiques et Aérodynamiques, Vernon, France
eva.cruck@dga.defense.gouv.fr

Abstract. We show how reachable sets of constrained continuous and simple hybrid systems may be computed using the minimum time-to-reach function. We present an algorithm for computing a discrete approximation to the minimum time-to-reach function, which we prove to be a converging underapproximation to the actual function. We use the discrete minimum time-to-reach function for simple hybrid systems to compute overapproximations of unsafe zones for aircraft in a sector of the Oakland Air Traffic Control Center, leading to the automatic generation of conflict-free aircraft maneuvers.

1 Introduction

It is well known that verification of system safety may be achieved by computing the *reachable set of states*, that is, the set of all states from which the system has a trajectory which enters the set of unsafe states (or target). If the initial state of the system is outside of this set, then the safety property is verified. The design of methods to efficiently compute this set for continuous and hybrid systems remains a tough problem, though progress has been made for hybrid systems with linear or affine dynamics, or for which the set representation can be simplified to, for example, polyhedra or ellipsoids [1, 11, 6]. In previous work of Mitchell, Bayen, and Tomlin [16], we have performed this reachable set computation using a convergent approximation of a level set function $J(x, t)$, which is the solution of a time varying Hamilton-Jacobi Equation (HJE), such that $\{x \in \mathbb{R}^N : J(x, t) \leq 0\}$ is the set of states from which the system has a trajectory which reaches the target set $\{x \in \mathbb{R}^N : J(x, 0) \leq 0\}$ in at most t time units.

In this paper, we consider the same reachability problem, using a different function to encode the reachable set: we define the *minimum time-to-reach function* $\theta_C^K(x)$ to be the minimum time for a trajectory of the system, starting at

---

[*] Research supported by DARPA under the Software Enabled Control Program (AFRL contract F33615-99-C-3014), by NASA under Grant NCC 2-5422, and by two Graduate Fellowships of the Délégation Générale pour l'Armement (France).

C.J. Tomlin and M.R. Greenstreet (Eds.): HSCC 2002, LNCS 2289, pp. 90–104, 2002.

state x, to reach the target set C while staying in a set K. The set of states from which the system has a trajectory which reaches the target set in at most t is thus $\{x \in \mathbb{R}^N : \theta_C^K(x) \leq t\}$. The minimum time-to-reach function has several interesting properties, which we will exploit here. First, the minimum time-to-reach function is known to exist and to be the unique Crandall-Evans-Lions viscosity solution ([12]) of a particular HJE (see Bardi [4]). Second, there exist numerical algorithms ([17, 10]) based on viability techniques (see Aubin [2, 3]) which compute guaranteed underapproximations of the minimum time-to-reach function, and therefore overapproximations of the reachable set, in the presence of constraints. These algorithms are based on discrete time, discrete state approximations of the continuous dynamics. Third, this function provides direct access to the "survival time" of the system within the reachable set, which is information that may readily be used for control purposes.

In this paper, we first define the minimum time-to-reach function in the context of both Hamilton-Jacobi equations and viability theory (set valued analysis). We present the first complete instantiation of an algorithm proposed by Saint-Pierre [18] in which we combine ideas from [8, 9] into a self-sufficient algorithm, which computes an underapproximation of this function. This algorithm actually computes the discrete minimum time-to-reach function for a discrete time, discrete state approximation of the continuous dynamics, whose trajectories we show to be "close", in a well-defined sense, to corresponding trajectories of the continuous dynamics. This discrete minimum time-to-reach function converges to the continuous minimum time-to-reach function as increments in the space and time step converge to zero: we generate proofs (inspired from [8, 9]) of well posedness and convergence. We provide a numerical validation of this algorithm by assessing its rate of convergence to the continuous function through two textbook examples (for which we know the continuous solution). In the second part of this paper, we consider the problem of maneuver synthesis in Sector 33 of the Oakland Air Traffic Control Center, which is one of the busiest sectors within this Center. We present an algorithm for computing the minimum time-to-reach function for hybrid and reset systems with one switch or reset. We then apply this algorithm to the generation of control policies for heading change or flight level change for sequences of aircraft.

Thus, the contributions of this paper are in the development and numerical implementation of a fast algorithm for computing a discrete underapproximation of the continuous minimum time-to-reach function, in the adaptation of the proofs of convergence of [8] to this special case, and in the extension of this method to the computation of guaranteed overapproximations of reachable sets for simple hybrid and reset systems (a recent previous extension has focussed on *impulse differential inclusions* [3]). Additional contributions are in the application of this algorithm to synthesizing safe maneuvers for aircraft in air traffic control. We show that the algorithms presented here, while less accurate than level set techniques, have advantages in the form of guaranteed set overapproximation, and survival time information.

2   Computing Reachable Sets of Continuous Systems

2.1   Reachability Using Minimum Time-to-Reach Functions

Let us consider the following control problem:

$$\begin{cases} \dot{x}(t) = f(x(t), u(t)), & t > 0 \\ x(0) = x \end{cases} \tag{1}$$

where $u(\cdot) \in \mathcal{U} := \{u : [0, +\infty[\rightarrow U, \text{ measurable}\}$ and U is a compact metric space, $x \in X = \mathbb{R}^N$, and f is continuous in u and Lipschitz-continuous in x. Following Aubin [2] we rewrite (1) in set valued form:

$$\begin{cases} \dot{x}(t) \in F(x(t)) := \{f(x, u)\}_{u \in U} \\ x(0) = x \end{cases} \tag{2}$$

The set of solutions of (2) (equivalently of (1)) is denoted $\mathcal{S}_F(x)$. Consider the following problem. Let $K \subset X$ be a constraint set and C be a closed set in K. Find the set of initial conditions x for which there exists a trajectory starting at x remaining in K and reaching C in finite time. In mathematical terms, we seek

$$W_C^K = \{x \in K : \exists x(\cdot) \in \mathcal{S}_F(x), \exists t \geq 0, x(t) \in C \wedge (\forall s < t, x(s) \in K)\} \tag{3}$$

We define the minimum time-to-reach function as:

$$\theta_C^K(x) = \inf_{x(\cdot) \in \mathcal{S}_F(x)} \inf\{t \in \mathbb{R}^+ : \quad x(t) \in C \quad \wedge \quad (\forall s < t, \ x(s) \in K)\} \tag{4}$$

Note that $\theta_C^K(x) = +\infty$ if all the trajectories originating at x leave K before reaching the target, or stay in K forever without reaching C.

Fact 1 W_C^K *may be computed using the minimum time-to-reach function:*

$$W_C^K = \mathrm{Dom}\left(\theta_C^K\right) := \{x \in K : \theta_C^K(x) < +\infty\} \tag{5}$$

where $\mathrm{Dom}(\cdot)$ *denotes the domain of definition of the function* θ_C^K, *or the set of points at which it is defined (here that is the set of points at which it is finite).*

2.2   Viscosity Solution of the Reachability Problem Using Viability

The minimum time-to-reach function $\theta_C^{\mathbb{R}^N}$ defined by (4) for (1) or (2) is known to be the viscosity solution of the following HJE (Bardi [4]):

$$\begin{cases} H(x, D\theta_C^{\mathbb{R}^N}) = 1 \text{ in } \Omega \backslash C \\ \theta_C^{\mathbb{R}^N} = 0 \qquad \text{in } \partial C \\ \theta_C^{\mathbb{R}^N}(x) \rightarrow +\infty \quad \text{as } x \rightarrow \partial\Omega \end{cases} \tag{6}$$

where $\Omega \supset C$ is an open set. Note that the proofs of Bardi [4] hold when there are no constraints, i.e. $K = X = \mathbb{R}^N$ here, and under local controllability assumptions. For a more general Hamilton-Jacobi framework, see Frankowska [13]. The Hamiltonian of the system is given by: $H(x, p) = \max_{u \in U}\{-p \cdot f(x, u)\}$. The function θ_C^K can also be characterized with the help of the *viability kernel* of an extended dynamics of our original system (see [10] for more details):

Definition 1. *For set-valued dynamics*[1] $F : X \rightsquigarrow X$ *and a set* $K \subset X$, *we define the* viability kernel *of* K *as:*

$$\mathrm{Viab}_F (K) = \{x \in K : \exists x(\cdot) \in S_F(x), \forall t \geq 0 \quad x(t) \in K\} \tag{7}$$

Intuitively, the viability kernel is the set of points for which there exists a solution to (2) staying in K forever. The following can be found in [9]:

Proposition 1. *Assume that in (2),* F *is uppersemicontinuous*[2] *with compact convex nonempty values and that* K *and* C *are closed. Then*

$$\mathrm{Epi}\left(\theta_C^K\right) = \mathrm{Viab}_\Phi\left(K \times \mathbb{R}^+\right) \tag{8}$$

where $\mathrm{Epi}\left(\theta_C^K\right) := \{(x,y) \in K \times \mathbb{R}^+ : y \geq \theta_C^K(x)\}$ *denotes the epigraph of the function* θ_K^C, *i.e. the set of points above its graph, and where*

$$\Phi(x) = \begin{cases} F(x) \times \{-1\} & \text{if } x \notin C \\ \overline{\mathrm{co}}\{F(x) \times \{-1\}, \{0,0\}\} & \text{if } x \in C \end{cases} \tag{9}$$

In (9), $\overline{\mathrm{co}}$ denotes the closure of the convex hull of the set between brackets (i.e. the closure of the smallest convex set containing it). Proposition 1 states that the set of points above the graph of the minimum time to reach function is the set of initial states $(x,y) \in K \times \mathbb{R}^+$ such that the trajectories $(x(\cdot), y(\cdot)) \in S_\Phi((x,y))$ reach $C \times \mathbb{R}^+$ in finite time. Even if we do not make direct use of (7,8,9) in the present paper, they have proved crucial in the development of the techniques used here. Indeed, Proposition 1 links the minimum time-to-reach function to the viability kernel and therefore enables the use of the *viability kernel algorithm* (Frankowska and Quincampoix [14]) whose numerical implementation (Saint-Pierre [17]) provides a guaranteed overapproximation of $\mathrm{Epi}\left(\theta_C^K\right)$. In subsequent work, Cardaliaguet and al. [8] tailored the viability kernel algorithm to the computation of the minimum time-to-reach function. In [18], Saint-Pierre proposes a further simplification this algorithm. In the next section, we present our numerical algorithm inspired by [18].

2.3   Approximation Algorithm

We present a proof of the convergence of the *underapproximation algorithm* for the minimum time-to-reach function under state constraints, θ_C^K, adapted from [9, 18] for our design. The inclusion of state constraints will allow us to ignore the problem of boundary conditions. It gives good insight into the approximation procedure: the algorithm computes the exact minimum time-to-reach function for a discrete time dynamics defined on a discrete state space. Hence, we begin by showing how we can define a fully discrete dynamics whose trajectories are *good* approximations of the trajectories of system (2) (in a sense that will be defined).

---

[1]   In the sequel, we shall use the arrow $\rightsquigarrow$ for "set valued" maps.
[2]   A set valued map $F : X \rightsquigarrow X$ with compact values is uppersemicontinuous iff $\forall x_0 \in X$, and $\forall \varepsilon > 0, \exists \eta > 0$ such that $\forall x \in x_0 + \eta \mathcal{B}, F(x) \subset F(x_0) + \varepsilon \mathcal{B}$.

Numerical Approximation of Continuous Dynamics. We endow X with the Euclidean norm $\|\cdot\|$, and we denote by $\mathcal{B}$ the unit ball under this norm. For $h > 0$, we set $X_h = \left(h\mathbb{N}/\sqrt{2}\right)^N$, where $\mathbb{N}$ is the set of natural numbers. Then $\forall x \in X$, $\exists x_h$ in the ball $x + h\mathcal{B}$. Hence, X_h is a discrete approximation of the state space X. The following theorem defines approximations of $S_F(x)$ of the system (2) by the set of trajectories $S_\Gamma(x_h)$ of discrete dynamics $\Gamma : X_h \rightsquigarrow X_h$.

Theorem 1 (Relationship between continuous and discrete trajectories). *Assume that $F : X \rightsquigarrow X$ is upper semicontinuous with nonempty convex compact values and is l-Lipschitz. Assume moreover that there exists $M > 0$ such that for all $x \in K$, $\sup_{y \in F(x)} \|y\| \leq M$. For a mesh $h > 0$ and a time step $\rho > 0$, we define discrete dynamics on X_h:*

$$x_h^{n+1} \in \Gamma_{\rho,h}(x_h^n) := [x_h^n + \rho\,(\,F(x_h^n) + r(\rho,h)\mathcal{B}\,)] \cap X_h, \qquad (10)$$

where $r(\rho,h) = lh + Ml\rho + 2\frac{h}{\rho}$, and we define the set of trajectories of this system as $S_{\Gamma_{\rho,h}}(x_h)$. Then a trajectory $x(\cdot)$ of system (2) defines trajectories of system (10) in the following way:

$$\forall \{x_h^n\} \in \{\{y_h^n\} : \forall n \in \mathbb{N},\ y_h^n \in (\,x(n\rho) + h\mathcal{B}\,)\}, \qquad \{x_h^n\} \in S_{\Gamma_{\rho,h}}(x_h), \quad (11)$$

and a trajectory $\{x_h^n\} \in S_{\Gamma_{\rho,h}}(x_h)$ is close to a trajectory $x(\cdot) \in S_F(x_h)$ in the following sense: $\forall t \geq 0$

$$\|x(t) - \hat{x}(t)\| \leq \begin{cases} \left(\,(\,M + r(\rho,h)\,)\rho + \frac{r(\rho,h)}{l}\right)(e^{lt} - 1) & \text{if } l > 0 \\ 2\frac{h}{\rho}t & \text{if } l = 0 \end{cases} \qquad (12)$$

where $\hat{x}(t) = x_h^n + \frac{x_h^{n+1} - x_h^n}{\rho}(t - n\rho)$, for $n \in \mathbb{N}$ and $t \in [n\rho, (n+1)\rho]$, represents a continuous trajectory interpolating points in $\{x_h^n\}$.

Proof: Please see Appendix. This theorem states that for all ρ and h, the dynamics (10) is an *overapproximation* of dynamics (2) in the following sense: all trajectories of system (2), when discretized with time step ρ and projected on X_h, are trajectories of (10); and all the trajectories of (10), when interpolated as in $\hat{x}(t)$ above, are approximations of trajectories of (2), with an upper bound on the error given by an increasing function of $\eta(\rho,h)$ (with $\eta(\rho,h) = 2h/\rho$ if $l = 0$) and of time. Therefore, the smaller the $\eta(\rho,h)$, the better the approximation. Moreover, $\eta(\rho,h)$ tends to 0 if and only if ρ, h and h/ρ tend to 0. This will be used in the approximation algorithm for the minimum time-to-reach function.

Approximation of the Minimum Time-to-Reach Function. We shall now define a fully discrete target problem which approximates the target problem defined for continuous time and state space, and shall prove relationships between the discrete minimum time-to-reach function and the continuous one. We shall use Θ to denote the discrete approximation of θ_C^K, its sub/superscripts will depend on context (and will always correspond to the sub/superscripts of θ).

We begin by defining a discrete approximation, and the sense in which discrete functions can converge to continuous functions.

Definition 2. *We say that a discrete function $\Psi_h : X_h \to \mathbb{R}$ is an* underapproximation *of a function $\theta : X \to \mathbb{R}$ if*

$$\forall x_h \in X_h, \quad \forall x \in (x_h + h\mathcal{B}), \qquad \Psi_h(x_h) \leq \theta(x),$$

and for a family (or a sequence) indexed by the set Ξ (containing elements called ξ) denoted $\{\Psi_{h,\xi}\}$, we write $\lim_{(h,\xi)\to(0^+,\xi_0)} \Psi_{h,\xi} = \theta$ if

$$\forall x \in X, \quad \lim_{(h,\xi)\to(0^+,\xi_0)} \sup_{x_h \in (x+h\mathcal{B})\cap X_h} \Psi_{h,\xi}(x_h) = \theta(x).$$

If moreover $\{\Psi_{h,\xi}\}$ is a underapproximation of θ for all $h > 0$ and all $\xi \in \Xi$, we say that it defines a converging underapproximation scheme *of θ.*

Theorem 2 (Discrete function is converging underapproximation of continuous). *Let $K \subset X$ be a closed set of constraints and $C \subset X$ be a closed target. Under the assumptions and notations of Theorem 1 and for $\rho > 0$ and $h > 0$, we denote $C_{\rho,h} = (C + (M\rho + h)\mathcal{B}) \cap X_h$ and $K_h = (K + h\mathcal{B}) \cap X_h$, and we define the discrete minimum time-to-reach function:*

$$\Theta_{C_{\rho,h}}^{K_h}(x_h) = \inf_{\{x_h^n\} \in S_{\Gamma_{\rho,h}}(x_h)} \inf\{n \in \mathbb{N} : x_h^n \in C_{\rho,h} \wedge \forall m < n, \, x_h^m \in K_h\} \quad (13)$$

Then $\left\{\Theta_{C_{\rho,h}}^{K_h}\right\}$ defines a converging underapproximation scheme of θ_C^K.

Corollary 1. *The minimum time-to-reach function θ_C^K can be underapproximated with use of a discrete function Θ^n, using the following algorithm:*

$$\Theta^0(x_h) = \begin{cases} 0 & \text{if } x_h \in K_h, \\ +\infty & \text{else} \end{cases} \qquad (14)$$

$$\Theta^{n+1}(x_h) = \begin{cases} 1 + \inf_{y_h \in \Gamma(x_h)} \Theta^n(y_h) & \text{if } x_h \notin C_{\rho,h}, \\ \Theta^n(x_h) & \text{else} \end{cases} \qquad (15)$$

Indeed, $\Theta_{C_{\rho,h}}^{K_h}(x_h) = \lim_{n \to +\infty} \Theta^n(x_h)$.

Proof of Theorem 2: Please see Appendix. The algorithm above provides a guaranteed underapproximation of the minimal time-to-reach function θ_C^K. The choice of the two parameters ρ and h is a matter of trial and error. However, when one of them is fixed, an interesting hint for setting the other is to minimize either $r(\rho, h)$ or $\eta(\rho, h)$ which appear in Theorem 1 and are indicators of the accuracy of the approximation by $\Gamma_{\rho,h}$.

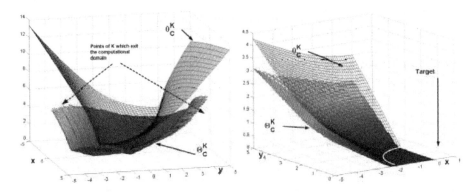

Fig. 1. Left: Numerical underapproximation of the value function of the double integrator problem (16), obtained by the the scheme presented in this paper. Computation realized on a 400×400 grid on $[-5, 5] \times [-5, 5]$, converged in 56 iterations, $\rho = 0.09$. **Right:** Numerical underapproximation of the value function of the wall pursuit evasion game (17). Computation realized on a 200×200 grid on $[-5, 0] \times [0, 5]$, converged in 36 iterations, $\rho = 0.09$. In both cases, three points out of four omitted in the plot for clarity. The numerical underapproximation of (17) is more accurate than that of (16). This is due to the zero Lipschitz constant of the dynamics of (17).

2.4   Numerical Validation

The previous section provides theoretical bounds for the error of the numerical approximation. However, as in Mitchell and al. [16], we need to assess how fast the method converges within these bounds.

Steering Problem (after Bryson [7]). The dynamical system for this problem is: $(\dot{x}, \dot{y}) = (y, u)$ where $u \in [-1, 1]$, $(x, y) \in \mathbb{R}^2$. The viscosity solution $\theta_{(0,0)}^{\mathbb{R}^2}$ of (6) corresponding for this dynamics is given by: ʹ

$$
\begin{cases}
\theta_{(0,0)}^{\mathbb{R}^2}(x, y) = -y + \sqrt{2y^2 - 4x} \text{ if } x + \frac{1}{2}y|y| \leq 0 \\
\theta_{(0,0)}^{\mathbb{R}^2}(x, y) = +y + \sqrt{2y^2 + 4x} \text{ if } x + \frac{1}{2}y|y| \geq 0
\end{cases}
\tag{16}
$$

The numerical results obtained from the underapproximation algorithm are compared to the viscosity solution $\theta_{(0,0)}^{\mathbb{R}^2}$ in Figure 1 (left). Clearly, the numerical result is below the analytical. The error is due to the Lipschitz constant of this example as related back to (12). We note here that Saint-Pierre [17] has developed powerful techniques to alleviate this problem. We did not implement them: they are computationally expensive and our goal here is fast overapproximations.

Wall pursuit evasion game (after Isaacs [15]). We treat this problem as a control problem by forcing the evader to run in one direction and reducing the space to the one quadrant. In this context: $(\dot{x}, \dot{y}) = (-w \cos d, \text{sign}(y) - w \sin d = 1 - w \sin d)$ with $(x, y) \in \mathbb{R}^- \times \mathbb{R}^+$: The pursuer has speed $w > 1$ and can move any direction d. Isaacs' *retrograde path equations* method enables reducing this problem to solving $(l + w\theta(x, y))^2 = x^2 + (y + \theta(x, y))^2$, which provides the viscosity solution (17) of equation (6), shown in Figure 1 (right), as well as its numerical underapproximation obtained with our algorithm.

$$\theta^{\mathbb{R}^- \times \mathbb{R}}_{B(0,l) \cap \mathbb{R}^- \times \mathbb{R}}(x, y) = \frac{1}{w^2 - 1} \left[-(lw - |y|) + \sqrt{(|y|w - l)^2 + (w^2 - 1)x^2} \right] \quad (17)$$

3   Application to Safety Analysis of Air Traffic Control

3.1   Conflict Resolution in Heavily Loaded Air Traffic Centers

We are interested in performing fast computations of safety zones of aircraft for Air Traffic Management systems. Guaranteed underapproximation of those sets is crucial: certification of a conflict resolution protocol always requires a proof of its safety. We will here show the application of our technique to aircraft conflict resolution problems very frequently encountered in the Sector 33 airspace of the Oakland ATC Center in Fremont, CA. The computational example presented below is extracted from a larger modeling and control project which we are working on in collaboration with NASA Ames and with Oakland ATC Center [5]. For the present study, only a subset of this model is used.

Sector 33 is one of the busiest high altitude sectors in the US. It is at the junction of jetways coming from and going to Los Angeles, San Francisco, Oakland, San Jose, Las Vegas and is a collector of traffic from the east coast. At waypoint COALDALE in this sector, aircraft coming from Las Vegas may frequently conflict with aircraft going to the east coast at the same flight level (*floor*).

We consider the following subproblem (the notations refer to Figure 2). Let the local flight plan of aircraft 1 be jetway 92 towards COALDALE and then jetway 58 towards San Francisco, while the flight plan of aircraft 2 is jetway 58 through COALDALE . If the aircraft are in danger of "losing separation", meaning coming closer than 5 nautical miles horizontally and 2000ft vertically to each other, the controller will either reroute horizontally or climb one of the aircraft (i.e. will provide only one discrete action). The goal here is to develop advisories for air traffic controllers, so that aircraft do not lose separation.

Let x be the planar relative coordinate of the aircraft 1 w.r.t. aircraft 2, v_{92} the velocity vector of aircraft 1 along jetway 92, and v_{58} the velocity vector of aircraft 2 along jetway 58. We allow uncertainty in speed (due to winds, gusts, inaccuracy of sensors), with uncertainty bound of Mach $M = 0.05$.

$$\dot{x} = v_{58} - (v_{92} + 0.05 \cdot c \cdot \mathcal{B}) \qquad \text{Mode 1} \qquad (18)$$

where c is the speed of sound and $\mathcal{B}$ is the unit ball in $\mathbb{R}^2$. We can now apply the results of the previous section. Let us consider aircraft 1 as the evader and compute the safe set of its allowed positions (i.e. for which no loss of separation can occur). The unsafe set is the set of points which can eventually enter a disk target C around aircraft 2 of radius 5 nautical miles. Let us denote $\theta^{\text{mode 1}}$ the minimal time-to-reach function for target C (there are no state constraints here). Then the safe set is $\mathbb{R}^2 \setminus \text{Dom}\left(\theta^{\text{mode 1}}\right)$.

Conflict resolution via heading change (hybrid model).

A possible controller choice is to make aircraft 1 "cut" between jetway 92 and jetway 58. This avoids the conflict and shortens the path of aircraft 1, and is the preferred option of the controllers in general. This can be modeled as a second mode of aircraft 1, now rotated by an angle ψ to the west:

$$\dot{\boldsymbol{x}} = \boldsymbol{v}_{58} - R_{\psi} \cdot (\boldsymbol{v}_{92} + 0.05 \cdot c \cdot \mathcal{B}) \qquad \text{Mode 2} \qquad (19)$$

where R_{ψ} is the standard rotation matrix of angle ψ. Let us denote $\theta^{\text{mode 2}}$ the minimal time function to reach C in this dynamics.

The controller's policy is the following: if aircraft 1 is safe in mode 1, stay in mode 1; else if it is safe in mode 2, switch to mode 2; if both modes are unsafe, switching can be used to increase the time during which the distance between the two aircraft is guaranteed to be greater than 5 nautical miles.

Denote by θ^{hybrid} the function representing the minimum guaranteed time before loss of separation, and by F_1 and F_2 the set valued dynamics associated to the two modes, and by $S_{F_1,F_2}(x,T)$ the set of trajectories originating at x for which switching from mode 1 to mode 2 occurs once. Then, at time T, we have:

$$\forall x \in X, \qquad \theta^{\text{hybrid}}(x) = \sup_{T>0} \inf_{x(\cdot) \in S_{F_1,F_2}(x,T)} \inf\{t > 0 : x(t) \in C\} \qquad (20)$$

with safe set $\mathbb{R}^2 \setminus \text{Dom}\left(\theta^{\text{hybrid}}\right)$. By definition, $\text{Dom}\left(\theta^{\text{hybrid}}\right) = \text{Dom}\left(\theta^{\text{mode 1}}\right) \cap \text{Dom}\left(\theta^{\text{mode 2}}\right)$ and $\forall x \in \mathbb{R}^2$, $\theta^{\text{hybrid}}(x) \geq \max\{\theta^{\text{mode 1}}, \theta^{\text{mode 2}}\}$. An algorithm for underapproximating θ^{hybrid} is presented in the next section.

Conflict resolution via floor climbing (reset model).

The second possible choice of the controller is to climb aircraft 1. It takes about 3 minutes to climb an aircraft from one floor to the next floor. If there are no aircraft on the next floor and there is enough time to climb the aircraft, then the problem is solved. Let us investigate the case in which there is another aircraft on the next floor (aircraft 3).

Let aircraft 1 be on floor 350 (35,000 ft) on jetway 92 towards COALDALE, aircraft 2 be on floor 350 on jetway 58 towards COALDALE and aircraft 3 on floor 370 (37,000) on jetway 58 towards COALDALE (see Figure 3). Given the positions of aircraft 2 and 3 on jetway 58 at their respective altitudes, we want to find the set of locations at which both collision cannot be avoided, and collision can be avoided by either climbing or staying at the same level. We assume that aircraft 2 and 3 are separated horizontally by a vector $\boldsymbol{\delta}$ (regardless of their altitude) and fly at the same speed (which is usually the case on high altitude jetways). If it takes T_{climb} seconds to climb from floor 350 to floor 370 and the horizontal speed during climbing is unchanged, let r be the following *reset function*:

$$r(\boldsymbol{x}) = \boldsymbol{x} + \boldsymbol{\delta} + T_{\text{climb}} \boldsymbol{v}_{92} \qquad (21)$$

Then climbing aircraft 1 from floor 350 to floor 370 is equivalent to a reset. Let us call $\boldsymbol{x}$ the relative position of aircraft 1 w.r.t. aircraft 2: if $\theta(\boldsymbol{x}) < T_{\text{climb}}$, there is not enough time to climb aircraft 1 without causing loss of separation with aircraft 2: the situation is unsafe. Otherwise, the aircraft can be climbed, and the algorithm in the next section will take this reset into account. Intuitively, the reset reinitializes the parameters by translating them by δ plus $T_{\text{climb}}v_{92}$, which is the ground distance needed to climb. As in the hybrid case, we will define θ^{reset} as the new minimal time-to-reach function which incorporates the possible reset within the execution of the automaton, and we will compute the set of points which are still unsafe when climbing is allowed, either because there is not enough time to climb, or the aircraft climbs to an unsafe zone on the next floor.

If we denote by $S_{F_1,r}(x,T)$ the set of trajectories originating at x for which resetting occurs at time T, we have

$$\forall x \in X, \qquad \theta^{\text{reset}}(x) = \sup_{T>0} \inf_{x(\cdot)\in S_{F_1,r}(x,T)} \inf\{t > 0 : x(t) \in C\} \qquad (22)$$

and the safe set is $\mathbb{R}^2 \setminus \text{Dom}\left(\theta^{\text{reset}}\right)$. An algorithm for underapproximating θ^{reset} is presented in the next section.

3.2   Computing Safe Sets for Hybrid and Reset Systems

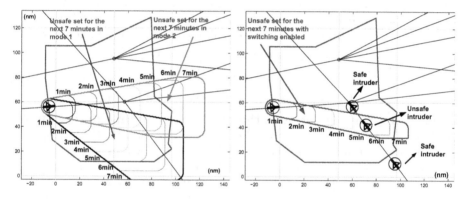

Fig. 2.   Result of the conflict avoidance protocol with hybrid switching enabled. Computation realized on a 350×350 grid. **Left:** Reachability computation for the next 7 minutes for both modes (superimposed). Isolines are in increments of one minute in relative coordinates (which is why the distance between the isolines seems bigger than the one minute achievable distance of one aircraft at Mach $M = 0.85$ in absolute coordinates). If the intruder is in the intersection of the two unsafe sets, it cannot avoid loss of separation with the set of two maneuvers. If it is in one of the unsafe sets, switching avoids loss of separation. Otherwise, any of the two modes is safe. **Right:** Same as left with switching enabled. Position of first and third intruder are safe relative to these two dynamics. The second intruder cannot avoid loss of separation with only these two maneuvers.

Guaranteed underapproximation of the survival time function for the hybrid model. The algorithm presented below stems from Corollary 1 and provides an underapproximation of θ^{hybrid}. It is based on the fact that, given that the system starts in mode 1 and may switch to mode 2 at any time, $\theta^{\text{hybrid}}(x) = \theta^{\text{mode 2}}(x)$ if $\theta^{\text{mode 2}}(x) \geq \theta^{\text{mode 1}}(x)$ because mode 2 guarantees safety longer than mode 1, otherwise $\theta^{\text{hybrid}}(x) \geq \theta^{\text{mode 1}}(x)$ since mode 1 is safer now, and switching to mode 2 later may increase the time for which the system is safe.

Theorem 3 (Approximation of the hybrid minimum time-to-reach function). *Let $C \subset X$ be a closed target. We assume that F_1 and F_2 satisfy the assumptions of Theorem 1. For $\rho > 0$, $h > 0$ and $i \in \{1, 2\}$, we define the fully discrete dynamics $\Gamma_{\rho,h}^i$ and the discrete minimum time-to-reach functions $\Theta_{\rho,h}^{\text{mode } i}$ as in Theorems 1 and 2. Let $S_{\rho,h} := \{x_h \in X_h : \ \Theta_{\rho,h}^{\text{mode 1}}(x_h) \leq \Theta_{\rho,h}^{\text{mode 2}}(x_h)\}$. Then a converging underapproximation scheme for θ^{hybrid} is given by $\Theta_{\rho,h}^{\text{hybrid}}(x_h) = \lim_{n \to +\infty} \Theta_{\rho,h}^n(x_h)$, where*

$$
\begin{bmatrix}
\Theta_{\rho,h}^0(x_h) = \sup\{\Theta_{\rho,h}^{\text{mode 1}}(x_h), \Theta_{\rho,h}^{\text{mode 2}}(x_h)\} \\
\Theta_{\rho,h}^{n+1}(x_h) = \begin{cases} 1 + \inf_{y_h \in \Gamma_{\rho,h}^1(x_h)} \Theta_{\rho,h}^n(y_h) & \text{if } x_h \notin S_{\rho,h} \\ \Theta_{\rho,h}^n(x_h) & \text{else} \end{cases}
\end{bmatrix}
\tag{23}
$$

Reset Models of Aircraft Climb. In the case of the reset model, the reasoning is similar to the hybrid case. Indeed, if a trajectory starts at x_0 with a reset at time T to x_1, we know that it cannot reach the target before $T + T_{\text{climb}} + \theta^{\text{mode 1}}(x_1)$. In order to avoid loss of separation during climbing, we set

$$
\theta^R(x) = \begin{cases} T_{\text{climb}} + \theta^{\text{mode 1}}(r(x)) & \text{if } \theta^{\text{mode 1}}(x) \geq T_{\text{climb}} \\ 0 & \text{else} \end{cases}
\tag{24}
$$

Then $\theta^R(x)$ plays the same role as $\theta^{\text{mode 2}}$ in the hybrid model.

Theorem 4 (Approximation of the reset minimum time to reach function). *Let $C \subset X$ be a closed target. We assume that F satisfies the assumptions of Theorem 1 and that the reset function $r : X \to X$ is λ-Lipschitz continuous. For $\rho > 0$, $h > 0$, we define $\Gamma_{\rho,h}$ and the discrete minimum time-to-reach function $\Theta_{\rho,h}(x_h)$ as in Theorem 1. We also define the discrete reset function*

$$
R_h(x_h) := (\ r(x_h) + (1 + \lambda)h\mathcal{B}\ ) \cap X_h
$$

Then a converging underapproximation scheme for θ^R is given by

$$
\Theta_{\rho,h}^R(x_h) := \begin{cases} \inf_{y_h \in R_h(x_h)} \Theta_{\rho,h}^{\text{mode 1}}(y_h) + \frac{T_{\text{climb}}}{\rho} & \text{if } \Theta_{\rho,h}^{\text{mode 1}}(x_h) \geq \frac{T_{\text{climb}}}{\rho}, \\ 0 & \text{else} \end{cases}
$$

Furthermore, if $S_h := \{x_h \in X_h : \ \Theta_{\rho,h}(x_h) < \Theta_{\rho,h}^R(x_h)\}$, then a converging underapproximation for θ^{reset} is given by $\Theta_{\rho,h}(x_h) = \lim_{n \to +\infty} \Theta^n(x_h)$, with

$$
\Theta_{\rho,h}^0(x_h) = \sup\{\Theta_{\rho,h}(x_h), \Theta_{\rho,h}^R(x_h)\}
\tag{25}
$$

$$
\Theta_{\rho,h}^{n+1}(x_h) = \begin{cases} 1 + \inf_{y_h \in \Gamma_{\rho,h}(x_h)} \Theta_{\rho,h}^n(y_h) & \text{if } x_h \notin S_h, \\ \Theta_{\rho,h}^n(x_h) & \text{else} \end{cases}
\tag{26}
$$

Proofs of Theorems 3 and 4 are not included here, but are available from the authors.

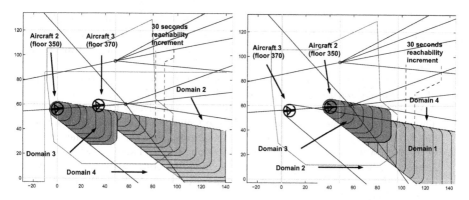

Fig. 3. Results of the conflict avoidance maneuver with reset enabled. Computation realized on a 350×350 grid with $T_{\text{climb}} = 3$min. Aircraft 2 and aircraft 1 are on floor 350. Aircraft 3 is on floor 370 approximately 35 miles ahead of (behind) aircraft 2. The different domains of the diagram have the following interpretation: if aircraft 1 is in Domain 1, there is no way conflict can be avoided by either climbing to 370 or staying on 350. If it is in Domain 2, it should stay there, for climbing will generate a conflict. In Domain 3, there is not enough time to climb, so conflict will occur on floor 350. In Domain 4, conflict can be avoided by climbing. Outside of these four domains, any altitude is safe. Each isoline represents a 30 sec. increment in the time to reach function w.r.t. the target (in relative dynamics).

4 Current Work

The version of our code used for the examples of this paper is designed in MAT-LAB. It is clear that the use of refinements proposed in [10] for the general viability kernel, such as local grid refinement and local Lipschitz constants, will improve the rate of convergence of the underapproximation algorithm. Yet even the simple code presented here provides guaranteed results, and its implementation for dimensions higher than 2, with reasonable computation time, should present few difficulties. In addition, while we have only presented the theorems for a single switch and reset here, we know the algorithm to be extendible to general hybrid systems, and we are currently working on this algorithm and proof.

References

[1] E. ASARIN, O. BOURNEZ, T. DANG, and O. MALER. Approximate reachability analysis of piecewise-linear dynamical systems. In B. Krogh and N. Lynch, editors, *Hybrid Systems: Computation and Control*, LNCS 1790, pages 21–31. Springer Verlag, 2000.

[2] J.-P. AUBIN. *Viability Theory*. Systems & Control: Foundations & Applications. Birkhäuser, 1991.

[3] J.-P. AUBIN, J. LYGEROS, M. QUINCAMPOIX, S. SASTRY, and N. SEUBE. Impulse differential inclusions: A viability approach to hybrid systems. Technical Report CUED/F-INFENG/TR.414, Department of Engineering - University of Cambridge, 2001.

[4] M. BARDI and I. CAPUZZO-DOLCETTA. *Optimal Control and Viscosity Solutions of Hamilton-Jacobi-Bellman Equations.* Birkäuser, 1997.

[5] A.M. BAYEN, H. SIPMA, C.J. TOMLIN, and G. MEYER. Delay Predictive Models of The National Airspace System using Hybrid Control Theory: Design, Simulation and Proofs. *Proceedings of the American Control Conference,* 8-10 May 2002.

[6] O. BOTCHKAREV and S. TRIPAKIS. Verification of hybrid systems with linear differential inclusions using ellipsoidal approximations. In B. Krogh and N. Lynch, editors, *Hybrid Systems: Computation and Control,* LNCS 1790, pages 73–88. Springer Verlag, 2000.

[7] A.E. BRYSON and Y.-C.HO. *Applied Optimal Control,Optimization, Estimation and Control.* Taylor and Francis, 1975.

[8] P. CARDALIAGUET, M. QUINCAMPOIX, and P. SAINT-PIERRE. Optimal Times for Constrained Nonlinear Control Problems without Local Controllability. *Applied Mathematics and Optimization,* 36:21–42, 1997.

[9] P. CARDALIAGUET, M. QUINCAMPOIX, and P. SAINT-PIERRE. Numerical Methods for Differential Games. In M. Bardi, T.E.S. Raghavan, and T. Parthasarathy, editors, *Stochastic and Differential Games: Theory and Numerical Methods,* Annals of the International Society of Dynamic Games. Birkhäuser, 1999.

[10] P. CARDALIAGUET, M. QUINCAMPOIX, and P. SAINT-PIERRE. Set-valued numerical analysis for optimal control and differential games. In M. Bardi, T.E.S. Raghavan, and T. Parthasarathy, editors, *Stochastic and Differential Games: Theory and Numerical Methods,* Annals of the International Society of Dynamic Games. Birkhäuser, 1999.

[11] A. CHUTINAN and B. H. KROGH. Approximating quotient transition systems for hybrid systems. In *Proceedings of the American Control Conference,* pages 1689–1693, Chicago, IL, 2000.

[12] M. G. CRANDALL, L. C. EVANS, and P.-L. LIONS. Some properties of viscosity solutions of Hamilton-Jacobi equations. *TransAMS,* 282(2):487–502, 1984.

[13] H. FRANKOWSKA. Lower Semicontinuous Solutions of Hamilton-Jacobi-Bellman Equations. *SIAM Journal of Control and Optimization,* 31(1):257–272, 1993.

[14] H. FRANKOWSKA and M. QUINCAMPOIX. Viability kernels of differential inclusions with constraints: Algorithm and applications. *Mathematics of Systems, Estimation and Control,* 1(3):371–388, 1991.

[15] R. ISAACS. *Differential Games.* Dover (reprint from John Wiley), 1999 (1965).

[16] I. MITCHELL, A.M. BAYEN, and C.J. TOMLIN. Validating a Hamilton-Jacobi approximation to hybrid system reachable sets. In M.D. Di Benedetto and A. Sangiovanni-Vincentelli, editors, *Hybrid Systems: Computation and Control,* LNCS 2034, pages 418–432. Springer Verlag, 2001.

[17] P. SAINT-PIERRE. Approximation of the Viability Kernel. *Applied Mathematics and Optimization,* 29:187–209, 1994.

[18] P. SAINT-PIERRE. Approche ensembliste des systèmes dynamiques, regards qualitatifs et quantitatifs. *Matapli, Société de Mathématiques Appliquées et Industrielles,* 66, 2001.

Appendix

Proof — [Theorem 1 - adapted from [10]]. In order to prove the first part, let $x_0 \in X$ and $x(\cdot) \in S_F(x_0)$. We claim that $x((n+1)\rho) \in G_\rho(x(n\rho))$ for all $n \in \mathbb{N}$. Indeed, $x((n+1)\rho) = x(n\rho) + \int_{n\rho}^{(n+1)\rho} \dot{x}(t)dt$ and since F is l-Lipschitz, and bounded by M, we have $\forall n \in \mathbb{N}$, $\forall t \in [n\rho, (n+1)\rho]$, $\dot{x}(t) \in F(x(t)) \subset F(x) + Mlt\,\mathcal{B}$. Furthermore, G_ρ is $(1+l\rho)$-Lipschitz. Hence,

$$\forall n \in \mathbb{N}, \quad \forall x_h^n \in (x(n\rho) + h\mathcal{B}) \cap X_h, \quad G_\rho(x(n\rho)) \subset G_\rho(x_h^n) + (1+l\rho)h\mathcal{B}$$

which completes the proof of the first part. We shall now prove the second part. Let $n \in \mathbb{N}$ and $t \in [n\rho, (n+1)\rho]$. The definition of $\hat{x}$ yields

$$\dot{\hat{x}}(t) \in F(x_h^n) + r(\rho, h)\mathcal{B} \tag{27}$$
$$\hat{x}(t) \in x_h^n + (\|F(x_h^n)\| + r(\rho, h))(t - n\rho)\mathcal{B} \tag{28}$$

Now since F is l-Lipschitz, $F(x_h^n) \subset F(\hat{x}(t)) + l\,\|\hat{x}(t) - x_h^n\|\,\mathcal{B}$. Hence, (27) yields

$$\dot{\hat{x}}(t) \in F(\hat{x}(t)) + (l(M + r(\rho, h))(t - n\rho) + r(\rho, h))\,\mathcal{B} \tag{29}$$

Let us set $\eta(\rho, h) = l(M + r(\rho, h))\rho + r(\rho, h)$. We have proved that $\dot{\hat{x}}(t) \in F(\hat{x}(t)) + \eta(\rho, h)\mathcal{B}$ for all t. Thanks to a theorem of Filippov[3], we know that there exists a trajectory $x(\cdot) \in S_F(x_h)$ such that

$$\forall t \geq 0, \quad \|x(t) - \hat{x}(t)\| \leq e^{lt} \left(\int_0^t \eta(\rho, h)e^{-ls}ds \right) \leq \begin{cases} \eta(\rho, h)\frac{(e^{lt}-1)}{l} & \text{if } l > 0 \\ 2\frac{h}{\rho}t & \text{if } l = 0 \end{cases} \tag{30}$$

which completes the proof. $\triangle$

Proof — [Theorem 2 - adapted from [10]] In order to prove that $\Theta_{C_{\rho,h}}^{K_h}$ is an under-approximation of θ_C^K, let $x_h \in K_h$ and let $x_0 \in x_h + h\mathcal{B}$ such that $\theta_C^K(x_0) < +\infty$. We denote $x(\cdot)$ an optimal trajectory in $S_F(x_0)$ originating at x_0. Then by the first part of Theorem 1, we can find trajectories $\{x_h^n\} \in S_{\Gamma_{\rho,h}}(x_h)$ such that $x_h^n \in (x(n\rho) + h\mathcal{B}) \cap X_h$. Now if $\theta_C^K(x) \in [n\rho, (n+1)\rho]$, **then** $x_h^n \in C_{\rho,h}$, and $x_h^m \in K_h$ for all $m < n$, which yields $\theta_C^K(x) \geq \rho\Theta_{C_{\rho,h}}^{K_h}(x_h)$ for all ρ, h. Thus, $\limsup_{h,\rho,\frac{h}{\rho}\to 0} \rho\Theta_{C_{\rho,h}}^{K_h}(x_h) \leq \theta_C^K(x)$. Now define two sequences $h_k \to 0$ and $\rho_k \to 0$ such that $\frac{h_k}{\rho_k} \to 0$ and

$$\mathcal{T} := \lim_{k \to +\infty} \rho_k \Theta_{C_{\rho_k,h_k}}^{K_{h_k}}(x_{h_k}) = \liminf_{\rho,h,\frac{h}{\rho}\to 0} \rho\Theta_{C_{\rho,h}}^{K_h}(x_h).$$

We shall prove that $\mathcal{T} \geq \theta_C^K(x)$. To this purpose, set $C_k := C_{\rho_k,h_k}$, $K_k := K_{h_k}$, and $\Gamma_k := \Gamma_{\rho_k,h_k}$. We denote by $\{x_k\}$ optimal trajectories for the fully discrete target problems with parameter k. Now let $x_k(\cdot) \in S_F(x_{h_k})$ denote the closest trajectories

---

[3] A consequence of the Filippov Theorem (Aubin [2, p.170]) is that if a function $y : \mathbb{R} \to X$ is such that $\dot{y}(t) \in F(y(t)) + \delta(t)\mathcal{B}$ for all t, then $\forall x_0 \in X, \exists x(\cdot) \in S_F(x_0)$ such that $\|x(t) - y(t)\| \leq e^{lt} \left(\|x_0 - y(0)\| + \int_0^t \delta(s)e^{-ls}ds \right)$ for all t.

as in Theorem 1. There exists a subsequence (again denoted) $x_k(\cdot)$ which converges[4] to some $x(\cdot) \in S_F(x)$ uniformly on the compact subsets of $\mathbb{R}^N$. By definition

$$\forall k \in \mathbb{N}, \; x_k(\rho_k N_{C_k}^{K_k}(x_{h_k})) \in C_k + (l\,(M + r(\rho_k, h_k))\,\rho_k + r(\rho_k, h_k))\,\frac{(e^{l(\rho_k N_{C_k}^{K_k}(x_{h_k}))} - 1)}{l}$$

Since C is closed, we have $x(T) \in C$. Moreover, the uniform convergence of $x^k(\cdot)$ to $x(\cdot)$ and the closedness of K ensures that $x(t) \in K$ if $t \leq T$. Thus, $\limsup_{h,\rho,\frac{h}{\rho} \to 0} \rho\Theta_{C_{\rho,h}}^{K_h}(x_h) \leq \theta_C^K(x)$ and $\limsup_{h,\rho,\frac{h}{\rho} \to 0} \rho\Theta_{C_{\rho,h}}^{K_h}(x_h) \geq \theta_C^K(x)$, meaning that $\limsup_{h,\rho,\frac{h}{\rho} \to 0} \rho\Theta_{C_{\rho,h}}^{K_h}(x_h) = \theta_C^K(x)$, which completes the proof.   △

---

[4] A consequence of Theorem 3.5.2 in [2, p.101] is that if a sequence of points y^n converges to y, then a sequence of trajectories $y^n(\cdot) \in S_F(y^n)$ admits a subsequence which converges to some $y(\cdot) \in S_F(y)$ uniformly on the compact subsets of $\mathbb{R}^+$.

On the Optimal Control Law for Linear Discrete Time Hybrid Systems

Alberto Bemporad[1,2], Francesco Borrelli[1], and Manfred Morari[1]

[1] Automatic Control Laboratory, ETH,
CH-8092 Zurich, Switzerland
Phone: +41 1 632-4158
Fax: +41 1 632-1211
bemporad,borrelli,morari@aut.ee.ethz.ch
[2] Dip. Ingegneria dell'Informazione
Università di Siena
Phone: +39 0577 234-631
Fax: +39 0577 234-632
bemporad@dii.unisi.it

Abstract. In this paper we study the solution to optimal control problems for discrete time linear hybrid systems. First, we prove that the closed form of the state-feedback solution to finite time optimal control based on quadratic or linear norms performance criteria is a time-varying piecewise affine feedback control law. Then, we give an insight into the structure of the optimal state-feedback solution and of the value function. Finally, we briefly describe how the optimal control law can be computed by means of multiparametric programming.

1 Introduction

Different methods for the analysis and design of controllers for hybrid systems have emerged over the last few years [31, 33, 11, 19, 26, 5]. Among them, the class of optimal controllers is one of the most studied. Most of the literature deals with optimal control of continuous-time hybrid systems and is focused on the study of necessary conditions for a trajectory to be optimal [32, 29], and on the computation of optimal or *sub-optimal* solutions by means of Dynamic Programming or the Maximum Principle [18, 20, 10, 30, 12]. Although some techniques for determining feedback control laws seem to be very promising, many of them suffer from the "curse of dimensionality" arising from the *discretization* of the state space necessary in order to solve the corresponding Hamilton-Jacobi-Bellman or Euler-Lagrange differential equations.

In this paper we study the solution to optimal control problems for linear discrete time hybrid systems. Our hybrid modeling framework is extremely general, in particular the control switches can be both internal, i.e., caused by the state reaching a particular boundary, and controllable (i.e., one can decide when to switch to some other operating mode). Even though interesting mathematical phenomena occurring in hybrid systems such as Zeno behaviors [25] do not exist

C.J. Tomlin and M.R. Greenstreet (Eds.): HSCC 2002, LNCS 2289, pp. 105–119, 2002.
© Springer-Verlag Berlin Heidelberg 2002

in discrete time, we have shown that for such a class of systems we can *character-ize* and *compute* the optimal control law *without gridding* the state space. In [3] we proposed a procedure for synthesizing piecewise affine optimal controllers for discrete time linear hybrid systems. The procedure, based on multiparametric programming, consists of finding the state-feedback solution to finite-time optimal control problems with performance criteria based on linear norms.

Sometimes the use of linear norms has practical disadvantages: A satisfactory performance may be only achieved with long time-horizons, with a consequent increase of complexity, and closed-loop performance may not depend smoothly on the weights used in the performance index, i.e., slight changes of the weights could lead to very different closed-loop trajectories, so that the tuning of the controller becomes difficult. This work is a step towards the characterization of the closed form of the state-feedback solution to optimal control problems for linear hybrid systems with performance criteria based on quadratic norms. First, we prove that the state-feedback solution to the finite time optimal control problem is a time-varying piecewise affine feedback control law (possibly defined over nonconvex regions). Then, we give an insight on the structure of the optimal state-feedback solution and of the value function. Finally, we briefly describe how the optimal control law can be computed by means of multiparametric programming.

The infinite horizon optimal controller can be approximated by implement-ing in a receding horizon fashion a finite-time optimal control law. The resulting state-feedback controller is stabilizing and respects all input and output con-straints. The implementation, as a consequence of the results presented here on finite-time optimal control, requires only the evaluation of a piecewise affine function. This opens up the route to use receding horizon techniques to control hybrid systems characterized by fast sampling and relatively small size. In col-laboration with different companies we have applied this type of optimal control design to a range of hybrid control problems, for instance in traction control [8].

2   Hybrid Systems

Several modeling frameworks have been introduced for discrete time hybrid sys-tems. Among them, *piecewise affine* (PWA) systems [31] are defined by parti-tioning the state space into polyhedral regions, and associating with each region a different linear state-update equation

$$x(t+1) = A_i x(t) + B_i u(t) + f_i$$
$$\text{if } \begin{bmatrix} x(t) \\ u(t) \end{bmatrix} \in \mathcal{X}_i \triangleq \{ [\begin{smallmatrix} x \\ u \end{smallmatrix}] : H_i x + J_i u \leq K_i \} \tag{1}$$

where $x \in \mathbb{R}^{n_c} \times \{0,1\}^{n_\ell}$, $u \in \mathbb{R}^{m_c} \times \{0,1\}^{m_\ell}$, $\{\mathcal{X}_i\}_{i=0}^{s-1}$ is a polyhedral partition of the sets of state+input space $\mathbb{R}^{n+m}$, $n \triangleq n_c + n_\ell$, $m \triangleq m_c + m_\ell$. In the special case $x \in \mathbb{R}^{n_c}$, $u \in \mathbb{R}^{m_c}$ (no binary states and inputs), we say that the PWA system (1) is continuous if the mapping $(x(t), u(t)) \mapsto x(t+1)$ is continuous. The double definition of the state-update function over common boundaries of sets $\mathcal{X}_i$ (the boundaries will also be referred to as *guardlines*) is a technical issue that arises only when the PWA mapping is discontinuous, and can be solved by allowing strict inequalities in the definition of the polyhedral cells in (1). PWA systems can model a large number of physical processes, such as systems with static nonlinearities, and can approximate nonlinear dynamics via multiple linearizations at different operating points.

Furthermore, we mention here linear complementarity (LC) systems [21, 35, 22] and extended linear complementarity (ELC) systems [13], max-min-plus-scaling (MMPS) systems [14], and mixed logical dynamical (MLD) systems [5]. Recently, the equivalence of PWA, LC, ELC, MMPS, and MLD hybrid dynamical systems was proven constructively in [23, 4]. Thus, the theoretical properties and tools can be easily transferred from one class to another. Each modeling framework has its advantages. For instance, stability criteria were formulated for PWA systems [24, 27] and control and verification techniques were proposed for MLD discrete time hybrid models [5, 7]. In particular, MLD models have proven successful for recasting hybrid dynamical optimization problems into mixed-integer linear and quadratic programs, solvable via branch and bound techniques [28].

MLD systems [5] allow specifying the evolution of continuous variables through linear dynamic equations, of discrete variables through propositional logic statements and automata, and the mutual interaction between the two. Linear dynamics are represented as difference equations $x(t+1) = Ax(t) + Bu(t)$, $x \in \mathbb{R}^n$. Boolean variables are defined from linear-threshold conditions over the continuous variables. The key idea of the approach consists of embedding the logic part in the state equations by transforming Boolean variables into 0-1 integers, and by expressing the relations as mixed-integer linear inequalities [5, 36].

By collecting the equalities and inequalities derived from the representation of the hybrid system we obtain the Mixed Logical Dynamical (MLD) system [5]

$$x(t + 1) = Ax(t) + B_1 u(t) + B_2 \delta(t) + B_3 z(t) \tag{2a}$$
$$E_2 \delta(t) + E_3 z(t) \leq E_1 u(t) + E_4 x(t) + E_5 \tag{2b}$$

where $x \in \mathbb{R}^{n_c} \times \{0,1\}^{n_\ell}$ is a vector of continuous and binary states, $u \in \mathbb{R}^{m_c} \times \{0,1\}^{m_\ell}$ are the inputs, $\delta \in \{0,1\}^{r_\ell}$, $z \in \mathbb{R}^{r_c}$ represent auxiliary binary and continuous variables respectively, which are introduced when transforming logic relations into mixed-integer linear inequalities, and A, B_{1-3}, E_{1-5} are matrices of suitable dimensions. We assume that system (2) is *completely well-posed* [5], which means that for all x, u within a bounded set the variables δ, z are uniquely determined, i.e., there exist functions F, G such that, at each time t, $\delta(t) = F(x(t), u(t))$, $z(t) = G(x(t), u(t))$. This allows one to assume that $x(t + 1)$ is uniquely defined once $x(t)$, $u(t)$ are given, and therefore that x-trajectories exist and are uniquely determined by the initial state $x(0)$ and input signal $u(t)$. It is clear that the well-posedness assumption stated above is usually guaranteed by the procedure used to generate the linear inequalities (2b), and therefore this hypothesis is typically fulfilled by MLD relations derived from modeling real-world plants through the tool HYSDEL [34].

In the next section we use the PWA modeling framework to derive the main properties of the state-feedback solution to finite time optimal control problem for hybrid systems. Thanks to the aforementioned equivalence between PWA and MLD systems, the latter will be used in Section 4 to compute the optimal control law.

3 Finite-Time Constrained Optimal Control

Consider the PWA system (1) subject to hard input and state constraints[1]

$$
\begin{aligned}
u_{\min} \leq u(t) \leq u_{\max}, \\
x_{\min} \leq x(t) \leq x_{\max}
\end{aligned}
\tag{3}
$$

for $t \geq 0$, and denote by constrained PWA system (CPWA) the restriction of the PWA system (1) over the set of states and inputs defined by (3),

$$
\begin{aligned}
x(t+1) = A_i x(t) + B_i u(t) + f_i \\
\text{if } \begin{bmatrix} x(t) \\ u(t) \end{bmatrix} \in \tilde{X}_i \triangleq \{[\begin{smallmatrix} x \\ u \end{smallmatrix}] : \tilde{H}_i x + \tilde{J}_i u \leq \tilde{K}_i\}
\end{aligned}
\tag{4}
$$

where $\{\tilde{X}_i\}_{i=0}^{s-1}$ is the new polyhedral partition of the sets of state+input space $\mathbb{R}^{n+m}$ obtained by intersecting the polyhedrons X_i in (1) with the polyhedron described by (3).

Define the following cost function

$$
J(U_0^{T-1}, x(0)) \triangleq \sum_{k=0}^{T-1} \|Q(x(k) - x_e)\|_p + \|R(u(k) - u_e)\|_p + \|P(x(T) - x_e)\|_p
\tag{5}
$$

and consider the finite-time optimal control problem (FTCOC)

$$
J^*(x(0)) \triangleq \min_{\{U_0^{T-1}\}} J(U_0^{T-1}, x(0))
\tag{6}
$$

$$
\text{s.t.} \begin{cases} x(t+1) = A_i x(t) + B_i u(t) + f_i \\ \text{if } \begin{bmatrix} x(t) \\ u(t) \end{bmatrix} \in \tilde{X}_i \end{cases}
\tag{7}
$$

where the column vector $U_0^{T-1} \triangleq [u'(0), \dots, u(T-1)']' \in \mathbb{R}^{mT}$, is the optimization vector and T is the time horizon. In (5), $\|Qx\|_p = x'Qx$ for $p = 2$ and $\|Qx\|_p = \|Qx\|_{1,\infty}$ for $p = 1, \infty$, where $R = R' \succ 0$, $Q = Q', P = P' \succeq 0$ if $p = 2$ and Q, R, P nonsingular if $p = \infty$ or $p = 1$.

---

[1] Although the form (3) is very common in standard formulation of constrained optimal control problems, the results of this paper also hold for the more general mixed constraints $Ex(t) + Lu(t) \leq M$ arising, for example, from constraints on the input rate $\Delta u(t) \triangleq u(t) - u(t-1)$.

We also need to recall the following definitions:

Definition 1. *A collection of sets* $R_1, \ldots, R_N$ *is a partition of a set* Θ *if* (i) $\bigcup_{i=1}^{N} R_i = \Theta$, (ii) $(R_i \backslash \partial R_i) \cap (R_j \backslash \partial R_j) = \emptyset$, $\forall i \neq j$, *where* ∂ *denotes the boundary. Moreover* $R_1, \ldots, R_N$ *is a polyhedral partition of a polyhedral set* Θ *if* $R_1, \ldots, R_N$ *is a partition of* Θ *and* R_i's *are polyhedral sets.*

Definition 2. *A function* $h(\theta) : \Theta \mapsto \mathbb{R}^k$, *where* $\Theta \subseteq \mathbb{R}^s$, *is* piecewise affine *(PWA) if there exists a partition* $R_1, \ldots, R_N$ *of* Θ *and* $h(\theta) = H^i \theta + k^i$, $\forall \theta \in R_i$, $i = 1, \ldots, N$.

Definition 3. *A function* $h(\theta) : \Theta \mapsto \mathbb{R}^k$, *where* $\Theta \subseteq \mathbb{R}^s$, *is PWA on polyhedrons (PPWA) if there exists a polyhedral partition* $R_1, \ldots, R_N$ *of* Θ *and* $h(\theta) = H^i \theta + k^i$, $\forall \theta \in R_i$, $i = 1, \ldots, N$.

In the following we need to distinguish between optimal control based on the 2-norm and optimal control based on the 1-norm or ∞-norm.

3.1   FTCOC - $p = 2$

Theorem 1. *The solution to the optimal control problem (5)-(7) is a PWA state feedback control law of the form*

$$u(x(k)) = F_i^k x(k) + G_i^k \text{ if } x(k) \in \mathcal{P}_i^k \triangleq \{x : \ x(k)' L_i^k x(k) + M_i^k x(k) \leq N_i^k\},$$
$$k = 0, \ldots, T - 1$$

$$(8)$$

where $\mathcal{P}_i^k$, $i = 1, \ldots, N_i$ *is a partition of the set* D^k *of feasible states* $x(k)$.

Proof: We will give the proof for $u(x(0))$, the same arguments can be repeated for $u(x(1)), \ldots, u(x(T-1))$.
Depending on the initial state $x(0)$ and on the input sequence $U = [\ u(0)', \ldots, u(k-1)']$ the state $x(k)$ is either infeasible or it belongs to a certain polyhedron $\tilde{\mathcal{X}}_i$. Suppose for the moment that there are no binary inputs, $m_\ell = 0$. The number of all possible locations of the state sequence $x(0), \ldots, x(T)$ is equal to s^{T+1}. Denote by v_i, $i = 1, \ldots, s^{T+1}$ the list of all possible switching sequences over the horizon T, and by v_i^k the k-th element of the sequence v_i, i.e., $v_i^k = j$ if $x(k) \in \tilde{\mathcal{X}}_j$.
Fix a certain v_i and constrain the state to switch according to the sequence v_i. Problem (5)-(7) becomes

$$J_{v_i}^*(x(0)) \triangleq \min_{\{U_0^{T-1}\}} J(U_0^{T-1}, x(0)) \tag{9}$$

$$\text{s.t.} \begin{cases} x(t+1) & = A_i x(t) + B_i u(t) + f_i \\ & \text{if } \begin{bmatrix} x(t) \\ u(t) \end{bmatrix} \in \tilde{\mathcal{X}}_i \\ x(k) \in \tilde{\mathcal{X}}_{v_i^k} & k = 0, \ldots, T \end{cases} \tag{10}$$

Problem (9)-(10) is equivalent to a finite time optimal control problem for a linear time-varying system with time-varying constraints and can be solved by using the approach of [6]. It's solution is the PPWA feedback control law

$$\tilde{u}^i(x(0)) = \tilde{F}^i_j x(0) + \tilde{G}^i_j, \quad \forall x(0) \in T^i_j, \quad j = 1, \dots, N_{ri} \tag{11}$$

where $\mathcal{D}^i = \bigcup_{j=1}^{N_{ri}} T^i_j$ is a polyhedral partition of the convex set $\mathcal{D}^i$ of feasible states $x(0)$ for problem (9)-(10). N_{ri} is the number of regions of the polyhedral partition of the solution and is a function of the number of constraints in problem (9)-(10). The upper-index i in (11) denotes that the input $\tilde{u}^i(x(0))$ is optimal when the switching sequence v_i is fixed.

The optimal solution $u(x(0))$ to the original problem (5)-(7) can be found by solving problem (9)-(10) for all v_i. The set $\mathcal{D}^0$ of all feasible states at time 0 is $\mathcal{D}^0 = \bigcup_{i=1}^{s^{T+1}} \mathcal{D}^i$ and, in general, is not convex.

As some initial states can be feasible for different switching sequences, the sets $\mathcal{D}^i$, $i = 1, \dots, s^{T+1}$, in general, can overlap. The solution $u(x(0))$ can be computed in the following way. For every polyhedron T^i_j in (11),

1. If $T^i_j \cap T^l_m = \emptyset$ for all $l \neq i$, $l = 1, \dots, s^{T-1}$, $m = 1, \dots, N_{r_l}$, then the switching sequence v_i is the only feasible one for all the states belonging to T^i_j and therefore the optimal solution is given by (11), i.e.

$$u(x(0)) = \tilde{F}^i_j x(0) + \tilde{G}^i_j, \quad \forall x \in T^i_j. \tag{12}$$

2. If T^i_j intersects one or more polyhedrons $T^{l_1}_{m_1}, T^{l_2}_{m_2}, \dots$, the states belonging to the intersection are feasible for more than one switching sequence v_i, v_{l_1}, v_{l_2}, $\dots$ and therefore the corresponding value functions $J^*_{v_i}(x(0))$, $J^*_{v_{l_1}}(x(0)), J^*_{v_{l_2}}(x(0))$, $\dots$ in (9) have to be compared in order to compute the optimal control law.

   Consider the simple case when only two polyhedrons overlap, i.e. $T^i_j \cap T^l_m \triangleq \tilde{T}^{i,l}_{j,m} \neq \emptyset$. We will refer to $\tilde{T}^{i,l}_{j,m}$ as a polyhedron of multiple feasibility. For all states belonging to $\tilde{T}^{i,l}_{j,m}$ the optimal solution is:

$$u(x(0)) = \begin{cases} \tilde{F}^i_j x(0) + \tilde{G}^i_j, & \forall x(0) \in \tilde{T}^{i,l}_{j,m} : J^*_{v_i}(x(0)) < J^*_{v_l}(x(0)) \\ \tilde{F}^l_m x(0) + \tilde{G}^l_m, & \forall x(0) \in \tilde{T}^{i,l}_{j,m} : J^*_{v_i}(x(0)) > J^*_{v_l}(x(0)) \\ \begin{cases} \tilde{F}^i_j x(0) + \tilde{G}^i_j \\ \tilde{F}^l_m x(0) + \tilde{G}^l_m \text{ or} \end{cases} & \forall x(0) \in \tilde{T}^{i,l}_{j,m} : J^*_{v_i}(x(0)) = J^*_{v_l}(x(0)) \end{cases} \tag{13}$$

Because $J^*_{v_i}(x(0))$ and $J^*_{v_l}(x(0))$ are quadratic functions on $\tilde{T}^i_j$ and $\tilde{T}^l_m$ respectively, the theorem is proved. In general, a polyhedron of multiple feasibility where n value functions intersect is partitioned into n subsets where in each one of them a certain value function is greater than all the others.

The proof can be repeated in the presence of binary inputs, $m_\ell \neq 0$. In this case the switching sequences v_i are given by all combinations of region indices

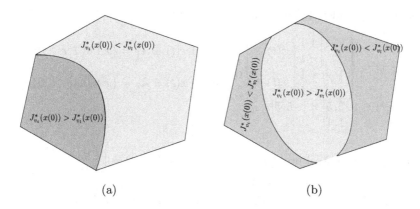

Fig. 1. Possible partitions corresponding to the optimal control law in case 2.d of Remark 1

and *binary inputs*, i.e. $i = 1, \ldots, (s * m_\ell)^{T+1}$. The continuous component of the optimal input is given by (12) or (13). Such an optimal continuous component of the input has an associated optimal sequence v_i which provides the remaining binary components of the optimal input.

$\square$

Remark 1. Let $\tilde{T}_{j,m}^{i,l}$ be a polyhedron of multiple feasibility and let $\mathcal{F} = \{x \in \tilde{T}_{j,m}^{i,l} : J_{v_i}^*(x) = J_{v_l}^*(x)\}$ be the set where the quadratic functions $J_{v_i}^*(x)$ and $J_{v_l}^*(x)$ intersect (for the sake of simplicity we consider the case where only two polyhedrons intersect). We distinguish four cases (sub-cases of case 2 in Theorem 1):

2.a $\mathcal{F} = \varnothing$, i.e., $J_{v_i}^*(x)$ and $J_{v_l}^*(x)$ do not intersect over $\tilde{T}_{j,m}^{i,l}$.
2.b $\mathcal{F} = \{x : Ux = P\}$ and $J_{v_i}^*(x)$ and $J_{v_l}^*(x)$ are tangent on $\mathcal{F}$.
2.c $\mathcal{F} = \{x : Ux = P\}$ and $J_{v_i}^*(x)$ and $J_{v_l}^*(x)$ are not tangent on $\mathcal{F}$.
2.d $\mathcal{F} = \{x : x'Yx + Ux = P\}$ with $Y \neq 0$.

In the first case $\tilde{T}_{j,m}^{i,l}$ is not further partitioned, the optimal solution in $\tilde{T}_{j,m}^{i,l}$ is either $\tilde{F}_j^i x(0) + \tilde{G}_j^i$ or $\tilde{F}_m^l x(0) + \tilde{G}_m^l$. In case 2.b, $\tilde{T}_{j,m}^{i,l}$ is not further partitioned but there are multiple optima on the set $Ux = P$. In case 2.c, $\tilde{T}_{j,m}^{i,l}$ is partitioned into two polyhedrons. In case 2.d $\tilde{T}_{j,m}^{i,l}$ is partitioned into two sets (not necessarily connected) as shown in Figure 1.

In the special case where case 2.c or 2.d occur but the control laws are identical, i.e., $F_j^i = F_m^l$ and $\tilde{G}_j^i = \tilde{G}_m^l$, we will assume that the set $\tilde{T}_{j,m}^{i,l}$ is not further partitioned.

Example 1. Consider the following simple system

$$
\begin{cases}
x(t+1) = \begin{cases}
\begin{bmatrix} 1 & 1 \\ 0 & 1 \end{bmatrix} x(t) + \begin{bmatrix} 0 \\ 1 \end{bmatrix} u(t) & \text{if } x(t) \in \mathcal{X}_1 = \{x : [0\ 1]x \geq 0\} \\
\begin{bmatrix} -1 & -1 \\ 3 & -1 \end{bmatrix} x(t) + \begin{bmatrix} 0 \\ 1 \end{bmatrix} u(t) & \text{if } x(t) \in \mathcal{X}_2 = \{x : [0\ 1]x < 0\}
\end{cases} \\
x(t) \in [-5,5] \times [-5,5] \\
u(t) \in [-1,1]
\end{cases}
\tag{14}
$$

and the optimal control problem (5)-(7), with $T = 1$, $Q = \begin{bmatrix} 1 & 0 \\ 0 & 1 \end{bmatrix}$, $R = 1$.

The possible switching sequences are $v_1 = \{1,1\}$, $v_2 = \{1,2\}$, $v_3 = \{2,1\}$, $v_4 = \{2,2\}$. The solution to problem (9)-(10) is depicted in Figure (2). In Figure 3(a) the four solutions are intersected, the white region corresponds to polyhedrons of multiple feasibility. The state-space partition of the optimal control law is depicted in Figure 3(b) (for lack of space, we do not report here the analytic expressions of the regions and the corresponding affine gains).

Theorem 2. *Suppose that the PWA system (1) is continuous, then the value function $J^*(x(0))$ in (7) is continuous.*

Proof: The continuity of the PWA system (1) implies the continuity of $J(U_0^{T-1}, x(0))$ in (5) as the composition of continuous functions. From the main results on sensitivity analysis [16], $J^*(x(0))$ is also continuous. $\square$

Theorem 3. *Assume $n_\ell = 0$, $m_\ell = 0$ (no discrete states and inputs). Suppose that the cost function $J(U_0^{T-1}, x(0))$ in (5) is continuous and that the optimizer $U_0^{T-1*}(x(0))$ is unique for all $x(0)$. Then the solution to the optimal control problem (5)-(7) is the PPWA state feedback control law*

$$
u(x(k)) = F_i^k x(k) + G_i^k \text{ if } x(k) \in \mathcal{P}_i^k \triangleq \{x : M_i^k x(k) \leq N_i^k\},
\tag{15}
$$
$$
k = 0, \dots, N-1
$$

Proof: : We will show that case 2.d in Remark 1 cannot occur by contradiction. Suppose case 2.d occurs. From the hypothesis the optimizer $u(x(0))$ is unique and from Theorem 1 the value function $J^*(x(0))$ is continuous on $\mathcal{F}$, this implies that $\tilde{F}_j^i x(0) + \tilde{G}_j^i = \tilde{F}_m^l x(0) + \tilde{G}_m^l$, $\forall x(0) \in \mathcal{F}$. That contradicts the hypothesis since the set $\tilde{\mathcal{F}}$ is not a hyperplane. The same arguments can be repeated for $u(x(k))$, $k = 1, \dots, N-1$. $\square$

Theorem 4. *Assume $n_\ell = 0$, $m_\ell = 0$ (no discrete states and inputs). Suppose that the cost function $J(U_0^{T-1}, x(0))$ in (5) is strictly convex with respect to U_0^{T-1} and x_0. Then, the solution to the optimal control problem (5)-(7) is a PPWA state feedback control law of the form (15). Moreover the solution $u(x(k))$ is continuous, $J^*(x(0))$ is convex and cases 2.c and 2.d in Remark 1 will never occur.*

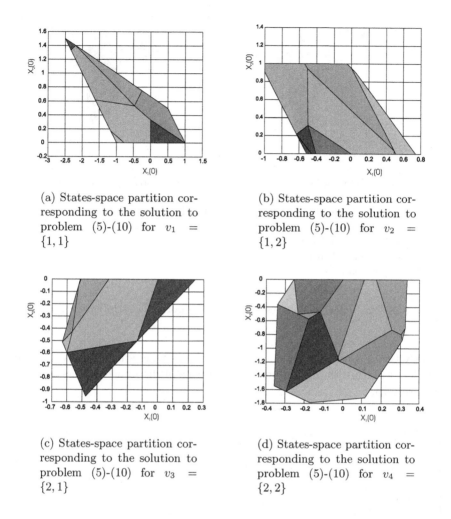

(a) States-space partition corresponding to the solution to problem (5)-(10) for $v_1 = \{1, 1\}$

(b) States-space partition corresponding to the solution to problem (5)-(10) for $v_2 = \{1, 2\}$

(c) States-space partition corresponding to the solution to problem (5)-(10) for $v_3 = \{2, 1\}$

(d) States-space partition corresponding to the solution to problem (5)-(10) for $v_4 = \{2, 2\}$

Fig. 2. First step for the solution of Example 1. Problem (5)-(10) is solved for different v_i, $i = 1, \ldots, 4$

Proof: The convexity of D_k and $J^*(x(0))$ and the continuity of $u(x(0))$ follow from the main theorems on sensitivity analysis [16]. Suppose cases 2.c or cases 2.d occur, then two (or more) value functions $J^*_{v_i}(x)$, $J^*_{v_l}(x)$ intersects over a polyhedron of multiple feasibility $\tilde{T}^{i,l}_{j,m}$. In $\tilde{T}^{i,l}_{j,m}$ the value function $J^*(x(0))$ is $\min\{J^*_{v_i}(x), J^*_{v_l}(x)\}$, which is not convex.   □

Remark 2. Theorem 2 relies on a rather weak uniqueness assumption. As the proof indicates, the key point is to exclude case 2d in Remark 1. Therefore, it is reasonable to believe that there are other conditions or problem classes which satisfy this structural property without claiming uniqueness. We are also

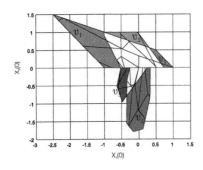 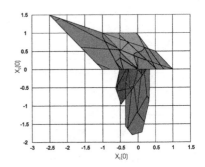

(a) Feasibility domain corresponding to the solution of Example 1 obtained by joining the solutions plotted in Figure 2. The white region corresponds to polyhedrons of multiple feasibility.

(b) State-space partition corresponding to the optimal control law of Example 1

Fig. 3. State-space partition corresponding to the optimal control law of Example 1

currently trying to identify and classify situations where it is usually the state transition structure that guarantees the absence of disconnected sets as shown in Figure 1(b).

Example 2. Consider the following simple system

$$
\begin{cases}
x(t+1) = \begin{cases}
\begin{bmatrix} 1 & 1 \\ 0 & 1 \end{bmatrix} x(t) + \begin{bmatrix} 0 \\ 1 \end{bmatrix} u(t) & \text{if } x(t) \in \mathcal{X}_1 = \{x : [0\ 1]x \geq 0\} \\
\begin{bmatrix} -1 & -1 \\ 0 & -1 \end{bmatrix} x(t) + \begin{bmatrix} 0 \\ 1 \end{bmatrix} u(t) & \text{if } x(t) \in \mathcal{X}_2 = \{x : [0\ 1]x < 0\}
\end{cases} \\
x(t) \in [-5, 5] \times [-5, 5] \\
u(t) \in [-1, 1]
\end{cases} \tag{16}
$$

and the optimal control problem (5)-(7), with $T = 1$, $Q = \begin{bmatrix} 1 & 0 \\ 0 & 1 \end{bmatrix}$, $R = 1$.

The possible switching sequences are $v_1 = \{1, 1\}$, $v_2 = \{1, 2\}$, $v_3 = \{2, 1\}$, $v_4 = \{2, 2\}$. In Figure 4(a) the white region corresponds to polyhedrons of multiple feasibility. The state-space partition of the optimal control law is depicted in Figure 4(b). Note that the feasible domain is convex and that the partition corresponding to the optimal control law is polyhedral.

The following proposition summarizes the properties enjoyed by the solution to problem (5)-(7) as a direct consequence of Theorems 1-3 and Remark 1

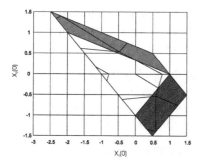

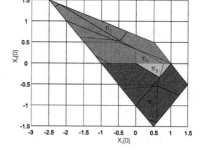

(a) Feasibility domain corresponding to the solution of
Example 2. The white region
corresponds to polyhedrons of
multiple feasibility.

(b) State-space partition corresponding to the optimal control law of Example 2

Fig. 4. State-space partition corresponding to the optimal control law of Example 2

Proposition 1.

1. $u(x(k))$ and $J^*(x(k))$ are, in general, discontinuous and D^k may be nonconvex.
2. $J^*(x(k))$ can be discontinuous only on a facet of a polyhedron of multiple
   feasibility.
3. If there exists a polyhedron of multiple feasibility with $\mathcal{F} = \{x : x'Yx + Ux = P\}$, $Y \neq 0$, then on $\mathcal{F}$ $u(x(k))$ is not unique, except possibly at isolated
   points.

3.2   FTCOC - $p = 1, \infty$

The results of the previous section can be extended to piecewise linear cost
functions, i.e., cost functions based on the 1-norm or the ∞-norm.

Theorem 5. *The solution to the optimal control problem (5)-(7) with $p = 1, \infty$
is a PPWA state feedback control law of the form (15), where $\mathcal{P}_i^k$, $i = 1, \ldots, N_i$
is a partition of the set D^k of feasible states $x(k)$.*

Proof: The proof is similar to the proof of Theorem 1. Fix a certain switching sequence v_i, consider the problem (5)-(7) and constrain the state to switch
according to the sequence v_i to obtain problem (9)-(10). Problem (9)-(10) can be
viewed as a finite time optimal control problem with performance index based on
1-norm or ∞-norm for a linear time varying system with time varying constraints
and can be solved by using the multiparameric linear program as described in [2].
It solution is a PPWA feedback control law

$$\tilde{u}^i(x(0)) = \tilde{F}_j^i x(0) + \tilde{G}_j^i, \quad \forall x \in \mathcal{T}_j^i, \quad j = 1, \ldots, N_{ri} \tag{17}$$

and the value function $J_{v_i}^*$ is piecewise affine and convex. The rest of the proof follows the proof of Theorem 1. Note that in this case the value functions to be compared are piecewise affine and not piecewise quadratic.   □

Theorem 6. *Suppose that the cost function $J(U_0^{T-1}, x(0))$ in (5) is convex with respect to U_0^{T-1} and x_0. Then the solution to the optimal control problem (5)-(7) is a PPWA and continuous state feedback control law of the form (15), where $D_k = \bigcup_i \mathcal{P}_i^k$ and $J^*(x(0))$ are convex and $u(x(0))$ is continuous.*

Proof: The proof is similar to the proof of Theorem 4.   □

4 Efficient Computation of the Solution

In the previous section the properties enjoyed by the solution to hybrid optimal control problems were investigated. Despite the fact that the proof is constructive (as shown in the figures), it is based on the enumeration of all the possible switching sequences of the hybrid system, the number of which grows exponentially with the time horizon. Although the computation is performed off line (the on-line complexity is the one associated with the evaluation of the PWA control law (15)), more efficient methods than enumeration are desirable. Here we show that MLD framework can be used in order to avoid enumeration. Consider the equivalent MLD system (2) of the PWA system (4). Problem (5)-(7) can be rewritten as:

$$\min_{\{U_0^{T-1}\}} J(U_0^{T-1}, x(0)) \triangleq \sum_{k=0}^{T-1} \|Ru(t)\|_p + \|Qx(t)\|_p + \|Px(T|t)\|_p \quad (18)$$

$$\text{subj. to} \begin{cases} x(k+1) = \Phi x(k) + G_1 v(k) + G_2 \delta(k) + G_3 z(k) \\ E_2 \delta(k) + E_3 z(k) \le E_1 v(k) + E_4 x(k) + E_5 \end{cases} \quad (19)$$

The optimal control problem in (18)-(19) can be formulated as a *Mixed Integer Quadratic Program* (MIQP) when the squared Euclidean norm $p = 2$ is used [5], or as a *Mixed Integer Linear Program* (MILP), when $p = \infty$ or $p = 1$ [3],

$$\min_{\varepsilon} \quad \varepsilon' H_1 \varepsilon + \varepsilon' H_2 x(0) + x(0)' H_3 x(0) + f_1' \varepsilon + f_2' x(0) + c$$

$$(20)$$

$$\text{subj. to } G\varepsilon \le S + Fx(0)$$

where $H_1, H_2, H_3, f_1, f_2, G, S, F$ are matrices of suitable dimensions, $\varepsilon = [\varepsilon_c', \varepsilon_d']$ where $\varepsilon_c, \varepsilon_d$ represent continuous and discrete variables, respectively and H_1, H_2, H_3, are null matrices if problem (20) is an MILP.

Given a value of the initial state $x(0)$, the MIQP (or MILP) (20) can be solved to get the optimal input $\varepsilon^*(x(0))$. Multiparametric programming [17, 15, 6, 9] can be used to efficiently compute the explicit form of the optimal state-feedback control law $u(x(k))$. By generalizing the result of [6] for linear systems to hybrid systems, the state vector $x(0)$, which appears in the objective function and in the linear part of the rhs of the constraints, can be handled as a vector of parameters. Then, for performance indices based on the ∞-norm or 1-norm, the optimization problem can be treated as a *multi-parametric MILP* (mp-MILP), while for performance indices based on the 2-norm, the optimization problem can be treated as a *multi-parametric MIQP* (mp-MIQP).

Solving an mp-MILP (mp-MIQP) amounts to expressing the solution of the MILP (MIQP) (20) as a function of the parameters $x(0)$. Two main approaches have been proposed for solving mp-MILP problems in [1, 15], while, to the authors' knowledge, there does not exist an efficient method for solving mp-MIQPs. An efficient algorithm for the solution of mp-MIQP problems arising from hybrid control problems that uses mp-QP solvers and dynamic programming is currently under development.

Acknowledgments

We thank Christos G. Cassandras for his constructive and helpful comments on the original manuscript.

References

[1] J. Acevedo and E.N. Pistikopoulos. A multiparametric programming approach for linear process engineering problems under uncertainty. *Ind. Eng. Chem. Res.*, 36:717–728, 1997.

[2] A. Bemporad, F. Borrelli, and M. Morari. Explicit solution of constrained $1/\infty$-norm model predictive control. In *Proc. 39th IEEE Conf. on Decision and Control*, December 2000.

[3] A. Bemporad, F. Borrelli, and M. Morari. Piecewise linear optimal controllers for hybrid systems. In *Proc. American Contr. Conf.*, pages 1190–1194, Chicago, IL, June 2000.

[4] A. Bemporad, G. Ferrari-Trecate, and M. Morari. Observability and controllability of piecewise affine and hybrid systems. *IEEE Trans. Automatic Control*, 45(10):1864–1876, 2000.

[5] A. Bemporad and M. Morari. Control of systems integrating logic, dynamics, and constraints. *Automatica*, 35(3):407–427, March 1999.

[6] A. Bemporad, M. Morari, V. Dua, and E.N. Pistikopoulos. The explicit linear quadratic regulator for constrained systems. *Automatica*, 38(1):3–20, 2002.

[7] A. Bemporad, F.D. Torrisi, and M. Morari. Optimization-based verification and stability characterization of piecewise affine and hybrid systems. In B. Krogh and N. Lynch, editors, *Hybrid Systems: Computation and Control*, volume 1790 of *Lecture Notes in Computer Science*, pages 45–58. Springer Verlag, 2000.

[8] F. Borrelli, A. Bemporad, M. Fodor, and D. Hrovat. A hybrid approach to traction control. In A. Sangiovanni-Vincentelli and M.D. Di Benedetto, editors, *Hybrid Systems: Computation and Control*, Lecture Notes in Computer Science. Springer Verlag, 2001.

[9] F. Borrelli, A. Bemporad, and M. Morari. A geometric algorithm for multiparametric linear programming. Technical Report AUT00-06, Automatic Control Laboratory, ETH Zurich, Switzerland, February 2000.

[10] M.S. Branicky and S.K. Mitter. Algorithms for optimal hybrid control. In *Proc. 34th IEEE Conf. on Decision and Control*, New Orleans, USA, December 1995.

[11] M.S. Branicky and G. Zhang. Solving hybrid control problems: Level sets and behavioral programming. In *Proc. American Contr. Conf.*, Chicago, Illinois USA, June 2000.

[12] M. Buss, O. von Stryk, R. Bulirsch, and G. Schmidt. Towards hybrid optimal control. *at*, 48:448–459, 200.

[13] B. De Schutter and B. De Moor. The extended linear complementarity problem and the modeling and analysis of hybrid systems. In P. Antsaklis, W. Kohn, M. Lemmon, A. Nerode, and S. Sastry, editors, *Hybrid Systems V*, volume 1567 of *Lecture Notes in Computer Science*, pages 70–85. Springer, 1999.

[14] B. De Schutter and T. van den Boom. Model predictive control for max-plus-linear systems. In *Proc. American Contr. Conf.*, pages 4046–4050, 2000.

[15] V. Dua and E.N. Pistikopoulos. An algorithm for the solution of multiparametric mixed integer linear programming problems. *Annals of Operations Research*, to appear.

[16] A V. Fiacco. *Introduction to sensitivity and stability analysis in nonlinear programming*. Academic Press, London, U.K., 1983.

[17] T. Gal. *Postoptimal Analyses, Parametric Programming, and Related Topics*. de Gruyter, Berlin, 2nd ed. edition, 1995.

[18] K. Gokbayrak and C.G. Cassandras. A hierarchical decomposition method for optimal control of hybrid systems. In *Proc. 38th IEEE Conf. on Decision and Control*, pages 1816–1821, Phoenix, AZ, December 1999.

[19] A Hassibi and S. Boyd. Quadratic stabilization and control of piecewise-linear systems. In *Proc. American Contr. Conf.*, Philadelphia, Pennsylvania USA, June 1998.

[20] S. Hedlund and A. Rantzer. Optimal control of hybrid systems. In *Proc. 38th IEEE Conf. on Decision and Control*, pages 3972–3976, Phoenix, AZ, December 1999.

[21] W.P.M.H. Heemels. *Linear complementarity systems: a study in hybrid dynamics*. PhD thesis, Dept. of Electrical Engineering, Eindhoven University of Technology, The Netherlands, 1999.

[22] W.P.M.H. Heemels, J.M. Schumacher, and S. Weiland. Linear complementarity systems. *SIAM Journal on Applied Mathematics*, 60(4):1234–1269, 2000.

[23] W.P.M.H. Heemels, B. De Schutter, and A. Bemporad. Equivalence of hybrid dynamical models. *Automatica*, 37(7):1085–1091, July 2001.

[24] M. Johannson and A. Rantzer. Computation of piece-wise quadratic Lyapunov functions for hybrid systems. *IEEE Trans. Automatic Control*, 43(4):555–559, 1998.

[25] K H Johansson, M Egerstedt, J Lygeros, and S Sastry. On the regularization of Zeno hybrid automata. *System & Control Letters*, 38:141–150, 1999.

[26] J. Lygeros, C. Tomlin, and S. Sastry. Controllers for reachability specifications for hybrid systems. *Automatica*, 35(3):349–370, 1999.

[27] D. Mignone, G. Ferrari-Trecate, and M. Morari. Stability and stabilization of piecewise affine and hybrid systems: An LMI approach. In *Proc. 39th IEEE Conf. on Decision and Control*, December 2000.

[28] G.L. Nemhauser and L.A. Wolsey. *Integer and Combinatorial Optimization*. Wiley, 1988.

[29] B. Piccoli. Necessary conditions for hybrid optimization. In *Proc. 38th IEEE Conf. on Decision and Control*, Phoenix, Arizona USA, December 1999.

On the Optimal Control Law for Linear Discrete Time Hybrid Systems 119

[30] P. Riedinger, F.Kratz, C. Iung, and C.Zanne. Linear quadratic optimization for hybrid systems. In *Proc. 38th IEEE Conf. on Decision and Control*, Phoenix, Arizona USA, December 1999.

[31] E.D. Sontag. Nonlinear regulation: The piecewise linear approach. *IEEE Trans. Automatic Control*, 26(2):346–358, April 1981.

[32] H.J. Sussmann. A maximum principle for hybrid optimal control problems. In *Proc. 38th IEEE Conf. on Decision and Control*, Phoenix, Arizona USA, December 1999.

[33] C.J. Tomlin, J. Lygeros, and S.S. Sastry. A game theoretic approach to controller design for hybrid systems. *Proceeding of IEEE*, 88, July 2000.

[34] F.D. Torrisi, A. Bemporad, and D. Mignone. HYSDEL - A language for describing hybrid systems. Technical Report AUT00-03, ETH Zurich, 2000. `http://control.ethz.ch/~hybrid/hysdel`.

[35] A.J. van der Schaft and J.M. Schumacher. Complementarity modelling of hybrid systems. *IEEE Trans. Automatic Control*, 43:483–490, 1998.

[36] H.P. Williams. *Model Building in Mathematical Programming*. John Wiley & Sons, Third Edition, 1993.

A Computational Framework for the Verification and Synthesis of Force-Guided Robotic Assembly Strategies

Michael S. Branicky[1] and Siddharth R. Chhatpar[2]

[1] Case Western Reserve University, Electrical Eng. and Computer Science,
Glennan 515B, 10900 Euclid Ave, Cleveland, OH 44106-7071, U.S.A
msb11@po.cwru.edu

[2] Case Western Reserve University, Mechanical and Aerospace Engineering,
Glennan 109, 10900 Euclid Ave, Cleveland, OH 44106, U.S.A
src2@po.cwru.edu

Abstract. Robotic assemblies are inherently hybrid systems. This paper pursues a class of multi-tiered peg-in-hole assemblies that we call *peg-in-maze* assemblies. These assemblies require a force-responsive, low-level controller governing physical contacts plus a decision-making, strategic-level supervisor monitoring the overall progress. To capture this dichotomy we formulate hybrid automata, where each state represents a different force-controlled *behavior* and transitions between states encode the high-level strategy of the assembly. Each of these behaviors is set in 6-dimensional space, and each dimension is parameterized by spring and damper values (an impedance controller). Our over-arching goal is to produce a computational framework for the verification and synthesis of such force-guided robotic assembly strategies. We investigate the use of two general hybrid systems software tools (HyTech and CEtool) for the verification of these strategies. We describe a computational environment developed at Case to help automate their synthesis. The implementation of these strategies on actual robotic assemblies is also described.

1 Introduction

Robotic assemblies are inherently hybrid systems [1] because they involve the making and breaking of contacts [2]. This paper pursues a class of such assemblies that we call *peg-in-maze* assemblies, which includes real-world examples such as clutch mating and gear meshing. These are multi-tiered versions of traditional *peg-in-hole* assembly problems. There are further complications due to the fact that the layers may move with respect to each other (allowing position uncertainties of the components that exceed the corresponding assembly clearances). Thus, successful assembly requires altering component locations through physical contact between the mating parts in a search for the next insertion hole. Once the hole is found, insertion may proceed. This already induces a layer-by-layer switching between search and insertion *behaviors*. Further complexity may

C.J. Tomlin and M.R. Greenstreet (Eds.): HSCC 2002, LNCS 2289, pp. 120–133, 2002.

arise if the assembly reaches a dead-end or JAM state, requiring the invocation of some other behavior (*backing_up*, *re-planning*, or *aborting*).

We have successfully automated example *peg-in-maze* assemblies using a two-level control in previous work, including a forward clutch (described below), reverse clutch, sun/planetary gear, torque converter, and several other assemblies [3] [4] [5]. To govern physical contacts, we use a parameterized family of low-level force-responsive algorithms known as natural admittance controllers [6]. To switch between different low-level controllers, invoke new behaviors, and monitor the overall progress of the assembly, we use a higher-level discrete-event supervisor [7]. Together, these two levels of control implement an assembly strategy that guides the assembly process from start to finish.

Both the strategy and the assembly process itself are hybrid systems. Any *run* of the system consists of continuous movements (such as searching for a hole or moving down until contact) that are governed by continuous control laws and discrete events (such as finding a hole or contacting a layer) that are processed by a logical decision maker. Thus, to formally model peg-in-maze assemblies and their associated assembly strategies, we must use a hybrid systems approach [8]. In this paper, we formulate hybrid automata [10] models of assemblies/strategies, where each state represents a different force-controlled behavior and transitions between states encode the high-level strategy of the assembly.

Our over-arching goal is to produce a computational framework for the verification and synthesis of such force-guided robotic assembly strategies. We investigate the use of two general hybrid systems software tools, HyTech and CEtool, for the verification of these strategies. Herein, we briefly describe the results obtained with these tools and our own C++ analysis algorithms specifically tailored to peg-in-maze problems.

Finally, we describe a computational environment developed at Case to help automate the synthesis and implementation of force-guided robotic assembly strategies. The tool includes a State Machine Editor for entering overall strategy and a Mode Editor for creating the underlying force-controlled behaviors. There is also a Code Generator and a Real-Time Monitor.

The paper is organized as follows. Section 2 describes peg-in-maze assemblies further and formulates the hybrid automaton representation of the strategies to automate them. Section 3 presents a simplified two-dimensional peg-in-maze assembly, which is used to fix ideas throughout. Section 4 describes the verification of assembly strategies using the general hybrid systems software tools. Section 5 outlines the computational environment for strategy synthesis and code generation, used for actual experiments. Finally, Sections 6–7 summarize results, conclusions, and future work.

2 Peg-in-Maze Assemblies and Assembly Strategies

In this section, we formulate hybrid automata models for peg-in-maze assemblies. We start by describing a real-world example, abstract this to a representative *prototype* assembly, and subsequently formulate our model.

(a)   (c)

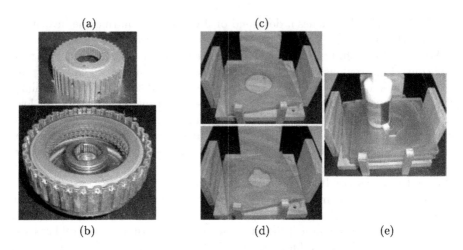

(b)   (d)   (e)

Fig. 1. (a,b) Forward clutch assembly; (c,d,e) Peg and layers in the prototype peg-in-maze assembly

The real-world assemblies we have investigated are from a Ford automatic transmission. One of them, insertion of a spline-toothed hub within a forward clutch assembly is described here. See Fig. 1(a,b). The forward-clutch housing, shown in Fig. 1(b), consists of a cylinder with five internal rings (clutch plates), each with spline teeth about the inner radius. These rings are each capable of sliding independently in the horizontal plane by up to 1.6 mm and rotating about a vertical axis. A cylindrical hub with teeth on its outer surface, shown in Fig. 1(a), is to be inserted within the housing of Fig. 1(b). However, the clutch plates are not, in general, aligned either radially or tangentially. The radial assembly clearance between the hub and a ring is 0.23 mm. Thus, the radial assembly uncertainty is more than six times larger than the clearance required for success. Additionally, the hub must align with the z-rotation of each spline ring within 5 mrads for successful assembly, even though the tooth spacing is 160 mrads.

The forward clutch mating and other assemblies cited in Section 1 belong to a special class that we call *peg-in-maze* assemblies, which are multi-tiered versions of the traditional peg-in-hole problem. We have also built a prototypical peg-in-maze assembly for illustration and experimentation purposes. See Fig. 1(c,d,e). This assembly abstracts the salient features and peculiarities of our example transmission assemblies. By construction, our prototype is analogous to the forward-clutch assembly problem. Namely, the clutch plates are represented by *layers* and the hub is represented by a keyed peg.

The prototype assembly has an unconventional peg-in-hole type structure. The female part is made up of five layers; each is a Plexiglas sheet, measuring 160×170×11 mm thick. These layers are stacked in a larger rectangular container, measuring 190×200 mm. Hence, the layers are capable of x-y sliding motion relative to each other and small rotations about the vertical axis. Each layer has a characteristically-shaped hole (circular, single-slotted, or double-slotted) cut in it through which the peg can pass, as shown in Fig. 1(c,d). The peg is cylindrical in shape, except for a small key (Fig. 1(e)). The structure has been made with large clearances (up to 11.5 mm) between the peg and the holes, however, the position eccentricities achievable by the holes (up to 42.5 mm) are much larger than the insertion clearances.

The assembly experiment starts with the peg on top of the first layer. The goal is to insert the peg through the holes on all the layers and reach the bottom of the box. To achieve insertion through all the layers, the peg should search for the hole on a layer and, finding it, move down to the next layer, and then repeat the search. The positions of the layers inside the container are arbitrary and hence the peg cannot be given a predetermined trajectory that will lead it straight to the holes. Trying to break down the complex scheme into simpler strategies, we can identify two distinct behaviors. One behavior (*Search*) is the search carried out to find the hole after contacting a layer, while the other (*Insert*) is to move down to contact another layer once alignment has been achieved. (There is also a *Layer Identification* behavior, not described here [8].) Although within a behavior the control law and search strategy are continuous, the transition between behaviors is a discontinuous jump. Hence, this problem falls under the domain of hybrid systems and should be treated as such. The hybrid automaton model of the controller for this peg-in-maze assembly is described below.

2.1   Discrete States and Events for the Peg-in-Maze

We have identified two primary behaviors for this assembly: *Search* and *Insert*, for each layer. Thus, in all there are 10 discrete states (for 5 layers) that the assembly can be in at any point of time. In addition, there is a START state, and the final ACCEPT state, making a total of 12 states. Other specialized routines, such as *Search Initialization,* are included as parts of the primary behaviors.

SEARCH **States:** In each SEARCH state, the controller moves the peg to perform a rectangular search for the hole (there is also a search in rotation for key-slot alignment and the aforementioned layer identification; see [5] [8]). In fact, each SEARCH state, S_i, itself consists of two functions, or substates, grouped together (Fig. 2(a)). Such hierarchical state machines can be represented using a formalism evocative of StateCharts [11].

On entering the SEARCH state, the controller shifts to the *Search Initialization* routine, and guides the peg to the center of the search area. In the *Rectangular Search* routine the controller moves the peg along a trajectory forming a rectangle of increasing side-length in the x-y plane (Fig. 2(b)). While searching, the peg is also controlled to maintain a downward force (z) on the layer. These movements are accomplished by moving the impedance controller's *attractor* [3].

If the peg finds the hole, the search is successful and the controller must shift to the corresponding INSERT state as the peg starts to move down through the

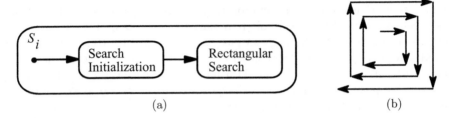

Fig. 2. (a) "StateChart" for SEARCH, (b) Simple rectangular search path in x-y plane

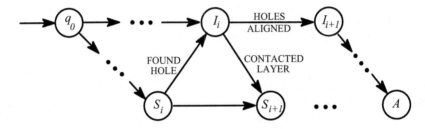

Fig. 3. Hybrid Automaton Representation

layer. To recognize this transition in the state of the assembly, the controller continuously runs an event-check routine. The event FOUND_HOLE can be distinguished by a sudden drop in the sensed force (along the vertical z). This spike in the sensed force is because the peg, while pushing against the layer, suddenly loses contact when it aligns with the hole.

INSERT **States:** When the controller is in an INSERT state it makes the peg move down through the hole to contact the next layer (again by moving the attractor). There are 2 events possible in this state. The event CONTACTED_LAYER is also distinguished by a sensed-force spike. The sensed force is nearly zero when the peg is not in contact with any layer and is moving down. But when the peg hits a layer, the sensed force suddenly shoots up.

If the holes on the current layer (that the peg is moving through) and the next layer are aligned, then the peg will move through the next layer without contacting it. Another event-check routine is used to signal this event: HOLES_ALIGNED. On recognition of this event, the controller shifts to the corresponding INSERT state and the peg continues to move down.

The hybrid automaton representation of this controller is shown in Fig. 3.

3 Detailed Example: Two-Dimensional Peg-in-Maze

A simplified two-dimensional version (Fig. 4) of our prototypical peg-in-maze assembly was used for exploring the simulation and verification of strategies.

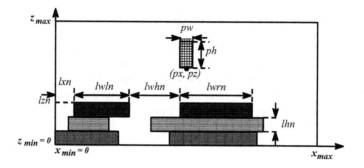

Fig. 4. Two-dimensional Peg-in-Maze Problem

The problem is reduced by two dimensions with the restriction that the peg can move only in the x or z direction (i.e., no y moves, no rotations). Correspondingly, the layers can only move with the peg in the x-direction. It is assumed there is no friction, so a layer will not move when the peg moves along the top of its surface.

3.1 Environment

The peg is represented by a fixed point, which is the center point on the bottom of the peg. The parameters for the peg include: x position (px), z position (pz), height (ph), and width (pw). Parameters for each layer are: lxn (offset from $x_{min} = 0$), $lwln$ (width of left shoulder), $lwhn$ (width of hole), $lwrn$ (width of right shoulder), exn (total eccentricity), lzn (z position of the top surface of the layer), and lhn (height). Here, n represents layer n. lxn should be no less than 0 and no greater than the total eccentricity of the layer (exn). Be aware that although there is no connection shown in Fig. 4 between the left shoulder and right shoulder of a layer, they are connected. So whenever one of them moves, the other moves with it.

3.2 Control Strategies

We build an event-based control strategy as described in Section 2.1, using the two previously identified controlled behaviors. One is to move the peg along the surfaces of layers, searching for holes using a constant velocity (*Search: x* direction movement only, using a constant velocity, v_x). Another is to move the peg down the hole once the hole is found (*Insert: z* direction movement only, using a constant velocity, v_z). We use an additional behavior to stop the movement of the peg once the task is successfully accomplished (the peg hits bottom of the box). Different control behaviors will be used when the peg is in different states. The *Search* behavior is itself made up of two distinct behaviors: *searchright* and *searchleft*. The peg is always made to search towards the right first. If it hits the right barrier without finding the hole, it will start searching to the left.

4   Verification of Assembly Strategies

General peg-in-maze problems are usually hard to solve analytically for lack of suitable tools to model both the hybrid nature of the system and underlying uncertainties. Here, we build a framework for computationally testing strategies for peg-in-maze problems [12]. This includes verification to prove properties of a strategy for a whole class of situations. Two software tools have been tried for this purpose: HyTech [13] [14] and CEtool [15].

4.1   HyTech

HyTech is a software tool that can automatically verify a certain class of hybrid systems, known as linear hybrid automata. Specifically, HyTech can symbolically compute the reachability sets of such systems starting from a set of initial conditions (even if the systems are non-deterministic). Thus, one can verify safety properties (e.g., *If the initial conditions are in set* INIT, *will the set* BAD *of undesirable states never be reached?*) and liveness properties (e.g., *If the initial conditions are in set* INIT, *will the state* SUCCESS *always be reachable?*). HyTech can also perform parametric analysis, in which it solves for constraints on the values of certain design parameters necessary and sufficient for the desired properties to hold.

In order to test control strategies easily, automata for the controller, the peg, and different layers have been separated. The search strategy is formalized in the controller automaton of Fig. 5. Similarly, automata are constructed for the peg and each layer (see [12]). These automata are not trivial. For instance, the peg automaton includes 3 MOVE_DOWN states (to move down to contact the first layer and then insert through the first and second layers), 6 SEARCH_LAYER states (for each layer: searching right on layer left shoulder, right on right shoulder, and left on right shoulder), a FINISHED state, a JAM state and a special CHECK state. The peg automaton enters the CHECK state whenever a movement can not be continued. For example, when the peg moves down and it hits an object it can not move down any further. In this situation, the peg automaton will issue the FORCEZ synchronization label, go to the CHECK state, and wait for feedback from the controller.

Using the strategy given, HyTech was used to evaluate the feasibility of the assembly tasks and calculate bounds on assembly times. Fig. 5 shows assemblies with different part geometry and particular initial conditions. Also shown are verification results on these assemblies.

As mentioned before, HyTech can only handle linear hybrid automata. Also, HyTech's calculation power is limited. Adding layers to HyTech will add more states, finally causing a state explosion that exceeds HyTech's calculation ability. To use HyTech more efficiently, one should try to keep the system description as small as possible. For example, one should share locations wherever possible, minimize the number of variables used, and use the strongest possible invariants. Simplifying the constants used also helps to speed up the analysis: integers should be used whenever possible.

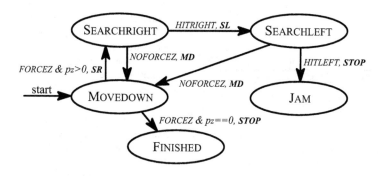

Fig. 5. The Controller Automaton

4.2   CEtool

CEtool is a software verification tool developed by a research group at Carnegie Mellon University. It is built on top of Matlab's Simulink toolbox; hence it has a GUI for entering models in a block-diagram fashion.

CEtool can handle so-called threshold-event-driven hybrid systems (TEDHS) because they support block diagram modeling. A TEDHS consists of three interconnected subsystems: (i) switched continuous systems (SCS) with piecewise constant inputs that select the continuous dynamics and continuous outputs, (ii) threshold event generators that take the continuous outputs of switched continuous systems and generate events when they cross certain thresholds, and (iii) finite state machines that are discrete transition systems.

The same control strategy as depicted by the finite automaton of Fig. 5 is encoded in a finite state machine (fsm). The fsm has six event inputs and one data output. The six events are: START, FORCEZ, NOFORCEZ, HITBOTTOM, HITRIGHT, and HITLEFT. The output q is connected to the SCS block. For different q values, the SCS block has different continuous dynamics. There are nine polyhedral threshold blocks (PTHB), $layer_1$, $hole_1$, $layer_2$, $hole_2$, $bottom$, x_{max}, exr, exl, and x_{min}. $layer_1$, $layer_2$, and $bottom$ mark the levels of layer one, two, and the bottom of the box. $hole_1$ and $hole_2$ mark the original positions of the two holes. x_{max} and x_{min} are the limits when the peg is searching for the first hole. exr and exl are the limits when the peg is in the first hole and is searching for the second hole. In each case, their constraints are given as the polyhedra $C\bar{x} \leq d$, where C is a matrix, $\bar{x} = [x\ z]'$, x is the x position of the peg, z is the z position of the peg, and d is a threshold vector.

The verification requirement for the system is (AF (AG ($fsm ==$ FINISH))) & (AG$\sim fsm ==$ JAM), which means the finite state machine will reach the FINISH state and stay there forever, and the JAM state will never be reached.

In CEtool, one can potentially verify bounds on assembly time also. For example, iterating the expression (AG ($\sim$ ($fsm ==$ FINISH $|$ $timer$))) can give us a lower bound on assembly time if we include the assembly time t as one of the state variables (with derivative equal to 1 in all modes) and adding a PTHB

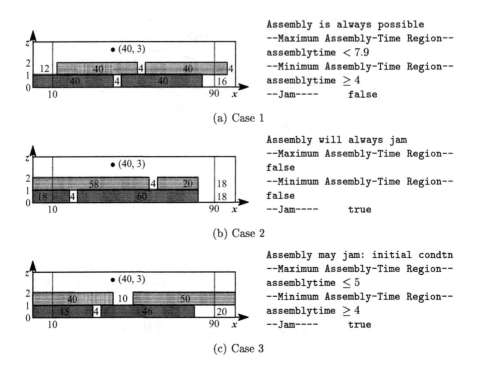

(a) Case 1

(b) Case 2

(c) Case 3

Fig. 6. Verification results for three different cases using HyTech

timer to check whether t is greater than a maximum lower bound. Similarly, the expression (AG ($fsm ==$ FINISH $|$ $timer$)) can be used to give us an upper bound on assembly time if the PTHB checks whether the assembly time t is less than a least upper bound. Unfortunately, CEtool did not converge on these two properties for the two-layer peg-in-maze assembly model.

A limitation of CEtool (in the version we downloaded, 1998) is that it does not allow the clock derivative constant to be parallel to any hyperplanes specified in the system. Thus, to use the tool to verify the system, we had to use the following *de-parallelization* trick to accommodate this constraint. When moving along the x-axis, for example, instead of setting the z velocity to zero, it was given a small negative value. Similarly, when moving down along the z-axis, instead of setting a zero x-velocity, a small positive value was tried. This latter *fix* caused a problem, however. If the peg finds the right wall of the hole, a NOFORCEZ event will be triggered and the peg goes to the MOVEDOWN state and tries to move down. But there is a small positive x-velocity when moving down, so the peg goes out of the region of the hole immediately and a FORCEZ event is falsely triggered. To solve this problem, the following changes can be made. The MOVEDOWN state in the finite state machine can be split into DOWN1 and DOWN2, and the NOFORCEZ event can likewise be split into two events. The NOFORCEZ1 event is triggered when the first hole is found; the NOFORCEZ2 event, when the second

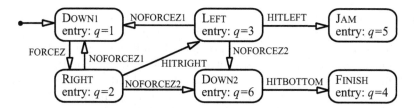

Fig. 7. *fsm* for verification

hole is found. The initial analysis region should be on the left of the first hole, so the problem will not happen with the first hole.

Another limitation is that CEtool does not allow resetting of continuous variables. For example, when the peg hits the layer, the z velocity has to be reset to zero. To model the reset and still keep the variable continuous, we can use another trick: *fast-time scale resetting*. That is, we add new states to the finite state machine to decelerate the velocities to zero quickly.

5   Assembly Strategy Synthesis and Code Generation

Our software synthesis framework is comprised of three levels or layers, as shown in Fig. 8. Each level of the framework addresses a fundamental problem associated with peg-in-maze/robotic assemblies and provides a solution for the same. The layers are implemented on separate platforms, and are independent subsystems by themselves, thus making it a truly heterogeneous system. The layers from bottom to top are explained briefly below. See [16] for more details.

5.1   Robot Client-Server (Lower Layer)

At the lowest level, we tackle the problem of controlling the robot. For this we need a set of commands. Different robot controllers have different command sets, and to compound the problem, the communication media for different robots vary. The framework is designed for a heterogeneous distributed platform with

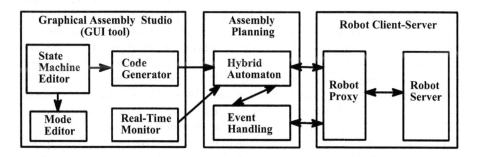

Fig. 8. System Diagram

multiple robots running on different controllers. We chose to follow the client-server paradigm to extend the object-oriented design beyond a single machine. The Robot Client-Server sub-system provides the following: (1) Generic Robot API, a universal command set to control any robot; (2) Robot Proxy, a local agent which acts as surrogate for a remote robot and hides communication details from the client; (3) Communication Architecture to handle different Inter-Process Communication (IPC) mechanisms; (4) Multi-Threaded Robot Server, residing locally in the platform hosting the real robot. The robot server handles multiple requests from more than one client concurrently.

5.2   Assembly Planning (Middle Layer)

Residing right above the Robot Client-Server is the Assembly Planning layer. Peg-in-maze assemblies are modeled as Hybrid Automata, or Hybrid State Machines. Jump conditions in the hybrid automata correspond to event sources in the framework. These events are identified and the transitions are triggered using the Event Handling Framework. Events include device, timer, software interrupts, digital input transitions, force feedback, operator input etc. The Event Handling Framework is based on the Delegation Model, an object oriented model for event handling. The Assembly Planning layer has the software implementation of these state machines. The uppermost layer, the Graphical Assembly Studio, automatically generates the main body of these state machines.

5.3   Graphical Assembly Studio, a GUI Tool (Upper Layer)

At the highest level resides the GUI tool, which we have named Graphical Assembly Studio. See Fig. 9. It comprises four main applications: State Machine Editor, Mode Editor, Code Generator, Real-Time Monitor. The state machine and mode editors are visual editors which allow the user to plan the assembly strategies in a WYSIWYG environment, and save assemblies as persistent objects. The State Machine Editor allows the user to (1) model the whole assembly as a hybrid automaton, (2) associate each location in the automaton with a mode, and (3) select from a library of registered events for transitions between locations. The Mode Editor is used to (1) select and customize predefined search patterns, (2) divide search patterns into neighborhoods and define primitive behaviors within them, (3) specify the subspace of the assembly, (4) specify other parameters specific to the search strategy, and (5) specify certain periodic behaviors, e.g. *jiggle*. The Code Generator parses these graphs to automatically generate C++ code, which forms the body of the state machine. This code becomes part of the middle-layer. The Real-Time Monitor is a useful application that allows the user to monitor assemblies as hybrid automata, when they actually execute. Active states are highlighted; events are visually noted.

Fig. 9(a) shows an assembly strategy for the forward clutch modeled as a hybrid automaton using the State Machine Editor. The rectangular blocks (MOVE_TO_FIRST, SPIRAL, MOVE_DOWN, STOP) are locations and are associated with corresponding strategy modes. The triangular blocks (HIT_LAYER,

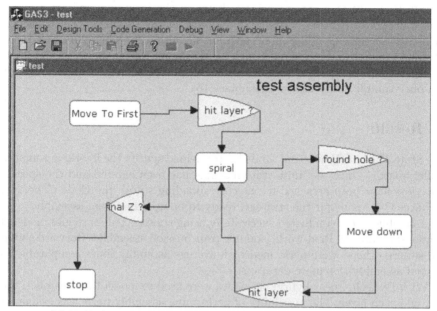

(a) Hybrid automaton model of forward clutch-assembly strategy

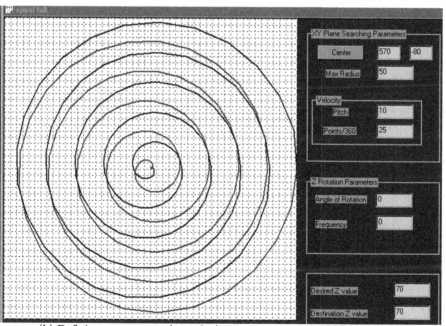

(b) Defining SPIRAL search mode (attractor trajectory and impedance controller parameters) using the Mode Editor

Fig. 9. Graphical Assembly Studio example screen captures

FOUND_HOLE, FINAL_Z) are transitions between the locations, and are selected from a library of registered events. A double-click on a location or a transition opens up the corresponding mode or event-definition for editing. For example, selecting the SPIRAL block would open up the Mode Editor shown in Fig. 9(b).

We used these tools to perform both the prototype peg-in-maze assembly and our example transmission assemblies [16].

6   Results

The State Machine Editor and Mode Editor helped specify the hybrid automaton model quickly. Once the finite state machine has been entered and the specific behaviors have been attached to the corresponding states, the Code Generator produces C++ code for the strategy, ready to be used in actual assembly.

Assemblies were conducted successfully using constructed strategies modeled as hybrid automata. Real-world example transmission assemblies (forward clutch and several others) were performed with average assembly times comparable to manual assembly (for more details, see [3] [4] [5]).

With HyTech, linear hybrid automata were used to model the controller, the peg, and each layer. The possibility of performing assembly tasks was evaluated under a variety of different geometries for whole sets of initial conditions (which encompassed all possible, a priori unknown, locations of the layers). Upper and lower bounds on assembly time were calculated. Also, velocity uncertainty was introduced and different strategies were tried. Finally, clock translation and linear phase-portrait approximation methods were used to convert nonlinear (force control) hybrid automata to linear hybrid automata (see [12]).

CEtool was used to simulate and verify peg-in-maze assemblies using both velocity and force control. The tool has limitations when applying it directly to peg-in-maze assemblies, but after modifications (*de-parallelization, fast-time scale resetting*), it dealt with the system correctly and gave satisfying results.

7   Future Work

In relation to verification of strategies, future work consists of extensions to higher dimensions, more realistic modeling, development of special purpose verification code, and incorporation of our hybrid systems modeling paradigm into control software tools. Due to the limitations of the general hybrid systems tools we used, a possible alternative is to write specific programs in a general language (e.g. C++) to verify the specific assemblies that one wants to solve. For verification, (in the two-dimensional case) a specialized analysis program would work as follows. For layer i (cf. Fig. 4), the peg can always find the hole if $pw < h_i$ and $l_i + h_i \geq l_{max}$ and $x_{min} + e_i + l_i \leq x_{max} - r_{max}$. If this condition is not satisfied, the peg can sometimes find the hole (i.e., for fortuitous initial conditions of the layers) if $pw < h_i$ and $x_{max} - r_i \geq x_{min} + l_{max}$ and $x_{min} + l_i \leq x_{max} - r_{max}$. Otherwise, the assembly is never possible. The conditions can be interpreted as follows: the peg can always find a hole if the hole is within the search limit of the peg, and the peg can sometimes find a hole if it is possible that the hole can be inside the search limit of the peg. The verification program was used to verify the three cases shown in Fig. 6(a,b,c) and gave the same results. More generally, one can use verification techniques based on linear programming.

Acknowledgements: NSF (DMI97-20309) and NIST (70NANB7H3024).

References

1. Branicky, M.S.: *Studies in Hybrid Systems: Modeling, Analysis, and Control.* Ph.D. Thesis, Electrical Engineering and Computer Science, M.I.T. (1995).
2. McCarragher, B.J., Asada, H.: The Discrete Event Modeling and Trajectory Planning of Robotic Assembly Tasks. *ASME J. of Dynamic Systems, Measurement and Control,* 117(3):394–400, (1995).
3. Newman, W.S., Branicky, M.S., Podgurski, H.A., Chhatpar, S.R., Huang, L., Swaminathan, J., Zhang, H.: Force-Responsive Robotic Assembly of Transmission Components. *Proc. IEEE Intl. Conf. Robotics & Automation,* Detroit, MI, pp. 2096–2102, (1999).
4. Newman, W.S., Branicky, M.S., Chhatpar, S.R., Huang, L., Zhang, H.: Impedance Based Assembly. *Video Proc. IEEE Intl. Conf. Robotics & Automation,* (1999).
5. Chhatpar, S.R.: *Experiments in Force-Guided Robotic Assembly.* M.S. Thesis, Electrical Engineering and Applied Physics, Case Western Reserve Univ. (1999).
6. Newman, W.S.: Stability and Performance Limits of Interaction Controllers. *ASME J. of Dynamic Systems, Measurement and Control,* 114(4):563–570, (1992).
7. Ramadge, P.J.G., Wonham, W.M.: The Control of Discrete Event Systems. *Proc. of the IEEE,* 77(1):81–98, (1989).
8. Chhatpar, S.R., Branicky, M.S.: A Hybrid Systems Approach to Force-Guided Robotic Assemblies. *Proc. IEEE Intl. Symp. on Assembly and Task Planning,* pp. 301–306, Porto, Portugal, (1999).
9. Branicky, M.S., Chhatpar, S.R.: A Computational Framework for the Simulation, Verification, and Synthesis of Force-Guided Robotic Assembly Strategies. *Proc. IEEE/RSJ Intl. Conf. Intelligent Robots & Systems,* pp. 1465–1470, Maui, (2001).
10. Henzinger, T.A.: The Theory of Hybrid Automata. *Proc. IEEE Symp. on Logic in Computer Science,* New Brunswick, (1996).
11. Harel, D.: Statecharts: A Visual Formalism for Complex Systems. *Science of Computer Programming,* 8:231–274, (1987).
12. Fu, Q.: *Simulation and Verification of Robotic Assembly Tasks.* M.S. Thesis, Electrical Engineering and Computer Science, Case Western Reserve Univ. (1999).
13. Henzinger, T.A., Ho, P-H., Toi, H.W.: HyTech: A Model Checker for Hybrid Systems. *Proc. Ninth Intl. Conf. on Computer-Aided Verification,* 1997. Lecture Notes in Computer Science, Vol. 1254. Springer, Berlin (1997) 460–463.
14. Henzinger, T.A., Ho, P-H., Toi, H.W.: HyTech: The Next Generation. *Proc. IEEE Real-time Systems Symp.,* pp. 56–65, (1995).
15. Chutinan, A.: *Hybrid System Verification Using Discrete Model Approximation.* Ph.D. Thesis, Electrical and Computer Engineering, Carnegie Mellon U. (1999).
16. Swaminathan, J.: *An Object-Oriented Application Framework for Peg-in-Maze Assemblies.* M.S. Thesis, Electrical Engineering and Computer Science, Case Western Reserve Univ. (1999).

A Comparison of Control Problems
for Timed and Hybrid Systems

Franck Cassez[1]*, Thomas A. Henzinger[2]**, and Jean-François Raskin[3]***

[1] IRCCyN, Ecole Centrale de Nantes, France
[2] EECS Department, University of California, Berkeley, USA
[3] Département d'Informatique, Université Libre de Bruxelles, Belgium

Abstract. In the literature, we find several formulations of the control problem for timed and hybrid systems. We argue that formulations where a controller can cause an action at any point in dense (rational or real) time are problematic, by presenting an example where the controller must act faster and faster, yet causes no Zeno effects (say, the control actions are at times $0, \frac{1}{2}, 1, 1\frac{1}{4}, 2, 2\frac{1}{8}, 3, 3\frac{1}{16}, \dots$). Such a controller is, of course, not implementable in software. Such controllers are avoided by formulations where the controller can cause actions only at discrete (integer) points in time. While the resulting control problem is well-understood if the time unit, or "sampling rate" of the controller, is fixed a priori, we define a novel, stronger formulation: the *discrete-time control problem with unknown sampling rate* asks if a sampling controller exists for *some* sampling rate. We prove that this problem is undecidable even in the special case of timed automata.

1   Introduction

Timed and hybrid systems are dynamical systems with both discrete and continuous components. A paradigmatic example of a hybrid system is a digital control program for an analog plant environment, like a furnace or an airplane: the controller state moves discretely between control modes, and in each control mode, the plant state evolves continuously according to physical laws. A natural model for hybrid systems is the *hybrid automaton*, which represents discrete components using finite-state machines and continuous components using real-numbered variables whose evolution is governed by differential equations or differential inclusions [ACH+95]. An interesting class of hybrid automata is the class of *rectangular automata* [HKPV98]: this is the most liberal generalization of *timed automata* [AD94] with interesting decidability properties. While in timed automata, all real-numbered variables are "clocks" with constant derivative 1, in

---

* Partially supported by the FNRS, Belgium, under grant 1.5.096.01.
** Partially supported by the DARPA SEC grant F33615-C-98-3614, the AFOSR MURI grant F49620-00-1-0327, the NSF Theory grant CCR-9988172, and the MARCO GSRC grant 98-DT-660.
*** Partially supported by a "Crédit aux chercheurs" from the Belgian National Fund for Scientific Research.

C.J. Tomlin and M.R. Greenstreet (Eds.): HSCC 2002, LNCS 2289, pp. 134–148, 2002.
© Springer-Verlag Berlin Heidelberg 2002

rectangular automata, the derivatives of all variables are bounded by constants from below and above. If the bounds on the derivative of a variable cannot change between control modes unless the variable is reset, then the rectangular automaton is called *initialized*.

The distinction between continuous evolutions of the plant state (which is given by the real-numbered variables of a hybrid automaton) and discrete switches of the controller state (which is given by the location, or control mode, of the hybrid automaton) permits a natural formulation of the *safety control problem*: given an unsafe set U of plant states, is there a strategy to switch the controller state in real time so that the plant can be prevented from entering U? In other words, the hybrid automaton specifies a set of possible control modes, together with the plant behavior resulting from each mode, and the control problem asks for deriving a switching strategy between control modes that keeps the plant out of trouble. A switch in control mode can be caused by two events: sensing of a particular plant state (e.g., "turn off the furnace when the heat hits x degrees"); or arrival of a particular time instant (e.g., "turn off the furnace after y seconds"). This can be formalized in several ways, and consequently, a variety of similar but different mathematical formulations of the safety control problem for timed and hybrid systems can be found in the literature (e.g., [HW92, AMP95, MPS95, Won97, HHM99, HK99, ABD+00, TLS00]). We classify various formulations, compare their relative strengths, and fill in some gaps that had been left open previously. In doing so, we focus on *safety* control purely for reasons of clarity; the treatment of more general control objectives is orthogonal to the issues studied here [dAHM01].

One fundamental distinction is between *dense-time* and *discrete-time* (or *sampling*) models of control. In dense-time models, the controller observes the plant state continuously, and may cause a control switch as soon as a particular plant state is encountered. In discrete-time models, while the plant evolves continuously, the controller observes the plant state only at regularly spaced time instants, and may cause a control switch only at those sampling points. With discrete-time models, we can further distinguish between *known* and *unknown* *sampling rate*. A control problem of the first kind asks: given a positive rational number β, can an unsafe plant state be prevented by a controller that samples the plant state every β seconds? The more general discrete-time control problem with unknown sampling rate asks: is there a rational number β such that an unsafe plant state be prevented by a controller with sampling rate β? For example, a discrete-time control problem may not be solvable with sampling rate of 10 *ms*, but it may be solvable with sampling rate of 5 *ms*.

Similarly, with dense-time models, we can distinguish between *known* and *unknown switch conditions*. A control problem of the first kind asks: for each control mode, given a set P of predicates on the plant state, can an unsafe plant state be prevented by a controller that watches the predicates in P and causes a mode switch only when the truth value of a predicate in P changes. The more general dense-time control problem with unknown switch conditions asks: is there a set P of predicates (typically chosen from some language) on the plant state such that an unsafe plant state be prevented by a controller choosing switch conditions from P? For example, a dense-time control problem may not be solvable by a controller that can switch mode by watching a sensor that indicates when a furnace hits a multiple of 10 degrees, but it may be solvable if the sensor has a granularity of 5 degrees.

The following three control problems have been studied in the literature: (1) The *known sampling rate* (known or unknown switch conditions) discrete-time control problem can be solved algorithmically for all rectangular automata [HK99] (see [HW92] for the timed case). (2) The *known switch conditions* dense-time control problem, while undecidable for general rectangular automata, is solvable for all initialized rectangular automata [HHM99]. (3) The *unknown switch conditions* dense-time control problem, while undecidable for initialized rectangular automata [HKPV98], is solvable for all timed automata [MPS95]. While none of these papers explicitly mention switch conditions, we obtain equivalent formulations in terms of switch conditions, which allow us to see that the three formulations (1)–(3) are of strictly increasing generality. Intuitively, if all switch conditions are known, then they are part of the hybrid automaton model, and the task of the controller is simply to disable or enable edge guards: at each plant state, the controller decides whether to cause a mode switch, or let an amount of time pass which is constrained only by the location invariant of the hybrid automaton. Since all timing constraints are already part of the model (in the form of location invariants and edge guards), this is also called *time-abstract control* [HHM99]. By contrast, in [MPS95, AMP95], the controller may strengthen the location invariants of the hybrid automaton model to achieve the control objective: at each plant state, the controller decides whether to cause a mode switch, or let an amount of time pass which is constrained by some new, derived predicate on the plant state. If the invariants are strengthened by polyhedral predicates, as in [AMP95, MPS95], this is called *polyhedral control*.

It is well-known that careless solutions of *dense-time* control problems may lead to unrealistic controllers that "stop time," either by blocking the progress of time altogether, or by causing mode switches at convergent points in time, say, $0, \frac{1}{2}, \frac{3}{4}, \frac{7}{8}, \ldots$ [Won97]. Such Zeno phenomena can be avoided by lifting the control objective from a safety objective to a combined safety and liveness objective ("always avoid unsafe states and let time progress for another unit") [dAHM01]. However, we show for the first time that dense-time control models are more seriously flawed: we present an example that can be controlled by a dense-time controller but not by any discrete-time controller with unknown sampling rate. The dense-time controller causes mode switches at divergent points in time, say, $0, \frac{1}{2}, 1, 1\frac{1}{4}, 2, 2\frac{1}{8}, 3, 3\frac{1}{16}, \ldots$, where the difference between adjacent time instants cannot be bounded from below. Such a controller is, of course, not implementable by software. This observation has led us to define the *unknown sampling rate* discrete-time control problem, which asks whether a discrete-time controller exists for *some* sampling rate, and if so, for a derivation of the sampling rate. We show that this problem is, surprisingly, undecidable even in the very special case of timed automata with known switching conditions. The undecidability proof is interesting, because it requires the encoding of unbounded integer values using the difference between two clocks.

We believe that our results have practical significance for two reasons. First, they put in question the usefulness of dense-time control formulations. Some authors insist, for example, that the number of dense-time control actions in a time unit is bounded from above [ABD+00]. But even such a bound does not prevent pathological examples like the one mentioned before, where there are no more than two control actions in any one time unit, yet the time intervals between control actions must get smaller and smaller. This can be avoided only if the time difference between control actions is bounded by a constant ε from below, which, however, fundamentally changes the control problem to a discrete-time problem with time unit ε. Second, our results show that even discrete-time control problems can be solved only when the sampling rate, or time unit, is fixed *a priori*. It follows that from a decidability point of view, the control of timed and hybrid systems is considerably more difficult than we thought when we embarked on our original goal of comparing different formulations found in the literature. (This, of course, does not affect the applicability of symbolic semi-decision procedures such as [Won97, ABD+00, TLS00, dAHM01]).

The paper is organized as follows. In Section 2, we recall the definitions of safety control for transition systems, as well as the definitions of timed and rectangular automata. In Section 3, we formulate and compare the four basic variations of the safety control problem for hybrid systems: known switch conditions vs. unknown switch conditions dense-time, and known sampling rate vs. unknown sampling rate discrete-time. We also show that a dense-time controller may exist in cases where no sampling rate exists. Section 4 contains the proof that the existence of digital controllers —i.e., the unknown sampling rate discrete-time control problem— is undecidable for timed automata.

2   Prerequisites

2.1   Labeled Transition Systems and Control

A *labeled transition system* S is a tuple $(Q, \Sigma, \rightarrow, Q_0)$, where Q is a (possibly infinite) set of states, Σ is a (possibly infinite) set of labels, $\rightarrow \subseteq Q \times \Sigma \times Q$ is a labeled transition relation, and $Q_0 \subseteq Q$ is a set of initial states. We write $q \xrightarrow{a} q'$ if $(q, a, q') \in \rightarrow$. A *run* of S is a finite sequence $\rho = q_0 a_0 q_1 a_1 \ldots q_n$ of states $q_i \in Q$ and labels $a_i \in \Sigma$ such that (1) $q_0 \in Q_0$ and (2) $q_i \xrightarrow{a_i} q_{i+1}$ for all $0 \le i < n$. We write $dest(\rho) = q_n$ for the final state of ρ. A state $q \in Q$ is *reachable in* S if there exists a run ρ of S such that $q = dest(\rho)$. A set $F \subseteq Q$ of states is *reachable in* S if there exists a state in F that is reachable in S.

Definition 1 (Reachability). *The* reachability problem *for a class C of labeled transition systems is the following: given a labeled transition system $S \in C$ and a set F of states of S, determine if F is reachable in S.*   □

The labels of a labeled transition system S can be interpreted as control actions. A label $a \in \Sigma$ is *enabled* at the state $q \in Q$ if $q \xrightarrow{a} q'$ for some state $q' \in Q$. We write $Enabled(q)$ for the labels that are enabled at q. A *control map* for S is a function $\kappa: Q \to 2^{\Sigma}$ that maps every state $q \in Q$ to a set $\kappa(q) \subseteq Enabled(q)$ of enabled labels. The *closed-loop system* $\kappa(S)$ is the labeled transition system $(Q, \Sigma, \to_{\kappa}, Q_0)$, where $q \xrightarrow{a}_{\kappa} q'$ iff $q \xrightarrow{a} q'$ and $a \in \kappa(q)$. The control map κ is *deadlock-free* for S if $\kappa(q) \neq \emptyset$ for every state q that is reachable in the closed-loop system $\kappa(S)$.

Definition 2 (Safety control). *The safety control problem for a class C of labeled transition systems is the following: given a labeled transition system $S \in C$ and a set F of states of S, determine if there exists a deadlock-free control map κ for S such that F is not reachable in the closed-loop system $\kappa(S)$.* $\square$

The *safety verification problem* is the special case of the safety control problem where $|\Sigma| = 1$. Note that the safety verification problem can be reduced to the non-reachability problem, and vice versa.

2.2   Timed and Rectangular Automata

Let X be a finite set of real-valued variables. A *valuation* for X is a function $v: X \to \mathbb{R}$. We write $[X \to \mathbb{R}]$ for the set of all valuations for X. For a set $V \subseteq [X \to \mathbb{R}]$ of valuations, and $x \in X$, define $V(x) = \{v(x) \mid v \in V\}$. Let $\bowtie \in \{<, \leq, >, \geq\}$, let $x_1, \ldots, x_n, x \in X$, and let $c_1, \ldots, c_n, c \in \mathbb{Z}$. A *rectangular inequality* over X is a formula of the form $x \bowtie c$; a *triangular inequality* over X is a formula of the form $x_1 - x_2 \bowtie c$; a *polyhedral inequality* over X is a formula of the form $c_1 x_1 + \cdots + c_n x_n \bowtie c$. A *rectangular predicate* over X is a conjunction of rectangular inequalities over X; the set of all rectangular predicates over X is denoted $Rect(X)$. A *polyhedral predicate* over X is a boolean combination of polyhedral inequalities over X. For a polyhedral predicate p over X, and a valuation v for X, we write $v(p)$ for the boolean value that is obtained from p by replacing each variable $x \in X$ with $v(x)$. The polyhedral predicate p defines the set $[\![p]\!] = \{v : X \to \mathbb{R} \mid v(p) = \text{true}\}$ of valuations.

Definition 3 (Rectangular automaton [HKPV98]). *A rectangular automaton H is a tuple $(L, X, \Sigma, \text{init}, E, \text{inv}, \text{flow})$. (1) L is a finite set of locations representing the discrete state of the automaton. (2) X is a finite set of real-valued variables representing the continuous state. We write $\dot{X} = \{\dot{x} \mid x \in X\}$ for the set of corresponding dotted variables, which represent first derivatives. (3) Σ is a finite set of events disjoint from $\mathbb{R}$. (4) init: $L \to Rect(X)$ is the initial condition. If the automaton starts in location ℓ, then each variable $x \in X$ has a value in the interval $[\![\text{init}(\ell)]\!](x)$. (5) $E \subseteq L \times Rect(X) \times \Sigma \times Rect(X) \times 2^X \times L$ is a finite set of edges. Every edge $(\ell, \gamma, \sigma, \alpha, U, \ell') \in E$ represents a change from location ℓ to location ℓ' with guard γ, label σ, and reset assignment α, which asserts that each variable $x \in U$ is nondeterministically reset to a value in the interval $[\![\alpha]\!](x)$, and each variable in $X \setminus U$ is left unchanged. (6) inv: $L \to Rect(X)$ is the invariant condition. The automaton can stay in location ℓ as long as each variable $x \in X$ has a value in the interval $[\![\text{inv}(\ell)]\!](x)$. (7) flow:*

$L \rightarrow Rect(\dot{X})$ is the flow condition. *We require that for every location* $\ell \in L$ *and variable* $x \in X$, *the interval* $[\![\text{flow}(\ell)]\!](\dot{x})$ *is bounded. If the automaton is in location* ℓ, *then each variable* $x \in X$ *can evolve nondeterministically with a derivative in the interval* $[\![\text{flow}(\ell)]\!](\dot{x})$. □

Definition 4 (Initialized rectangular automaton). *An* initialized rectangular automaton *is a rectangular automaton that satisfies the following: for all edges* $(\ell, \gamma, \sigma, \alpha, U, \ell') \in E$ *and variables* $x \in X$, *if* $[\![\text{flow}(\ell)]\!](x) \neq [\![\text{flow}(\ell')]\!](x)$, *then* $x \in U$. *In other words, every time the bounds on the derivative of a variable change between two locations, the variable is reset.* □

Definition 5 (Timed automaton). *A* timed automaton *is an initialized rectangular automaton such that (1)* $\text{flow}(\ell) \equiv \wedge_{x \in X}(\dot{x} = 1)$ *for all locations* $\ell \in L$, *and (2)* $\alpha \equiv \wedge_{x \in U}(x = 0)$ *for all edges* $(\ell, \gamma, \sigma, \alpha, U, \ell') \in E$. *In other words, all variables advance at the rate of time —they are called* clocks— *and variables can be reset only to 0.*[1] □

Let H be a rectangular automaton with locations L and variables X. The state space of H is $L \times [X \rightarrow \mathbb{R}]$; that is, every state $\langle \ell, v \rangle$ of H consists of a discrete part $\ell \in L$ and a continuous part $v \colon X \rightarrow \mathbb{R}$. A *polyhedral* (resp. *rectangular*) *state predicate* pred for H is a function that maps every location in L to a polyhedral (resp. rectangular) predicate pred(ℓ) over X. Note that the initial and invariant conditions of H are rectangular state predicates for H. The polyhedral state predicate pred defines the set $[\![\text{pred}]\!] = \{ \langle \ell, v \rangle \in L \times [X \rightarrow \mathbb{R}] \mid v \in [\![\text{pred}(\ell)]\!] \}$ of states. A state set $P \subseteq L \times [X \rightarrow \mathbb{R}]$ is *polyhedral* if there exists a polyhedral state predicate pred such that $[\![\text{pred}]\!] = P$. We define three semantics for rectangular automata. The first two permit location changes at all real-valued points in time; the third only at multiples of a fixed sampling unit.

Definition 6 (Dense-time semantics). *The* dense-time semantics *of a rectangular automaton* $H = (L, X, \Sigma, \text{init}, E, \text{inv}, \text{flow})$ *is the labeled transition system* $S_H^{dense} = (Q, \Sigma_{dense}, \rightarrow_{dense}, Q_0)$, *where* $Q = [\![\text{inv}]\!]$ *and* $\Sigma_{dense} = \Sigma \cup \mathbb{R}_{>0}$ *and* $Q_0 = [\![\text{init}]\!]$, *and* $\rightarrow_{dense}$ *is defined as follows. (1) Discrete transitions for each event* $\sigma \in \Sigma$: *let* $\langle \ell, v \rangle \xrightarrow{\sigma}_{dense} \langle \ell', v' \rangle$ *iff there exists an edge* $(\ell, \gamma, \sigma, \alpha, U, \ell') \in E$ *such that* $v \in [\![\gamma]\!]$, *and* $v'(x) \in [\![\alpha]\!](x)$ *for all* $x \in U$, *and* $v'(x) = v(x)$ *for all* $x \in X \backslash U$. *(2) Continuous transitions for each duration* $\delta \in \mathbb{R}_{>0}$: *let* $\langle \ell, v \rangle \xrightarrow{\delta}_{dense} \langle \ell', v' \rangle$ *iff* $\ell = \ell'$ *and for each variable* $x \in X$, *there exists a differentiable function* $f_x \colon [0, \delta] \rightarrow [\![\text{inv}(\ell)]\!](x)$ *such that (i)* $f_x(0) = v(x)$, *(ii)* $f_x(\delta) = v'(x)$, *and (iii)* $\dot{f}_x(t) \in [\![\text{flow}(\ell)]\!](x)$ *for all* $0 < t < \delta$. □

The time-abstract semantics hides the duration of continuous transitions.

---

[1] Unlike [AD94], we do not allow triangular inequalities in the definition of a timed automaton. However, every timed automaton with triangular inequalities can be transformed into one that accepts the same timed language and has only rectangular predicates.

Definition 7 (Time-abstract semantics). *Let* $H = (L, X, \Sigma, \mathrm{init}, E, \mathrm{inv}, \mathrm{flow})$ *be a rectangular automaton and* $S_H^{dense} = (Q, \Sigma_{dense}, \rightarrow_{dense}, Q_0)$ *its dense-time semantics. The time-abstract semantics of* H *is the labeled transition system* $S_H^{abstr} = (Q, \Sigma_{abstr}, \rightarrow_{abstr}, Q_0)$, *where* $\Sigma_{abstr} = \Sigma \cup \{time\}$ *and* $\rightarrow_{abstr}$ *is defined as follows. (1) For each* $\sigma \in \Sigma$, *let* $q \xrightarrow{\sigma}_{abstr} q'$ *iff* $q \xrightarrow{\sigma}_{dense} q'$. *(2) Let* $q \xrightarrow{time}_{abstr} q'$ *iff* $q \xrightarrow{\delta}_{dense} q'$ *for some duration* $\delta \in \mathbb{R}_{>0}$. □

If we assume that discrete transitions alternate with continuous transitions of a fixed duration β, then we obtain a discrete-time semantics with time unit β. The *sampling semantics*, with sampling unit β, further assumes that all discrete transitions (i.e., location changes) represent moves of the controller, and all continuous transitions (i.e., variable evolutions) represent moves of the plant. The intuition behind this semantics is that the plant evolves continuously, observed by a digital controller whose control decisions are separated by time β.[2]

Definition 8 (Sampling semantics). *Let* $H = (L, X, \Sigma, \mathrm{init}, E, \mathrm{inv}, \mathrm{flow})$ *be a rectangular automaton and* $S_H^{dense} = (Q, \Sigma_{dense}, \rightarrow_{dense}, Q_0)$ *its dense-time semantics. Let* $\beta \in \mathbb{Q}_{>0}$ *be a sampling unit. The* β-*sampling semantics of* H *is the labeled transition system* $S_H^{sample}(\beta) = (Q \times \{Control, Plant\}, \Sigma_{sample}, \rightarrow_{sample}, Q_0 \times \{Control\})$, *where* $\Sigma_{sample} = \Sigma \cup \{\beta\}$ *and* $\rightarrow_{sample}$ *is defined as follows. (1) Discrete control transitions for each* $\sigma \in \Sigma$: *let* $\langle q, Control \rangle \xrightarrow{\sigma}_{sample} \langle q', Plant \rangle$ *iff* $q \xrightarrow{\sigma}_{dense} q'$. *(2) Continuous plant transitions of fixed duration* $\beta \in \mathbb{Q}_{>0}$: *let* $\langle q, Plant \rangle \xrightarrow{\beta}_{sample} \langle q', Control \rangle$ *iff* $q \xrightarrow{\beta}_{dense} q'$. □

3   Control of Timed and Rectangular Automata

3.1   Dense-Time Control

In dense-time control, the controller can make a decision to change location — i.e., to switch control mode— at every real-valued time instant $t \in \mathbb{R}_{\geq 0}$. We distinguish between dense-time control with known switch conditions [HHM99] and unknown switch conditions [AMP95, MPS95, AMPS98].

Known switch conditions. A known switch conditions dense-time controller decides in every state either to issue a control action or to let time pass. If the controller issues a control action σ, then an edge with label σ is taken. In location ℓ, if the controller lets time pass, then an arbitrary positive amount of time $\delta \in \mathbb{R}_{>0}$ is selected so that the invariant of ℓ is not violated. As the actual amount of time that will pass is not decided by the controller, the model is time-abstract.

Definition 9 (Known switch conditions dense-time safety control). *The* known switch conditions dense-time safety control problem *for a class* $\mathcal{C}$ *of rectangular automata is the following: given a rectangular automaton* $H \in \mathcal{C}$ *and*

---

[2] The sampling semantics of [HK99] is more general in that it allows more than one discrete transition between two continuous transitions of duration β. All results presented here apply also to that case.

a rectangular state predicate fin *for H, solve the safety control problem for the time-abstract semantics* S_H^{abstr} *and state set* [[fin]]; *that is, determine if there exists a deadlock-free control map* κ *for* S_H^{abstr} *such that* [[fin]] *is not reachable in the closed-loop system* $\kappa(S_H^{abstr})$.   □

Unknown switch conditions. An unknown switch conditions dense-time controller controls a rectangular automaton by strengthening the invariants and guards that appear in the automaton. In particular, in location ℓ, such a controller may let time pass up to some upper bound, which can be stronger than the invariant of ℓ. In order to synthesize control maps, the constraints added by the controller cannot be arbitrary, but must be expressible in some language. Following [AMPS98], we consider constraints that can be expressed as polyhedral predicates. This is captured by the notion of a polyhedral control map.

Let $H = (L, X, \Sigma, \mathsf{init}, E, \mathsf{inv}, \mathsf{flow})$ be a rectangular automaton, and let κ be a control map for the dense-time semantics S_H^{dense}. For a state set $P \subseteq L \times [X \rightarrow \mathbb{R}]$ and an event $\sigma \in \Sigma$, define $Post_H^{\sigma}(P) = \{q' \mid \exists q \in P.\ q \xrightarrow{\sigma}_{dense} q'\}$ and $Post_{\kappa,H}^{\sigma}(P) = \{q' \mid \exists q \in P.\ q \xrightarrow{\sigma}_{dense} q'$ and $\sigma \in \kappa(q)\}$. Furthermore, define $Post_H^{time}(P) = \{q' \mid \exists q \in P,\ \delta \in \mathbb{R}_{>0}.\ q \xrightarrow{\delta}_{dense} q'\}$ and $Post_{\kappa,H}^{time}(P) = \{q' \mid \exists q \in P,\ \delta \in \mathbb{R}_{>0}.\ q \xrightarrow{\delta}_{dense} q'$ and $\delta \in \kappa(q)\}$. Note that if P is polyhedral, then $Post_H^{\sigma}(P)$ is a polyhedral state set of H for all events $\sigma \in \Sigma$, and $Post_H^{time}(P)$ is also a polyhedral state set of H [ACH+95]. A control map κ for the dense-time semantics S_H^{dense} is *polyhedral* if the following two conditions are satisfied. (1) For every event $\sigma \in \Sigma$, there exists a polyhedral state set P_σ of H such that for every polyhedral state set P of H, we have $Post_{\kappa,H}^{\sigma}(P) = Post_H^{\sigma}(P \cap P_\sigma)$. (2) There exists a polyhedral state set P_{time} of H such that for every polyhedral state set P of H, we have $Post_{\kappa,H}^{time}(P) = Post_H^{time}(P) \cap P_{time}$. Note that the polyhedral state set P_σ can be used to strengthen edge guards, while P_{time} can be used to strengthen location invariants.

Definition 10 (Unknown switch conditions dense-time safety control). *The* unknown switch conditions dense-time safety control problem *for a class C of rectangular automata is the following: given a rectangular automaton $H \in C$ and a rectangular state predicate* fin *for H, determine if there exists a deadlock-free polyhedral control map κ for the dense-time semantics S_H^{dense} such that the state set* [[fin]] *is not reachable in the closed-loop system $\kappa(S_H^{dense})$.*   □

It is easy to see that if the answer to the known switch conditions dense-time control problem $\langle H, \mathsf{fin} \rangle$ is YES, then the answer to the unknown switch conditions dense-time control problem $\langle H, \mathsf{fin} \rangle$ is also YES. Indeed, if the answer to the known (resp. unknown) switch conditions dense-time control problem $\langle H, \mathsf{fin} \rangle$ is YES, then we can constructively strengthen the guards (resp. both invariants and guards) of H with a finite set of polyhedral predicates such that the resulting hybrid automaton $\kappa(H)$ (which may no longer be rectangular) is non-blocking and contains no reachable states in [[fin]].

3.2   Discrete-Time Control

In discrete-time control, the controller samples the plant state once every β time units, for some sampling unit $\beta \in \mathbb{Q}_{>0}$, and issues control actions at these points in time. Control actions, as before, may cause a change in location. Between control actions the plant evolves for β time units without interruption. We distinguish between discrete-time control with a known sampling unit β [HK99], and the more ambitious problem of synthesizing a suitable sampling unit, which has not been studied before.

Definition 11 (Known sampling rate discrete-time safety control). *The known sampling rate discrete-time safety control problem for a class $\mathcal{C}$ of rectangular automata is the following: given a rectangular automaton $H \in \mathcal{C}$, a sampling unit $\beta \in \mathbb{Q}_{>0}$, and a rectangular state predicate* fin *for H, solve the safety control problem for the sampling semantics $S_H^{sample}(\beta)$ and state set* [[fin]]; *that is, determine if there exists a deadlock-free control map κ for $S_H^{sample}(\beta)$ such that* [[fin]] *is not reachable in the closed-loop system $\kappa(S_H^{sample}(\beta))$.*   □

Definition 12 (Unknown sampling rate discrete-time safety control). *The* unknown sampling rate discrete-time safety control problem *for a class $\mathcal{C}$ of rectangular automata is the following: given a rectangular automaton $H \in \mathcal{C}$ and a rectangular state predicate* fin *for H, determine if there exist a sampling unit $\beta \in \mathbb{Q}_{>0}$ and a deadlock-free control map κ for the sampling semantics $S_H^{sample}(\beta)$ such that the state set* [[fin]] *is not reachable in the closed-loop system $\kappa(S_H^{sample}(\beta))$.*   □

3.3   Comparison between Dense-Time and Discrete-Time Control

To compare the different classes of controllers we first recall what is known about the decidability of the various control problems defined above. The results from the literature are summarized in Table 1. For all decidable entries, suitable control maps can be synthesized algorithmically. Next we study two examples that shed some light on the relative merits of the different models.

Unknown sampling rate discrete-time control is not as powerful as dense-time control. Our definitions of dense-time control ignore Zeno phenomena; for example, a controller that blocks the progress of time by causing control actions at convergent points in time, such as $0, \frac{1}{2}, \frac{3}{4}, \frac{7}{8}, \ldots$, is considered legal. Zeno phenomena have been studied extensively, and are usually avoided either by lifting the control objective from safety to liveness [Won97, dAHM01], or by assumption, as in [AMPS98], where it is imposed that every loop in the control structure of a hybrid automaton must contain a clock that is reset to 0 and then tested to be greater than 1 ("strongly non-zeno automata"). However, dense-time control models are more seriously flawed: we present a timed automaton H that can be controlled by a dense-time controller, but there is no sampling unit,

	KSC	USC	KSR	USR
Timed automata	$\sqrt{}$ [MPS95]	$\sqrt{}$ [MPS95]	$\sqrt{}$ [HW92]	?
Initialized rectangular automata	$\sqrt{}$ [HHM99]	$\times$ [HKPV98]	$\sqrt{}$ [HK99]	?
Rectangular automata	$\times$ [HHM99]	$\times$ [HKPV98]	$\sqrt{}$ [HK99]	?

Table 1. Decidability results for safety control problems. KSC stands for "known switch conditions dense-time"; USC for "unknown switch conditions dense-time"; KSR for "known sampling rate discrete-time"; USR for "unknown sampling rate discrete-time"; $\sqrt{}$ stands for decidable, $\times$ for undecidable, and ? for previously open. In the next section, it will be shown that all three previously open problems are undecidable (cf. Corollary 1).

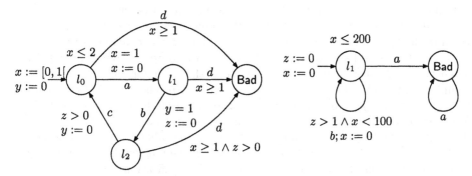

Fig. 1. A timed automaton that cannot be controlled by any sampling controller, no matter how small the sampling unit, but can be controlled by a dense-time controller (cf. Theorem 1).

Fig. 2. A timed automaton that cannot be controlled by any time-abstract controller, but can be controlled by a sampling controller (cf. Theorem 2).

however small, such that H can be controlled by a sampling controller. The dense-time controller issues control actions at divergent points in time, such as $0, \frac{1}{2}, 1, 1\frac{3}{4}, 2, 2\frac{7}{8}, 3, 3\frac{15}{16}, \ldots$, but the difference between adjacent time instants cannot be bounded from below.

Consider the timed automaton of Figure 1. The control objective is to avoid the location Bad. Thus, the controller must keep the automaton looping in locations l_0, l_1, and l_2. To do so, let us show that the controller must leave location l_2 faster and faster. The first time that the automaton enters l_0, the variables x and y have the values x_0 and y_0, respectively, where $x_0 < 1$ and $y_0 = 0$. To keep looping, the controller must ensure that $x \leq 1$ when reentering location l_0. We now describe the evolution of the value of x at the successive times location l_0 is entered: by x_i and y_i, we denote the values of x and y, respectively, when entering l_0 after i iterations of the loop. The loop consists in taking successively the edges labeled by a, b, and c. When crossing a, we have $x = 1$, and when entering l_1, we have $x = 0$ and y equals the amount of time δ_i^0 spent by the automaton in location l_0. The automaton stays in location l_1 for time $\delta_i^1 = 1 - \delta_i^0$, and then the edge labeled by b is crossed. The automaton stays in location l_2 for time $\delta_i^2 > 0$. So the value of x when reentering l_0 is $x_{i+1} = x_i + \delta_i^2$. Remember that the value of x must be less or equal to 1 when entering location l_0 in order to avoid being forced to go to the Bad location. So we must have $\sum_{i=1}^{\infty} \delta_i^2 < 1 - x_0$. Such a converging sequence of δ_i^2 can be enforced by a dense-time controller with unknown switch conditions. This controller imposes the additional invariant $x < 1$ on l_2, and the d edges are labeled with the guard false, ensuring that they can never be taken. It is not difficult to see that this new automaton is non-blocking and cannot visit the Bad location. Note that our controller only takes three control actions per time unit, and so is not excluded by the definition of control given in [ABD+00], which requires the number of control actions per time unit to be bounded from above. As a direct consequence of the discussion above, the automaton of Figure 1 modified with the additional invariant $x < 1$ on location l_2 is controllable by a dense time controller with known switch conditions.

Now let us establish that there does not exist a sampling controller that can avoid the location Bad, no matter how small the sampling unit. If we fix the sampling unit to be $\beta \in \mathbb{Q}_{>0}$, then the automaton reaches for the first time l_2 with $x_0 = \beta$ and $y_0 = 0$. Then, after each iteration of the loop, when entering l_0 the value of x has grown by β (the time spent in location l_2). Thus, after n iterations of the loop, for $n = \min_j(j \cdot \beta > 1 - \beta)$, the value of x when entering l_0 is strictly greater than 1. Thus only the d edge leaving l_0 can be taken, leading to the Bad location. Finally, let us note that this justification is still valid when considering the automaton of Figure 1 modified with the additional invariant $x < 1$ on location l_2.

Theorem 1. *There exist a timed automaton H and a rectangular state predicate* fin *such that the answer to the known switch conditions dense-time safety control problem $\langle H, \text{fin} \rangle$ is* YES, *and the answer to the unknown sampling rate discrete-time safety control problem $\langle H, \text{fin} \rangle$ is* NO. $\qquad\square$

Known switch conditions dense-time control is not as powerful as discrete-time control. Let us now consider the timed automaton of Figure 2. The control objective is again to avoid the location Bad. The automaton is not known switch conditions dense-time controllable. In fact, when entering for the first time l_1, we have $z = 0$, and the controller can decide either to take the edge labeled by a, or to let time pass. The decision to take the edge labeled by a is excluded, as this would lead directly to the Bad location. Unfortunately, the controller cannot allow time to pass either. In fact, if the controller chooses to let time pass, then it agrees to wait for an undetermined amount of time, including delays $100 \leq \delta \leq 200$. If $\delta = 200$, then the automaton reaches a state where only a is enabled, which leads to the Bad location. This means that this simple system cannot be controlled by a dense-time controller with known switch conditions. On the other hand, the automaton is controllable by an unknown switch conditions dense-time controller. A simple way to control the automaton is to add the invariant $x < 100$ to location l_1, and to add the guard false to the edge labeled by a. The automaton can also be controlled by a discrete-time controller with a sampling unit $\beta < 100$.

Theorem 2. *There exist a timed automaton H, a sampling unit β, and a rectangular state predicate* fin *such that the answer to the known sampling rate discrete-time safety control problem $\langle H, \beta, \text{fin} \rangle$ is* YES, *and the answer to the known switch conditions dense-time safety control problem $\langle H, \text{fin} \rangle$ is* No. □

4   Unknown Sampling Rate Control Is Undecidable

We establish the undecidablity of the unknown sampling rate discrete-time safety control problem for the restricted class of timed automata. Actually, we prove the undecidability of a weaker question, namely, the unknown-rate discrete-time reachability problem.

Definition 13 (Unknown-rate discrete-time reachability). *The* unknown-rate discrete-time reachability problem *for a class C of rectangular automata is the following: given a rectangular automaton $H \in C$ and a rectangular state predicate* fin *for H, determine if there exists a sampling unit $\beta \in \mathbb{R}_{>0}$ such that the state set $[\![\text{fin}]\!]$ is not reachable in the sampling semantics $S_H^{sample}(\beta)$.* □

Our main result is the following.

Theorem 3. *The unknown-rate discrete-time reachability problem is undecidable for timed automata.* □

As non-reachability can be reduced to safety control, we obtain the following.

Corollary 1. *The unknown sampling rate discrete-time safety control problem is undecidable for timed automata.*

To establish Theorem 3, we reduce the control state reachability problem for two-counter machines to the unknown-rate discrete-time reachability problem for timed automata. The former is well-known to be undecidable, thus implying the undecidability of the latter. A two-counter machine M consists of two counters (initially 0) and a finite sequence of instructions, each taken from the following: increment a counter; test a counter for zero and branch conditionally; decrement a counter if its value is not zero. Given M and a control state u of M, we construct a timed automaton H_M and a location l_u of H_M such that the execution of M reaches u iff there exists a sampling unit $\beta \in \mathbb{Q}_{>0}$ such that a state with discrete part l_u is reachable in the sampling semantics $S_{H_M}^{sample}(\beta)$. The key property of H_M is that if the automaton is sampled every $\frac{1}{b}$ time units, for some $b \in \mathbb{Q}_{>0}$, then it can simulate the execution of M as long as the counter values are less than $\lfloor b \rfloor$. When a counter overflow occurs, then H_M goes into a terminal location different from l_u. If the execution of M reaches u, then it does so with some maximal counter values, and H_M can reach l_u for a sufficiently large choice of b. On the other hand, if the execution of M does not reach u, then H_M cannot reach l_u for any choice of b.

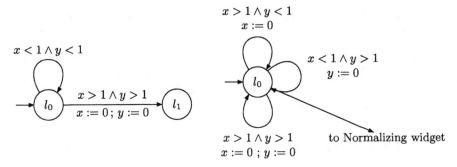

Fig. 3. Widget for zero testing   **Fig. 4.** Idling widget

Configuration encoding. First we need to decide how to encode the configurations of the counter machine M. A configuration of M consists of a control state and two counter values $c_1, c_2 \in \mathbb{N}$. The control state w of M is directly encoded by a location l_w of H_M. A counter value c is encoded by the difference between two clocks x and y. Recall that H_M is sampled every $\frac{1}{b}$ time units. If clocks are always reset to 0, then the clock difference $x - y$ is a multiple of $\frac{1}{b}$ at every state in every run of the sampling semantics $S_{H_M}^{sample}(\frac{1}{b})$. Moreover, we constrain the values of x and y to lie in the interval $I_b = [0, \frac{\lfloor b+1 \rfloor}{b}]$; then $|x - y| \in I_b$. We encode counter value c using only clock values $x, y \in I_b$, and impose the following on the automaton H_M:

- If $x \geq y$, then $c = (x - y) \cdot b$.
- If $x < y$, then $c = \left(\frac{\lfloor b+1 \rfloor}{b} - (y - x) \right) \cdot b$.

In this way the maximal counter value we can encode with $x, y \in I_b$ is exactly $\lfloor b \rfloor$. Note that when $x < y$, we cannot encode the counter value 0. Thus, $c = 0$ is always encoded with $x \geq y$.

We now give widgets for encoding the three types of instructions of the counter machine, and a widget for what we call "normalization" of the encoding. As we want our result to be as general as possible, and *robust* in the sense of [HR00], we avoid the use of equality in the rectangular predicates of H_M (the proof, especially the widget for zero testing, would be somewhat easier if the use of equality were allowed).

Zero testing. We assume two clocks x and y encoding counter value c with $x \geq y$. A widget for zero testing without using equality is shown in Figure 3. More formally, there exists $\frac{1}{b} \in \mathbb{Q}_{>0} \setminus \frac{1}{\mathbb{N}}$ such that the state $\langle l_1, x = 0, y = 0 \rangle$ is reachable from $\langle l_0, x, y \rangle$ in the sampling semantics $S_{H_M}^{sample}(\frac{1}{b})$ iff $x = y$ in l_0. This gives us a way to test if $c = 0$ when its value is encoded by $(x - y) \cdot b$. As we will see in the next paragraph, we can restrict ourselves to zero testing when $x \geq y$. In the sequel we assume $\frac{1}{b} \in \mathbb{Q}_{>0} \setminus \frac{1}{\mathbb{N}}$, so that value 1 is never hit for both x and y at any sampling point of any run.

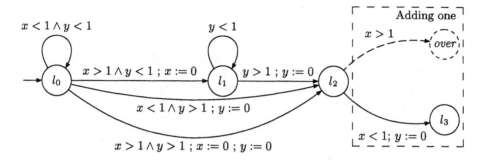

Fig. 5. Widget for normalizing (and incrementing) the encoding of a counter value

Normalizing the encoding. Before addressing the encoding of incrementing and decrementing a counter, we give a widget for obtaining a normal form for the encoding of counter value c. By *normal form* we mean that $c = (x - y) \cdot b$ can be written in a unique manner with $y = 0$ and $x \geq y$. The widget for normalization is shown in Figure 5 (the dashed box contains extra material that will be dealt with later). If either $x \geq y$ and $c = (x-y)\cdot b$, or $x < y$ and $c = \left(\frac{\lfloor b+1 \rfloor}{b} - (y-x)\right)\cdot b$, then the counter value c is in normal form when entering location l_2, that is, $y = 0$ and $x \geq y$.

Incrementing a counter. To add one to counter value c encoded by clocks x and y, we first normalize the encoding of c using the widget of Figure 5. To increment c we need to let time pass until the next edge transition, that is, we need to wait $\frac{1}{b}$ time units in location l_2. Thus we add a single edge from l_2 to l_3 resetting y; see Figure 5 inside the dashed box.

Decrementing a counter. To decrement a counter value we use a slightly modified version of the widget for normalization, namely, an anti-normal form: encode counter value c with $x = 0$ and $y > 0$, and after $\frac{1}{b}$ time units reset x.

Counter overflow and idling. Counter overflows are dealt with when adding one to a counter. The dashed transition to location *over* in Figure 5 corresponds to a counter overflow. Finally, we have to manage concurrently two counters C_1 and C_2. While C_1 is updated, time elapses, and we need to keep the value of C_2. This is done by using an *idling* widget, shown in Figure 4, for the counter that is not in the instruction to be performed. An instruction of the counter machine involving C_1 is encoded by the synchronous composition of the appropriate widget for C_1 and the idling widget for C_2. This completes the proof sketch for Theorem 3.

References

[ABD⁺00] E. Asarin, O. Bournier, T. Dang, O. Maler, and A. Pnueli. Effective synthesis of switching controllers for linear systems. In *Proc. IEEE*, 88:1011–1025, 2000.

[ACH⁺95] R. Alur, C. Courcoubetis, N. Halbwachs, T.A. Henzinger, P.-H. Ho, X. Nicollin, A. Olivero, J. Sifakis, and S. Yovine. The algorithmic analysis of hybrid systems. *Theoretical Computer Science*, 138:3–34, 1995.

[AD94] R. Alur and D.L. Dill. A theory of timed automata. *Theoretical Computer Science*, 126:183–235, 1994.

[AMP95] E. Asarin, O. Maler, and A. Pnueli. Symbolic controller synthesis for discrete and timed systems. In *Hybrid Systems II*, LNCS 999, pp. 1–20. Springer, 1995.

[AMPS98] E. Asarin, O. Maler, A. Pnueli, and J. Sifakis. Controller synthesis for timed automata. In *IFAC Symp. System Structure and Control*, pp. 469–474. Elsevier, 1998.

[dAHM01] L. de Alfaro, T.A. Henzinger, and R. Majumdar. Symbolic algorithms for infinite-state games. In *CONCUR: Concurrency Theory*, LNCS 2154, pp. 536–550. Springer, 2001.

[HHM99] T.A. Henzinger, B. Horowitz, and R. Majumdar. Rectangular hybrid games. In *CONCUR: Concurrency Theory*, LNCS 1664, pp. 320–335. Springer, 1999.

[HK99] T.A. Henzinger and P.W. Kopke. Discrete-time control for rectangular hybrid automata. *Theoretical Computer Science*, 221:369–392, 1999.

[HKPV98] T.A. Henzinger, P.W. Kopke, A. Puri, and P. Varaiya. What's decidable about hybrid automata? *J. Computer and System Sciences*, 57:94–124, 1998.

[HR00] T.A. Henzinger and J.-F. Raskin. Robust undecidability of real-time and hybrid systems. In *Hybrid Systems: Computation and Control*, LNCS 1790, pp. 145–159. Springer, 2000.

[HW92] G. Hoffmann and H. Wong-Toi. The input-output control of real-time discrete-event systems. In *RTSS: Real-time Systems Symp.*, pp. 256–265. IEEE, 1992.

[MPS95] O. Maler, A. Pnueli, and J. Sifakis. On the synthesis of discrete controllers for timed systems. In *STACS: Theoretical Aspects of Computer Science*, LNCS 900, pp. 229–242. Springer, 1995.

[TLS00] C. Tomlin, J. Lygeros, and S. Sastry. A game-theoretic approach to controller design for hybrid systems. In *Proc. IEEE*, 88:949–970, 2000.

[Won97] H. Wong-Toi. The synthesis of controllers for linear hybrid automata. In *CDC: Conf. Decision and Control*, pp. 4607–4612. IEEE, 1997.

Hybrid Control Loops, A/D Maps, and Dynamic Specifications

J.M. Davoren[1], T. Moor[1], and A. Nerode[2]

[1] Research School of Information Sciences and Engineering
Australian National University, Canberra ACT 0200 AUSTRALIA
j.m.davoren@anu.edu.au, thomas.moor@anu.edu.au
[2] Department of Mathematics, Cornell University
Ithaca NY 14853 USA
anil@math.cornell.edu

Abstract. We re-examine the basic hybrid control set-up of a continuous plant in a closed feedback loop with a finite state control automaton and an interface consisting of an A/D map and a D/A map. We address the question of how dynamic specifications can be formulated independently of a particular A/D map, and of the effect of refining an A/D map. The main contribution of this paper is that it extends the framework of supervisory controller synthesis for hybrid systems to include more general dynamic specifications, and demonstrates how to employ known results to solve these synthesis problems.

1 Introduction

The basic hybrid control configuration consists of a continuous plant in a closed feedback loop with a finite state supervisory controller, linked by an interface consisting of an A/D map and a D/A map, converting a continuous plant output signal into a discrete controller input signal, and converting a discrete controller output signal into an input to the continuous plant, respectively [16, 12, 7, 5]. Of a particular interest here is the task of controller design; e.g. [7, 16, 9, 4] study classes of control problems in which the continuous plant and D/A map are given, and the task is to construct an A/D map and a supervisory controller so that the closed-loop system fulfills various specifications. Once the A/D map has been constructed, the overall plant exhibits discrete event inputs and outputs. Language inclusion specifications can then be addressed by tools from DES theory (e.g. [14, 15]) and/or within the framework of Willem's behavioural systems theory (e.g. [17]). Consequences for the hybrid control configuration are drawn in [7] and [10], respectively.

In this paper, we re-examine the basic hybrid control configuration and address how control objectives can be stated independently from a particular A/D map, including a discussion on what effects one may expect from refining an A/D map. This matter is of a specific interest whenever a controller synthesis procedure involves A/D map refinement; this is the case in e.g. [7, 16, 4, 9].

C.J. Tomlin and M.R. Greenstreet (Eds.): HSCC 2002, LNCS 2289, pp. 149–163, 2002.
© Springer-Verlag Berlin Heidelberg 2002

On the technical side, we use behavioural systems theory as a framework for our discussion as it cleanly accommodates both motion in continuous space and time, and discrete execution sequences. In that theory, a *dynamical system* is a triple $(T, W, \mathfrak{B})$, where $T \subseteq \mathbb{R}$ is the *time axis*, W is the *signal space*, and $\mathfrak{B} \subseteq W^T := \{ f \mid f \colon T \to W \}$ is the *behaviour*. Functions $f \colon T \to W$ are trajectories, and the behaviour $\mathfrak{B}$ is viewed as the set of all trajectories compatible with the phenomena modelled; trajectories not in $\mathfrak{B}$ cannot occur. Typically, a behaviour $\mathfrak{B}$ is defined to be a solution set of a more detailed model; e.g. an ODE for the continuous case. For our purposes, we also consider a behaviour $\mathfrak{B}$ to express *dynamic specifications*, where the trajectories in $\mathfrak{B}$ are those deemed acceptable or permissible for that specification, and those not in $\mathfrak{B}$ are unacceptable or prohibited. With respect to the plant dynamics, our behavioural specifications are similar to the language specifications from DES theory: we ask the closed-loop behaviour to be a subset of the dynamic specification behaviour. However, in contrast to DES theory, we also need to address the continuous aspects of our hybrid control configuration. Therefore, we investigate continuous-time, continuous-space dynamic specifications as behaviours over $T = \mathbb{R}_0^+ := [0, \infty)$ and $X \subseteq \mathbb{R}^n$. The principal case is piecewise-continuous functions $\mathbf{x} \colon \mathbb{R}_0^+ \to X$, since this is what can be generated by a switched plant. For an A/D map from X into Y, with Y finite, we then ask what it means for continuous dynamic specification to be *captured* by a discrete behaviour, over time axis $T = \mathbb{N}$, with words/sequences $\mathbf{y} \in Y^{\mathbb{N}}$, using the A/D map and a language specification. This puts us into a position where we can discuss the effects of A/D map refinement with respect to the task of capturing a given continuous dynamic specification.

The body of the paper is organised as follows. Section 2 consists of mathematical preliminaries. In Section 3, we give a transition system representation of a switched plant coupled with an A/D map, which models the uncontrolled plant when viewed through the lens of the A/D map. In Section 4, we assemble the hybrid closed-loop and show the formal relationship between the hybrid control configuration and hybrid automata models [1, 2]. In Section 5, we formulate the supervisory control problem, and give several illustrative examples of continuous behavioural specifications. Section 6 introduces the notion of a continuous behavioural specification being *captured* by an A/D map together with a discrete behaviour. A/D map refinement as it occurs within supervisory controller synthesis procedures is discussed in Section 7. In Section 8, we show how – in principle – we can solve the control problem for continuous dynamic specifications by using the notion of capturing and drawing from known results on strategic A/D map-refinement and DES-style supervisory controller synthesis.

2   Preliminaries

We adopt the notation from set-valued analysis [3] in writing $r \colon X \rightsquigarrow Y$ to mean $r \colon X \to 2^Y$ is a *set-valued function*, with set-values $r(x) \subseteq Y$ for each $x \in X$, possibly $r(x) = \varnothing$, or equivalently, $r \subseteq X \times Y$ is a *relation*. The *domain* of a set-valued map is $\mathrm{dom}(r) := \{x \in X \mid r(x) \neq \varnothing\}$. The expressions $y \in r(x)$ and $(x, y) \in r$ are synonymous. Every set-valued map $r \colon X \rightsquigarrow Y$ has an *inverse* or *converse* $r^{-1} \colon Y \rightsquigarrow X$ given by: $x \in r^{-1}(y)$ iff $y \in r(x)$.

A set-valued map $\alpha \colon X \rightsquigarrow Y$ is *total* if $\mathrm{dom}(\alpha) = X$. A total map α defines a *cover* of the set X as follows: for each $y \in Y$, define the set $A_y := \alpha^{-1}(y) \subseteq X$. Then by the totalness condition, we have $X = \bigcup_{y \in Y} A_y$, so the family of sets $\{A_y\}_{y \in Y}$ gives a cover of X. We call the sets A_y the *cells* of the cover α. The cover is *finite* if the *range*, $\mathrm{ran}(\alpha) := \mathrm{dom}(\alpha^{-1})$, is a finite set. A cover α defines an equivalence relation on X of indistinguishability by cover cells: $x \simeq_\alpha x'$ iff $\alpha(x) = \alpha(x')$. A special case of a cover map is when $\alpha \colon X \to Y$ is a (single-valued) total function, in which case the cells A_y for $y \in Y$ are *partition blocks* of the equivalence relation $\simeq_\alpha$.

Given a space $X \subseteq \mathbb{R}^n$, we shall use the term *continuous behaviour* to refer to continuous-time, continuous-space behaviours $\mathfrak{C} \subseteq X^{\mathbb{R}_0^+}$. Note that functions $\mathbf{x} \colon \mathbb{R}_0^+ \to X$ in $\mathfrak{C}$ need not be continuous as maps. Given any set W, we shall use the term *discrete behaviour* to refer to discrete-time behaviours $\mathfrak{B} \subseteq W^{\mathbb{N}}$.

A *transition system* is a structure $\mathcal{S} = (S, W, \delta, S_0)$ where S is a non-empty set of states; W is the external alphabet; $\delta \colon S \times W \rightsquigarrow S$ is the (possibly not deterministic) transition relation; and $S_0 \subseteq S$ is a set of initial states. If $|S| \in \mathbb{N}$ and $|W| \in \mathbb{N}$, then $\mathcal{S}$ is called a *finite state automaton*. Recall that W^* is the set of all finite words over the alphabet W, including the empty word ϵ.

A *state execution sequence* of a transition system $\mathcal{S}$ is a pair of sequences $(\mathbf{s}, \mathbf{w}) \in S^{\mathbb{N}} \times W^{\mathbb{N}}$ or $(\mathbf{s}, \mathbf{w}) \in S^* \times W^*$ such that $\mathbf{s}(0) \in S_0$ and $\mathbf{s}(k + 1) \in \delta(\mathbf{s}(k), \mathbf{w}(k))$ for all $k < \mathrm{len}(\mathbf{s})$. A state $s \in S$ is $\mathcal{S}$-*reachable* if there exists a state execution sequence $(\mathbf{s}, \mathbf{w})$ and a $k \leq \mathrm{len}(\mathbf{s})$ such that $s = \mathbf{s}(k)$. A transition system $\mathcal{S}$ has the *non-blocking* property if for every $\mathcal{S}$-reachable state $s \in S$, there exists $w \in W$ such that $\delta(s, w) \neq \varnothing$.

Define the *discrete full state behaviour* of $\mathcal{S}$ to be the set $\mathfrak{B}_{\mathrm{st}}(\mathcal{S}) \subseteq (S^{\mathbb{N}} \times W^{\mathbb{N}})$ of all infinite state execution sequences of $\mathcal{S}$, and the *discrete external behaviour* of $\mathcal{S}$ to be the set $\mathfrak{B}_{\mathrm{ex}}(\mathcal{S}) := \mathcal{P}_W \mathfrak{B}_{\mathrm{st}}(\mathcal{S})$, where $\mathcal{P}_W \colon S \times W \to W$ is the natural projection map. Given a discrete behaviour $\mathfrak{B} \subseteq W^{\mathbb{N}}$, we say that a transition system $\mathcal{S} = (S, W, \delta, S_0)$ is a *state machine realization* of $\mathfrak{B}$, written $\mathcal{S} \cong \mathfrak{B}$, if $\mathfrak{B}_{\mathrm{ex}}(\mathcal{S}) = \mathfrak{B}$. In order to ensure that the restriction to only infinite sequences in the full state behaviour and external behaviour does not result in any loss in the representation of $\mathcal{S}$, care must be taken to ensure that $\mathcal{S}$ is non-blocking.

Let $\mathcal{S} = (S, W, \delta, S_0)$ and $\mathcal{Q} = (Q, W, \gamma, Q_0)$ be two transition systems over a common external alphabet W. Their *synchronous parallel composition* is the system $\mathcal{S} \parallel \mathcal{Q} := (S \times Q, W, \lambda, S_0 \times Q_0)$, where $(s', q') \in \lambda((s, q), w)$ if and only if $s' \in \delta(s, w)$ and $q' \in \gamma(q, w)$.

3   Switched Plants and A/D Maps

A switched plant is a control system which consists of a finite number of vector fields, with the system switching between one vector field and another. The control input to a switched plant is via discrete input events which select which vector field is to be active.

Definition 1. *A switched plant is a system* $\text{SP} = (U, X, F)$, *where* U *is a finite control (input) alphabet,* $X \subseteq \mathbb{R}^n$ *is the plant state space (equipped with standard Euclidean topology), and* $F\colon U \times X \to \mathbb{R}^n$ *is a function defining a finite family of (time-invariant) differential equations* $\dot{x} = F_u(x)$, *where for each* $u \in U$, *the* u *vector field is* $F_u := F(u, -)\colon X \to \mathbb{R}^n$.

For example, a switched plant may arise from a continuous control system $\dot{x} = f(x, v)$ and finitely many state feedback control laws $g_u\colon X \to V$. More generally, one can also consider controllers with their own dynamics, and form a switched plant from finitely many continuous closed-loop systems.

In order to ensure that the state trajectories of a switched plant are well-defined, we assume that the vector fields F_u are locally Lipschitz continuous, and that the state space X is open. Then from each initial condition $x_0 \in X$, each differential equation $\dot{x} = F_u(x)$ has a unique maximal integral curve in X on a well defined maximal interval of time $[0, T_u(x_0))$, where $T_u(x_0) \in \mathbb{R}_0^+ \cup \{\infty\}$. We denote this maximal curve by $\Phi_u(x_0, -)\colon [0, T_u(x_0)) \to X$. In the case of $T_u(x_0) < \infty$, it is well known that $\Phi_u(x_0, -)$ escapes from any *bounded* subset of X at some time less than or equal to $T_u(x_0)$.

Definition 2. *An* A/D *map on a space* X *is a total set-valued map* $\alpha\colon X \rightsquigarrow Y$ *where* Y *is a finite set, with cover cells* $A_y \subseteq X$ *for* $y \in Y$.

For any A/D map $\alpha\colon X \rightsquigarrow Y$, we can assume without loss of generality that Y contains a distinguished element $\ddagger \notin \text{ran}(\alpha)$ with the property that $A_\ddagger = \alpha^{-1}(\ddagger) = \varnothing$. In what follows, we use the "dummy" symbol $\ddagger$ as an output symbol indicating that a trajectory will make no more switches.

Definition 3. *Given* $\text{SP} = (U, X, F)$ *and an* A/D *map* $\alpha\colon X \rightsquigarrow Y$, *we define the transition system model* $\mathcal{S}_{\text{SP}\triangleright\alpha} := (S, W, \delta, S_0)$ *as follows:*

- $S := X \times \mathbb{R}_0^+ \times U \times Y$

- $W := U \times Y$

- *for* $(\mu, \nu) \in U \times Y$, *define:* $(x', \tau', u', y') \in \delta((x, \tau, u, y), (\mu, \nu))$ *iff*
  either **(i):** $y \neq \ddagger$ and $\nu \neq \ddagger$ and $u' = \mu$ and $y' = \nu$ and $y' \neq y$ and $x' = \Phi_\mu(x, \tau' - \tau) \in A_\nu$ and $\Phi_\mu(x, t) \in A_y$ for all $t \in [0, \tau' - \tau]$,
  or **(ii):** $y \neq \ddagger$ and $\nu = \ddagger$ and $u' = \mu$ and $y' = \nu$ and $\Phi_\mu(x, t) \in A_y$ for all $t \in [0, \infty)$,
  or else **(iii):** $y = \ddagger$ and $\nu = \ddagger$ and $u' = \mu$ and $y' = \nu$.

- $S_0 = S$

For an infinite state execution sequence $(\mathbf{s}, \mathbf{w}) \in \mathfrak{B}_{\text{st}}(\mathcal{S}_{\text{SP}\triangleright\alpha})$, *we identify the sequence elements by writing* $\mathbf{s}(i) = (x_i, \tau_i, u_i, y_i)$, *and* $\mathbf{w}(i) = (\mu_i, \nu_i)$, *for each* $i \in \mathbb{N}$. *Let* $\mathfrak{B}_{\text{SP}\triangleright\alpha} := \mathfrak{B}_{\text{ex}}(\mathcal{S}_{\text{SP}\triangleright\alpha})$.

The discrete behaviour $\mathfrak{B}_{\text{SP}\triangleright\alpha} \subseteq (U \times Y)^{\mathbb{N}}$ is the *uncontrolled* external behaviour of the plant SP with discrete inputs U, when viewed through the lens of the A/D map α to give discrete outputs Y. The piecewise-continuous state trajectories of the uncontrolled system $(\mathrm{SP} \triangleright \alpha)$ can be recovered from the infinite state execution sequences in $\mathfrak{B}_{\mathrm{st}}(\mathcal{S}_{\mathrm{SP} \triangleright \alpha})$, as follows.

Define a map $\rho \colon \mathfrak{B}_{\mathrm{st}}(\mathcal{S}_{\mathrm{SP} \triangleright \alpha}) \to X^{\mathbb{R}_0^+}$ such that for each $(\mathbf{s}, \mathbf{w}) \in \mathfrak{B}_{\mathrm{st}}(\mathcal{S}_{\mathrm{SP} \triangleright \alpha})$, the function $\rho(\mathbf{s}, \mathbf{w}) \colon \mathbb{R}_0^+ \to X$ is given by:

$$\rho(\mathbf{s}, \mathbf{w})(t) = \Phi_{\mu_i}(x_i, t - \tau_i) \tag{1}$$

for all $i \in \mathbb{N}$, for all $t \in [\tau_i, \tau_{i+1})$ if $\nu_i \neq \ddagger$, and for all $t \in [\tau_i, \infty)$ if $\nu_i = \ddagger$. Then define:

$$\mathfrak{C}_\rho(\mathcal{S}_{\mathrm{SP} \triangleright \alpha}) := \{\rho(\mathbf{s}, \mathbf{w}) \in X^{\mathbb{R}_0^+} \mid (\mathbf{s}, \mathbf{w}) \in \mathfrak{B}_{\mathrm{st}}(\mathcal{S}_{\mathrm{SP} \triangleright \alpha})\} \tag{2}$$

Observe that for a state trajectory $\rho(\mathbf{s}, \mathbf{w})$ of $(\mathrm{SP} \triangleright \alpha)$, the i-th segment during the interval $[\tau_i, \tau_{i+1})$ consists of the flow according to input $\mu_i \in U$ starting from state x_i, with the whole segment lying within the cell A_{y_i}, up to and including the starting point x_{i+1} of the next segment, reached at time τ_{i+1}, and that point x_{i+1} lies in the overlap of cells $A_{y_i} \cap A_{y_{i+1}}$, where $y_{i+1} = \nu_i \in Y$ is the output for stage i.

4   The Hybrid Closed-Loop and Hybrid Automata Models

Given a switched plant $\mathrm{SP} = (U, X, F)$ and an A/D map $\alpha \colon X \rightsquigarrow Y$, the transition system $\mathcal{S}_{\mathrm{SP} \triangleright \alpha}$ over $W = U \times Y$ is able to accept any input events from U without blocking. This property is referred to as *I/S/- plant* form, and technically requires that for all reachable states $s \in S$ and all inputs $u \in U$, there exists an output $y \in Y$ and an $s' \in S$ such that $(s, (u, y), s') \in \delta$. Similarly, a potential controller that is modeled by a transition system $\mathcal{Q} = (Q, U \times Y, \gamma, Q_0)$ is said to be in *I/S/- controller form* if it at any time accepts any output event from Y as generated by the plant. Here the technical requirement is that $\mathcal{Q}$ is non-blocking and that for all reachable states $q \in Q$, for all transitions $(q, (u, y), q') \in \gamma$ and for all controller inputs (plant outputs) $y' \in Y$, there exists $q'' \in Q$ such that $(q, (u, y'), q'') \in \gamma$. Obviously, the parallel composition of a system in I/S/- plant from with one in I/S/- controller form is non-blocking, and this motivates the following definition of admissible supervisory controllers for switched plants:

Definition 4. *Given a switched plant* $\mathrm{SP} = (U, X, F)$ *and A/D map* $\alpha \colon X \rightsquigarrow Y$, *an* admissible supervisory controller *for the uncontrolled system* $(\mathrm{SP} \triangleright \alpha)$ *is a transition system* $\mathcal{Q} = (Q, W, \gamma, Q_0)$ *over* $W = U \times Y$ *that is in I/S/- controller form. The* closed-loop hybrid system *is the transition system* $\mathcal{S}_{\mathrm{SP} \triangleright \alpha} \parallel \mathcal{Q}$. *Let* $\mathfrak{B}_{\mathrm{sup}} := \mathfrak{B}_{\mathrm{ex}}(\mathcal{Q})$. *The discrete external behaviour of the closed-loop system is*

$$\mathfrak{B}_{\mathrm{ex}}(\mathcal{S}_{\mathrm{SP} \triangleright \alpha} \parallel \mathcal{Q}) = \mathfrak{B}_{\mathrm{SP} \triangleright \alpha} \cap \mathfrak{B}_{\mathrm{sup}}$$

From a state execution sequence $(\mathbf{s}, \mathbf{q}, \mathbf{w}) \in \mathfrak{B}_{\mathrm{st}}(\mathcal{S}_{\mathrm{SP} \triangleright \alpha} \parallel \mathcal{Q})$ of the closed-loop, we can recover a piecewise-continuous state trajectory $\rho(\mathbf{s}, \mathbf{q}, \mathbf{w}) \colon \mathbb{R}_0^+ \to X$

in the same way as for execution sequences of $\mathcal{S}_{\mathrm{SP}\triangleright\alpha}$. Let $\mathfrak{C}_\rho(\mathcal{S}_{\mathrm{SP}\triangleright\alpha} \parallel \mathcal{Q})$ denote the set of all piecewise-continuous trajectories recovered from the state execution sequences of the closed-loop hybrid system.

The closed-loop system can be readily shown to be an instance of the standard hybrid automaton model [1, 2].

Definition 5. *A hybrid automaton is a system* $\mathcal{H} = (Q, E, X, F, D, R)$ *where:*
- Q *is a finite set of* discrete control modes;
- $E\colon Q \rightsquigarrow Q$ *is the* discrete transition relation;
- $X \subseteq \mathbb{R}^n$ *is the* continuous state space;
- $F\colon Q \times X \rightarrow \mathbb{R}^n$ *defines a finite family of* vector fields $F_q : X \rightarrow \mathbb{R}^n$, *where* $F_q := F(q, -)$ *for each* $q \in Q$;
- $D\colon Q \rightsquigarrow X$ *defines the* mode domain $D_q := D(q) \subseteq X$ *for each* $q \in Q$;
- $R\colon X \times E \rightsquigarrow X$ *is the set-valued* reset map.

A function $\mathbf{x}\colon \mathbb{R}_0^+ \rightarrow X$ *is a* state trajectory *of* $\mathcal{H}$ *if there exists a discrete index set* $I = \mathbb{N}$ *or* $I = \{0, 1, \ldots, m\}$, *a non-decreasing time-point sequence* $(\tau_i)_{i \in I}$, *with* $\tau_0 = 0$, *a sequence of discrete modes* $(q_i)_{i \in I}$, *and two sequences of continuous states* $(x_i)_{i \in I}$ *and* $(\tilde{x}_i)_{i \in I}$, *the first starting from* $x_0 := \mathbf{x}(0)$, *such that for all* $i \in I$ *and for all* $t \in [\tau_i, \tau_{i+1})$, *the following conditions hold:*

(1.) $\mathbf{x}(t) = \Phi_{q_i}(x_i, t - \tau_i)$ *and* $\mathbf{x}(t) \in D_{q_i}$

(2.)   *if* $i < \sup(I)$ *then* $\tilde{x}_i := \lim_{t \rightarrow \tau_{i+1}^-} \Phi_{q_i}(x_i, t - \tau_i)$ *and* $\tilde{x}_i \in D_{q_i}$

(3.)   *if* $i < \sup(I)$ *then* $(q_i, q_{i+1}) \in E$

(4.)   *if* $i < \sup(I)$ *then* $x_{i+1} \in R(\tilde{x}_i, (q_i, q_{i+1}))$

(5.)   *if* $i = \sup(I)$ *then* $\tau_{i+1} = \infty$

Let $\mathfrak{C}(\mathcal{H}) \subseteq X^{\mathbb{R}_0^+}$ *denote the set of all state trajectories of* $\mathcal{H}$.

For each discrete transition $(q, q') \in E$, the component reset map is $R_{q,q'} := R(-, q, q') : X \rightsquigarrow X$, and the so-called *guard region* is $G_{q,q'} := \mathrm{dom}(R_{q,q'}) \subseteq X$.

Proposition 1. *Given a closed-loop system formed from* SP, α *and* $\mathcal{Q}$, *define the hybrid automaton* $\mathcal{H}\,(\mathrm{SP}, \alpha, \mathcal{Q}) = (\hat{Q}, E, X, \hat{F}, D, R)$ *as follows:*
- $\hat{Q} := \{(q, u, y) \in Q \times U \times Y \mid (\exists q' \in Q)\,(q, (u, y), q') \in \gamma\}$
- $\hat{F}\colon \hat{Q} \times X \rightarrow \mathbb{R}^n$ *given by* $\hat{F}((q, u, y), x) = F(u, x)$ *for all* $(q, u, y) \in \hat{Q}$ *and* $x \in X$
- *for each* $(q, u, y) \in \hat{Q}$, *the mode domain* $D_{(q,u,y)} = A_y$
- $E\colon \hat{Q} \rightsquigarrow \hat{Q}$ *given by:*

$$((q, u, y), (q', u', y')) \in E \text{ iff } (q, (u, y), q') \in \gamma \text{ and } A_y \cap A_{y'} \neq \varnothing \qquad (3)$$

- *for each* $((q, u, y), (q', u', y')) \in E$, *the reset relation is*

$$R_{(q,u,y),(q',u',y')} := \{(x, x') \in X \times X \mid x \in A_y \cap A_{y'} \text{ and } x' = x\} \qquad (4)$$

Then

$$\mathfrak{C}(\mathcal{H}(\mathrm{SP}, \alpha, \mathcal{Q})) = \mathfrak{C}_\rho(\mathcal{S}_{\mathrm{SP}\triangleright\alpha} \parallel \mathcal{Q})$$

This result shows that every hybrid closed-loop can be represented as a hybrid automaton with simple membership-testing resets.

5   Continuous Behaviours as Dynamic Specifications for Supervisory Controller Synthesis

We address the following class of supervisory controller synthesis problems.

Synthesis Problem: *Given a switched plant SP and a continuous behavioural specification $\mathfrak{C}_{\text{spec}}$, construct an A/D map α and a discrete supervisor $\mathcal{Q}$ such that the closed-loop behaviour fulfills the following behavioural inclusion:*

$$\mathfrak{C}_\rho(\mathcal{S}_{\text{SP}\triangleright\alpha} \parallel \mathcal{Q}) \subseteq \mathfrak{C}_{\text{spec}}. \tag{5}$$

This quite general notion of a continuous dynamic specification gives us a means to place conditions on the evolution of a dynamical system without referring to a model of the system itself; trajectories $x \in \mathfrak{C}_{\text{spec}}$ are deemed acceptable, while trajectories $x \notin \mathfrak{C}_{\text{spec}}$ are deemed unacceptable. To indicate the broad scope of this notion of a specification, we give several illustrative examples.

Example 1: notions of stability. Convergence of trajectories to an equilibrium point $x^\star \in X$ is a necessary condition for asymptotic stability. Consider the continuous behavioual specification:

$$\mathfrak{C}_{\text{conv}} := \{\mathbf{x} \colon \mathbb{R}_0^+ \to X \mid \lim_{t \to \infty} \mathbf{x}(t) = x^\star\} \tag{6}$$

Note that the specification $\mathfrak{C}_{\text{conv}}$ does *not* require $x^\star$ to actually be an equilibrium. This further condition can be expressed by:

$$\mathfrak{C}_{\text{equi}} := \{\mathbf{x} \colon \mathbb{R}_0^+ \to X \mid \mathbf{x}(0) = x^\star \;\Rightarrow\; (\forall t \in \mathbb{R}_0^+)\, \mathbf{x}(t) = x^\star\}. \tag{7}$$

Obviously, we can combine the two specifications by taking their intersection: the specification $\mathfrak{C}_{\text{equi}} \cap \mathfrak{C}_{\text{conv}}$ requires $x^\star$ to be an equilibrium to which all trajectories converge.

Example 2: circular motion. An elementary example of hybrid controller synthesis is given in [16], where the control objective is to enforce a clockwise circular motion in the plane $\mathbb{R}^2$. While [16] refers to a particular A/D map in order to formalise this objective, we give an alternative characterisation as a continuous dynamic specification independent of any A/D map. Let $TL := \{l \colon \mathbb{R}_0^+ \to \mathbb{R}_0^+ \mid l$ is monotone, unbounded, continuous$\}$ be the set of *time-lag* functions, and consider the clockwise circular reference trajectory $\mathbf{r} \colon \mathbb{R}_0^+ \to \mathbb{R}^2$ given by $\mathbf{r}(t) = (\cos(t), -\sin(t))$. Then define:

$$\mathfrak{C}_{\text{circ}} := \{\mathbf{x} \colon \mathbb{R}_0^+ \to X \mid (\exists l \in TL)(\forall t \in \mathbb{R}_0^+)\; \mathbf{r}(l(t))^\top \mathbf{x}(t) > 0\} \tag{8}$$

Visually, think of the reference $\mathbf{r}(t)$ as the orthogonal to the separator in a revolving door, rotating clockwise. The "lag" function l allows the revolver to rotate at arbitrary angular velocities, while the inequality ensures that a trajectory $\mathbf{x}$ must stay on the same side of the separator at all times. Intuitively, any person within such a revolving door will be forced to make "steady progress" in a clockwise circular motion, since the separator will only allow "a quarter lap forth and back" relative to the reference trajectory.

Example 3: static safety. The classic form of a safety property consists of specifying a set $Bad \subseteq X$, and requiring that no trajectory ever enters Bad. Consider:

$$\mathfrak{C}_{\text{safe}} := \{\, \mathbf{x} \colon \mathbb{R}_0^+ \to X \mid (\forall t \in \mathbb{R}_0^+)\, \mathbf{x}(t) \notin Bad \,\} \qquad (9)$$

This type of specification is *static* rather than *dynamic* in the sense that it does not change over time. We will return to these examples after introducing the notion of capturing in the following section.

6   A/D Maps and Discrete Behaviours

Our task here is to formulate the notion of using an A/D map $\alpha \colon X \rightsquigarrow Y$ together with a discrete behaviour $\mathfrak{B} \subseteq Y^{\mathbb{N}}$ to "capture" or "enforce" a continuous dynamic specification $\mathfrak{C}_{\text{spec}} \subseteq X^{\mathbb{R}_0^+}$. Recall that $\ddagger \in Y$ is a distinguished symbol which we use to indicate that no more switches will occur.

Definition 6. *Let* $TP := \{\tau \colon \mathbb{N} \to \mathbb{R}_0^+ \mid \tau(0) = 0 \wedge (\forall i \in \mathbb{N})\, \tau(i) < \tau(i+1)\,\}$ *be the set of (strictly increasing) time-point sequences. Given an A/D map* $\alpha \colon X \rightsquigarrow Y$ *and a discrete behaviour* $\mathfrak{B} \subseteq Y^{\mathbb{N}}$, *define:*

$$
\begin{aligned}
\mathcal{C}(\alpha, \mathfrak{B}) := \{\, \mathbf{x} \colon \mathbb{R}_0^+ \to X \mid\ & (\exists \mathbf{y} \in \mathfrak{B})(\exists \tau \in TP)(\forall i \in \mathbb{N}) \\
& \big[\, \text{if } \mathbf{y}(i) \neq \ddagger \ \text{then} \ (\forall t \in [\tau(i), \tau(i+1)))\ \mathbf{x}(t) \in A_{\mathbf{y}(i)} \\
& \text{and if } \mathbf{y}(i) \neq \ddagger \ \text{and also } \mathbf{y}(i+1) = \ddagger \\
& \text{then} \ (\forall t \in [\tau(i), \infty))\ \mathbf{x}(t) \in A_{\mathbf{y}(i)} \,\big] \,\}
\end{aligned}
\qquad (10)
$$

Given a continuous behaviour $\mathfrak{C} \subseteq X^{\mathbb{R}_0^+}$, *we say that the pair* $(\alpha, \mathfrak{B})$ *captures* $\mathfrak{C}$, *if* $\mathcal{C}(\alpha, \mathfrak{B}) \subseteq \mathfrak{C}$.

The idea is that the continuous behaviour $\mathcal{C}(\alpha, \mathfrak{B})$ includes all and only the trajectories $\mathbf{x} \colon \mathbb{R}_0^+ \to X$ that respect the sequence order of some $\mathbf{y} \in \mathfrak{B}$ considered as a sequence of regions on X via α. To illustrate how an A/D map and a discrete behaviour together capture a continuous behaviour, we continue with our examples.

Ad Example 1: notions of stability. The requirement expressed by $\mathfrak{C}_{\text{conv}}$ depends on the actual topology on X referred to in the expression $\lim_{t \to \infty} \mathbf{x}(t) = x^\star$. Generalising the notion of a limit to cover arbitrary topological spaces (e.g. *Moore-Smith convergence*, [8], §20.IX), the condition is fulfilled if for any open set V containing $x^\star$, there exists a τ such that $\mathbf{x}(t) \in V$ for all $t > \tau$. In the case of the Euclidean topology on X, this cannot be captured by any pair $(\alpha, \mathfrak{B})$ where the signal space Y is finite. However, we can look more broadly at other topologies on X. Fix an A/D map $\alpha \colon X \rightsquigarrow Y$ and consider the finite topology $\mathcal{T}_\alpha \subseteq 2^X$ generated by taking all finite unions and intersections of the α-cells A_y for $y \in Y$. For the most basic case where α defines a finite partition, the open sets in the topology $\mathcal{T}_\alpha$ are just the cells closed under unions. Let $A_{y^\star}$ be the cell such that $x^\star \in A_{y^\star}$, and let:

$$\mathfrak{B}^\alpha_{\mathrm{conv}} := \{\mathbf{y} \in Y^{\mathbb{N}} \mid (\exists i \in \mathbb{N})[\, \mathbf{y}(i) = y^\star \wedge (\forall j > i)\, \mathbf{y}(j) = \ddagger\,\} \tag{11}$$

Then $(\alpha, \mathfrak{B}^\alpha_{\mathrm{conv}})$ captures $\mathfrak{C}_{\mathrm{conv}}$. For the more general case where α is a finite cover with overlaps, we can also capture $\mathfrak{C}_{\mathrm{conv}}$, but have to replace α with a *refinement* β such that $\mathcal{T}_\beta = \mathcal{T}_\alpha$, where the cells of β are the *join-irreducibles* in $\mathcal{T}_\alpha$ as a lattice of sets (see also [12]). For the equilibrium specification $\mathfrak{C}_{\mathrm{equi}}$, it is also clear that it cannot be captured via any finite range A/D map. However, what can be captured is a weaker version of $\mathfrak{C}_{\mathrm{equi}}$ already relativised to α by replacing true equality $=$ with $\simeq_\alpha$ in Equation (7).

Ad Example 2: circular motion. Consider an A/D map α based on the four quadrants of $\mathbb{R}^2$, similar to [16]. More precisely, let $A_1 = \{(x_1, x_2) \mid x_1 > 0,\ x_2 \geq 0\}$, $A_2 = \{(x_1, x_2) \mid x_1 \leq 0,\ x_2 > 0\}$, $A_3 = \{(x_1, x_2) \mid x_1 < 0,\ x_2 \leq 0\}$, $A_4 = \{(x_1, x_2) \mid x_1 \geq 0,\ x_2 < 0\}$, and, in order to partition the entire $\mathbb{R}^2$, let $A_0 = \{(0, 0)\}$. Denote the corresponding single-valued A/D map by $\alpha \colon Y \to \mathbb{R}^2$, where $Y = \{0, 1, 2, 3, 4\}$. Let

$$\mathfrak{B}^\alpha_{\mathrm{circ}} := (1432)^\omega \cup (4321)^\omega \cup (3214)^\omega \cup (2143)^\omega \tag{12}$$

Then $(\alpha, \mathfrak{B}^\alpha_{\mathrm{circ}})$ captures $\mathfrak{C}_{\mathrm{circ}}$.

Ad Example 3: static safety. Consider any A/D map $\alpha \colon X \rightsquigarrow Y$ such that for some $Y_{Bad} \subseteq Y$, we have $Bad \subseteq \bigcup_{y \in Y_{Bad}} A_y$. Then define:

$$\mathfrak{B}^\alpha_{\mathrm{safe}} := \{\mathbf{y} \colon \mathbb{N} \to Y \mid (\forall i \in \mathbb{N})\, \mathbf{y}(i) \notin Y_{Bad}\} \tag{13}$$

Then $(\alpha, \mathfrak{B}^\alpha_{\mathrm{safe}})$ captures $\mathfrak{C}_{\mathrm{safe}}$.

To resume our study of the notion of *capturing*, fix an A/D-map $\alpha \colon X \rightsquigarrow Y$ and a discrete behaviour $\mathfrak{B} \subseteq Y^{\mathbb{N}}$. It is clear that the set of all dynamic specifications $\mathfrak{C}$ that are captured by the pair $(\alpha, \mathfrak{B})$ forms a complete lattice, with the usual set-theoretic operations. Moreover, $(\alpha, \mathfrak{B})$ captures $\mathfrak{C}_1 \cap \mathfrak{C}_2$ iff $(\alpha, \mathfrak{B})$ captures $\mathfrak{C}_1$ and $(\alpha, \mathfrak{B})$ captures $\mathfrak{C}_2$.

Also observe directly from Definition 6 that the operator $\mathcal{C}(\alpha, \cdot)$ distributes over arbitrary unions in the second argument; i.e. if $\mathfrak{B}_i \subseteq Y^{\mathbb{N}}$ for $i \in I$, then: $\mathcal{C}(\alpha, \bigcup_{i \in I} \mathfrak{B}_i) = \bigcup_{i \in I} \mathcal{C}(\alpha, \mathfrak{B}_i)$. Consequently, for a fixed A/D-map and a fixed behaviour $\mathfrak{C} \subseteq X^{\mathbb{R}_0^+}$, the set of all discrete behaviours $\mathfrak{B} \subseteq Y^{\mathbb{N}}$ such that the pair $(\alpha, \mathfrak{B})$ captures $\mathfrak{C}$ forms a complete upper semi-lattice w.r.t. the usual set-theoretic operations. In particular, there uniquely exists a *largest* or *least restrictive* discrete behaviour $\mathfrak{B} \subseteq Y^{\mathbb{N}}$ such that $(\alpha, \mathfrak{B})$ captures $\mathfrak{C}$.

Some immediate consequences of the observed lattice structure are summarized as follows:

Proposition 2. *For any A/D map* $\alpha\colon X \rightsquigarrow Y$ *and continuous behaviour* $\mathfrak{C} \subseteq X^{\mathbb{R}_0^+}$, *define:*

$$\mathcal{B}(\alpha, \mathfrak{C}) := \bigcup\{\mathfrak{B} \subseteq Y^{\mathbb{N}} \mid \mathcal{C}(\alpha, \mathfrak{B}) \subseteq \mathfrak{C}\} \tag{14}$$

Then, for all $\mathfrak{B}' \subseteq Y^{\mathbb{N}}$, *we have:* $\mathcal{C}(\alpha, \mathfrak{B}') \subseteq \mathfrak{C}$ *if and only if* $\mathfrak{B}' \subseteq \mathcal{B}(\alpha, \mathfrak{C})$. *Furthermore, the following inclusions hold for all* $\mathfrak{C}$ *and* $\mathfrak{B}$:

$$\mathcal{C}(\alpha, \mathcal{B}(\alpha, \mathfrak{C})) \subseteq \mathfrak{C}, \qquad \mathfrak{B} \subseteq \mathcal{B}(\alpha, \mathcal{C}(\alpha, \mathfrak{B})). \tag{15}$$

7 Refining A/D Maps

If the supervisory controller synthesis fails for a given A/D map one may consider a finer A/D-map.

Definition 7. *Let* $\alpha\colon X \rightsquigarrow Y$ *and* $\beta\colon X \rightsquigarrow Z$ *be two A/D maps, with cover cells* $A_y = \alpha^{-1}(y) \subseteq X$ *for* $y \in Y$ *and* $B_z = \beta^{-1}(z) \subseteq X$ *for* $z \in Z$. *We say* β *is a* refinement *of* α, *written* $\alpha \Subset \beta$, *if for each* $y \in Y$, *there exists* $z_1, z_2, \ldots, z_m \in Z$ *such that*

$$A_y = B_{z_1} \cup B_{z_2} \cup \cdots \cup B_{z_m} \tag{16}$$

and for each $z \in Z$, *there exists* $y \in Y$ *such that*

$$B_z \subseteq A_y \tag{17}$$

When $\alpha \Subset \beta$, *define a set-valued map* $\theta_{\alpha\beta}\colon Y \rightsquigarrow Z$ *by:* $z \in \theta_{\alpha\beta}(y)$ *iff* $B_z \subseteq A_y$ *or* $y = z = \ddagger$. *Then* $A_y = \bigcup\{B_z \mid z \in \theta_{\alpha\beta}(y)\}$ *for all* $y \in Y$.

Proposition 3. *Fix a continuous behaviour* $\mathfrak{C} \subseteq X^{\mathbb{R}_0^+}$, *an A/D map* $\alpha\colon X \rightsquigarrow Y$, *and a discrete behaviour* $\mathfrak{B} \subseteq Y^{\mathbb{N}}$ *such that* $(\alpha, \mathfrak{B})$ *captures* $\mathfrak{C}$. *Let* $DS := \{\kappa\colon \mathbb{N} \to \mathbb{N} \mid \kappa(0) = 0 \wedge (\forall i \in \mathbb{N})\, \kappa(i) < \kappa(i+1)\}$ *be the set of strictly increasing discrete-time stretch maps. Now for any A/D map* $\beta\colon X \rightsquigarrow Z$ *such that* $\alpha \Subset \beta$, *define:*

$$\mathcal{B}^{\beta}(\alpha, \mathfrak{B}) := \{\mathbf{z} \in Z^{\mathbb{N}} \mid (\exists \mathbf{y} \in \mathfrak{B})(\exists \kappa \in DS)(\forall j \in \mathbb{N})$$
$$\mathbf{z}|_{[\kappa(j),\kappa(j+1))} \subseteq (\theta_{\alpha\beta}(\mathbf{y}(j)))^* \}. \tag{18}$$

Then $(\beta, \mathcal{B}^{\beta}(\alpha, \mathfrak{B}))$ *captures* $\mathfrak{C}$.

In defining the candidate $\mathcal{B}^{\beta}(\alpha, \mathfrak{B}) \subseteq Z^{\mathbb{N}}$, we collect all infinite sequences $\mathbf{z}$ that can be decomposed in a sequence of finite words $\mathbf{z}|_{[\kappa(i),\kappa(i+1))}$ such that: (a) each finite word corresponds to a single cover cell $\mathbf{y}(i)$ of α; and that (b) this labelling generates an infinite sequence $\mathbf{y}$ which lies inside the original discrete specification $\mathfrak{B} \subseteq Y^{\mathbb{N}}$.

Proof. To show $(\beta, \mathcal{B}^\beta(\alpha, \mathfrak{B}))$ captures $\mathfrak{C}$, fix an arbitrary $\mathbf{x} \in \mathcal{C}(\beta, \mathcal{B}^\beta(\alpha, \mathfrak{B}))$. Then there exists a sequence $\mathbf{z} \in \mathcal{B}^\beta(\alpha, \mathfrak{B})$ and a $\tau \in TP$ such that for all $i \in \mathbb{N}$, if $\mathbf{z}(i) \neq \ddagger$ then $\mathbf{x}(t) \in B_{\mathbf{z}(i)}$ for all $t \in [\tau(i), \tau(i{+}1))$, and if $\mathbf{z}(i) \neq \ddagger$ but $\mathbf{z}(i{+}1) = \ddagger$ then $\mathbf{x}(t) \in B_{\mathbf{z}(i)}$ for all $t \in [\tau(i), \infty)$. Now by Equation (18), $\mathbf{z} \in \mathcal{B}^\beta(\alpha, \mathfrak{B})$ means there is a witness $\mathbf{y} \in \mathfrak{B}$ and a function $\kappa \in DS$ such that $\mathbf{z}|_{[\kappa(j), \kappa(j{+}1))} \subseteq (\theta_{\alpha\beta}(\mathbf{y}(j)))^*$ for all $j \in \mathbb{N}$. And from the definition of $\theta_{\alpha\beta}$, we know that $B_{\mathbf{z}(k)} \subseteq A_{\mathbf{y}(j)}$ for all $k \in [\kappa(j), \kappa(j{+}1)) = \{\kappa(j), \kappa(j){+}1, \dots, \kappa(j{+}1){-}1\}$. We now define a new function $\hat{\tau} \colon \mathbb{N} \to \mathbb{R}_0^+$ by $\hat{\tau}(j) := \tau(\kappa(j))$. Since τ and κ are both strictly increasing, then so is $\hat{\tau}$, and also $\hat{\tau}(0) = \tau(\kappa(0)) = \tau(0) = 0$. Hence $\hat{\tau} \in TP$. We want to show that $\mathbf{x} \in \mathcal{C}(\alpha, \mathfrak{B})$ with witnesses $\mathbf{y} \in \mathfrak{B}$ and $\hat{\tau} \in TP$; then since $(\alpha, \mathfrak{B})$ captures $\mathfrak{C}$, we would have $\mathbf{x} \in \mathfrak{C}$, as required. So now fix any $j \in \mathbb{N}$ and suppose that $\mathbf{y}(j) \neq \ddagger$. Then $\mathbf{z}(k) \neq \ddagger$ for all $k \in [\kappa(j), \kappa(j + 1))$. Fix any $t \in [\hat{\tau}(j), \hat{\tau}(j{+}1)) = [\tau(\kappa(j)), \tau(\kappa(j{+}1)))$. Then for some $k \in [\kappa(j), \kappa(j{+}1))$, we must have $\mathbf{x}(t) \in B_{\mathbf{z}(k)}$, and thus also $\mathbf{x}(t) \in A_{\mathbf{y}(j)}$. For the other case, suppose that $\mathbf{y}(j) \neq \ddagger$ but $\mathbf{y}(j + 1) = \ddagger$. Then $\mathbf{z}(k) \neq \ddagger$ and $\mathbf{z}(\kappa(j + 1)) = \ddagger$. Fix any $t \in [\hat{\tau}(j), \infty) = [\tau(\kappa(j)), \infty)$. Then we must have $\mathbf{x}(t) \in B_{\mathbf{z}(\kappa(j))}$, and hence $\mathbf{x}(t) \in A_{\mathbf{y}(j)}$, as required. Since $\mathbf{x}$ was arbitrary, we conclude that $(\beta, \mathcal{B}^\beta(\alpha, \mathfrak{B}))$ captures $\mathfrak{C}$.

8 Applying DES and Discrete Behavioural Approaches to Controller Synthesis

In tackling the general synthesis problem formulated in Section 5, we can build on previous work in [7, 16, 5], first starting by seeking to find an A/D map α and a discrete dynamic specification $\mathfrak{B}^\alpha_{\mathrm{spec}}$ such that $(\alpha, \mathfrak{B}^\alpha_{\mathrm{spec}})$ captures $\mathfrak{C}_{\mathrm{spec}}$. The synthesis problem can then be restated purely in terms of the discrete behaviours, $\mathfrak{B}_{\mathrm{SP} \triangleright \alpha}$ and $\mathfrak{B}^\alpha_{\mathrm{spec}}$: find an admissible discrete supervisor with induced behaviour $\mathfrak{B}_{\mathrm{sup}}$ such that the discrete-time closed-loop behaviour $\mathfrak{B}_{\mathrm{cl}} = \mathfrak{B}_{\mathrm{SP} \triangleright \alpha} \cap \mathfrak{B}_{\mathrm{sup}}$ lies within $\mathfrak{B}^\alpha_{\mathrm{spec}}$. The admissibility requirement for $\mathfrak{B}_{\mathrm{sup}}$ is that it have a transition system realisation in $I/S/-$ controller form. Up to minor notational variations, this restated control problem has been extensively studied in [10, 11, 13]. We provide a terse summary of the main results, in order to show how the broader scope of this contribution relates to the literature.

Fix a switched plant $\mathrm{SP} = (U, X, F)$ and an A/D map $\alpha \colon X \rightsquigarrow Y$, so the induced external behaviour $\mathfrak{B}_{\mathrm{SP} \triangleright \alpha} \subseteq (U \times Y)^{\mathbb{N}}$. Let $\mathfrak{B}^\alpha_{\mathrm{spec}}$ be a discrete dynamic specification. We refer to the pair $(\mathfrak{B}_{\mathrm{SP} \triangleright \alpha}, \mathfrak{B}^\alpha_{\mathrm{spec}})$ as a *discrete-time supervisory control problem* and ask for an admissible supervisor that enforces $\mathfrak{B}^\alpha_{\mathrm{spec}}$ when interconnected with $\mathfrak{B}_{\mathrm{SP} \triangleright \alpha}$. We give a formal definition of this problem and its solutions.

Definition 8. *Let $\mathfrak{B}_{\mathrm{sup}} \subseteq (U \times Y)^{\mathbb{N}}$.*
- *$\mathfrak{B}_{\mathrm{sup}} \subseteq W^{\mathbb{N}}$ to said to be* generically implementable *if for all $k \in \mathbb{N}$,*
  $(\mathbf{u}, \mathbf{y})|_{[0,k]} \in \mathfrak{B}_{\mathrm{sup}}|_{[0,k]}$, $(\tilde{\mathbf{u}}, \tilde{\mathbf{y}})|_{[0,k]} \in W^{k+1}$, $\tilde{\mathbf{u}}|_{[0,k]} = \mathbf{u}|_{[0,k]}$, $\tilde{\mathbf{y}}|_{[0,k)} = \mathbf{y}|_{[0,k)}$
  implies $(\tilde{\mathbf{u}}, \tilde{\mathbf{y}})|_{[0,k]} \in \mathfrak{B}_{\mathrm{sup}}|_{[0,k]}$.

- *The two behaviours $\mathfrak{B}_{\text{SP}\triangleright\alpha}$ and $\mathfrak{B}_{\text{sup}} \subseteq W^{\mathbb{N}}$ are said to be* nonconflicting *if $\mathfrak{B}_{\text{SP}\triangleright\alpha}|_{[0,k]} \cap \mathfrak{B}_{\text{sup}}|_{[0,k]} = (\mathfrak{B}_{\text{SP}\triangleright\alpha} \cap \mathfrak{B}_{\text{sup}})|_{[0,k]}$ for all $k \in \mathbb{N}$.*
- *The behaviour $\mathfrak{B}_{\text{sup}}$ is said to* enforce *the discrete dynamic specification $\mathfrak{B}_{\text{spec}}^{\alpha} \subseteq Y^{\mathbb{N}}$ if $(\mathbf{u}, \mathbf{y}) \in \mathfrak{B}_{\text{SP}\triangleright\alpha} \cap \mathfrak{B}_{\text{sup}}$ implies $\mathbf{y} \in \mathfrak{B}_{\text{spec}}^{\alpha}$.*

The behaviour $\mathfrak{B}_{\text{sup}}$ solves the control problem $(\mathfrak{B}_{\text{SP}\triangleright\alpha}, \mathfrak{B}_{\text{spec}}^{\alpha})$ *if it satisfies each of these three conditions.* [1]

Note that formally, the trivial behaviour $\mathfrak{B}_{\text{sup}} = \varnothing$ solves $(\mathfrak{B}_{\text{SP}\triangleright\alpha}, \mathfrak{B}_{\text{spec}}^{\alpha})$, leading to an empty closed-loop behaviour; obviously, this is undesirable. In response, we ask for the prospective supervisor to be as least restrictive as possible. This line of thought is similar to that of DES supervisory control theory [14, 15]. In fact, [10, 11] show that a key result of [14, 15] naturally carries over to the hybrid case: a *least restrictive supervisor* $\mathfrak{B}_{\text{sup}}^{\uparrow}$ that solves $(\mathfrak{B}_{\text{SP}\triangleright\alpha}, \mathfrak{B}_{\text{spec}}^{\alpha})$ always exists uniquely.

Proposition 4. *The behaviour*

$$\mathfrak{B}_{\text{sup}}^{\uparrow} := \bigcup \{\mathfrak{B}_{\text{sup}} \subseteq (U \times Y)^{\mathbb{N}} | \ \mathfrak{B}_{\text{sup}} \ solves \ (\mathfrak{B}_{\text{SP}\triangleright\alpha}, \mathfrak{B}_{\text{spec}}^{\alpha})\} \qquad (19)$$

is a itself a solution of $(\mathfrak{B}_{\text{SP}\triangleright\alpha}, \mathfrak{B}_{\text{spec}}^{\alpha})$. We denote the closed-loop behaviour of $\mathfrak{B}_{\text{SP}\triangleright\alpha}$ under least restrictive supervisory control by $\mathfrak{B}_{\text{cl}}^{\uparrow} := \mathfrak{B}_{\text{SP}\triangleright\alpha} \cap \mathfrak{B}_{\text{sup}}^{\uparrow}$.

In particular, there exists a solution to $(\mathfrak{B}_{\text{SP}\triangleright\alpha}, \mathfrak{B}_{\text{spec}}^{\alpha})$ with non-empty closed-loop behaviour if and only if $\mathfrak{B}_{\text{cl}}^{\uparrow} \neq \varnothing$.

Unfortunately, very stringent conditions apply to the underlying continuous dynamics Φ when the synthesis is to be carried out directly, based on $\mathfrak{B}_{\text{SP}\triangleright\alpha}$, or, for that matter, on $\mathcal{S}_{\text{SP}\triangleright\alpha}$ and α. Prospective candidates here are cases in which Φ is linear in both state and time; i.e. straight line evolution, and α a polyhedral partition. On the other hand, if both $\mathfrak{B}_{\text{SP}\triangleright\alpha}$ and $\mathfrak{B}_{\text{spec}}^{\alpha}$ were realized by finite automata, the least restrictive supervisor could readily be computed drawing from slightly modified methods from DES theory; e.g. [14, 15, 11]. These procedures typically compute a finite automaton realisation of the least restrictive closed-loop $\mathfrak{B}_{\text{cl}}^{\uparrow}$. The latter automaton can also be employed as a supervisor; we give detailed account to this interpretation in [11] from a technical application perspective. A formal conversion to a finite state transition system $\mathcal{Q}$ in I/S/-controller form is straight-forward.

However, while in our framework we may assume $\mathfrak{B}_{\text{spec}}^{\alpha}$ to be realised as a finite automaton, this assumption in general will not hold up for $\mathfrak{B}_{\text{SP}\triangleright\alpha}$. Consequently, [7, 6, 10, 13] suggest to approximately realize $\mathfrak{B}_{\text{SP}\triangleright\alpha}$ by a suitable finite automata and then to carry out the synthesis for the problem $(\mathfrak{B}_{\text{ca}}, \mathfrak{B}_{\text{spec}}^{\alpha})$, where $\mathfrak{B}_{\text{ca}} \subseteq (U \times Y)^{\mathbb{N}}$ denotes the external behaviour induced by the approximate automata realisation. In this approximation-based approach, two main

---

[1] The notion here of *generic implementability* corresponds to *implementability w.r.t. a particular plant* as defined in [10], and it can been seen that the alternative formulation leads to precisely the same closed-loop behaviours. The specification $\mathfrak{B}_{\text{spec}}$ in the notation of [10, 11] is related to the $\mathfrak{B}_{\text{spec}}^{\alpha}$ above by $\mathfrak{B}_{\text{spec}} = \{(\mathbf{u}, \mathbf{y}) | \ \mathbf{y} \in \mathfrak{B}_{\text{spec}}^{\alpha}\}$

issues present themselves. First, the approximation needs to be sufficiently accurate in order to allow for a successful controller synthesis; we come back to this issue below. Second, assuming that a supervisor could be synthesised for the approximation, one needs to guarantee that desired closed-loop properties are retained when the supervisor is connected to the actual hybrid plant. The second issue is commonly dealt with by requiring that the approximation must be conservative in the sense that it predicts at least all those trajectories on which the actual hybrid plant can evolve. Within our framework this requirement can be stated as the behavioural inclusion $\mathfrak{B}_{\mathrm{SP}\triangleright\alpha} \subseteq \mathfrak{B}_{\mathrm{ca}}$ and, indeed, this forms a sufficient condition for resolving the second issue:

Proposition 5. *Assume that $\mathfrak{B}^{\alpha}_{\mathrm{spec}}$, $\mathfrak{B}_{\mathrm{ca}}$ and $\mathfrak{B}_{\mathrm{sup}}$ can all be realised by finite automata. Suppose $\mathfrak{B}_{\mathrm{sup}}$ solves the problem $(\mathfrak{B}_{\mathrm{ca}}, \mathfrak{B}^{\alpha}_{\mathrm{spec}})$ and suppose $\mathfrak{B}_{\mathrm{SP}\triangleright\alpha} \subseteq \mathfrak{B}_{\mathrm{ca}}$. Then $\mathfrak{B}_{\mathrm{sup}}$ is also a solution of $(\mathfrak{B}_{\mathrm{SP}\triangleright\alpha}, \mathfrak{B}^{\alpha}_{\mathrm{spec}})$. Furthermore, $\mathfrak{B}_{\mathrm{ca}} \cap \mathfrak{B}_{\mathrm{sup}} = \varnothing$ if and only if $\mathfrak{B}_{\mathrm{SP}\triangleright\alpha} \cap \mathfrak{B}_{\mathrm{sup}} = \varnothing$.*

Recall that on the approximation level, the least restrictive closed-loop behaviour – and hence a realisation $\mathcal{Q}$ in I/S/- controller form – can be computed by methods from DES theory. If $\mathfrak{B}_{\mathrm{sup}} \cong \mathcal{Q}$ is found to enforce a nontrivial closed-loop behaviour $\mathfrak{B}_{\mathrm{ca}} \cap \mathfrak{B}_{\mathrm{sup}} \neq \varnothing$, then by the result above, this realises a solution of our discrete-time supervisory control problem $(\mathfrak{B}_{\mathrm{SP}\triangleright\alpha}, \mathfrak{B}^{\alpha}_{\mathrm{spec}})$. We can conclude from $\mathfrak{B}_{\mathrm{cl}} \subseteq \mathfrak{B}^{\alpha}_{\mathrm{spec}}$ that the hybrid closed loop consisting of SP, α and $\mathcal{Q}$ fulfills the continuous dynamic specification $\mathfrak{C}_{\mathrm{spec}}$ in the sense of Eq. (5), and thus the original control problem given by SP and $\mathfrak{C}_{\mathrm{spec}}$ has also been solved.

If $\mathfrak{B}_{\mathrm{sup}} \cong \mathcal{Q}$ enforces the trivial closed-loop behaviour $\mathfrak{B}_{\mathrm{ca}} \cap \mathfrak{B}_{\mathrm{sup}} = \varnothing$, we distinguish two subcases. First, there may exist no solution for the original problem, in which case we can't complain about failure in finding one. Second, it could be that the chosen A/D map was too coarse and therefore gives a prospective supervisor too little measurement information for it to be able to drive the system according to the continuous dynamic specification. In the latter case, we want to have another attempt with a refined A/D map β, with $\alpha \Subset \beta$. Various methods of A/D map refinement have been discussed in the literature, mostly based on a backward reachability analysis, and the reader is kindly referred to [7, 16, 5, 4]. As worked out in Section 6, discrete dynamic representations of specifications depend on the A/D map. More precisely, when moving from α on to β, we also replace $\mathfrak{B}^{\alpha}_{\mathrm{spec}}$ by $\mathcal{B}^{\beta}(\alpha, \mathfrak{B}^{\alpha}_{\mathrm{spec}})$, as in Eq. 18. In particular, the refinement procedure suggested in [7] for partitions lends itself to the proposed setting.

9   Discussion and Conclusion

The framework developed here has two main advantages from the perspective of controller synthesis. First, after a cover refinement, we still refer to the same continuous dynamic specification $\mathfrak{C}_{\mathrm{spec}}$, the latter serving as a formal platform to express the relation between the two control problems stated for α and β, respectively. Thus we make clear that if it is a cover refinement that finally leads to the successful synthesis of a supervisor, then it is in fact the original control objective that we fulfil with our closed-loop design. Second, for any fixed A/D map α, our restated control problem still refers to the "full" hybrid dynamics: although $\mathfrak{B}_{\mathrm{SP}\triangleright\alpha}$ is defined on a discrete-time axis, it refers to the transition system $\mathcal{S}_{\mathrm{SP}\triangleright\alpha}$ over the full hybrid state space, and continuous evolution is recovered by Eq. 1, Section 3. Contrast this with [7], where once the A/D partition is fixed, the treatment of the restated control problem exclusively refers to the so-called *DES Plant*, which is realized as a finite automaton and can be seen to be a rather coarse abstraction. In fact, [13, 10, 11] suggest an ordered family of *l-complete approximations* $\mathfrak{B}_l$, $l \in \mathbb{N}$, where $\mathfrak{B}_{\mathrm{SP}\triangleright\alpha} \subseteq \mathfrak{B}_{l+1} \subseteq \mathfrak{B}_l$, and the DES Plant according to [7] corresponds to the coarsest case $l = 0$. On the other hand, [13, 10, 11] do not discuss the potential gain of accuracy that lies in the refinement of the A/D map. Our current contribution is seen to strategically combine the strengths of both views: the A/D map refinement suggested by [7, 16] as well as the option to increase accuracy for a fixed A/D map suggested by [13, 10, 11].

References

[1] R. Alur, C. Courcoubetis, N. Halbwachs, T.A. Henzinger, P.-H. Ho, X. Nicollin, A. Olivero, J. Sifakis, and S. Yovine. The algorithmic analysis of hybrid systems. *Theoretical Computer Science*, 138:3–34, 1995.

[2] R. Alur, T.A. Henzinger, G. Lafferriere, and G. Pappas. Discrete abstractions of hybrid systems. *Proceedings of the IEEE*, 88:971–984, July 2000.

[3] J-P. Aubin and H. Frankowska. *Set-Valued Analysis*. Birkhäuser, Boston, 1990.

[4] J. M. Davoren and T. Moor. Logic-based design and synthesis of controllers for hybrid systems. Technical report, RSISE, Australian National University, July 2000. Submitted for publication.

[5] J.M. Davoren and A. Nerode. Logics for hybrid systems. *Proceedings of the IEEE*, 88:985–1010, July 2000.

[6] B. A. Krogh J. E. R. Cury and T. Niinomi. Synthesis of supervisory controllers for hybrid systems based on approximating automata. *IEEE Transactions on Automatic Control, Special issue on hybrid systems*, 43:564–568, 1998.

[7] X. Koutsoukos, P. J. Antsaklis, J. A. Stiver, and M. D. Lemmon. Supervisory control of hybrid systems. *Proceedings of the IEEE*, 88:1026–1049, July 2000.

[8] K. Kuratowski. *Topology*, volume 1. Academic Press, New York, 1966.

[9] T. Moor and J. M. Davoren. Robust controller synthesis for hybrid systems using modal logic. In M. D. Di Benedetto and A. Sangiovanni-Vincentelli, editors, *Hybrid Systems: Computation and Control (HSCC'01)*, volume 2034 of *LNCS*, pages 433–446. Springer-Verlag, 2001.

[10] T. Moor and J. Raisch. Supervisory control of hybrid systems within a behavioural framework. *Systems and Control Letters*, 38:157–166, 1999.

[11] T. Moor, J. Raisch, and S. D. O'Young. Discrete supervisory control of hybrid systems based on l-complete approximations. in print, scheduled 2002.

[12] A. Nerode and W. Kohn. Models for hybrid systems: Automata, topologies, controllability, observability. In R. Grossman *et al.*, editor, *Hybrid Systems*, LNCS 736, pages 297–316. Springer-Verlag, 1993.

[13] J. Raisch and S. D. O'Young. Discrete approximation and supervisory control of continuous systems. *IEEE Transactions on Automatic Control, Special issue on hybrid systems*, 43:569–573, 1998.

[14] P. J. Ramadge and W. M. Wonham. Supervisory control of a class of discrete event systems. *SIAM J. Control and Optimization*, 25:206–230, 1987.

[15] P. J. Ramadge and W. M. Wonham. The control of discrete event systems. *Proceedings of the IEEE*, 77:81–98, 1989.

[16] J. A. Stiver, P. J. Antsaklis, and M. D. Lemmon. Interface and controller design for hybrid systems. In P.J. Antsaklis, W. Kohn, A. Nerode, and S. Sastry, editors, *Hybrid Systems II*, LNCS 999, pages 462–492. Springer-Verlag, 1995.

[17] J. C. Willems. Paradigms and puzzles in the theory of dynamic systems. *IEEE Transactions on Automatic Control*, 36:258–294, 1991.

Switching and Feedback Laws for Control of Constrained Switched Nonlinear Systems

Nael H. El-Farra and Panagiotis D. Christofides

Department of Chemical Engineering
University of California
Los Angeles, CA 90095-1592
farra@ucla.edu, pdc@seas.ucla.edu

Abstract. A hybrid nonlinear control strategy is developed for switched nonlinear systems whose constituent subsystems are subject to input constraints. The key feature of this strategy is the integrated synthesis, via multiple control Lyapunov functions, of "lower-level" bounded nonlinear feedback control laws together with "upper-level" switching laws that orchestrate the transitions between the constituent modes and their respective controllers. The control laws enforce asymptotic stability in the continuous modes and provide an explicit characterization of the stability region associated with each mode, in terms of the magnitude of the constraints. The switching scheme is then constructed to coordinate the switching between the stability regions of the different modes in a way that respects input constraints and guarantees stability of the overall switched closed-loop system.

1 Introduction

There are many examples in the chemical process industries where the dynamical properties of the process depend on a more or less intricate interaction between discrete and continuous variables. In many of these applications, the continuous behavior arises from the underlying fundamental physico-chemical phenomena and is conveniently described by continuous-time differential equations. However, discrete phenomena superimposed on the continuous dynamics often constitute an important part of the picture as well and make a significant contribution to the overall system response. Such phenomena may arise, for example, in the form of inherent discontinuities in the basically continuous dynamics as a consequence of the system moving through state space (e.g., phase changes, flow reversals). Alternatively, it may arise from instrumentation with discrete actuators and sensors (e.g., on/off valves, binary sensors, motors with constant speed), digital regulatory control, or in the form of logical functions for supervisory and safety control. It is well understood at this stage that the interaction of discrete events with even very simple continuous dynamical systems can lead to complex dynamics and, occasionally, to very undesirable outcomes.

Even though theory for the analysis and control of purely continuous-time systems exists and, to a large extent, is well-developed, similar techniques for

C.J. Tomlin and M.R. Greenstreet (Eds.): HSCC 2002, LNCS 2289, pp. 164–178, 2002.

combined discrete-continuous systems are limited at present primarily due to the difficulty of extending the available concepts and tools to treat the hybrid nature of these systems and their changing dynamics, which makes them more difficult to describe, analyze, or control. Motivated by these challenges as well as the abundance of situations where hybrid systems arise in practice, significant research efforts have focused on hybrid systems over the last decade, covering a broad spectrum of problems including, for example, modeling [1], simulation [1, 8], optimization [9], and control [15, 4, 2, 16].

A class of hybrid systems that has attracted significant attention recently, because it can model several practical control problems that involve integration of supervisory logic-based control schemes and feedback control algorithms, is the class of switched (or multi-modal) systems. For this class, results have been developed for stability analysis using the tools of multiple Lyapunov functions (MLFs), for linear [17] and nonlinear systems [18, 3, 22], and the concept of dwell time [10]; the reader may refer to [13, 5] for a survey of results in this area. These results have motivated the development of methods for control of various classes of switched systems (see, e.g., [21, 23, 11, 19]). Most of the available results in this direction, however, have focused on control of switched linear systems and have not dealt with the problems arising when the constituent subsystems are subject to hard input constraints. Significant research therefore remains to be done in the direction of nonlinear control of constrained switched systems, especially since the majority of practical switched systems exhibit inherently nonlinear dynamics and are subject to input constraints. Motivated by these considerations, we present in this work a nonlinear control strategy for a broad class of switched nonlinear systems with input constraints, that accounts for the interactions between the"lower-level" constrained continuous dynamics with the "upper-level" discrete or logical components. The key idea of this approach is the coupling between the switching logic and the stability regions arising from the limitations imposed by input constraints on the dynamics of the constituent modes of the switched system. The proposed approach involves the integrated synthesis, via multiple Lyapunov functions, of lower-level bounded nonlinear continuous control laws and upper-level switching laws that orchestrate the transitions between the constituent control modes to guarantee stability of the switched closed-loop system.

The manuscript is organized as follows: We initially cast switched nonlinear systems as variable structure or "multi-modal" systems in which each mode is governed by continuous dynamics, whereas the transitions between the modes are controlled by discrete events. Then, using multiple control Lyapunov functions, one for each continuous mode, we synthesize a family of bounded nonlinear controllers that enforce the desired stability and performance properties within each individual dynamical mode in the presence of input constraints. The controller synthesis procedure yields also an explicit characterization of the stability region associated with each mode. Finally, we derive a set of switching rules that orchestrate the transition between the constituent modes and their respective controllers, in a way that ensures asymptotic stability in the overall constrained switched closed-loop system.

2   Preliminaries

2.1   Class of Systems

We consider the class of switched nonlinear systems represented by the following state-space description:

$$\dot{x}(t) = f_{\sigma(t)}(x(t)) + G_{\sigma(t)}(x(t))u_{\sigma(t)}$$
$$\sigma(t) \in \mathcal{I} = \{1, \cdots, N\} \tag{1}$$

where $x(t) \in \mathbb{R}^n$ denotes the vector of continuous-time state variables, $u(t) = [u_1(t) \cdots u_m(t)]^T \in \mathcal{U} \subset \mathbb{R}^m$ denotes the vector of control inputs taking values in a nonempty compact convex subset of $\mathbb{R}^m$, $\sigma : [0, \infty) \rightarrow \mathcal{I}$ is the switching signal which is assumed to be a piecewise continuous (from the right) function of time, i.e. $\sigma(t_k) = \lim_{t \rightarrow t_k^+} \sigma(t)$ for all k, implying that only a finite number of switches is allowed on any finite interval of time. $\sigma(t)$, which takes values in the finite index set $\mathcal{I}$, represents a discrete state that indexes the vector field $f(\cdot)$, the matrix $G(\cdot)$, and the control input $u(\cdot)$, which altogether determine $\dot{x}$. For each value that σ assumes in $\mathcal{I}$, the temporal evolution of the continuous state, x, is governed by a different set of differential equations. Systems of the form of (1) are therefore referred to as multi-modal, or of variable structure. They consist of a finite family of N continuous-time nonlinear subsystems (or modes) and some rules for switching between them. These rules define a switching sequence that describes the temporal evolution of the discrete state. Throughout the paper, we use the notations t_{i_k} and t_{i_k+1} to denote, the k-th times that the i-th subsystem is switched in and out, respectively, i.e. $\sigma(t_{i_k}^+) = \sigma(t_{i_k+1}^-) = i$. With this notation, it is understood that the continuous state evolves according to $\dot{x} = f_i(x) + G_i(x)u_i$ for $t_{i_k} \leq t < t_{i_k+1}$. Note that for all $k \in Z_+$, $i_k = i$. We denote by $\mathcal{T}_{i,in}$ the set of switching times at which the i-th subsystem is switched in, i.e. $\mathcal{T}_{i,in} = \{t_{i_1}, t_{i_2}, \cdots\}$. Similarly, $\mathcal{T}_{i,out}$ denotes the set of switching times at which the i-th subsystem is switched out, i.e. $\mathcal{T}_{i,out} = \{t_{i_1+1}, t_{i_2+1}, \cdots\}$. Note that both of these sets maybe finite or infinite, depending on whether a finite or infinite number of switching is allowed over the infinite time interval.

It is assumed that all entries of the vector functions $f_i(x)$, and the $n \times m$ matrices $G_i(x)$, are sufficiently smooth on $\mathbb{R}^m$ and that $f_i(0) = 0$ for all $i \in \mathcal{I}$. We also assume that the state x does not jump at the switching instants, i.e. the solution $x(\cdot)$ is everywhere continuous.

Note that changes in the discrete state $\sigma(t)$ (i.e. transitions between the continuous dynamical modes) may, in general, be a function of time, state, or both. When changes in $\sigma(t)$ depend only on inherent process characteristics, the switching is referred to as autonomous. However, when $\sigma(t)$ is chosen by some higher process such as a controller or human operator, then the switching is controlled. In this paper, we focus exclusively on controlled switching where mode transitions are decided and executed by some higher-level supervisor. This class of systems arises naturally, for example, in the context of coordinated supervisory and feedback control of chemical process systems.

2.2 Stability Analysis of Switched Systems via Multiple Lyapunov Functions

One of the main tools for analyzing the stability of switched nonlinear systems is that of multiple Lyapunov functions (MLFs) (see, e.g., [3]). In many respects, MLF theory extends the classical Lyapunov analysis for continuous-time nonlinear systems to switched systems. This extension is quite natural given the view of switched systems as a finite collection of continuous-time nonlinear systems with discrete events that govern the transition between them. Unlike classical Lyapunov theory, however, MLF theory provides additional conditions that account for the changing dynamics of switched systems.

Preparatory for its use in control of switched systems, we will briefly review in this section the main idea of MLF analysis. To this end, consider the switched system of (1), with $u_i(t) \equiv 0$, $i = 1, \cdots, N$, and suppose that we can find a family of Lyapunov-like functions $\{V_i : i \in 1, \cdots, N\}$, each associated with the vector field $f_i(x)$. A Lyapunov-like function for the system $\dot{x} = f_i(x)$, with equilibrium point $0 \in \Omega_i \subset \mathbb{R}^n$, is a real-valued function $V_i(x)$, with continuous partial derivatives, defined over the region Ω_i, satisfying the conditions: 1) positive definiteness: $V_i(0) = 0$ and $V_i(x) > 0$ for $0 \neq x \in \Omega_i$, and 2) negative definite derivative: for $x \in \Omega_i$, $\dot{V}_i = \frac{\partial V_i(x)}{\partial x} f_i(x) \leq 0$. The following theorem provides sufficient conditions for stability.

Theorem 1 ([5], see also [3]). *Given the N-switched nonlinear system of (1), with $u_i(t) \equiv 0$, $i = 1, \cdots, N$, suppose that each vector field f_i has an associated Lyapunov-like function V_i in the region Ω_i, each with equilibrium point $x_{eq} = 0$, and suppose $\bigcup_i \Omega_i = \mathbb{R}^n$. Let $\sigma(t)$ be a given switching sequence such that $\sigma(t)$ can take on the value of i only if $x(t) \in \Omega_i$, and in addition*

$$V_i(x(t_{i_k})) \leq V_i(x(t_{i_{k-1}})) \tag{2}$$

where t_{i_k} denotes the k-th time that the vector field f_i is switched in, i.e., $\sigma(t_{i_k}^-) \neq \sigma(t_{i_k}^+) = i$. Then, the system of (1), with $u_i(t) \equiv 0$, $i = 1, \cdots, N$, is Lyapunov stable.

Remark 1. Note, from the definition of a Lyapunov-like function, that V_i is monotonically non-increasing on every time interval where the i-th subsystem is active and that the set Ω_i represents the part of the state space where $\dot{V}_i \leq 0$. The idea of Theorem 1 above is that even if there exists such a Lyapunov function for each subsystem f_i individually (i.e. each mode is stable), restrictions must be placed on the switching scheme to guarantee stability of the overall switched system. In fact, it is easy to construct examples of globally asymptotically stable systems and a switching rule that sends all trajectories to infinity (see [3] for some classical examples). A sufficient condition to guarantee stability is to require, as in (2), that for every mode i, the value of V_i at the beginning of each interval on which the i-th subsystem is active exceed the value at the beginning of the next interval on which the i-th subsystem is active (see Fig.1). Some variations and generalizations of this result are discussed in [22, 18].

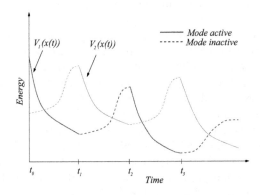

Fig. 1. Stability analysis using multiple Lyapunov functions.

Remark 2. When the condition of (2) is modified to the following:

$$V_i(x(t_{i_k+1})) < V_i(x(t_{i_{k-1}+1})) \qquad (3)$$

the Lyapunov functions, V_i are said to satisfy the sequence non-increasing condition. This is a stronger notion than the Lyapunov-like condition of Theorem 1 and is used to prove asymptotic stability (see, e.g., [17, 4, 13]).

3   Nonlinear Control of Switched Systems

Having reviewed, in the previous section, how multiple Lyapunov functions can be used to analyze the stability of switched nonlinear systems without control inputs (or systems for which a controller has already been designed), we proceed in this section to use the MLF framework as a tool for control of switched nonlinear systems with input constraints. For purely continuous-time systems, the idea of using a candidate Lyapunov function for designing feedback has been used extensively, though made explicit only relatively recently with the introduction of the concept of a control Lyapunov function:

Definition 1 ([20]). *A control Lyapunov function (CLF) for a nonlinear control system of the form $\dot{x} = f(x) + G(x)u$ is a smooth, proper, and positive* *definite function $V : \mathbb{R}^n \to \mathbb{R}$ with the property that for every fixed $x \neq 0$, there exists admissible values $u_1 \cdots u_m$ for the controls such that:*

$$\inf_{u \in \mathcal{U}} \{L_f V + L_{g_1} V u_1 + \cdots + L_{g_m} V u_m\} < 0 \qquad (4)$$

where $L_f V = \frac{\partial V}{\partial x} f(x)$, g_i is the i-th column of the matrix G.

The importance of the CLF concept is that, when a CLF is known, a stabilizing control law can be selected from a choice of explicit expressions such as those in (e.g., [14]). In the context of control of switched systems, a generalization of this concept, similar to the MLF idea, is that of multiple control Lyapunov functions (MCLFs). The idea is to use a family of control Lyapunov functions, one for each subsystem, to: a) design a family of nonlinear feedback controllers that stabilize the individual subsystems, and b) design a set of stabilizing switching laws that orchestrate the transition between the constituent modes and their respective controllers. In many ways, the relationship between the concepts of CLF and MCLFs parallels that between classical Lyapunov functions and MLFs.

3.1   Problem Formulation

Consider the switched nonlinear system of (1) where each vector of control inputs, u_i, is constrained in the interval $[-u_{max}, u_{max}]$ for $i = 1, \cdots, N$ (i.e., $|u_i| \leq u_{max}$). Given that switching is controlled by some higher-level supervisor, the problem we focus on is how to orchestrate switching between the various subsystems in a way that respects the constraints and guarantees closed-loop stability. To this end, we formulate the following control objectives. The first is to synthesize a family of N bounded nonlinear feedback control laws of the form

$$u_i = -k_i(V_i, u_{max})(L_{G_i} V_i)^T, i = 1, \cdots, N \qquad (5)$$

that: 1) enforce asymptotic stability, for the individual closed-loop subsystems, and 2) provide, for each mode, an explicit characterization of the set of admissible initial conditions starting from where this mode is guaranteed to be stable in the presence of constraints. Referring to the $L_G V$ controller of (5), we note that $k_i(V_i, u_{max})$ is a scalar nonlinear gain function that depends on the Lyapunov function V_i and the constraints u_{max}, and is to be designed so that $|u_i| \leq u_{max}$. $(L_{G_i} V_i)^T$ is a row vector of the form $[L_{g_{i,1}} V_i \cdots L_{g_{i,m}} V_i]$. For simplicity, we consider only the case of state feedback in this paper. The case of output feedback can be treated using the controller-observer combination approach proposed in [7]. The second objective is to identify explicitly a set of switching laws to orchestrate the transition between the constituent modes and their respective controllers in a way that respects input constraints and guarantees asymptotic stability of the constrained switched closed-loop system. These switching laws essentially provide the supervisor with the set of switching times for which activating a given mode is deemed safe, which in turn determines the time-course of the discrete state $\sigma(t)$. In order to proceed with the design of the controllers, we need to impose the following assumption on the system of (1).

Assumption 1. *For every $i \in \mathcal{I}$, a CLF, V_i, exists for the system $\dot{x} = f_i(x) + G_i(x)u_i$.*

3.2   Switching and Feedback Laws

This section contains the main result of this paper. Theorem 2 below provides a formula for the bounded nonlinear feedback controllers used to stabilize the constituent subsystems and states precise switching conditions that guarantee the desired properties in the constrained switched closed-loop system. The proof of this Theorem is given in the appendix.

Theorem 2. *Consider the switched nonlinear system of (1), for which assumption 1 holds, under the following family of bounded nonlinear feedback controllers:*

$$u_i = -k_i(V_i, u_{max})(L_{G_i}V_i)^T, \; i = 1, \cdots, N \tag{6}$$

where

$$k_i(\cdot, \cdot) = \begin{cases} \dfrac{L_{f_i}V_i + \sqrt{(L_{f_i}V_i)^2 + (u_{max}|(L_{G_i}V_i)^T|)^4}}{(|(L_{G_i}V_i)^T|)^2[1 + \sqrt{1 + (u_{max}|(L_{G_i}V_i)^T|)^2}]} & , |(L_{G_i}V_i)^T| \neq 0 \\[4mm] 0 & , |(L_{G_i}V_i)^T| = 0 \end{cases} \tag{7}$$

Let $\Phi_i(u_{max})$ be the largest set of x, containing the origin, such that $\forall \, 0 \neq x \in \Phi_i(u_{max})$:

$$L_{f_i}V_i < u_{max}|(L_{G_i}V_i)^T| \tag{8}$$

Also, let $\Omega_i^*(u_{max})$ be the largest invariant subset of $\Phi_i(u_{max})$ and assume, without loss of generality, that $x(0) \in \Omega_i^*(u_{max})$ for some $i \in \mathcal{I}$. If, at any given time T, the following conditions hold:

$$x(T) \in \Omega_j^*(u_{max}) \tag{9}$$

$$V_j(x(T)) < V_j(x(t_{j_*+1})) \tag{10}$$

for some $j \in \mathcal{I}$, $j \neq i$, where t_{j_*+1} is the time when the j-th subsystem was last switched out, i.e. $\sigma(t_{j_*+1}^+) \neq \sigma(t_{j_*+1}^-) = j$, then setting $\sigma(T^+) = j$ guarantees that the switched closed-loop system is asymptotically stable in the presence of constraints.

Remark 3. Theorem 2 proposes a hierarchical approach for control of nonlinear switched systems with input constraints. The key aspect of this approach is the integrated synthesis, via multiple control Lyapunov functions, of "lower-level" continuous controllers that stabilize the constituent subsystems and "upper-level" switching laws that coordinate the transitions between these subsystems and their respective controllers in a way that respects the constraints and guarantees stability of the constrained switched closed-loop system. Figure 2 shows a pictorial representation of the proposed integrated synthesis of switching laws and feedback controllers. Regarding the practical applications of this theorem, one must initially identify all the modes of the switched system. A control Lyapunov function is then constructed for each mode and used to: a) synthesize, via (6), the stabilizing bounded nonlinear controller for that mode, and b) construct, with the aid of (8), the associated stability region for that mode. Once these tasks are completed, one proceeds with the implementation of the switching strategy. This is done by initializing the closed-loop system within the stability region of the desired initial mode of operation and implementing the corresponding controller. Then, the switching laws of (9)-(10) are checked on line, to determine if it's possible to switch to a particular mode at a particular time. If the conditions are satisfied, then we can safely switch to the target mode and its controller. If the conditions are not satisfied, however, then the current mode is kept active until any future time that the target mode becomes feasible.

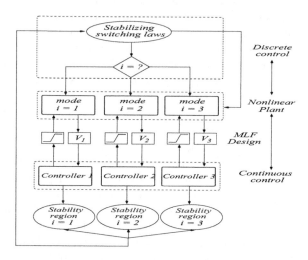

Fig. 2. Proposed control strategy for switched nonlinear systems of the form of (1).

Remark 4. Referring to the family of N nonlinear feedback controllers given in (6)-(7), we note that they are synthesized, via multiple control Lyapunov functions, by reshaping the nonlinear gain of the bounded $L_G V$ controller proposed in [14], in order to accommodate arbitrary input constraints. With $u_{max} = 1$, the controller of (6) reduces to that given in [14]. Each of these controllers is continuous at the origin provided that the corresponding CLF satisfies the small control property (see [14] for details).

Remark 5. The use of bounded nonlinear controllers of the form of (6) to stabilize the constituent modes is motivated by the fact that this class of controllers account explicitly for the problem of input constraints. Specifically, each of these controllers provides an explicit characterization of the region of admissible initial conditions starting from where closed-loop stability of the corresponding subsystem is guaranteed with the available control action (stability region). This characterization can be obtained from the set of inequalities given in (8). For each subsystem, the corresponding inequality describes an open and unbounded region in the state space, $\Phi_i(u_{max})$, where the corresponding control law satisfies the constraints and the associated Lyapunov function, V_i, decreases monotonically. It is important to note that even though a trajectory starting in $\Phi_i(u_{max})$ will move from one Lyapunov surface to an inner Lyapunov surface with lower energy (because $\dot{V}_i < 0$), there is no guarantee that the trajectory will remain forever in $\Phi_i(u_{max})$ since it is not necessarily a region of invariance. Once the trajectory leaves $\Phi_i(u_{max})$, however, there is no guarantee that $\dot{V}_i < 0$. Therefore, to guarantee that $\dot{V}_i$ remains negative for all times during which the i-th mode is active, we confine the initial conditions to the largest invariant set $\Omega_i^*(u_{max})$ within $\Phi_i(u_{max})$. This set, which is also parameterized by the constraints, represents an estimate of the stability region associated with each mode. This idea of constructing a region of invariance within the region described by the inequality of (8), in order to guarantee closed-loop stability, was first introduced in [6] where it was used in the context of robustly stabilizing continuous-time uncertain nonlinear systems via bounded control (see [12] for details on how to construct these invariant sets).

Remark 6. The two switching rules of (9)-(10) determine, implicitly, the times when switching from mode i to mode j is permissible. The first rule tracks the temporal evolution of the continuous state, x, and requires that, at the desired time for switching, the continuous state reside within the stability region associated with the subsystem that is to be activated (see Fig.3 for a schematic representation of the proposed switching strategy). This ensures that, once this subsystem is activated, its Lyapunov function continues to decay for as long as that mode remains active. Note that this condition applies at every time that the supervisor considers switching from one mode to another. In contrast, the second switching rule of (10) applies only when the target mode j (considered for possible activation) has been previously activated. In this case, (10) requires that the gain in V_j from the last "switch out" to the current "switch in" be less than unity. Note that if each of the N modes is activated only once during the course of operation (i.e. we never switch back to a mode that was activated previously), the second condition is automatically satisfied. Furthermore, for the case when only a finite number of switches (over the infinite time interval) is considered, this condition can be relaxed by allowing switching to take place even when the value V_j at the desired switching time is larger than its value when mode j was last switched in, as long as the increase is finite. The rationale for this owes to the fact that these finite increases in V_j (resulting from switching back to mode j) will be overcome when the system eventually settles in the "final" mode whose controller forces its Lyapunov function to continue to decay as time tends to infinity, thus asymptotically stabilizing the overall system.

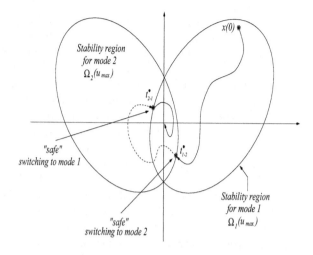

Fig. 3. Proposed switching strategy.

Remark 7. Note that the switching rule of (10) is different from that of (3). In the latter, the gain in V_j from last "switch out" to current "switch in" is allowed to exceed unity provided that the value of V_j at the end of each interval on which the j-th subsystem is active exceeds the value at the end of the next such interval. The condition of (3), though less restrictive than that of (10), is not suited for deciding whether switching to mode j at some time T is permissible, because it requires a priori knowledge of how x evolves in time, or at least what value x will take when mode j is to be disengaged in the future. Equation (10), in contrast, depends only on the current (and past) switching times for the target mode. Nonetheless, it is possible to replace the condition of (10) by that of (3) provided that every time that we switch back to mode j (whenever rule 1 is satisfied), the mode (and its controller) is allowed by the supervisor to remain active for a sufficiently long time interval such that at the end of that interval, (3) holds.

Remark 8. Referring to the definitions of the sets Ω_i (given in Theorem 1) and Φ_i (given in Theorem 2), the following parallels and differences are to be noted. For a given mode, both sets describe regions in the state space where $\dot{V}_i < 0$. However, in the case of Φ_i, it is the use of feedback control that makes $\dot{V}_i$ negative since the unforced dynamics of each mode are allowed to be unstable. Note also that in the case of Ω_i's, the union of these sets covers the entire state space. Therefore, the system trajectory is guaranteed to belong to some Ω_i at any time instance. In this case, the autonomous switching sequence (which is assumed to be fixed a priori) partitions the state space into a number of neighboring regions where each mode dwells. In contrast, the sets $\Phi_i \subset \mathbb{R}^n$ arise due to the limitations that input constraints impose on the feasible initial conditions starting from where each mode is stabilizable with the available control action. In the absence of constraints, each of the Φ_i's is allowed to cover all of $\mathbb{R}^n$. The state space therefore is not partitioned into neighboring regions where each mode is confined; rather, the regions described by Φ_i's can be overlapping implying that a given mode is allowed to remain active even if x crosses into the stability region of another mode. The union of Φ_i's therefore does not necessarily span all of $\mathbb{R}^n$, thus leaving parts of the state space, starting from where none of the constituent modes is stabilizable with the given constraints. Since neither Ω_i nor Φ_i is necessarily a region of invariance, it is possible for trajectories starting within these regions to leave the region at some point. However when this happens in the case of Theorem 1, the trajectory simply enters another Ω_i whose associated mode becomes (autonomously) active, thus preserving stability. In the case of Theorem 2, on the other hand, the trajectory can possibly enter the uncontrollable part (outside of all the Φ_i's). Furthermore, since the switching sequence in Theorem 2 is assumed to be controlled (and not autonomous) by some supervisor in order to achieve some higher objective, there is no guarantee, even if the trajectory simply crosses into another Φ_i, that this will occur at the time deemed, by the supervisor, as appropriate for switching. These considerations together motivate working with the invariant sets, Ω_i^*'s, when implementing the switching laws.

Remark 9. It is important to note that the switching scheme proposed in Theorem 2 is only sufficient to guarantee closed-loop stability. If the conditions in (9)-(10) are satisfied at a given time instance, then we conclude that it is "safe" to switch from the current mode/controller combination to the one for which the conditions hold. However, it is not necessary to switch at that time to maintain closed-loop stability. The reason for this is the fact that the initial condition belongs to the closed-loop stability region of at least one of the modes. So, even if switching doesn't take place, the trajectory of the system will remain in this set and stabilize at the desired equilibrium point. However, in many practical situations, changes in operational conditions and requirements motivate the need to switch between the various dynamical modes.

Remark 10. Note that it is possible for more than one subsystem (j) to satisfy the switching rules given in (9)-(10). This can happen when x lies within the intersection of several stability regions (the Ω_i^*'s). In this case, Theorem 2 guarantees only that a switch from the current mode to any of these modes is safe but does not decide which one to pick since they all guarantee stability. The decision to pick a particular mode to switch to is made by the supervisor based on the particular operational requirements of the process.

4   Acknowledgment

Financial support, in part by UCLA through Chancellor's Fellowship for N. H. El-Farra, NSF, CTS-0129571, and AFOSR, is gratefully acknowledged.

References

[1] P. I. Barton and C. C. Pantelides. Modeling of combined discrete/continuous processes. *AIChE Journal*, 40:966–979, 1994.

[2] A. Bemporad and M. Morari. Control of systems integrating logic, dynamics and constraints. *Automatica*, 35:407–427, 1999.

[3] M. S. Branicky. Multiple Lyapunov functions and other analysis tools for switched and hybrid systems. *IEEE Trans. Automat. Contr.*, 43:475–482, 1998.

[4] M. S. Branicky, V. S. Borkar, and S. K. Mitter. A unified framework for hybrid control: model and optimal control theory. *IEEE Trans. Automat. Control.*, 43:31–45, 1998.

[5] R. A. Decarlo, M. S. Branicky, S. Petterson, and B. Lennartson. Perspectives and results on the stability and stabilizability of hybrid systems. *Proceedings of the IEEE*, 88:1069–1082, 2000.

[6] N. H. El-Farra and P. D. Christofides. Integrating robustness, optimality, and constraints in control of nonlinear processes. *Chem. Eng. Sci.*, 56:1841–1868, 2001.

[7] N. H. El-Farra and P. D. Christofides. Robust near-optimal output feedback control of nonlinear systems. *Int. J. Contr.*, 74:133–157, 2001.

[8] R. L. Grossman, A. Nerode, A. P. Ravn, and H. Rischel. *Hybrid systems*, volume 736 of *Lecture Notes in Computer Science*. Springer-Verlag, New York, 1993.

[9] I. E. Grossmann, S. A. van den Heever, and I. Harjukoski. Discrete optimization methods and their role in the integration of planning and scheduling. In *Proceedings of 6th International Conference on Chemical Process Control*, pages 124–152, Tucson, AZ, 2001.

[10] J. P. Hespanha and A. S. Morse. Stability of switched systems with average dwell time. In *Proceedings of 38th IEEE Conference on Decision and Control*, pages 2655–2660, Phoenix, AZ, 1999.

[11] B. Hu, X. Xu, P. J. Antsaklis, and A. N. Michel. Robust stabilizing control law for a class of second-order switched systems. *Syst. Contr. Lett.*, 38:197–207, 1999.

[12] H. K. Khalil. *Nonlinear Systems*. Macmillan Publishing Company, New York, second edition, 1996.

[13] D. Liberzon and A. S. Morse. Basic problems in stability and design of switched systems. *IEEE Control Systems Magazine*, 19:59–70, 1999.

[14] Y. Lin and E. D. Sontag. A universal formula for stabilization with bounded controls. *Systems & Control Letters*, 16:393–397, 1991.

[15] J. Lygeros, D. N. Godbole, and S. S. Sastry. A game theoretic approach to hybrid system design. In *Lecture Notes in Computer Science*, volume 1066, pages 1–12, Alur, R. and T. Henzinger Eds., Berlin: Springer, 1996.

[16] D. Mignone, A. Bemporad, and M. Morari. A framework for control, fault detection, state estimation, and verification of hybrid systems. In *Proceedings of American Control Conference*, pages 134–139, San Diego, CA, 1999.

[17] P. Peleties and R. DeCarlo. Asymptotic stability of m-switched systems using lyapunov-like functions. In *Proceedings of American Control Conference*, pages 1679–1684, Boston, MA, 1991.

[18] S. Pettersson and B. Lennartson. Stability and robustness for hybrid systems. In *Proceedings of 35th IEEE Conference on Decision and Control*, pages 1202–1207, Kobe, Japan, 1996.

[19] A. V. Savkin, E. Skafidas, and R. J. Evans. Robust output feedback stabilizability via controller switching. *Automatica*, 35:69–74, 1999.

[20] E. D. Sontag. A lyapunov-like characterization of asymptotic controllability. *SIAM J. Contr. & Opt.*, 21:462–471, 1983.

[21] M. A. Wicks, P. Peleties, and R. A. DeCarlo. Switched controller synthesis for the quadratic stabilization of a pair of unstable linear systems. *European J. Contr.*, 4:140–147, 1998.

[22] H. Ye, A. N. Michel, and L. Hou. Stability theory for hybrid dynamical systems. *IEEE Trans. Automat. Contr.*, 43:461–474, 1998.

[23] M. Zefran and J. W. Burdick. Design of switching controllers for systems with changing dynamics. In *Proceedings of 37th IEEE Conference on Decision and Control*, pages 2113–2118, Tampa, FL, 1998.

5   Appendix

Proof (of Theorem 2). To prove this theorem , we proceed in two steps. In the first step we show, for each individual mode (without switching), that, starting from any initial condition within the set Ω_i^*, the corresponding feedback control law asymptotically stabilizes the closed-loop subsystem. In the second step, we use this fact together with the MLF stability result of Theorem 1 to show that the switching laws of (9)-(10) enforce asymptotic stability in the switched closed-loop system, starting from any initial condition that belongs to any of the sets Ω_i^*.

Step 1: Consider the i-th subsystem of the switched nonlinear system of (1) for which assumption 1 holds. Substituting the control law of (6), evaluating the time-derivative of the Lyapunov function along the closed-loop trajectories, and using the fact that $|(L_{G_i} V_i)^T|^2 = (L_{G_i} V_i)(L_{G_i} V_i)^T$, we obtain

$$\dot{V}_i = L_{f_i} V_i + L_{G_i} V_i u_i$$

$$= L_{f_i} V_i - L_{G_i} V_i \left(\frac{L_{f_i} V_i + \sqrt{(L_{f_i} V_i)^2 + (u_{max}|(L_{G_i} V_i)^T|)^4}}{|(L_{G_i} V_i)^T|^2 \left[1 + \sqrt{1 + (u_{max}|(L_{G_i} V_i)^T|)^2}\right]} \right) (L_{G_i} V_i)^T$$

$$= \frac{L_{f_i} V_i \sqrt{1 + (u_{max}|(L_{G_i} V_i)^T|)^2} - \sqrt{(L_{f_i} V_i)^2 + (u_{max}|(L_{G_i} V_i)^T|)^4}}{\left[1 + \sqrt{1 + (u_{max}|(L_{G_i} V_i)^T|)^2}\right]}$$

$$\tag{11}$$

It is clear from the last equality that when $L_{f_i} V_i < 0$, we have $\dot{V}_i < 0$. Furthermore, when $0 < L_{f_i} V_i < u_{max}|(L_{G_i} V_i)^T|$, we have $(L_{f_i} V_i)^2 < (u_{max}|(L_{G_i} V_i)^T|)^2$ and therefore

$$-\sqrt{(L_{f_i} V_i)^2 + (u_{max}|(L_{G_i} V_i)^T|)^4} < -L_{f_i} V_i \sqrt{1 + (u_{max}|(L_{G_i} V_i)^T|)^2} \tag{12}$$

Substituting the above estimate into the expression for $\dot{V}_i$ in (11), we have that $\dot{V}_i < 0$. To summarize, we see that whenever $L_{f_i} V_i < u_{max}|(L_{G_i} V_i)^T|$, we have

$\dot{V}_i < 0$. Since Ω_i^* is the largest invariant set where this inequality holds, then starting from any initial state $x(0) \in \Omega_i^*$, we have that

$$\dot{V}_i < 0 \ \forall \ x \neq 0, \ \ i = 1, \cdots, N \tag{13}$$

which implies that the closed-loop subsystems are asymptotically stable.

Step 2: Consider now the switched closed-loop system and, without loss of generality, suppose that $x(0) \in \Omega_i^*$ for some $i \in \mathcal{I}$. Then it follows from (13) above and the invariance of Ω_i^* that the Lyapunov function for this mode, V_i, decays monotonically, along the trajectories of the closed-loop system, for as long as mode i is to remain active, i.e. for all times such that $\sigma(t) = i$. If at any time T, such that $x(T) \in \Omega_j^*$ for some $j \in \mathcal{I}$, $j \neq i$, we set $\sigma(T^+) = j$ (i.e. activate mode j and its respective controller), then using the same argument, it is clear that the corresponding Lyapunov function for this mode, V_j, will also decay monotonically for as long as we keep $\sigma(t) = j$. Note that T, which is the time that mode i is switched out, is not known a priori but is rather determined by the evolution of the closed-loop continuous state. By tracking the closed-loop trajectory in this manner, we conclude that, starting from any $x(0) \in \Omega_i^*$ for any $i \in \mathcal{I}$ and as long as the i-th mode (and its controller) is activated only at a time when $x(t) \in \Omega_i^*$, we have that for all $i_k \in \mathcal{I}$, $k \in Z_+$

$$\dot{V}_{\sigma(t_{i_k})} < 0 \ \ \forall \ t \in [t_{i_k}, t_{i_k+1}) \tag{14}$$

where t_{i_k} and t_{i_k+1} refer, respectively, to the times that the i-th mode is switched in and out for the k-th time, by the supervisor. Furthermore, from (10), we have that for any admissible switching time t_{i_k}

$$V_i(x(t_{i_k})) < V_i(x(t_{i_{k-1}+1})) \tag{15}$$

which consequently implies that

$$V_i(x(t_{i_k})) < V_i(x(t_{i_{k-1}})) \tag{16}$$

since $V_i(x(t_{i_{k-1}+1})) < V_i(x(t_{i_{k-1}}))$ from (14). Using (14)-(16), a direct application of the MLF result of Theorem 2.3 in [3] can be performed to conclude that the switched closed-loop system, under the switching laws of Theorem 2, is Lyapunov stable. To prove asymptotic stability, we note from the strict inequality in (16) that for every (infinite) sequence of switching times $t_{i_1}, t_{i_2}, \cdots$ such that $\sigma(t_{i_k}^+) = i$, the sequence $V_{\sigma(t_{i_1})}, V_{\sigma(t_{i_2})}, \cdots$ is decreasing and positive, and therefore has a limit $L \geq 0$. We have

$$0 = L - L = \lim_{k \to \infty} V_{\sigma(t_{i_{k+1}}^+)}(x(t_{i_{k+1}+1})) - \lim_{k \to \infty} V_{\sigma(t_{i_k}^+)}(x(t_{i_k+1}))$$

$$= \lim_{k \to \infty} \left[V_i(x(t_{i_{k+1}+1})) - V_i(x(t_{i_k+1})) \right] \tag{17}$$

Note that the term in brackets in the above equation is strictly negative for all nonzero x and zero only when $x = 0$. Therefore, there exists a function α of class $\mathcal{K}$ (i.e. continuous, increasing, and zero at zero) such that

$$\left[V_i(x(t_{i_{k+1}+1})) - V_i(x(t_{i_k+1})) \right] \leq -\alpha(|x(t_{i_k+1})|) \tag{18}$$

Substituting the above estimate into (17), we have

$$0 = \lim_{k \to \infty} \left[V_i(x(t_{i_{k+1}+1})) - V_i(x(t_{i_k+1})) \right]$$
$$\leq \lim_{k \to \infty} \left[-\alpha(|x(t_{i_k+1})|) \right] \leq 0$$

$$(19)$$

which implies that $x(t)$ converges to the origin, which together with Lyapunov stability, implies that the switched closed-loop system is asymptotically stable.

Quantized Stabilization of Two-Input Linear Systems: A Lower Bound on the Minimal Quantization Density*

Nicola Elia[1] and Emilio Frazzoli[2]

[1] Dept. of Electrical and Computer Engineering, Iowa Sate University
nelia@iastate.edu
[2] Dept. of Aeronautical and Astronautical Engineering,
University of Illinois at Urbana-Champaign
frazzoli@uiuc.edu

Abstract. In this paper we derive a lower bound on the density of the coarsest quantizer that quadratically stabilizes a two-input linear discrete time system. This result describes how much improvement could be expected in terms of reduced quantization density by using two inputs instead of one to quadratically stabilize the system. A by-product result is that the optimal quantizer is radially logarithmic. This is a generalization of the logarithmic quantizer obtained in previous work.

1 Introduction

Understanding what is the minimal information to achieve a given goal is a central problem in several disciplines dealing with complex systems. Examples include control over communication networks, active vision, autonomous vehicles, and more generally, the design of hybrid systems. In these situations it is necessary to quantize the system's input and output as coarsely as possible in order to reduce complexity while maintaining an acceptable performance level.

The basic problem we address in this paper is that of finding the coarsest quantizer that quadratically stabilizes a two input system. This paper contains preliminary results that extend those of [1] valid for single input systems. The problem of stabilization with quantized feedback, and its variations, have been studied by several researchers in the recent past. The approach of [1] has been extended in [3] to continuous time systems with the introduction of a dwell-time constraint, and in [2] to include bounded energy gain performance. In [4] several quantized stabilization strategies were analyzed and compared for singe-input single-state systems. In [5] a scheme based on a time varying quantizer was shown to stabilize the system. [7,8] focused on the symbolic dynamical aspects of system with quantized state-space. On the related problem of feedback stabilization over communication channels, [6] has provided the bit rate needed to stabilize a linear

---

* This research has been supported by NSF under the Career Award grant number ECS-0093950

C.J. Tomlin and M.R. Greenstreet (Eds.): HSCC 2002, LNCS 2289, pp. 179–193, 2002.

discrete-time system. This result has been later extended in [9] to include noisy channel effects. See also [11,10,12] for related work.

The paper is organized as follows. In Section 2, we define the problem, provide definitions of density of quantization and covering, and introduce a natural classification of the Control Lyapunov Functions for a multi-input system. For a p-input system, there are at most p types of CLFs. In Section 3, we describe the main result of the paper which is developed in the subsequent sections. In Section 4 and 5 we search for the coarsest quantizer over the Type_1, and Type_2 class respectively. In Section 4, we show that no improvement can be achieved on the existing single input result. In Section 5, we first derive a one-parameter parameterization of the Type_2 CLFs for a given system (two parameter if we search over all systems). We then develop a lower bound on the density of the coarsest quantizer over all type_2 CLFs. Finally, in Section 6, we present the conclusions.

2 Preliminaries

Consider the linear discrete time system governed by the following equation:

$$x^+ = Ax + Bu \tag{1}$$

where $x \in \mathbb{R}^n \triangleq X$, x^+ denotes the system state at the next discrete-time, $A \in \mathbb{R}^{n \times n}$, and $B \in \mathbb{R}^{n \times p}$ with full column rank. The system is assumed unstable, but stabilizable. For simplicity, and without loss of generality, we further assume that the system is completely unstable, i.e., all the eigenvalues of A are strictly greater than 1. We use the notation $\lambda_i^u(A)$ to denotes one of the unstable eigenvalue of A.

In this paper we will restrict our attention to the two-input case, $p = 2$.

Since the system is stabilizable and linear, it is quadratically stabilizable, i.e., there is a control input u, function of x, that makes a quadratic function of the state a Lyapunov function for the closed loop system. Such Lyapunov functions are called Control Lyapunov Functions (CLF). For LTI systems, given a CLF, it is always possible to find a stabilizing control in the form of a linear static state-feedback control.

Given a quadratic CLF $V(x) = x'Px$ with $P > 0$ (P is always assumed to be symmetric in this paper) we follow [1], and select a set of fixed control values such that $V(x)$ is still a Lyapunov function for the system, i.e., it decreases along the system's trajectories. In particular, we ask that for any $x \neq 0$

$$\Delta V(x) \triangleq V(x^+) - V(x) < 0.$$

More precisely, we want to solve the following problem

Problem 1. For a given CLF $V(x) = x'Px$, $P > 0$, we want to find a set

$$\mathcal{U} = \{u_i \in \mathbb{R}^2 : i \in Z\}$$

and a function $f : X \to \mathcal{U}$, such that for any $x \in X$, $x \neq 0$

$$\Delta V(x) = V(Ax + Bf(x)) - V(x) < 0$$

We call f the quantizer. f induces a partition in the state-space of the system, where equivalence classes of states are given by $\Omega_i = \{x \in X \mid f(x) = u_i\}$.

2.1   Quantization and Covering Density

We next define the notion of quantization density for a quantizer g. It is convenient to use polar coordinates. The following definition is the natural extension of the one-dimensional case of [1].

Definition 1. *Given $V(x) = x'Px$, $P > 0$, a CLF for System (1), let $\mathcal{Q}(V)$ denote the set of all quantizers that solve Problem 1. For $g \in \mathcal{Q}(V)$ and $0 < \epsilon \leq 1$, denote $\#g[\epsilon]$ as the number of elements (of $\mathcal{U}$) in an annular region $R(\epsilon)$ centered at the origin bounded by the radii ϵ, and $\frac{1}{\epsilon}$,*

$$R_\epsilon = \left\{ (r, \theta) \mid r \in \left[\epsilon, \frac{1}{\epsilon} \right], \, \theta \in [0, 2\pi) \right\}.$$

Define $\eta_g = \limsup\limits_{\epsilon \to 0} \dfrac{\#g[\epsilon]}{\ln \frac{1}{\epsilon}}$; η_g is called the quantization density (of g).

A quantizer f is said to be coarsest *for $V(x)$ if it has the smallest density of quantization, i.e.,*

$$f = \arg \inf_{g \in \mathcal{Q}(V)} \eta_g$$

It is worth pointing out that the above definition allows us to measure quantizers for which the number of quantization values, although infinite, grows logarithmically in radial direction, rather than linearly. Under this measure, the density of any radially uniform quantizer is infinity, and the density of any radially finite quantizer is zero.

Note also that the density is unbounded if in any annulus the number of levels is infinite. This prevents cartesian logarithmic quantizers to have bounded density. A cartesian logarithmic quantizer has levels given by the cartesian product of the levels of two independent logarithmic quantizers, one for each input channel. Thus, the quantization levels accumulate on both axes. The implication of the definition of density we adopt, is that we are looking for quantizers that are more efficient than any cartesian logarithmic quantizer. This is in line with quantization results in information theory [13].

A quantizer which is *coarsest* for $V(x)$ need not be unique, since different sets $\mathcal{U}$ may satisfy the asymptotic property, and for the same $\mathcal{U}$, there may be different ways to define the function f mapping X into $\mathcal{U}$. Moreover, a quantizer which is *coarsest* for $V(x)$ may not be an element of $\mathcal{Q}(V)$. At any rate, since the quantizer induces a partition on X, the density of quantization induces a measure of coarseness on the partitions in the state-space X.

Definition 2. *The density of the coarsest quantizer over all $V \in \mathcal{CLF}$ is defined as*

$$\eta^* = \inf_{V \in \mathcal{CLF}} \inf_{g \in \mathcal{Q}(V)} \eta_g$$

In [1], it was shown that $\eta^* = \dfrac{4}{\ln\left(\dfrac{\prod |\lambda_i^u(A)| + 1}{\prod |\lambda_i^u(A)| - 1}\right)}$ for single input systems.

As in [1], the main idea in the derivation of $\mathcal{U}$ and f is to consider the CLF as a robust Lyapunov function where, for a given fixed control value, we are interested in finding the set of all states (uncertainty set) for which $\Delta V(x)$ is negative. Thus, any set of the partition associated with a fixed control value u_0, must be a subset of the uncertainty set associated to u_0.

We will see next that the uncertainty sets for a given CLF are ellipsoids. Even though, in some cases the ellipsoids degenerate into infinite strips (at least for some of the coordinates), we usually face the fact that the ellipsoids need to overlap on non-empty (relative-)interior sets in order to guarantee that the quantizer makes the Lyapunov function decreasing for any non-zero state. Thus, associated to any quantizer there is a covering of X which includes the partition of X induced by the quantizer f. The density of a covering is defined similarly to Definition 1, with the number of levels replaced by the number of uncertainty sets.

2.2 Classification of CLFs

In this section, we provide a simple classification of all the (quadratic) CLFs for system (1).

Definition 3. *A CLF for system (1) is said to be a CLF of $Type_J$ if the number of strictly positive eigenvalues of $A'PA - P$ equals J.*

With a slight abuse of notation we denote by $Type_J$ the set of all CLF of $Type_J$.

It follows that any CLF for system (1) can belong to only one of possible p-Types, where p is the total number of inputs.

Lemma 1. *The set of all (quadratic) CLFs for system (1) denoted by $\mathcal{CLF}$ is given by*

$$\mathcal{CLF} = \biguplus_{J=1}^{p} Type_J$$

where $\biguplus$ means disjoint union.

Proof. V being a CLF means that for any x we can find $u \in \mathbb{R}^p$ that makes

$$\Delta V(x) = V(Ax + Bu) - V(x) = x'(A'PA - P)x + 2x'A'PBu + u'B'PBu < 0$$

However, for any $x \in \{span\{A'PB\}\}^{\perp}$, $x'A'PBu = 0$ for all $u \in \mathbb{R}^p$. Notice that $dim\{span\{A'PB\}\}^{\perp} \geq n-p$. Thus, for any $x \in \{span\{A'PB\}\}^{\perp}$, $\Delta V(x) = x'(A'PA - P)x + u'B'PBu < 0$, for some u.

Since $B'PB$ is positive definite, the above condition implies that $x'(A'PA - P)x < 0$ for all $x \in \{span\{A'PB\}\}^{\perp}$. Therefore, $(A'PA - P)$ must have at least $n - p$ strictly negative eigenvalues, and thus $V \in \text{Type}_J$ for some $J \le p$.   □

3   Main Results

In this section we summarize the main results of the paper which are derived later. Motivated by the classification of Section 2.2 we first show that, if we restrict our attention to Type_1 CLFs (assuming they exist) then the coarsest quantizer is given by the coarsest quantizer of [1], for an equivalent single input system obtained by making the p input channels linearly dependent with each other. So to say, that having more than one input does not improve the optimal quantization density of the quantizer, when we restrict the CLF to be of Type_1. We then study Type_2. Searching partitions over this class is considerably more difficult. Thus, we derive a lower bound on the achievable densities of quantization over Type_2 instead. We find that

$$\eta^* \ge \frac{4}{ln\left(\dfrac{\sqrt{\prod |\lambda_i^u(A)|}+1}{\sqrt{\prod |\lambda_i^u(A)|}-1}\right)}.$$

4   Search over Type_1 CLFs

In this section we assume that the set Type_1 is not empty, and show that the result of [1] for a single input cannot be improved by the presence of more than one input.

Theorem 1. *If $V(x) = x'Px$, $P > 0$, is a CLF of $Type_1$ for system (1). Then $V(x)$ is also a CLF for the single input system*

$$x^+ = Ax + \bar{B}w \tag{2}$$

obtained by replacing B with $\bar{B} = B\Pi$ where $\Pi = (B'PB)^{-1}B'PAv$, and v denotes the eigenvector associated with the only positive eigenvalue of $A'PA - P$. Moreover the coarsest quantizer for system (1), and such a V, is given by

$$f(x) = \Pi \bar{f}(x)$$

where $\bar{f}(x)$ is the coarsest quantizer for system (2).

Proof. Since $V(x) = x'Px$ is of Type_1, let v denote the eigenvector associate with the only positive eigenvalue of $A'PA - P$. We need only to study $\Delta V(x)$ along the v direction, since for any $x \perp v$ $\Delta V(x, 0) < 0$. Let $x = \alpha v$ for $\alpha \in \mathbb{R}$. Then

$$\Delta V(\alpha, u) = \alpha^2 v'(A'PA - P)v + 2u'B'PAv\alpha + u'B'PBu$$

Since V is a CLF there is a u for which $\Delta V(\alpha, u) < 0$. For such a u, we can find the set of all α, by solving the second order equation in α, $\Delta V(\alpha, u) = 0$. The solutions are given by

$$\alpha^{(1)/(2)} = \frac{-v'A'PBu \pm \sqrt{v'A'PBuu'B'PAv - v'(A'PA - P)vu'B'PBu}}{v'(A'PA - P)v}$$

and $\Delta V(\alpha, u) < 0$ for all $\alpha \in (\alpha^{(1)}, \alpha^{(2)})$. Consider the ratio between the two solutions defined as follows

$$\rho(u) = \frac{\alpha^{(2)}}{\alpha^{(1)}} = \frac{1 + \sqrt{1 - \frac{v'(A'PA-P)vu'B'PBu}{u'B'PAvv'A'PBu}}}{1 - \sqrt{1 - \frac{v'(A'PA-P)vu'B'PBu}{u'B'PAvv'A'PBu}}}$$

We want to find the u that maximizes $\rho(u)$. Due to the scale invariance in u, the maximization of $\rho(u)$ will provide us with a coarsest logarithmic state-space partition. It is easy to see (the details are left to the reader) that $\rho(u)$ is maximized if $\dfrac{u'B'PAvv'A'PBu}{u'B'PBu}$ is maximized. Noting that $B'PB > 0$ since B has full column rank, we obtain that $\bar{u} = -(B'PB)^{-1}B'PAv$ is the unique maximizing solution that guarantees that $\Delta V(\alpha, u_0) < 0$ for $\alpha \in (\alpha^{(1)}, \alpha^{(2)})$.

If we define $\rho = \sup_u \rho(u)$, then, we have that

$$\rho = \frac{1 + \sqrt{1 - \frac{v'(A'PA-P)v}{v'A'PB(B'PB)^{-1}B'PAv}}}{1 - \sqrt{1 - \frac{v'(A'PA-P)v}{v'A'PB(B'PB)^{-1}B'PAv}}}$$

If we let $\Pi = (B'PB)^{-1}B'PAv$ then $\bar{B} = B\Pi \in \mathbb{R}^{n,1}$ is the resulting single input matrix with the property that

$$v'A'PB(B'PB)^{-1}B'PAv = v'A'P\bar{B}(\bar{B}'P\bar{B})^{-1}\bar{B}'PAv.$$

This means that the same ρ can be achieved by replacing B with $\bar{B}$. Since ρ is the basis of the logarithmic partition, this implies that the best quantizer for system (1) associated with $V \in \text{Type}_1$ is not coarser than the quantizer acting on the single input channel $\bar{B}$.

Let $\bar{f}(x)$ be such quantizer for system (2). Then, the quantizer for system (1) is given by

$$f(x) = \Pi\bar{f}(x)$$

where $\Pi = (B'PB)^{-1}B'PAv$.   □

5   Search over Type$_2$ CLFs

We begin by making a preliminary change of coordinates. Since we deal with CLF of the form $V(x) = x'Px$, with $P > 0$, let $x = P^{-1/2}z$, $\bar{A} = P^{1/2}AP^{-1/2}$, and $\bar{B} = P^{1/2}B$. In the new coordinate system, we have that

$$\Delta V(z, u) = z'(\bar{A}'\bar{A} - I)z + 2z'\bar{A}'\bar{B}u + u'\bar{B}'\bar{B}u$$

Since $V(z, u)$ is a Type$_2$ CLF, $\bar{A}'\bar{A} - I$ has only two positive eigenvalues. This also means that $\bar{A}$ has only two singular values greater than 1. Let $\mathsf{V} = [v_1, v_2]$ where v_1 and v_2 are the eigenvectors associated with the only two positive eigenvalues of $\bar{A}'\bar{A} - I$. Note, for future reference, that $\mathsf{V}'\mathsf{V} = I$.

There is no loss of generality in studying $\Delta V(z, u)$ when $z \in span\{v_1, v_2\}$, since for $z \in \{span\{v_1, v_2\}\}^{\perp}$, $\Delta V(z, 0) < 0$. Thus we can consider

$$\Delta V(\xi, u) = \xi'\mathsf{V}'(\bar{A}'\bar{A} - I)\mathsf{V}\xi + 2\xi'\mathsf{V}'\bar{A}'\bar{B}u + u'\bar{B}'\bar{B}u$$

where $\xi \in \mathbb{R}^2$.

Finally, we change the coordinates once more to the following ones. Let $y = \Sigma^{1/2}\xi$, where $\Sigma = \mathsf{V}'(\bar{A}'\bar{A} - I)\mathsf{V}$. Note that Σ is positive definite by assumption, and diagonal by construction. Then, in the new variables,

$$\Delta V(y, u) = y'y + 2y'\Sigma^{-1/2}\mathsf{V}'\bar{A}'\bar{B}u + u'\bar{B}'\bar{B}u \tag{3}$$

where $y \in Y = \mathbb{R}^2$.

Based on the above equation, we define the following mapping from Y to $U = \mathbb{R}^2$, the space of control vectors.

$$u = -(\bar{B}'\bar{B})^{-1}\bar{B}'\bar{A}\mathsf{V}\Sigma^{-1/2}y \overset{\triangle}{=} K_{GD}\, y, \tag{4}$$

K_{GD} is the controller that makes $\Delta V(y, u)$ decreasing the most for any given y. By using K_{GD}, we have that $\Delta V(y, K_{GD}y) = -y'Qy$, where

$$Q = \Sigma^{-1/2}\mathsf{V}'\bar{A}'\bar{B}(\bar{B}'\bar{B})^{-1}\bar{B}'\bar{A}\mathsf{V}\Sigma^{-1/2} - I.$$

Note that $Q > 0$. This follows from the assumption on V being Type$_2$ CLF, and our construction.

Lemma 2. K_{GD} *is invertible, and*

$$(K_{GD})^{-1} = -(Q + I)^{-1}\Sigma^{-1/2}\mathsf{V}\bar{A}'\bar{B}$$

Proof. The first claim follows immediately, if we look at Equation (3), since otherwise for all $y \in Null\{\bar{B}'\bar{A}\Sigma^{-1/2}\}$, $\Delta V(y, u) > 0$ for all u, contradicting the assumption that $V \in$ Type$_2$.
   From $u = -(\bar{B}'\bar{B})^{-1}\bar{B}'\bar{A}\mathsf{V}\Sigma^{-1/2}y$, left multiply both sides by $\Sigma^{-1/2}\mathsf{V}'\bar{A}'\bar{B}$ to obtain $\Sigma^{-1/2}\mathsf{V}'\bar{A}'\bar{B}u = -\Sigma^{-1/2}\mathsf{V}'\bar{A}'\bar{B}(\bar{B}'\bar{B})^{-1}\bar{B}'\bar{A}\mathsf{V}\Sigma^{-1/2}y$.
   However, $\Sigma^{-1/2}\mathsf{V}'\bar{A}'\bar{B}(\bar{B}'\bar{B})^{-1}\bar{B}'\bar{A}\mathsf{V}\Sigma^{-1/2} = Q + I$, which is invertible. Thus $y = -(Q + I)^{-1}\Sigma^{-1/2}\mathsf{V}'\bar{A}'\bar{B}u$. $\square$

Note that, for any $u_0 \neq 0$, the unique $y_0 = (K_{GD})^{-1}u_0$ is the one for which $\Delta V(y_0, u_0)$ is decreasing the most. The important point of the above lemma is that Y and U can be seen as equivalent spaces. Thus any quantization of U will correspond to a quantization of Y, and any partition or covering of Y will correspond to a partition or covering of U.

We are now ready to state the following theorem which characterizes the set of states in Y for which $V(y, u_0) < 0$ for any given fixed u_0.

Theorem 2. *For any $u_0 \neq 0$, let $y_0 = (K_{GD})^{-1} u_0$, and let*

$$\mathcal{N}(u_0) = \{y \in \mathbb{R}^2 \mid \Delta V(y, u_0) < 0\}.$$

Then

1) *$\mathcal{N}(u_0)$ is a disc centered at $c = (Q + I)y_0$ and of radius $r = |(Q + Q^2)^{1/2} y_0|$.*

2) *$\mathcal{N}(u_0)$ has the following (radial) scaling property $\mathcal{N}(\alpha u_0) = \alpha \mathcal{N}(u_0)$ for any $\alpha \in \mathbb{R}, \alpha \geq 0$.*

3) *Finally, let $\mathcal{C}$ be the locus of the centers of unit radius $\mathcal{N}(\cdot)$. Then, $\mathcal{C}$ is an ellipsoid described as follows.*

$$\mathcal{C} = \left\{ c = (I + Q^{-1})^{1/2} \nu \mid \nu \in \mathbb{R}^2, |\nu| = 1 \right\}.$$

Proof. By completing the square in Equation (3), we obtain

$$\Delta V(y, u_0) = -y'Qy + |(\bar{B}'\bar{B})^{-1/2} \bar{B}' \bar{A} V \Sigma^{-1/2} y + (\bar{B}'\bar{B})^{1/2} u_0|^2.$$

Let $y = y_0 + y_1$, where $y_0 = (K_{GD})^{-1} u_0$, then

$$\Delta V(y_0 + y_1, u_0) = -y_0'Q y_0 - y_1'Q y_1 - 2y_1'Q y_0 + |(\bar{B}'\bar{B})^{-1/2} \bar{B}' \bar{A} V \Sigma^{-1/2} y_1|^2$$
$$= -y_0'Q y_0 + y_1'y_1 - 2y_1'Q y_0.$$

We can further complete the squares to obtain the following equation.

$$\Delta V(y_0 + y_1, u_0) = |y_1 - Q y_0|^2 - y_0'(Q + Q^2)y_0.$$

Therefore, in the Y-coordinate system, $\mathcal{N}(u_0)$ has the following representation.

$$\mathcal{N}(u_0) = \left\{ y = y_0 + y_1 \mid |y_1 - Q y_0|^2 < |(Q + Q^2)^{1/2} y_0|^2 \right\}.$$

Not surprisingly, $y = y_0 \neq 0$ is contained in the set, but note that also

$$y = c \overset{\triangle}{=} y_0 + Q y_0 \in \mathcal{N}(u_0), \text{ for } y_0 \neq 0.$$

This means that, for any u_0 (and associated y_0), $\mathcal{N}(u_0)$ is a disc centered at c of radius $r = |(Q + Q^2)^{1/2} y_0|$. This proves 1).

The scaling property follows immediately from the linearity of both c and r in y_0 and u_0.

As for 3), $\mathcal{C}$, the locus of the centers of unit radius $\mathcal{N}$, is given by

$$\mathcal{C} = \left\{ c = (I + Q)y_0 \mid \text{ for } y_0 \text{ such that } |(Q + Q^2)^{1/2} y_0| = 1 \right\}$$

or equivalently, if we let $\nu = (Q + Q^2)^{1/2} y_0$ and rearrange, $\mathcal{C}$ is given by

$$\mathcal{C} = \left\{ c = (I + Q^{-1})^{1/2} \nu \mid \nu \in \mathbb{R}^2, |\nu| = 1 \right\}.$$

$\square$

We want to point out that the characterization of the uncertainty sets in Y given by the above theorem is the natural generalization in the two input setting of the characterization of the uncertainty sets in the single input case obtained in [1]. In [1], it was shown that the relevant uncertainty sets were those in $Y = Range(K_{GD})$. Since K_{GD} had a one-dimensional range the sets were just segments with the scaling property. In the present case, we still have that $Y = Range(K_{GD})$. However, Y is bi-dimensional, and thus the sets are balls and they are subject to the directionally different scaling factors represented by $\mathcal{C}$. The problem of finding a quantizer or a covering is sensibly more complex in this case. We need to search over all $\mathcal{C}$, and all coverings. The search over all $\mathcal{C}$ is greatly simplified by the next theorem.

Theorem 3. *Given any $V \in Type_2$, the volume of $\mathcal{C}$, denoted by $Vol(\mathcal{C})$ is always greater than or equal to the product of the unstable eigenvalues of A.*

Proof. $Q = \Sigma^{-1/2} V' \bar{A}' \bar{B} (\bar{B}' \bar{B})^{-1} \bar{B}' \bar{A} V \Sigma^{-1/2} - I$. Consider $V' \bar{A}' \bar{B} (\bar{B}' \bar{B})^{-1} \bar{B}' \bar{A} V$. Let R be such that $\bar{A} V = \bar{B} R$. This implies that $R = (\bar{B}' \bar{B})^{-1} \bar{B}' \bar{A} V$, where $(\bar{B}' \bar{B})^{-1} \bar{B}'$ is the left inverse of $\bar{B}$. Hence, $V' \bar{A}' \bar{B} (\bar{B}' \bar{B})^{-1} \bar{B}' \bar{A} V = V' \bar{A}' \bar{B} R = V' \bar{A}' \bar{A} V$ and $Q = \Sigma^{-1/2} V' \bar{A}' \bar{A} V \Sigma^{-1/2} - I = \Sigma^{-1/2} \left(V' \bar{A}' \bar{A} V - \Sigma \right) \Sigma^{-1/2} = \Sigma^{-1/2} V' V \Sigma^{-1/2} = \Sigma^{-1}$.

Therefore, $I + Q^{-1} = I + \Sigma = V' \bar{A}' \bar{A} V$ and $\lambda_i \left\{ (I + Q^{-1})^{1/2} \right\} = \Sigma(i,i) + 1 = \lambda_i^{1/2} \left\{ V' \bar{A}' \bar{A} V \right\} = \sigma_i \left\{ \bar{A} V \right\}, \quad i = 1, 2$

Thus, the product of the eigenvalues of $(I + Q^{-1})^{1/2}$ is given by the product of the singular values of $\bar{A} V$. Since $\Sigma(i,i) > 0$, for $i = 1, 2$, $(V(x) \in Type_2)$ then $\sigma_i \left\{ \bar{A} V \right\} > 1$ for $i = 1, 2$. Therefore,

$$\prod_{i=1,2} \lambda_i \left\{ (I + Q^{-1})^{1/2} \right\} = \prod_{i=1,2} \Sigma(i,i) + 1 = \prod_{i=1,2} \sigma_i \left\{ \bar{A} V \right\} \geq \prod_{i=1..n} \sigma_i \left\{ \bar{A} \right\}$$

$$= \prod_{i=1..n} |\lambda_i \left\{ A \right\}| = |\det(A)|. \qquad \square$$

Remark 1. We will consider ellipsoids $\mathcal{C}$ of volume equal to $|\det A|$. We don't need to consider those $\mathcal{C}$ whose volume is strictly greater than $|\det A|$. Having larger volume, but allowing for the same uncertainty, they will lead to denser coverings and partitions, as we will see.

Remark 2. The above theorem is transforming the problem of searching over all $type_2$ CLFs and over all systems with the same product of unstable eigenvalues, into a one-parameter search, the eccentricity of $\mathcal{C}$. In fact $\mathcal{C}$ can be described as an ellipsoid centered at the origin with axes of size λ_M and λ_m respectively, with $\lambda_M \geq \lambda_m > 1$. We can assume, without loss of generality, that the major axis is horizontal and the minor one is vertical in the cartesian plane. Also, we identify a specific ellipsoid $\mathcal{C}$ by $\mathcal{C}(\lambda_M, \lambda_m)$.

We introduce the following notation and definitions useful in the rest of the paper.

A unit ball centered at c_0 is denoted by $\Delta(c_0) = \{y \in Y \,|\, |y - c_0|^2 \leq 1\}$.
A unit ball centered at $c \in \mathcal{C}$ is denoted by $\Delta_{\mathcal{C}}(c) = \Delta(c)$, for $c \in \mathcal{C}$.
The set of unit balls centered on $\mathcal{C}$ is defined as $\Delta_{\mathcal{C}} = \{\Delta_{\mathcal{C}}(c) \,|\, c \in \mathcal{C}\}$.

From the radial scaling property we have that, if $c \in \mathcal{C}(\lambda_M, \lambda_m)$, then the largest uncertainty ball centered at αc has radius α for any $\alpha \geq 0$. We denote such sets by

$$\Delta_{\mathcal{C}}(c, \alpha) = \alpha \Delta_{\mathcal{C}}(c) \tag{5}$$

We make the following definitions to introduce the notion of a covering of Y compatible with $\mathcal{C}$.

Definition 4.

A covering of Y, is a set $\Omega = \{\Omega_i, i \in \mathbb{Z}\}$, such that $Y = \bigcup \Omega_i$.
A covering, Ω, of Y is compatible with $\mathcal{C}(\lambda_M, \lambda_m)$ if $\Omega_i = \Delta_{\mathcal{C}(\lambda_M, \lambda_m)}(c_i, \alpha_i)$.
The set of all covering of Y compatible with $\mathcal{C}(\lambda_M, \lambda_m)$ is denoted by $\mathcal{W}$.

Note that any covering of Y compatible with $\mathcal{C}(\lambda_M, \lambda_m)$ will need the uncertainty sets to overlap on a non empty interior set since they are balls. From a covering we can then derive a partition. However the search over all coverings seems very difficult. In this paper, we look for a lower bound on the density of the coarsest covering instead. The idea is to consider special subsets (Rays) of Y for which the coarsest partition can be computed, and to use this density as a lower bound on the whole space.

5.1   Coarsest Partition of Rays

In this section we consider problem of finding a minimal density partition of a Ray. As already anticipated, rays are the basic elements in our construction. For a given angle θ, the ray associated with θ is defined as follows,

$$Ray(\theta) = \{(r, \theta) \,|, r \geq 0\}$$

Given $\mathcal{C}(\lambda_M, \lambda_m)$, and a covering, Ω, of Y compatible with $\mathcal{C}(\lambda_M, \lambda_m)$, then, the induced covering of $Ray(\theta)$ compatible with $\mathcal{C}(\lambda_M, \lambda_m)$ is defined naturally to be

$$g(\theta) = \Omega \bigcap Ray(\theta).$$

To simplify the notation we will omit θ when unnecessary.

Assumption 1. *All the coverings are assumed to be compatible with $\mathcal{C}(\lambda_M, \lambda_m)$.*

The density of the covering g is defined according to Definition 1.

Definition 5. *A covering, f, of $Ray(\theta)$ is said to be* coarsest *if it has the smallest covering density*

$$f = \arg \inf_{g \in W \cap Ray(\theta)} \eta_g.$$

Note that f may not be unique. Next theorem provides f and η_f.

Theorem 4. *Let*

$$\psi(\theta) = -\arctan \frac{\left(\frac{1}{\lambda_M^2} - \frac{1}{\lambda_m^2}\right) \sin 2\theta}{2\left(1 - \frac{\cos^2 \theta}{\lambda_m^2} - \frac{\sin^2 \theta}{\lambda_M^2}\right)}, \tag{6}$$

$$\rho(\theta) = \frac{1 + \sqrt{1 - \frac{(\lambda_M^2 - 1)(\lambda_m^2 - 1)}{\lambda_m^2(\lambda_M^2 - 1) - (\lambda_M^2 - \lambda_m^2)\cos^2\theta}}}{1 - \sqrt{1 - \frac{(\lambda_M^2 - 1)(\lambda_m^2 - 1)}{\lambda_m^2(\lambda_M^2 - 1) - (\lambda_M^2 - \lambda_m^2)\cos^2\theta}}}, \tag{7}$$

and

$$r_0(\theta + \psi(\theta)) = \left(\frac{\cos^2(\theta + \psi(\theta))}{\lambda_M^2} + \frac{\sin^2(\theta + \psi(\theta))}{\lambda_m^2}\right)^{-\frac{1}{2}}.$$

Consider the following set of uncertainty balls

$$\Omega_f = \left\{\Delta_{\mathcal{C}(\lambda_M, \lambda_m)}(c, \alpha_i) \mid \alpha_i = \rho^i(\theta),\ i \in \mathbb{Z}\right\},$$

where $c = (r_0(\theta + \psi(\theta)), \theta + \psi(\theta)) \in \mathcal{C}(\lambda_M, \lambda_m)$, and $\Delta_{\mathcal{C}}(c, \alpha)$ is defined in Equation (5). Then, $f = \Omega_f \cap Ray(\theta)$, and

$$\eta_f = \frac{2}{\ln \rho(\theta)}. \tag{8}$$

Proof. We want to point out that the problem of finding f and η_f is not difficult because it is about finding the covering for a one dimensional object. It is not surprising that, the derivation of this result is similar to that developed for the single input case in [1]. Thus, we only sketch the proof here.

The basic idea of the proof is to find the largest subset of $Ray(\theta)$ that can be covered by a unit uncertainty ball. We only need to consider unit balls because of the scaling property. Once we have found the most covering unit ball, we can appropriately scale it to cover the entire Ray.

For convenience, we describe the center of any unit ball offset by the angle θ, i.e., the center of the ball is given by $c = (r_0(\theta + \psi), \theta + \psi)$, where $r_0(\theta + \psi) = \left(\frac{\cos^2(\theta + \psi)}{\lambda_M^2} + \frac{\sin^2(\theta + \psi)}{\lambda_m^2}\right)^{-\frac{1}{2}}$.

Let the unit ball centered at $(r_0(\theta + \psi), \theta + \psi)$ be denoted by $B_0(\theta, \psi)$. We assume, without loss of generality, that $B_0(\theta, \psi) \cap Ray(\theta) \neq \emptyset$, $\psi = 0$ always satisfies this conditions.

Let $x^{(1)/(2)} \in Ray(\theta)$ denote the boundary points of the intersection $B_0(\theta, \psi) \cap Ray(\theta)$. Then $x^{(1)//(2)}$ are given by the following expression

$$x^{(1)(2)} = r_0(\theta + \psi) \cos \psi \pm \sqrt{r_0^2(\theta + \psi) \cos^2 \psi - r_0^2(\theta + \psi) + 1}$$

Consider their ratio,

$$\rho(\theta, \psi) = \frac{1 + \sqrt{1 - \left(1 - \frac{1}{r_0^2(\theta + \psi)}\right)\frac{1}{\cos^2(\psi)}}}{1 - \sqrt{1 - \left(1 - \frac{1}{r_0^2(\theta + \psi)}\right)\frac{1}{\cos^2(\psi)}}} \tag{9}$$

Note that, under the assumption of nonempty intersection, and given that $r_0(\theta + \psi) > 1$, $\rho(\theta, \psi) \geq 1$. We can then optimize over ψ to obtain the largest ratio. It is not difficult to see that

$$\psi(\theta) = \arg\max_{\psi} \rho(\theta, \psi) = \arg\max_{\psi} \left[1 - \left(1 - \frac{1}{r_0^2(\theta + \psi)}\right)\frac{1}{\cos^2(\psi)}\right]$$

the details are left to the reader.

From standard trigonometric equalities, the above optimization can be rewritten as follows

$$\psi(\theta) =$$
$$\arg\max_{\psi} \left[\frac{1}{r_0^2(\theta)} + \left(\frac{\cos^2 \theta}{\lambda_m^2} + \frac{\sin^2 \theta}{\lambda_M^2} - 1\right)\tan^2 \psi - \left(\frac{1}{\lambda_M^2} - \frac{1}{\lambda_m^2}\right)\sin(2\theta)\tan \psi\right]$$

Simple differentiation leads to the optimal ψ shown in Equation (6).

Substituting $\psi(\theta)$ into Equation (7), after some rearrangements, we obtain $\rho(\theta)$ given by Equation (7).

Now, if we select the sequence of uncertainty balls along the $Ray(\theta + \psi(\theta))$, and with centers at $(r_0(\theta + \psi(\theta))\rho^i(\theta), \theta + \psi(\theta))$, as described in the theorem statement, then we can cover the whole $Ray(\theta)$. Note that such covering is the coarsest since $\rho(\theta)$ is optimal and the balls are scaled so that there is no overlapping on non empty relative interior sets.

Given $\rho(\theta)$ and Ω_f it is easy to obtain f and η_f, left to the reader.   □

Expressed in words, the theorem is saying that associated to any θ there is another direction $\theta + \psi(\theta)$ locus of the centers of the uncertainty balls that cover $Ray(\theta)$ in the most efficient way. The covering is indeed a partition and is the coarsest achievable given $\mathcal{C}(\lambda_M, \lambda_m)$.

5.2   A Lower Bound on the Density of the Coarsest Quantizer

In this section we derive a lower bound on the coarsest covering of Y, based on the result of Theorem 4. We need to introduce a new function:

$$\varphi(t) = \arctan\sqrt{\frac{r_0^2(t)}{1 - r_0^2(t)}}.$$

$\varphi(t)$ has the following meaning. For a given angle t, consider $B_0(t)$, the unit uncertainty ball centered at $c = (r_0(t), t) \in \mathcal{C}(\lambda_M, \lambda_m)$. Then $2\varphi(t)$ is the angle of the cone tangent to $B_0(t)$ with vertex at the origin. Such cone can be equivalently identified with the set $\{\Delta(c, \alpha) \mid \alpha \geq 0\}$, where $\Delta(c, \alpha)$ is defined by Equation (5).

Theorem 5. *Given $\mathcal{C}(\lambda_M, \lambda_m)$, then any covering of Y compatible with $\mathcal{C}(\lambda_M, \lambda_m)$ has a density greater than $\underline{\eta} = 2\eta_{f(0)} = \dfrac{4}{\ln\left(\dfrac{\lambda_M + 1}{\lambda_M - 1}\right)}$, where $\eta_{f(0)}$ is the coarsest density of the covering of $Ray(0)$.*

Proof. The idea is to show that the positive and negative directions of the major axis need separate covering. We begin by considering the function $\varphi(t)$. $\varphi(t)$ is maximized when $t = \pi/2 + k\pi, k = 0, 1, 2, \ldots$, i.e., when t coincides with the minor axis direction. This coincides with our intuition, that the unit uncertainty ball centered on the minor axis will subtend the largest angle cone.

Therefore, $\varphi(t) \leq \arctan\sqrt{\dfrac{\lambda_m^2}{\lambda_m^2 - 1}} = \varphi\left(\dfrac{\pi}{2}\right) < \dfrac{\pi}{2}$, and $2\varphi(t) < \pi$. This means that no ball in any covering of Y compatible with any $\mathcal{C}$ can include points in Y which are symmetric with respect to the origin. In particular, no points on the positive and the negative directions of the major axis can be covered by the same uncertainty ball. Thus, any covering of Y compatible with any $\mathcal{C}$, requires two different sets of balls to cover the two opposite directions of the major axis. The reason for selecting the major axis direction is due to the fact that $\rho(\theta)$ in Theorem 4 is maximized at $\theta = k\pi$, i.e., along the major axis. Hence, any covering of Y compatible with any $\mathcal{C}(\lambda_M, \lambda_m)$ must have a density of at least

$$\underline{\eta} = 2\eta_{f(0)} = \frac{4}{\ln\left(\dfrac{\lambda_M + 1}{\lambda_M - 1}\right)}.$$

$\square$

Remark 3. Recall that the Volume of $\mathcal{C}$ is equal to $\prod |\lambda_i^u(A)|$. Thus, $\lambda_M = \dfrac{\prod |\lambda_i^u(A)|}{\lambda_m}$, and $\lim\limits_{\lambda_m \to 1} \underline{\eta} = \lim\limits_{\lambda_m \to 1} \dfrac{4}{\ln\left(\dfrac{\prod |\lambda_i^u(A)| + \lambda_m}{\prod |\lambda_i^u(A)| - \lambda_m}\right)} = \dfrac{4}{\ln\left(\dfrac{\prod |\lambda_i^u(A)| + 1}{\prod |\lambda_i^u(A)| - 1}\right)}$.

The last term is just the density of the coarsest quantizer in the single input case. In other words, the single-input result is recovered as the Lyapunov function $V(x) = x'Px$ moves toward the boundary of the Type$_2$ set. The limit as λ_m goes to 1 corresponds to a function, which is on the boundary of the Type$_1$ and Type$_2$ sets, but it does not belong to either of the two sets, since it is not strictly decreasing for all the system's states ($A'PA - P \geq 0$ instead of > 0).

Remark 4. We can obtain a lower bound on the density of any covering of Y compatible with any $\mathcal{C}$ using the fact that the minimal value of λ_M is obtained when $\lambda_M = \lambda_m = \sqrt{\prod |\lambda_i^u(A)|}$. Thus, any covering of Y compatible with any $\mathcal{C}$ must have a density of at least $\eta = \dfrac{4}{\ln\left(\dfrac{\sqrt{\prod |\lambda_i^u(A)|} + 1}{\sqrt{\prod |\lambda_i^u(A)|} - 1}\right)}$.

This result, together with Theorem 1, implies that $\eta^* \geq \dfrac{4}{\ln\left(\dfrac{\sqrt{\prod |\lambda_i^u(A)|} + 1}{\sqrt{\prod |\lambda_i^u(A)|} - 1}\right)}$.

6   Conclusions

In this paper we have derived a lower bound on the density of the coarsest quantizer that quadratically stabilizes a two-input linear discrete time system. This result describes how much improvement could be expected in terms of reduced quantization density by using two inputs instead of one to quadratically stabilize the system. The lower bound is expressed only in terms of the unstable eigenvalues of the system. The proposed lower bound is not tight and there is room for improvement, which will be explored in future research. A by-product result is that the optimal quantizer is radially logarithmic, which is a generalization of the logarithmic quantizer obtained in [1].

6.1   Acknowledgments

The authors wish to thank S.K Mitter and A. Megretski for the interesting discussions and useful suggestions.

References

1. N. Elia, and S. K. Mitter, "Stabilization of linear systems with limited information", IEEE Transactions on Automatic Control, Vol.46, No. 9, pp. 1384 -1400, Sept. 2001.
2. N. Elia "Design of hybrid systems with guaranteed performance", Proceedings of the 39th IEEE Conference on Decision and Control, Vol. 1 pp. 993-998, 2000
3. H. Ishii, B. A. Francis, "Stabilizing a linear system by switching control with dwell time", Proceedings of the 2001 American Control Conference, Vol. 3 pp.1876 -1881, 2001.
4. F. Fagnani, S. Zampieri, "Stability anaysis and synthesis for scalar linear systems with a quantized feedback" preprint 2001.
5. R. W. Brockett, D. Liberzon, "Quantized feedback stabilization of linear systems", IEEE Transactions on Automatic Control, Vol. 45 No. 7, pp.1279 -1289, July 2000
6. S. Tatikonda, A. Sahai, and S. K. Mitter, "Control of LQG Systems under Communication Constraints," 37th Conference on Control and Decision Systems, Tampa Fl. 1998, pp. 1165-1170.
7. J. Lunze, "Qualitative Modeling of Linear Dynamical Systems with Quantized State Measurements," Automatica Volume 30, Number 3, pp. 417-432, 1994.

8. J. Lunze, B. Nixdorf, and Schröder, "Deterministic Discrete-Event Representation of Continuous-Variable Systems," Automatica, Vol 35, pp. 395-406, 1999.
9. A. Sahai, "Anytime Information Theory", Ph.D. Thesis M.I.T. Nov. 2000.
10. W. S. Wong, R. W. Brockett, "Systems with finite communication bandwidth constraints. II. Stabilization with limited information feedback", IEEE Transactions on Automatic Control, Vol. 44, No, 5, pp. 1049 -1053, May 1999.
11. W. S. Wong, R. W. Brockett, "Systems with finite communication bandwidth constraints. I. State estimation problems", IEEE Transactions on Automatic Control, Vol. 42 No. 9, pp. 1294 -1299, Sept. 1997.
12. V. Borkar, and S.K. Mitter, "LQG Control with Communication Constraints", LIDS Report number LIDS-P-2326, M.I.T. 1995.
13. T. M. Cover, and J. A. Thomas, "Elements of information theory" Wiley series in telecommunications Wiley, New York, 1991.

Analysis of Discrete-Time PWA Systems with Logic States

Giancarlo Ferrari-Trecate, Francesco A. Cuzzola, and Manfred Morari

Automatic Control Laboratory,
ETH - Swiss Federal Institute of Technology, ETL,
CH-8092 Zürich, Switzerland,
Tel. +41-1-6327812, Fax +41-1-6321211
{ferrari,cuzzola,morari}@aut.ee.ethz.ch

Abstract In this paper we consider discrete-time piecewise affine hybrid systems with Boolean inputs, outputs and states and we show that they can be represented in a canonical form where the logic variables influence the switching between different submodels but not the continuous-valued dynamics. We exploit this representation for studying Lagrange stability and developing performance analysis procedures based on linear matrix inequalities. Moreover, by using arguments from dissipativity theory for nonlinear systems, we generalize our approach to solve the H_∞ analysis problem.

Keywords: Piecewise Affine Systems, Mixed Logic Dynamical systems, Hybrid Systems, Stability, H_∞, Linear Matrix Inequalities.

1 Introduction

In the area of hybrid systems, stability analysis has been one of the most considered topics. The fact that a hybrid system can switch between different dynamics according to logic rules, makes the problem of designing stability tests difficult and, depending on the modeling framework considered, various solutions have been proposed in the literature [6,14,17]. In this work we focus on discrete-time Piece-Wise Affine (PWA) systems, whose state-space representation is

$$\begin{bmatrix} x_c \\ x_\ell \end{bmatrix}(k+1) = \tilde{A}_i \begin{bmatrix} x_c \\ x_\ell \end{bmatrix}(k) + \tilde{B}_i \begin{bmatrix} u_c \\ u_\ell \end{bmatrix}(k) + \tilde{a}_i \tag{1a}$$

$$\begin{bmatrix} y_c \\ y_\ell \end{bmatrix}(k) = \tilde{C}_i \begin{bmatrix} x_c \\ x_\ell \end{bmatrix}(k) + \tilde{D}_i \begin{bmatrix} u_c \\ u_\ell \end{bmatrix}(k) + \tilde{c}_i \tag{1b}$$

$$\text{for } \begin{bmatrix} x \\ u \end{bmatrix}(k) \in \tilde{\mathcal{X}}_i, \tag{1c}$$

where, $x = [x_c{}^T, x_\ell{}^T]^T$ is the state, $u = [u_c{}^T, u_\ell{}^T]^T$ is the input and $y = [y_c{}^T, y_\ell{}^T]^T$ is the output. State, input and output are partitioned in the continuous components $x_c \in \mathbb{R}^{n_c}$, $u_c \in \mathbb{R}^{m_c}$, $y_c \in \mathbb{R}^{p_c}$ and logic components $x_\ell \in$

C.J. Tomlin and M.R. Greenstreet (Eds.): HSCC 2002, LNCS 2289, pp. 194–208, 2002.

$\{0,1\}^{n_\ell}$, $u_\ell \in \{0,1\}^{m_\ell}$, $y_\ell \in \{0,1\}^{p_\ell}$. Each affine subsystem $(\tilde{A}_i, \tilde{B}_i, \tilde{a}_i, \tilde{C}_i, \tilde{D}_i, \tilde{c}_i)$, $i = 1, \ldots, \tilde{s}$ is defined on a *cell* $\tilde{\mathcal{X}}_i \subset \mathbb{R}^{n_c} \times \{0,1\}^{n_\ell} \times \mathbb{R}^{m_c} \times \{0,1\}^{m_\ell}$ that is a (not necessarily closed) polyhedron. The cells satisfy $\tilde{\mathcal{X}}_i \cap \tilde{\mathcal{X}}_j = \emptyset$, $\forall i \neq j$, and their union defines the admissible set of states and inputs $\tilde{\mathbb{X}} = \bigcup_{i=1}^{\tilde{s}} \tilde{\mathcal{X}}_i$.

Under mild assumptions, the state-space form (1) provides a unified representation for many classes of discrete-time hybrid systems such as Mixed Logic Dynamical (MLD) systems [2], Linear Complementarity, Extended Linear Complementarity and Min-Max Plus Scaling systems [13]. PWA systems arise also when considering either linear constrained or MLD models regulated by a Model Predictive Control (MPC) scheme. Indeed, in [1,4] it has been shown that, under mild assumptions, the resulting closed-loop systems has the form (1) and can be computed in closed form. It is then apparent that stability/performance tests for PWA models can be exploited either for investigating stability/performance of all the above classes of hybrid systems or for checking the *a posteriori* stability/performance obtained via an MPC law.

In a PWA system, the coupling between logic and dynamics is realized through the following features. First, the state-update and output maps can be discontinuous across the boundaries of the cells; second, the use of logic inputs u_ℓ, outputs y_ℓ and states x_ℓ allows one to model automata and finite state machines in the PWA form [3].

Algorithms for checking stability of PWA systems without logic states have been proposed in [9]. However, the presence of logic states either does not allow to apply directly such algorithms or makes them overly conservative. Moreover, in many practical cases, one is interested in studying the stability of the continuous-valued part x_c of the state (that usually represents physical quantities) without imposing the convergence of the logical part x_ℓ to a constant value. Indeed, this allows considering also cases in which x_c reaches the equilibrium thanks to the switching of the logic state. This stability concept, called *Lagrange stability* [12], is the one considered in this work.

The design of algorithms for testing Lagrange stability is achieved in two steps. First, in Section 2, we show that every PWA system can be written in a canonical form, termed PWA Logic Canonical (PWA-LC) form that is suitable for analyzing Lagrange stability. This is done by recalling the equivalence between MLD and PWA forms [2] and by showing that every MLD system admits an equivalent PWA-LC representation. Furthermore we prove, under a well-posedness assumption, that also the converse holds, *i.e.*, every PWA-LC system can be written in the PWA form. In Section 3, various stability tests for PWA-LC systems with different degrees of conservativeness are proposed. In particular, similarly to [14,17], we synthesize Piece-Wise Quadratic (PWQ) Lyapunov functions by solving Linear Matrix Inequalities (LMIs).

Finally, in Section 4, we consider the H_∞ analysis problem and exploit passivity theory for discrete-time nonlinear systems [16] in order to synthesize suitable PWQ storage functions via LMI procedures. For the sake of brevity we omit all the proofs and we refer the interested reader to [10] for the details.

2   Logic Canonical Form of Discrete-Time PWA Systems

We consider discrete-time hybrid systems in the Mixed Logic Dynamical form that are described through the formulas [3]

$$
\begin{bmatrix} x_c \\ x_\ell \end{bmatrix}(k+1) = \begin{bmatrix} A_{cc} & A_{c\ell} \\ A_{\ell c} & A_{\ell\ell} \end{bmatrix} \begin{bmatrix} x_c \\ x_\ell \end{bmatrix}(k) + \begin{bmatrix} B_{1,cc} & B_{1,c\ell} \\ B_{1,\ell c} & B_{1,\ell\ell} \end{bmatrix} \begin{bmatrix} u_c \\ u_\ell \end{bmatrix}(k) + \begin{bmatrix} B_{2,c\ell} \\ B_{2,\ell\ell} \end{bmatrix} \delta(k) + \begin{bmatrix} B_{3,cc} \\ B_{3,\ell c} \end{bmatrix} z(k)
$$
(2a)

$$
\begin{bmatrix} y_c \\ y_\ell \end{bmatrix}(k) = \begin{bmatrix} C_{cc} & C_{c\ell} \\ C_{\ell c} & C_{\ell\ell} \end{bmatrix} \begin{bmatrix} x_c \\ x_\ell \end{bmatrix}(k) + \begin{bmatrix} D_{1,cc} & D_{1,c\ell} \\ D_{1,\ell c} & D_{1,\ell\ell} \end{bmatrix} \begin{bmatrix} u_c \\ u_\ell \end{bmatrix}(k) + \begin{bmatrix} D_{2,c\ell} \\ D_{2,\ell\ell} \end{bmatrix} \delta(k) + \begin{bmatrix} D_{3,cc} \\ D_{3,\ell c} \end{bmatrix} z(k)
$$
(2b)

$$
E_2\delta(k) + E_3 z(k) \le \begin{bmatrix} E_{1,c} & E_{1,\ell} \end{bmatrix} \begin{bmatrix} u_c \\ u_\ell \end{bmatrix}(k) + \begin{bmatrix} E_{4,c} & E_{4,\ell} \end{bmatrix} \begin{bmatrix} x_c \\ x_\ell \end{bmatrix}(k) + E_5
$$
(2c)

where $\delta \in \{0,1\}^{r_\ell}$ and $z \in \mathbb{R}^{r_c}$ represent auxiliary binary and continuous variables respectively. The overall state, input and output vectors will be denoted with x, u and y. The continuous-valued and logic components of the state can be obtained by using the projection operators $\mathcal{C}(x) = x_c$ and $\mathcal{L}(x) = x_\ell$. A thorough description of MLD systems and of their modeling capabilities can be found in [3,2]. All constraints on state, input, and auxiliary variables are summarized in the inequality (2c). Note that, despite the fact that equations (2a)-(2b) are linear, nonlinearity is hidden in the integrality constraints over binary variables. In this paper we consider MLD systems that are *completely well-posed* [3], such that, for given $x(t)$ and $u(t)$, the values of $\delta(t)$ and $z(t)$ are uniquely determined through the inequalities (2c). In other words, the inequalities (2c) implicitly define the maps $Z(x(t), u(t)) = z(t)$ and $\Delta(x(t), u(t)) = \delta(t)$. This assumption is not restrictive and is always satisfied when real plants are described in the MLD form [3].

In order to study the relations between different representations for hybrid systems we use the following definition

Definition 1 *Consider two discrete-time systems Σ_1 and Σ_2 in state-space form. The system Σ_1 is equivalent to Σ_2 if all the trajectories $x(k)$, $u(k)$, $y(k)$ compatible with the state-space equations Σ_1 are also compatible with Σ_2. Two classes of systems are strongly equivalent if for each system in the first class there exists an equivalent system in the second class and vice-versa.*

Consider now the following class of hybrid systems.

Definition 2 *A PWA system in the Logic Canonical form (PWA-LC system) is described by the state-space equations*

$$
\begin{bmatrix} x_c \\ x_\ell \end{bmatrix}(k+1) = A_i \begin{bmatrix} x_c \\ x_\ell \end{bmatrix}(k) + B_i \begin{bmatrix} u_c \\ u_\ell \end{bmatrix}(k) + a_i
$$
(3a)

$$
\begin{bmatrix} y_c \\ y_\ell \end{bmatrix}(k) = C_i \begin{bmatrix} x_c \\ x_\ell \end{bmatrix}(k) + D_i \begin{bmatrix} u_c \\ u_\ell \end{bmatrix}(k) + c_i
$$
(3b)

$$
for \begin{bmatrix} x_c \\ u_c \end{bmatrix}(k) \in \mathcal{X}_i, \quad x_\ell(k) = \bar{x}_{\ell,i}, \quad u_\ell(k) = \bar{u}_{\ell,i}
$$
(3c)

where $i = 1, 2, \ldots, s$ *and the matrices appearing in (3a)-(3b) have the block structure*

$$A_i = \begin{bmatrix} F_{cc,i}, & 0 \\ 0 & 0 \end{bmatrix}, \quad B_i = \begin{bmatrix} G_{cc,i} & 0 \\ 0 & 0 \end{bmatrix}, \quad a_i = \begin{bmatrix} a_{c,i} \\ a_{\ell,i} \end{bmatrix} \tag{4}$$

$$C_i = \begin{bmatrix} H_{cc,i} & 0 \\ 0 & 0 \end{bmatrix}, \quad D_i = \begin{bmatrix} L_{cc,i}, & 0 \\ 0 & 0 \end{bmatrix}, \quad c_i = \begin{bmatrix} c_{c,i} \\ c_{\ell,i} \end{bmatrix} \tag{5}$$

$$F_{cc,i} \in \mathbb{R}^{n_c \times n_c}, \quad G_{cc,i} \in \mathbb{R}^{n_c \times m_c}, \quad H_{cc,i} \in \mathbb{R}^{p_c \times n_c}, \quad L_{cc,i} \in \mathbb{R}^{p_c \times n_c},$$
$$a_{c,i} \in \mathbb{R}^{n_c}, \quad a_{\ell,i} \in \{0,1\}^{n_\ell}, \quad c_{c,i} \in \mathbb{R}^{p_c}, \quad c_{\ell,i} \in \{0,1\}^{p_\ell}.$$

In (3c) the cells $\mathcal{X}_i \subset \mathbb{R}^{n_c} \times \mathbb{R}^{m_c}$ *are (not necessarily closed) polyhedra. Moreover,* $\bar{x}_{\ell,i}$ $\bar{u}_{\ell,i}$ *are vectors with binary entries, i.e.* $\bar{x}_{\ell,i} \in \{0,1\}^{n_\ell}$, $\bar{u}_{\ell,i} \in \{0,1\}^{m_\ell}$.

The set of admissible continuous states and inputs for a PWA-LC systems is $X = \bigcup_{i=1}^{s} \mathcal{X}_i$ and, as it is apparent from (3c), a constant logic state $\bar{x}_{\ell,i}$ and input $\bar{u}_{\ell,i}$ are associated to each cell $\mathcal{X}_i$. Note that the state and output trajectories of a PWA-LC system can be non-unique, since it may happen that a state x and an input u satisfy the condition (3c) for different values of the index i. However, as pointed out in [3], non-uniqueness is often due to modeling errors, rather than to intrinsic properties of the system and therefore it is sensible to restrict the attention to the class of *completely well-posed* PWA-LC systems.

Definition 3 *A PWA-LC system is completely well posed if, for each pair* (x, u), *satisfying* $[x_c{}^T, u_c{}^T]^T \in X$, *there exists a unique index* i *such that* $[x_c{}^T, u_c{}^T]^T \in \mathcal{X}_i$, $x_\ell = \bar{x}_{\ell i}$ *and* $u_\ell = \bar{u}_{\ell i}$.

Remark 1 *Note that a completely well-posed PWA-LC systems is equivalent to a PWA systems in the form (1). In fact, by choosing*

$$\tilde{\mathcal{X}}_i = \left\{ (x, u) : [x_c^T, u_c^T]^T \in \mathcal{X}_i, x_\ell = \bar{x}_{\ell i}, u_\ell = \bar{u}_{\ell i} \right\},$$

from the well-posedness of the PWA-LC form it follows that $\tilde{\mathcal{X}}_i \cap \tilde{\mathcal{X}}_j = \emptyset, \forall i \neq j$. *Then, by choosing the matrices in (1a)-(1b) equal to the corresponding ones in (3a)-(3b) the equivalence follows.*

Compared to the model (1), PWA-LC systems have two additional features. First, the dynamics of the continuous-valued components x_c and y_c is not influenced by the binary states x_ℓ and inputs u_ℓ (in particular, the logic input u_ℓ contributes only in determining the switching between different cells); second, to the i-th subsystem corresponds a unique vector with binary entries

$$v_i = \left[x_\ell(k)^T \; x_\ell(k+1)^T \; y_\ell(k)^T \; u_\ell(k)^T \right]^T. \tag{6}$$

In fact, if the index i is fixed, condition (3c) ensures the uniqueness of $x_\ell(k)$ and $u_\ell(k)$ whereas $x_\ell(k+1)$ and $y_\ell(k)$ depend only on the displacements $a_{\ell,i}$ and $c_{\ell,i}$ that are time-independent.

The following theorem clarifies the relations between MLD and PWA-LC systems. In the sequel, we always assume that a PWA-LC system is completely well-posed.

Theorem 1 *For every MLD system (2) there exists an equivalent PWA-LC system (3).*

The proof of Theorem 1, which can be found in [10], is constructive and provides an algorithm for obtaining the PWA-LC form of an MLD system. Moreover, since, under minor assumptions, the class of PWA systems is strongly equivalent to the class of MLD systems [2], Theorem 1 guarantees that every PWA system can be written in the PWA-LC form. The converse follows from Remark 1. Finally, in [13] it was shown that the class of PWA systems is strongly equivalent (under mild assumptions) to the classes of hybrid systems in the Linear Complementarity, Extended Linear Complementarity and Min-Max Plus Scaling forms. Therefore, all such classes of hybrid systems are strongly equivalent to the class of PWA-LC systems.

Example 1 *Consider the PWA system (1a) where $\tilde{s} = 4$, $n_c = 2$, $n_\ell = 1$ (i.e. the state vector is $[x_{c,1}, x_{c,2}, x_\ell]^T$) and the matrices are*

$$\tilde{A}_1 = \left[\begin{array}{c|c} \bar{A}_1 & 0 \\ 0 \\ \hline 0 \; 0 & 1 \end{array}\right], \; \tilde{a}_1 = \left[\begin{array}{c} \bar{a}_1 \\ 0 \end{array}\right], \; \tilde{B}_1 = \left[\begin{array}{c} 0 \\ 0 \\ 0 \end{array}\right], \; \bar{A}_1 = 0.8 \cdot \left[\begin{array}{cc} \cos(-\frac{\pi}{8}) & -\sin(-\frac{\pi}{8}) \\ \sin(-\frac{\pi}{8}) & \cos(-\frac{\pi}{8}) \end{array}\right], \; \bar{a}_1 = \left[\begin{array}{c} 0 \\ 0 \end{array}\right], \quad (7)$$

$$\tilde{A}_2 = \left[\begin{array}{c|c} \bar{A}_2 & 0 \\ 0 \\ \hline 0 \; 0 & 1 \end{array}\right], \; \tilde{a}_2 = \left[\begin{array}{c} \bar{a}_2 \\ 0 \end{array}\right], \; \tilde{B}_2 = \left[\begin{array}{c} 0 \\ 0 \\ 0 \end{array}\right], \; \bar{A}_2 = 0.8 \cdot \left[\begin{array}{cc} \cos(\frac{\pi}{9}) & -\sin(\frac{\pi}{9}) \\ \sin(\frac{\pi}{9}) & \cos(\frac{\pi}{9}) \end{array}\right], \; \bar{a}_2 = \left[\begin{array}{c} 0 \\ 0 \end{array}\right], \quad (8)$$

$$\tilde{A}_3 = \left[\begin{array}{c|c} \bar{A}_3 & 0 \\ 0 \\ \hline 0 \; 0 & 0 \end{array}\right], \; \tilde{a}_3 = \left[\begin{array}{c} \bar{a}_3 \\ 0 \end{array}\right], \; \tilde{B}_3 = \left[\begin{array}{c} 0 \\ 0 \\ 0 \end{array}\right], \; \bar{A}_3 = 0.8 \cdot \left[\begin{array}{cc} \cos(-\frac{\pi}{6}) & -\sin(-\frac{\pi}{6}) \\ \sin(-\frac{\pi}{6}) & \cos(-\frac{\pi}{6}) \end{array}\right], \; \bar{a}_3 = \left[\begin{array}{c} 0 \\ 0 \end{array}\right], \quad (9)$$

$$\tilde{A}_4 = \left[\begin{array}{c|c} \bar{A}_5 & 0 \\ 0 \\ \hline 0 \; 0 & 0 \end{array}\right], \; \tilde{a}_4 = \left[\begin{array}{c} \bar{a}_4 \\ 1 \end{array}\right], \; \tilde{B}_4 = \left[\begin{array}{c} 0 \\ 0 \\ 0 \end{array}\right], \; \bar{A}_4 = 0.8 \cdot \left[\begin{array}{cc} \cos(\frac{\pi}{18}) & -\sin(\frac{\pi}{18}) \\ \sin(\frac{\pi}{18}) & \cos(\frac{\pi}{18}) \end{array}\right], \; \bar{a}_4 = \left[\begin{array}{c} 0 \\ 0 \end{array}\right]. \quad (10)$$

Consider the regions

$$\mathcal{R}_1 = \{(x_{c,1}, x_{c,2}) : -x_{c,1} + x_{c,2} \leq 0, \; x_{c,1} \leq 1, \; x_{c,2} \geq 0\} \tag{11}$$
$$\mathcal{R}_2 = \{(x_{c,1}, x_{c,2}) : -2.14 x_{c,1} + x_{c,2} \leq 0, \; 0.7 x_{c,1} + x_{c,2} \leq 1.7, \; x_{c,1} - x_{c,2} < 0\} \tag{12}$$
$$\mathcal{R}_3 = \{(x_{c,1}, x_{c,2}) : x_{c,2} < 0, \; 0 \leq x_{c,1} \leq 1, \; -0.47 x_{c,1} - x_{c,2} \leq 0.2\} \tag{13}$$

that partition the continuous state space as shown in Figure 1. The cells $\tilde{\mathcal{X}}_i$ are given by

$$\tilde{\mathcal{X}}_1 = \mathcal{R}_1 \times \{0\}, \qquad\qquad \tilde{\mathcal{X}}_2 = \mathcal{R}_1 \times \{1\},$$
$$\tilde{\mathcal{X}}_3 = (\mathcal{R}_2 \times \{0\}) \bigcup (\mathcal{R}_2 \times \{1\}), \quad \tilde{\mathcal{X}}_4 = (\mathcal{R}_3 \times \{0\}) \bigcup (\mathcal{R}_3 \times \{1\}).$$

The PWA system admits an equivalent representation in the PWA-LC form (3a) with 6 subsystems characterized by the following matrices

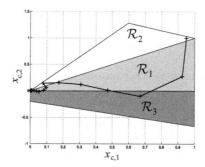

Fig. 1. A state trajectory $(x_{c,1}(k), x_{c,2}(k))$ for the PWA system in Example 1.

$$A_1 = \left[\begin{array}{c|c} \bar{A}_1 & 0 \\ & 0 \\ \hline 0\ 0 & 0 \end{array}\right], \quad A_2 = \left[\begin{array}{c|c} \bar{A}_2 & 0 \\ & 0 \\ \hline 0\ 0 & 0 \end{array}\right], \quad A_3 = \left[\begin{array}{c|c} \bar{A}_4 & 0 \\ & 0 \\ \hline 0\ 0 & 0 \end{array}\right], \tag{14}$$

$$A_4 = \left[\begin{array}{c|c} \bar{A}_4 & 0 \\ & 0 \\ \hline 0\ 0 & 0 \end{array}\right], \quad A_5 = \left[\begin{array}{c|c} \bar{A}_3 & 0 \\ & 0 \\ \hline 0\ 0 & 0 \end{array}\right], \quad A_6 = \left[\begin{array}{c|c} \bar{A}_3 & 0 \\ & 0 \\ \hline 0\ 0 & 0 \end{array}\right] \tag{15}$$

$$a_1 = \left[\begin{array}{c} \bar{a}_1 \\ 0 \end{array}\right], \quad a_2 = \left[\begin{array}{c} \bar{a}_2 \\ 1 \end{array}\right], \quad a_3 = \left[\begin{array}{c} \bar{a}_4 \\ 1 \end{array}\right], \quad a_4 = \left[\begin{array}{c} \bar{a}_4 \\ 1 \end{array}\right], \quad a_5 = \left[\begin{array}{c} \bar{a}_3 \\ 0 \end{array}\right], \quad a_6 = \left[\begin{array}{c} \bar{a}_3 \\ 0 \end{array}\right], \tag{16}$$

$$B_i = [\, 0\ 0\ |\ 0\,]^T, \quad i = 1, \dots, 6. \tag{17}$$

The cells of the PWA-LC system are given by

$$\mathcal{X}_1 = \mathcal{X}_2 = \mathcal{R}_1, \quad \mathcal{X}_3 = \mathcal{X}_4 = \mathcal{R}_3, \quad \mathcal{X}_5 = \mathcal{X}_6 = \mathcal{R}_2 \tag{18}$$

$$\bar{x}_{\ell,1} = \bar{x}_{\ell,3} = \bar{x}_{\ell,6} = 0, \quad \bar{x}_{\ell,2} = \bar{x}_{\ell,4} = \bar{x}_{\ell,5} = 1. \tag{19}$$

The trajectory of the continuous states $(x_{c,1}(k), x_{c,2}(k))$ stemming from $x(0) = [0.95, 1, 0]^T$ is depicted in Figure 1. Note that, by construction, every trajectory $(x_{c,1}(k), x_{c,2}(k))$ approaching the origin does not settle in a single cell but switches continuously among different cells.

3   Stability Analysis for PWA-LC Systems

In this section we analyze the stability property of autonomous PWA-LC systems. Such models, in view of Definition 2, can be written in the following form:

$$x(k + 1) = A_i x(k) + a_i, \quad \text{for} \quad \mathcal{C}(x(k)) \in \mathcal{X}_i \quad \mathcal{L}(x(k)) = \bar{x}_{\ell,i} \tag{20}$$

where $\mathcal{C}(x)$ belongs to the set of admissible states $\mathbb{X} = (\bigcup_{i=1}^{s} \mathcal{X}_i) \subseteq \mathbb{R}^{n_c}$, the cells $\{\mathcal{X}_i\}_{i=1}^{s}$ are polyhedra and the matrices A_i and a_i have the block structure

$$A_i = \left[\begin{array}{cc} A_{c,i} & 0 \\ 0 & 0 \end{array}\right], \quad a_i = \left[\begin{array}{c} a_{c,i} \\ a_{\ell,i} \end{array}\right], \quad A_{c,i} \in \mathbb{R}^{n_c \times n_c}, \ a_{c,i} \in \mathbb{R}^{n_c \times 1}. \tag{21}$$

According to the notation in [14], we call $\mathcal{I} = \{1, 2, \ldots, s\}$ the set of indices of the state space cells of the autonomous PWA system (20). $\mathcal{I}$ is partitioned as $\mathcal{I} = \mathcal{I}_0 \cup \mathcal{I}_1$, where $\mathcal{I}_0$ are the indices of the cells whose closure contains the origin and $\mathcal{I}_1 := \mathcal{I} \backslash \mathcal{I}_0$.

We assume that the origin $x_c = 0$ is contained in $\mathbb{X}$, and that it is an equilibrium of the system (20), i.e.

$$\mathcal{C} \left(A_i \begin{bmatrix} 0 \\ \bar{x}_{\ell,i} \end{bmatrix} (k) + a_i \right) = 0, \ \forall i \in \mathcal{I}_0. \tag{22}$$

From equations (21) and (22) it is also apparent that if $x_c = 0$ is an equilibrium, then we have $a_{c,i} = 0$, $\forall i \in \mathcal{I}_0$. Moreover, it is important to stress that this does not imply that the logic state $x_\ell(k)$ has a constant value but only that $x_\ell(k) \in \{\bar{x}_{\ell,i}, i \in \mathcal{I}_0\}$.

Hereafter we focus on the Lagrange stability [12] of the origin of (20), i.e. on the stability of the continuous-valued part x_c of the state vector.

Definition 4 *Let $\mathbb{X}_0 \subseteq \mathbb{X}$ such that $0 \in \mathbb{X}_0$. The equilibrium $x_c = 0$ is **exponentially stable** on $\mathbb{X}_0$ if there exist two coefficients $K > 0$, $0 < \gamma < 1$ and a time instant $\bar{k}$ such that, for all initial states $x(0)$ satisfying $\mathcal{C}(x(0)) \in \mathbb{X}_0$ then $\|x_c(k)\|^2 \leq K\gamma^k \|x_c(0)\|^2$, $\forall k > \bar{k}$.*

Note that in (1), the set $\mathbb{X}$ is possibly defined by polyhedral constraints on the state trajectory $x_c(k)$. Therefore, when focusing on stability on a set $\mathbb{X}_0$ it is natural to introduce the next Assumption.

Assumption 1 *The free evolution of the state trajectory for the PWA-LC system (20) stemming from an initial state $x(0)$ satisfying $\mathcal{C}(x(0)) \in \mathbb{X}_0$ fulfills the condition $\mathcal{C}(x(k)) \in \mathbb{X} \ \forall k \in \mathbb{N}_+$.*

In order to analyze the stability of $x_c = 0$, we will exploit a particular class of Lyapunov functions with the structure:

$$V(x_c) = x_c^T P_i(x_c) x_c, \quad \forall x_c \in \mathcal{X}_i \tag{23}$$

where

$$P_i : \mathcal{X}_i \to \mathbb{R}^{n_c \times n_c}, \forall i \in \mathcal{I} \tag{24}$$

$$x_c^T P_i(x_c) x_c > 0, \quad \forall x_c \in \mathcal{X}_i \backslash \{0\}, \forall i \in \mathcal{I} \tag{25}$$

and $\forall i \in \mathcal{I}$, $\sup_{x_c \in \mathcal{X}_i} |\lambda_{max}(P_i(x_c))| < +\infty$, $\sup_{x_c \in \mathcal{X}_i} |\lambda_{min}(P_i(x_c))| < +\infty$ and $\forall x_c \in \mathcal{X}_i$ $P_i(x_c) = P_i(x_c)^T$ ($\lambda_{max}(P)$ and $\lambda_{min}(P)$ denote the largest and the smallest eigenvalues, respectively, of a real and symmetric matrix P). Note that (23) does not imply that the matrices $P_i(x)$ are positive definite because the inequality is required to hold only for the points in the i-th region. Moreover the assumption on the maximum and minimum eigenvalues avoids that $|x_c^T(k) P_i(x_c(k)) x_c(k)|$ goes to infinity for some sequence $x_c(k) \in \mathcal{X}_i$, $k = 0, \ldots, +\infty$ that converges to a limit point belonging to the boundary of $\mathcal{X}_i$. Obviously, in order to guarantee these requirements on the eigenvalues, possible choices of matrices $P_i(\cdot)$ are

1. continuous functions on $\mathcal{X}_i$ if $\mathcal{X}_i$ is bounded;
2. constant matrices if the $\mathcal{X}_i$ is unbounded.

As shown in [9] in discrete-time, the function $V(x_c)$ used to prove stability of the origin can be discontinuous across the cell boundaries. More precisely, we do not need to require the continuity of $V(x_c)$ on the whole state-space $\mathbb{X}$ to prove the stability, as long as the number of cells is finite. For this reason we introduce the following Assumption.

Assumption 2 *The cardinality $|\mathcal{I}|$ of the set $\mathcal{I}$ is finite.*

In order to check the stability it is possible to resort to the procedure reported in the following theorem.

Theorem 2 *Let Assumption 2 hold. Let $\mathbb{X}_0$ be a set of initial states satisfying Assumption 1. The equilibrium $x_c = 0$ of (1) is exponentially stable on $\mathbb{X}_0$ if there exists a function $V(x_c)$ as in (23) possessing a negative forward difference $\Delta V(k+1, k) = V(x_c(k+1)) - V(x_c(k)), \forall k \geq 0$:*

$$\Delta V(k+1, k) = x_c(k+1)^T P_i(x_c(k+1))x_c(k+1) - x_c(k)^T P_j(x_c(k))x_c(k) < 0, \tag{26}$$

where $x_c(k) \neq 0$ and i, j are the indices such that $x_c(k) \in \mathcal{X}_j$, $x_\ell(k) = \bar{x}_{\ell,j}$, $x_c(k+1) \in \mathcal{X}_i$, $x_\ell(k+1) = \bar{x}_{\ell,i}$.

Remark 2 *Note that if, for a fixed $0 < \gamma \leq 1$, we can substitute the condition (26) with*

$$V(x_c(k+1)) - \gamma V(x_c(k)) =$$
$$= x_c(k+1)^T P_i(x_c(k+1))x_c(k+1) - \gamma x_c(k)^T P_j(x_c(k))x_c(k) < 0, \tag{27}$$

where $x_c(k) \neq 0$ and $x_c(k) \in \mathcal{X}_j$, $x_\ell(k) = \bar{x}_{\ell,j}$, $x_c(k+1) \in \mathcal{X}_i$, $x_\ell(k+1) = \bar{x}_{\ell,i}$, then it is possible to state that there exists a coefficient $\bar{\gamma}$, $0 < \bar{\gamma} < \gamma$ such that

$$\forall k \in \mathbb{N}_+, \|x_c(k)\|^2 < K\bar{\gamma}^k \|x_c(0)\|^2 \tag{28}$$

where K is a suitable positive coefficient. Therefore, γ represents a strict upper bound on the minimum degree of exponential stability.

3.1   LMI Algorithms for Exponential Stability Analysis

In this section we investigate numerical procedures to check the stability conditions (25) and (26). We first impose a convenient structure to the Lyapunov function used in (25) and (26). More precisely, we will adopt one of the following alternatives:

i) $P_i(x_c) = P_i \ \forall x_c \in \mathcal{X}_i$: this class of Lyapunov functions, which leads to the so-called Piecewise Quadratic (PWQ) stability, has been studied for continuous-time PWA systems without logic states in [14];

$ii)$ $P_i(x_c) = \sum_{j=0}^{N} P_{i(j)} \rho_{i(j)}(x_c)$ where $\rho_{i(j)} : \mathcal{X}_i \longrightarrow [0,1]$, $j = 1, 2, \ldots, N$ are (bounded) basis-functions [15] for $P_i(\cdot)$ and $P_{i(1)}, P_{i(2)}, \ldots, P_{i(N)}$ are parameter matrices. A similar class of Lyapunov functions has been proposed for continuous-time nonlinear systems in [15].

It is apparent that the stability tests obtained from choice $ii)$ are less conservative than those exploiting choice $i)$ We point out that all these tests can be translated into an LMI form [18] by replacing (25) and (26) with the following more conservative conditions:

$a)$ $P_i(x_c) > 0$, $\forall i \in \mathcal{I}$, $\forall x_c \in \mathcal{X}_i$ (29)

$b)$ $(A_{c,j} x_c + a_{c,j})^T P_i (A_{c,j} x_c + a_{c,j})(A_{c,j} x_c + a_{c,j}) - \gamma x_c^T P_j(x_c) x_c < 0$ (30)
$\forall j \in \mathcal{I}$, $\forall x_c \in \mathcal{X}_j \backslash \{0\}$, and $A_{c,j} x_c + a_{c,j} \in \mathcal{X}_i$, $a_{\ell,j} = \bar{x}_{\ell,i}$

where $0 < \gamma \leq 1$ represents a strict upper bound on the minimal degree of exponential stability. As one can easily note, inequalities (29)-(30) are LMI conditions both in case $i)$ and in the case $ii)$. Unfortunately, in general and even when the state-space $\mathbb{X}$ is bounded, one has to deal with an infinite-dimensional LMI problem or, in other words, it is necessary to deal with a Parameterized LMI (PMI) problem that can be reduced to a finite-dimensional LMI problem by resorting to various techniques based either on gridding of the parameter space [19] or on multiconvexity concepts [11].

3.2 Relaxation of Finite-Dimensional LMI Tests for Exponential Stability

In the previous subsection we proposed two stability tests based on the conditions (25) and (26). In this subsection we focus on the tests associated with Lyapunov functions of type (23) with the structure corresponding to the case $i)$. In fact, for this case, it is possible to obtain stability tests that do not require gridding and that are computationally less expensive. For the sake of simplicity, we assume that:

$$a_i^c = 0, \forall i \in \mathcal{I}. \tag{31}$$

It is easy to verify that conditions (29)-(30) are satisfied, for a given $0 < \gamma \leq 1$, if the following alternative inequalities are met:

$a)$ $P_i > 0$, $\forall i \in \mathcal{I}$ (32)

$b)$ $A_{c,j}^T P_i A_{c,j} - \gamma P_j < 0$, $\forall (i,j) \in \mathcal{W}$ (33)

where

$$\mathcal{W} = \left\{ (i,j) | j, i \in \mathcal{I}, x_c \in \mathcal{X}_j, \mathcal{C} \left(A_j \begin{bmatrix} x_c \\ \bar{x}_{\ell,j} \end{bmatrix} + a_j \right) \in \mathcal{X}_i \text{ and } a_{\ell,j} = \bar{x}_{\ell,i} \right\}. \tag{34}$$

The set $\mathcal{W}$, which represents all possible switches between subsystems in a single time-step, can be found by resorting first to the equivalence between MLD systems and PWA-LC systems and then by applying reachability analysis procedures available for MLD systems (see [2]). We point out that the computational burden for the determination of $\mathcal{W}$ is usually negligible compared to the one required for solving the LMIs (32)-(33).

Remark 3 *Lagrange stability is defined in terms of the continuous-valued part of the state x_c. However, this does not mean that it is independent of the evolution of the logic part of the state x_ℓ. Indeed, since from (20)-(21) it holds that $x_\ell(k + 1) = a_{\ell,i}$, the dynamics of x_ℓ influences the LMIs (32)-(33) since it contributes in defining the minimal set $\mathcal{W}$ of one-step switches.*

Following the rationale of [14] we note that the LMIs (32)-(33) are actually valid on the whole state space, even though they would be required to hold in a single cell only *i.e.* for $\mathcal{C}(x) \in \mathcal{X}_i$. We can remove some conservativeness by deriving from (25) and (26) some alternative conditions by exploiting the so-called S-Procedure (see *e.g.* [23]). More precisely, it is possible to reduce conservativeness if we can find matrices F_i and G_{ij} such that

$$P_i - F_i > 0, \ \forall i \in \mathcal{I} \tag{35}$$

$$A_{c,j}^T P_i A_{c,j} - \gamma P_j + G_{ij} < 0, \ \forall (i,j) \in \mathcal{W} \tag{36}$$

$$x_c^T F_j x_c \geq 0, \quad x_c^T G_{ij} x_c \geq 0 \quad \text{if} \ x_c \in \mathcal{X}_j. \tag{37}$$

Note that we do not require the matrices F_i and G_{ij} to be positive or negative definite, we only require that the quadratic forms take on the signs mentioned above in the corresponding cells. From the assumptions on the matrices F_i and G_{ij} it follows that the fulfillment of the LMIs (35)-(36) implies the fulfillment of (29)-(30).

As for the issue of finding suitable matrices F_i and G_{ij} fulfilling the requirement (37) and how to remove the assumption (31) we refer the interested reader to [14]

Example 2 *We analyze the Lagrange stability of the PWA-LC system considered in Example 1. The minimal set of one step switches $\mathcal{W}$ that can be found by means of the reachability analysis procedure described in [5] is*

$$\mathcal{W} = \{(1,1),(3,1),(2,2),(5,2),(2,3),(4,3),(2,4),(4,4),(1,5),(6,5),(1,6),(6,6)\} \tag{38}$$

By solving the LMIs (35)-(37) it has been possible to prove that the equilibrium $x_c = 0$ is exponentially stable on $\mathbb{X}$ with degree of exponential stability $\gamma \leq 0.49001$.

4   Performance Analysis Techniques

In this section we consider the H_∞ analysis problem for discrete-time PWA systems with logic states and show how it can be addressed by resorting to LMI-based algorithms. The rationale for our derivation hinges on the use of passivity theory for nonlinear systems [16]. As will be clear, the proposed LMI techniques can also be adapted to consider different performance indices.

We point out that an important application of the H_∞ performance analysis tests is the performance *analysis* of MPC for both linear and MLD systems. This can be done by exploiting the explicit PWA form of the closed-loop system [4,1].

Notation: The symbol $*$ will be used in some matrix expressions to induce a symmetric structure. For example, if L and R are symmetric matrices, then

$$
\begin{bmatrix} L + M + * & * \\ N & R \end{bmatrix} := \begin{bmatrix} L + M + M^T & N^T \\ N & R \end{bmatrix}. \tag{39}
$$

4.1 H_∞ Performance of Piecewise Affine Systems

Consider the augmented autonomous PWA-LC system

$$
\begin{aligned}
x(k+1) &= A_i x(k) + B_i w(k) + a_i \\
z(k) &= C_i x(k) + D_i w(k)
\end{aligned}, \quad \mathcal{C}(x(k)) \in \mathcal{X}_i \quad \mathcal{L}(x(k)) = \bar{x}_{\ell,i} \tag{40}
$$

where the system matrices have the block structure

$$
A_i = \begin{bmatrix} A_{c,i} & 0 \\ 0 & 0 \end{bmatrix}, \quad B_i = \begin{bmatrix} B_{c,i} \\ 0 \end{bmatrix}, \quad a_i = \begin{bmatrix} a_{c,i} \\ a_{\ell,i} \end{bmatrix},
$$
$$
A_{c,i} \in \mathbb{R}^{n_c \times n_c}, \; B_{c,i} \in \mathbb{R}^{n_c \times m}, \; a_{c,i} \in \mathbb{R}^{n_c \times 1}
$$
$$
C_i = \begin{bmatrix} C_{c,i} & 0 \end{bmatrix}, \; C_{c,i} \in \mathbb{R}^{r \times n_c}, D_i \in \mathbb{R}^{r \times m}. \tag{41}
$$

In the model (40), w represents a disturbance signal and z is a penalty output that can model, for instance, tracking errors. The Assumption 1 has to be modified in order to take into account the effects of the disturbance signal w as follows.

Assumption 3 *The evolution of the state trajectory for the PWA-LC system (40) stemming from an initial state $x(0)$ satisfying $\mathcal{C}(x(0)) \in \mathbb{X}_0$ and due to a disturbance signal $w(k), k \in \mathbb{N}_+$ satisfies the condition $\mathcal{C}(x(k)) \in \mathbb{X} \; \forall k \in \mathbb{N}_+$.*

As done in Section 3.2 to simplify the exposition we assume $a_{c,i} = 0, \forall i \in \mathcal{I}$.

We focus on the disturbance attenuation problem in an H_∞ framework: given a real number $\gamma > 0$, the exogenous signal w is attenuated by γ if, starting from a state x_0 satisfying $\mathcal{C}(x(0)) = 0$, for each integer $N \geq 0$ and for every non null $w \in l_2([0, N], \mathbb{R}^m)$ it holds

$$
\sum_{k=0}^{N} \|z(k)\|^2 < \gamma^2 \sum_{k=0}^{N} \|w(k)\|^2. \tag{42}
$$

Note that, as usual in the control of nonlinear systems [16], performance indices defined over a finite time horizon are considered.

A discrete-time nonlinear system (e.g. the PWA system (40)) is *strictly dissipative* with supply rate $W : \mathbb{R}^r \times \mathbb{R}^m \to \mathbb{R}$ [7] if there exists a non-negative function $V : \mathbb{R}^{n_c} \to \mathbb{R}$ termed *storage function* such that

$$\forall w(k) \in \mathbb{R}^m, \forall k \geq 0, \quad V(x_c(k+1)) - V(x_c(k)) < W(z(k), w(k)) \tag{43}$$

and $V(0) = 0$.
Condition (43), is the so-called *dissipation inequality* that can be equivalently represented through the condition [16,22]:

$$\forall w(k), \forall N \geq 0, \forall x_0 : \mathcal{C}(x_0) \in \mathbb{X}, \quad V(x_c(N+1)) - V(x_c(0)) < \sum_{k=0}^{N} W(z(k), w(k)) \tag{44}$$

where $x_c(0) = \mathcal{C}(x_0)$. Hereafter, we concentrate on finite gain dissipative PWA systems with the following supply rate

$$W_\infty(z, w) = \gamma^2 \|w\|^2 - \|z\|^2, \gamma > 0. \tag{45}$$

In fact, the supply rate $W_\infty(z, w)$ is related to the H_∞ performance of the PWA system. Other types of performance analysis procedures can be derived by considering alternative types of supply rate functions (see e.g. [18]).
An important issue is represented by the structure of the storage function used to test this performance criterion. The considerations reported in Section 3.1 about the structure of a Lyapunov function that can be used for stability tests, are valid also for the problem of selecting the structure of the candidate storage function.

4.2 H_∞ Analysis for PWA Systems

We first establish some preliminary facts on the H_∞ norm of a PWA-LC system for which the origin is PWQ stable

Lemma 1 *Let Assumptions 3 and 2 hold. Assume that there exists matrices P_i fulfilling the LMIs (32)-(33) and set $\mathcal{C}(x_0) = 0$. Then, the H_∞ constraint (42) is satisfied $\forall \gamma > \gamma_0$ where*

$$\gamma_0 = \left(\tilde{C}^2 \bar{\gamma}^2 + \tilde{D}^2 \right)^{1/2} \tag{46}$$

and

$$\begin{array}{c} \tilde{C} := \sup_{i \in \mathcal{I}} \|C_{c,i}\| \quad \tilde{D} := \sup_{i \in \mathcal{I}} \|D_i\| \\ \bar{\gamma} := \frac{\bar{L}_1 + (\bar{L}_1^2 + 4\bar{L}_2)^{1/2}}{2} \quad \bar{L}_1 := \frac{2L_1 \bar{P}}{\sigma} \quad \bar{L}_2 := \frac{L_2 \bar{P}}{\sigma} \\ L_1 := \sup_{i \in \mathcal{I}} \|A_{c,i}\| \|B_{c,i}\| \quad L_2 := \sup_{i \in \mathcal{I}} \|B_{c,i}\|^2 \quad \bar{P} := \sup_{i \in \mathcal{I}} \|P_i\|. \end{array} \tag{47}$$

The next result, which is a generalization of the classical Bounded Real Lemma [20,21,16] to PWA-LC systems, allows us to analyze the H_∞ performance of a PWA system with logic states.

Lemma 2 *Let Assumptions 2 and 3 hold. Consider the system (40) and an initial state $x(0)$ such that $C(x(0)) = 0$. If there exists a function $V(x_c) = x_c^T P_i(x_c) x_c \ \forall x_c \in \mathcal{X}_i$ of type (23) satisfying the dissipativity inequality (43) with supply rate (45), then the H_∞ performance condition (42) is satisfied. Furthermore, the equilibrium $x_c = 0$ of the system (40) is exponentially stable on $\mathbb{X}_0$.*

4.3   Solution Procedures for Performance Analysis Tests

The conservativeness of the performance condition (43) with supply rate (45) depends strictly on the structure adopted for the matrices $P_i(\cdot)$: some possible choices are reported in Section 3.1.

It is also worthwhile stressing that the performance analysis condition (43) is satisfied if the following inequality is fulfilled

$$M_{ji}(x_c(k), w(k)) < 0, \tag{48}$$

where $x_c(k) \in \mathcal{X}_j \setminus \{0\}$, $x_c(k+1) = A_{c,j} x_c(k) + B_{c,j} w(k) \in \mathcal{X}_i$ and

$$M_{ji}(x_c(k), w(k)) := \tag{49}$$

$$\begin{bmatrix} A_{c,j}^T P_i(x_c(k+1)) A_{c,j} - P_j(x_c(k)) + C_{c,j}^T C_{c,j} & * \\ D_j^T C_{c,j} + B_{c,j}^T P_i(x_c(k+1)) A_{c,j} & B_{c,j}^T P_i(x_c(k+1)) B_{c,j} + D_j^T D_j - \gamma^2 I \end{bmatrix}$$

Obviously, it is possible to reduce the condition (48) to a PMI problem that, as pointed out in Section 3.1, can be solved by resorting to classical techniques like the gridding method.

Furthermore, by assuming that the matrices $P_i(\cdot)$ are independent of the state (case i) of Section 3.1), condition (48) becomes

$$P_i > 0, \ \forall i \in \mathcal{I} \qquad \bar{M}_{ji} < 0 \ \forall (i,j) \in \mathcal{W} \tag{50}$$

where

$$\bar{M}_{ji} := \begin{bmatrix} A_{c,j}^T P_i A_{c,j} - P_j + C_{c,j}^T C_{c,j} & * \\ D_j^T C_{c,j} + B_{c,j}^T P_i A_{c,j} & B_{c,j}^T P_i B_{c,j} + D_j^T D_j - \gamma^2 I \end{bmatrix}. \tag{51}$$

Furthermore, similarly to what has been proposed in the previous section about the stability analysis procedure, it is possible to reduce the conservativeness of the LMIs (50) by relaxing these inequalities with matrices F_i and G_{ij} satisfying the requirements (37).

5   Conclusions

In this paper we first showed that a PWA system can be represented in a logic canonical form that is particularly advantageous for investigating both Lagrange stability and performance of PWA systems with logic states. Then, analogously to the techniques developed in [9], we derived stability tests for PWA-LC systems based on LMI theory. Moreover, we extended our results to the H_∞ analysis problem by means of classical dissipative concepts for nonlinear discrete-time systems. Future research will focus on the adaptation of the procedure proposed in [8] for the synthesis of state-feedback controllers, to the case of PWA-LC systems. Also Model Predictive Control (MPC) schemes for PWA-LC systems are under development.

Acknowledgments

This research has been supported by the Swiss National Science Foundation.

References

1. A. Bemporad, F. Borrelli, and M. Morari. Optimal controllers for hybrid systems: Stability and explicit form. *Proc. 39th Conference on Decision and Control*, December 2000.
2. A. Bemporad, G. Ferrari-Trecate, and M. Morari. Observability and Controllability of Piecewise Affine and Hybrid Systems. *IEEE Transactions on Automatic Control*, 45(10):1864–1876, 2000.
3. A. Bemporad and M. Morari. Control of Systems Integrating Logic, Dynamics, and Constraints. *Automatica*, 35(3):407–427, March 1999.
4. A. Bemporad, M. Morari, V. Dua, and E. N. Pistikopoulos. The explicit linear quadratic regulator for constrained systems. In *American Control Conference*, Chicago, IL, June 2000.
5. A. Bemporad, F.D. Torrisi, and M. Morari. Optimization-Based Verification and Stability Characterization of Piecewise Affine and Hybrid Systems. In Springer Verlag Lecture Notes in Computer Science, editor, *Proceedings 3rd International Workshop on Hybrid Systems, Pittsburgh, PA, USA*, 2000.
6. M.S. Branicky. Multiple Lyapunov functions and other analysis tools for switched and hybrid systems. *IEEE Trans. Autom. Control*, 43(4):475–482, April 1998.
7. C. I. Byrnes and W. Lin. Passivity and absolute stabilization of a class of discrete-time nonlinear systems. *Automatica*, 31(2):263–268, 1995.
8. F. A. Cuzzola and M. Morari. A Generalized Approach for Analysis and Control of Discrete-Time Piecewise Affine and Hybrid Systems. In A. Sangiovanni-Vincentelli and M. Di Benedetto, editors, *Hybrid Systems: Computation and Control, Proceedings 4th International Workshop on Hybrid Systems*, Lecture Notes in Computer Science 2034, pages 189–203. Springer-Verlag, 2001.
9. G. Ferrari-Trecate, F. A. Cuzzola, D. Mignone, and M. Morari. Analysis of Discrete-Time Piecewise Affine and Hybrid Systems. Technical Report AUT01-16, Automatic Control Laboratory, ETH Zurich, 2001. Provisionally accepted for the publication in *Automatica*.
10. G. Ferrari-Trecate, F. A. Cuzzola, and M. Morari. Analysis of Discrete-Time PWA Systems with Boolean Inputs, Outputs and States. Technical Report AUT01-21, Automatic Control Laboratory, ETH Zurich, 2001.
11. P. Ghainet, P. Apkarian, and M. Chilali. Affine parameter-dependent Lyapunov functions and real parametric uncertainty. *IEEE Transactions on Automatic Control*, 41(3):436–442, 1996.
12. A. Hassibi, S. P. Boyd, and J. P. How. A Class of Lyapunov Functionals for Analyzing Hybrid Dynamical Systems. In *Proc. of the American Control Conference*, pages 2455 – 2460, 1999.

13. W.P.M.H. Heemels, B. De Schutter, and A. Bemporad. On the Equivalence of Classes of Hybrid Systems: Mixed Logical Dynamical and Complementarity Systems. *Automatica*, 37(7):1085–1091, 2000.
14. M. Johannson and A. Rantzer. Computation of piecewise quadratic Lyapunov functions for hybrid systems. *IEEE Trans. Autom. Control*, 43(4):555–559, 1998.
15. T. A. Johansen. Computation of Lyapunov functions for smooth nonlinear systems using convex optimisation. *Automatica*, 36(11):1617–1626, 2000.
16. W. Lin and C. I. Byrnes. H_∞ Control of Discrete-Time Nonlinear Systems. *IEEE Transactions on Automatic Control*, 41(4):494–510, 1996.
17. A. Pettersson and B. Lennartson. Exponential Stability of Hybrid Systems Using Piecewise Quadratic Lyapunov Functions Resulting in LMIs. In *IFAC, 14th Triennial World Congress, Beijing, P.R. China*, 1999.
18. C. W. Scherer, P. Gahinet, and M. Chilali. Multi-Objective Output-Feedback Control via LMI Optimization. *IEEE Transactions on Automatic Control*, 42(7):896–911, 1997.
19. H. D. Tuan, E. Ono, P. Apkarian, and S. Hosoe. Nonlinear H_∞ Control for an Integrated Suspension System via Parametrized Linear Matrix Inequality Characterizations. *IEEE Transactions on Control System Technology*, 9(1):175–185, 2001.
20. A. J. Van der Schaft. The H_∞ control problem: A state space approach. *System & Control Letters*, 16:1–8, 1991.
21. A. J. Van der Schaft. L_2-gain analysis of nonlinear systems and nonlinear H_∞ control. *IEEE Transactions on Automatic Control*, 37:770–784, 1992.
22. J. C. Willems. Dissipative dynamic systems. *Arch. Rational Mechanics Analysis*, 45:321–393, 1972.
23. V. A. Yakubovich. S-Procedure in nonlinear control theory. *Vestnik Leninggradskogo Universiteta, Ser. Matematika*, pages 62–77, 1971.

Modeling and Control of Co-generation Power Plants: A Hybrid System Approach

Giancarlo Ferrari-Trecate[1], Eduardo Gallestey[2], Paolo Letizia[1],
Matteo Spedicato[1], Manfred Morari[1], and Marc Antoine[3]

[1] Institut für Automatik,
ETH - Swiss Federal Institute of Technology, ETL,
CH-8092 Zürich, Switzerland,
Tel. +41-1-6327812, Fax +41-1-6321211
{ferrari,letizia,spedicat,morari}@aut.ee.ethz.ch
[2] ABB Corporate Research Ltd.
eduardo.gallestey@ch.abb.com
[3] ABB Power Automation Ltd.
marc.antoine@ch.abb.com

Abstract. In this paper the optimization of a combined cycle power plant is accomplished by exploiting hybrid systems, i.e. systems evolving according to continuous dynamics, discrete dynamics, and logic rules. The possibility of turning on/off the gas and steam turbine, the operating constraints (minimum up and down times) and the different types of start up of the turbines characterize the hybrid behavior of a combined cycle power plant. In order to model both the continuous/discrete dynamics and the switching between different operating conditions we use the framework of Mixed Logic Dynamical systems. Next, we recast the economic optimization problem as a Model Predictive Control (MPC) problem, that allows us to optimize the plant operations by taking into account the time variability of both prices and electricity/steam demands. Because of the presence of integer variables, the MPC scheme is formulated as a mixed integer linear program that can be solved in an efficient way by using commercial solvers.

1 Introduction

In the last decade, the electric power industry has been subject to deep changes in structure and organization. From the technological side, the use of combined cycle power plants (CCPP) became more and more popular because of their high efficiency. A typical CCPP is composed of a gas cycle and a steam cycle. The gas cycle is fed by fuel and produces electric power through the expansion of the gas in the gas turbine; the steam cycle is supplied with the output exhaust gas from the gas turbine and generates both electricity and steam for the industrial processes. From the economic side, the liberalization of the energy market promoted the need of operating CCPPs in the most efficient way, that is by maximizing the profits due to the sales of steam and electricity and by minimizing the operating costs.

C.J. Tomlin and M.R. Greenstreet (Eds.): HSCC 2002, LNCS 2289, pp. 209–224, 2002.
© Springer-Verlag Berlin Heidelberg 2002

In this paper we consider the problem of optimizing the short-term operation of a CCPP, i.e. to optimize the plant on an hourly basis over a time horizon that may vary from few hours to one day [23]. A large stream of research in the power systems area focused on this problem. The usual recipe is to recast the economic optimization into the minimization of a cost functional and to account for the physical model of the plant through suitably defined constraints. The results available in the literature differ both in the *features* of the CCPP modeled and in the *scope* of optimization.

In [23], [13], [24] the CCPP is assumed in a standard operating condition and optimal scheduling of the resources is performed via non linear programming techniques. The main limitation is that the possibility of turning on/off the turbines is not considered and therefore it is not possible to determine the optimal switching strategy. The discrete features of a CCPP (i.e. the fact that turbines can be turned on/off, the minimum up and down time constraints and the priority constraints in start up sequences) can be captured by using binary decision variables along with continuous-valued variables describing physical quantities (e.g. mass, energy and flow rates).

In [21] binary variables are introduced to model the on/off status of the devices and the corresponding optimization problem is solved through the use of genetic algorithms. The same modeling feature is considered in [16] where the automatic computation of the optimal on/off input commands (fulfilling also operational priority constraints) is accomplished through Mixed Integer Linear Programming (MILP). However in both papers, the modeling of the CCPP is done in an ad-hoc fashion and the generalization to plants with different topologies and/or specifications seems difficult. Moreover, other important features such as minimum up and down times or the behavior during start up are neglected. A fairly complete model of a thermal unit, using integer variables for describing minimum up/down time constraints, ramp constraints and different startup procedures, is given in [2]. The behaviour of the unit is then optimized by solving MILP problems. Even if this approach could be adapted for modeling a single turbine of a CCPP, no methodological way for describing the coordination between different turbines is provided.

The aim of this paper is to show how both the tasks of modeling and optimization of CCPPs can be efficiently solved by resorting to hybrid system methodologies. Hybrid systems recently have attracted the interest of many researchers, because they can capture in a single model the interaction between continuous and discrete-valued dynamics. Various models for hybrid system have been proposed [18], [20], [6] and the research focused on the investigation of basic properties such as stability [5], [17], controllability and observability [3], and the development of control [4] [20], state estimation [11] and verification, [1] schemes.

We will use discrete-time hybrid systems in the Mixed Logical Dynamical (MLD) form [4] for two reasons. First, they provide a general framework for modeling many discrete features of CCPPs, including the coordination and prioritization between different devices; second, they are suitable to be used in on-line optimization schemes [4].

In Section 2 we briefly recall the basic features of MLD systems and in Section 3 we describe the CCPP plant we consider (the "Island" CCPP). In Section 3.2 it is shown how to model in the MLD form both the continuous and discrete features of the plant. The operation optimization is then described in Section 4. We show how to recast the economic optimization problem in a Model Predictive Control (MPC) scheme for MLD systems that can be solved via Mixed Integer Liner Programming (MILP). The use of piecewise affine terms in the cost functional allows us to consider various economic factors as the earnings due to selling of the electric power and steam, the fixed running costs, the start up costs and the cost due to aging of plant components. Finally in Section 5 the most significant control experiments are illustrated and in Section 5.1 the computational burden of the optimization procedure is discussed.

2   Hybrid Systems in the MLD Form

The derivation of the MLD form of a hybrid system involves basically three steps [4]. The first one is to associate with a logical statement S, that can be either true or false, a binary variable $\delta \in \{0,1\}$ that is 1 if and only if the statement holds true. Then, the combination of elementary statements $S_1, ..., S_q$ into a compound statement via the Boolean operators AND ($\wedge$), OR ($\vee$), NOT ($\sim$) can be represented as linear inequalities over the corresponding binary variables δ_i, $i = 1, ..., q$.

An example would be the condition $a^T x \leq 0$:

$$[a^T x \leq 0] \Leftrightarrow [\delta = 1]$$

where $x \in X \subseteq R^n$ is a continuous variable and X is a compact set. If one defines m and M as lower and upper bounds on $a^T x$ respectively, the inequalities

$$\begin{cases} a^T x \leq M - M\delta \\ a^T x \geq \varepsilon + (m - \varepsilon)\delta \end{cases}$$

assign the value $\delta = 1$ if and only if the value of x satisfies the threshold condition. Note that $\varepsilon > 0$ is a small tolerance (usually close to the machine precision) introduced to replace the strict inequalities by non-strict ones.

The second step is to represent the product between linear functions and logic variables by introducing an auxiliary variable $z = \delta a^T x$. Equivalently, z is uniquely specified through the mixed integer linear inequalities

$$\begin{cases} z \leq M\delta \\ z \geq m\delta \\ z \leq a^T x - m(1 - \delta) \\ z \geq a^T x - M(1 - \delta) \end{cases}$$

The third step is to include binary and auxiliary variables in an LTI discrete-time dynamic system in order to describe in a unified model the evolution of the continuous and logic components of the system.

The general MLD form of a hybrid system is [4]

$$x(t+1) = Ax(t) + B_1u(t) + B_2\delta(t) + B_3z(t) \tag{1a}$$
$$y(t) = Cx(t) + D_1u(t) + D_2\delta(t) + D_3z(t) \tag{1b}$$
$$E_2\delta(t) + E_3z(t) \leq E_1u(t) + E_4x(t) + E_5 \tag{1c}$$

where $x = \begin{bmatrix} x_c^T & x_l^T \end{bmatrix}^T \in R^{n_c} \times \{0,1\}^{n_l}$ are the continuous and binary states, $u = \begin{bmatrix} u_c^T & u_l^T \end{bmatrix}^T \in R^{m_c} \times \{0,1\}^{m_l}$ are the inputs, $y = \begin{bmatrix} y_c^T & y_l^T \end{bmatrix}^T \in R^{p_c} \times \{0,1\}^{p_l}$ the outputs, and $\delta \in \{0,1\}^{r_l}$, $z \in R^{r_c}$ represent auxiliary binary and continuous variables, respectively. All constraints on the states, the inputs, the z and δ variables are summarized in the inequalities (1c). Note that, although the description (1a)-(1b)-(1c) seems to be linear, non linearity is hidden in the integrality constraints over the binary variables.

MLD systems are a versatile framework to model various classes of systems. For a detailed description of such capabilities we defer the reader to [4], [3]. The discrete-time formulation of the MLD system allows to develop numerically tractable schemes for solving complex problems, such as stability [7], state estimation [11], and control [4]. In particular, MLD models were proven successful for recasting hybrid dynamic optimization problems into mixed-integer linear and quadratic programs solvable via branch and bound techniques.

In this paper, for the optimization of the plant we propose a predictive control scheme (*Model Predictive Control - MPC*) which is able to stabilize MLD systems on desired reference trajectories while fulfilling operating constraints.

In order to automatize the procedure for representing a hybrid system in the MLD form (1a)-(1b)-(1c), the compiler HYSDEL (HYbrid System DEscription Language), that generates the matrices of the MLD model starting from a high-level description of the dynamic and logic of the system, was developed at ETH, Zürich [27].

3   Hybrid Model of a Combined Cycle Power Plant

The cogeneration combined cycle power plant Island consists of four main components: a gas turbine, a heat recovery steam generator, a steam turbine and a steam supply for a paper mill.

We adopted the simplified input/output description of the plant presented in [24] and represented in Figure 1. Note that the heat recovery steam generator does not appear in Figure 1 because it is hidden in the "steam turbine" block. The plant has two continuous-valued inputs (u_1 and u_2), and two binary inputs (u_{l1} and u_{l2}):

- u_1 is the set point for the gas turbine load (in percent). The permitted operation range for the gas turbine is in the interval $[u_{1,\min}, u_{1,\max}]$;
- u_2 is the steam mass flow to the paper mill. The permitted range for the steam flow is in the interval $[u_{2,\min}, u_{2,\max}]$;

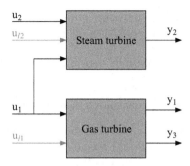

Fig. 1. Block diagram of the Island power plant.

  – u_{l1} and u_{l2} are, respectively, the on/off commands for the gas and steam
    turbines; the "on" command is associated with the value one.

In the Island plant the inputs u_1 and u_2 are independent and all possible combinations within the admissible ranges are permitted. The binary input variables
must fulfill the logic condition

$$u_{l2} = 1 \quad \Rightarrow \quad u_{l1} = 1 \tag{2}$$

which defines a priority constraint between the two turbines: The steam turbine
can be switched on/off only when the gas turbine is on, otherwise the steam
turbine must be kept off.

The output variables of the model are:

  – the fuel consumption of the gas turbine, y_1 [kg/s];
  – the electric power generated by the steam turbine, y_2 [MW];
  – the electric power generated by the gas turbine, y_3 [MW];

Since we aim at optimizing the plant hourly, we chose a sampling time of one
hour and we assume that the inputs are constant within each sampling interval.
As reported in [24], an input/output model of the plant

$$y_1(k+1) = f_1(u_1(k)) \tag{3}$$
$$y_2(k+1) = f_2(u_1(k), u_2(k)) \tag{4}$$
$$y_3(k+1) = f_3(u_1(k)) \tag{5}$$

where the maps f_1, f_2 and f_3 can be either affine or piecewise affine and are
obtained by interpolating experimental data. In particular, the use of piecewise
affine input/output relations allows to approximate nonlinear behaviours in an
accurate way.

3.1 Hybrid Features of the Plant

The features which suggest modeling the Island power plant as a hybrid system
are the following:

- the presence of the binary inputs u_{l1} and u_{l2};
- the turbines have different start up modes, depending on how long the turbines have been kept off;
- electric power, steam flow and fuel consumption are continuous valued quantities evolving with time.

Furthermore, the following constraints have to be taken into account:

- the operating constraints on the minimum amount of time for which the turbines must be kept on/off (the so-called minimum up/down times);
- the priority constraint (2). This condition, together with the previous one, leads to constraints on the sequences of logic inputs which can be applied to the system;
- the gas turbine load u_1 and the steam mass flow u_2 are bounded.

Finally one would also like to describe the piecewise affine relations (3)-(5) in the model of the CCPP.

3.2   The MLD Model of the Island Plant

All the features of the Island power plant mentioned in Section 3.1 can be captured by a hybrid model in the MLD form. For instance, the possibility to incorporate piecewise affine relations in the MLD model is discussed in [4,3] and the modeling of priority constraints like (2) is detailed in [4]. Moreover the possibility of incorporating bounds on the inputs is apparent from the inequalities (1c). In the following we show, as an example, how to derive the MLD description of the different types of start up for the turbines. We focus on the steam turbine only, since the procedure is exactly the same for the gas turbine.

Typical start up diagrams show that the longer the time for which a turbine is kept off, the longer the time required before producing electric power when it is turned on. This feature can be modeled, in an approximate way, as a delay between the time instant when the command on is given and the instant when the production of electric power begins.

	$time\ spent\ off\ (h)$	$delay\ (h)$
normal start up	$[0, 8]$	1
hot start up	$]8, 60]$	2
warm start up	$]60, 120]$	3
cold start up	$]120, +\infty[$	4

Table 1. Types of start up procedures for the steam turbine

In our model we consider the four different types of start up procedures for the steam and gas turbines, that are reported in Table 1. In order to take into account in the MLD model the different start up procedures, it is necessary to introduce three clocks with reset (which are state variables), five auxiliary logic variables δ, and three auxiliary real variables z.

The clocks are defined as follows:

- ξ_{on} stores the consecutive time during which the turbine produces electric power. If the turbine is producing electric power, ξ_{on} is increased according to the equation

$$\xi_{on}(k+1) = \xi_{on}(k) + 1 \tag{6}$$

otherwise it is kept equal to zero;
- ξ_{off} stores the consecutive time during which the turbine does not produce electric power. So, if the turbine is off or does not produce electric power (as in a start up phase), ξ_{off} is increased according to the equation

$$\xi_{off}(k+1) = \xi_{off}(k) + 1 \tag{7}$$

otherwise it is kept equal to zero;
- ξ_d, when it is positive, stores the delay that must occur between the turning on command and the actual production of electric power. If the turbine is turned on, ξ_d starts to decrease according to the law

$$\xi_d(k+1) = \xi_d(k) - 1 \tag{8}$$

and the energy generation will begin only when the condition $\xi_d < 0$ is fulfilled. Otherwise, if the turbine is off, ξ_d stores the delay corresponding to the current type of start up. In view of Table 1, the value of ξ_d is given by the following rules:

$$\text{if } u_{l2} = 0 \text{ and if } \begin{cases} \xi_{off} \leq 8h & \Rightarrow & \xi_d = 0 \\ 8h < \xi_{off} \leq 60h & \Rightarrow & \xi_d = 1 \\ 60h < \xi_{off} \leq 120h & \Rightarrow & \xi_d = 2 \\ \xi_{off} > 120h & \Rightarrow & \xi_d = 3 \end{cases} \tag{9}$$

The procedure of deriving the MLD form of the clocks ξ_{on}, ξ_{off} and ξ_d by introducing auxiliary logic (δ) and real (z) variables with the corresponding mixed-integer linear inequalities is reported in [26]. Clocks with reset in an MLD form are also discussed in [10].

The complete MLD model, capturing all the hybrid features of the Island plant described in Section 3.1, involves 12 state variables, 25 δ-variables and 9 z-variables [26]. The 103 inequalities stemming from the representation of the δ and z variables are collected in the matrices E_i, $i = 1, ..., 5$ of (1c) and are not reported here due to the lack of space. Some significant simulations which test the correctness of the MLD model of the Island power plant are also available in [26].

4   Plant Optimization

The control technique we use to optimize the operation of the Island power plant is the Model Predictive Control (MPC) [22], [4]. The main idea of MPC is to use a model of the plant (the MLD model in our case) to *predict* the future evolution of the system within a fixed prediction horizon. Based on this prediction, at each time step k the controller selects a sequence of future command inputs through an on-line optimization procedure, which aims at minimizing a suitable cost function, and enforces fulfillment of the constraints. Then, only the first sample of the optimal sequence is applied to the plant at time k and at time $k + 1$, the whole optimization procedure is repeated. This on-line "re-planning" provides the desired feedback control action.

Economic optimization is achieved by designing the inputs of the plant that minimize a cost functional representing the operating costs. The terms composing the cost functional we consider are described in Section 4.1. In particular, some terms appearing in the cost functional are naturally non linear and in Section 4.2 we will show how to recast them into a linear form by using suitably defined auxiliary optimization variables. This allows reformulating the MPC problem as a Mixed Integer Linear Programming (MILP) problem, for which efficient solvers exist [12].

4.1   Cost Functional

The following cost functional is minimized

$$
J = C_{dem} + C_{change} + C_{fuel} + C_{start\ up} + \\
+ C_{fixed} - E + C_{start\ up\ gas} + C_{fixed\ gas}
\tag{10}
$$

Let k and M be respectively the current time instant and the length of the control horizon. We use the notation $f(t|k)$ for indicating a time function, defined for $t \geq k$, that depends also on the current instant k. Then, the terms appearing in (10) have the following meaning:

- C_{dem} is the penalty function for not meeting the electric and steam demands over the prediction horizon:

$$
C_{dem} = \sum_{t=k}^{k+M-1} k_{dem\ el}(t|k)\, |y_2(t|k) + y_3(t|k) - d_{el}(t|k)| + \\
+ \sum_{t=k}^{k+M-1} k_{dem\ st}(t|k)\, |u_2(t|k) - d_{st}(t|k)|
$$

where $k_{dem\ el}(t|k)$ and $k_{dem\ st}(t|k)$ are suitable positive weight coefficients; $d_{el}(t|k)$ and $d_{st}(t|k)$, $t = k, ..., k + M - 1$ represent, respectively, the profile of the electric and steam demands within the prediction horizon. Both the coefficients and the demands are assumed to be known over the prediction horizon. In actual implementation they are usually obtained by economic forecasting. The values of $k_{dem\ el}(t|k)$ and $k_{dem\ st}(t|k)$ weigh the fulfillment of the electric power demand and the fulfillment of the steam demand, respectively.

– C_{change} is the cost for changing the operation point between two consecutive time instants:

$$C_{change} = \sum_{t=k}^{k+M-2} k_{\Delta u_1}(t|k)\,|u_1(t+1|k) - u_1(t|k)| +$$
$$+ \sum_{t=k}^{k+M-2} k_{\Delta u_2}(t|k)\,|u_2(t+1|k) - u_2(t|k)|$$

where $k_{\Delta u_1}(t|k)$, $k_{\Delta u_2}(t|k)$ are the positive weights.

– C_{fuel} takes into account the cost for fuel consumption (represented in the model by the output y_1).

$$C_{fuel} = \sum_{t=k}^{k+M-1} k_{fuel}(t|k)y_1(t|k)$$

where $k_{fuel}(t|k)$ is the price of the fuel.

– $C_{start\ up}$ is the cost for the start up of the steam turbine. In fact, during the start up phase, no energy is produced and an additional cost related to fuel consumption is paid. $C_{start\ up}$ is then given by

$$C_{start\ up} = \sum_{t=k}^{k+M-2} k_{start\ up}(t|k)(\max\{[u_{l1}(t+1|k) - u_{l1}(t|k)], 0\}$$

where $k_{start\ up}(t|k)$ represents the positive weight coefficient. Note that

$$\max\{[u_{l1}(t+1|k) - u_{l1}(t|k)], 0\}$$

is equal to one only if the start up of the steam turbine occurs, otherwise it is always equal to zero. Since, as discussed in Section 3.2, different start up modes are allowed, $k_{start\ up}(t|k)$ should increase as the delay between the "on" command and the production of electric power increases (see Table 1).

– C_{fixed} represents the fixed running cost of the steam turbine. It is non zero only when the device is on and it does not depend on the level of the steam flow u_2. C_{fixed} is given by

$$C_{fixed} = \sum_{t=k}^{k+M-1} k_{fixed}(t|k)u_{l1}(t|k)$$

where k_{fixed} represents the fixed cost (per hour) due to the use of the turbine. Note that C_{fixed} causes the steam turbine to be turned on only if the earnings by having it running are greater than the fixed costs.

– E represents the earnings from the sales of steam and electricity; this term has to take into account that the surplus production can not be sold:

$$E = \sum_{t=k}^{k+M-1} p_{el}(t|k)(\min[y_2(t|k) + y_3(t|k), d_{el}(t|k)]) +$$
$$\sum_{t=k}^{k+M-1} p_{st}(t|k)(\min[u_2(t|k), d_{st}(t|k)])$$

where $p_{el}(t|k)$ and $p_{st}(t|k)$ represent, respectively, the prices for electricity and steam.

- $C_{start\ up\ gas}$ is the start up cost for the gas turbine. It plays the same role as the term $C_{start\ up}$ and is defined through the logic input u_{l2}. $C_{start\ up\ gas}$ is given by

$$C_{start\ up\ gas} = \sum_{t=k}^{k+M-2} k_{start\ up\ gas}(t|k) \max\{[u_{l2}(t+1|k) - u_{l2}(t|k)], 0\}$$

where $k_{start\ up\ gas}(t|k)$ is a positive weight.

- $C_{fixed\ gas}$, represents the fixed running cost of the gas turbine (is analogous to C_{fixed}):

$$C_{fixed\ gas} = \sum_{t=k}^{k+M-1} k_{fixed\ gas}(t|k) u_{l2}(t|k) \tag{11}$$

where $k_{fixed\ gas}(t|k)$ is a positive weight.

4.2   Constraints and Derivation of the MILP

The constraints of the optimization problem are the system dynamics expressed in the MLD form (1a)-(1c). Thus, the overall optimization problem can be written as

min J

subject to $x(k|k) = x_k$ and for $t = k,...,k + M$

$$x(t+1|k) = Ax(t|k) + B_1 u(t|k) + B_2 \delta(t|k) + B_3 z(t|k) \tag{12}$$

$$y(t|k) = Cx(t|k) + D_1 u(t|k) + D_2 \delta(t|k) + D_3 z(t|k)$$

$$E_2 \delta(t|k) + E_3 z(t|k) \le E_1 u(t|k) + E_4 x(t|k) + E_5$$

where the state x_k of the system at time k enters through the constraint $x(k|k) = x_k$ and the optimization variables are $\{u(t|k)\}_{t=k}^{k+M-1}$, $\{\delta(t|k)\}_{t=k}^{k+M-1}$, $\{z(t|k)\}_{t=k}^{k+M-1}$.

In the following, for a signal $p(t|k)$ we denote with $\underline{p}_k$ the vector

$$\underline{p}_k = [p(k|k) \cdots p(k + M - 1|k)]'. \tag{13}$$

Then, the optimization problem (12) can be written as follows:

min J

subject to $x(k|k) = x_k$ and for $t = k,...,k + M$

$$\underline{x}_{k+1} = T_x x_k + T_u \underline{u}_{Tk} + T_\delta \underline{\delta}_k + T_z \underline{z}_k \tag{14}$$

$$\underline{y}_k = C_C \underline{x}_{k+1} + D_{D1} \underline{u}_k + D_{D2} \underline{\delta}_k + D_{D3} \underline{z}_k + \tilde{C} x_k$$

$$E_{E2} \underline{\delta}_k + E_{E3} \underline{z}_k \le E_{E1} \underline{u}_k + E_{E4} \underline{x}_{k+1} + E_{E5},$$

where the entries of matrices T_x, T_u, T_δ and T_z can be computed by successive substitutions involving the equation

$$x(t) = A^{t-k}x_k + \sum_{i=0}^{t-k-1} A^i[B_1 u(t-1-i) + B_2\delta(t-1-i) + B_3 z(t-1-i)]$$

(15)

that gives the state evolution of the MLD system. Also the E_{E_i} matrices, $i = 1, ..., 5$ can be found by exploiting (15).

The optimization problem (14) is a mixed integer *nonlinear* program because of the nonlinearities appearing in the terms C_{dem}, C_{change}, $C_{start\ up}$, E and $C_{start\ up\ gas}$. However the non linearities in the cost functional are of a special type. In fact, both the absolute value appearing in C_{dem} and C_{change}, and the min / max functions appearing in E, $C_{start\ up}$ and $C_{start\ up\ gas}$ are piecewise affine maps and the optimization of a piecewise affine cost functional subject to linear inequalities can be always formulated as an MILP by suitably introducing further binary and continuous optimization variables [9]. The case of the cost functional J is even simpler because, by using the fact that all the weight coefficients are positive, it is possible to write J as a linear function of the unknowns without increasing the number of binary optimization variables. For details we defer the reader to [8,19].

5   Control Experiments

In this section, we demonstrate the effectiveness of the proposed optimization procedure through some simulations.

The input/output equations describing the plant are given by (3)-(5) where

$$f_1(u_1) = 0.0748 \cdot u_1 + 2.0563 \tag{16}$$
$$f_2(u_1, u_2) = 0.62 \cdot u_1 - 0.857 \cdot u_2 + 29.714 \tag{17}$$
$$f_3(u_1) = 1.83 \cdot u_1 - 0.0012 \tag{18}$$

The permitted range for u_1 and u_2 are summarized in Table 2. For the Island plant, the affine models (16) and (18) are sufficiently accurate [24], whereas equation (17) is a crude approximation of the nonlinear behaviour and has a maximum error of 2%. We highlight again the fact that a more precise MLD

Input	Minimum	Maximum
u_1	50%	100%
u_2	2 kg/s	37 kg/s

Table 2. Upper and lower bounds on the inputs

model could be obtained by using more accurate (and complex) piecewise affine approximations for the function f_2.

For a specified profile of the electric and steam demands, the optimizer chooses the optimal inputs in order to track the demands and at the same time minimize the operating costs. In particular the performance of the control action can be tuned by using suitable values of the weight coefficients appearing in the cost functional J. For example, the fulfillment of the electric power demand can be enforced in spite of the fulfillment of the steam demand if the ratio $k_{dem\ el}/k_{dem\ st}$ is high enough. In fact, due to the typical running of a combined cycle power plant, high values of both electric power and steam mass flow cannot be produced simultaneously because, in order to fulfill an high power demand, part of the steam must be used for running the steam turbine and cannot be supplied to the paper mill.

The turbines are switched on/off respecting the operating constraints (the minimum up and down times and the different types of start up). The use of different start up procedures implies that a minimum prediction horizon of five hours should be adopted in order to enable each type of start up. In fact the prediction horizon should be longer than the maximum delay that can occur between the command "on" and the production of electric power (which is four hours for a cold start up).

The control experiment we present was conducted over four days and a prediction horizon M of 24 hours was adopted. The profile of the electric demand is a scaled version of the one reported in the "IEEE reliability test" [15]. As is apparent from Figure 2(a), it has the feature that the demand during the week end differs from the one during the working days. Moreover the electricity prices are chosen proportionally to the profile of the electricity demand. The steam demand is constant and assumed to be near to the maximum level that can be generated by the plant (see Figure 3(b)).

Different start up costs for different start up procedures have been used. As remarked in Section 4.1, this can be done by properly choosing the weight coefficients $k_{start\ up}$ and $k_{start\ up\ gas}$. The admissible values for $k_{start\ up}$ and $k_{start\ up\ gas}$ are summarized in Table 3. In order to illustrate how the startup coefficients are assigned, we focus on the gas turbine, being the procedure analogous for the steam turbine. If, at time k, the gas turbine is off, the type of startup is determined by the value of the counter ξ_d (see formula (9)). Then, the numerical values of $k_{start\ up}(t|k)$, $t = k, \ldots, k+M-1$, are determined according to Table 3 and by assuming that only one startup will occur in the control horizon. For instance, if $t_{off}(k) = 60$ an "hot startup" should occur if the turbine is turned on in the next hour and a "warm startup" should occur if the turbine is tuned on in the next 60 houres. Then, if $M < 60$, the values $k_{start\ up}(k|k) = 58$ and $k_{start\ up}(t|k) = 115$, $t = k+1, \ldots, k+M-1$ are used for determining the optimal inputs at time k. This guarantees that at least the first startup of the turbine within the control horizon is correctly penalized.

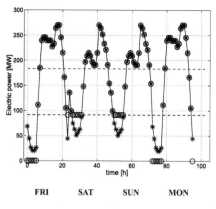

(a) Electric power demanded (stars and solid line) and produced by both the turbines (circles).

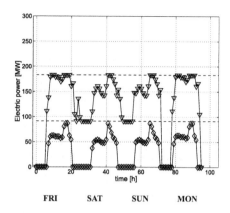

(b) Electric power produced by the steam turbine (diamonds) and by the gas turbine (triangles).

Fig. 2. Control experiment over 4 days with $M = 24$ hours. The horizontal dashed line represents the maximum and minimum electric power that can be produced by the gas turbine.

‖NORMAL start up‖	$k_{start\ up} = 30$ ‖	$k_{start\ up\ gas} = 30$ ‖
‖HOT start up	$k_{start\ up} = 58$ ‖	$k_{start\ up\ gas} = 58$ ‖
‖WARM start up	$k_{start\ up} = 115$‖	$k_{start\ up\ gas} = 115$‖
‖COLD start up	$k_{start\ up} = 152$‖	$k_{start\ up\ gas} = 152$‖

Table 3. Weights for the startup of the gas and steam turbines

The other weight coefficients have the constant values

$$k_{dem\ el} = 20\ [\mathrm{MW}], \quad k_{fuel} = 0.02\ \left[\frac{\mathrm{kg}}{\mathrm{s}}\right], \quad k_{dem\ st} = 1\ \left[\frac{\mathrm{kg}}{\mathrm{s}}\right], \quad k_{fixed} = 1,$$
$$k_{\Delta u_1} = 0.001, \qquad k_{fixed\ gas} = 1, \qquad k_{\Delta u_2} = 0.001, \qquad p_{st} = 0.2$$

Note, in particular, that the fulfillment of the electric demand has an higher priority than the fulfillment of the steam demand because it holds $k_{dem\ el} \gg k_{dem\ st}$.

At time $k = 0$ the two turbines are assumed to have been off for one hour.

By looking at the electric power produced by each turbine (depicted in Figure 2(b)) and the sequence of logic inputs (Figure 3(a)), one notes that at early morning of Friday and Monday the gas turbine is kept off because the demand is significantly below the minimum level that can be produced by the plant (the dashed line in Figure 2(a)). On the other hand, during Friday and Saturday night, the gas turbine is kept on because the drop in demand is not big enough. From Figures 2(b) and 3(a) it is also apparent that the steam turbine is turned on when required.

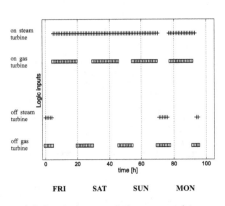

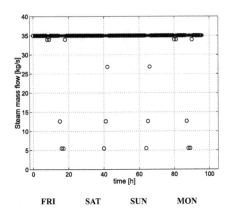

(a) Logic input of the gas turbine (squares) and of the steam turbine.

(b) Steam demanded (stars) and supplied (circles).

Fig. 3. Control experiment over 4 days with $M = 24$ hours.

5.1   Computational Complexity

It is well known that MILP problems are NP-complete and their computational complexity strongly depends on the number of integer variables [25]. Therefore, the computational burden must be analyzed in order to decide about possibility of optimizing the CCPP on-line.

We considered the case study reported in Section 5, by using different prediction horizons M. At every time instant, an MILP problem with $(46 \cdot M - 4)$ optimization variables ($(27 \cdot M)$ of which are integer), and $(119 \cdot M - 8)$ mixed integer linear constraints was solved. The computation times (average and worst cases) needed for solving the MILPs, on a Pentium II-400 (running Matlab 5.3 for building the matrices defining the MILP and running CPLEX for solving it) are reported in Table 4.

M	Average times [s]	Worst case times [s]
2	0.7705	0.8110
3	1.1335	1.2720
5	2.0996	4.4860
9	4.7323	9.7040
24	33.6142	101.7370

Table 4. Computational times for solving the MILP (14)

Note that the computation times increase as the prediction horizon M becomes longer. However, the solution to the optimization problem took at most 102 s, a time much shorter than the sampling time of one hour.

6   Conclusions

The main goal of this paper is to show that hybrid systems in the MLD form provide a suitable framework for modeling CCPPs. In particular, many features like the possibility of switching on/off the turbines, the presence of minimum up and down times, priority constraints between turbines and different startup procedures can be captured by an MLD model. We point out that also other characteristics, like ramp constraints or nonlinear input/output relations (approximated by piecewise affine functions), can be easily incorporated in the MLD description.

Then, the optimization of the operation can be recasted into an MPC problem that can be efficiently solved by resorting to MILP solvers. The economic factors we considered in the definition of the cost functional are not the only possible choices. In fact different piecewise affine terms, reflecting other performance criteria could be added without changing the structure of the resulting optimization problem [9]. For instance the asset depreciation due to plant aging can be incorporated by exploiting lifetime consumption models [14].

References

1. R. Alur, T. A. Henzinger, and P. H. Ho. Automatic symbolic verification of embedded systems. *IEEE Trans. on Software Engineering*, 22(3):181–201, March 1996.
2. J.M. Arroyo and A.J. Conejo. Optimal response of a thermal unit to an electricity spot market. *IEEE Trans. on Power Systems*, 15(3):1098–1104, 2000.
3. A. Bemporad, G. Ferrari-Trecate, and M. Morari. Observability and Controllability of Piecewise Affine and Hybrid Systems. *IEEE Trans. on Automatic Control*, 45(10):1864–1876, 2000.
4. A. Bemporad and M. Morari. Control of systems integrating logic, dynamics, and constraints. *Automatica*, 35(3):407–427, 1999.
5. M.S. Branicky. Multiple Lyapunov functions and other analysis tools for switched and hybrid systems. *IEEE Trans. on Automatic Control*, 43(4):475–482, 1998.
6. M.S. Branicky, W.S. Borkar, and S.K. Mitter. A unified framework for hybrid control: model and optimal control theory. *IEEE Trans. on Automatic Control*, 43(1):31–45, 1998.
7. G. Ferrari-Trecate, F.A. Cuzzola, D. Mignone, and M. Morari. Analysis and control with performance of piecewise affine and hybrid systems. *Proc. American Control Conference*, pages 200–205, 2001.
8. G. Ferrari-Trecate, E. Gallestey, P. Letizia, M. Spedicato, M. Morari, and M. Antoine. Modeling and control of co-generation power plants: A hybrid system approach. Technical report, AUT01-18, Automatic Control Laboratory, ETH Zurich, 2001.
9. G. Ferrari-Trecate, P. Letizia, and M. Spedicato. Optimization with piecewise-affine cost functions. Technical report, AUT00-13, Automatic Control Laboratory, ETH Zurich, 2001.
10. G. Ferrari-Trecate, D. Mignone, D. Castagnoli, and M. Morari. Mixed Logic Dynamical Model of a Hydroelectric Power Plant. *Proceedings of the 4th International Conference: Automation of Mixed Processes: Hybrid Dynamic Systems ADPM, Dortmund, Germany*, 2000.

11. G. Ferrari-Trecate, D. Mignone, and M. Morari. Moving horizon estimation for hybrid systems. *IEEE Trans. on Automatic Control*, 2002. to appear.
12. R. Fletcher and S. Leyffer. A mixed integer quadratic programming package. Technical report, Department of Mathematics, University of Dundee, Scotland, U.K., 1994.
13. C. A. Frangopoulos, A. I. Lygeros, C. T. Markou, and P. Kaloritis. Thermoeconomic operation optimization of the Hellenic Aspropyrgos Refinery combined-cycle cogeneration system. *Applied Thermal Engineering*, 16(12):949–958, 1996.
14. E. Gallestey, A. Stothert, M. Antoine, and S. Morton. Model predictive control and the optimisation of power plant load while considering lifetime consumption. *IEEE Trans. on Power Systems*, 2001. To appear.
15. C. Grigg and P. Wong. The IEEE Reliability Test System-1996. *IEEE Trans. on Power Systems*, 14(3):1010–1020, August 1999.
16. K. Ito and R. Yokoyama. Operational strategy for an industrial gas turbine cogeneration plant. *International Journal of Global Energy Issues*, 7(3/4):162–170, 1995.
17. M. Johannson and A. Rantzer. Computation of piecewise quadratic Lyapunov functions for hybrid systems. *IEEE Trans. on Automatic Control*, 43(4):555–559, 1998.
18. G. Labinaz, M.M. Bayoumi, and K. Rudie. A Survey of Modeling and Control of Hybrid Systems. *Annual Reviews of Control*, 21:79–92, 1997.
19. P. Letizia. Controllo di impianti cogenerativi mediante sistemi ibridi, 2001. M. Sc. thesis, Universita' degli Studi di Pavia.
20. J. Lygeros, C. Tomlin, and S. Sastry. Controllers for reachability specifications for hybrid systems. *Automatica*, 35(3):349–370, 1999.
21. D. A. Manolas, C. A. Frangopoulos, T. P. Gialamas, and D. T. Tsahalis. Operation optimization of an industrial cogeneration system by a genetic algorithm. *Energy Conversion Management*, 38(15-17):1625–1636, 1997.
22. M. Morari, J. Lee, and C. Garcia. *Model Predictive Control*. Prentice Hall, Draft Manuscript, 2001.
23. K. Moslehi, M. Khadem, R. Bernal, and G. Hernandez. Optimization of multiplant cogeneration system operation including electric and steam networks. *IEEE Trans. on Power Systems*, 6(2):484–490, 1991.
24. K. Mossig. Load optimization. Technical report, ABB Corporate Research, Baden (Zurich), 2000.
25. G.L. Nemhauser and L.A. Wolsey. *Integer and Combinatorial Optimization*. Wiley, 1988.
26. M. Spedicato. Modellizzazione di impianti cogenerativi mediante sistemi ibridi, 2001. M. Sc. thesis, Universita' degli Studi di Pavia.
27. F. D. Torrisi, A. Bemporad, and D. Mignone. HYSDEL - A Tool for Generating Hybrid Models. Technical report, AUT00-03, Automatic Control Laboratory, ETH Zurich, 2000.

Exploiting Implicit Representations in Timed Automaton Verification for Controller Synthesis

Robert P. Goldman, David J. Musliner, and Michael J.S. Pelican*

Automated Reasoning Group, Honeywell Laboratories, 3660 Technology Drive,
Minneapolis, MN 55418, USA
{goldman, musliner, pelican}@htc.honeywell.com

Abstract. Automatic controller synthesis and verification techniques promise to revolutionize the construction of high-confidence software. However, approaches based on explicit state-machine models are subject to extreme state-space explosion and the accompanying scale limitations. In this paper, we describe how to exploit an implicit, transition-based, representation of timed automata in controller synthesis. The CIRCA Controller Synthesis Module (CSM) automatically synthesizes hard real-time, reactive controllers using a transition-based implicit representation of the state space. By exploiting this implicit representation in search for a controller and in a customized model checking verifier, the CSM is able to efficiently build controllers for problems with very large state spaces. We provide experimental results that show substantial speed-up and orders-of-magnitude reductions in the state spaces explored. These results can be applied to other verification problems, both in the context of controller synthesis and in more traditional verification problems.

1 Introduction

This paper describes techniques for exploiting implicit representations in timed automaton controller synthesis. We show how reachability search exploits the implicit representation to substantially improve its efficiency. We have developed and implemented a system, the CIRCA Controller Synthesis Module (CSM), for automatic synthesis and execution of hard real-time discrete controllers. Unlike previous, game-theoretic algorithms [2, 8], the CSM derives its controller "on-the-fly" [14]. The CSM exploits a feature- and transition-based implicit representation of its state space, both in searching for the controller and in checking its correctness. Finally, the CSM generates memoryless and clockless controllers. These design elements substantially decrease the number of states that must be explored in the synthesis process.

The CSM is a component of the CIRCA architecture for intelligent control of mission-critical real-time autonomous systems [10, 11]. To permit on-line

---

* This material is based upon work supported by DARPA/ITO and the Air Force Research Laboratory under Contract No. F30602-00-C-0017.The authors thank Stavros Tripakis for many helpful suggestions. Thanks also to our anonymous referees.

C.J. Tomlin and M.R. Greenstreet (Eds.): HSCC 2002, LNCS 2289, pp. 225–238, 2002.

reconfiguration, CIRCA has concurrently-operating controller synthesis (planning) and control (plan-execution) subsystems. The CSM uses models of the world (plant and environment) to automatically synthesize hard real-time safety-preserving controllers (plans). Concurrently a separate Real-Time Subsystem (RTS) executes the controllers, enforcing response time guarantees. The concurrent operation means that the computationally expensive methods used by the CSM will not violate the tight timing requirements of the controllers.

This paper discusses how the CSM's controller synthesis algorithm interacts with a model-checking reachability search algorithm that exploits the implicit representation. This technique substantially improves verification efficiency; by two orders of magnitude for large examples. We start by introducing the CIRCA CSM and its transition- and feature-based representation. Then we outline the forward search algorithm that the CSM uses to synthesize controllers, pointing out the role played by timed automaton verification. Next we explain how to formulate the execution semantics of the CIRCA model as a construction of sets of timed automata. The timed automaton model provides the semantics, but does not provide a practical approach for verification. We describe methods for model-checking that exploit CIRCA's implicit, transition-based, state space representation. We conclude with a comparison to related work in controller synthesis and AI planning.

2   The Controller Synthesis Module

CIRCA's CSM automatically synthesizes real-time reactive discrete controllers that guarantee system safety when run on CIRCA's Real-Time Subsystem (RTS). The CSM takes in a description of the processes in the system's environment, represented as a set of time-constrained transitions that modify world features. Discrete states of the system are modeled as sets of feature-value assignments. Thus the transition descriptions, together with specifications of initial states, implicitly define the set of possible system states.

For example, Fig. 1 shows several transitions taken from a problem where CIRCA is to control the Cassini spacecraft in Saturn Orbital Insertion [4, 12]. This figure also includes the initial state description.

The CSM reasons about transitions of three types:

Action transitions represent actions performed by the RTS. These parallel the operators of a conventional planning system. Associated with each action is a worst case execution time, an *upper bound* on the delay before the action occurs.

Temporal transitions represent uncontrollable processes, some of which may need to be preempted. See Sect. 2.1 for the definition of "preemption" in this context. Associated with each temporal transition is a *lower bound* on its delay. Transitions whose lower bound is zero are referred to as "events," and are handled specially for efficiency reasons.

```
;; The action of switching on an Inertial Reference Unit (IRU).
ACTION start_IRU1_warm_up
   PRECONDITIONS: '((IRU1 off))
   POSTCONDITIONS: '((IRU1 warming))
   DELAY: <= 1

;; The process of the IRU warming.
RELIABLE-TEMPORAL warm_up_IRU1
   PRECONDITIONS: '((IRU1 warming))
   POSTCONDITIONS: '((IRU1 on))
   DELAY: [45 90]

;; Sometimes the IRUs break without warning.
EVENT IRU1_fails
   PRECONDITIONS: '((IRU1 on))
   POSTCONDITIONS: '((IRU1 broken))

;; If the engine is burning while the active IRU breaks,
;; we have a limited amount of time to fix the problem before
;; the spacecraft will go too far out of control.
TEMPORAL fail_if_burn_with_broken_IRU1
   PRECONDITIONS: '((engine on)(active_IRU IRU1) (IRU1 broken))
   POSTCONDITIONS: '((failure T))
   DELAY: >= 5
```

Fig. 1. Example transition descriptions given to CIRCA's planner.

Reliable temporal transitions represent continuous processes that may need
   to be employed by the CIRCA agent. Reliable temporal transitions have both
   upper and lower bounds on their delays.

While in the worst case an implicit representation is not superior to explicit
state space enumeration, in practice there are substantial advantages. In many
problems, vast sub-spaces of the state space are unreachable, either because of
the control regime, or because of consistency constraints. The use of an implicit representation, together with a constructive search algorithm, allow us to
avoid enumerating the full state space. The transition-centered representation
allows us to conveniently represent processes that extend over multiple states.
For example, a single transition (e.g., warming up a piece of equipment) may be
extended over multiple discrete states. A similar representational convenience
is often achieved by multiplying together many automata, but expanding the
product construction restores the state explosion. Finally, in this paper we show
how the transition-based implicit representation can be exploited in a verifier.

2.1   CSM Algorithm

Given problem representations as above, the controller synthesis (planning)
problem can be posed as *choosing a control action for each reachable discrete*

state (feature-value assignment) of the system. Note that this controller synthesis problem is simpler than the general problem of synthesizing controllers for timed automata. In particular, CIRCA's controllers are memoryless and cannot reference clocks. This restriction has two advantages: first, it makes the synthesis problem easier and second, it allows us to ensure that the controllers we generate are actually realizable in the RTS.

Since the CSM focuses on generating *safe* controllers, a critical issue is making failure states unreachable. In controller synthesis, this is done by the process we refer to as *preemption*. A transition t is preempted in a state s iff some other transition t' from s must occur before t could possibly occur. The CSM achieves preemption by choosing a control action that is fast enough that it is guaranteed to occur before the transition to be preempted.[1]

The controller synthesis algorithm is as follows:

1. Choose a state from the set of reachable states (at the start of controller synthesis, only the initial state(s) is(are) reachable).
2. For each uncontrollable transition enabled in this state, choose whether or not to preempt it. Transitions that lead to failure states *must* be preempted.
3. Choose a control action or no-op for that state.
4. Invoke the verifier to confirm that the (partial) controller is safe.
5. If the controller is *not* safe, use information from the verifier to direct backtracking.
6. If the controller *is* safe, recompute the set of reachable states.
7. If there are no unplanned reachable states (reachable states for which a control action has not been chosen), terminate successfully.
8. If some unplanned reachable states remain, loop to step 1.

During the course of the search algorithm, the CSM will use the verifier module after each assignment of a control action (see step 4). This means that the verifier will be invoked before the controller is complete. At such points we use the verifier as a conservative heuristic by treating all unplanned states as if they are "safe havens." Unplanned states are treated as absorbing states of the system, and any verification traces that enter these states are regarded as successful. Note that this process converges to a sound and complete verification when the controller synthesis process is complete. When the verifier indicates that a controller is *unsafe*, the CSM will query it for a path to the distinguished failure state. The set of states along that path provides a set of candidate decisions to revise.

For those familiar with designs for game-theoretic synthesis of controllers for timed systems [2, 8], the CSM algorithm is the same in its purpose. One difference is that the CSM algorithm works starting from an initial state and building forward by search. The game-theoretic algorithms, on the other hand, typically use a fixpoint operation to find a controllable subspace, starting from unsafe states (or other synthesis failures). Another difference is that the CSM

---

[1] Note that in some cases a reliable temporal transition, e.g., the warming up of the backup IRU, can be the transition that preempts a failure.

algorithm heavily exploits its implicit state space representation. Because of these features, for many problems, the CSM algorithm is able to find a controller without visiting large portions of the state space.

Two further remarks are worth making. The first is that the search described here is *not* made blindly. We use a domain-independent heuristic, providing limited lookahead, to direct the search. We do not have space to describe that heuristic here; it is based on one developed for AI planning [9]. Without heuristic direction, even small synthesis problems can be too challenging. The second is that we have developed an alternative method of search that works by divide-and-conquer rather than reasoning forward [6]. For many problems, this supplies a substantial speed-up. Again, we do not have space to discuss this approach in depth here.

3   Modeling for Verification

The CSM algorithm described above operates entirely in the discrete domain of the timed problem. This ensures that the controllers may be easily implemented automatically. However, a path-dependent computation is required to determine how much time remains on a transition's delay when it applies to two or more states on a path. The CSM uses a timed automaton verification system to ensure that the controllers the CSM builds are safe. In this section, we discuss a formal model of the RTS, expressed in terms of timed automata. The following section describes how to reason about this model efficiently.

3.1   Execution Semantics

The controllers of the CIRCA RTS are not arbitrary pieces of software; they are intentionally very limited in their computational power. These limitations serve to make controller synthesis computationally efficient and make it simpler to build an RTS that provides timing guarantees. The controller generated by the CSM is compiled into a set of *Test-Action Pairs* (TAPs) to be run by the RTS. Each TAP has a boolean test expression that distinguishes between states where a particular action is and is not to be executed. Note that these test expressions do not have access to any clocks. A sample TAP for the Saturn Orbit Insertion domain is given in Fig. 2.

The set of TAPs that make up a controller are assembled into a loop and scheduled to meet all the TAP deadlines. Note that in order to meet deadlines, this loop may contain multiple copies of a single TAP. The deadlines are computed from the delays of the transitions that the control actions must preempt.

3.2   Timed Automata

Now that we have a sense of the execution semantics of CIRCA's RTS, we briefly review the modeling formalism, timed automata, before presenting the model itself.

```
#<TAP 2>
 Tests: (AND (IRU1 BROKEN)
             (OR (AND (ACTIVE_IRU NONE) (IRU2 ON))
                 (AND (ACTIVE_IRU IRU1) (ENGINE ON))))
 Acts : select_IRU2
```

Fig. 2. A sample Test-Action Pair and TAP schedule loop from the Saturn Orbit Insertion problem.

Definition 1 (Timed Automaton [3].). *A timed automaton A is a tuple $\langle S, s^i, \mathcal{X}, \mathcal{L}, \mathcal{E}, \mathcal{I} \rangle$ where S is a finite set of locations; s^i is the initial location; $\mathcal{X}$ is a finite set of clocks; $\mathcal{L}$ is a finite set of labels; $\mathcal{E}$ is a finite set of edges; and $\mathcal{I}$ is the set of invariants. Each edge $e \in \mathcal{E}$ is a tuple (s, L, ψ, ρ, s') where $s \in S$ is the source, $s' \in S$ is the target, $L \subseteq \mathcal{L}$ are the labels, $\psi \in \Psi_{\mathcal{X}}$ is the guard, and $\rho \subseteq \mathcal{X}$ is a clock reset. Timing constraints ($\Psi_{\mathcal{X}}$) appear in guards and invariants and clock assignments. In our models, all clock constraints are of the form $c_i \le k$ or $c_i > k$ for some clock c_i and integer constant k. Guards dictate when the model may follow an edge, invariants indicate when the model must leave a state. In our models, all clock resets re-assign the corresponding clock to zero; they are used to start and reset processes. The state of a timed automaton is a pair: $\langle s, C \rangle$. $s \in S$ is a location and $C : \mathcal{X} \to \mathbf{Q} \ge 0$ is a clock valuation, that assigns a non-negative rational number to each clock.*

It often simplifies the representation of a complex system to treat it as a product of some number of simpler automata. The labels $\mathcal{L}$ are used to synchronize edges in different automata when creating their product.

Definition 2 (Product Automaton). *Given two automata A_1 and A_2, $A_1 = \langle S_1, s_1^i, \mathcal{X}_1, \mathcal{L}_1, \mathcal{E}_1, \mathcal{I}_1 \rangle$ and $A_2 = \langle S_2, s_2^i, \mathcal{X}_2, \mathcal{L}_2, \mathcal{E}_2, \mathcal{I}_2 \rangle$, their product A_p is $\langle S_1 \times S_2, s_p^i, \mathcal{X}_1 \cup \mathcal{X}_2, \mathcal{L}_1 \cup \mathcal{L}_2, \mathcal{E}_p, \mathcal{I}_p \rangle$, where $s_p^i = (s_1^i, s_2^i)$ and $\mathcal{I}(s_1, s_2) = \mathcal{I}(s_1) \wedge \mathcal{I}(s_2)$. The edges are defined by:*

1. *for $l \in \mathcal{L}_1 \cap \mathcal{L}_2$, for every $\langle s_1, l, \psi_1, \rho_1, s_1' \rangle \in \mathcal{E}_1$, and $\langle s_2, l, \psi_2, \rho_2, s_2' \rangle \in \mathcal{E}_2$, $\mathcal{E}_p$ contains $\langle (s_1, s_2), l, \psi_1 \cup \psi_2, \rho_1 \cup \rho_2, (s_1', s_2') \rangle$.*
2. *for $l \in \mathcal{L}_1 \setminus \mathcal{L}_2$, for $\langle s_1, l, \psi_1, \rho_1, s_1' \rangle \in \mathcal{E}_1$ and $s_2 \in S_2$, $\mathcal{E}_p$ contains $\langle (s_1, s_2), l, \psi_1, \rho_1, (s_1', s_2) \rangle$. Likewise for $l \in \mathcal{L}_2 \setminus \mathcal{L}_1$.*

3.3 Modeling CIRCA with Timed Automata

We give the semantics of CSM models in terms of sets of interacting timed automata (see Fig. 3). Using multiple automata allows us to accurately capture the interaction of multiple, simultaneously operating processes. The starting

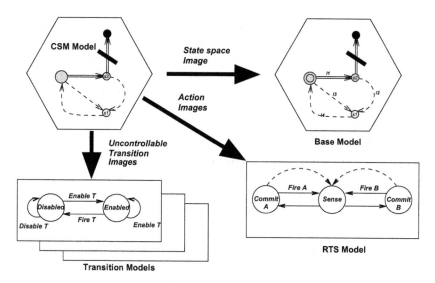

Fig. 3. The verifier model and its relation to the CSM model.

point of the translation is the CIRCA plan-graph, constructed by the CIRCA CSM:

Definition 3 (Plan Graph). $\mathcal{P} = \langle S, E, \vec{F}, \vec{V}, \phi, I, T, \iota, \eta, p, \pi \rangle$ *where*

1. S *is a set of states.*
2. E *is a set of edges.*
3. $\vec{F} = [f_0...f_m]$ *is a vector of features (in a purely propositional domain, these will be propositions).*
4. $\vec{V} = [\mathcal{V}_0...\mathcal{V}_m]$ *is a corresponding vector of sets of values ($\mathcal{V}_i = \{v_{i0}...v_{ik_i}\}$) that each feature can take on.*
5. $\phi : S \mapsto \vec{V}$ *is a function mapping from states to unique vectors of value assignments.*
6. $I \subset S$ *is a distinguished subset of initial states.*
7. $T = U \cup A$ *is the set of transitions, made up of an uncontrollable (U) subset, the temporals and reliable temporals, and a controllable (A) subset, the actions. Each transition, t, has an associated delay (Δ_t) lower and upper bound: $lb(\Delta_t)$ and $ub(\Delta_t)$. For temporals $ub(\Delta_t) = \infty$, for events $lb(\Delta_t) = 0, ub(\Delta_t) = \infty$.*
8. ι *is an interpretation of the edges: $\iota : E \mapsto T$.*
9. $\eta : S \mapsto 2^T$ *is the* enabled *relationship — the set of transitions enabled in a particular state.*
10. $p : S \mapsto A \cup \epsilon$ *(where ϵ is the "action" of doing nothing) is the actions that the CSM has planned. Note that p will generally be a partial function.*
11. $\pi : S \mapsto 2^U$ *is a set of preemptions the CSM expects.*

For every CIRCA plan graph, $\mathcal{P}$, we construct a timed automaton model, $\theta(\mathcal{P})$. $\theta(\mathcal{P})$ is the product of a number of individual automata. There is one automaton, which we call the *base model*, that models the feature structure of the domain. There is an *RTS model* that models the actions of the CIRCA agent. Finally, for every uncontrollable transition, there is a separate timed automaton modeling that process. Proper synchronization ensures that the base machine state reflects the effect of the transitions and that the state of the other automata accurately indicate whether or not a given process will (may) be underway.

Definition 4 (Translation of CIRCA Plan Graph).
$\theta(\mathcal{P}) = \beta(\mathcal{P}) \times \rho(\mathcal{P}) \times \prod_{u \in U(\mathcal{P})} \upsilon(u)$ *where* $\beta(\mathcal{P})$ *is the base model;* $\rho(\mathcal{P})$ *is the RTS model; and* $\upsilon(u)$ *is the automaton modeling the process that corresponds to uncontrollable transition* u.

Definition 5 (Base model). $\beta(\mathcal{P}) = \langle \theta(S), \{l^0\}, \emptyset, \Sigma(\mathcal{P}), \theta_E(\mathcal{P}), I_\top \rangle$ *where:*

1. $\theta(S) = \{\theta(s) \mid s \in S\} \cup \{l^\mathcal{F}, l^0\}$ *is the image under* θ *of the state set of* $\mathcal{P}$. *This image contains a location for each state in* $\mathcal{P}$, *as well as a distinguished failure location,* $l^\mathcal{F}$, *and initial location,* l^0.
2. $\Sigma(\mathcal{P})$ *is the label set; it is given as Definition 6.*
3. $\theta_E(\mathcal{P})$ *is the edge set of the base model. It is given as Definition 7.*

Note that there are no clocks in the base machine; all timing constraints will be handled by other automata in the composite model. Thus, the invariant for each state in this model is simply $\top$. We have notated this vacuous invariant as $I_\top$. Similarly, all of the edges have a vacuous guard. The labels of the translation model ensure that the other component automata synchronize correctly.

Definition 6 (Label set for $\theta(\mathcal{P})$).
$\Sigma(\mathcal{P}) = \{\mathbf{e}_u, \mathbf{d}_u, \mathbf{f}_u \mid u \in U\} \, (1) \cup \{\mathbf{f}_a \mid a \in A\} \, (2) \cup \{\mathbf{r}_a\}$

The symbols in (1) are used to synchronize the automata for uncontrollable transitions with the base model. The symbols in (2) together with the distinguished reset symbol $\mathbf{r}_a$ are used to synchronize the automaton modeling the RTS with the base model. The base model edge set, $\theta_E(\mathcal{P})$, captures the *effect* on the agent and environment of the various transitions.

Definition 7 (Base model edge set). $\theta_E(\mathcal{P})$ *is made up of the following subsets of edges:*[2]

(1) $\left\{ \langle l^0, \theta_\sigma(init, s), \theta(s) \rangle \mid s \in I \right\}$
(2) $\left\{ \langle \theta(s), \{\mathbf{f}_u\}, l^\mathcal{F} \rangle \mid s \in S, u \in \pi(s) \right\}$
(3) $\left\{ \langle \theta(s), \{\mathbf{f}_u\} \cup \theta_\sigma(u, s'), \theta(s') \rangle \mid s \in S, u \notin \pi(s), s' \in u(s) \right\}$
(4) $\left\{ \langle \theta(s), \{\mathbf{c}_a\}, s \rangle \mid s \in S, a = p(s) \right\}$
(5) $\left\{ \langle \theta(s), \{\mathbf{f}_a\} \cup \theta_\sigma(a, s'), \theta(a(s)) \rangle \mid s \in S, a \in \eta(s), s' \in a(s) \right\}$
(6) $\left\{ \langle \theta(s), \{\mathbf{f}_a\}, l^\mathcal{F} \rangle \mid s \in S, a \notin \eta(s) \right\}$

---

[2] The clock resets of these transitions are all $\emptyset$, and the guards are all $\top$, so we have omitted them.

Edge set (1) is merely a set of initialization edges, that carry the base model from its distinguished single initial location to the image of each of the initial states of $\mathcal{P}$. (2) takes the base model to its distinguished failure location, $l^{\mathcal{F}}$, when a preemption fails. (3) captures the effects of the uncontrollable transitions the CSM didn't preempt. (4) synchronizes with the RTS transitions that capture the RTS committing to execute a particular action (i.e., the test part of the TAP). (5) captures the effects of a successfully-executed action. (6) captures a failure due to a race condition. Event sets $\theta_\sigma(t, s)$ are used to capture the effects on the various processes of going to s by means of t.

Definition 8.

$$\theta_\sigma(t, s) = \{\mathbf{e}_u \mid u \in \eta(s)\} \cup \{\mathbf{d}_u \mid u \neq t \land u \notin \eta(s)\} \cup \{\mathbf{r}_a\}$$

The symbol set $\theta_\sigma(t, s)$ contains an enable symbol for each u enabled in s, and a disable symbol for each u not enabled in s. The addition of the symbol $\mathbf{r}_a$ ensures that the RTS machine will "notice" the state transition.

There will be one automaton, $\upsilon(u)$ for every uncontrollable transition, u. Each such model will have two states, enabled, e_u, and disabled, d_u, and transitions for enabling, disabling, and firing: $\mathbf{e}_u, \mathbf{d}_u$, and $\mathbf{f}_u$, respectively (see Fig. 3). It will also have a clock, c_u, and the guards and invariants will be derived from the timing constraints on u:

Definition 9 (Uncontrollable Transition Automata).

$$\upsilon(u) = \langle\{e_u, d_u\}, d_u, \{c_u\}, \{\mathbf{e}_u, \mathbf{d}_u, \mathbf{f}_u\}, E(\upsilon(u)), I\rangle$$

$$\begin{aligned}
E(\upsilon(u)) = \{ &\langle d_u, \{\mathbf{d}_u\}, \top, \emptyset, d_u\rangle, \langle d_u, \{\mathbf{e}_u\}, \top, c_u := 0, e_u\rangle, \\
&\langle e_u, \{\mathbf{e}_u\}, \top, \emptyset, e_u\rangle, \langle e_u, \{\mathbf{d}_u\}, \top, \emptyset, d_u\rangle, \\
&\langle e_u, \{\mathbf{f}_u\}, c_u \geq lb(\Delta_u), \emptyset, d_u\rangle \}
\end{aligned}$$

$$I(e_u) = c_u \leq ub(\Delta_u) \text{ and } I(d_u) = \top$$

The model of the RTS, ρ, contains all of the planned actions in a single automaton. Execution of each planned action is captured as a two stage process: first the process of committing to the action (going to the state c_a), and then the action's execution (returning to s_0 through transition $\mathbf{f}_a$).

Definition 10 (RTS Model).

$$\begin{aligned}
\rho = \langle &\{s_0\} \cup \{c_a \mid a \in p\}, s_0, \{c_{RTS}\}, \\
&\{\mathbf{r}_a\} \cup \{c_a, \mathbf{f}_a \mid a \in p\}, \\
&\{\langle s_0, \{c_a\}, c_{RTS} \leq 0, c_{RTS} := 0, c_a\rangle, \\
&\langle c_a, \{\mathbf{f}_a\}, c_{RTS} \geq ub(\Delta_a), c_{RTS} := 0, s_0\rangle, \\
&\langle c_a, \{\mathbf{r}_a\}, c_{RTS} < ub(\Delta_a), c_{RTS} := 0, s_0\rangle, \\
&\langle c_a, \{\mathbf{r}_a\}, c_{RTS} < ub(\Delta_a), \emptyset, c_a\rangle \mid a \in p\} \\
&\{I(c_a) = c_{RTS} \leq ub(\Delta_a), I(s_0) = c_{RTS} \leq 0\}\rangle
\end{aligned}$$

There are two classes of safety violations the verifier must detect. The first is a failure to successfully preempt some nonvolitional transition. This case is caught by transitions (2) of Definition 7. The second is a race condition: here the failure is to plan a for state s but not complete it before an uncontrolled process brings the world to another state, s', that does not satisfy the preconditions of a. The latter case is caught by transitions (6) of Definition 7.[3]

4   Exploiting the Model in Verification

A direct implementation of the above model will suffer a state space explosion. To overcome this, we have built a CIRCA-specific verifier (CSV) able to exploit CIRCA's implicit state-space representation. The CSV constructs its timed automata, *both the individual automata and their product*, in the process of computing reachability. This on-the-fly computation relies on the factored representation of the discrete state space and on the limitations of CIRCA's RTS.

The efficiency gains from our factored state representation come in the computation of successor states. A naive implementation of the search would compute all of the locations (distinct discrete states) of the timed automaton up front, but many of those might be unreachable. We compute the product automaton lazily, rather than before doing the reachability search, thus constructing only reachable states.

The individual automata, as well as their product, are computed on-the-fly. The timed automaton formalism permits multiple automata to synchronize in arbitrary ways. However, CIRCA automata synchronize in only limited ways. There will be only one "primary transition" that occurs in any state of the CIRCA product automaton: either a controlled transition that is part of the RTS automaton, or a single uncontrolled transition. Thus we may dispense with component transitions and their labels.

The transitions that synchronize with the primary transition are of three types:

1. updates to the world automaton, recording the effect (the postconditions) of the primary jump on the discrete state of the world;
2. enabling and disabling jumps that set the state of uncontrolled transitions in the environment;
3. a jump that has the effect of activating the control action planned for the new state.

Accordingly, we can very efficiently implement a lazy successor generation for a set of states $S = \langle s, \mathbf{C} \rangle$, where s is a discrete state and $\mathbf{C}$ is a symbolic representation of a class of clock valuations, in our case a difference-bound matrix. When one needs to compute the successor locations for the location s, one

---

[3] Checking for the race condition is not fully implemented in our current version; its implementation is in progress as of this writing.

Table 1. Comparison of run times with different search strategies (Forward and DAP), timed automaton verifier (RTA) versus CIRCA-specific verifier (CSV). Times are given in milliseconds.

Scenario	Size	Forward			DAP		
		Kronos	RTA	CSV	Kronos	RTA	CSV
1	1920	9288	190	188	22431	483	417
2	72	6777	173	124	7070	385	309
3	100	4765	114	97	4399	783	385
4	560	5619	138	156	5599	366	288
5	3182592	∞	∞	∞	∞	∞	16278
6	40304	16983	762	568	506897	3035	1349
7	191232	258166	23030	25194	12919	4102	1833
8	191232	14637	652	533	436450	1157849	79855
9	991232	231769	21923	15474	∞	∞	2254
10	448512	∞	1063321	466631	∞	∞	5661
11	411136	∞	1064518	444657	∞	∞	5571
12	193536	37500	2585	1568	321626	3382	1626
13	129024	56732	3453	2933	77022	9958	1218
14	4592	16025	478	427	20220	1251	1036
15	7992	4680	183	176	75941	7672	5568
16	768	11535	426	337	13983	859	621
17	120	5730	100	368	5695	754	680
18	2880	16425	1349	1102	28922	2484	1669
19	192	6474	170	117	5715	331	308
20	768	9016	303	246	6870	564	416

need only compute a single outgoing edge for the RTS transition and make one outgoing edge for each uncontrollable transition.

Making the outgoing edges is a matter of (again lazily) building the successor locations and determining the clock resets for the edge. The clocks that must be reset are: (a) For each uncontrolled transition that is enabled in the successor location, but not enabled in the source location, s, add a clock reset for the corresponding transition; (b) If the action planned for the successor location is different from the action planned for the source location, reset the action clock. These computations are quite simple to make and much easier than computing the general product construction.

Our experimental results show that the CSV substantially improves performance over KRONOS [15] and also over a conventional model checker (denoted "RTA") that we built into CIRCA before developing the CSV. Table 1 contains comparison data between the conventional verifiers and the CSV, for two different search strategies.[4] The columns marked "forward," correspond to the algorithm described in this paper. The columns marked "DAP" correspond to the divide-and-conquer alternative [6]. The times, given in milliseconds, are for

---

[4] The problems are available at: http://www.htc.honeywell.com/projects/ants/

runs of the CSM on a Sun UltraSparc 10, SPARC v. 9 processor, 440 MHz, with 1 gigabyte of RAM. An ∞ indicates a failure to find an automaton within a 20 minute (i.e., $t > 1,200,000$) time limit.

To give a sense of the raw size of the problems, the "Size" column presents a worst-case bound on the number of *discrete* states for the final verification problem of each scenario. This value is computed by multiplying the number of possible CSM world model states (for the base model) times the number of transition model states ($2^{|U|}$) times the number of RTS model states ($|A| + 1$).

Using the forward search strategy, the CSV is faster on 16 out of 20 scenarios. Using DAP, the CSV is faster on all 20 trials. The probability of these occurring, if the CSV and the conventional verifier were equally likely to win on any given trial, is .0046 and .000019, respectively. Table 1 indicates a speed-up of two orders of magnitude on the larger scenarios, numbers 9-11, using DAP.

Table 2 shows the state space reductions achieved by exploiting the implicit representation. This table compares the total number of states visited by each verifier in the course of controller synthesis.

A few facts should be noted: A verifier will be run many times in the course of synthesizing a controller. To minimize this, a number of cheaper tests filter controller synthesis choices in advance of verification, in order to avoid verification search whenever possible. The comparison is only with KRONOS used *as a component of the CSM*, not KRONOS as a general verification tool. Finally, the computations done by KRONOS and RTA are of a special-purpose product model that is slightly simpler and *less* accurate than the CSV's model.

5   Related Work

Asarin, Maler, Pneuli and Sifakis (AMPS) [2, 8] independently developed a game-theoretic method of synthesizing real-time controllers. This work stopped at the design of the algorithm and derivation of complexity bounds; to our knowledge it was not implemented. The AMPS approach has been implemented for the special case of automatically synthesizing schedulers [1]. The "planning as model checking" [5] approach is similar to work on game-theoretic controller synthesis, but limited to purely discrete systems.

Kabanza [7]'s SIMPLAN is very similar to our CSM. However, SIMPLAN adopts a discrete time model and uses domain-specific heuristics.

Tripakis and Altisen (TA) [14] have independently developed a controller synthesis algorithm for discrete and timed systems, that also uses forward search with on-the-fly generation of the state space. Note that on-the-fly synthesis has been part of the CIRCA system since its conception in the early 1990s [10, 11]. TA's on-line synthesis has some different features from ours. They allow for multiple control actions in a single state, and they allow the controller to consult clocks. TA's implicit representation of the state space is based on composition of automata, as opposed to our feature and transition approach. We hope to compare performance of CIRCA and a recent implementation of the TA algorithm [13].

Table 2. Comparison of state spaces explored with different search strategies (Forward and DAP), timed automaton verifier (RTA) versus CIRCA-specific verifier (CSV). Units are verifier state objects, i.e., a location × a difference-bound matrix.

Scenario	Forward RTA	Forward CSV	DAP RTA	DAP CSV
1	30	30	30	33
2	34	34	33	33
3	15	15	15	15
4	18	18	18	18
5	153147	229831	170325	3069
6	122	120	500	54
7	2826	5375	631	83
8	146	131	301165	24065
9	4361	4799	163133	259
10	219885	129329	184972	871
11	219885	129329	189184	871
12	585	513	509	99
13	685	675	1782	93
14	106	106	141	142
15	17	17	1054	1389
16	117	101	131	116
17	27	27	29	25
18	284	290	355	269
19	18	18	18	18
20	63	60	33	34

TA do not have a fully on-the-fly algorithm for timed controller synthesis. Their algorithm requires the initial computation of a quotient graph of the automata, in turn requiring a full enumeration of the discrete state space. The disadvantages of such an approach can be seen by considering the state space sizes of some examples, given in   Table 1. We do not need to pre-enumerate the quotient, since we build only a clockless reactive controller and so can use the cruder time abstraction, which we compute on-the-fly. Note that this means that there are some controllers that TA (and AMPS) can find, that we cannot. However, clockless reactive controllers are easy to implement automatically, and this is not true of controllers that employ clocks. Also, and again because of the size of the state space, we use heuristic guidance in our state space search.

6   Conclusions

In this paper, we have presented the CIRCA controller synthesis algorithm, provided a timed automaton model for CIRCA CSM problems, and shown how a CIRCA-specific verifier (CSV) algorithm can exploit the features of the model. The CSV shows dramatic speed-up over a general-purpose verification algorithm.

While our model was developed for CIRCA, it is a general model for supervisory control of timed automata, and could readily be used in other applications.

References

[1] K. Altisen, G. Goessler, A. Pnueli, J. Sifakis, S.Tripakis, and S.Yovine. A framework for scheduler synthesis. In *Proceedings of the 1999 IEEE Real-Time Systems Symposium (RTSS '99)*, Phoenix, AZ, December 1999. IEEE Computer Society Press.

[2] E. Asarin, Oded Maler, and Amir Pneuli. Symbolic controller synthesis for discrete and timed systems. In Panos Antsaklis, Wolf Kohn, Anil Nerode, and Shankar Sastry, editors, *Proceedings of Hybrid Systems II*. Springer Verlag, 1995.

[3] C. Daws, A. Olivero, S. Tripakis, and S. Yovine. The tool Kronos. In *Hybrid Systems III*, 1996.

[4] Erann Gat. News from the trenches: An overview of unmanned spacecraft for AI. In Illah Nourbakhsh, editor, *AAAI Technical Report SSS-96-04: Planning with Incomplete Information for Robot Problems*. American Association for Artificial Intelligence, March 1996.

[5] Fausto Giunchiglia and Paolo Traverso. Planning as model-checking. In *Proceedings of ECP-99*. Springer Verlag, 1999.

[6] Robert P. Goldman, David J. Musliner, Kurt D. Krebsbach, and Mark S. Boddy. Dynamic abstraction planning. In *Proceedings of the Fourteenth National Conference on Artificial Intelligence*, pages 680–686, Menlo Park, CA, July 1997. American Association for Artificial Intelligence, AAAI Press/MIT Press.

[7] Froduald Kabanza. On the synthesis of situation control rules under exogenous events. In Chitta Baral, editor, *Theories of Action, Planning, and Robot Control: Bridging the Gap*, number WS-96-07, pages 86–94. AAAI Press, 1996.

[8] Oded Maler, Amir Pneuli, and Joseph Sifakis. On the synthesis of discrete controllers for timed systems. In Ernst W. Mayr and Claude Puech, editors, *STACS 95: Theoretical Aspects of Computer Science*, pages 229–242. Springer Verlag, 1995.

[9] Drew McDermott. Using regression-match graphs to control search in planning. *Artificial Intelligence*, 109(1 − 2):111–159, April 1999.

[10] David J. Musliner, Edmund H. Durfee, and Kang G. Shin. CIRCA: a cooperative intelligent real-time control architecture. *IEEE Transactions on Systems, Man and Cybernetics*, 23(6):1561–1574, 1993.

[11] David J. Musliner, Edmund H. Durfee, and Kang G. Shin. World modeling for the dynamic construction of real-time control plans. *Artificial Intelligence*, 74(1):83–127, March 1995.

[12] David J. Musliner and Robert P. Goldman. CIRCA and the Cassini Saturn orbit insertion: Solving a prepositioning problem. In *Working Notes of the NASA Workshop on Planning and Scheduling for Space*, October 1997.

[13] Stavros Tripakis, January 2002.

[14] Stavros Tripakis and Karine Altisen. On-the-fly controller synthesis for discrete and dense-time systems. In J. Wing, J. Woodcock, and J. Davies, editors, *Formal Methods 1999*, volume I of *Lecture Notes in Computer Science*, pages 233–252. Springer Verlag, Berlin, 1999.

[15] S. Yovine. Kronos: A verification tool for real-time sytems. In *Springer International Journal of Software Tools for Technology Transfer*, volume 1, October 1997.

Computation of Root-Mean-Square Gains of Switched Linear Systems*

João P. Hespanha

University of California, Santa Barbara, CA 93106-9560, USA
hespanha@ece.ucsb.edu

Abstract. In this paper we compute the root-mean-square (RMS) gain of a switched linear system when the interval between consecutive switchings is large. The algorithm proposed is based on the fact that a given constant γ provides an upper bound on the RMS gain whenever there is a separation between the stabilizing and the antistabilizing solutions to a set of γ-dependent algebraic Riccati equations. The motivation for this problem is the application of robust stability tools to the analysis of hybrid systems.

1 Introduction

A switched linear system is defined by a linear differential equation for which the matrices that appear in the right-hand-side are piecewise constant. The times at which these matrices are discontinuous are called "switching times." Formally, to define a switched linear system one considers a family of n-dimensional, m-input, k-output minimal realizations

$$\{(A_p, B_p, C_p, D_p) : p \in \mathcal{P}\},\tag{1}$$

parameterized by an index set $\mathcal{P}$, together with a family of piecewise constant signals $\mathcal{S} := \{\sigma : [0, \infty) \to \mathcal{P}\}$. For a given signal $\sigma \in \mathcal{S}$, one can then define the following linear time-varying system

$$\dot{x} = A_\sigma x + B_\sigma u, \qquad\qquad y = C_\sigma x + D_\sigma u.\tag{2}$$

The signal σ is called a *switching signal* and the times at which it is discontinuous are called *switching times*. Between switching times the dynamics of (2) are time-invariant. Typically switching signals are generated by a supervisory logic and different values of σ correspond to distinct modes of operation [1].

For different switching signals σ, the system (2) has different properties. However, it is useful to study properties of this system that remain invariant for every σ in a particular set of switching signals $\mathcal{S}$. A property that has been extensively investigated for several sets of switching signals is stability. We say

---

* This material is based upon work supported by the National Science Foundation under Grant No. ECS-0093762.

C.J. Tomlin and M.R. Greenstreet (Eds.): HSCC 2002, LNCS 2289, pp. 239–252, 2002.

that (2) is *uniformly exponentially stable over* $\mathcal{S}$ when the state transition matrix $\Phi_\sigma(t, \tau)$ of the homogeneous switched system $\dot{z} = A_\sigma z$ can be bounded by[1]

$$\|\Phi_\sigma(t, \tau)\| \leq ce^{-\lambda(t-\tau)}, \qquad\qquad \forall t, \tau \geq 0, \quad \forall \sigma \in \mathcal{S},$$

where the constants $c, \lambda > 0$ are chosen independently of σ in $\mathcal{S}$. In [2, 3, 4, 5, 6, 7, 8, 9, 10] conditions are presented that guarantee stability of (2) for every set of switching signals $\mathcal{S}$. It is also well known (cf., e.g., [11]) that (2) is uniformly exponentially stable as long as $\mathcal{S}$ only contains signals with consecutive switching times separated by a sufficiently long interval. In particular, defining $\mathcal{S}[\tau_D]$, $\tau_D > 0$ to be the set of all switching signals with interval between consecutive discontinuities no smaller than τ_D, there exists a $\tau_D^* > 0$ so that (2) is uniformly exponentially stable over any $\mathcal{S}[\tau_D]$, $\tau_D \geq \tau_D^*$. The minimum interval τ_D between consecutive switching times is called the *dwell-time*. In [12] it is shown that uniform exponential stability is preserved when the set of switching signals is enlarged to contain signals that occasionally have dwell times smaller than τ_D, provided that this does not happen on-the-average (*slow-switching on-the-average*). The reader is referred to [13, 1] for a discussion of these and related results.

Surprisingly, there has been relatively little work on the study of input-output properties that remain invariant over sets of switching signals. For example, little is known under what conditions a switched system like (2) satisfies an *Integral Quadratic Constrain* (IQC) [14]:

$$\int_0^\infty [y(t)'\ u(t)'] M \begin{bmatrix} y(t) \\ u(t) \end{bmatrix} dt \geq 0, \qquad\qquad \forall u \in \mathcal{L}_2, \qquad (3)$$

for every $\sigma \in \mathcal{S}$. In (3), y is computed along solutions to (2) with $x(0) = 0$. This type of constrain provides a general framework to address performance and robustness of interconnected systems and has therefore been receiving significant attention in the context of unswitched system. It is therefore timely to study conditions under which IQCs remain invariant over specific classes of switching signals. In the recent paper [15] the authors study passivity-like IQCs with

$$M = M_{\delta, \rho} := \begin{bmatrix} -\delta^2 I & I \\ I & -\rho^2 I \end{bmatrix}, \qquad\qquad \delta, \rho \geq 0,$$

for switched hybrid systems. When

$$M = M_\gamma := \begin{bmatrix} -I & 0 \\ 0 & \gamma^2 I \end{bmatrix}, \qquad\qquad \gamma > 0$$

we obtain another IQC whose importance has long been recognized as it can be used to characterize the RMS gain of a systems. In this paper we study this

---

[1] Given a vector a and a matrix A we denote by $\|a\|$ and $\|A\|$ the Euclidean norm of a and the largest singular value of A, respectively. Given a vector or matrix-valued measurable signal z defined on $[0, \infty)$, we denote by $\|z\|_2$ the $\mathcal{L}_2$-norm $\left(\int_0^\infty \|z(t)\| dt\right)^{\frac{1}{2}}$ of z. The set of all signals z for which $\|z\|_2$ is finite is denoted by $\mathcal{L}_2$.

IQC for switched systems. RMS gains of switched system are typically needed to evaluate the performance of closed-loop systems with hybrid controllers or processes. This analysis also finds application in the use of robust control techniques in the stability analysis of hybrid systems.

Given a set of switching signals $\mathcal{S}$, we define the *RMS gain of* (2) *over* $\mathcal{S}$ to be the smallest scalar $\mathfrak{g}_\mathcal{S} \geq 0$ for which (3) holds with $M = M_{\mathfrak{g}_\mathcal{S}}$, for every $\sigma \in \mathcal{S}$. To be more precise,

$$\mathfrak{g}_\mathcal{S} := \inf\{\gamma \geq 0 : \|y\|_2 \leq \gamma \|u\|_2, \ \forall u \in \mathcal{L}_2, \ \sigma \in \mathcal{S}\},$$

where y is computed along solutions to (2) with $x(0) = 0$. The RMS gain $\mathfrak{g}_\mathcal{S}$ can be viewed as a "worst-case" energy amplification gain for the switched system, *over all possible input and switching signals.*

When (2) is uniformly exponentially stable over $\mathcal{S}$, the RMS gain $\mathfrak{g}_\mathcal{S}$ is known to be finite. Since both slow dwell-time switching and slow-switching on-the-average result in exponential stability, both these forms of slow switching result in a finite RMS gain $\mathfrak{g}_\mathcal{S}$. In [16, 12, 17] one can find upper bounds on RMS gains over appropriately defined sets of switching signals that satisfy the slow-switching properties mentioned above. However, these bounds are typically very conservative and prompted us to compute the precise value of the RMS gain under slow-switching.

The RMS gain over the set of switching signals $\mathcal{S}[\tau_D]$ with dwell-time $\tau_D > 0$ is a monotone decreasing function of τ_D. This is simply because, given two dwell-times $\tau_{D_1} \leq \tau_{D_2}$, we have that $\mathcal{S}[\tau_{D_1}] \supset \mathcal{S}[\tau_{D_2}]$. One can then ask: *What is the smallest RMS gain that can be obtained for* (2) *by increasing the dwell-time?* To answer this question we define the *slow-switching RMS gain*, by

$$\mathfrak{g}_{\text{slow}} := \inf_{\tau_D > 0} \mathfrak{g}_{\mathcal{S}[\tau_D]}. \tag{4}$$

Since every $\mathcal{S}[\tau_D]$, $\tau_D > 0$ contains the constant switching signals $\sigma(t) = p$, $t \geq 0$, $p \in \mathcal{P}$, $\mathfrak{g}_{\text{slow}}$ is necessarily larger or equal to the RMS gains of all the "unswitched systems," i.e.,

$$\mathfrak{g}_{\text{slow}} \geq \mathfrak{g}_{\text{static}} := \sup_{p \in \mathcal{P}} \|C_p(sI - A_p)^{-1} B_p + D_p\|_\infty, \tag{5}$$

where $\|T(s)\|_\infty$ denotes the $\mathcal{H}_\infty$-norm of a transfer matrix $T(s)$. We recall that $\|T(s)\|_\infty$ is numerically equal to the RMS gain of any linear time-invariant system with transfer matrix $T(s)$. Until recently, it was believed that the inequality in (5) was actually an equality. This would mean that, by switching sufficiently slow, one would recover the RMS gains of the "unswitched systems," which are realization independent. It turns out that this is not true and the above inequality is often strict. The following simple example illustrates this and also provides some intuition on the difficulties introduced by switching: Consider a SISO switched system

$$\dot{x} = A_\sigma x + b_\sigma u, \qquad\qquad y = c_\sigma x, \tag{6}$$

for which the switching signal σ takes values in the set $\mathcal{P} := \{1, 2\}$ and both unswitched systems have $\mathcal{H}_\infty$-norm (and therefore RMS gain) equal to one, i.e.,

$$\|c_p(sI - A_p)^{-1}b_p\|_\infty = 1, \qquad\qquad p \in \mathcal{P}. \qquad (7)$$

Consider also the switching signal

$$\sigma(t) := \begin{cases} 1 & t < 1 \\ 2 & t \geq 1 \end{cases} \qquad\qquad t \geq 0. \qquad (8)$$

Since σ has a single discontinuity, it belongs to every family of switching signals $\mathcal{S}[\tau_D]$, $\tau_D > 0$. Take now the following probe input signal with $\mathcal{L}_2$-norm equal to one:

$$u(t) := \begin{cases} 1 & t < 1 \\ 0 & t \geq 1 \end{cases} \qquad\qquad t \geq 0. \qquad (9)$$

The output of (6) corresponding to the switching signal (8) and the input (9) is given by

$$y(t) = \begin{cases} c_1\left(\int_0^t e^{A_1(t-\tau)}d\tau\right)b_1 & 0 \leq t < 1 \\ c_2\left(\int_0^1 e^{A_1(t-\tau)}d\tau\right)b_1 & t \geq 1 \end{cases} \qquad t \geq 0.$$

It turns out that c_2 can be chosen arbitrarily large without violating (7), provided that b_2 is sufficiently small. Therefore, by appropriate choice of c_2, the $\mathcal{L}_2$-norm of y can actually be very large (in particular larger than 1) for a unit-norm input, *even though we are switching between two systems with RMS gain equal to one.* The intuition behind this example is that for $t < 1$ the input energy is "stored" in the system through one realization (perhaps through a "large" b_1) and then it is "released" to the output for $t \geq 1$ through a different realization (perhaps through a "large" c_2). From this example, we conclude that even for very slow switching (in the extreme a single switch), the RMS gain of a switched system can be arbitrarily larger than the RMS gains of the "unswitched systems." Moreover, the RMS gain of a switched system is realization dependent and cannot be determined just from the transfer functions of the systems being switched. The goal of this paper is then to compute the slow-switching RMS gain $\mathfrak{g}_{\text{slow}}$ defined by (4).

For linear time-invariant systems, the RMS gain can be determined by solving algebraic Riccati equations. In particular, it is well known (*Bounded-real Lemma*) that the RMS gain is smaller than a given constant $\gamma > 0$ if and only if an algebraic Riccati equation of the form

$$S(P; \gamma) := A'_\gamma P + P A_\gamma + P R_\gamma P + Q_\gamma = 0, \qquad (10)$$

has a positive definite solution P, where A_γ, Q_γ, and R_γ are appropriately defined γ-dependent $n \times n$ real matrices with Q_γ and R_γ symmetric and positive semidefinite (cf. Theorem 1 in Sect. 3 for details). This allows one to determine the precise value of the RMS gain of a system using a bisection algorithm to find the smallest value of γ for which a positive definite solution to (10) exists [18]. Although in general algebraic Riccati equations have more than one solution, in order to determine the RMS gain of a linear system it is sufficient to find one of these solutions. However, to determine the RMS gain of a switched system, we have to pay special attention to the multiple solutions to the algebraic Riccati equations involved. We shall see below that the condition for the slow-switching RMS gain of a switched system to be smaller than γ requires a separation between *all* the stabilizing and *all* the antistabilizing solutions to the algebraic Riccati equations of the systems being switched.

The remaining of this paper is organized as follows: In Sect. 2 we derive a general formula for the RMS gain of a switched system in terms of the solution to a differential Riccati equation. This prompts us to investigate the solutions to differential Riccati equations, which is done in Sect. 3. In Sect. 4 we determine upper and lower bounds on the RMS gain of a switched system over the set $\mathcal{S}_1$ of switching signals with no more than one discontinuity. We then show in Sect. 5 that these same bounds are also valid for the slow-switching RMS gain. A bisection-type algorithm to compute it is given in Sect. 6. Section 7 contains final conclusions and directions for future research.

2   Computation of RMS Gains

To determine the RMS gain of (2) over $\mathcal{S}$ we consider the following optimization problem:

$$J(\gamma, \sigma) := \lim_{T \to \infty} \sup_{u \in \mathcal{L}_2} \int_0^T \|y(\tau)\|^2 - \gamma^2 \|u(\tau)\|^2 d\tau, \qquad \gamma \geq 0, \ \sigma \in \mathcal{S},$$

where y is computed along solutions to (2) with $x(0) = 0$. The RMS gain of (2) over $\mathcal{S}$ is then given by

$$\mathfrak{g}_{\mathcal{S}} := \inf\{\gamma \geq 0 : J(\gamma, \sigma) \leq 0, \ \forall \sigma \in \mathcal{S}\}. \tag{11}$$

Note that because the system is linear, when $J(\gamma, \sigma) > 0$ we must actually have $J(\gamma, \sigma) = +\infty$, which means that $J(\gamma, \sigma) \leq 0$ in (11) could be replaced by $J(\gamma, \sigma) < \infty$. It is also sufficient to consider the case $\gamma > \|D_p\|$, $p \in \mathcal{P}$ as the RMS gain is always larger or equal to any of the high frequency gains $\|D_p\|$ because of (5).

We shall use dynamic programming to compute $J(\gamma, \sigma)$ for a given $\sigma \in \mathcal{S}$ and $\gamma > \|D_p\|$, $p \in \mathcal{P}$. To this effect let us define the following finite-horizon "cost-to-go:"

$$V(x_0, t; T, \gamma, \sigma) := \sup_{u \in \mathcal{L}_2, x(t) = x_0} \int_t^T \|y(\tau)\|^2 - \gamma^2 \|u(\tau)\|^2 d\tau.$$

The corresponding dynamic-programming equation is given by[2]

$$-V_t = \sup_{u \in \mathbb{R}} \|Cx_0 + Du\|^2 - \gamma^2 \|u\|^2 + V_x(Ax_0 + Bu)$$

$$= V_x A x_0 + x_0' C' C x_0 + \left(\frac{1}{2}V_x B + x_0' C' D\right) X^{-1} \left(\frac{1}{2}B'V_x' + D'Cx_0\right), \quad (12)$$

where $X_p := \gamma^2 I - D_p' D_p > 0$. Since for a fixed σ we are dealing with a linear time-varying system, we can restrict our attention to costs-to-go of the form $V(x_0, t; T, \gamma, \sigma) = x_0' P(t) x_0$, $t \geq 0$ with $P(t)$ real symmetric. Replacing this in (12) we obtain

$$0 = x_0' \left(\dot{P} + PA_\sigma + A_\sigma' P + C_\sigma' C_\sigma + (PB_\sigma + C_\sigma' D_\sigma) X_\sigma^{-1} (B_\sigma' P + D_\sigma' C_\sigma)\right) x_0,$$

for every x_0, which (because of symmetry) actually implies that

$$-\dot{P} = PA_\sigma + A_\sigma' P + C_\sigma' C_\sigma$$
$$+ (PB_\sigma + C_\sigma' D_\sigma) X_\sigma^{-1} (B_\sigma' P + D_\sigma' C_\sigma) = S_\sigma(P; \gamma), \quad (13)$$

where

$$S_p(P; \gamma) := P\bar{A}_p + \bar{A}_p P + Q_p + PR_p P, \qquad p \in \mathcal{P}, \quad (14)$$

with

$$\bar{A}_p := A_p + B_p X_p^{-1} D_p' C_p, \quad R_p := B_p X_p^{-1} B_p' \quad Q_p := C_p'(I + D_p X_p^{-1} D_p') C_p.$$

Moreover,

$$P(T) = 0, \quad (15)$$

since $V(x_0, T; T, \gamma, \sigma) = 0$ for every x_0. Since (13) is locally Lipschitz, we conclude that $J(\gamma, \sigma) < \infty$ if and only if the unique solution to the final value problem (13)–(15) exists on every interval $[0, T)$, $T > 0$. Therefore

$$\mathfrak{g}_\mathcal{S} = \inf \left\{ \gamma \geq 0 : \text{solution to (13)–(15) exists on } [0, T), \forall T > 0, \sigma \in \mathcal{S} \right\}. \quad (16)$$

To compute the RMS gain of a switched system we must then study the existence of solution to a differential Riccati equation. We do this in the following section.

3   Differential Riccati Equations

We start by considering the following *algebraic Riccati equation*

$$S(P) := A'P + PA + PRP + Q = 0, \quad (17)$$

---

[2] For simplicity we dropped the subscript $\sigma(t)$ from all matrices and the dependence of $(x_0, t; T, \gamma, \sigma)$ on V. We denote the partial derivatives of V with respect to t and x by V_t and V_x, respectively.

where A, Q, and R are $n \times n$ real matrices with Q and R symmetric. Associated with this equation one defines a $2n \times 2n$ *Hamiltonian matrix* by

$$H := \begin{bmatrix} A & R \\ -Q & -A' \end{bmatrix}.$$

In the sequel, we say that a matrix P^- is a *stabilizing* solution to the algebraic Riccati equation (17) if P^- is real, symmetric, positive definite, and $A + RP^-$ is asymptotically stable. We say that P^+ is an *antistabilizing* solution to (17) if P_+ is real, symmetric, positive definite, and $-(A + RP^+)$ is asymptotically stable. The following theorem is a consequence of several well known results on algebraic Riccati equations.

Theorem 1. *Consider a minimal realization $(\bar{A}, \bar{B}, \bar{C}, \bar{D})$ with $\bar{A}$ asymptotically stable and*

$$\|\bar{C}(sI - \bar{A})^{-1}\bar{B} + \bar{D}\|_\infty < \gamma \tag{18}$$

for some $\gamma > 0$. Then $\|D\| < \gamma$ and there exist stabilizing and antistabilizing solutions P^- and P^+, respectively, to the algebraic Riccati equation (17) with

$$A := \bar{A} + \bar{B}\bar{X}^{-1}\bar{D}'\bar{C}, \qquad\qquad R := \bar{B}\bar{X}^{-1}\bar{B}',$$
$$Q := \bar{C}'(I + \bar{D}\bar{X}^{-1}\bar{D}')\bar{C}, \qquad\qquad X := \gamma^2 I - \bar{D}'\bar{D}.$$

Moreover, $P_+ - P_- > 0$ [3] and these solutions can be computed by

$$P^- = P_2^-(P_1^-)^{-1}, \qquad\qquad P^+ = P_2^+(P_1^+)^{-1}, \tag{19}$$

where the columns of $[\, P_1^{-'} \; P_2^{-'}\,]'$ and $[\, P_1^{+'} \; P_2^{+'}\,]'$ are chosen to form bases for the stable and antistable invariant[4] subspaces of H, respectively. The matrices P_1^- and P_1^+ above are guaranteed to be nonsingular.

Consider now the final-value solution to the following differential Riccati equation

$$-\dot{P} = S(P) = A'P + PA + PRP + Q, \qquad P(t_0) = P_0, \qquad t \le t_0. \tag{20}$$

The following theorem is inspired by results from [19] and [20, Chapter 3].

---

[3] Given a symmetric matrix Q we write $Q > 0$, $Q \ge 0$, $Q < 0$, and $Q \le 0$ when Q is positive definite, positive semidefinite, negative definite, and negative semidefinite, respectively. We write $Q \not\ge 0$ when Q is nonsingular and not positive semidefinite (therefore Q must have at least one strictly negative eigenvalue). Similarly, $Q \not\le 0$ means that Q is nonsingular and not negative semidefinite.

[4] Let H be a matrix with characteristic polynomial $\alpha(s) = \alpha^-(s)\alpha^0(s)\alpha^+(s)$, where all roots of the polynomials $\alpha^-(s)$, $\alpha^+(s)$, and $\alpha^0(s)$ have negative, positive, and zero real parts, respectively. The *stable* and *antistable* invariant subspaces of H are defined to be $\operatorname{Ker}\alpha^-(H)$ and $\operatorname{Ker}\alpha^+(H)$, respectively.

Theorem 2. *Suppose that there exist stabilizing and antistabilizing solutions to (17) with $P^+ - P^- > 0$.*

(i) *When $P_0 - P^+$ is nonsingular, the solution $\Pi(t; P_0)$ to (20) is given by $\Pi(t; P_0) = P^+ + \Lambda(t)^{-1}$, $t \leq t_0$, with*

$$\Lambda(t) := e^{(A+RP^+)(t-t_0)} \left((P_0 - P^+)^{-1} + (P^+ - P^-)^{-1} \right)$$
$$e^{(A+RP^+)'(t-t_0)} - (P^+ - P^-)^{-1} \quad (21)$$

on the interval $\mathcal{I}$ on which Λ is nonsingular.

(ii) *When $R \geq 0$ and $P_0 - P^+ < 0$ the solution $\Pi(t; P_0)$ to (20) exists globally for $t \leq t_0$ and $\Pi(t; P_0) \to P^-$ as $t \to -\infty$. The same result holds when $R \leq 0$ and $P_0 - P^+ > 0$.*

(iii) *When $R \geq 0$ and $P_0 - P^+ \nleq 0$, the solution $\Pi(t; P_0)$ to (20) has finite escape time. The same result holds when $R \leq 0$ and $P_0 - P^+ \ngeq 0$.*

The proof of this Theorem can be found in [21].

4   RMS Gain of Single-Switch Systems

In this section we consider the set $\mathcal{S}_1$ of switching signals with no more than one discontinuity. Using the results from the previous section we compute bounds on the RMS gain $\mathfrak{g}_{\mathcal{S}_1}$ of (2) over $\mathcal{S}_1$:

Theorem 3. *Assume that the realizations in (1) are minimal. Given any $\gamma > \mathfrak{g}_{static}$,*

$$\exists p, q \in \mathcal{P} \quad P_q^+ - P_p^- \nleq 0 \quad \Rightarrow \quad \mathfrak{g}_{\mathcal{S}_1} \geq \gamma \quad (22)$$
$$\forall p, q \in \mathcal{P} \quad P_q^+ - P_p^- > 0 \quad \Rightarrow \quad \mathfrak{g}_{\mathcal{S}_1} \leq \gamma, \quad (23)$$

where P_p^+ and P_p^-, $p \in \mathcal{P}$ respectively denote the stabilizing and antistabilizing solutions to the algebraic Riccati equation $S_p(P; \gamma) = 0$, with S_p defined by (14).

Before proving Theorem 4, it is interesting to note that the condition in (23) that gives the upper bound on the RMS gain requires a separation between *all* the stabilizing and *all* the antistabilizing solutions to the algebraic Riccati equations of the systems being switched. Note that for $p = q$, the fact that the qth system has RMS gain smaller than γ already guarantees that $P_q^+ - P_q^- > 0$ (cf. Theorem 1). However, this is not enough for $\mathfrak{g}_{\mathcal{S}_1}$ to be smaller or equal to γ. Indeed, we need all the stabilizing solutions P_p^- to be "smaller" than all the antistabilizing solutions P_q^+.

Proof (Theorem 3). To prove (22) we show that when $P_q^+ - P_p^- \nleq 0$ for some $p, q \in \mathcal{P}$, the RMS gain $\mathfrak{g}_{\mathcal{S}_1}$ given by (16) must be larger or equal to γ because the solution to (13)–(15) does not exist for some $T > 0, \sigma \in \mathcal{S}$. To this effect suppose that there are $p, q \in \mathcal{P}$ for which $P_q^+ - P_p^- \not\geq 0$ and take

$$\sigma(t) := \begin{cases} q & t < T_{\text{switch}} \\ p & t \geq T_{\text{switch}} \end{cases} \qquad t \geq 0, \qquad (24)$$

for some $T_{\text{switch}} > 0$. Because $R_p \geq 0$ and $-P_p^+ < 0$ (cf. Theorem 1), we conclude from Theorem 2 (ii) that the solution to (13)–(15) exists for every $t \in [T_{\text{switch}}, T)$. Moreover, if σ where equal to p for all times, we would actually have $P(t) \to P_p^-$ as $t \to -\infty$. This means that by choosing T sufficiently large, it is possible to have $P(T_{\text{switch}})$ sufficiently close to P_p^- so that $P_q^+ - P(T_{\text{switch}}) \not\geq 0$. Here, we are using the fact that the set $\{P : P_q^+ - P \not\geq 0\}$ is open and therefore if $P(T_{\text{switch}})$ is sufficiently close to the element P_p^- of this set, it must be inside the set. Once it is known that T is chosen such that $P_q^+ - P(T_{\text{switch}}) \not\geq 0$, by applying Theorem 2 to solve (13)–(15) for $t \leq T_{\text{switch}}$, we conclude from (iii) that the solution is actually only defined in an interval $(T_{\text{escape}}, T_{\text{switch}}]$ of finite length. Because of time invariance, we can choose T sufficiently large so that $T_{\text{escape}} > 0$. So the solution to (13)–(15) does not exist globally. This finishes the proof of (22).

To prove (23) we show directly that when $P_q^+ - P_p^- > 0$ for every $p, q \in \mathcal{P}$, we have $\|y\|_2 \leq \gamma \|u\|_2$ for every input and switching signals. To this effect pick arbitrary $u \in \mathcal{L}_2$, $\sigma \in \mathcal{S}_1$ and define

$$v(t) := V(x(t), t) + \int_0^t \|y(\tau)\|^2 - \gamma^2 \|u(\tau)\|^2 d\tau, \qquad t \geq 0,$$

where x and y are evaluated along a solution to (2) and $V(x, t) := x'P(t)x$, $t \geq 0$. Here, $P(t)$ denotes a time-varying continuous real symmetric matrix with the property that on any interval on which σ is constant we have

$$-\dot{P} = S_\sigma(P; \gamma). \qquad (25)$$

To construct such $P(t)$ we use the fact that because $\sigma \in \mathcal{S}_1$, the switching signal must be of the form (24) (possibly with $p = q$ if it is actually constant). Suppose then that for $t > T_{\text{switch}}$ we set $P(t)$ constant and equal to P_p^-, and for $t \leq T_{\text{switch}}$, $P(t)$ is defined by the final value problem

$$-\dot{P} = S_q(P; \gamma), \qquad P(T_{\text{switch}}) = P_p^-.$$

The function $P(t)$ is well defined for every $t \leq T_{\text{switch}}$ because $P_p^- - P_q^+ < 0$ (cf. Theorem 2 (ii)). By construction this choice of $P(t)$ does satisfy (25) on every interval on which σ is constant. From (25) and (12)–(13) it is straightforward to conclude that on any such interval we have $\dot{v} \leq 0$. We then conclude that v decreases between discontinuities of σ and is continuous at the switching time T_{switch}. Therefore $v(t) \leq v(0) = x(0)'P(0)x(0), \forall t \geq 0$. For a zero initialization of (2) we then conclude that $v(t) \leq 0, \forall t \geq 0$, or equivalently that

$$\int_0^t \|y(\tau)\|^2 - \gamma^2 \|u(\tau)\|^2 d\tau \leq -V(x(t), t), \qquad \forall t \geq 0.$$

Since $u \in \mathcal{L}_2$, $\lim_{t\to\infty} x(t) = 0$ and therefore

$$\int_0^\infty \|y(\tau)\|^2 - \gamma^2\|u(\tau)\|^2 d\tau \leq 0.$$

This concludes the proof since it shows that indeed $\|y\|_2 \leq \gamma \|u\|_2$.   ∎

5   Slow-Switching RMS Gain

In this section we show that the upper and lower bounds provided by Theorem 3 on the RMS gain $\mathfrak{g}_{\mathcal{S}_1}$ of (2) over $\mathcal{S}_1$ also hold for the slow-switching RMS gain $\mathfrak{g}_{\text{slow}}$ of (2). For simplicity, in this section we assume that the set $\mathcal{P}$ is finite, i.e., that we are switching among a finite number of systems. However, it would be straightforward to replace this assumption by uniformity conditions on the systems being switched, e.g., compactness of the family of realizations $\{A_p, B_p, C_p, D_p : p \in \mathcal{P}\}$.

Theorem 4. *Assume that the realizations in* (1) *are minimal and* $\mathcal{P}$ *is finite. Given any* $\gamma > \mathfrak{g}_{\text{static}}$

$$\exists p, q \in \mathcal{P} \quad P_q^+ - P_p^- \not\geq 0 \qquad \Rightarrow \qquad \mathfrak{g}_{\text{slow}} \geq \gamma \tag{26}$$

$$\forall p, q \in \mathcal{P} \quad P_q^+ - P_p^- > 0 \qquad \Rightarrow \qquad \mathfrak{g}_{\text{slow}} \leq \gamma, \tag{27}$$

where P_p^+ *and* P_p^-, $p \in \mathcal{P}$ *respectively denote the stabilizing and antistabilizing solutions to the algebraic Riccati equation* $S_p(P; \gamma) = 0$, *with* S_p *defined by* (14).

Proof (Theorem 4). To prove (26) note that for any $\tau_D > 0$, $\mathcal{S}_1 \subset \mathcal{S}[\tau_D]$ and therefore $\mathfrak{g}_{\mathcal{S}_1} \leq \mathfrak{g}_{\text{slow}}$. From Theorem 3 we then conclude that

$$\exists p, q \in \mathcal{P} \quad P_q^+ - P_p^- \not\geq 0 \qquad \Rightarrow \qquad \mathfrak{g}_{\mathcal{S}_1} \geq \gamma \qquad \Rightarrow \qquad \mathfrak{g}_{\text{slow}} \geq \mathfrak{g}_{\mathcal{S}_1} \geq \gamma.$$

To prove (27) assume that $P_q^+ - P_p^- > 0$ for every $p, q \in \mathcal{P}$ and therefore that we can select a positive constant ϵ and matrices $P_{(p,q)}$, $p, q \in \mathcal{P}$ such that

$$\|P - P_p^-\| \leq \epsilon \quad \Rightarrow \quad P_q^+ > P_{(p,q)} \geq P, \qquad \forall p, q \in \mathcal{P}. \tag{28}$$

In practice, $P_{(p,q)}$ can be any matrix sufficiently close to P_p^- so that $P_q^+ > P_{(p,q)} > P_p^-$ and ϵ a sufficiently small positive constant so that for any P such that $\|P - P_p^-\| \leq \epsilon$ we still have $P_{(p,q)} \geq P$.

Since $P_{(p,q)} - P_q^+ < 0$, we conclude from Theorem 2 (ii) that the solution to the final value problem

$$-\dot{P} = S_q(P; \gamma), \qquad\qquad P(T) = P_{(p,q)}, \tag{29}$$

exists globally and converges to P_q^- as $t \to -\infty$. Pick now a constant τ_D sufficiently large so that $\|P(t) - P_q^-\| \leq \epsilon$, $\forall t \leq T - \tau_D$ regardless of the choices for

p and q in (29). We show next that the RMS gain over $\mathcal{S}[\tau_D]$ is smaller or equal to γ and therefore so is the slow-switching RMS gain $\mathfrak{g}_{\text{slow}}$.

Pick arbitrary $u \in \mathcal{L}_2$, $\sigma \in \mathcal{S}_1$ and define

$$v(t) := V(x(t), t) + \int_0^t \|y(\tau)\|^2 - \gamma^2 \|u(\tau)\|^2 d\tau, \qquad t \geq 0,$$

where x and y are evaluated along a solution to (2) and $V(x, t) := x'P(t)x$, $t \geq 0$. Here, $P(t)$ denotes a time-varying symmetric matrix with the property that on any interval (t_1, t_2) on which σ is constant and equal to q we have

$$-\dot{P} = S_q(P; \gamma), \qquad\qquad P(t_2) = P_0, \qquad\qquad (30)$$

where P_0 is chosen equal to P_q^- in case $t_2 = \infty$ and equal to $P_{(p,q)}$ when $t_2 < \infty$, with p being the value of σ immediately after t_2. Note that in the former case (which occurs only when t_1 is the last switching time), $P(t)$ is constant for $t > t_1$. In the latter case, the solution to (30) is well defined for every $t \leq t_2$ because $P_{(p,q)} - P_q^+ < 0$ (cf. Theorem 2 (ii)).

As in the proof of Theorem 3, we conclude that $\dot{v} \leq 0$ on any interval on which σ is constant. However, now $v(t)$ is discontinuous at switching times. In particular, if σ switches from q to p at time t_2, we have

$$\lim_{\tau \downarrow t_2} v(\tau) - \lim_{\tau \uparrow t_2} v(\tau) = x(t_2)'(\bar{P} - P_{p,q})x(t_2),$$

where $\bar{P}$ is either equal to P_p^- in case t_2 is the last switching time or the solution at time t_2 of a final value problem of the form

$$-\dot{P} = S_p(P; \gamma), \qquad\qquad P(t_3) = P_{(\bar{p}, p)},$$

for some $\bar{p} \in \mathcal{P}$ and with $t_3 \geq t_2 + \tau_D$. However, we selected τ_D sufficiently large so that $\|P(t_2) - P_p^-\| \leq \epsilon$. Therefore we always have $\|\bar{P} - P_p^-\| \leq \epsilon$ whether or not t_2 is the last switching time. From this and (28) we conclude that $\bar{P} - P_{p,q} \leq 0$ and therefore

$$\lim_{\tau \downarrow t_2} v(\tau) - \lim_{\tau \uparrow t_2} v(\tau) = x(t_2)'(\bar{P} - P_{p,q})x(t_2) \leq 0.$$

This means that even at points of discontinuity of v this signal decreases and therefore also here $v(t) \leq v(0)$, $\forall t \geq 0$. As in the proof of Theorem 3 we can then conclude that $\|y\|_2 \leq \gamma \|u\|_2$ for a zero initialization of (2). This finishes the proof since we showed that the RMS gain over $\mathcal{S}[\tau_D]$ is indeed no larger than γ. ∎

Remark 1. The proof of (27) actually provides a bound on the dwell-time τ_D to have the RMS gain over $\mathcal{S}[\tau_D]$ smaller or equal to γ. In general, if the separation between the stabilizing and antistabilizing is large, we can choose the ϵ in (28) large and therefore have an RMS gain no larger than γ even for small τ_D.

6   Computation of the Slow-Switching RMS Gain

Theorem 4 suggests the following bisection algorithm to compute the slow-switching RMS gain $\mathfrak{g}_{\mathrm{slow}}$ of (2):

> 1. *Select a tolerance ϵ, an upper bound γ_{up} and a lower bound γ_{low} on $\mathfrak{g}_{\mathrm{slow}}$ (e.g., $\gamma_{\mathrm{low}} := \mathfrak{g}_{\mathrm{static}}$ and γ_{up} taken from [12])*
> 2. *If $\gamma_{\mathrm{up}} - \gamma_{\mathrm{low}} \leq 2\epsilon$ then stop (the RMS gain $\mathfrak{g}_{\mathrm{slow}}$ is away from $\frac{\gamma_{\mathrm{up}} + \gamma_{\mathrm{low}}}{2}$ by less than ϵ)*
> 3. *Otherwise set $\gamma = \frac{\gamma_{\mathrm{up}} + \gamma_{\mathrm{low}}}{2}$ and*
>
> $$\text{If} \quad \exists p, q \in \mathcal{P} \quad P_q^+ - P_p^- \not\geq 0 \quad \text{then set} \quad \gamma_{\mathrm{low}} = \gamma$$
> $$\text{If} \quad \forall p, q \in \mathcal{P} \quad P_q^+ - P_p^- > 0 \quad \text{then set} \quad \gamma_{\mathrm{up}} = \gamma$$
>
> *and go back to step 2*

The previous algorithm only fails if there is a positive-length interval of values for γ on which all $P_q^+ - P_p^- \geq 0$ but at least one of these matrices has an eigenvalue exactly at the origin. Generically, this should not happen over an interval of positive length since an infinitely small perturbation on γ should make the eigenvalue become either positive or negative. However, even when this happens one can still use algorithms similar to the one above to compute the following upper and lower bounds on $\mathfrak{g}_{\mathrm{slow}}$:

$$\sup\{\gamma > \mathfrak{g}_{\mathrm{static}} : \exists p, q \in \mathcal{P}, \ P_q^+ - P_p^- \not\geq 0\}$$
$$\leq \mathfrak{g}_{\mathrm{slow}} \leq \inf\{\gamma > \mathfrak{g}_{\mathrm{static}} : P_q^+ - P_p^- > 0, \ \forall p, q \in \mathcal{P}\}.$$

Remark 2. The verification of the matrix-inequality conditions in step 3 is computationally simple when $\mathcal{P}$ is a finite set. Indeed, when $\mathcal{P}$ has n elements, in the worst case the verification of this conditions requires the computation of the stabilizing and anti-stabilizing solutions to n algebraic Riccati equations (e.g., using (19) in Theorem 1) and then verifying if $n(n-1)$ matrices are positive definite. However, if $\mathcal{P}$ is a continuum (i.e., when one can switch among an infinitely large family of systems) the above algorithm may not be practical.

7   Conclusions

We presented a method to compute the slow-switching RMS gain of a switched linear system. The algorithm proposed uses the fact that a given constant γ provides an upper bound on the RMS gain whenever there is a separation between *all* the stabilizing and *all* the antistabilizing solutions to the algebraic Riccati equations of the systems being switched. We are now in the process of expressing this condition in the form of Linear Matrix Inequalities. The motivation is to construct efficient algorithms that can be used to design switching controllers that minimize the RMS gain of the closed-loop.

Acknowledgments

The author would like to thank Dr. G. Zhai for finding an error in previous related work and for subsequent discussions that lead to the results presented here, and also to Dr. D. Liberzon for several comments that found their way into the final version of the paper. The reference [20] was graciously provided by Dr. E. Jonckheere.

References

[1] J. P. Hespanha, *Encyclopedia of Life Support Systems*, ch. Stabilization Through Hybrid Control. UNESCO, Feb. 2001. Submitted.

[2] A. P. Molchanov and Y. S. Pyatnitskiy, "Criteria of asymptotic stability of differential and difference inclusions encountered in control theory," *Syst. & Contr. Lett.*, vol. 13, pp. 59–64, 1989.

[3] K. S. Narendra and J. Balakrishnan, "A common Lyapunov function for stable LTI systems with commuting A-matrices," *IEEE Trans. on Automat. Contr.*, vol. 39, pp. 2469–2471, Dec. 1994.

[4] L. Gurvits, "Stability of linear inclusions—part 2," tech. rep., NECI, Dec. 1996.

[5] T. M. Yoshihiro Mori and Y. Kuroe, "A solution to the common Lyapunov function problem for continuous-time systems," in *Proc. of the 36th Conf. on Decision and Contr.*, vol. 3, pp. 3530–3531, Dec. 1997.

[6] W. P. Dayawansa and C. F. Martin, "A converse Lyapunov theorem for a class of dynamical systems which undergo switching," *IEEE Trans. on Automat. Contr.*, vol. 44, pp. 751–760, Apr. 1999.

[7] D. Liberzon, J. P. Hespanha, and A. S. Morse, "Stability of switched linear systems: a Lie-algebraic condition," *Syst. & Contr. Lett.*, vol. 37, pp. 117–122, June 1999.

[8] R. N. Shorten and K. S. Narendra, "Necessary and sufficient conditions for the existence of a common quadratic Lyapunov function for two stable second order linear time-invariant systems," in *Proc. of the 1999 American Contr. Conf.*, pp. 1410–1414, June 1999.

[9] R. N. Shorten and K. S. Narendra, "Necessary and sufficient conditions for the existence of a common quadratic Lyapunov function for m stable second order linear time-invariant systems," in *Proc. of the 2000 Amer. Contr. Conf.*, pp. 359–363, June 2000.

[10] A. A. Agrachev and D. Liberzon, "Lie-algebraic stability criteria for switched systems," *SIAM J. Contr. Optimization*, vol. 40, no. 1, pp. 253–269, 2001.

[11] A. S. Morse, "Supervisory control of families of linear set-point controllers—part 1: exact matching," *IEEE Trans. on Automat. Contr.*, vol. 41, pp. 1413–1431, Oct. 1996.

[12] J. P. Hespanha and A. S. Morse, "Stability of switched systems with average dwell-time," in *Proc. of the 38th Conf. on Decision and Contr.*, pp. 2655–2660, Dec. 1999.

[13] D. Liberzon and A. S. Morse, "Basic problems in stability and design of switched systems," *IEEE Contr. Syst. Mag.*, vol. 19, pp. 59–70, Oct. 1999.

[14] A. Megretski and A. Rantzer, "System analysis via integral quadratic constraints," *IEEE Trans. on Automat. Contr.*, vol. 42, pp. 819–830, June 1997.

[15] M. Žefran, F. Bullo, and M. Stein, "A notion of passivity for hybrid systems." To appear in the 40th IEEE Conf. on Dec. and Control., Dec. 2001.

[16] J. P. Hespanha, *Logic-Based Switching Algorithms in Control*. PhD thesis, Yale University, New Haven, CT, 1998.

[17] G. Zhai, B. Hu, K. Yasuda, and A. N. Michel, "Disturbance attenuation properties of time-controlled switched systems." Submitted to publication., 2001.

[18] K. Zhou, J. C. Doyle, and K. Glover, *Robust and Optimal Control*. New Jersey: Prentice Hall, 1996.

[19] J. C. Willems, "Least squares stationary optimal control and the algebraic Riccati equation," *IEEE Trans. on Automat. Contr.*, vol. AC-16, pp. 621–634, Dec. 1971.

[20] J. M. Rodriguez-Canabal, *The Geometry of the Riccati Equation*. PhD thesis, University of Southern California, Los Angeles, CA, June 1972.

[21] J. P. Hespanha, "Computation of $\mathcal{L}_2$-induced norms of switched linear systems," tech. rep., University of California, Santa Barbara, CA, Oct. 2001.

Mode Estimation of Probabilistic Hybrid Systems

Michael W. Hofbaur[1,2*] and Brian C. Williams[1]

[1] MIT Space Systems and Artificial Intelligence Laboratories
77 Massachusetts Ave., Rm-37-381, Cambridge MA 02139, USA,
williams@mit.edu

[2] Graz University of Technology, Department of Automatic Control,
Inffeldgasse 16c/2, A-8010 Graz, Austria,
hofbaur@irt.tu-graz.ac.at

Abstract. Model-based diagnosis and mode estimation capabilities excel at diagnosing systems whose symptoms are clearly distinguished from normal behavior. A strength of mode estimation, in particular, is its ability to track a system's discrete dynamics as it moves between different behavioral modes. However, often failures bury their symptoms amongst the signal noise, until their effects become catastrophic.

We introduce a hybrid mode estimation system that extracts mode estimates from subtle symptoms. First, we introduce a modeling formalism, called *concurrent probabilistic hybrid automata* (cPHA), that merge hidden Markov models (HMM) with continuous dynamical system models. Second, we introduce *hybrid estimation* as a method for tracking and diagnosing cPHA, by unifying traditional continuous state observers with HMM belief update. Finally, we introduce a novel, any-time, any-space algorithm for computing approximate hybrid estimates.

1 Introduction

The year 2000 was kicked off with two missions to Mars, following on the heals of the highly successful Mars Pathfinder mission. Mars Climate Orbiter burned up in the Martian atmosphere. After extensive investigation it was found that a units error in a small forces table introduced a small, but indiscernible fault that, over a lengthy time period, caused the loss of the orbiter. The problem of misinterpreting a system's dynamics was punctuated later in the year when the Mars Polar Lander vanished without a trace. After months of analysis, the failure investigation team concluded that the vehicle most likely crashed into Mars, because it incorrectly shutdown its engine at 40 meters above the surface. This failure, like the orbiter, resulted from a misinterpretation of the vehicle's dynamics, in this case, due to a faulty software monitor.

The above case study is a dramatic instance of a common problem – increasingly complex systems are being developed, whose failure symptoms are nearly

---

* Supported by NASA under contract NAG2-1388.

C.J. Tomlin and M.R. Greenstreet (Eds.): HSCC 2002, LNCS 2289, pp. 253–266, 2002.

indiscernible, up until a catastrophic result occurs. To tackle this problem we address two issues. First, these failures are manifest through a coupling between a system's continuous dynamics, and its evolution through different behavior modes. We address this issue by developing hybrid monitoring and diagnosis capabilities that are able to track a system's behavior, along both its continuous state evolution and its discrete mode changes. Second, failures may generate symptoms that are initially on the same scale as sensor and actuator noise. To discover these symptoms, we use statistical methods to separate the noise from the true dynamics.

We address this challenge by extending the deductive mode estimation capabilities of the Livingstone system[1], to reason about continuous dynamics, using classical methods for state estimation[2]. After a motivating example, we discuss traditional methods for separately estimating discrete and continuous behaviors. We then introduce a modeling formalism, called *concurrent probabilistic hybrid automata* (cPHA), that merges hidden Markov models (HMM) with continuous dynamical system models. A cPHA provides a modeling framework that captures probabilistic mode transitions, This is unlike most traditional hybrid modeling frameworks, for example, [3,4,5,6], which define mode transitions to be deterministic, or do not explicitly specify probabilities for transitions.

Next, we introduce a method, called *hybrid mode estimation*, that tracks and diagnoses cPHA, by creating a hybrid HMM observer. The observer uses the results of continuous state estimates to estimate a system's mode changes, and coordinates the actions of a set of continuous state observers. This approach is similar to work pursued in multi-model estimation[7,8,9]. However, we provide a novel any-time, any-space algorithm for computing approximate hybrid estimates, which allows us to track concurrent automata that have a large number of possible modes.

Several approaches have been recently introduced for hybrid system diagnosis, including approaches that bridge methods from model-based diagnosis and multi-model filtering (e.g. [10,11,12]), and less traditional methods, such as dynamic Bayesian networks[13] or particle filters[14]. Most of these methods, however, do not deal with autonomous mode transitions of the system under investigation. Our paper remedies this situation and provides one possible path towards a unified framework for monitoring and diagnosing hybrid systems.

2   Example: BIO-Plex

Our application is the BIO-Plex Test Complex at NASA Johnson Space Center, a five chamber facility for evaluating biological and physiochemical life support technologies. It is an artificial, biosphere-type, closed environment, which must robustly provide all the air, water, and most of the food for a crew of four without interruption. Plants are grown in plant growth chambers, where they provide food for the crew, and convert the exhaled CO_2 into O_2. In order to maintain a closed-loop system, it is necessary to control the resource exchange between the chambers, without endangering the crew. For the scope of this paper, we restrict our evaluation to the sub-system dealing with CO_2 control in the plant growth chamber (PGC), shown in Fig. 1.

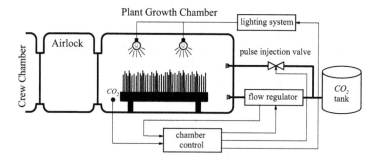

Fig. 1. BIO-Plex plant growth chamber

The system is composed of several components, such as a flow regulator that provides continuous CO_2 supply, a pulse injection valve that provides a means for increasing the CO_2 concentration rapidly, a lighting system and the plant growth chamber, itself. The control system maintains a plant growth optimal CO_2 concentration of 1200 ppm during the day phase of the system (20 hours/day). This CO_2 level is unsuitable for humans, hence the gas concentration is lowered to 500 ppm, whenever crew members request to enter the chamber for harvesting, re-planting or other service activities. Safety regulations require that the system inhibit high volume gas injection via the pulse-injection path, while crew members are in the PGC. Sensors are available to record entry and exit of crew members. However, sensors are known to fail. In this paper we demonstrate how hybrid estimation provides a robust backup strategy that detects the presence of crew members, based on the slight change in the gas balance that is caused by the exhaled CO_2.

Hybrid estimation schemes are key to tracking system operational modes, as well as, detecting subtle failures and performing diagnoses. For instance, a partial lighting failure has impact on the gas conversion rate due to lower photosynthesis activity. The failure leads to behavior that is similar to crew members entering the PGC. A hybrid estimation scheme should correctly discriminate among different operational and failure modes of each system component, based on the overall system operation.

3   Traditional Estimation

To model a hybrid system, we start by using a *hidden Markov model (HMM)* to describe discrete stochastic changes in the system. We then fold in the continuous dynamics, by associating a set of continuous dynamical equations with each HMM state. To avoid confusion in terminology, we refer to the HMM state as the system's mode, and reserve the term state to refer to the state of a probabilistic hybrid automaton. We develop a hybrid estimation capability by generalizing traditional methods for estimating HMM states and continuous state-variables.

3.1   Estimating HMMs

For an HMM, estimation is framed as a problem of belief-state update, that is, the problem of determining the probability distribution $b_{(k)}$ over modes $\mathcal{M}$ at time-step k. The probability of being in a mode m_i at time-step k is denoted $b_{(k)}[m_i]$.

Definition 1. A *Hidden Markov Model (HMM)* can be described by a tuple $\langle \mathcal{M}, \mathcal{Y}_d, \mathcal{U}_d, P_\Theta, P_T, P_O \rangle$. $\mathcal{M}$, $\mathcal{Y}_d$ and $\mathcal{U}_d$ denote finite sets of *feasible modes* m_i, *observations* y_{di} and *control values* u_{di}, respectively. The *initial state function*, $P_\Theta[m_i]$, denotes the probability that m_i is the initial mode. The *mode transition function*, $P_T(m_i|u_d, m_j)$, describes the probability of transitioning from mode $m_{j,(k-1)}$ to $m_{i,(k)}$ at time-step k, given a discrete control action $u_{d,(k-1)}$. The *observation function* $P_O(y_d|m_i)$ describes the probability that a discrete value y_d is observed, given the mode m_i.

Standard belief update for an HMM is an incremental process that determines the belief-state $b_{(k)}$ at the current time-step, given the current observations $y_{d,(k)}$, and the belief-state $b_{(k-1)}$ and discrete control action $u_{d,(k-1)}$ from the previous time-step. Belief update is a two step process. First, it uses the previous belief-state and the probabilistic transition function to predict the belief-state, denoted $b_{(\bullet k)}[m_i]$. Then it adjusts this prediction to account for the current observations at time-step k, resulting in the final belief-state $b_{(k)}[m_i]$:

$$b_{(\bullet k)}[m_i] = \sum_{m_j \in \mathcal{M}} P_T(m_i|u_{d,(k-1)}, m_j)b_{(k-1)}[m_j] \tag{1}$$

$$b_{(k)}[m_i] = \frac{b_{(\bullet k)}[m_i]P_O(y_{d,(k)}|m_i)}{\sum_{m_j \in \mathcal{M}} b_{(\bullet k)}[m_j]P_O(y_{d,(k)}|m_j)}, \tag{2}$$

3.2   Estimating Continuous Variables

The state of a continuous dynamic system is traditionally estimated using a state observer. In this paper we use a discrete-time model for the continuous dynamics and estimate the behavior with discrete-time extended Kalman filters[2]. This model selection is motivated by our overall goal: building a hybrid estimator for a supervisory control system that operates on a discrete-time basis.

Definition 2. We describe a *discrete-time model (DTM)* as a tuple $\langle \mathbf{x}, \mathbf{y}, \mathbf{u}, \mathbf{v}_s,$ $\mathbf{v}_o, \mathbf{f}, \mathbf{g}, T_s, \mathbf{Q}, \mathbf{R} \rangle$. $\mathbf{x}, \mathbf{y}, \mathbf{u}$ denote the vectors of *independent state-variables* $x_1,$ $\dots, x_n$, *observed variables* $y_1, \dots, y_{m_i}$ and *control variables* $u_1, \dots, u_{m_o}$ respectively. The function $\mathbf{f}$ specifies the dynamic evolution $\mathbf{x}_{(k)} = \mathbf{f}(\mathbf{x}_{(k-1)}, \mathbf{u}_{(k-1)}) +$ $\mathbf{v}_{s,(k-1)}$ and the function $\mathbf{g}$ determines the observed variables $\mathbf{y}_{(k)} = \mathbf{g}(\mathbf{x}_{(k)},$

$\mathbf{u}_{(k)}) + \mathbf{v}_{o,(k)}$. The exogenous inputs $\mathbf{v}_s$ and $\mathbf{v}_o$ represent additive state disturbances and measurement noise. We assume that these disturbances can be modeled as a random, uncorrelated sequence with zero-mean and Gaussian distribution, and specify them by the covariance matrices $E[\mathbf{v}_{s,(k)}\mathbf{v}_{s,(k)}{}^T] =: \mathbf{Q}$ and $E[\mathbf{v}_{o,(k)}\mathbf{v}_{o,(k)}{}^T] =: \mathbf{R}$. T_s denotes the *sampling-rate*, so that the time-step, k, denotes the time point, $t_k = kT_s$, assuming the initial time point $t_0 = 0$.

The disturbances and imprecise knowledge about the initial state $\mathbf{x}_{(0)}$ make it necessary to estimate the state[1] by its mean $\hat{\mathbf{x}}_{(k)}$ and covariance matrix $\mathbf{P}_{(k)}$. We use an extended Kalman filter for this purpose, which updates its current state, like an HMM observer, in two steps. The first step uses the model to predict the state $\hat{\mathbf{x}}_{(\bullet k)}$ and its covariance $\mathbf{P}_{(\bullet k)}$, based on the previous estimate $\langle \hat{\mathbf{x}}_{(k-1)}, \mathbf{P}_{(k-1)} \rangle$, and the control input $\mathbf{u}_{(k-1)}$:

$$\hat{\mathbf{x}}_{(\bullet k)} = \mathbf{f}(\hat{\mathbf{x}}_{(k-1)}, \mathbf{u}_{(k-1)}) \tag{3}$$

$$\mathbf{A}_{(k-1)} = \left. \frac{\partial \mathbf{f}}{\partial \mathbf{x}} \right|_{\hat{\mathbf{x}}_{(k-1)}, \mathbf{u}_{(k-1)}} \tag{4}$$

$$\mathbf{P}_{(\bullet k)} = \mathbf{A}_{(k-1)} \mathbf{P}_{(k-1)} \mathbf{A}_{(k-1)}^T + \mathbf{Q}. \tag{5}$$

This one-step ahead prediction leads to a prediction residual $\mathbf{r}_{(k)}$ with covariance matrix $\mathbf{S}_{(k)}$

$$\mathbf{r}_{(k)} = \mathbf{y}_{(k)} - \mathbf{g}(\hat{\mathbf{x}}_{(\bullet k)}, \mathbf{u}_{(k)}) \tag{6}$$

$$\mathbf{C}_{(k)} = \left. \frac{\partial \mathbf{g}}{\partial \mathbf{x}} \right|_{\hat{\mathbf{x}}_{(\bullet k)}, \mathbf{u}_{(k)}} \tag{7}$$

$$\mathbf{S}_{(k)} = \mathbf{C}_{(k)} \mathbf{P}_{(\bullet k)} \mathbf{C}_{(k)}^T + \mathbf{R}. \tag{8}$$

The second filter step calculates the Kalman filter gain $\mathbf{K}_{(k)}$, and refines the prediction as follows:

$$\mathbf{K}_{(k)} = \mathbf{P}_{(\bullet k)} \mathbf{C}_{(k)}^T \mathbf{S}_{(k)}^{-1} \tag{9}$$

$$\hat{\mathbf{x}}_{(k)} = \hat{\mathbf{x}}_{(\bullet k)} + \mathbf{K}_{(k)} \mathbf{r}_{(k)} \tag{10}$$

$$\mathbf{P}_{(k)} = \left[\mathbf{I} - \mathbf{K}_{(k)} \mathbf{C}_{(k)} \right] \mathbf{P}_{(\bullet k)}. \tag{11}$$

The output of the extended Kalman filter is a sequence of mean/covariance pairs $\langle \hat{\mathbf{x}}_{(k)}, \mathbf{P}_{(k)} \rangle$ for $\mathbf{x}_{(k)}$.

4   Concurrent Probabilistic Hybrid Automata

We extend hidden Markov models by incorporating discrete-time difference equations and algebraic equations for each mode to capture the dynamic evolution of the system. This leads to a hybrid model with probabilistic transitions. More specifically, we define our automaton model as:

---

[1] Throughout this paper we assume that the discrete-time models under investigation are observable in the sense of control theory.

Definition 3. A *discrete-time probabilistic hybrid automaton (PHA)* $\mathcal{A}$ can be described as a tuple $\langle \mathbf{x}, \mathbf{w}, F, T, \mathcal{X}_d, \mathcal{U}_d, T_s \rangle$:

- $\mathbf{x}$ denotes the hybrid *state variables* of the automaton,[2] composed of $\mathbf{x} = \{x_d\} \cup \mathbf{x}_c$. The discrete variable x_d denotes the *mode* of the automaton and has finite domain $\mathcal{X}_d$. The *continuous state variables* $\mathbf{x}_c = \{x_{c1}, \ldots, x_{cn}\}$ capture the dynamic evolution of the automaton with domain $\mathbb{R}^n$. $\mathbf{x}$ denotes the *hybrid state* of the automaton, while $\mathbf{x}_c$ denotes the *continuous state*.
- The set of *I/O variables* $\mathbf{w} = \mathbf{u}_d \cup \mathbf{u}_c \cup \mathbf{y}_c$ of the automaton is composed of disjoint sets of discrete input variables $\mathbf{u}_d = \{u_{d1}, \ldots, u_{dm_d}\}$ (called *command variables*), continuous *input variables* $\mathbf{u}_c = \{u_{c1}, \ldots, u_{cm_i}\}$, and continuous *output variables* $\mathbf{y}_c = \{y_{c1}, \ldots, y_{cm_o}\}$. The I/O variables have domain $\mathcal{U}_d$, $\mathbb{R}^{m_i}$ and $\mathbb{R}^{m_o}$, respectively.
- $F : \mathcal{X}_d \to F_{DE} \cup F_{AE}$ specifies the *continuous evolution* of the automaton in terms of *discrete-time difference equations* F_{DE} and *algebraic equations* F_{AE} for each mode $x_d \in \mathcal{X}_d$. T_s denotes the sampling period of the discrete-time difference equations.
- The finite set, T, of *transitions* specifies the probabilistic discrete evolution of the automaton in terms of tuples $\langle \tau_i, c_i \rangle \in T$. Each *transition function* τ_i has an associated Boolean *guard condition* $c_i : \mathbb{R}^n \times \mathcal{U}_d \to \{\text{true}, \text{false}\}$ and specifies the probability mass function over target modes $x_d \in \mathcal{X}_d$.

Fig. 2 visualizes the probabilistic transitions $T = \{\langle \tau_1, c_1 \rangle, \langle \tau_2, c_2 \rangle\}$ for a PHA with 4 modes $\mathcal{X}_d = \{m_1, m_2, m_3, m_4\}$, where m_2 and m_4 represent failure modes. The transition function τ_2 specifies a transition from mode m_1 to mode m_3 with probability p_3 or to mode m_4 with probability p_4, whenever its associated guard c_2 is satisfied.

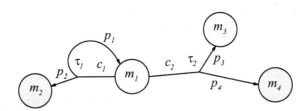

Fig. 2. Probabilistic mode transition

Complex systems are modeled as a composition of concurrently operating PHA that represent the individual system components. A *concurrent probabilistic hybrid automata (cPHA)* specifies this composition as well as its interconnection to the outside world:

---

[2] When clear from context, we use lowercase bold symbols, such as $\mathbf{v}$, to denote a *set* of variables $\{v_1, \ldots, v_l\}$, as well as a *vector* $[v_1, \ldots, v_l]^T$ with components v_i.

Definition 4. A *concurrent probabilistic hybrid automaton (cPHA)* $\mathcal{CA}$ can be described as a tuple $\langle A, \mathbf{u}, \mathbf{y}_c, \mathbf{v}_s, \mathbf{v}_o, N_x, N_y \rangle$:

- $A = \{\mathcal{A}_1, \mathcal{A}_2, \ldots, \mathcal{A}_l\}$ denotes the finite set of PHAs that represent the components $\mathcal{A}_i$ of the cPHA (we denote the components of a PHA $\mathcal{A}_i$ by $x_{di}, \mathbf{x}_{ci}, \mathbf{u}_{di}, \mathbf{u}_{ci}, \mathbf{y}_{ci}, F_i$, etc.).
- The *input variables* $\mathbf{u} = \mathbf{u}_d \cup \mathbf{u}_c$ of the automaton consists of the sets of discrete input variables $\mathbf{u}_d = \mathbf{u}_{d1} \cup \ldots \cup \mathbf{u}_{dl}$ (command variables) and continuous input variables $\mathbf{u}_c \subseteq \mathbf{u}_{c1} \cup \ldots \cup \mathbf{u}_{cl}$.
- The *output variables* $\mathbf{y}_c \subseteq \mathbf{y}_{c1} \cup \ldots \cup \mathbf{y}_{cl}$ specify the observed output variables of the cPHA.
- The observation process is subject to (mode dependent[3]) additive Gaussian *sensor noise*. $N_y : \mathcal{X}_d \to \mathbb{R}^{m \times m}$ specifies the disturbance $\mathbf{v}_o$ in terms of the covariance matrix $\mathbf{R}$.
- N_x specifies (mode dependent) additive Gaussian *disturbances* that act upon the continuous state variables $\mathbf{x}_c = \mathbf{x}_{c1} \cup \ldots \cup \mathbf{x}_{cl}$. $N_x : \mathcal{X}_d \to \mathbb{R}^{n \times n}$ specifies the disturbance $\mathbf{v}_s$ in terms of the covariance matrix $\mathbf{Q}$.

Definition 5. The *hybrid state* $\mathbf{x}_{(k)}$ of a cPHA at time-step k specifies the mode assignment $\mathbf{x}_{d,(k)}$ of the mode variables $\mathbf{x}_d = \{x_{d1}, \ldots, x_{dl}\}$ and the continuous state assignment $\mathbf{x}_{c,(k)}$ of the continuous state variables $\mathbf{x}_c = \mathbf{x}_{c1} \cup \ldots \cup \mathbf{x}_{cl}$.

Interconnection among the cPHA components $\mathcal{A}_i$ is achieved via shared continuous I/O variables $w_c \in \mathbf{u}_{ci} \cup \mathbf{y}_{ci}$ only. Fig. 3 illustrates a simple example composed of 2 PHAs.

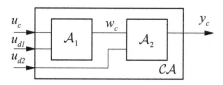

Fig. 3. Example cPHA composed of two PHAs

A cPHA specifies a mode dependent discrete-time model for a plant with command inputs $\mathbf{u}_d$, continuous inputs $\mathbf{u}_c$, continuous outputs $\mathbf{y}_c$, mode $\mathbf{x}_d$, continuous state variables $\mathbf{x}_c$ and disturbances $\mathbf{v}_s, \mathbf{v}_o$. The continuous evolution of $\mathbf{x}_c$ and $\mathbf{y}_c$ can be described by

$$\mathbf{x}_{c,(k)} = \mathbf{f}_{(k)}\big(\mathbf{x}_{c,(k-1)}, \mathbf{u}_{c,(k-1)}\big) + \mathbf{v}_{s,(k-1)} \tag{12}$$

$$\mathbf{y}_{c,(k)} = \mathbf{g}_{(k)}\big(\mathbf{x}_{c,(k)}, \mathbf{u}_{c,(k)}\big) + \mathbf{v}_{o,(k)}. \tag{13}$$

The functions $\mathbf{f}_{(k)}$ and $\mathbf{g}_{(k)}$ are obtained by symbolically solving the set of equations $F_1(x_{d1,(k)}) \cup \ldots \cup F_l(x_{dl,(k)})$ given mode $\mathbf{x}_{d,(k)} = [x_{d1,(k)}, \ldots, x_{dl,(k)}]^T$.

---

[3] E.g. sensors can experience different magnitudes of disturbances for different modes.

Consider the cPHA in Fig. 3 with $\mathcal{A}_1 = \langle\{x_{d1}, x_{c1}\}, \{u_{d1}, u_c, w_c\}, F_1, T_1,$
$\{m_{11}, m_{12}\}, \ldots\rangle$ and $\mathcal{A}_2 = \langle\{x_{d2}\}, \{u_{d2}, w_c, y_c\}, F_2, T_2, \{m_{21}, m_{22}\}, \ldots\rangle$, where
F_1 and F_2 provide for a cPHA mode $\mathbf{x}_{d,(k)} = [m_{11}, m_{21}]^T$ the equations
$F_1(m_{11}) = \{x_{c1,(k)} = -0.5x_{c1,(k-1)} + u_{c,(k-1)}, w_c = x_{c1}\}$ and $F_2(m_{21}) = \{w_c = 4y_c\}$. This leads to the discrete-time model

$$x_{c1,(k)} = -0.5x_{c1,(k-1)} + u_{c,(k-1)} + v_{s,(k-1)} \tag{14}$$

$$y_{c,(k)} = 0.25x_{c1,(k)} + v_{o,(k)}. \tag{15}$$

Definition 6. A *trajectory* of a cPHA $\mathcal{CA}$ for a given input sequence $\{\mathbf{u}_{(0)}, \mathbf{u}_{(1)},$
$\ldots, \mathbf{u}_{(k)}\}$ is represented by a sequence of hybrid states $\{\mathbf{x}_{(0)}, \mathbf{x}_{(1)}, \ldots, \mathbf{x}_{(k)}\}$ and
can be observed in terms of the sequence of observations $\{\mathbf{y}_{c,(0)}, \mathbf{y}_{c,(1)}, \ldots, \mathbf{y}_{c,(k)}\}$.

5 Hybrid Estimation

To detect the onset of subtle failures, it is essential that a monitoring and diagnosis system be able to accurately extract the hybrid state of a system from a signal that may be hidden among disturbances, such as measurement noise. This is the role of a hybrid observer. More precisely:

Hybrid Estimation Problem: Given a cPHA $\mathcal{CA}$, a sequences of observations $\{\mathbf{y}_{c,(0)}, \mathbf{y}_{c,(1)}, \ldots, \mathbf{y}_{c,(k)}\}$ and control inputs $\{\mathbf{u}_{(0)}, \mathbf{u}_{(1)}, \ldots, \mathbf{u}_{(k)}\}$, estimate the most likely hybrid state $\hat{\mathbf{x}}_{(k)}$ at time-step k.

A *hybrid state estimate* $\hat{\mathbf{x}}_{(k)}$ consists of a *continuous state estimate*, together with the associated *mode*. We denote this by the tuple $\hat{\mathbf{x}}_{(k)} := \langle\mathbf{x}_{d,(k)}, \hat{\mathbf{x}}_{c,(k)}, \mathbf{P}_{(k)}\rangle$, where $\hat{\mathbf{x}}_{c,(k)}$ specifies the mean and $\mathbf{P}_{(k)}$ the covariance for the continuous state variables $\mathbf{x}_c$. The likelihood of an estimate $\hat{\mathbf{x}}_{(k)}$ is denoted by the *hybrid belief-state* $h_{(k)}[\hat{\mathbf{x}}]$.

The hybrid observer is composed of two components. The first component, an extended Kalman filter bank, maintains several continuous state estimates. The second component, a hybrid Markov observer, controls the filter bank by selecting trajectory candidates for estimation and ranking the estimated trajectories according to their belief-state. In the following we specify this operation in more detail and show (a) how the filter bank uses information from the hybrid Markov observer to guide continuous state estimation, and (b) how results from the filter bank guide the hybrid Markov observer.

5.1 Continuous State Estimation

Continuous state estimation is performed by a bank of extended Kalman filters which track the set of trajectories under consideration and provides an estimate $\langle\hat{\mathbf{x}}_{i,(k)}, \mathbf{P}_{i,(k)}\rangle$ and residual $\langle\hat{\mathbf{r}}_{i,(k)}, \mathbf{S}_{i,(k)}\rangle$ for each trajectory. The filter bank is controlled by the hybrid Markov observer that performs the mode estimation.

5.2   Mode Estimation - Hybrid Markov Observer

To extend HMM-style belief update to hybrid estimation, we must account for two ways in which the continuous dynamics influences the system's discrete modes. First, mode transitions depend on changes in continuous state variables (autonomous transitions), as well as discrete events injected via $\mathbf{u}_d$. To account for this influence we specify the hybrid probabilistic transition function P_T to depend on continuous state $\mathbf{x}_c$. Second, the observation of the output variables $\mathbf{y}_{c,(k)}$ offers important evidence that can significantly shape the hybrid state probabilities. To account for this influence we specify the hybrid probabilistic observation function P_O to depend on $\hat{\mathbf{x}}$ and $\mathbf{u}_c$.

A major difference between hybrid estimation and an HMM-style belief-state update, as well as multi-model estimation, is, however, that hybrid estimation tracks a set of trajectories, whereas standard belief-state update and multi-model estimation aggregate trajectories which share the same mode. This difference is reflected in the first of the following two recursive functions which define our hybrid estimation scheme:

$$h_{(\bullet k)}[\hat{\mathbf{x}}_i] = P_T(\mathbf{m}_i|\hat{\mathbf{x}}_{j,(k-1)}, \mathbf{u}_{d,(k-1)})h_{(k-1)}[\hat{\mathbf{x}}_j] \tag{16}$$

$$h_{(k)}[\hat{\mathbf{x}}_i] = \frac{h_{(\bullet k)}[\hat{\mathbf{x}}_i]P_O(\mathbf{y}_{c,(k)}|\hat{\mathbf{x}}_{i,(k)}, \mathbf{u}_{c,(k)})}{\sum_j h_{(\bullet k)}[\hat{\mathbf{x}}_j]P_O(\mathbf{y}_{c,(k)}|\hat{\mathbf{x}}_{j,(k)}, \mathbf{u}_{c,(k)})} \tag{17}$$

$h_{(\bullet k)}[\hat{\mathbf{x}}_i]$ denotes an intermediate hybrid belief-state, based on transition probabilities only. Hybrid estimation determines for each $\hat{\mathbf{x}}_{j,(k-1)}$ at the previous time-step $k-1$ the possible transitions, thus specifying candidate trajectories to be tracked by the filter bank. Filtering provides the new hybrid state $\hat{\mathbf{x}}_{i,(k)}$ and adjusts the hybrid belief-state $h_{(k)}[\hat{\mathbf{x}}_i]$ based on the hybrid probabilistic observation function $P_O(\mathbf{y}_{c,(k)}|\hat{\mathbf{x}}_{i,(k)}, \mathbf{u}_{c,(k)})$.

The next three subsections complete the story by outlining techniques for calculating the hybrid probabilistic transition function P_T and the hybrid probabilistic observation function P_O, as well as providing a tractable algorithmic formulation for hybrid estimation.

5.3   Hybrid Probabilistic Transition Function

A mode transition $\mathbf{m}_j \rightarrow \mathbf{m}_i$ involves transitions $\langle \tau_{l\eta}, c_{l\eta} \rangle \in \mathcal{T}_l$ for each component $\mathcal{A}_l$ of the cPHA[4]. Given that the automaton component is in mode $x_{dl,(k-1)} = m_j$, the probability $P_{T l\eta}$ that it will take a transition to $x'_{dl,(k-1)} = m_i$ is the probability that its guard $c_{l\eta}$ is satisfied times the probability of transition $\tau_{l\eta}(m_i)$, given that the guard $c_{l\eta}$ is satisfied. We assume independence of component transitions, therefore, we obtain P_T by taking the product of all components' $P_{T l\eta}$.

For a PHA $\mathcal{A}_l$, the guard $c_{l\eta}$ is a constraint over continuous variables $\mathbf{x}_{cl}$ and the discrete command inputs $\mathbf{u}_{dl}$. The guard $c_{l\eta}$ is of the form $[b^- \leq q_{cl\eta}(\mathbf{x}_{cl}) <$

---

[4] For symmetry, we also treat the non-transition $m_j \rightarrow m_j$ of a PHA $\mathcal{A}_l$ as a transition.

$b^+] \wedge q_{dl\eta}(\mathbf{u}_{dl})$, where $q_{cl\eta}(\cdot)$ is a nonlinear function, b^- and b^+ denote two boundary values, and $q_{dl\eta}(\cdot)$ is a propositional logic formula. Assuming independence of $\mathbf{x}_{cl,(k)}$ and $\mathbf{u}_{dl,(k)}$ allows us to determine both constraints separately as follows: The probability $P(c_{cl\eta})$ that the guard inequality $b^- \leq q_{cl\eta}(\mathbf{x}_{cl}) < b^+$ is satisfied, can be expressed by the volume integral over the multi-variable Gaussian distribution of the continuous state estimate $\{\hat{\mathbf{x}}_{cl}, \mathbf{P}_l\}$ for component $\mathcal{A}_l$

$$P(c_{cl\eta}) = \frac{|\mathbf{P}_l|^{-1/2}}{(2\pi)^{n/2}} \int \cdots \int_{\mathcal{Q}} e^{-(\mathbf{z}-\hat{\mathbf{x}}_{cl})^T \mathbf{P}_l^{-1}(\mathbf{z}-\hat{\mathbf{x}}_{cl})/2} dz_1 \ldots dz_n \qquad (18)$$

where $\mathcal{Q} \subset \mathbb{R}^n$ denotes the domain of states that satisfy the guard inequality. Our current implementation calculates this cumulative distribution using a Monte Carlo[15] approach that checks the guard inequality on a sufficiently large set of normally distributed state samples with mean $\hat{\mathbf{x}}_{cl}$ and covariance matrix $\mathbf{P}_l$. An open research issue is to compute $P(c_{cl\eta})$ more efficiently, through a combination of restricting and approximating the function $q_{cl\eta}$.

The discrete constraint $q_{dl\eta}(\mathbf{u}_d)$ has probability $P(c_{dl\eta}) = 1$ or $P(c_{dl\eta}) = 0$, according to its truth value. The assumed independence of the continuous state and the discrete input leads to

$$P_{Tl\eta} = P(c_{cl\eta})P(c_{dl\eta})\tau_{l\eta}(m_i) \qquad (19)$$

5.4   Hybrid Probabilistic Observation Function

The extended Kalman filters calculate state estimates for the continuous state $\hat{\mathbf{x}}_{c,(k)}$. This involves calculating the measurement residual $\mathbf{r}_{(k)}$ (Eq. 6) and its associated covariance matrix $\mathbf{S}_{(k)}$ (Eq. 8). From this estimate we can calculate $P_{\mathcal{O}}(\mathbf{y}_{(k)}|\hat{\mathbf{x}}_{(k)}, \mathbf{u}_{c,(k)})$ using the standard relation for the multi-variable Gaussian probability density function without normalization[5]:

$$P_{\mathcal{O}}(\mathbf{y}_{(k)}|\hat{\mathbf{x}}_{(k)}, \mathbf{u}_{c,(k)}) = e^{-\mathbf{r}_{(k)}^T \mathbf{S}_{(k)}^{-1} \mathbf{r}_{(k)}/2} \qquad (20)$$

5.5   Tracking the Most Likely Trajectories

Tracking all possible trajectories of a system is almost always intractable because the number of trajectories becomes too large after only a few time steps. As an example consider a cPHA with 10 components. The components have on average 5 modes and each mode has on average 3 successor states. This cPHA represents an automaton with $5^{10} \approx 10000000$ modes and hybrid estimation, as formulated above, lead to $(3^{10})^k$ trajectories to be tracked at time-step k. Fig. 4 visualizes this blowup for a single hybrid estimation step.

---

[5] We omit the normalization term $\frac{|\mathbf{S}_{(k)}|^{-1/2}}{(2\pi)^{n/2}}$ as our any-time any-space estimation algorithm requires $0 \leq P_{\mathcal{O}} \leq 1$. Normalization is already ensured by Eq. 17. Furthermore, [7] explicitly suggest this change based on the observation that the normalization term has nothing to do with the identification of the correct mode.

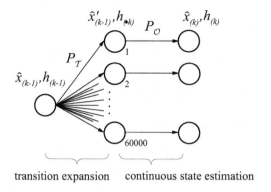

transition expansion   continuous state estimation

Fig. 4. Hybrid Estimation at time-step k with single estimate $\hat{\mathbf{x}}_{(k-1)}$.

The problem of exponential growth is a well known drawback of full hypothesis multi-model estimation and lead to the development of approximative schemes, such as the generalized pseudo-Bayesian and the interacting multiple model algorithm[8] and adaptive extensions[9,16]. These algorithms slow the effect of the exponential growth by merging the estimates. However, in general they are not effective enough to cope with many hybrid estimation problems as the number of hypotheses at each time-step is still beyond their scope (e.g. $3^{10} \approx 60000$ in the "small" example above).

We address this problem with an any-time, any-space solution that dynamically adjusts the number of trajectories tracked in order to fit within the processor's computational and memory limits. The Livingston system[1] successfully utilized such a focusing scheme for model-based diagnosis and configuration management. This approach succeeds because a small subset of the set of possible modes of a system is typically sufficient to cover most of the probability space. For hybrid estimation we adopt an analogous scheme that enumerates a focused subset of the possible trajectories by framing hybrid estimation as *beam search* that maintains the fringe $\mathbf{X}_{(k)} = \{\hat{\mathbf{x}}_{1,(k)}, \ldots, \hat{\mathbf{x}}_{m,(k)}\}$ of the m most likely trajectories. Key to this approach is an any-time, any-space enumeration scheme that provides, at each time-step k, the focussed subset of most likely states $\{\hat{\mathbf{x}}_{1,(k)}, \ldots, \hat{\mathbf{x}}_{m,(k)}\}$, without having to calculate a prohibitively large number of hybrid state estimates $\hat{\mathbf{x}}_{i,(k)}$.

In our modeling framework, we assume that the mode transitions of the system's components are independent of each other. Therefore, we consider possible mode transitions for a hybrid estimate $\hat{\mathbf{x}}_{i,(k-1)}$ and the discrete (command) input $\mathbf{u}_{(k-1)}$ componentwise. This allows us to formulate enumeration as best-first search, using A* (Fig. 5 shows the corresponding search tree for a fringe size of 1). Best-first search expands search tree nodes in increasing order of their utility $f(n)$. We define the utility of a node n as $f(n) = f_1(n) + f_2(n)$, where

$$f_1(n) = -\ln(h_{(k-1)}[\hat{\mathbf{x}}_j]) - \sum_{i=1}^{\nu} \ln(P_i), \quad P_i = \begin{cases} P_{Ti} & i = 1, \ldots, l \\ P_{\mathcal{O}} & i = l+1 \end{cases} \qquad (21)$$

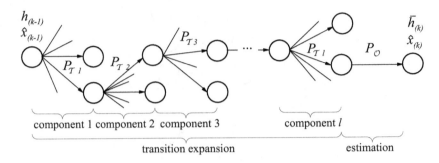

Fig. 5. Search Tree for Hybrid Estimation at time-step k

denotes the cost of the path from a root node (state estimate $\hat{\mathbf{x}}_{j,(k-1)}$ with initial cost $-\ln(h_{(k-1)}[\hat{\mathbf{x}}_j])$) to a node within the search tree (e.g. considering transitions in components $1, \ldots, \nu$, whenever $\nu \leq l$). $f_2(n)$ estimates the cost for the best path from node n to a goal node by considering the best transitions for the remaining components, more specifically[6]

$$f_2(n) = \sum_{i=\nu+1}^{l} -\ln(\max_{\eta} P_{Ti\eta}). \tag{22}$$

The search is optimal and complete, as $f_2(n)$ *never overestimates* the cost to reach a goal (i.e. f_2 is a *admissible heuristic*). It provides, at each time-step k, the most likely successor states $\{\hat{\mathbf{x}}_{1,(k)}, \hat{\mathbf{x}}_{2,(k)}, \ldots\}$ of the fringe $\mathbf{X}_{(k-1)}$ together with the un-normalized hybrid belief $\bar{h}_{i,(k)} = h_{(\bullet k)}[\hat{\mathbf{x}}_i] P_{O}(\mathbf{y}_{c,(k)}|\hat{\mathbf{x}}_{i,(k)}, \mathbf{u}_{c,(k)})$ in consecutive order.

6   Example Continued

We demonstrate hybrid mode estimation for two operational conditions of the BIO-Plex system: (1) detection of crew entry into the PGC ($m_{p4} \to m_{p5}$) and (2) a failure of the lighting system that reduces the light intensity in the PGC by 20% ($m_{l2} \to m_{l4}$). The dynamic behavior of the CO_2 concentration (in ppm) at the modes m_{p4} and m_{p5} with operational lighting system (m_{l2}), for instance, is governed by ($T_s = 1$ [min]):

$$
\begin{aligned}
x_{c1,(k)} &= u_{c,(k-1)} \\
x_{c2,(k)} &= x_{c2,(k-1)} + 11.8373[f(x_{c,(k-1)}) + x_{c1,(k-1)} + h_{c,(k-1)}] \\
y_{c1,(k)} &= x_{c1,(k)} \\
y_{c2,(k)} &= x_{c2,(k)} \\
f(x_{c,(k)}) &= -1.4461 \cdot 10^{-2} \left[72.0 - 78.89 e^{-\frac{x_{c,(k)}}{400.0}} \right],
\end{aligned}
$$

---

[6] The maximum value for the probabilistic observation function ($P_O = 1$) can be omitted as $\ln(1) = 0$.

where h_c accounts for the exhaled CO_2 ($m_{p4} : h_c = 0, m_{p5} : h_c = 0.3$). The noisy measurement of the controlled CO_2 concentration (black) and its estimation (red/gray) are given in the left graph of Fig. 6. The crew enters the PGC at time step 900 and cause an adaption of the gas injection. Hybrid mode estimation filters this noisy measurement and detects the mode change immediately at $k = 901$. The light fault is then injected at time-step 1100 and diagnosed 17 time-steps later. The graphs to the right in Fig. 6 show the mode of the leading trajectory estimate for the plant growth chamber and the lighting system.

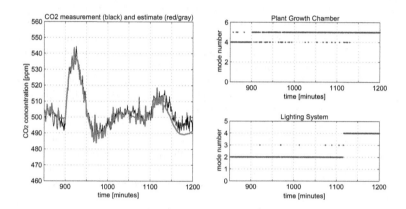

Fig. 6. Estimation results for BIO-Plex scenarios

7   Implementation and Discussion

The implementation of our hybrid estimation scheme is written in Common LISP. The hybrid estimator uses a cPHA description and performs estimation, as outlined above. Although designed to operate online, we used the estimator to determine the hybrid state of the PGC based on input data gathered from simulating a subset of NASA JSC's CONFIG model for the BIO-Plex system.

Optimized model-based estimation schemes, such as Livingstone[1], utilize *conflicts* to focus the search operation. A conflict is a (partial) mode assignment that makes a hypothesis very unlikely. The decompositional model-based learning system, Moriarty[17], introduced an algebraic version of conflicts, called *dissents*. We are currently reformulating dissents for hybrid systems and investigate their incorporation in the search scheme. This will lead to an overall framework for hybrid estimation that unifies our previous work on Livingstone and Moriarty.

A novel capability of discrete model-based diagnosis methods is the ability to handle *unknown modes* where no assumption is made about the behavior of one or several components of the system. We are in the process of incorporating this novel capability of model-based diagnosis into our estimation scheme by calculating partial filters. The filters are based on causal analysis of the specified components and their interconnection within the cPHA model. Incorporating unknown modes provides a robust estimation scheme that can cope with unmodeled situations and partial information.

References

1. Williams, B., Nayak, P.: A model-based approach to reactive self-configuring systems. In: Proc. of the 13th Nat. Conf. on Artificial Intelligence (AAAI-96). (1996)
2. Anderson, B., Moore, J.: Optimal Filtering. Prentice Hall (1979)
3. Branicky, M.: Studies in Hybrid Systems: Modeling, Analysis, and Control. PhD thesis, Department of Electrical Engineering and Computer Science, MIT (1995)
4. Henzinger, T.: The theory of hybrid automata. In: Proc. of the 11th Annual IEEE Symposium on Logic in Computer Science (LICS '96) (1996) 278–292
5. Hu, J., Lygeros, J., Sastry, S.: Towards a theory of stochastic hybrid systems. In Lynch, N., Krogh, B., eds.: Hybrid Systems: Computation and Control. Lecture Notes in Computer Science, 1790. Springer (2000) 160–173
6. Nancy Lynch, Roberto Segala, F.V.: Hybrid I/O automata revisited. In M.D. Di Benedetto, A.S.V., ed.: Hybrid Systems: Computation and Control, HSCC 2001. Lecture Notes in Computer Science, 2034. Springer Verlag (2001) 403–417
7. Maybeck, P., Stevens, R.: Reconfigurable flight control via multiple model adaptive control methods. IEEE Transactions on Aerospace and Electronic Systems **27** (1991) 470–480
8. Bar-Shalom, Y., Li, X.: Estimation and Tracking. Artech House (1993)
9. Li, X., Bar-Shalom, Y.: Multiple-model estimation with variable structure. IEEE Transactions on Automatic Control **41** (1996) 478–493
10. McIlraith, S., Biswas, G., Clancy, D., Gupta, V.: Towards diagnosing hybrid systems. In: Proc. of the 10th Internat. Workshop on Principles of Diagnosis. (1999) 194–203
11. Narasimhan, S., Biswas, G.: Efficient diagnosis of hybrid systems using models of the supervisory controller. In: Proc. of the 12th Internat. Workshop on Principles of Diagnosis. (2001) 127–134
12. Zhao, F., Koutsoukos, X., Haussecker, H., Reich, J., Cheung, P.: Distributed monitoring of hybrid systems: A model-directed approach. In: Proc. of the Internat. Joint Conf. on Artificial Intelligence (IJCAI'01). (2001) 557–564
13. Lerner, U., Parr, R., Koller, D., Biswas, G.: Bayesian fault detection and diagnosis in dynamic systems. In: Proc. of the 17th Nat. Conf. on Artificial Intelligence (AAAI'00). (2000)
14. McIlraith, S.: Diagnosing hybrid systems: a Bayseian model selection approach. In: Proc. of the 11th Internat. Workshop on Principles of Diagnosis. (2000) 140–146
15. Robert, C., Casella, G.: Monte Carlo Statistical Methods. Springer-Verlag (1999)
16. Hanlon, P., Maybeck, P.: Multiple-model adaptive estimation using a residual correlation Kalman filter bank. IEEE Transactions on Aerospace and Electronic Systems **36** (2000) 393–406
17. Williams, B., Millar, B.: Decompositional, model-based learning and its analogy to diagnosis. In: Proc. of the 15th Nat. Conf. on Artificial Intelligence (AAAI-98). (1998)

Symmetry Reduction of a Class of Hybrid Systems*

Jianghai Hu and Shankar Sastry

Department of Electrical Engineering & Computer Sciences
University of California at Berkeley
{jianghai,sastry}@eecs.berkeley.edu

Abstract. The optimal control problem for a class of hybrid systems (switched Lagrangian systems) is studied. Some necessary conditions of the optimal solutions of such a system are derived based on the assumption that there is a group of symmetries acting uniformly on the domains of different discrete modes, such that the Lagrangian functions, the guards, and the reset maps are all invariant under the action. Lagrangian reduction approach is adopted to establish the conservation law of certain quantities for the optimal solutions. Some examples are presented. In particular, the problems of optimal collision avoidance (OCA) and optimal formation switching (OFS) of multiple agents moving on a Riemannian manifold are studied in some details.

1 Motivation

In this paper we study the optimal control problem of a class of hybrid systems which we called *switched Lagrangian systems*. Roughly speaking, a switched Lagrangian system is a hybrid system with a set of discrete modes, and associated with each discrete mode, a domain which is a manifold (possibly with boundary) together with a Lagrangian function defined on it. The continuous state of the system evolves within one of the domains, and upon hitting certain subsets (*guards*), can trigger a jump in the discrete mode, in which case the continuous state is reset inside the domain of the new discrete mode according to some prescribed rules (*reset maps*). Thus a typical execution of the system can be partitioned into a number of curves in distinctive domains. The cost of the execution is then the sum of the costs of these curves, with the cost of each curve being the integral along it of the corresponding Lagrangian function. Given two points which might lie in different domains, we try to find the executions that steer the system from one point to the other with minimal cost.

If there is only one discrete mode, then the problem is a classical variational problem whose solutions are characterized by the Euler-Lagrangian equations [1] in any coordinate system of the domain. In particular, if the Lagrangian function

---

* This research is partially supported by DARPA under grant F33615-98-C-3614, by the project "Sensor Webs of SmartDust: Distributed Processing/Data Fusion/Inferencing in Large Microsensor Arrays" under grant F30602-00-2-0538.

C.J. Tomlin and M.R. Greenstreet (Eds.): HSCC 2002, LNCS 2289, pp. 267–280, 2002.

is quadratic and positive definite on each fiber, it can be used to define a riemannian metric on the domain, and the optimal solutions are geodesics under this metric [5]. For a general system with multiple discrete modes, these conclusions still hold for the segments of an optimal solution restricted on each individual domain. Overall speaking, however, it is usually a very tricky issue to determine how these individual segments can be pieced together to form an optimal solution, especially when the guards and the reset maps are complicated. In [11], it is shown that if all the Lagrangian functions are quadratic and positive definite, then, under some additional mild assumptions, successive segments must satisfy at the switching points a necessary condition that is analogous to the *Snell Law* in optics, provided that segments of optimal solutions in different domains are thought of as light rays traveling in heterogeneous media.

In this paper, we try to derive necessary conditions on an optimal solution that apply *both* on its segments inside each domain *and* at its switching points where discrete jumps occur. We do so under the additional assumption that the switched Lagrangian system admits a group of symmetries, i.e., there exists a Lie group G acting uniformly on all of the domains, with respect to which the Lagrangian functions, the guards, and the reset maps are invariant. By using perturbations generated by the group action, we can establish through variational analysis the conservation law of certain quantities (*momentum maps*) taking values in the dual of the Lie algebra of G throughout the duration of the optimal solution. It should be pointed out that this approach has extensive applications in geometry and mechanics when the underlying state space is smooth, and is often presented from the more elegant symplectic point of view in the literature [1, 12]. What is new in this paper is its reformulation and application in the context of switched Lagrangian systems, which are nonsmooth in nature. This nonsmoothness also justifies the Lagrangian point of view adopted here.

The results in this paper will be illustrated through examples. Two important examples are the *Optimal Collision Avoidance* (OCA) and the *Optimal Formation Switching* (OFS) of multiple agents moving on a Riemannian manifold [10]. In either case, one has to steer a group of agents from a starting configuration to a destination configuration on the manifold with minimal cost, such that their joint trajectory satisfies certain separation constraints throughout the process. We will show how these two problems can be formulated as the optimal control problems for suitably chosen switched Lagrangian systems, and how the conserved quantities can be derived for various choices of the Riemannian manifold.

A price we pay for the general applicability of the necessary conditions is that they in general only partially characterize the optimal solutions, since the number of symmetries presented in a system is usually much smaller than the dimensions of the domains, and that the conserved quantities are usually not integrable. Nonetheless, in certain simple cases, the derived necessary conditions can indeed help to characterize the optimal solutions completely [10].

In this paper, we only consider holonomic motions of the agents. For nonholonomic motion planning, see [2, 6]. Some relevant results can also be found in [4, 13], to name a few.

This paper is organized as following. In Section 2, we define the notions of switched Lagrangian systems, G-symmetry, and their optimal control problem. In Section 3, Lagrangian variational approach is adopted to derive a necessary condition for the optimal solutions. Two important examples of switched Lagrangian systems, the OCA and the OFS problems on Riemannian manifolds, are introduced in Section 4. In particular, we study the cases when the underlying manifold is $\mathbf{SO}_n$ and the Grassmann manifold. Finally, some concluding remarks are presented in Section 5.

2   Switched Lagrangian Systems

First we define the notions of switched Lagrangian systems and their executions. For the definition of general hybrid systems, see [8].

Definition 1 (Switched Lagrangian Systems). *A switched Lagrangian system $\mathcal{H}$ is specified by the following:*

1. *A set Γ of discrete modes;*
2. *For each $l \in \Gamma$, a domain M_l which is a manifold, possibly with boundary ∂M_l, and a Lagrangian function $L_l : TM_l \to \mathbb{R}$ defined on the tangent bundle of M_l. We assume that the domains M_l, $l \in \Gamma$, are disjoint, and write $M = \cup_{l \in \Gamma} M_l$;*
3. *A set of discrete transitions $E_d \subset \Gamma \times \Gamma$;*
4. *For each $(l_1, l_2) \in E_d$, a subset $D_{(l_1,l_2)} \subset M_{l_1}$, called the* guard *associated with the discrete transition (l_1, l_2), and a continuous transition relation $E_c(l_1, l_2) \subset D_{(l_1,l_2)} \times M_{l_2}$ such that for each $q_1 \in D_{(l_1,l_2)}$, there exists at least one $q_2 \in M_{l_2}$ with $(q_1, q_2) \in E_c(l_1, l_2)$. In other words, $E_c(l_1, l_2)$ specifies a one-to-many map from $D_{(l_1,l_2)}$ to M_{l_2}.*

Definition 2 (Hybrid Executions). *A* hybrid execution *(or simply a* path*) of $\mathcal{H}$ defined on some time interval $[t_0, t_1]$ can be described as the following: there is a finite partition of $[t_0, t_1]$, $t_0 = \tau_0 \leq \ldots \leq \tau_{m+1} = t_1$, $m \geq 0$, and a succession of discrete modes $l_0, \ldots, l_m \in \Gamma$ and arcs $\gamma_0, \ldots, \gamma_m$, such that*

- *$(l_j, l_{j+1}) \in E_d$ for $j = 0, \ldots, m - 1$;*
- *$\gamma_j : [\tau_j, \tau_{j+1}] \to M_{l_j}$ is a continuous and piecewise C^∞ curve[1] in M_{l_j} for $j = 0, \ldots, m$;*
- *For each $j = 0, \ldots, m-1$, $\gamma_j(\tau_{j+1}) \in D_{(l_j, l_{j+1})}$, and $(\gamma_j(\tau_{j+1}), \gamma_{j+1}(\tau_{j+1})) \in E_c(l_j, l_{j+1})$.*

We will denote such a path by γ, and call $\gamma_0, \ldots, \gamma_m$ the *segments* of γ. The *cost* of γ is defined by

$$J(\gamma) = \sum_{j=0}^{m} \int_{\tau_j}^{\tau_{j+1}} L_{l_j}(\dot{\gamma}_j) \, dt.$$

---

[1] All curves in this paper are assumed to be continuous and piecewise C^∞.

Intuitively speaking, a path is the trajectory of a point moving in M such that whenever the point is in M_{l_1} and it reaches a point in a guard, say, $q_1 \in D_{(l_1, l_2)}$, it has the option of jumping to a point q_2 in M_{l_2} according to the continuous transition relation $(q_1, q_2) \in E_c(l_1, l_2)$, and continuing its motion in M_{l_2}, and so on. We call such a jump a *transition*, which consists of a discrete transition $l_1 \rightarrow l_2$ and a continuous transition $q_1 \rightarrow q_2$. Note that during a transition, there is possibly more than one position the point can jump to due to two reasons: guards for different discrete transitions may intersect; and for a single discrete transition, the continuous transition relation is a one-to-many map.

It is allowed in the definition of the path γ that some of $\tau_0, \dots, \tau_{m+1}$ are identical, implying that more than one transition may occur at the same epoch, though in a sequential way. This can cause trouble since it is possible that all the legitimate transitions from a certain point lead to infinite number of jumps occurring at the same epoch, thus blocking the system from further evolving. This kind of hybrid systems is usually called *blocking*. To ensure that the switched Lagrangian systems studied in this paper are nonblocking, we make the following (usually stronger) assumption.

Assumption 1 (Connectness) *Assume that the switched Lagrangian system $\mathcal{H}$ is connected in the sense that for any two points $a, b \in M$, there exists at least one path γ connecting them.*

The problem of interest to us can be formulated as

Problem 1 (Optimal Control on $\mathcal{H}$) *Given $a, b \in M$ and a time interval $[t_0, t_1]$, find the path (or paths) from a to b defined on $[t_0, t_1]$ with minimal cost.*

Assumption 1 alone can not guarantee the existence of solutions to Problem 1, which requires some completeness conditions on the space consisting of all the paths from a to b defined on $[t_0, t_1]$. In addition, in the context of hybrid systems, one needs to ensure that the solutions are not *zeno* (i.e., exhibiting infinite number of transitions within a finite time interval). These difficulties are side-stepped in this paper by the following assumption.

Assumption 2 (Existence of Solutions) *Assume that $\mathcal{H}$ is chosen such that solutions to Problem 1 exist.*

We focus on a special class of switched Lagrangian systems. Let G be a Lie group.

Definition 3 (G-symmetry). *A switched Lagrangian system $\mathcal{H}$ is G-symmetric if it has the following properties:*

- *G acts on the domain M_l from the left for each $l \in \Gamma$. We shall denote this smooth action uniformly by $\Phi : G \times M_l \rightarrow M_l$ for all l;*
- *For each discrete transition $(l_1, l_2) \in E_d$, the guard $D_{(l_1, l_2)}$ and the continuous transition relation $E_c(l_1, l_2)$ are both invariant under the action of G, i.e., for any $g \in G$, $\Phi(g, D_{(l_1, l_2)}) \subset D_{(l_1, l_2)}$, and $(q_1, q_2) \in E_c(l_1, l_2)$ if and only if $(\Phi(g, q_1), \Phi(g, q_2)) \in E_c(l_1, l_2)$;*

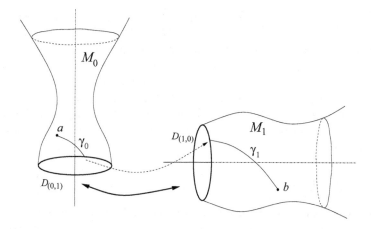

Fig. 1. An example of an $\mathbf{S}^1$-symmetric switched Lagrangian system.

– *For each $l \in \Gamma$, the Lagrangian function L_l is invariant under G, i.e., $L_l \circ d\Phi_g = L_l$, $\forall g \in G$. Here $\Phi_g : M_l \to M_l$ is the map defined by $\Phi_g : q \mapsto \phi(g, q)$, $\forall q \in M_l$, and $d\Phi_g : TM_l \to TM_l$ is its tangential map.*

Assumption 3 (G-symmetry of $\mathcal{H}$) *There is a Lie group G such that the switched Lagrangian system $\mathcal{H}$ is G-symmetric.*

We illustrate the above concepts by two simple examples.

Example 1. Shown in Figure 1 is an example of a switched Lagrangian system that is $\mathbf{S}^1$-symmetric. Here $\Gamma = \{0, 1\}$, and the domains of the two discrete modes are two disjoint surfaces of revolution M_0 and M_1 in $\mathbb{R}^3$, each with a boundary obtained as the cross section of the surface with a plane perpendicular to its rotational axis. Let $E_d = \{(0, 1), (1, 0)\}$, $D_{(0,1)} = \partial M_0$, $D_{(1,0)} = \partial M_1$. Define the continuous transition relation $E_c(0, 1)$ as the graph of a map φ from ∂M_0 to ∂M_1 that is invariant under the rotations, i.e., φ rotates the circle ∂M_0 by a certain angle and "fits" it into ∂M_1. Define $E_c(1, 0)$ to be the graph of φ^{-1}. Let M_0 be equipped with the riemannian metric inherited from $\mathbb{R}^3$, and define a Lagrangian function L_0 on it by $L_0(v) = \frac{1}{2}\|v\|_q^2$, $\forall v \in T_q M_0$, where $\|\cdot\|_q$ is the norm on the tangent space $T_q M_0$ determined by the riemannian metric. In the following we shall simply write $L_0 = \frac{1}{2}\|\cdot\|^2$. Similarly $L_1 = \frac{1}{2}\|\cdot\|^2$, where the norm now corresponds to the riemannian metric on M_1 inherited from $\mathbb{R}^3$. The action of $\mathbf{S}^1 = \{z \in \mathbb{Z} : \|z\| = 1\}$ on M_0 can be defined as: each $e^{j\theta} \in \mathbf{S}^1$ corresponds to a rotation of M_0 along its axis by an angle θ. Similarly for the action of $\mathbf{S}^1$ on M_1. By properly choosing the directions of rotation in the above definitions, one can easily check that the resulting system $\mathcal{H}$ is $\mathbf{S}^1$-symmetric.

Example 2. Consider the following system $\mathcal{H}$. Let $\Gamma = \{0, 1\}$. For each $l \in \Gamma$, $M_l = \{l\} \times (\mathbb{R}^2 \setminus \{0\}) \subset \mathbb{R}^3$ is a plane with the origin removed, and the

Lagrangian function L_l is defined in the polar coordinate of $M_l \simeq \mathbb{R}^2 \setminus \{0\}$ as: $L_l(v) = \frac{1}{2}v^t A_l(r)v$, for $v = (\dot{r}, \dot{\theta})^t \in T_q M_l$, $q \in M_l$. Here $A_l(r)$ is a 2-by-2 positive definite matrix whose entries are smooth functions of r, and $A_l(r) \to \infty$ as $r \to 0$. Let $E_d = \{(0,1),(1,0)\}$, $D_{(0,1)} = M_0$, $D_{(1,0)} = M_1$. Choose $E_c(0,1) = \{((0,x),(1,x)) : x \in \mathbb{R}^2, x \neq 0\}$, $E_c(1,0) = \{((1,x),(0,x)) : x \in \mathbb{R}^2, x \neq 0\}$. Therefore, a point moving in $\mathcal{H}$ can freely switch between two copies of $\mathbb{R}^2 \setminus \{0\}$ with different Lagrangian functions. $\mathbf{S}^1$ acts on M_l, $l \in \Gamma$, in the following way. Each $e^{j\theta} \in \mathbf{S}^1$ corresponds to a rotation counterclockwise of M_l by an angle of θ. $\mathcal{H}$ thus defined can be verified to be $\mathbf{S}^1$-symmetric.

3   Conservation Laws

Suppose we are given a switched Lagrangian system $\mathcal{H}$ that satisfies the assumptions in the previous section. We shall now derive necessary conditions that optimal solutions to Problem 1 must satisfy.

Since $\mathcal{H}$ is G-symmetric, an important observation is

Proposition 1. *If γ is a path of $\mathcal{H}$ defined on $[t_0, t_1]$, then for each C^∞ curve $g : [t_0, t_1] \to G$, $g\gamma$ is also a path of $\mathcal{H}$ defined on $[t_0, t_1]$.*

To be precise, $g\gamma$ is defined in the following way. Let $\tau_0, \ldots, \tau_{m+1}$ and $l_0, \ldots, l_m$ be as in the definition of γ, and let $\gamma_0, \ldots, \gamma_m$ be the corresponding segments of γ. Then $g\gamma$ is a sequence of arcs, $g\gamma_j \triangleq \Phi_g(\gamma_j) = \Phi(g(\cdot), \gamma_j(\cdot))$, $j = 0, \ldots, m$, whose intervals of definition and corresponding discrete modes coincide with those of γ_j, $j = 0, \ldots, m$, respectively. The proof of Proposition 1 is straightforward, hence omitted.

Assume that for given $a, b \in M$, γ is an optimal solution to Problem 1 defined on $[t_0, t_1]$ connecting a and b. Denote with $c_e : [t_0, t_1] \to G$ the constant map mapping every $t \in [t_0, t_1]$ to the identity $e \in G$. Let g be a *proper variation* of c_e, i.e., $g : (-\epsilon, \epsilon) \times [t_0, t_1] \to G$ is a C^∞ map satisfying $g(\cdot, t_0) = g(\cdot, t_1) = g(0, \cdot) \equiv e$ for some small positive number ϵ. Then for each $s \in (-\epsilon, \epsilon)$, $g_s(\cdot) \triangleq g(s, \cdot)$ is a C^∞ curve in G both starting and ending at e, hence by Proposition 1 can be used to define a path $\gamma_s = g_s\gamma$ in $\mathcal{H}$ that starts from a and ends in b. Note that $\gamma_0 = \gamma$ since $g_0 = c_e$. Define $J(s) = J(\gamma_s)$, $s \in (-\epsilon, \epsilon)$. Then a necessary condition for γ to be optimal is that J achieves its minimum at $s = 0$, which in turn implies $\frac{dJ}{ds}(0) = 0$.

For each $(s, t) \in (-\epsilon, \epsilon) \times [t_0, t_1]$, introduce the notations

$$\dot{g}_s(t) = \dot{g}(s, t) = \frac{\partial g}{\partial t}(s, t), \quad g'_s(t) = g'(s, t) = \frac{\partial g}{\partial s}(s, t),$$

where we follow the convention in [5] of using dot and prime to indicate differentiations with respect to time t and variation parameter s respectively. Both $\dot{g}(s, t)$ and $g'(s, t)$ are tangent vectors of G at $g(s, t)$. We pull them back via left multiplication to the tangent space of G at the identity e. Thus we define

$$\xi_s(t) = \xi(s, t) = g(s, t)^{-1}\dot{g}(s, t),$$
$$\eta_s(t) = \eta(s, t) = g(s, t)^{-1}g'(s, t).$$

Here to simplify notation we use $g(s,t)^{-1}\dot{g}(s,t)$ to denote $dm_{g(s,t)^{-1}}[\dot{g}(s,t)]$ (for any $g \in G$, $m_g : G \to G$ stands for the left multiplication by g, while dm_g is its tangent map). Similarly for $g(s,t)^{-1}g'(s,t)$. This kind of notational simplifications will be carried out in the following without further explanation. Both $\xi(s,t)$ and $\eta(s,t)$ belong to $\mathfrak{g} = T_eG$, the Lie algebra of G. The fact that g is a proper variation implies that $g'(\cdot, t_0) = g'(\cdot, t_1) = 0$, hence $\eta(\cdot, t_0) = \eta(\cdot, t_1) = 0$. Moreover, $g(0, \cdot) = e$ implies that $\dot{g}(0, \cdot) = 0$, hence $\xi(0, \cdot) = 0$.

Lemma 1. *Let $\xi'(s,t) = \frac{\partial \xi}{\partial s}(s,t)$ and $\dot{\eta}(s,t) = \frac{\partial \eta}{\partial t}(s,t)$. Then*

$$\xi' = \dot{\eta} + [\xi, \eta] \tag{1}$$

for all $(s,t) \in (-\epsilon, \epsilon) \times [t_0, t_1]$, where $[\xi, \eta]$ is the Lie bracket of ξ and η.

Proof. A general proof can be found in, for example, [3]. In the case when G is a matrix Lie group, the proof is particularly simple ([12]): differentiating $\xi = g^{-1}\dot{g}$ with respect to s and $\eta = g^{-1}g'$ with respect to t, we get

$$\xi'(s,t) = -g^{-1}g'g^{-1}\dot{g} + g^{-1}\frac{\partial^2 g}{\partial s \partial t} = -\eta\xi + g^{-1}\frac{\partial^2 g}{\partial s \partial t},$$

$$\dot{\eta}(s,t) = -g^{-1}\dot{g}g^{-1}g' + g^{-1}\frac{\partial^2 g}{\partial s \partial t} = -\xi\eta + g^{-1}\frac{\partial^2 g}{\partial s \partial t}.$$

Their difference gives $\xi' - \dot{\eta} = \xi\eta - \eta\xi = [\xi, \eta]$.

Define

$$w(t) = \xi_0'(t) = \xi'(0,t), \quad \forall t \in [t_0, t_1]. \tag{2}$$

By letting $s = 0$ in (1), we have $w = \dot{\eta}_0 + [\xi_0, \eta_0] = \dot{\eta}_0$ since $\xi_0 = 0$. So $\int_{t_0}^{t_1} w(t)\, dt = \eta_0(t_1) - \eta_0(t_0) = 0$. Conversely, for each C^∞ map $w : [t_0, t_1] \to \mathfrak{g}$ with $\int_{t_0}^{t_1} w(t)\, dt = 0$, we can define $\alpha(t) = \int_{t_0}^t w(t)\, dt$, which satisfies $\alpha(t_0) = \alpha(t_1) = 0$. By choosing $g(s,t) = \exp[s\alpha(t)]$, where $\exp$ is the exponential map of G, one can verify that g is indeed a proper variation of c_e such that $w = \xi_0'$, where $\xi = g^{-1}\dot{g}$. Therefore,

Lemma 2. *The necessary and sufficient condition for a C^∞ map $w : [t_0, t_1] \to \mathfrak{g}$ to be realized as $w = \xi_0'$ where $\xi = g^{-1}\dot{g}$ for some C^∞ proper variation g of c_e is*

$$\int_{t_0}^{t_1} w(t)\, dt = 0. \tag{3}$$

Suppose one such g is chosen. For each $(s,t) \in (-\epsilon, \epsilon) \times [t_0, t_1]$, and each segment γ_j of γ, $j = 0, \ldots, m$, we have[2]

$$L_{l_j}[\frac{d}{dt}(g_s\gamma_j)] = L_{l_j}[\dot{g}_s\gamma_j + g_s\dot{\gamma}_j] = L_{l_j}[g_s(\xi_s\gamma_j + \dot{\gamma}_j)] = L_{l_j}[\xi_s\gamma_j + \dot{\gamma}_j], \tag{4}$$

---

[2] Since γ_j is only piecewise C^∞, this and all equations that follow should be understood to hold only at those t where $\dot{\gamma}_j$'s are well defined.

where the last equality follows by the G-invariance of L_{l_j}. Here $\dot{g}_s\gamma_j$ denotes $d\Phi^{\gamma_j}(\dot{g}_s)$, where $d\Phi^{\gamma_j}$ is the differential of the map $\Phi^{\gamma_j} : G \to M_{l_j}$ that maps each $g \in G$ to $\Phi(g, \gamma_j)$, and $g_s\dot{\gamma}_j$ denotes $d\Phi_{g_s}(\dot{\gamma}_j)$. Both $\dot{g}_s\gamma_j$ and $g_s\dot{\gamma}_j$ are tangent vectors in $T_{g_s\gamma_j}M_{l_j}$. The cost of $\gamma_s = g_s\gamma$ is then

$$J(s) = \sum_{j=0}^{m} \int_{\tau_j}^{\tau_{j+1}} L_{l_j}[\xi_s\gamma_j + \dot{\gamma}_j]\,dt. \tag{5}$$

For a vector space V, denote with $(\cdot, \cdot) : V^* \times V \to \mathbb{R}$ the natural pairing between V and its dual V^*, i.e., $(f, v) = f(v), \forall f \in V^*, v \in V$. Differentiating (5) with respect to s at $s = 0$, and using the fact that $\xi_0 = 0$ and $\xi_0' = \omega$, we have

$$J'(0) = \sum_{j=0}^{m} \int_{\tau_j}^{\tau_{j+1}} ((dL_{l_j})_{\dot{\gamma}_j}, d\Phi^{\gamma_j}(\omega))\,dt = \sum_{j=0}^{m} \int_{\tau_j}^{\tau_{j+1}} ((d\Phi^{\gamma_j})^*(dL_{l_j})_{\dot{\gamma}_j}, \omega)\,dt. \tag{6}$$

Here $(dL_{l_j})_{\dot{\gamma}_j}$ is in fact the differential at $\dot{\gamma}_j$ of the restriction of L_{l_j} on the fiber $T_{\gamma_j}M_{l_j}$. We identify the tangent space at $\dot{\gamma}_j$ of $T_{\gamma_j}M_{l_j}$ with $T_{\gamma_j}M_{l_j}$ itself, so $d\Phi^{\gamma_j}(\omega) \in T_{\gamma_j}M_{l_j}$ and $(dL_{l_j})_{\dot{\gamma}_j} \in T^*_{\gamma_j}M_{l_j}$. In addition, $(d\Phi^{\gamma_j})^* : T^*_{\gamma_j}M_{l_j} \to \mathfrak{g}^*$ is the dual of $d\Phi^{\gamma_j} : \mathfrak{g} \to T_{\gamma_j}M_{l_j}$ defined by

$$((d\Phi^{\gamma_j})^*f, v) = (f, d\Phi^{\gamma_j}(v)), \ \forall f \in T^*_{\gamma_j}M_{l_j}, \ v \in \mathfrak{g}. \tag{7}$$

From (6) and Lemma 2, the condition that $J'(0) = 0$ for all g is equivalent to that

$$\sum_{j=0}^{m} \int_{\tau_j}^{\tau_{j+1}} ((d\Phi^{\gamma_j})^*(dL_{l_j})_{\dot{\gamma}_j}, \omega)\,dt = 0, \tag{8}$$

for all C^∞ map $\omega : [t_0, t_1] \to \mathfrak{g}$ such that $\int_{t_0}^{t_1} \omega\,dt = 0$. Since $(d\Phi^{\gamma_j})^*(dL_{l_j})_{\dot{\gamma}_j}$ is piecewise continuous (though not necessarily continuous) in $\mathfrak{g}^*$, (8) implies that $(d\Phi^{\gamma_j})^*(dL_{l_j})_{\dot{\gamma}_j}$ is constant for all t and all j whenever $\dot{\gamma}_j$'s are well defined, for otherwise one can always choose an ω with $\int_{t_0}^{t_1} \omega\,dt = 0$ such that (8) fails to hold. Therefore,

Theorem 1 (Noether). *Suppose γ is an optimal solution to Problem 1, and let $\gamma_0, \ldots, \gamma_m$ be its segments. Then there exists a constant $\nu_0 \in \mathfrak{g}^*$ such that*

$$(d\Phi^{\gamma_j})^*(dL_{l_j})_{\dot{\gamma}_j} = \nu_0, \quad \forall t \in [\tau_j, \tau_{j+1}], \ j = 0, \ldots, m. \tag{9}$$

A simple way of writing equation (9) is $(d\Phi^\gamma)^*dL_{\dot{\gamma}} \equiv \nu_0$.

If for each $l \in \Gamma$, there is a riemannian metric $\langle \cdot, \cdot \rangle_l$ on M_l such that $L_l = \frac{1}{2}\|\cdot\|_l^2$, then under the canonical identification of $T_{\gamma_j}M_{l_j}$ with $T^*_{\gamma_j}M_{l_j}$ via the metric $\langle \cdot, \cdot \rangle_l$, $(dL_{l_j})_{\dot{\gamma}_j}$ is identified with $\dot{\gamma}_j$, and equation (9) becomes

$$(d\Phi^{\gamma_j})^*\dot{\gamma}_j = \nu_0, \quad \forall t \in [\tau_j, \tau_{j+1}], \ j = 0, \ldots, m, \tag{10}$$

where $(d\Phi^{\gamma_j})^* : T_{\gamma_j}M_{l_j} \to \mathfrak{g}^*$ now is defined by

$$((d\Phi^{\gamma_j})^*u, v) = \langle u, d\Phi^{\gamma_j}(v)\rangle_{l_j}, \ \forall u \in T_{\gamma_j}M_{l_j}, \ v \in \mathfrak{g}. \tag{11}$$

Example 3. Consider Example 1 with a, b as shown in Figure 1. Then an optimal solution γ from a to b consists of two segments $\gamma_0 \subset M_0$ and $\gamma_1 \subset M_1$. It can be shown that for γ_0, the conserved quantity ν_0 is the component of the angular momentum $(\gamma_0 - c_0) \times \dot{\gamma}_0 \in \mathbb{R}^3$ along the rotational axis of M_0. Here c_0 is an arbitrary point on the rotational axis. Similarly we can obtain the conserved quantity for γ_1. Theorem 1 states that these two quantities are identical.

4   OCA and OFS Problems

In this section, we will describe very briefly two related classes of switched Lagrangian systems. For more details, see [9, 10].

Let M be a C^∞ Riemannian manifold[3]. Denote with $\langle \cdot, \cdot \rangle$ the riemannian metric and with $\| \cdot \|$ the associated norm on TM. The arc length of a curve $\alpha : [t_0, t_1] \rightarrow M$ is defined as $\int_{t_0}^{t_1} \|\dot{\alpha}(t)\| \, dt$. The distance between two arbitrary points q_1 and q_2 in M, which we denote as $d_M(q_1, q_2)$, is by definition the infimum of the arc length of all the curves connecting q_1 and q_2. A geodesic in M is a locally distance-minimizing curve. In this paper, we always assume that M is connected and complete, and that all the geodesics are parameterized proportionally to arc length.

Let $L : TM \rightarrow \mathbb{R}$ be a smooth nonnegative function that is convex on each fiber. As an example one can take $L = \frac{1}{2}\| \cdot \|^2$. For each curve $\alpha : [t_0, t_1] \rightarrow M$, its *cost* is defined as $J(\alpha) = \int_{t_0}^{t_1} L[\dot{\alpha}(t)] \, dt$.

Consider an (ordered) k-tuple of points of M, $\langle q_i \rangle_{i=1}^k = (q_1, \dots, q_k)$. We say that $\langle q_i \rangle_{i=1}^k$ satisfies the *r-separation condition* for some positive r if and only if $d_M(q_i, q_j) \geq r$ for all $i \neq j$. Let $\langle a_i \rangle_{i=1}^k$ and $\langle b_i \rangle_{i=1}^k$ be two k-tuples of points of M, each of which satisfies the r-separation condition. $\langle a_i \rangle_{i=1}^k$ is called the *starting position* and $\langle b_i \rangle_{i=1}^k$ the *destination position*. Let $h = (h_1, \dots, h_k)$ be a k-tuple of curves in M defined on $[t_0, t_1]$ such that $h_i(t_0) = a_i, h_i(t_1) = b_i$, for $i = 1, \dots, k$. h is said to be *collision-free* if the k-tuple $\langle h_i(t) \rangle_{i=1}^k$ satisfies the r-separation condition for each $t \in [t_0, t_1]$.

Problem 2 (OCA) *Among all collision-free $h = \langle h_i \rangle_{i=1}^k$ that start from $\langle a_i \rangle_{i=1}^k$ at time t_0 and end at $\langle b_i \rangle_{i=1}^k$ at time t_1, find the one (or ones) minimizing*

$$J(h) = \sum_{i=1}^{k} \lambda_i J(h_i). \tag{12}$$

Here $\langle \lambda_i \rangle_{i=1}^k$ is a k-tuple of positive numbers.

To introduce the second problem we need some notions. Let $\langle q_i \rangle_{i=1}^k$ be a k-tuple of points of M satisfying the r-separation condition. Then a graph (V, E) can be constructed as following: the set of vertices is $V = \{1, \dots, k\}$; the set

---

[3] M here should not be confused with M in Section 2, where it is used to denote the union of the domains of $\mathcal{H}$.

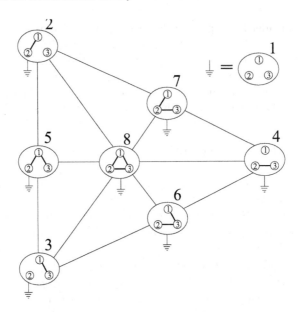

Fig. 2. Formation adjacency graph ($k = 3$, $M = \mathbb{R}^2$).

E of edges is such that an edge e_{ij} between vertex i and vertex j exists if and only if $d_M(q_i, q_j) = r$. (V, E) is called the *formation pattern* of $\langle q_i \rangle_{i=1}^k$. Let $h = \langle h_i \rangle_{i=1}^k$ be a collision-free k-tuple of curves in M defined on $[t_0, t_1]$. Then for each $t \in [t_0, t_1]$, the formation pattern of h at time t is defined to be the formation pattern of $\langle h_i(t) \rangle_{i=1}^k$.

Depending on M, r, and k, not all graphs with k vertices can be realized as the formation pattern of some $\langle q_i \rangle_{i=1}^k$. Two possible formation patterns are called *adjacent* if one is a strict subgraph of the other. This adjacency relation can be used to define a graph G_{adj} called the *formation adjacency graph*, whose set of vertices is the set of all possible formation patterns, and whose set of edges is such that an edge exists between two formation patterns if and only if they are adjacent. Figure 2 shows G_{adj} in the case $M = \mathbb{R}^2$ and $k = 3$, where the attachments of the "ground" symbol to vertices $2, \ldots, 8$ signal their adjacency with vertex 1.

Now we are ready to define the OFS problem.

Problem 3 (OFS) *Let G'_{adj} be a connected subgraph of G_{adj} such that the formation patterns of $\langle a_i \rangle_{i=1}^k$ and $\langle b_i \rangle_{i=1}^k$ are both vertices of G'_{adj}. Among all collision-free h that start from $\langle a_i \rangle_{i=1}^k$, end in $\langle b_i \rangle_{i=1}^k$, and satisfy the additional constraint that the formation pattern of h at any time $t \in [t_0, t_1]$ belongs to the vertices of G'_{adj}, find the one (or ones) minimizing the cost (12).*

For some choices of G'_{adj}, the OFS problem may not have a solution for all $\langle a_i \rangle_{i=1}^k$ and $\langle b_i \rangle_{i=1}^k$. This difficulty is removed if we assume that G'_{adj} is *closed*, i.e., for each formation pattern (V, E) belonging to the vertices of G'_{adj}, any formation pattern (V', E') containing (V, E) as a subgraph is also a vertex of G'_{adj}. In the example shown in Figure 2, one can choose G'_{adj} to be the subgraph obtained by removing vertices 1, 2, 3, 4 and all the edges connected to them, thus imposing the constraint that all three agents, each of which is of radius $\frac{r}{2}$, have to "contact" one another either directly or indirectly via the third agent at any time in the joint trajectory. As another example, G'_{adj} can be taken to the subgraph of G_{adj} consisting of vertices 2, 5, 7, 8, and all the edges among them. So agent 1 and agent 2 are required to be bound together at all time, and the OFS problem becomes the optimal collision avoidance between agent 3 and this two-agent subsystem.

The OFS (hence OCA) problem can be naturally described as a switched Lagrangian system $\mathcal{H}$. Its discrete modes correspond to the vertices of G'_{adj}, i.e., the allowed formation patterns. For each such formation pattern (V, E), the corresponding domain is the subset of $M^{(k)} = M \times \ldots \times M$ consisting of points $(q_1, \ldots, q_k)$ such that $d_M(q_i, q_j) = r$ if $e_{ij} \in E$ and $d_M(q_i, q_j) \geq r$ otherwise, and the Lagrangian function is given by $\sum_{i=1}^{k} \lambda_i L \circ dP_i$, where dP_i is the differential of the projection P_i of $M^{(k)}$ onto its i-th component. The set E_d of discrete transitions is exactly the set of edges of G'_{adj}. For each discrete transition, its guard is the intersection of the domain of the source discrete mode with that of the target discrete mode, its continuous transition relation is given by the graph of the identity map. One anomaly of this definition is that the domains of different discrete modes may intersect each other. But this can be removed by introducing an additional index dimension, as is the case in Example 2.

We make the following two assumptions:

1. $\Phi : G \times M \to M$ is a C^∞ left action of a Lie group G on M by isometries.
2. The function L is G-invariant.

As before, for each $g \in G$, define $\Phi_g : M \to M$ to be the map $q \mapsto gq$, $\forall q \in M$. Similarly, for each $q \in M$ define $\Phi^q : G \to M$ to be the map $g \mapsto gq$, $\forall g \in G$. Therefore, for each $g \in G$, the first assumption implies that Φ_g is an isometry of M, while the second assumption implies that $L \circ d\Phi_g = L$. A very important observation is that, under these two assumptions, the switched Lagrangian system $\mathcal{H}$ is G-symmetric. Therefore, by Theorem 1 we have

Theorem 2. *Suppose $h = \langle h_i \rangle_{i=1}^k$ is an optimal solution to the OCA (or OFS) problem. Then there exists a constant $\nu_0 \in \mathfrak{g}^*$ such that*

$$\nu \triangleq \sum_{i=1}^{k} \lambda_i (d\Phi^{h_i})^* dL_{\dot{h}_i} \equiv \nu_0 \tag{13}$$

for all $t \in [t_0, t_1]$ where $\dot{h}_i$'s are well defined.

Example 4 ($G = \mathbf{SO}_n$, $M = \mathbf{S}^{n-1}$). Let $M = \mathbf{S}^{n-1} = \{(x_1, \ldots, x_n)^t \in \mathbb{R}^n : x_1^2 + \ldots + x_n^2 = 1\}$ be the unit $(n-1)$-sphere, and let $G = \mathbf{SO}_n = \{Q \in \mathbb{R}^{n \times n} :$

$Q^t Q = I, \det Q = 1\}$ be the group of orientation-preserving n-by-n orthogonal matrices. G acts on M by left matrix multiplication. For each $q \in \mathbf{S}^{n-1}$, the tangent space $T_q \mathbf{S}^{n-1} = \{v \in \mathbb{R}^n : v^t q = 0\}$ is equipped with the standard metric $\langle u, v \rangle = u^t v, \forall u, v \in T_q \mathbf{S}^{n-1}$, which is invariant under the action of $\mathbf{SO}_n$. The Lie algebra of $\mathbf{SO}_n$, $\mathfrak{so}_n$, is the set of all n-by-n skew-symmetric matrices, i.e., $\mathfrak{so}_n = \{X \in \mathbb{R}^{n \times n} : X + X^t = 0\}$, where the Lie bracket is given by $[X, Y] = XY - YX, \forall X, Y \in \mathfrak{so}_n$. Choose $L = \frac{1}{2}\|\cdot\|^2$. Suppose that $h = \langle h_i \rangle_{i=1}^k$ is a k-tuple of curves on $\mathbf{S}^{n-1}$ that solves the OCA (or OFS) problem. At any time $t \in [t_0, t_1]$, let $u \in T_{h_i} \mathbf{S}^{n-1}$ and $v \in \mathfrak{so}_n$ be arbitrary. Then

$$\langle u, d\Phi^{h_i} v \rangle = \langle u, v h_i \rangle = u^t v h_i = \operatorname{tr}(u^t v h_i) = \operatorname{tr}(h_i u^t v) = \langle u h_i^t, v \rangle_F,$$

where $\langle \cdot, \cdot \rangle_F$ is the Frobenius inner product on $\mathbb{R}^{n \times n}$ defined by $\langle X, Y \rangle_F = \operatorname{tr}(X^t Y)$ for any two n-by-n matrices X and Y. Since v is skew-symmetric, it is easily checked that $\langle u h_i^t, v \rangle_F = \frac{1}{2}\langle u h_i^t - h_i u^t, v \rangle_F$. Therefore

$$((d\Phi^{h_i})^* u, v) = \langle u, d\Phi^{h_i} v \rangle = \frac{1}{2}\langle u h_i^t - h_i u^t, v \rangle_F, \quad \forall v \in \mathfrak{so}_n. \tag{14}$$

Note that $u h_i^t - h_i u^t$ is skew-symmetric, hence belongs to $\mathfrak{so}_n$. We use the restriction of $\frac{1}{2}\langle \cdot, \cdot \rangle_F$ to establish a metric on $\mathfrak{so}_n$, hence identifying $\mathfrak{so}_n^*$ with $\mathfrak{so}_n$. Then equation (14) can be written as

$$(d\Phi^{h_i})^* u = u h_i^t - h_i u^t.$$

Hence the conservation law (13) becomes

$$\sum_{i=1}^k \lambda_i (\dot{h}_i h_i^t - h_i \dot{h}_i^t) \equiv \nu_0 \in \mathfrak{so}_n, \tag{15}$$

If we write each h_i in coordinates as $h_i = (h_{i,1}, \dots, h_{i,n})^t \in \mathbf{S}^{n-1} \subset \mathbb{R}^n$, then (15) is equivalent to $\sum_{i=1}^k \lambda_i (\dot{h}_{ij_1} h_{ij_2} - h_{ij_1} \dot{h}_{ij_2}) \equiv C_{j_1 j_2}, \forall t \in [t_0, t_1], 1 \le j_1 < j_2 \le n$, where $C_{j_1 j_2}$'s are constants in $\mathbb{R}$. In particular, if $n = 2$ ($M = \mathbf{S}^2$, $G = \mathbf{SO}_3$), then equation (15) can be written compactly as $\sum_{i=1}^k \lambda_i (h_i \times \dot{h}_i) \equiv \Omega_0$ for some $\Omega_0 \in \mathbb{R}^3$, where $\times$ is the vector product. This is exactly the conservation of total angular momentum.

Example 5 (Grassmann Manifold). Let $\mathbf{O}_n$ be the set of orthogonal n-by-n matrices equipped with the standard metric inherited from $\mathbb{R}^{n \times n}$, which can be shown to be bi-invariant. Let p be an integer such that $1 \le p \le n$. Define H_p to be the subgroup of $\mathbf{O}_n$ consisting of all those matrices of the form $\begin{bmatrix} Q_p & 0 \\ 0 & Q_{n-p} \end{bmatrix}$, where Q_p and Q_{n-p} are p-by-p and $(n-p)$-by-$(n-p)$ orthogonal matrices respectively. Let $G_{n,p} = \{QH_p : Q \in \mathbf{O}_n\}$ be the set of all left cosets of H_p in $\mathbf{O}_n$. Alternatively, $G_{n,p}$ is the set of all equivalence classes of the equivalence relation $\sim$ defined on $\mathbf{O}_n$ by: $\forall P, Q \in \mathbf{O}_n$, $P \sim Q$ if and only if $P = QA$ for some $A \in H_p$.

Elements in $G_{n,p}$ are denoted by $[[Q]] = QH_p = \{QA : A \in H_p\}, \forall Q \in \mathbf{O}_n$, and correspond in a one-to-one way to the set of all p-dimensional subspaces of $\mathbb{R}^n$. As a quotient space of $\mathbf{O}_n$, $G_{n,p}$ admits a natural differential structure, and is called the Grassmann manifold. At each $Q \in \mathbf{O}_n$, the tangent space of $\mathbf{O}_n$ can be decomposed as the direct sum of two parts: the vertical space $\mathrm{vert}_Q\mathbf{O}_n$ and the horizontal space $\mathrm{hor}_Q\mathbf{O}_n$. $\mathrm{vert}_Q\mathbf{O}_n$ is the tangent space of QH_p at Q, which consists of all those matrices of the form $Q \begin{bmatrix} Y & 0 \\ 0 & Z \end{bmatrix}$ for some p-by-p skew symmetric matrix Y and some $(n-p)$-by-$(n-p)$ skew symmetric matrix Z; $\mathrm{hor}_Q\mathbf{O}_n$ is the orthogonal complement in $T_Q\mathbf{O}_n$ of $\mathrm{vert}_Q\mathbf{O}_n$, and consists of all those matrices of the form $Q \begin{bmatrix} 0 & -X^t \\ X & 0 \end{bmatrix}$ for some $(n-p)$-by-p matrix X. Define a metric on $\mathrm{hor}_Q\mathbf{O}_n$ by

$$\langle Q \begin{bmatrix} 0 & -X_1^t \\ X_1 & 0 \end{bmatrix}, Q \begin{bmatrix} 0 & -X_2^t \\ X_2 & 0 \end{bmatrix} \rangle = \frac{1}{2}\langle Q \begin{bmatrix} 0 & -X_1^t \\ X_1 & 0 \end{bmatrix}, Q \begin{bmatrix} 0 & -X_2^t \\ X_2 & 0 \end{bmatrix} \rangle_F = \mathrm{tr}(X_1^t X_2),$$
(16)

for all $X_1, X_2 \in \mathbb{R}^{(n-p)\times p}$. An important observation is that $\mathrm{hor}_Q\mathbf{O}_n$ provides a representation of the tangent space of $G_{n,p}$ at $[[Q]]$, and the metric defined in (16) is independent of the choice of Q in $[[Q]]$, as long as one equates $Q \begin{bmatrix} 0 & -X^t \\ X & 0 \end{bmatrix}$ in $\mathrm{hor}_Q\mathbf{O}_n$ with $Q \begin{bmatrix} 0 & -X^t \\ X & 0 \end{bmatrix} A$ in $\mathrm{hor}_{QA}\mathbf{O}_n$ for arbitrary $A \in H_p$. Note that here we use the fact that the metric on $\mathbf{O}_n$ is bi-invariant. Therefore, (16) induces a metric on $G_{n,p}$, which is easily verified to be invariant with respect to the action of $\mathbf{O}_n$. Under this metric, the distance between $[[Q_1]]$ and $[[Q_2]]$, $Q_1, Q_2 \in \mathbf{O}_n$, can be calculated as $\sqrt{\sum_{i=1}^{p} \theta_i^2}$, where $\cos\theta_i$, $i = 1, \ldots, p$, are the singular values of the p-by-p matrix $[I_p\ 0]\, Q_1^t Q_2 \begin{bmatrix} I_p \\ 0 \end{bmatrix}$. Here I_p is the p-by-p identity matrix ([7]).

Suppose $L = \frac{1}{2}\|\cdot\|^2$. Let $h = \langle h_i \rangle_{i=1}^{k}$ be a k-tuple of curves in $G_{n,p}$ which is a solution to the OCA (or OFS) problem. For each $i = 1, \ldots, k$, let q_i be a *lifting* of h_i in $\mathbf{O}_n$, i.e. q_i is a curve in $\mathbf{O}_n$ such that $[[q_i(t)]] = h_i(t), \forall t \in [t_0, t_1]$. In other words, $q_i(t)$ is an orthogonal matrix in $\mathbf{O}_n$ whose first p columns span the subspace $h_i(t) \in G_{n,p}$. Also implicit in this definition is that q_i is continuous and piecewise C^∞. At any time $t \in [t_0, t_1]$, from the previous paragraph we can identify $T_{h_i}G_{n,p}$ with $\mathrm{hor}_{q_i}\mathbf{O}_n$. So for any $u \in T_{h_i}G_{n,p} \subset T_{q_i}\mathbf{O}_n$ and $v \in \mathbf{o}_n$,

$$\langle u, d\Phi^{h_i}v \rangle_{T_{h_i}G_{n,p}} = \langle u, P_{q_i}(vq_i) \rangle_{\mathrm{hor}_{q_i}\mathbf{O}_n} = \langle u, vq_i \rangle_{T_{q_i}\mathbf{O}_n} = \langle uq_i^{-1}, v \rangle_{\mathbf{o}_n}.$$

Here for clarity we indicate in the subscript the associated tangent space of each inner product. P_{q_i} is defined as the orthogonal projection of $T_{q_i}\mathbf{O}_n$ onto the subspace $\mathrm{hor}_{q_i}\mathbf{O}_n$. More specifically, each $w \in T_{q_i}\mathbf{O}_n$ can be written as $q_i \begin{bmatrix} Y & -X^t \\ X & Z \end{bmatrix}$ for some p-by-p skew symmetric matrix Y, $(n-p)$-by-$(n-p)$ skew symmetric matrix Z, and $(n-p)$-by-p matrix X, then $P_{q_i}(w) = q_i \begin{bmatrix} 0 & -X^t \\ X & 0 \end{bmatrix}$.

As a result, we see that $(d\Phi^{h_i})^*u = uq_i^{-1} = uq_i^t, \forall u \in \mathbf{T}_{h_i}G_{n,p}$. Finally, notice that $\dot{h}_i = P_{q_i}(\dot{q}_i)$. Therefore, the conserved quantity is

$$\nu_0 = \sum_{i=1}^{k} \lambda_i P_{q_i}(\dot{q}_i)q_i^t \in \mathbf{o}_n. \qquad (17)$$

5   Conclusions

We study the optimal control problem of switched Lagrangian systems with a group of symmetries. Necessary conditions are given for the optimal solutions. In particular, we show that the OCA and the OFS problems for multiple agents moving on a Riemannian manifold are special occasions of such a problem. Several examples are presented to illustrate the results.

References

[1] V. I. Arnold, K. Vogtmann, and A. Weinstein. *Mathematical Methods of Classical Mechanics, 2nd edition.* Springer-Verlag, 1989.

[2] A. Bicchi and L. Pallottino. Optimal planning for coordinated vehicles with bounded curvature. In *Proc. Work. Algorithmic Foundation of Robotics (WAFR'2000)*, Dartmouth, Hanover, NH, 2000.

[3] A. M. Bloch, P. S. Krishnaprasad, J. E. Marsden, and T. S. Ratiu. The Euler-Poincare equations and double bracket dissipation. *Comm. Math. Phys.*, 175(1):1–42, 1996.

[4] J. C. P. Bus. The lagrange multiplier rule on manifolds and optimal control of nonlinear systems. *SIAM J. Control and Optimization*, 22(5):740–757, 1984.

[5] M. P. de Carmo. *Riemannian Geometry.* Birkhäuser Boston, 1992.

[6] J. P. Desai and V. Kumar. Nonholonomic motion planning for multiple mobile manipulators. In *Proc. IEEE Int. Conf. on Robotics and Automation*, volume 4, pages 20–25, Albuquerque, NM, 1997.

[7] A. Edelman, T. A. Arias, and S. T. Smith. The geometry of algorithms with orthogonality constraints. *SIAM J. Matrix Anal. and Appl.*, 20(2):303–353, 1998.

[8] John Lygeros et al. *Hybrid Systems: Modeling, Analysis and Control.* ERL Memorandum No. UCB/ERL M99/34, Univ. of California at Berkeley, 1999.

[9] J. Hu, M. Prandini, and S. Sastry. Hybrid geodesics as optimal solutions to the collision-free motion planning problem. In *Proc. Hybrid Systems: Computation and Control, 4th Int. Workshop (HSCC 2001)*, pages 305–318, Rome, Italy, 2001.

[10] J. Hu and S. Sastry. Optimal collision avoidance and formation switching on Riemannian manifolds. In *Proc. 40th IEEE Int. Conf. on Decision and Control*, Orlando, Florida, 2001.

[11] J. Hu and S. Sastry. Geodesics of manifolds with boundary: a case study. unpublished, 2002.

[12] J. E. Marsden and T.S. Ratiu. *Introduction to Mechanics and Symmetry, 2nd edition.* Springer-Verlag, 1994.

[13] H. J. Sussmann. A maximum principle for hybrid optimal control problems. In *Proc. 38th IEEE Int. Conf. on Decision and Control*, volume 1, pages 425–430, Phoenix, AZ, 1999.

Bisimulation Based Hierarchical System Architecture for Single-Agent Multi-modal Systems

T. John Koo and Shankar Sastry

Department of Electrical Engineering and Computer Sciences
University of California at Berkeley
Berkeley, CA 94720
{koo,sastry}@eecs.berkeley.edu

Abstract. In this paper, a hierarchical system architecture for single-agent multi-modal systems is proposed. The layered system is designed to promote proof obligations so that system specification at one level of granularity conforms with that at another level and vice versa. The design principle for the construction of the hierarchy is based on bisimulation with respect to reachability specifications. Therefore, a higher-level system and a lower-level system are bisimilar. Our approach is illustrated by designing a system architecture for controlling an autonomous agent.

1 Introduction

Control of multi-agent systems focus on the control of individual agents to accomplish a mission collectively, while satisfying their dynamic equations and inter-agent formation constraints, for an underlying communication protocol being deployed. Advances in embedded software, computation, communication, and new methods of distributed sensing and actuation are revolutionizing the development of advanced control technologies for distributed, multi-agent systems. These advances also enable the conduct of missions deemed impossible in the recent past.

Imposing a hierarchical structure on the system architecture has been used for solving the control problem of large-scale systems[5,15,17,19]. A desired hierarchical structure should not only provide manageable complexity but also promote verification. There are several approaches to understanding a hierarchy depending on the design perspective. In particular, two distinct approaches have been shown in [20] for the design and analysis of AHS [19]. One approach to the meaning of hierarchy is to adopt *one-world* semantics, and the other approach is referred to as *multi-world* semantics.

In one-world semantics for hierarchical systems as shown in [18], a higher-level expression is interpreted in a process called *semantic flattening*: the expression is first compiled into lower-level expression and then interpreted. In other words, an interpretation at each level is semantically complied into a single interpretation at the lowest-level in the *imperative* world. Furthermore, semantic flattening

C.J. Tomlin and M.R. Greenstreet (Eds.): HSCC 2002, LNCS 2289, pp. 281–293, 2002.

implies that checking any high-level truth-claim can be performed by an automatic procedure if there is a facility for automatically verifying the lowest-level interpretation. This approach provides a unique interpretation to system description and verification. However, a major drawback to one-world semantics is that higher-level syntax and truth-claims have to be reformulated if there are some changes at any of the lower levels. The advantage of using one-world semantics for hierarchical systems is gained at the heavy cost of a rigidity of framework that makes it unsuitable for most complex and heterogeneous system. On the other hand, in multi-world semantics for hierarchical systems, an expression at each level is interpreted at the same level. Therefore, checking the truth-claim at that level is performed in its own *declarative* world. This approach conforms with common system design practice. However, relating these disconnected worlds together is a nontrivial task. In the following, we will present a multi-agent system to motivate our discussion on the design of hierarchical system architecture.

Consider a mission of controlling a group of autonomous agents in the pursuit of multiple evaders. Assume that each agent is a UAV equipped with necessary computation, communication, and sensing capabilities to accomplish the mission. Different approaches have been proposed in solving the pursuit-evasion game either in deterministic [14,16] or probabilistic framework [7,8] based on complete or partial information about the environment. In the common setting of the game, the game is performed on a finite graph $G = (S, E)$ with node $s \in S$ and all allowed motions for the players are represented by edges $e \in E \subseteq S \times S$ connecting the nodes. Each node may be occupied by more than one agent. The game is then performed on the discrete graph G, and each action of an agent depends on a discrete event generated from a given strategy. Depending on the level of centralization and the nature of the game, a specific set of strategies can be selected to accomplish the mission. In the game, an evader is *captured* if the evader and one of the pursuers occupy the same node.

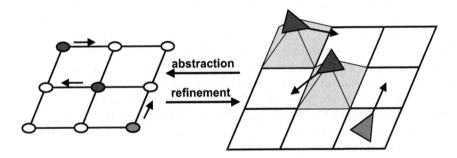

Fig. 1. A hierarchical system for solving the Pursuit-Evasion game is designed as a two-layered system in which decision-making procedures for solving the game on the discrete graph are performed at the top level and motions being generated in the physical world by agents are exhibited at the bottom level.

However, the actual game is taken place in a continuous space $X \subseteq \mathbb{R}^3$ by the agents. In order to implement the discrete game in the continuous space X, one has to construct a partition of X which contains a finite number of cells X_j for $j = 1, \ldots, M$ with each cell corresponding to a node on the graph G. Furthermore, for an agent, each allowed motion on the graph has to be refined to feasible motions by exhibiting multi-modal behaviors. Hence, the system is designed as a two-layered system in which decision-making procedures for solving the game on the discrete graph are performed at the top level and motions being generated in the physical world by agents are exhibited at the bottom level. Between these two worlds, state information at the bottom level is being abstracted at the top level and control information at the top level is being refined at the bottom level.

To achieve high level of mission reliability, it is desirable that the layered system is designed to promote proof obligations so that system specification at one level of granularity *conforms* with system specification at another level. Consider two levels of a system and system specification at a lower-level conforms with system specification at a higher-level. Hence, there is a tight relation between the levels since each detailed state at the lower-level corresponds to an abstract state at the higher-level, and each transition at the lower-level corresponds to a transition at the higher-level. This relation is captured mathematically by the notion of *simulation*. If system specification at the higher-level conforms with system specification at the lower-level, the detailed system at the lower level and the abstracted system at the higher level are called *bisimilar*.

In this paper, we are interested in the design of a hierarchical system architecture for a single-agent multi-modal system based on bisimulation with respect to reachability specification. Therefore, if the abstracted system at the top level, which utilizes the graph G, and the detailed system at the bottom level, which is a hybrid system containing a collection of control modes, are bisimilar with respect to reachability specification, then the reachability problem for the hybrid system can be converted to an equivalent reachability problem on the finite graph G. If, in addition, the equivalent problem can be performed in a computationally feasible way, then the reachability problem for the hybrid system is *decidable*. An agent model inspired by the motion capability of helicopter is used as an example to demonstrate the effectiveness of the proposed concepts for solving the control system design problem.

2   Single-Agent Multi-modal Systems

Given the motion capability of an agent, we assume that there exist control strategies such that a finite number of directions of motion can be generated. Any control strategy may utilize a single controller or a sequence of controllers for generating the motion directions. In this paper, we consider that an agent can only move in a horizontal plane and assume that it has five possible motion directions. In general, depending on the choice on a control strategy, one can have different sets of motion directions. However, we will show that the feasible motion directions would affect the construction of the partition which are used for abstracting state from detailed system to abstracted system.

2.1 Hybrid Automaton

Motivated by an design example of a helicopter based UAV shown in [10], we consider that the detailed system is modeled as a multi-modal system with five control modes citeKPS01. In each control mode, there is a closed-loop dynamics embedded. The system can further be modeled as a hybrid automaton citeLTS99. As depicted in Figure 2, the hybrid automaton H which models the multi-modal system is defined as a collection $H = (Q \times X, \Sigma, Y, Init, f, h, I, G, R)$ where $Q = \{q_1, q_2, q_3, q_4, q_5\}$, $X \subseteq \mathbb{R}^3$ and $\Sigma = \{\sigma_1, \sigma_2, \sigma_3, \sigma_4, \sigma_5\}$, $Y \subseteq \mathbb{R}^3$, with the hybrid state $(q, x) \in Q \times X$, the input $\sigma \in \Sigma$, and the output $y \in Y$. Let

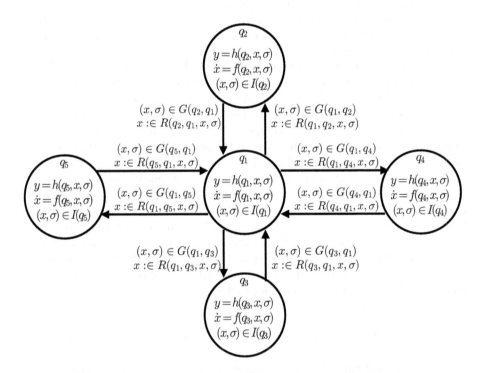

Fig. 2. Hybrid automaton models the multi-modal behaviors of an agent.

$x = [p_x, p_y, p_z]$ to specify the location of an agent in the state space X. The vector field is defined by

$$f(q, x, \sigma) = \begin{cases} (0,0,0) & \text{if } q = q_1, \\ (\epsilon_2, 0, 0) & \text{if } q = q_2, \\ (-\epsilon_3, 0, 0) & \text{if } q = q_3, \\ (0, \epsilon_4, 0) & \text{if } q = q_4, \\ (0, -\epsilon_5, 0) & \text{if } q = q_5 \end{cases}$$

where $\epsilon_i > 0$ for $i = 2, 3, 4, 5$. The output map is defined by $h(q, x, \sigma) = x$ for $q \in Q$. The invariant is defined by

$$I(q_i) = X \times \{\sigma_i\} \quad \text{for } i = 1, \ldots, 5.$$

The guard and the reset relation are defined by

$$\begin{cases} G(q_i, q_j) = X \times \{\sigma_j\} \\ R(q_i, q_j, x) = \{x\} \end{cases}, \qquad \begin{array}{l} \text{for } (i, j) \in \{(1,2), (2,1), (1,3), (3,1) \\ (1,4), (4,1), (1,5), (5,1)\}. \end{array}$$

The initial set is defined by $Init = \{q_1\} \times X$. When the multi-modal system is in q_1 mode, since the vector field is a zero vector the continuous state x remains the same. If there is an input σ_2, the guard $G(q_1, q_2)$ is enabled and the discrete state becomes q_2 and p_x keeps increasing while p_y, p_z remain the same. This is because in control mode q_2, the first component of the vector field is a positive number and the other components are zero. If we use the North-East-Down coordinate system for defining x, y, z axes, then when the system is in q_2 mode the agent is moving in north direction and hence when the system is in q_4 mode the agent is moving in east direction. The situations are similarly defined for the system being in q_3 and q_5 modes.

After defining the motion capability of an agent, we are interested in the issues related to reachability. Consider $x', x'' \in X$, σ_i-labeled transition is defined as $x' \xrightarrow{\sigma_i} x''$ iff there exists $\delta \geq 0$, and a curve $x : [0, \delta] \to \mathbb{R}^n$ with $x(0) = x', x(\delta) = x''$ and for all $t \in [0, \delta]$ it satisfies $\dot{x}(t) = f(q_i, x(t), \sigma_i)$. Notice that the continuous transitions are time-abstract transitions, in the sense that the time it takes to reach one state from another is ignored. Now, we define another transition relation which is used for taking a transition from q_1 to q_i then back to q_1. Therefore, after taking the transition, the state of the multi-modal system is always q_1. Consider $x', x'' \in X$, σ_i-labeled cyclic transition is defined as $x' \xrightarrow{\sigma_i} x''$ iff $x' \xrightarrow{\sigma_i} x'' \xrightarrow{\sigma_i} x''$. The above definitions of transition relations are motivated by the similar definitions defined in [1] for timed automata.

2.2 Partition and Its Induced Equivalence Relation

Having the transition relations defined, we can start discussing the partition of the continuous space. To address this issue, we consider an equivalence relation $\sim$ over the state space X. Consider that the continuous space X is decomposed into a finite number of cells X_j for $j = 1, \ldots, m$ and we denote the family of subsets X as $\pi = \{X_j\}$. Define $\mathcal{I} = \{1, \ldots, m\}$. If we require that each location of an agent in the space can belong to exactly one cell, π should be a *partition* of X which satisfies the following properties:

$$X = \bigcup_{j \in \mathcal{I}} X_j, \tag{2.1}$$

$$X_i \cap X_j = \emptyset, \qquad \forall i \neq j. \tag{2.2}$$

Therefore, the cells of the partition π *cover* the space X and *do not overlap*. Here, the induced equivalence relation is called *cell equivalence*, which is defined over the space X. For two locations $x', x'' \in X$, $x' \sim x''$ if $\exists j \in \mathcal{I}$ such that $x', x'' \in X_j$.

However, in order to obtain a *stable* partition [1], the motion capability of an agent has to be taken into consideration. Consider the multi-modal system, the partition is designed by putting a two-dimensional grid over the state space and each boundary of a cell is parallel to exactly one possible motion direction. Therefore, we obtain a partition π composed of rectangular cells and each cell is a Cartesian product of two half-open intervals. The partition is depicted in Figure 3.

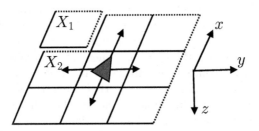

Fig. 3. Graphical illustration of the partition and the possible agent motion directions.

Given a cell $X_j \in \pi$, define $\mathcal{I}_j = \{i \in \mathcal{I} \setminus \{j\}| \ |\partial X_j \cap \partial X_i| > 1\}$. Thus, every $X_i \in \pi$ is *adjacent* to X_j for $i \in \mathcal{I}_j$. Hence we have the following lemma concerning the local motion capability of the agent.

Lemma 1 (Local Motion Capability). *Given a cell $X_j \in \pi$ and an adjacent cell $X_i \in \pi$ with $i \in \mathcal{I}_j$, $\exists \sigma \in \Sigma \ \forall x' \in X_j \ \exists x'' \in X_i$ such that $x' \overset{\sigma}{\Rightarrow} x''$.*
Proof: Given the partition, due to the definition of adjacent cells, there are only four possible adjacent cells for each cell. For an adjacent cell, since there exists exactly one motion direction that parallel to each boundary, one can simply pick a motion direction that could make an agent go towards the adjacent cell. Due to the simple reachability property of the multi-modal system, one can easily show that an agent could start from any where within the cell and could reach some where inside the adjacent cell in some time.

Therefore, if an agent starts at any location $x' \in X_j$, then it can move to any adjacent cells X_i of cell X_j and reach some location $x'' \in X_i$ in some time. By construction, the reachability computation of the hybrid automaton is greatly simplified. Therefore, sophisticated reach set computation is avoided.

3   Bisimulation

Consider an agent starting from a location in a cell $X_S \in \pi$ and we are interested in determining whether it can reach a final cell $X_F \in \pi$. Now, we define a transition system which preserve the reachability property of the multi-modal system. A transition system $T = (X, \Sigma, \Rightarrow, X_S, X_F)$ is constructed to consist of a set X of states, an alphabet Σ of events, a transition relation $\Rightarrow \subseteq X \times \Sigma \times X$, a set $X_S \subseteq X$ of initial states, and a set $X_F \subseteq X$ of final states. The σ_i-labeled cyclic transition $(x', \sigma_i, x'') \in \Rightarrow$ is simply denoted as $x' \Rightarrow x''$. The transition system is infinite since the cardinality of X is infinite. Given an equivalence relation $\sim \subseteq X \times X$ which partitions the state space into a number of equivalence classes. Let $X/\sim = \{X_j\}$ denote the quotient space. For a region X' we denote by $X'/\sim$ the collection of all equivalence classes which intersect X'. If a set is a union of equivalence classes, it is called a $\sim$-block.

Definition 1 (Bisimulation). *Given $T = (X, \Sigma, \Rightarrow, X_S, X_F)$, and $\sim$ an equivalence relation over X, $\sim$ is called a bisimulation if:*

1. X_S is a union of equivalence classes;

2. X_F is a union of equivalence classes;

3. For all $\sigma \in \Sigma$, if X' is a $\sim$-block, $Pre_\sigma(X') = \{x' \in X | \exists x'' \in X' : x' \Rightarrow x''\}$ is a $\sim$-block.

By using Definition 1, we can show that the equivalence relation defined in previous section is a bisimulation.

Theorem 1 (Bisimulation). *The equivalence relation $\sim$ is a bisimulation.*
Proof: By construction, each cell in the partition π is an equivalence class. Therefore, X_S, X_F are $\sim$-blocks since $X_S, X_F \in \pi$. For all $\sigma \in \Sigma$ and for every $\sim$-block X', the predecessor set defined by $Pre_\sigma(X')$ is a $\sim$-block since by Lemma 1 the predecessor can only be the union of all adjacent cells of X'. Hence the result.

The complexity of the reachability problem is reduced by using special quotient transition systems. The quotient transition system is defined as $T/\sim = (X/\sim, \Sigma, \Rightarrow_\sim, X_S/\sim, X_F/\sim)$ where the transition relation $\Rightarrow_\sim$ on the quotient space is defined as follows: for $X_1, X_2 \in X/\sim$, $X_1 \Rightarrow_\sim X_2$ iff there exists $x' \in X_1$ and $x'' \in X_2$ such that $x' \Rightarrow x''$. $T/\sim$ is a reachability preserving quotient system. Since the cardinality of $X/\sim$ is finite, $T/\sim$ is called *finite*. Furthermore, we have the following result.

Theorem 2 (Bisimular Systems). *T and $T/\sim$ are bisimilar.*

T and $T/\sim$ accept the same language [6]. Furthermore, the checking reachability for the detailed system T can be equivalently performed on the finite, discrete, quotient graph. Since the quotient graph is finite, the reachability algorithm will terminate. Given the partition, since the equivalent reachability

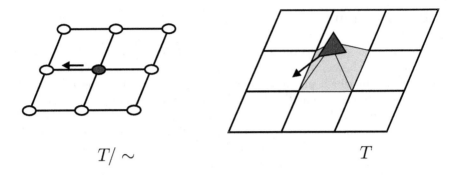

Fig. 4. $T/\sim$ and T are bisimilar.

problem on the finite graph can be performed in a computationally feasible way, the reachability problem for the hybrid system is decidable.

In the next section, we will show how to use the quotient transition system to construct a hierarchical system architecture for the single-agent multi-modal system.

4   System Architecture

In this section, we are interested in the design of a hierarchical system architecture for the single-agent multi-modal system by considering the transition system T and its reachability preserving quotient transition system $T/\sim$. Hence, a two-layered system architecture is naturally suggested. The abstracted system, N, on the top layer is associated with $T/\sim$ whereas the detailed system, M, on the bottom layer is associated with T. The hierarchical system F is the composition of the two systems, *i.e.* $F = N\|M$.

However, there are two technical issues have to be addressed before the design of the hierarchical system can take place. First, two transition systems have different notions of time. This is because the continuous transitions defined are *time-abstract*. However, it does take some time for the continuous state to make a transition. Therefore, although T and $T/\sim$ accept the same language, the time accepting an event could be badly mismatched. Second, the use of transition systems is mainly for reachability analysis but they are not suitable to be used as system models to perform actual computation.

For the first issue, we suggest to use a synchronization scheme for keeping a close correspondence between two layers so that state transitions can be synchronized. Next, since $T/\sim$ is a purely discrete transition system, it literary suggests that finite automaton would be sufficient to be used to represent the quotient transition system for performing actual computation, and since T exhibits hybrid behaviors, hybrid automaton could be used to model the transition system. Therefore, the proposed hierarchical system is composed of a finite automaton and a hybrid automaton. To simplify future discussion on system composition, we will use the hybrid formalism to express the finite automaton. Regarding the formal treatment of the composition of hybrid automata, please refer to [2].

4.1   A Design Example

In this design example, we assume that there are only 4 equivalence classes in a partition and initially an agent is located at $x \in X_S = X_1$.

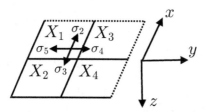

Fig. 5. Four equivalence classes, namely X_1, X_2, X_3, X_4, are illustrated. An agent is located in X_1 and it is capable of moving in four different directions

For the quotient transition system $T/\sim$, we associate it with a hybrid automaton N which is a collection $N = (S, P \times \Sigma, S \times \Sigma, Init_N, f_N, h_N, I_N, G_N, R_N)$ where the state $s \in S = \{s_1, s_2, s_3, s_4\}$, the input $(p, \sigma) \in P \times \Sigma$ with $P = \{p_1, p_2, p_3, p_4\}$, the output $(s, \delta) \in S \times \Sigma$, the initial set $Init_N = \{s_1\}$, the vector field $f_N(s, p, \sigma) = \emptyset$, the output map $h_N(s, p, \sigma) = (s, \sigma)$, the invariant $I_N(s) = \emptyset$, the reset map $R_N(s_i, s_j) = \emptyset \ \forall i, j \in \{1, 2, 3, 4\}$, and the guard $G_N(s_i, s_j) = \{p_i\} \times \{\delta_{ij}\}$ with

$$
\delta_{ij} = \begin{cases}
\sigma_2 & \text{for } (i,j) \in \{(2,1), (4,3)\} \\
\sigma_3 & \text{for } (i,j) \in \{(1,2), (3,4)\} \\
\sigma_4 & \text{for } (i,j) \in \{(1,3), (2,4)\} \\
\sigma_5 & \text{for } (i,j) \in \{(3,1), (4,2)\}
\end{cases}.
$$

Each state s_i represents an equivalence class X_i for $i \in \{1, 2, 3, 4\}$. For each s_i, there is also a corresponding state p_i provided from the bottom layer as an input to N for synchronizing the two layers.

For the transition system T, we associate it with a hybrid automaton M. Since σ_i-*labeled cyclic transition* is introduced in the construction of the transition system, the hybrid automaton H has to be augmented in order to be able to accept the same language as T does. Consider M is composed of two hybrid automata K and H, i.e. $M = K \| H$. Hybrid automaton K is a collection $K = (P, X \times \Sigma, P \times \Sigma, Init_K, f_K, h_K, I_K, G_K, R_K)$ where the state $p \in P = \{p_1, p_2, p_3, p_4, p_{12}, p_{21}, p_{13}, p_{31}, p_{42}, p_{24}, p_{43}, p_{34}\}$, the input $(x, \delta) \in X \times \Sigma$, the output $(p, \sigma) \in P \times \Sigma$, the initial set $Init_K = \{p_1\}$, the vector field $f_K(p, x, \delta) = \emptyset$, the invariant $I_K(p) = \emptyset$, the reset map $R_K(p_i, p_j) = \emptyset$ $\forall i, j \in \{1, 2, 3, 4\}$, the output map $h_K(p_i, x, \delta) = (p_i, \sigma_1)$ $\forall i \in \{1, 2, 3, 4\}$,

$$
\begin{aligned}
h_K(p_{12}, x, \delta) &= (p_1, \sigma_3), \; h_K(p_{21}, x, \delta) = (p_2, \sigma_2), \\
h_K(p_{13}, x, \delta) &= (p_1, \sigma_4), \; h_K(p_{31}, x, \delta) = (p_3, \sigma_5), \\
h_K(p_{42}, x, \delta) &= (p_4, \sigma_5), \; h_K(p_{24}, x, \delta) = (p_2, \sigma_4), \\
h_K(p_{43}, x, \delta) &= (p_4, \sigma_2), \; h_K(p_{34}, x, \delta) = (p_3, \sigma_3),
\end{aligned}
$$

and the guard $G_K(s_i, s_{ij}) = \{\delta_{ij}\}$ with

$$
\delta_{ij} = \begin{cases}
\sigma_2 & \text{for } (s_i, s_{ij}) \in \{(p_2, p_{21}), (p_4, p_{43})\} \\
\sigma_3 & \text{for } (s_i, s_{ij}) \in \{(p_1, p_{12}), (p_3, p_{34})\} \\
\sigma_4 & \text{for } (s_i, s_{ij}) \in \{(p_1, p_{13}), (p_2, p_{24})\} \\
\sigma_5 & \text{for } (s_i, s_{ij}) \in \{(p_3, p_{31}), (p_4, p_{42})\}
\end{cases} ,
$$

or the guard $G_K(s_{ij}, s_j) = X_j$ $\forall i, j \in \{1, 2, 3, 4\}$.

To implement the σ-*labeled cyclic transition*, for each possible transition from p_i to p_j an intermediate state p_{ij} are introduced so that two different symbols σ and σ_1 can be emitted via the output to the hybrid automaton H. To explain the idea, the following scenario is considered. Assume that the system starts from p_1 and the output is (p_1, σ_1). Now, there is an input σ_4 and hence an transition from p_1 to an intermediate state p_{13} is enabled. At p_{13}, the output is (p_1, σ_4). Therefore, the symbol σ_4 can enable the evolution of the continuous state in H. Before the condition $x \in X_3$, p_1 is still being indicated at the output. When $x \in X_3$, a transition from p_{13} to p_3 is enabled and the output becomes (p_3, σ_1). Hence, $M = K \| H$ can be used to generate the transition system T.

We have shown the construction of a hierarchical system $F = N \| M$. Since N and M accept the same language, every sequence accepted by N would also be accepted by M. Hence, checking reachability of the system can be equivalently performed on the finite, discrete graph. Furthermore, in execution, the architecture guarantees that two different worlds residing in two different layers are synchronized. Between these two worlds, state information at the bottom level is abstracted at the top level and control information at the top level is refined at the bottom level.

4.2   System Realization

We have described the construction of a hierarchical system architecture which promotes proof obligations while conforming with common design practice. Here, we are interested in the realization of the system design. Control laws and decision-making procedures can be considered as the basic components for the construction of the hierarchical system. To realize a system design, component-based design provides a clean way to integrate heterogeneous models by hierarchical nesting of parallel and serial composition of components. A semantics gives meaning to components and their interconnections. A collection of semantics models which are useful for system design have been codified in [12] as *models of computation* (MOCs). Here, we outline some of the most useful MOCs, such as continuous-time (CT), finite-sate machine (FSM), and discrete-event (DE). CT models represented by differential equations are excellent for modeling physical systems. Execution in FSM is a strictly ordered sequence of state transitions and FSM models are amenable to in-depth formal analysis. In DE model, an event consists of a value and a time stamp. There is no global clock tick in DE, but there is a globally consistent notion of time.

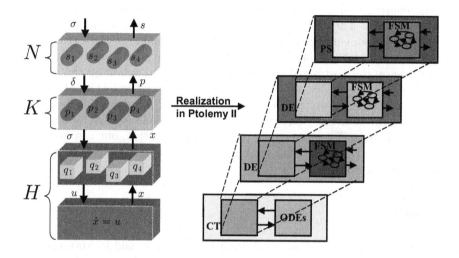

Fig. 6. Hierarchical system architecture for single-agent multi-modal systems and its realization in Ptolemy II [11] by hierarchical aggregating components.

For the proposed hierarchical system architecture for single-vehicle multi-modal systems, we suggest a realization of the system by hierarchical aggregating components such that components are hierarchically refined. As depicted in Figure 6, there are four levels of hierarchy introduced. At each level of hierarchy, a MOC is chosen to govern the interaction between components. The hybrid automaton H is realized by mixing FSM and CT together to exhibit multi-modal behaviors. The interaction between H and K is governed by DE since events consisting of values and time stamps are exchanged between components. The FSM models the abstracted system N which interacts with the detailed system M in DE domain. Since the interaction between N and any component at higher levels is pure asynchronous, a specific MOC such as publisher-subscriber (PS) could be used.

5   Conclusion

In this paper, a hierarchical system architecture for single-agent multi-modal systems has been proposed. The design principle for the construction of the hierarchy is based on bisimulation and therefore a higher-level system and a lower-level system are bisimilar. The layered system is designed to promote proof obligations so that system specification at one level of granularity *conforms* with system specification at another level and vice versa. Hence, it can be guaranteed that the system is correct by construction with respect to a given set of specifications. Our approach is illustrated on designing a system architecture for executing a mission of controlling a single autonomous agent. We have shown that the construction of a transition system and the corresponding quotient transition system. They both capture the reachability properties of the agent within the environment but at different levels of granularity. Furthermore, we have shown that both systems bisimilar. Thus, one can guarantee that for every action made on the abstracted system there is a refined action on the detailed system; for every event occurred on the detailed system there is an abstracted event on the abstracted system. However, for any concurrent game being played by multiple players, one may have to use alternating simulation[3,4] for obtaining a useful abstraction. Therefore, with this simulation notion, one can guarantee that for any game being played at the higher-level there is a corresponding game played at the lower-level.

Acknowledgments

The authors would like to thank G. J. Pappas, H. J. Kim, and R. Majumdar for stimulating discussions and valuable comments. This work is supported by the DARPA SEC grant, F33615-98-C-3614.

References

1. R. Alur and D. Dill. A theory of time automata. *Theoretical Computer Science*, 126:183-235, 1994.
2. R. Alur and T.A. Henzinger. Modularity for timed and hybrid systems. In *Proceedings of the Eighth International Conference on Concurrency Theory (CONCUR)*, pages 74-88, 1997.
3. R. Alur, T.A. Henzinger, O. Kupferman, and M.Y. Vardi. Alternating refinement relations. In *Proceedings of the Tenth International Conference on Concurrency Theory (CONCUR)*, pages 163-178, 1998.
4. L. de Alfaro, T.A. Henzinger, and R. Majumdar. Symbolic algorithms for infinite-state games. In *Proceedings of the 12th International Conference on Concurrency Theory (CONCUR)*, 2001.
5. Datta N. Godbole, John Lygeros, and Shankar S. Sastry. Hierarchical hybrid control: an IVHS case study. In *Proceedings of the 33th IEEE Conference on Decision and Control*, pages 1592-1597, 1994.

6. T.A. Henzinger. Hybrid automaton with finite bisimulstions. In Z. Fülöp and F. Gécseg, editors, *ICALP 95: Automata, Languages, and Programming*, pages 324-335, Springer-Verlag, 1995.

7. J. P. Hespanha, H. J. Kim, and S. Sastry. Multiple-agent probabilistic pursuit-evasion games. In *Proceedings of IEEE Conference on Decision and Control*, pages 2432-2437, Phoenix, Arizona, December 1999.

8. H. J. Kim, R. Vidal, H. Shim, O. Shakernia, and S. Sastry. A hierarchical approach to probabilistic pursuit-evasion games with unmanned ground and aerial vehicles. In *Proceedings of IEEE Conference on Control and Decision*, Orlando, Florida, December 2001.

9. T. J. Koo, G. Pappas, and S.Sastry. Mode switching synthesis for reachability specifications. In M. D. Di Benedetto and A. Sangiovanni-Vincentelli, editors, *Hybrid Systems: Computation and Control*, Lecture Notes in Computer Science, Vol. 2034, pages 333-346, Springer Verlag, 2001.

10. T. J. Koo, B. Sinopoli, A. Sangiovanni-Vincentelli, and S. Sastry. A formal approach to reactive system design: a UAV flight management system design example. In *Proceedings of IEEE International symposium on Computer-Aided Control System Design*, pages 522-7, Kohala Coast, Hawaii, September 1999.

11. E. A. Lee. Overview of the ptolemy project. Technical Report UCB/ERL M01/11, University of California, Berkeley, 2001.

12. E. A. Lee and A. Sangiovanni-Vincentelli. A Framework for Comparing Models of Computation. *IEEE Transactions on Computer-Aided Design of Integrated Circuits and Systems*, 17(12):1217-1229, December 1998.

13. J. Lygeros, C. Tomlin, S. Sastry. Controllers for reachability specifications for hybrid systems, Automatica, Volume 35, Number 3, March 1999.

14. N. Megiddo, S. L. Hakimi, M. R. Garey, D.S. Johnson, and C. H. Papadimitriou. The complexity of searching a graph. *Journal of the ACM*, 35(1):18-44, January 1988.

15. A. Pant, P. Seiler, T. J. Koo, and J. K. Hedrick. Mesh stability of unmanned aerial vehicle clusters. In *Proceedings of American Control Conference*, pages 62-68, Arlington, Virginia, June, 2001.

16. T. D. Parsons. Pursuit-evasion in a graph. In Y. Alani and D. R. Lick, editors, *Theory and Application of Graphs*, pages 426-441, Springer-Verlag, 1976.

17. S. Sastry, G. Meyer, C. Tomlin, J. Lygeros, D. Godbole, and G. Pappas. Hybrid control in air traffic management systems. In *Proceedings of the 1995 IEEE Conference in Decision and Control*, pages 1478-1483, New Orleans, LA, December 1995.

18. M.P. Singh. Multiagent systems. A theoretical framework for intentions, know-how, and communications. Berlin, Germany: Springer-Verlag, 1994.

19. P. Varaiya. Smart Cars on Smart Roads: Problems of Control, *IEEE Transactions on Automatic Control*, 38(2):195-207, February 1993.

20. P. Varaiya. A question about hierarchical systems, *System Theory: Modeling, Analysis and Control*, T. Djaferis and I. Schick (eds), Kluwer, 2000.

Qualitative Modeling and Heterogeneous Control
of Global System Behavior[*]

Benjamin Kuipers[1] and Subramanian Ramamoorthy[2]

[1] Computer Science Department, University of Texas at Austin, Austin, Texas 78712 USA.
kuipers@cs.utexas.edu
[2] Electrical and Computer Engineering Department, University of Texas at Austin,
Austin, Texas 78712, and
National Instruments Corp., 11500 N. Mopac Expwy, Building B,
Austin, Texas 78759 USA.
s.ramamoorthy@ni.com

Abstract. Multiple model approaches to the control of complex dynamical systems are attractive because the local models can be simple and intuitive, and global behavior can be analyzed in terms of transitions among local operating regions. In this paper, we argue that the use of qualitative models further improves the strengths of the multiple model approach by allowing each local model to describe a large class of useful non-linear dynamical systems. In addition, reasoning with qualitative models naturally identifies weak sufficient conditions adequate to prove qualitative properties such as stability. We demonstrate our approach by building a global controller for the free pendulum. We specify and validate local controllers by matching their structures to simple generic qualitative models. This process identifies qualitative constraints on the controller designs, sufficient to guarantee the desired local properties and to determine the possible transitions between local regions. This, in turn, allows the continuous phase portrait to be abstracted to a simple transition graph. The degrees of freedom in the design that are unconstrained by the qualitative description remain available for optimization by the designer for any other purpose.

1 Introduction

Multiple model approaches to the control of complex dynamical systems are attractive because the local models can be simple and intuitive, and global behavior can be analyzed in terms of transitions among local operating regimes [1].

In this paper, we argue that the use of qualitative models further improves the strengths of the multiple model approach by allowing each local model to describe a large class of useful non-linear dynamical systems [2]. In addition, reasoning with qualitative models naturally identifies weak sufficient conditions adequate to prove qualitative properties such as stability. Since a qualitative model only constrains certain aspects

* This work has taken place in the Intelligent Robotics Lab at the Artificial Intelligence Laboratory, The University of Texas at Austin. Research of the Intelligent Robotics lab is supported in part by NSF grants IRI-9504138 and CDA 9617327, and by funding from Tivoli Corporation.

C.J. Tomlin and M.R. Greenstreet (Eds.): HSCC 2002, LNCS 2289, pp. 294–307, 2002.

of a real system, the remaining degrees of freedom are available for optimization according to any criterion the designer chooses.

We use the QSIM framework for representing qualitative differential equations (QDEs) and doing qualitative simulation to predict the set of all possible behaviors of a QDE and initial state [2]. A QDE is a qualitative abstraction of a set of ODEs, in which the domain of each variable is described in terms of a finite, totally ordered set of *landmark values,* and an unknown function may be described in terms of regions of monotonic behavior and tuples of corresponding landmark values it passes through. Qualitative simulation predicts a transition graph of qualitative states guaranteed to describe all solutions to all ODE models consistent with the given QDE. By querying QSIM output with a temporal logic model-checker, we can prove universal statements in temporal logic as theorems about sets of dynamical systems described by the QDE [3].

Because it is consistent with nonlinear models, a simple and intuitive QDE model can cover a larger region of the state space than would be possible for a linear ODE. Because a QDE model can express incomplete knowledge, it can be formulated even when the model is not fully specified, and it can express sufficient conditions for a desired guarantee while leaving other degrees of freedom unspecified. These properties are helpful in abstracting the continuous state space of the system to a compact and useful transition graph.

1.1   Abstraction from Continuous to Discrete States

The discrete transition-graph representation is important for reasoning about large-scale hybrid systems, because it allows the analyst to focus on which large-granularity state the system is in rather than on its detailed dynamics. The representation facilitates analysis of the system using temporal logic and automata theory [4], and building hierarchical representations for knowledge of dynamics [5].

We decompose the state space into a set of regions with disjoint interiors, though boundary points may be shared. To be useful, the description of the dynamical system, restricted to each region, should be significantly simpler than the description of the global system. Each region is then abstracted to a node in the transition-graph model.

A transition from one node to another represents the existence of a trajectory between the corresponding regions through their common boundary in the continuous state space. Consider the set of continuous trajectories with initial states in the region. If all of those trajectories stay within the region, then the abstracted node has no outgoing transitions. If some trajectories cross the region's boundary and pass into other regions, then the abstracted model includes transitions to each of the corresponding nodes.

QSIM predicts all possible behaviors of a system, given a QDE model and a qualitative description of its initial state. Therefore, if the region can be characterized by a qualitative description, and if the dynamical system restricted to that region can be described by a QDE, then qualitative simulation can infer the corresponding transitions.

Qualitative modeling and simulation is not a "magic bullet" for proving properties of arbitrary nonlinear and heterogeneous systems. However, it does provide a much

more expressive language for describing the qualitative and semi-quantitative properties of classes of non-linear dynamical systems, and inferring properties of the sets of
all possible behaviors of those systems. It provides more flexibility and power for a designer to specify intended properties of a dynamical system. It also provides tools for
proving that a qualitatively specified design achieves its desired goals.

1.2   Example: The Free Pendulum

The free pendulum (Figure 1) is a simple but non-trivial non-linear dynamical system.
The task of balancing the pendulum in the upright position is widely used as a textbook
exercise in control, and as a target for machine learning methods that learn dynamical control laws. The inverted pendulum is also an important practical model for tasks
ranging from robot walking to missile launching.

We demonstrate our approach by building a global controller for the free pendulum.
We specify and validate local controllers by matching their structures to simple generic
qualitative models. The qualitative framework of QSIM allows us to generalize simple
familiar systems like the damped harmonic oscillator ("damped spring"), by replacing
linear terms with monotonic functions. Either by using QSIM or analytically (as we
do in this paper), it is not difficult to prove useful qualitative properties of the damped
spring and important variants such as the spring with negative damping.

There is an open-ended set of local models that have desirable properties to be
incorporated into a heterogeneous hybrid model. We explore some simple but useful
examples here. The set of useful transitions among local models is also currently open-
ended, but may turn out in the end to be finite, at least under qualitative description. We
provide some useful examples here, but no suggestion yet about the limits of such a set.

This process identifies qualitative constraints on the controller designs, adequate to
guarantee the desired local properties and to determine the possible transitions between
local regions. This, in turn, allows the continuous phase portrait to be abstracted to a
simple transition graph.

2   Qualitative Properties of Damped Oscillators

Before addressing the pendulum, we need to prove a couple of useful lemmas about the
properties of two generic qualitative models: the spring with damping friction and the
spring with negative damping.

Consider the familiar mass-spring system. The key fact about springs is Hooke's
Law, which says that the restoring force exerted by a spring is proportional to its displacement from its rest position. If x represents the spring's displacement from rest,
then

$$F = ma = m\ddot{x} = -k_1 x.$$

We add a damping friction force to the linear model by adding a term proportional
to $\dot{x}$ and opposite in direction. (Real damping friction is often non-linear.)

$$F = ma = m\ddot{x} = -k_1 x - k_2 \dot{x}.$$

Rearranging and renaming the constants, we get a linear model of the damped spring:

$$\ddot{x} + b\dot{x} + cx = 0. \tag{1}$$

The linear model is easy to solve, but it embodies simplifying assumptions that are often unrealistic. By generalizing linear terms in equation (1) to monotonic functions, and allowing the functions to be described qualitatively rather than specified precisely, we get a model

$$\ddot{x} + f(\dot{x}) + g(x) = 0$$

that encompasses a large number of precise ODE models, including ones that are much more realistic descriptions of the world.

To make qualitative simulation possible, we must restrict our attention to "reasonable" functions, which are defined below along with some useful concepts for expressing qualitative models.

Definition 1. *Where* $[a, b] \subseteq \Re^*$, *the function* $f : [a, b] \rightarrow \Re^*$ *is a* reasonable function *over* $[a, b]$ *if*

1. *f is continuous on $[a, b]$,*
2. *f is continuously differentiable on (a, b),*
3. *f has only finitely many critical points in any bounded interval,*
4. *The one-sided limits $\lim_{t \to a^+} f'(t)$ and $\lim_{t \to b^-} f'(t)$ exist in $\Re^*$. Define $f'(a)$ and $f'(b)$ to be equal to these limits.*

Definition 2. *M^+ is the set of reasonable functions $f : [a, b] \rightarrow \Re^*$ such that $f' > 0$ over (a, b).*

Definition 3. *M_0^+ is the set of $f \in M^+$ such that $f(0) = 0$.*

Definition 4. *$[x]_0 = sign(x) \in \{+, 0, -\}$.*

Here we establish the important qualitative properties of the monotonic "damped spring" model.

Lemma 1. *Let $A \subseteq \Re^2$ include $(0, 0)$ in its interior, and let S be a system governed by the QDE*

$$\ddot{x} + f(\dot{x}) + g(x) = 0 \tag{2}$$

for every $(x, \dot{x}) \in A$, where f and g are reasonable functions such that $f \in M_0^+$ and $[g(x)]_0 = [x]_0$. Then for any trajectory $(x(t), \dot{x}(t))$ of S that lies entirely within A,

$$\lim_{t \to \infty} (x(t), \dot{x}(t)) = (0, 0).$$

Proof: We rewrite equation (2) as

$$\dot{x}_1 = f_1(x_1, x_2) = x_2 \\ \dot{x}_2 = f_2(x_1, x_2) = -f(x_2) - g(x_1) \tag{3}$$

Because g is a reasonable function, we know that $g'(0)$ is defined. Since $[g(x)]_0 = [x]_0$, we conclude that $g(0) = 0$ and $g'(0) > 0$. Any fixed-point of equation (3) must satisfy $\dot{x}_1 = \dot{x}_2 = 0$, which implies that the only fixed point is at $x_1 = x_2 = 0$.

By the stable manifold theorem [6], the qualitative behavior of the nonlinear system (3) around the fixed point at $(0, 0)$ is the same as that of its local linearization:

$$\dot{x}_1 = x_2 \\ \dot{x}_2 = -f'(0)x_2 - g'(0)x_1 \tag{4}$$

The eigenvalues of (4) are

$$\lambda_{1,2} = \frac{1}{2}\left[-f'(0) \pm \sqrt{f'(0)^2 - 4g'(0)} \right].$$

Because $f'(0), g'(0) > 0$, the eigenvalues have negative real parts, so $(0, 0)$ is an asymptotically stable fixed point. When the "friction force" term f' is small relative to the "spring force" term g', the eigenvalues will be complex, in which case $(0, 0)$ will be a spiral attractor.

Because $[g(x)]_0 = [x]_0$, the "spring force" is always a restoring force, so we can define a Lyapunov function

$$V(x, \dot{x}) = \frac{1}{2}\dot{x}^2 + \int_0^x g(x) \, dx \tag{5}$$

and show that $V(x, \dot{x}) \geq 0$, that $V = 0$ only at $(0, 0)$, and that $\frac{d}{dt}V \leq 0$. This means that S is asymptotically stable at $(0, 0)$, and that A can contain no limit cycles.

Together, this tells us that any trajectory $(x(t), \dot{x}(t))$ that enters A eventually terminates at $(0, 0)$, for any reasonable functions f and g such that $f \in M_0^+$ and $[g(x)]_0 = [x]_0$.   □

Now we establish similar properties for another monotonic generalization of the "damped spring", but with negative damping.

Lemma 2. *Let $A \subseteq \Re^2$ include $(0, 0)$ in its interior, and let S be a system governed by the QDE*

$$\ddot{x} - f(\dot{x}) + g(x) = 0 \tag{6}$$

for every $(x, \dot{x}) \in A$, where f and g are reasonable functions such that $f \in M_0^+$ and $[g(x)]_0 = [x]_0$. Then $(0, 0)$ is the only fixed point of S in A, and it is unstable. Furthermore, A cannot contain a limit cycle.

Proof: The proof of this Lemma is very similar to the previous one. We rewrite equation (6) as

$$\dot{x}_1 = f_1(x_1, x_2) = x_2 \\ \dot{x}_2 = f_2(x_1, x_2) = f(x_2) - g(x_1) \tag{7}$$

As before, because g is a reasonable function, we know that $g'(0)$ is defined. Since $[g(x)]_0 = [x]_0$, we conclude that $g(0) = 0$ and $g'(0) > 0$.

Any fixed-point of equation (7) must satisfy $\dot{x}_1 = \dot{x}_2 = 0$, so the only fixed point is at $x_1 = x_2 = 0$.

As before, the qualitative behavior of the nonlinear system (7) around the fixed point at $(0, 0)$ is the same as that of its local linearization:

$$\begin{aligned} \dot{x}_1 &= x_2 \\ \dot{x}_2 &= f'(0)x_2 - g'(0)x_1 \end{aligned} \tag{8}$$

The eigenvalues of (8) are

$$\lambda_{1,2} = \frac{1}{2}\left[f'(0) \pm \sqrt{f'(0)^2 - 4g'(0)} \right].$$

In this case, since $f'(0) > 0$, the eigenvalues have positive real parts, and $(0, 0)$ is an unstable fixed point. If the "friction force" term f' is small relative to the "spring force" term g', then the eigenvalues will be complex, so $(0, 0)$ will be a spiral repellor.

By the Bendixon negative criterion [6], there can be no periodic orbits contained in A because

$$\frac{\partial f_1}{\partial x_1} + \frac{\partial f_2}{\partial x_2} = f'(x_2)$$

is always positive over A. That is, A cannot contain a limit cycle.

Therefore, except for the unstable fixed-point at $(0, 0)$ itself, any trajectory $(x(t), \dot{x}(t))$ that starts in A, eventually leaves A, for any reasonable functions f and g such that $f \in M_0^+$ and $[g(x)]_0 = [x]_0$. □

In this context, like that of Lemma 1, we can interpret $V(x, \dot{x})$ from equation (5) as representing the total energy of the system, but here we can show that energy is increasing steadily except at isolated points.

2.1 Proof by Qualitative Simulation

These Lemmas establishing the properties of the monotonic spring models were proved by hand to make this paper self-contained, and because these models are generic and useful.

It is also possible to generate proofs of these and similar statements automatically from the QSIM QDE models. The Guaranteed Coverage Theorem states that every real behavior of every model described by the QDE is predicted by QSIM [7,2]. Then we can use a temporal logic model-checker to establish whether the predicted behavior tree is a model of a specified statement in temporal logic. For universal statements, the completeness of the model-checker and QSIM Guaranteed Coverage combine to show that a positive response from the model-checker implies that the temporal logic statement is a theorem for all behaviors of all dynamical systems consistent with the given QDE [3].

This method of deriving the necessary lemmas using QSIM makes it possible to generalize this approach to more complex models as in [8].

3   A Controller for the Pendulum

By appealing to the qualitative properties of solutions to these very general models, we can give a simple and natural derivation for a controller for the pendulum, able to pump it up and stabilize it in the inverted position.

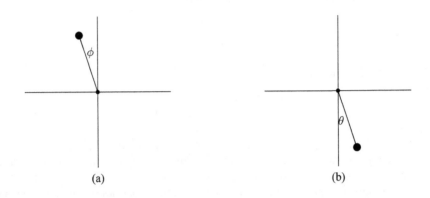

(a)   (b)

Fig. 1. Local models of the pendulum (where $\phi = \theta - \pi$): (a) $\phi = 0$ at the unstable fixed-point, and (b) $\theta = 0$ at the stable fixed-point.

3.1   Stabilizing the Inverted Pendulum

The pendulum is a mass on a rigid, massless rod, attached to a fixed pivot. The variable ϕ measures the angular position counter-clockwise from the vertical (Figure 1(a)). We consider only $\phi \in (-\pi/2, +\pi/2)$.[1]

The angular acceleration due to gravity is $k \sin \phi$, and there is a small amount of damping friction $-f(\dot{\phi})$, where $f \in M_0^+$. A control action $u(\phi, \dot{\phi})$ exerts angular acceleration at the pivot. The resulting model of the pendulum is:

$$\ddot{\phi} + f(\dot{\phi}) - k \sin \phi + u(\phi, \dot{\phi}) = 0. \tag{9}$$

Our goal is to design $u(\phi, \dot{\phi})$ so that the system is asymptotically stable at $(\phi, \dot{\phi}) = (0, 0)$.

Lemma 1 provides a simple sufficient condition: make the pendulum behave like a monotonic damped spring. We define the controller for the **Balance** region to be:

$$u(\phi, \dot{\phi}) = g(\phi) \text{ such that } [g(\phi) - k \sin \phi]_0 = [\phi]_0. \tag{10}$$

Since $k \sin \phi$ increases monotonically with ϕ over $(-\pi/2, +\pi/2)$, $g(\phi)$ must increase at least as fast in order to ensure that $[g(\phi) - k \sin \phi]_0 = [\phi]_0$.

---

[1] The derivation here applies over the larger interval $(-\pi, +\pi)$, but the maximum control force is required at $\phi = \pm\pi/2$. The controller design problem is less interesting if the controller is powerful enough to lift the pendulum directly to $\phi = 0$ from any value of ϕ.

We can get faster convergence by augmenting the natural damping $f(\dot{\phi})$ with a damping term $h(\dot{\phi})$ included in the control law, giving us

$$u(\phi, \dot{\phi}) = g(\phi) + h(\dot{\phi}) \text{ where } [g(\phi) - k \sin \phi]_0 = [\phi]_0 \text{ and } h \in M_0^+(\dot{\phi}). \quad (11)$$

If there is a bound u_{max} on the control action u, then the limiting angle ϕ_{max} beyond which the controller cannot restore the pendulum to $\phi = 0$ is given by the constraint

$$u_{max} = k \sin \phi_{max}. \quad (12)$$

The maximum velocity $\dot{\phi}_{max}$ that the **Balance** controller can tolerate at $\phi = 0$ is then determined by the constraint

$$\frac{1}{2}\dot{\phi}_{max}^2 = \int_0^{\phi_{max}} g(\phi) - k \sin \phi \, d\phi \quad (13)$$

which represents the conversion of the kinetic energy of the system (9) at $(0, \dot{\phi}_{max})$ into potential energy at $(\phi_{max}, 0)$.

Therefore, we define the region of applicability for the **Balance** controller by the ellipse

$$\frac{\phi^2}{\phi_{max}^2} + \frac{\dot{\phi}^2}{\dot{\phi}_{max}^2} \leq 1. \quad (14)$$

Note that the shapes of the non-linear functions g and h are only very weakly constrained. The qualitative constraints in (11) provide weak sufficient conditions guaranteeing the stability of the inverted pendulum controller. However, there is plenty of freedom available to the designer to select the properties of g and h to optimize any desired criterion.

3.2 Pumping Up the Hanging Pendulum

With no input, the stable state of the pendulum is hanging straight down. We use the variable θ to measure the angular position counter-clockwise from straight down (Figure 1(b)). The goal is to pump energy into the pendulum, swinging it progressively higher, until it reaches the region where the inverted pendulum controller can balance it in the upright position.

Angular acceleration due to gravity is $-k \sin \theta$. As before, damping friction is $-f(\dot{\theta})$, where $f \in M_0^+$, and the control action exerts an angular acceleration $u(\theta, \dot{\theta})$ at the pivot. The resulting model of our system is:

$$\ddot{\theta} + f(\dot{\theta}) + k \sin \theta + u(\theta, \dot{\theta}) = 0. \quad (15)$$

Without control action, since $[\sin \theta]_0 = [\theta]_0$ over $-\pi < \theta < \pi$, the model exactly matches the monotonic damped spring model of Lemma 1, so we know that it is asymptotically stable at $(\theta, \dot{\theta}) = (0, 0)$. Unfortunately, this is not where we want it.

Fortunately, Lemma 2 gives us a sufficient condition to transform the stable attractor at $(0, 0)$ into an unstable repellor. We define the controller for the **Pump** region so that the system is modeled by a spring with negative damping, pumping energy into the system. That is, define

$$u(\theta, \dot{\theta}) = -h(\dot{\theta}) \text{ such that } h - f \in M_0^+ \qquad (16)$$

Starting with any perturbation from $(0, 0)$, this controller will pump the pendulum to higher and higher swings. Lemma 2 is sufficient to assure us that there are no limit cycles in the region $-\pi < \theta < \pi$ to prevent the trajectory from approaching $\theta = \pi$ so the **Balance** control law can stabilize it in the inverted position.

3.3   The Spinning Pendulum

The **Spin** region represents the behavioral mode of the pendulum when it is spinning freely at high speed. In the **Spin** region, a simple qualitative controller augments the natural friction of the system with additional damping, to slow the system down toward the two other regions.

$$u(\theta, \dot{\theta}) = f_2(\dot{\theta}) \text{ such that } f_2 \in M_0^+. \qquad (17)$$

3.4   Bounding the Pump and Spin Regions

One might ask whether the **Pump** controller could be so aggressive that the pendulum would overshoot the **Balance** region entirely. Even with augmented damping by the **Spin** controller, it might be possible to get a limit cycle that alternates between the **Pump** and **Spin** regions. (While the analogy is not perfect, this is one aspect of how the van der Pol oscillator works.)

We can avoid this problem by defining a suitable boundary between the **Pump** and **Spin** regions, and showing that the **Pump** and **Spin** controllers together define a sliding mode controller [9], forcing nearby trajectories to converge to the boundary.

A boundary with the desired properties is the separatrix of the same pendulum,

$$\ddot{\theta} + k \sin \theta = 0 \qquad (18)$$

without damping friction or control action. It turns out that this boundary will lead straight into the heart of the **Balance** region (Figure 2).

A *separatrix* is a trajectory that starts at an unstable fixed-point of the system and ends at another fixed-point. In the case of the pendulum, the separatrices are the trajectories where the pendulum starts upright and at rest, then swings around once and returns to the upright position, at rest. It is the locus of points $(\theta, \dot{\theta})$ such that the total energy of the system is exactly equal to the potential energy of the motionless pendulum in the upright position.

$$KE + PE = \frac{1}{2}\dot{\theta}^2 + \int_0^\theta k \sin \theta \, d\theta = 2k$$

Evaluating the integral and simplifying, we get an equation $s(\theta, \dot{\theta}) = 0$ that defines the separatrix, i.e., the boundary between **Spin** ($s > 0$) and **Pump** ($s < 0$).

$$s(\theta, \dot{\theta}) = \frac{1}{2}\dot{\theta}^2 - k(1 + \cos \theta) = 0. \qquad (19)$$

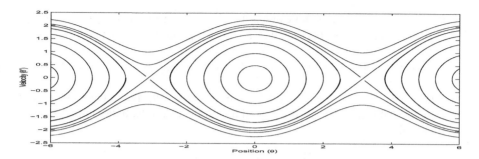

Fig. 2. The $(\theta, \dot{\theta})$ phase portrait of the undamped pendulum. The **Balance** region is an ellipse around the saddle point at $(\pi, 0)$. The **Pump** region is contained within the separatrices, and the **Spin** region is outside the separatrices.

We use the method for defining a sliding mode controller from [9] to ensure that trajectories always approach $s = 0$.

Differentiating (19) and substituting for $\ddot{\theta}$, we get:

$$\dot{s} = \dot{\theta} \, \ddot{\theta} + k \sin \theta \, \dot{\theta}$$
$$= \dot{\theta} \left(-f(\dot{\theta}) - k \sin \theta - u(\theta, \dot{\theta})\right) + k \sin \theta \, \dot{\theta}$$
$$= -\dot{\theta} f(\dot{\theta}) - \dot{\theta} \, u(\theta, \dot{\theta})$$

Now, examine the **Pump** region, inside the separatrix where $s < 0$, and substitute the **Pump** control law (16) for $u(\theta, \dot{\theta})$.

$$\dot{s}_{pump} = -\dot{\theta} f(\dot{\theta}) + \dot{\theta} \, h(\dot{\theta}) \text{ where } h - f \in M_0^+$$
$$= \dot{\theta} \, (h - f)(\dot{\theta})$$
$$\geq 0$$

Similarly, for the **Spin** region where $s > 0$, substituting its control law (17).

$$\dot{s}_{spin} = -\dot{\theta} f(\dot{\theta}) - \dot{\theta} f_2(\dot{\theta}) \text{ where } f_2 \in M_0^+$$
$$= -\dot{\theta}(f + f_2)(\dot{\theta})$$
$$\leq 0$$

This shows that the **Pump** control law moves the system toward the separatrix from the inside, and the **Spin** control law approaches the separatrix from the outside: the existing control laws define a sliding mode controller with the separatrix $s = 0$ as the attractor. Once the system gets sufficiently close to the boundary, it will follow the separatrix, directly into the **Balance** region. In particular, it is impossible for an aggressive **Pump** controller to overshoot the **Balance** region.

3.5   Heterogeneous Control of the Free Pendulum

We have derived local control laws for the three relevant regions. The region definition for **Balance** takes priority over the defining relations for **Pump** or **Spin**.

- **Balance**: $(\phi, \dot\phi) \approx (0, 0)$, more precisely $\phi^2/\phi^2_{max} + \dot\phi^2/\dot\phi^2_{max} \leq 1$ from equation (14). Stabilize the unstable saddle by adding a "spring-like" attractive force:

$$u(\phi, \dot\phi) = g(\phi) + h(\dot\phi) \text{ such that } [g(\phi) - k\sin\phi]_0 = [\phi]_0 \text{ and } h \in M_0^+(\dot\phi).$$

- **Pump**: $s(\theta, \dot\theta) < 0$, where s is defined in equation (19). Pump the system away from the stable attractor at $(0, 0)$ by adding to the controller a destabilizing "anti-frictional" force:

$$u(\theta, \dot\theta) = -h(\dot\theta) \text{ such that } h - f \in M_0^+.$$

- **Spin**: $s(\theta, \dot\theta) > 0$, where s is defined in equation (19). Slow down a quickly spinning pendulum by augmenting the (small) natural friction of the system with a "friction-like" damping control:

$$u(\theta, \dot\theta) = f_2(\dot\theta) \text{ such that } f_2 \in M_0^+.$$

We have shown that the qualitative constraints associated with each local law are sufficient to guarantee that its local performance is as desired. We need to demonstrate that the continuous behavior of the controlled pendulum can be abstracted to the discrete transition model consisting of the operating regions of the controller.

$$\textbf{Pump} \quad \nrightarrow \quad \textbf{Spin}$$
$$\searrow \qquad \swarrow$$
$$\textbf{Balance}$$

- **Pump $\nrightarrow$ Spin**. Since the boundary $s = 0$ between **Pump** and **Spin** is the attractor for a sliding mode controller, in theory no trajectory can cross from one side of the boundary to the other. In practice, the trajectory will "chatter" around the boundary. The boundary can be made fuzzy to eliminate discontinuous changes in control action, but in any case, the trajectory can be kept very close to the boundary [9].
- **Pump $\rightarrow$ Balance**. The discussion in section 3.4 shows that $s(\theta, \dot\theta)$ increases throughout **Pump**. Therefore, the maximum amplitude θ_{max} of the pendulum's swings, where $\dot\theta = 0$, must increase. Since these values are determined by $s = -k(1 + \cos\theta_{max})$, the value of θ_{max} must increase in absolute value, toward $\pm\pi$. Lemma 2 says that **Pump** contains no fixed point or limit cycle. Therefore, eventually the extremal point $(\theta_{max}, 0)$ will lie within the region of applicability of the **Balance** controller (14), which will capture the trajectory, bringing it to the fixed point at $(\theta, \dot\theta) = (\pi, 0)$ (i.e., $(\phi, \dot\phi) = (0, 0)$).
- **Spin $\rightarrow$ Balance**. Similarly, we have shown that $s(\theta, \dot\theta)$ decreases throughout **Spin**. Therefore, the minimum velocity $\dot\theta_{min}$, which occurs where $\theta = \pi$ (i.e., $\phi = 0$), must also decrease in absolute value. The extremal point $(\pi, \dot\theta_{min})$ will eventually fall within the region of applicability of the **Balance** controller (14), which will capture the trajectory and bring it to the desired fixed-point.
- **Balance**. Lemma 1 guarantees that, once the system's trajectory enters **Balance**, it cannot leave. Therefore, there are no outgoing transitions from the **Balance** region.

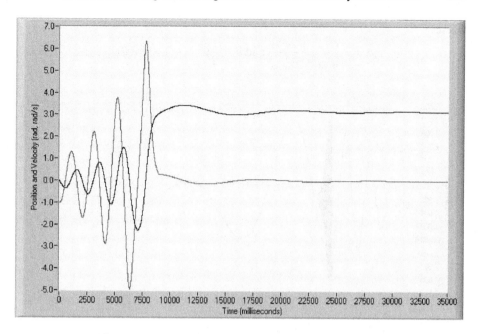

Fig. 3. $\theta(t)$ and $\dot{\theta}(t)$ as the heterogeneous controller pumps a weakly-powered pendulum from $\theta = 0$ to $\theta = \pi$.

Figure 3 shows an example behavior as a very weak controller pumps the pendulum up from $\theta = 0$ and balances it at $\phi = 0$. We define an instance of the pendulum model and the local control laws:

$$\textbf{Plant}: \quad \ddot{\theta} + c\dot{\theta} + k\sin\theta + u(\theta, \dot{\theta}) = 0 \quad c = 0.01 \quad k = 10 \quad u_{max} = 4$$
$$\textbf{Balance}: u = (c_{11} + k)(\theta - \pi) + c_{12}\dot{\theta} \quad c_{11} = 0.4 \; c_{12} = 0.3$$
$$\textbf{Spin}: \quad u = c_2\dot{\theta} \qquad\qquad\qquad\quad c_2 = 0.5$$
$$\textbf{Pump}: \quad u = -(c + c_3)\dot{\theta} \qquad\qquad\;\; c_3 = 0.5$$

The plant model is chosen with normal gravity, slight friction, and a maximum control action too weak to lift the pendulum directly up. The local control laws are all linear for simplicity, though they could be designed to be nonlinear. The controllers are defined so that the desired behavior is guaranteed as long as the parameters c_i are all positive. The specific values for the c_i are chosen to ensure that $u < u_{max}$.

Given the maximum control action u_{max} and the gain $c_{11} + k$ of the **Balance** controller, we can determine the bounds $\phi_{max} = 0.4$ and $\dot{\phi}_{max} = 0.3$ for the **Balance** region from equations (12) and (13), respectively. We define the switching strategy to be

If $\alpha \le 1$ then **Balance**
else if $s < 0$ then **Pump**
else **Spin**

where

$$\alpha = \frac{\phi^2}{\phi_{max}^2} + \frac{\dot{\phi}^2}{\dot{\phi}_{max}^2} \text{ and } s = \frac{1}{2}\dot{\theta}^2 - k(1 + \cos\theta).$$

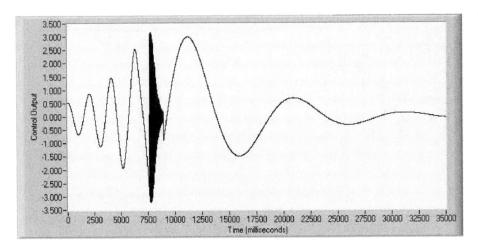

Fig. 4. The control action $u(t)$ shows chattering along the sliding mode.

Because of the sharp transitions among regions, the control action $u(t)$ "chatters" back and forth across the **Spin-Balance** interface (Figure 4). A "dead zone" along the boundary where $u = 0$ produces a virtually identical behavior, but without chatter in the control action. Fuzzy boundaries would presumably have the same effect.

4   Discussion

4.1   Regions with Fuzzy Boundaries

In some cases, it is convenient to have local models and corresponding regions that overlap, or have gradual rather than sharp boundaries. Such regions can be described by fuzzy set membership functions. In the simplest case, the continuous state space can be decomposed into *pure* regions, where only one membership function is non-zero, and *overlap* regions, where two (or perhaps a small finite number of) regions have non-zero membership functions. The dynamical system in an overlap region is the weighted average of the overlapping local models, weighted by the values of the membership functions.

The qualitative QDE formalism is particularly useful for representing overlap regions, since not only the local models, but even more, the shapes of the membership functions in the overlap region may be only partially known or specified. QSIM can establish which properties of the local models, and of the overlapping membership functions, are sufficient to guarantee that trajectories through an overlap region can be abstracted to a transition from one pure region to another. Kuipers and Åström [8] demonstrated this for controllers for a simple water tank and for a highly nonlinear chemical reaction.

4.2   Feedback Linearization

Feedback linearization [10] designs a control law for a system to add a term compensating for the non-linearities in the system, making the sum linear and therefore suitable for well-understood control methods. The problem is that this approach demands precise knowledge of the nonlinear system.

In our qualitative method, we make the much weaker requirement that the sum of the nonlinear system and the controller be monotonic. This may be achievable even with incomplete knowledge of the original system, for example with bounding envelopes around unknown functions. Incomplete knowledge in this form will reduce the remaining degrees of freedom available for optimization, but it will not affect the qualitative guarantee of stability.

4.3   Conclusions

By using qualitative models, we make it possible to express incomplete knowledge of the dynamics of the uncontrolled plant, and to separate the properties of the controller needed to provide qualitative guarantees from the remaining degrees of freedom that can be used for optimization. Qualitative models can also express natural nonlinear models, allowing the use of larger and more natural local models in a multiple-model framework. Furthermore, QSIM can be used to prove the necessary properties of generic qualitative models, or of the specific models that describe the controlled system. These features are illustrated by the design of a heterogeneous controller for the free pendulum.

References

1. Murray-Smith, R., Johansen, T.A.: Multiple Model Approaches to Modelling and Control. Taylor and Francis, UK (1997)
2. Kuipers, B.J.: Qualitative Reasoning: Modeling and Simulation with Incomplete Knowledge. MIT Press, Cambridge, MA (1994)
3. Shults, B., Kuipers, B.: Proving properties of continuous systems: qualitative simulation and temporal logic. Artificial Intelligence **92** (1997) 91–129
4. Alur, R., Courcoubetis, C., Halbwachs, N., Henzinger, T.A., Ho, P.H., Nicollin, X., Olivero, A., Sifakis, J., Yovine, S.: The algorithmic analysis of hybrid systems. Theoretical Computer Science **138** (1995) 3–34
5. Varaiya, P.: A question about hierarchical systems. In Djaferis, T., Schick, I., eds.: System Theory: Modeling, Analysis and Control. Kluwer (2000)
6. Guckenheimer, J., Holmes, P.: Nonlinear Oscillations, Dynamical Systems, and Bifurcations of Vector Fields. Springer-Verlag, Berlin (1983)
7. Kuipers, B.: Qualitative simulation. Artificial Intelligence **29** (1986) 289–338
8. Kuipers, B.J., Åström, K.: The composition and validation of heterogeneous control laws. Automatica **30** (1994) 233–249
9. Slotine, J.J., Li, W.: Applied Nonlinear Control. Prentice Hall, Englewood Cliffs NJ (1991)
10. Friedland, B.: Advanced Control System Design. Prentice-Hall (1996)

An Approach to Model-Based Diagnosis of Hybrid Systems

Sriram Narasimhan and Gautam Biswas

Vanderbilt University
Department of Electrical Engineering and Computer Science
Box 1679, Station B
Nashville, TN 37235.
{nsriram, biswas}@vuse.vanderbilt.edu

Abstract. The need for reliability and robustness in present day systems requires that they possess the capability for accommodating faults in the controlled plant. Fault accommodation requires tight integration of online fault detection, isolation, and identification with the system control loop. This paper develops an effective fault diagnosis scheme for plants that mainly exhibit continuous behavior, but include supervisory control making the overall dynamic behavior hybrid in nature. We use hybrid bond graph models to develop diagnosis algorithms that combine hybrid behavior tracking, mode estimation, and qualitative-quantitative reasoning techniques. The effectiveness of the approach is demonstrated with example scenarios generated from a three- and five-tank systems with control valves and sources that can be turned on and off by supervisory control.

1   Introduction

The need for reliability and robustness in present day complex systems requires that they possess the capability for accommodating faults in the controlled plant. Fault accommodation combines fault detection, isolation, and identification [1] with the determination of appropriate control actions to mitigate the effect of the faults and help maintain nominal system operation. The fault diagnosis task must be performed on line, and has to be tightly integrated with the system control loop. This motivates online model-based approaches to diagnosis that provide sufficient information for fault adaptations by the supervisory controller.

Aircraft subsystems, chemical processes, and manufacturing plants combine continuous dynamics with discrete supervisory control. Therefore, overall system behavior is necessarily *hybrid.*Discrete changes in the system can be attributed to supervisory controller input (*controlled jumps*) and changes defined by internal variables crossing threshold values (*autonomous jumps*)[1]. Fig. 1(a) presents a simple example of such a system: three tanks with flow sources, connecting

---

[1] Autonomous jumps are often attributed to modeling simplifications introduced to avoid complex non-linearities in system behavior [9].

C.J. Tomlin and M.R. Greenstreet (Eds.): HSCC 2002, LNCS 2289, pp. 308–322, 2002.

pipes, and outlet pipes. The valves on all the pipes and sources are commanded by signals from the supervisory controller. The upper connecting pipes between the tanks become active only when the fluid levels reach pre-defined heights. They represent autonomous transitions.

Model-based diagnosis starts with a framework that links system behavior to system components and parameters. Most real systems are equipped with a limited number of sensors to track system behavior, and analytic redundancy methods have to be applied to derive non-local interaction between potential faults and observations. These techniques have been applied to a variety of schemes used in the diagnosis of discrete [2], discrete event [3] and continuous systems [1,4,5]. They have also been applied to hybrid system diagnosis, using a single continuous model with complex non-linearities, or abstracting the continuous dynamics to a discrete event model. Complex nonlinearities complicate the analysis and they may introduce numerical convergence problems. Discrete event abstractions lead to loss of critical information, such as fault transient characteristics. Further, methods to identify the set of events that describe both nominal and faulty behavior is often a computationally challenging task bringing to question the scalability of such approaches [6]. Hybrid system analyses require the use of multiple models of the system. As a result, appropriate model selection and switching has to be performed at run time to execute tasks like simulation, monitoring, control, and fault isolation. This paper discusses a model-based diagnosis

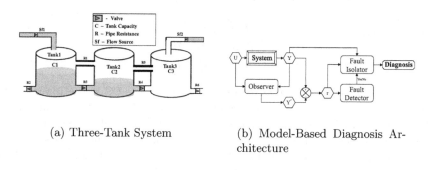

(a) Three-Tank System   (b) Model-Based Diagnosis Architecture

Fig. 1.

methodology for hybrid systems that builds on our previous work in continuous system diagnosis [5]. Since the overall goal is fault accommodation, the diagnosis algorithm has to be:(i) online, (ii) employ analytic redundancy methods since the number of sensors are small, (iii) based on analysis of fault transients so that faults can be quickly isolated and identified.

2   The Hybrid Diagnosis System

A complete diagnosis scheme for the type of systems displayed in Fig. 1(a) must consider faults in the plant and the supervisory controller. A faulty controller issues commands that are in conflict with the desired functionality. We do not deal with these faults in this paper, and make the assumption that the controller has no faults. A lot of work in the FDI community has dealt with fault isolation filter design using structured and directional residual methods that mainly apply to additive faults [1]. When dealing with multiplicative faults (e.g., changes in the plant parameters) that affect the dynamic response of the system, researchers have resorted to parameter estimation techniques that are often computationally complex and hard to implement online. Our focus in this paper is on plant component faults. We assume that these faults can be parameterized, and a fault is represented as a persistent step change in a plant parameter value. In dynamic systems, a step change in a parameter value causes a *transient response* that is superimposed on the nominal plant dynamics. In previous work, we have developed qualitative schemes to characterize and analyze these transients to solve the fault isolation problem in a way that mitigates some of the problems of the numerical schemes [5,11]. We extend these schemes for continuous diagnosis to address the more complex problem of hybrid diagnosis.

We restrict ourselves to systems whose models can be described as piecewise linear hybrid dynamical models. These models are sufficient to describe a large class of engineered systems [6]. The discrete time state space parameterized model of a hybrid system is given by

$$x(t+1) = A_{q(t)}(P)x(t) + B_{q(t)}(P)u(t)$$
$$q(t+1) = \delta(q(t), \pi(x(t)), \sigma(t))$$
$$y(t) = C_{q(t)}(P)x(t) + D_{q(t)}(P)u(t),$$

where $x(t) \in R^n$ is the state vector of the plant, $u(t) \in R^m$ is the input to the plant, and $q(t) \in I$ is the discrete mode that can take on a finite number of values. The system matrices A, B, C, and D are functions of the physical plant parameters, P. For such systems it has been shown that the state space can be divided into polyhedral regions, where each region corresponds to a mode of system operation [6].

In our work, we are interested in diagnosing *step changes* in a single deviated parameter $p_i \in P$. Our model-based approach (Fig. 1(b)) uses a *hybrid observer* to track nominal system behavior, a fault detection mechanism, and a fault isolation and identification unit. The observer uses a quantitative hybrid model of the plant to follow a hybrid trajectory. The mode of operation, q, and the continuous state vector in that mode, x defines the system state. Mode changes are defined by controlled and autonomous changes. For controlled transitions, it is assumed that the controller signals are input to the diagnosis system. Autonomous changes are defined by events that are functions of system variables. Mode identification is complicated by measurement noise and imperfections in the system models. The resulting inaccuracies and delay in the observer can affect the accuracy and precision in predicting autonomous transitions. Mode transitions require computation of the new mode of system operation, and the initial state in the new mode using the *reset* function. We have adopted a combination of a hybrid automata and Kalman filtering approach to design our *hybrid observer* [7]. Small differences, attributed to minor imperfections in the model and noise in the measurements, are compensated for in the observer mechanism. When the differences become significant, the *fault detection unit* signals the presence of a fault, and this triggers the *fault isolation unit*, which generates candidate faults and refines them by analyzing subsequent measurements from the system.

3   Modeling Hybrid Systems

Our approach to modeling hybrid systems is based on an extended form of bond graphs [8], called *Hybrid Bond Graphs* (HBG). Bond graphs present a methodology for energetic modeling of physical systems. A bond graph is made up of capacitors and inertias, dissipative elements, and ideal sources of effort and flow, (ii) 0− *and* 1− *junctions* (correspond to parallel and series connections, respectively) that define the interconnectivity between components, and (iii) *bonds* that represent the energy transfer pathways in the system. System behavior is based on component characteristics and the principles of continuity and conservation of energy that are imposed by the junction relations. Extensions to hybrid systems require the introduction of discrete changes into the model configuration. In the HBG framework, discontinuities in behavior are dealt with at a *meta-model* level, where the energy model embodied in the bond graph scheme is frozen for a time instant, and discontinuous model configuration changes are executed as instantaneous junction switching. The switched junctions act as idealized switches that turn energy connections on and off, and do not violate the physical principles of energy conservation [9]. Hybrid Bond Graphs can be formally defined as:

$$HBG = \{BG, M\}, \tag{1}$$

where BG is a continuous bond graph model, $M = \{M_1, M_2, \ldots M_k\}$, are a set of finite state machines, with each $M_i \in M$ being assigned to a switched junction of the HBG. Each finite state machine M_i is formally defined as:

$M = (Q, \sum, \delta, \mu, q_0)$
$Q = \{q_1, q_2, \ldots, q_n\}$ is the finite set of states
$\sum = \sum_c \bigcup \sum_a$ is the set of discrete events,
$\sum_c$ is the finite set of controller events,
$\sum_a : \{f_a(x) > 0\}$, where x is the continuous state vector,
$\delta : Q \times \sum \to Q$ is the transition function,
$\mu : Q \to \{on, off\}$ is the output function, and
$q_0 \in Q$ is the initial state.

A system mode transition occurs when one or more automata M_i undergo a state transition. The sequence of transitions establish the *on/off* state of all the individual switched junctions, and defines a new mode q for the system. The switching conditions are specified so that each combination of junction states correspond to a polyhedron in the state space. If only one automata triggers at a point in time, each polyhedron is adjacent to at most n polyhedra, where n is the number of switched junctions. After the discrete mode transition, system behavior evolution is again continuous till another point in time when a M_i changes state. Assigning individual automata to each switched junction provides a compact representation of the system model across all its nominal modes of operation.

Fig. 2 represents the HBG model of the three-tank system (Fig. 1(a)). The three tanks are modeled as capacitors, and the pipes are modeled as simple resistances. Some junction states are determined by controlled signals. Others, such as junction 4 and 6, whose on-off transitions depend on the height of the liquid column, are autonomous. Hybrid automata models (e.g., [10]), traditional

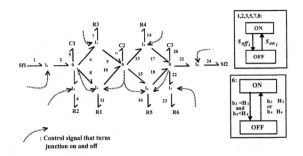

Fig. 2. Hybrid Bond Graph Model of Three-Tank System

computational models used in hybrid systems community are easily derived from HBG models of a system. Typically a linear hybrid automaton is defined as:

$$A = (X, V, flow, inv, init, E, jump, \Sigma, syn),$$

where X is the real-valued state vector, V is the finite set of system modes, *flow* describes the equations governing X in each mode, *inv* assigns an invariant condition to each mode, and *init* assigns initial conditions to each mode (a mode is initiated if and only if it's initial conditions are true), E describes a finite set of mode switches represented as a directed edge between two modes, *jump* represents the change in values of X after a mode switch, Σ describes the finite set of events, and *syn* assigns an event to each mode switch.

The hybrid automata model A is easily derived from a HBG model by setting $X = \{$a subset of effort and flow variables in the bond graph $BG\}$, $V = \{\mu(M_1), \mu(M_2), \dots, \mu(M_k)\}$, where (μ) takes on two values *on/off* as described earlier. Hence the automata has a total of 2^k modes. For each mode, *flow* can be obtained by deriving the bond graph for that mode and then deriving the state space equations from the bond graph. $inv = !\Sigma$. Events Σ force transitions in the FSM's, and hence the system can stay in a mode only when these events do not occur. $init = \Phi$. $E = \bigcup \delta(M_i) \forall M_i \in M$. $jump = previous(X)$. There is no change to the state as a result of a mode change. $\Sigma = \bigcup \Sigma(M_i) \forall M_i \in HBG$. $syn = \bigcup \delta(M_i) \forall M_i \in M$.

We use the HBG models of our hybrid system to derive hybrid automata models for the system. Within each state of the automata (i.e., mode of the system). we can derive (i) state space equations, (ii) temporal causal graphs, and input output equations from the corresponding BG model. Each of these models are employed for different tasks in our diagnosis engine.

4   Fault Isolation

In previous work, we have developed a qualitative reasoning scheme based on the analyses of *transients* caused by step changes in parameter values for fault isolation in continuous systems [5]. This methodology uses a framework developed by AI researchers, where the fault isolation task is broken into two parts: (i) *hypothesis generation* and (ii) *hypothesis refinement*. The hypothesis refinement algorithm uses a progressive monitoring technique that we describe in more detail later. Qualitative reasoning schemes provide efficient means for initial hypotheses generation and refinement, but lack precision for fault identification. To overcome this problem, we combine qualitative reasoning with least squares based parameter estimation techniques for fault isolation and identification [11].

The fault isolation task in hybrid systems is complex because the discrete mode transitions cause changes in the model and may cause discrete changes in variable values. The residual analysis scheme must, therefore, include mode identification techniques to achieve correct fault isolation. However, the occurrence of a fault invalidates the system model and, therefore, the mapping between the state space and the measured variables. Hence the state estimates made by the observer may no longer be correct. Abrupt faults (i.e., step changes) may produce a discontinuous jump in the values of the state and output variables. This abrupt change may result in a sudden transition from one mode to another. For example, an abrupt decrease in the capacitance of tank 1 (Fig. 1(a)) (caused by an object falling into the tank) would cause a sudden discontinuous increase in the pressure. The increase may render pipe R1 to become active changing the system mode, and therefore, the system model. In addition, the polyhedral boundary region definitions are functions of system parameter values. A fault, i.e., a change in a parameter value, can, therefore, cause a change in the polyhedral partition of the state space. Therefore, autonomous mode transitions may no longer be correctly predicted after the occurrence of a fault. Therefore, designing of fault observers becomes a nontrivial task. In our work, we mitigate this problem to some extent by using qualitative tracking schemes.

A second problem with hybrid fault isolation is that the fault may be detected only after mode transitions have occurred. Therefore, the current system model does not provide the right set of constraints for initial hypothesis generation. To solve this problem, one has to introduce a fast *roll back* process to determine the possible modes in which the fault could have occurred. Solving the fault isolation problem requires determining the mode along with the parameter value change that explains the observed discrepancies in system behavior. The residual analysis task for hypothesis refinement requires a fast *roll forward* process to determine the current mode of the system. Multiple hypotheses may be generated, and the fault identification process then determines the true fault. The

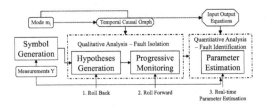

Fig. 3. Hybrid Fault Isolation and Identification

overall scheme for hybrid diagnosis is illustrated in Fig. 3. Like the continuous case, we overcome limitations of quantitative schemes by combining robust qualitative reasoning mechanisms with quantitative techniques. The fault isolation methodology for hybrid systems is broken down into three steps:

A fast *roll back process* using qualitative reasoning techniques to generate possible fault hypotheses. Since the fault could have occurred in a mode earlier than the current mode, fault hypotheses need to be characterized as a two-tuple *(mode, fault parameter)*, where mode indicates the mode in which the fault occurs, and fault parameter is the parameter of an implicated component whose deviation possibly explains the observed discrepancies in behavior.

A quick *roll forward process* using progressive monitoring techniques to refine the possible fault candidates. The goal is to retain only those candidates whose fault signatures are consistent with the current sequence of measurements. After the occurrence of a fault, the observer's predictions of autonomous mode transitions may no longer be correct, therefore, determining the consistency of fault hypotheses also requires the fault isolation unit to roll forward to the correct current mode of system operation.

A *real-time parameter estimation process* using quantitative parameter estimation schemes. The qualitative reasoning schemes are inherently imprecise. As a result, a number of fault hypotheses may still be active after Step 2. We employ least squares based estimation techniques on the input-output form of the system model to estimate consistent values of the fault parameter that is consistent with the sequence of measurements made on the system.

4.1   Hypotheses Generation Using Roll Back Process

Since the fault could have occurred in a mode that is different from the mode in which the fault is detected, we need to consider previous modes when generating hypotheses. Without knowledge of the current mode, it is not possible to determine, what modes the system could have been in previously (using the pre operator defined in [6]).

Lemma 1 (Fault Mode) *If we assume that the observer can accurately track the system under nominal conditions, then the mode in which the fault occurred has to be part of the observer mode trajectory.*

Lemma 1 implies that it is sufficient to generate hypotheses only in modes in the observer predicted trajectory. We can further restrict this using diagnosability studies to determine that any fault must manifest itself in the form of significant transients within k modes. This defines the roll back process for hybrid diagnosis.

Definition 1 (k Diagnosability) *A system is said to be k diagnosable if the effects of any fault manifest themselves within k mode transitions.*

Hypotheses generation within a mode is based on a back propagation algorithm performed on the temporal causal graph (TCG) derived from the bond graph model in that mode. In the TCG, we start at the node(s) corresponding to these discrepancy(s) expressed as + or $-^2$ and propagate them against the direction of arrows. When we traverse an edge that contains a parameter, we include that parameter as a fault candidate (See [5] for more details). Let $BackProp(q,\delta)$ denote the back propagation algorithm performed on the TCG model of the system in mode q with initial symbolic discrepancies δ.

Suppose $\{q_1, q_2, \ldots, q_n\}$ is the observed mode trajectory of the system. q_n is the mode in which the fault was detected. Let δ_n denote the symbolic discrepancies detected. $Reset(q_1,q_2,\delta_n)$ denotes the reset function when the system transitions from mode q_1 to mode q_2. Let $InverseReset$ denote the inverse of the $Reset$ function. Hypotheses generation (hybrid back propagation) algorithm is summarized as:

$\delta_{current} = \delta_n$

For mode = 1 to k

$BackProp(q_{n-mode-1}, \quad \delta_{current})$

$\delta_{current} = InverseReset(q_{n-mode}, q_{n-mode-1}, \delta_{current})$

We first run back propagation in the mode in which the fault is detected using the observed discrepancies and generate candidates in that mode. Then we go back in the observer predicted mode trajectory and generate candidates in each of those modes. Note that the TCG in each of these modes is different. Discrepancies are propagated back across modes by applying constraints specified by the appropriate reset functions. Note that the sign of the propagation may be undetermined (both + and −) because of the ambiguity of qualitative arithmetic.

---

^{2} The algorithm for generating symbolic discrepancies is described in [12]

In such cases we have to propagate both + and - values across the mode for hypotheses generation in the previous mode. Note that backward propagation is applied only once, immediately after a fault has been detected.

Definition 2 (Fault Hypotheses) *A fault hypothesis is defined as the pair (q_i, p_j) where q_i represents the mode in which the fault occurred and p_j represents the deviating parameter.*

4.2   Hypotheses Refinement Using Roll Forward Process

Qualitative hypothesis refinement compares signatures generated from the model against the symbolic representation of the measurement transient as it evolves in time. Inconsistent fault hypothesis are dropped as the tracking progresses. To generate signatures, we need to determine the current mode of the system and derive the system model in the mode using the hybrid bond graph. Since the system state is unknown after the occurrence of a fault, the hypotheses refinement needs to solve the mode identification problem. Using the assumption that the controller signals are known, the controlled transitions that have occurred between the hypothesized fault mode (for each candidate hypothesis) and current time are known. We apply these known mode changes to get a hypothesized current mode. We call this a quick *roll forward* process.

Lemma 2 (Sequence of Mode Transitions) *A sequence of k mode transitions occurring in any order would drive the system to the same final mode if the system starts in the same initial mode.*

Lemma 2 can be justified by looking at the representation of a mode in the hybrid bond graph. Since each junction state is dependent only on its local automata, the order in which the junction states are changed does not matter. Note some sequences may not be physically valid. For example, if the level of fluid in tank 1 is below the pipe R1 and is decreasing, we cannot assume that the autonomous transition that makes R1 active will occur next.

For each fault hypothesis (q_i, p_j) we need to determine what the current mode is. In order to do this we first determine all controlled transitions that occurred since the time the system was in mode q_i and current time. If this set is given by $\{\Sigma_1, \Sigma_2, \ldots, \Sigma_n\}$, then we can hypothesize the current mode as $q_{current} = \delta \ldots (\delta (\delta (q_i, \Sigma_1), \Sigma_2), \ldots, \Sigma_n)$.

The qualitative progressive monitoring techniques used for hypotheses refinement within a mode is discussed in section 4.2. Let ProgressiveMonitoring $((q_i, p_j), q_{current})$ denote the results of progressive monitoring on fault candidate (q_i, p_j) in mode $q_{current}$. If the progressive monitoring indicates that the predictions based on the hypothesized fault do not match the observed output, we cannot drop the hypothesis because our hypothesized current mode may not be the right current mode. Since we have complete knowledge of controlled transitions, the implication is that some autonomous transition could have occurred in the system (due to the effects of the fault) that the observer could not predict.

In order to determine the possible autonomous transitions, we define a qualitative forward prediction operator (inverse of the pre operator defined in [6]) to identify which modes the system may have reached from the current hypothesized mode. The operator looks at the fault signature for different variables and determines if a possible autonomous transition is consistent with a predicted signature. This restricts the number of autonomous changes we need to consider. Let HypothesizeAutonomous(q) denote the possible autonomous transitions out of mode q.

We apply each of these selected autonomous transitions in turn to generate a new mode. In each of these new modes we repeat the qualitative hypotheses refinement process. We keep hypothesizing autonomous transitions till the total number of transitions from the hypothesized fault mode to the hypothesized current mode exceeds k, at which point we drop the candidate if there is still a discrepancy. As discussed before this k is a function of the diagnosability measure. This approach will eventually lead us to the correct current mode based on Lemma 2.

The hypotheses refinement algorithm for each fault hypothesis (q_i, p_j) is:
$q_{current} = \delta \ldots (\delta (\delta (q_i, \Sigma_1), \Sigma_2), \ldots, \Sigma_n)$
if $!ProgressiveMonitoring((q_i, p_j), q_{current})$
$\Sigma_a = $ HypothesizeAutonomous ($q_{current}$)
For each $\Sigma \ \varepsilon \ \Sigma_a$
$q_{current} = \delta (q_{current}, \Sigma)$
Repeat step 2.

We next discuss the qualitative hypotheses refinement process within a mode (progressive monitoring).

Qualitative Hypotheses Refinement in Continuous Regions As discussed, faults are represented as step changes in parameter values, and the occurrence of faults produces transients in system behavior. Previous work has shown that discontinuous changes in variable values can only occur at the point of failure, thus system behavior is continuously differentiable before and after the occurrence of a fault. Therefore, the transient response in a measurement after the time point of failure, t_0, can be approximated by the Taylor series expansion. If $r(t_0)$ is the value of the residual signal just after the occurrence of the fault, the kth order Taylor series expansion for $r(t)$, $t \geq t_0$ is given by

$$r(t) = r(t_0) + r'(t_0)\frac{(t - t_0)}{1!} + r''(t_0)\frac{(t - t_0)^2}{2!} + \cdots + r^k(t_0)\frac{(t - t_0)^k}{k!} + R_k(t),$$

where $R_k(t)$ is a remainder term based on higher order derivatives of r and $r^k = \frac{\partial^k r}{\partial t^k}$

For most well behaved functions the series converges, therefore, the Taylor series is a good approximation of the true signal $r(t)$ when t is close to t_0. The analysis of transient dynamics by interpreting the signal as a Taylor series approximation is the basis for describing the fault transient signal as a *fault signature*.

Qualitative fault isolation is based on the comparison of the fault signatures with measurements made on the system. Performing this analysis quantitatively is an intractable problem. When a fault occurs, the exact magnitude of parameter value changes is unknown, so derivative values in the fault signature have to be computed from subsequent measurements. To address this problem, we use a *qualitative constraint analysis* scheme, developed for the fault isolation task.

In the qualitative framework, individual measurements are labeled as normal (0), above normal (+) and below normal (−). Similarly, derivatives take on values, increasing (+), steady (0), and decreasing(−). The fault signature in the qualitative framework then is the sequence of +,0, or − magnitude and k derivative values computed at the point of failure, t_0. This fault signature is the basis for qualitative transient analysis using the progressive monitoring scheme.

Lemma 3 (Qualitative Transient Analysis) *Transient dynamics are captured by evaluation of the direction of abrupt change at the point of failure (if it occurs), and the signs of the derivatives of the signal after the onset of a fault.*

Fault detection triggers the fault isolation mechanism. The hypothesis generation algorithms, implemented as a two-step process, fault hypothesis generation followed by fault signature generation for each hypothesis, is described in detail in [5] An observer, defined in terms of a set of fault signatures, one for each measurement, is designed for each fault hypothesis.

Comparing the fault signature with the feature vector obtained from the evolving transient data is the basis of a *progressive monitoring* scheme for tracking signal transients [5].

Lemma 4 (Progressive Monitoring) *Qualitative magnitude and slope of a fault transient are matched against a qualitative fault signature by starting in a sequence from a discontinuous magnitude and first order change to a succession of higher order derivatives.*

Comparing the ith and $(i+1)^{th}$ terms in the Taylor series, one can establish $|r^i(t_0)| \geq |r^{(i+1)}(t_0)|(t\text{-}t_o)/(i+1)$ for some period of time t. As t increases, the inequality reverses and the higher order derivative starts dominating the lower one. Lemma 4 provides the basis for progressive monitoring of signal dynamics using higher order derivatives. Starting from the point of failure, t_0, the signal magnitude in response to the fault, $r(t_0)$ determines the signal value. Immediately after that the first derivative of the signal dominates the dynamic behavior because small values of $(t-t_o)$ dominate higher powers $(t-t_o)^i$ in the Taylor series. As t increases, higher order derivatives in succession increasingly contribute to the dynamics of the signal.

4.3   Fault Identification Using Real-Time Parameter Estimation

In other work ([11]), we have derived limited discriminatory capabilities of the qualitative progressive monitoring scheme. This often leads to multiple fault hypotheses as the diagnostic result. Even if the fault isolation is unique, we still need to identify the fault. For this we use real-time parameter estimation using the least squares estimation method. A fault observer is triggered for each fault hypothesis that is still valid. Note that each remaining hypothesis has a current mode associated with it. We symbolically derive the parameterized input output equation model of the system from the bond graph model in that mode using Mason's gain rule. We substitute nominal values for all component parameters except the implicated fault hypotheses . This gives us an input output model in terms of inputs (u), measurements (y), and the fault parameter p_i. The least squares estimate is run on each fault observer, to estimate p_i. If this estimation does not converge, we may drop that corresponding hypothesis. If it converges, then we have identified the fault. In case of transitions during the estimation, we can switch modes and derive the new input output models and continue the estimation in the new mode.

5   Experiments

Fig. 4 illustrates a sample run of our diagnosis engine on the three-tank system (Fig. 1(a)). The three pressure values at the bottom of each tank are measured. We keep all the controlled pipes open at all time steps. The sources are opened at time step 20. The source into tank1 is shut off at time step 60. The source into tank 3 is shut off at time step 70. We introduce a clog in the outlet pipe from tank 1 (called Drain West) at time step 30 by changing the resistance value R2 from 1 to 10.

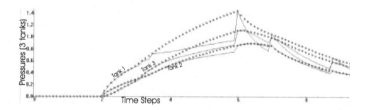

Fig. 4. Sample Run

The plot shows the actual system output as circles and the estimated observer output as solid lines. The observer tracks controlled and autonomous changes like the pipe R2 going active at time steps 32. Fault detection is triggered at time step 39. Note that the observer is unable to track system behavior after the occurrence of the fault.

Hypotheses generation and quick roll back (with $k = 1$) are initiated on the initial discrepancy: tank 1 pressure below nominal. This produces the following hypotheses in the current mode q_1(all open) and in the previous mode q_2 (all but

R5 open): C1-, R2+, C2-, R1-, C3-, R5+, R3+, R4+, and R6+ (Fig. 1(a)). The quick roll forward brings the predictions back to the current mode for all the candidates. Hypothesis refinement is initiated considering all measurement discrepancies. All the C candidates predict a discontinuous change in the pressures, which we do not see, so they are eliminated. To continue tracking, we have to hypothesize autonomous transitions for some candidates (R1 and R5) in q_1, and continue progressive monitoring. The signatures still do not match and so these hypotheses are also dropped. R2+ and R6+, the remaining candidates cannot be distinguished by qualitative analysis. The parameter estimation procedure is initiated, and the estimate converges for the left drain (R2+) to a new resistance value = 10.43. For R6+, parameter estimation does not converge.

Table 1. Experiments on Three-Tank amd Five-Tank Systems

System	Measurements	Fault (original value, new value)	Qualitative Diagnosis (Steps)	Parameter Estimated (Steps)
Three-Tank	h2,h3	C2- (1,0.2)	C2- (2)	0.21 (15)
Three-Tank	h2,h3	R1+ (1,5)	R1+ (8), R12- (8)	4.978 (16), NC
Three-Tank	h2,h3	R23- (1,0.2)	R23- (6)	0.195 (16)
Five-Tank	h2,h3,h4	C2- (1,0.2)	C2- (2)	0.203 (21)
Five-Tank	h2,h3,h4	C4+ (1,5)	C4+ (2)	4.967 (21)
Five-Tank	h2,h3,h4	R5- (1,0.2)	R5- (10), R12+ (10)	0.191 (22), NC
Five-Tank	h2,h3,h4	R34+ (1,5)	R34+ (7)	5.023 (20)

Table 1 summarizes the results of a set of experiments on a three-tank and five-tank system. The results indicate that the diagnosis algorithm scales well. For capacitance faults, the qualitative analysis can isolate the true fault using discontinuity detection. Signature orders of 3 and 5 were used for the three-tank and five-tank system respectively. The parameter estimation also identifies the correct fault magnitude. For resistive faults, the qualitative diagnosis takes longer but still converges to the correct fault hypothesis (NC implies Non-convergence for corresponding fault hypothesis). In some cases, parameter estimation is required to isolate the correct fault.

6   Discussions and Conclusion

This paper has developed a model-based approach to fault detection, isolation, and identification for hybrid systems. Our work is motivated by the fault accommodation task that requires that the diagnosis tasks be performed online while the system is in operation. We have described the complexities of tracking and analyzing hybrid behavior under faulty conditions: (i) changes in the model, (ii) the current system mode may be unknown, and (iii) since the model is faulty, the observer cannot reliably predict autonomous transitions. This would normally lead to exhaustive search techniques to solve the fault isolation and identification problem. By introducing qualitative reasoning mechanisms, we have developed computationally simple operators that perform the equivalent of a pre and post operations defined for piecewise linear hybrid systems.

Our work contrasts the approach of Lunze [4], who maps hybrid behaviors into discrete spaces for fault diagnosis applications. This requires exhaustive pre-enumeration of trajectories to derive the automata for tracking system behavior, and does not easily scale up to large systems. On the other hand, Ferrari-Trecate et al. [13], use a mixed integer logic model formulation to solve the fault detection and isolation problem as an optimization problem. In their work, deriving mixed logic dynamic model for a general system is non-trivial. Also the computational complexity of their optimization methods makes it unsuitable for online applications.

In future work, we plan to formalize our approach in defining the pre and post operator for tracking hybrid behavior under a variety of fault conditions. We are currently working on more complex systems, like the aircraft fuel transfer system and NASA's bioplex system to demonstrate the effectiveness of our approach.

Acknowledgments: The DARPA/ITO SEC program (F30602-96-2-0227) and The Boeing Company have supported the activities described in this paper. We would like to thank Dr. Gabor Karsai, Tivadar Szemethy, and Eric Manders for their help.

References

1. Gertler, J., Fault detection and isolation using parity relations. Control Engineering Practice, 1997. 5(5): p. 653-661.
2. Kleer, J.D., An assumption-based truth maintenance system. Artificial Intelligence, 1987. 28: p. 197-224.
3. Sampath, M., et al., Failure diagnosis using discrete event models. IEEE Transactions on Control Systems Technology, 1996. 4: p. 105-124.
4. Lunze, J., A timed discrete event abstraction of continuous variable systems. International Journal of Control, 1999. 72(13): p. 1147-1164.
5. Mosterman, P.J. and G. Biswas, Diagnosis of continuous valued systems in transient operating regions. IEEE Transactions on Systems, Man, and Cybernetics, 1999. 29: p. 554-565.
6. Koutsoukos, X. and P. Antsaklis, Hierarchical control of piecewise linear hybrid dynamical systems based on discrete abstractions, Technical Report, 2001.
7. Narasimhan, S., Biswas, G., Karsai, G., Pasternak, T., and Zhao, F., 2000. Building Observers to Handle Fault Isolation and Control Problems in Hybrid Systems, Proc. 2000 IEEE Intl. Conference on Systems, Man, and Cybernetics, Nashville, TN, pp. 2393-2398.
8. R.C. Rosenberg, and D.C. Karnopp. Introduction to physical system dynamics, McGraw-Hill, 1983.
9. Mosterman, P.J. and G. Biswas. Towards procedures for systematically deriving hybrid models of complex systems. Third International Workshop on Hybrid Systems: Computation and Control. 2000.

10. R. Alur, C. Courcoubetis, T.A. Henzinger, and P.-H. Ho. "Hybrid Automata – an algorithmic approach to specification and verification of hybrid systems", Hybrid Systems I, Lecture Notes in Computer Science 736, pp. 209-229, Springer-Verlag, 1994.
11. Manders E.J., S. Narasimhan, G. Biswas, and P.J. Mosterman. A combined qualitative/quantitative approach for efficient fault isolation in complex dynamic systems. 4th Symposium on Fault Detection, Supervision and Safety Processes, pp. 512-517, 2000.
12. Manders E.J., P.J. Mosterman, and G. Biswas. Signal to symbol transformation techniques for robust diagnosis in TRANSCEND, Tenth International Workshop on Principles of Diagnosis, Loch Awe, Scotland, pp. 155-165, 1999.
13. Ferrari-Trecate G., D. Mignone and M. Morari. Moving Horizon Estimation for Hybrid Systems, IEEE Transactions on Automatic Control, To Appear, 2002.

Information-Based Alpha-Beta Search and the Homicidal Chauffeur

Todd W. Neller[*]

Department of Computer Science, Gettysburg College,
Gettysburg, PA, 17325, USA.
tneller@gettysburg.edu

Abstract. The standard means of applying a discrete search to a continuous or hybrid system is the uniform discretization of control actions and action timing. Such discretization is fixed a priori and does not allow search to benefit from information gained at run-time. This paper introduces Information-Based Alpha-Beta Search, a new algorithm that preserves and benefits from the continuous or hybrid nature of the search. In a novel merging of alpha-beta game-tree search and information-based optimization, Information-Based Alpha-Beta Search makes trajectory-sampling decisions dynamically based on the maximum-likelihood of search pruning. The result is a search algorithm which, while incurring higher computational overhead for the optimization, manages to so increase the quality of the sampling, that the net effect is a significant increase in performance. We present a new piecewise-parabolic variant of the algorithm and provide empirical evidence of its performance relative to random and uniform discretizations in the context of a variant of the homicidal chauffeur game.

1 Motivation

Locally optimal ("greedy") control decisions are not necessarily globally optimal control decisions for many systems. Some sort of "lookahead" facility is necessary to derive optimal or approximately optimal control policies. Tree-based search techniques have proven powerful for lookahead in some complex discrete systems, but are not easily applied to continuous or hybrid systems. One reason is that an a priori discretization of control actions is necessary. A good discretization is often not easy to discern.

We introduce a new technique which performs discretization dynamically during search according to maximum-likelihood reasoning. This technique lifts the burden of discretization from the control engineer and, as we shall see, can outperform standard discretization approaches. Thus the primary contribution of this paper is a technique that enables both easier and better use of search techniques for lookahead in continuous and hybrid control systems. The remainder of this section relates these thoughts in greater detail.

---

[*] This work was done both at the Stanford Knowledge Systems Laboratory with support by NASA Grant NAG2-1337, and at Gettysburg College.

C.J. Tomlin and M.R. Greenstreet (Eds.): HSCC 2002, LNCS 2289, pp. 323–336, 2002.

Many optimal control techniques seek to optimize some performance measure by steepest ascent or descent of the measure's gradient. While locally optimal, such "greedy" control actions are not necessarily optimal with respect to finite or infinite time-horizons. In discrete systems, this is easily illustrated with the game of chess. If the performance measure is based on material advantage, the player who employs a greedy policy falls victim to a clever opponent's sacrifices where short-term material advantage is followed by a stronger counter-attack. The player with foresight looks beyond the immediate gain to the ramifications of that gain.

For continuous systems, we may imagine a pursuit-evasion game in which the evader wants to avoid prolonged close proximity with a slightly faster pursuer. The greedy evader immediately in front of the pursuer will seek to maintain as much distance from the pursuer as possible by running away in the same direction of pursuit. The evader with foresight looks beyond the immediate situation to see that charging towards the pursuer and then breaking to the side will put it behind the pursuer. A temporary increase in proximity makes possible a significant decrease in proximity as the pursuer struggles to turn and renew pursuit. For hybrid systems, we may imagine a pursuit-evasion game with environmental constraints (e.g. dangerous airspace, terrain features, etc.).

From these examples, we can see the performance benefit of global "looka-head" versus local "greedy" policies. In situations where we have a small, finite state space (or a continuous or hybrid state space approximable as such), we can apply dynamic programming to compute a globally optimal control policy. However, such situations are rare in practice. With an increase in the dimensionality of a state space, either the necessary memory or the granularity of the discretization grows *exponentially*, making such approaches infeasable.

However, in the case where (1) an approximate continuous or hybrid simulation model can be derived for the system, (2) limited lookahead with this model enables better performance, and (3) a sampling of the *action space* (i.e. space of possible control input vectors) is adequate to inform a good decision, we can benefit from tree-search techniques. Such techniques sample possible *sequences of control actions* and use that sample to approximate optimal behavior.

From any given state, a sample of possible control actions and an assumed delay before the next action yields a sample of possible future states. These future states may in turn be used to generate a sample of further future states until we reach a search stopping condition. The result is a discrete search tree which can be used to approximate the utility of a sample of control actions. The best of these actions in turn approximates the optimal control action.

One drawback to standard search approaches is that they assume that the actions (i.e. control inputs) are discretized *a priori* into a finite set of actions. Finding a good discretization of control inputs is often not a trivial task. By committing to a fixed or *static* action discretization, standard approaches cannot *dynamically* adapt the sampling at run-time in order to improve the quality of the discretization.

To illustrate this, we turn again to the pursuit-evasion example. Suppose the evader samples a few possible directions for evasion and looks ahead at branching trees of possible trajectories in these directions. Lookahead indicates that some directions are especially good. In greatest likelihood, the evader will find better control actions closer to those sampled actions which appear best. This intuitive sort of dynamic sampling behavior is *not possible in pre-existing search formalisms*.

This paper introduces a new formalism for hybrid games, and a new and powerful technique which works with a subset of such games: Information-Based Alpha-Beta Search. Not only does the algorithm preserve the continuous or hybrid nature of control actions in search, but it also reaps performance benefits from this preservation.

2 Alpha-Beta Search

In this section, we describe the game-tree search technique commonly known as "alpha-beta search" or "minimax search with alpha-beta pruning". Before introducing basic concepts of game-tree search, it is important to motivate the use of such algorithms and place them in context.

At heart, artificial intelligence (AI) search algorithms are a form of *optimization*. The primary distinction between search algorithms and other forms of optimization is that search algorithms optimize utility (i.e. performance index) over *sequences of actions* (i.e. control vector sequences). Unlike optimal control formulations of multi-stage problems, AI search does not assume a finite number of stages. However, by computational necessity, the search is often biased towards shorter sequences of actions. Any process which can benefit from examining the ramifications of short sequences of control decisions can benefit from this form of optimization.

A classical AI game-tree search problem definition concerns discrete system dynamics and consists of three components: (1) an *initial state* (including system state and current player), (2) a *successor function* (a mapping from states to sets of possible future states[1], and (3) a *utility function* (a mapping from states to the value of being in that state). (1) and (2) define the state space. An alternate formalism we use breaks component (2) into two parts: (2a) an *operator function* (a mapping from states to sets of legal actions), and (2b) a mapping from states and actions to resulting states. We prefer this formalism as it is often easier to define possible states indirectly by defining possible actions.

A classical AI game-tree search algorithm typically works as follows: We begin with a set of unsearched states consisting of the initial state (1). Iteratively, we choose and remove a state from our unsearched state set, evaluate its utility, generate possible future states, and add these to the unsearched state set. At any time, the search algorithm has searched a portion of the search tree and may modify its valuation of actions by propogating utilities up the tree. Since states

---

[1] When a state maps to an empty set, the state is said to be *terminal*.

can be repeated in the tree, a specific state at a position in the tree is called a *node*. Different algorithms will vary in how they choose the next unsearched state. Since most search trees cannot be searched exhaustively, different algorithms also have different stopping conditions.

Although the *minimax* algorithm can be used to evaluate a game search tree (i.e. game tree), this process can be made significantly more efficient for zero-sum games through a technique called *alpha-beta pruning*. During search, if one can prove through zero-sum constraints that rational play will never lead to a node, search from that node can be "pruned" (i.e. discontinued).

Since we assume a zero-sum game, we can have a single utility associated with each node. One player (MAX) seeks to maximize this utility, and the other (MIN) seeks to minimize it. Assume without loss of generality that at the initial search node (or *root*), it is MAX's turn. At each search node, we keep track of two values α and β. Along the path (i.e. sequence of actions) from the root to a node, α is the best score for MAX, and β is the best score for MIN. Put another way, play along that path guarantees a score of *at least* α and *at most* β. At the root node, these are $-\infty$ and ∞ respectively.

To compute MAX-Value(s, α, β):

1. If state s is terminal or triggers a terminating condition of search, then return the utility of s.
2. For each legal action a of MAX in state s:
   (a) Let state s' be the result of action a in state s.
   (b) Set α equal to the greater of α and MIN-Value(s', α, β).
   (c) If α is greater than or equal to β, then "prune" search and return β.
3. Return α.

To compute MIN-Value(s, α, β):

1. If state s is terminal or triggers a terminating condition of search, then return the utility of s.
2. For each legal action a of MIN in state s:
   (a) Let state s' be the result of action a in state s.
   (b) Set β equal to the lesser of β and MAX-Value(s', α, β).
   (c) If β is less than or equal to α, then "prune" search and return α.
3. Return β.

A player MAX will take the action corresponding to the successor state with the greatest MIN-Value. Although other terminating conditions of search are often employed, we will use the simplest throughout: a limitation on the *depth* of search – the maximum length of an action sequence. The number of possible actions in a state is called the *breadth* of search.

This discrete search algorithm assumes a discrete dynamical system. For any state, there are a finite number of actions which result in a finite number of successor states. In order to apply such an algorithm to a continuous or hybrid dynamical system, we must first approximate the system as a discrete system through a process called *discretization*.

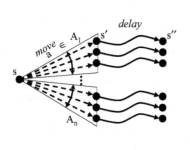

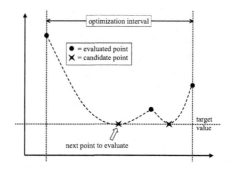

(a) DASAT Hybrid System Game

(b)   Parabolic   Information-Based Optimization

Fig. 1.

There are two types of discretization which must occur: (1) discretization of actions, and (2) discretization of action timing. For (1), it is common practice to discretize a continuum of possible control inputs with a uniform sampling. For (2), it is common to pick a fixed time interval Δt for which the control inputs hold as simulation advances to the next successor state.

It is often not obvious what constitutes a good decision for either type of discretization. Worse yet, by committing to such a discretization before search, it is not possible to reap the benefit of information obtained during search to form a better discretization. In the next section, we describe a more general game formalism which assumes a fixed (static) discretization for action timing, but allows an adaptive (dynamic) discretization for control actions.

3   DASAT Hybrid System Game

In this section, we present a formalism for hybrid system games called *DASAT hybrid system games*, and a subclass of such games that can be searched with our new techniques. DASAT stands for <u>D</u>ynamic <u>A</u>ction discretization with <u>S</u>tatic <u>A</u>ction <u>T</u>iming discretization.

Formally, a *DASAT hybrid system game* is defined as a 7-tuple

$$\{S, s_0, \mathbf{A}, p, l, m, d\}$$

where

- S is the hybrid state space[1] with a finite number of finite discrete variable domains, and a finite-dimensional continuous space,
- $s_0 \in S$ is the initial state,
- $\mathbf{A}$ is a finite set $\{A_1, \ldots, A_n\}$ of continuous action regions indexed $\{1, \ldots, n\}$,

- p is the number of players,
- $l : S \times \{1, \ldots, p\} \rightarrow \mathbf{A}'$ where $\mathbf{A}' \subset \mathbf{A}$ is a *legal move* function mapping from a state and player number to a finite set of legal continuous action regions which contain points representing all legal actions that may be executed in that state by that player,
- $m : S \times \mathbf{a}^p \rightarrow S \times \Re^p$ is a *move* function mapping from a state and simultaneous player actions (region index, region point pairs) to a resulting state and the utility of the combined actions for each player,
- $d : S \rightarrow S \times \Re^p$ is a *delay* function mapping from a state to the resulting state and the utility of the trajectory segment for each player. This delay governs the hybrid evolution of the system through time between moves.

This formalism is visualized in Figure 1(a). For any state s in our hybrid state space S, there are a finite number of action regions $\{A_1, \ldots, A_n\}$. Each region can be thought of as a closed, contiguous set of allowable control input vectors. Let a be an action (e.g. a single control input vector) from one of these action regions. The *move* function maps s and a to s', applying an instantaneous transition to system state, and computing the associated change in utility. The *delay* function maps s' to s'', simulating the evolution of the hybrid system over some time interval $\Delta t \geq 0$. Overall, the system state evolves through both moments of action (moves) and periods of inaction (delays).

The total utility of any finite trajectory is computed as the sum of the trajectory move and delay utilities. In this time-invariant formalism, time can easily be encoded in a continuous clock variable, and time variant behavior can thus be easily achieved.

This formalism is very general in both its dynamics and game-theoretical form. Indeed, in the latter respect, it is too general for the application of alpha-beta search. Two restrictions are necessary to define a class of DASAT hybrid system games for which the techniques of this paper are applicable: (1) The zero-sum constraint of the player score function must be preserved in the *move* and *delay* functions, and (2) a single player must be allowed to move at a time. For (2), we can include the current player in the state, and have the *legal move* function only allow a "null" move for all other players. An example of these restrictions in practice is presented in the following section.

4   Homicidal Chauffeur Game Variant

In this section we present a variant of the *homicidal chauffeur game*[2,3]. The differences in this variation are (1) fixed time delays between actions, (2) a different cost function, and (3) game theoretic information structure (i.e. who knows what when). Regarding (1), the homicidal chauffeur game is a *differential game*[2]. In our variant, we have a fixed discretization of action timing. Regarding (2), the homicidal chauffeur game has only two player utilities representing capture and non-capture. In our variant, utility is calculated by integrating inverse distance of a trajectory to the origin (pursuer) over time. Regarding (3), the homicidal

Chauffeur game as a differential game has both players acting at once. In our variant, players take actions in turn with complete knowledge of previous actions.

The homicidal chauffeur game is a pursuit-evasion game in which a chauffeur in a circular car with limited turning radius seeks to hit a slower pedestrian who can change direction instantly. Speed and maneuverability are asymmetric. In our variant, the object of the pursuer/evader is to minimize/maximize their inverse distance integrated over time.

The pursuer can choose a value $u^1 \in [-1, 1]$ where -1 and 1 are extreme left and right turns respectively. The evader chooses any angle u^2. The pursuer and evader travel at constant velocities 1 and v_2 respectively. Let us assume an (x_1, x_2) coordinate frame relative to the pursuer. The pursuer faces the positive x_2-axis. Then the system evolves according to:

$$\dot{x}_1 = -u^1 x_2 + v_2 \sin(u^2), \qquad \dot{x}_2 = -1 + u^1 x_1 + v_2 \cos(u^2)$$

For our information structure, we assume that the pursuer chooses u^1 immediately after the evader chooses u^2 with knowledge of that choice. There is then a finite, positive delay Δt before the evader again chooses u^2. The system evolution is piecewise continuous with discrete controller transitions.

This game is not as general as it could be. In particular, we could have multiple ranges of control inputs and hybrid rather than continuous dynamics. This problem was chosen because (1) it is well known, and (2) it is easily visualizable to validate results.

Within our formalism, the hybrid states consists of two continuous variables (x_1 and x_2) and one discrete variable (p, the current player). Continuous action regions are $A_1 = [-1, 1]$, $A_2 = [-\pi, \pi]$, and A_3 is a "null move" singleton set with any value. The legal move function maps all states and player i to the singleton action region set A_i when the current player is i, and maps to A_3 otherwise. Suppose i is the current player: The move function changes u^i according to a_i (the ith action of the action vector). The move function also changes the current player and has no utility change. The delay function simulates the system forward Δt_i time units. The delay function also has zero-sum utility change (positive for pursuer, negative for evader) according to the inverse distance between players integrated over Δt_i. After the evader acts and before the pursuer acts we have no delay ($\Delta t_1 = 0$). After the pursuer acts and before the evader acts we have a fixed positive Δt_2 which was set to 0.1.

We now turn our attention to a new class of algorithms suited to this subclass of DASAT hybrid system games.

5   DASAT Alpha-Beta Search

In our new approach to search, we redefine MAX-Value and MIN-Value as follows (changes underlined):
To compute MAX-Value(s, α, β):

1. If state s is terminal or triggers a terminating condition of search, then return the utility of the trajectory to s.

2. While we have not yet reached our breadth limit:
   (a) *Choose a continuous action region A_i and a legal action $a \in A_i$ of MAX in state s.*
   (b) Let state s' be the result of the move function of state s and action a.
   (c) Let state s'' be the result of the delay function of state s'.
   (d) Set α equal to the greater of α and MIN-Value(s'', α, β).
   (e) If α is greater than or equal to β, then "prune" search and return β.
3. Return α.

To compute MIN-Value(s, α, β):

1. If state s is terminal or triggers a terminating condition of search, then return the utility of the trajectory to s.
2. While we have not yet reached our breadth limit:
   (a) *Choose a continuous action region A_i and a legal action $a \in A_i$ of MIN in state s.*
   (b) Let state s' be the result of the move function of state s and action a.
   (c) Let state s'' be the result of the delay function of state s'.
   (d) Set β equal to the lesser of β and MAX-Value(s'', α, β).
   (e) If β is less than or equal to α, then "prune" search and return α.
3. Return β.

Note that there are essentially three major differences between this search and classical alpha-beta search. The first is a result of our formalism for computing utility changes through discrete actions and simulation delays. The second is a result of the fact that there are potentially infinite actions we could choose. The italicized step is the dynamic action discretization step of DASAT Alpha-Beta Search. The third is a result of our alternate formalism for generating state successors in search. We first instantaneously apply an action (e.g. change a control input). We then simulate the effect on the system for a duration fixed by our delay function.

Finally, we note that since this is a two-player zero-sum game, we can simply use the first element of the DASAT game utility vector. Thus player 1 is MAX, and player 2 is MIN.

In this framework, there are many possible techniques for dynamic discretization. The first technique we use for comparison is to dynamically choose a fixed uniform sampling. This serves as a control to tell us what we gain by performing sampling dynamically. The second technique we use is a random sampling. As we shall see, this simple stochastic technique has its advantages as well. The third technique relies on a class of maximum-likelihood-based optimization techniques called information-based optimization. We describe this type of optimization in the next section.

6   Information-Based Optimization

We defer the details of our information-based optimization algorithm to [4] and provide only an overview for brevity. Information-based optimization is a type of global optimization that seeks to achieve a *target value* by, at each step of optimization, evaluating the point *most likely* to have that value *given previous evaluations*.

We provide a brief sketch of this optimization in Figure 1(b). Given a set of evaluated points, we wish to choose the next point for evaluation which has greatest likelihood of having our desired target value. In our parabolic variant, we assume that (1) the unknown function is most likely piecewise parabolic, and (2) smaller magnitude constants for quadratic terms are more likely than greater magnitude constants.

Then for single-dimensional functions, we may compute candidate points between prior evaluated points by finding the intersections of the target line and tangential parabolas which pass through adjacent evaluated points. We then choose the candidate point associated with the parabola having a quadratic term of minimum magnitude. In Figure 1(b), we prefer the left candidate as it is associated with the least "steep" parabola. For single-dimensional functions, interval end points are initially chosen.

7   Information-Based Alpha-Beta Search

In Section 5, we noted that there are a variety of ways one can dynamically choose which actions to evaluate from a continuum of actions. Commonly, one performs a static uniform discretization. Information-Based Alpha-Beta Search chooses the next action according to information-based optimization, where (1) actions are evaluated by the MAX- or MIN-Values of resulting states, and (2) the target value for optimization is the pruning value β or α.

Information-based optimization chooses an action to evaluate. A subtree search takes place to evaluate the quality of this action, which is then used in the selection of the next action, and so forth. At every node, Information-Based Alpha-Beta Search uses prior subtree searches from that node to choose the next action most likely to lead to pruning. MAX (MIN) seeks actions which will most-likely have a score of β (α), the pruning limit. Initially, this pruning limit is infinite and Information-Based Alpha-Beta Search always chooses the middle of the largest gap between evaluated points.

Since an optimization is performed at each search node, there is considerable computational overhead in this approach. However, we will see in the next section that under certain circumstances, this computationally intensive process is compensated for by the quality of the sampling and/or the quality of the pruning.

8   Results

The following empirical study supports conclusions of the initial empirical study of Information-Based Alpha-Beta Search in the context of magnetic levitation control [5, ch. 4].

The most important parameters of search are search breadth (b) and depth (d) as the computational cost is bounded above by a constant times b^d. Each experiment varies either breadth or depth of search.

Since there are many possible problem parameters and initial conditions, we arbitrarily chose the following fixed parameters for our experimentation: $\Delta t = 0.1$, $\beta = 0.34$, and $v_2 = 0.8^2$. In all trials, initial x_1 and x_2 values were chosen on a uniform 20×20 grid from $[-2, -2]$ to $[2, 2]$. For each initial state (x_1, x_2) we play two algorithms against each other and compare their resulting scores, times for computation, and number of nodes expanded. More specifically, one algorithm as the evader performs a search, and takes the action recommended by search. The next algorithm then does the same as the pursuer, and this is repeated for fours turns of play. We then repeat the trial with the algorithms switched.

In this empirical study, means and 90% confidence intervals for the means were computed with 10000 bootstrap resamples. Graphs for experiments where breadth or depth are varied have circles representing resampled means and lines representing 90% confidence intervals for the means.

The first important parameter we vary is search breadth, i.e. the number of actions we sample at each node. We hold search depth fixed at 6.

Varying search breadth and comparing Information-Based Alpha-Beta Search with DASAT alpha-beta search with random discretization, we generally see a *time versus score tradeoff*. See Figure 2. Information-based discretization consistently outscores random discretization as we would expect. The magnitude of the score difference lessens with increase in search breadth. Optimization is more costly per node than random selection, but random selection must search nearly exponentially more nodes with the increase in breadth. While random discretization performs faster for small breadths, there is no statistically significant difference for larger breadths.

Varying search breadth and comparing Information-Based Alpha-Beta Search with DASAT alpha-beta search with uniform discretization, we generally see the *same scores but with nearly exponential savings in time* as the breadth increases. See Figure 3. For almost all breadths, we see no significant statistical difference in score. However, information-based discretization results in significantly greater pruning. This pruning more than compensates for the computational cost of the optimization, and yields nearly exponential savings in time with the increase in search breadth.

To understand why information-based and uniform discretizations yield such similar scores, we review the behavior of information-based optimization at the start of search. Search starts with $\alpha = -\infty$ and $\beta = \infty$, resulting in a sampling where the next point is always chosen from the middle of the largest gap between previous points. The sampled points are then identical for both methods when $b = 2, 3, 5, 9, 17, \ldots, 2^i + 1$ where i is a non-negative integer. At other times, the

---

[2] The choice of β with respect to v_2 is only significant in the context of the original homicidal chauffeur game.

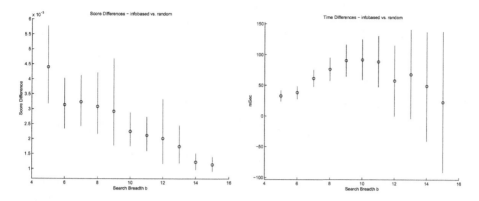

Fig. 2. Score and time difference confidence intervals for information-based versus random discretization with varying search breadth

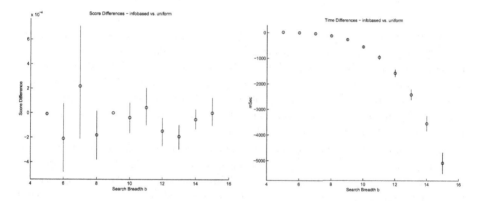

Fig. 3. Score and time difference confidence intervals for information-based versus uniform discretization with varying search breadth

resulting sampling is not uniform and thus scores are somewhat worse (without statistical significance in most cases).

A simple modification we could make to our algorithm is to choose a uniform discretization *with an information-based ordering of evaluations* whenever $\alpha = -\infty$ and $\beta = \infty$. A more interesting and potentially significant question would be whether the maximum-likelihood decision process of information-based optimization could efficiently make use of our knowledge of breadth b. Should our choice of the next point for evaluation seek also to increase the likelihood of pruning in future iterations?

The next important parameter we vary is search depth, i.e. the length of the action sequences (and thus the time horizon) we consider in search. We hold search breadth fixed at 10.

Varying search depth and comparing Information-Based Alpha-Beta Search with DASAT alpha-beta search with random discretization, we again generally

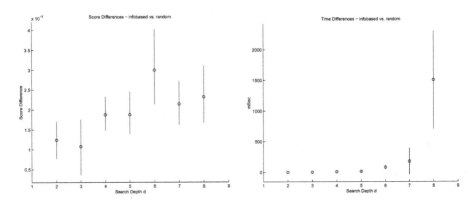

Fig. 4. Score and time difference confidence intervals for information-based versus random discretization with varying search depth

see a *time versus score tradeoff*. See Figure 4. Information-based discretization consistently outscores random discretization as we would expect. The difference in score increases with depth. We do observe an exponential decrease in the relative number of nodes searched as we increase depth using information-based discretization. However, the quality of the pruning does not compensate for the computational cost of optimization, and the overall run-time difference increases nearly exponentially for higher search depths.

In summary, we observe consistently better scores from information-based discretization, but random discretization appears to be significantly more efficient for higher search depths. One could imagine an interesting hybrid of the two, where search at greater depths is performed stochastically and more crucial decisions shallower in search are performed with information-based optimization.

Varying search depth and comparing Information-Based Alpha-Beta Search with DASAT alpha-beta search with uniform discretization, we again generally see the *same scores but with nearly exponential savings in time* as the depth increases. See Figure 5. For almost all depths, we see no significant statistical difference in score. However, as we increase search depth, we observe a clear exponential decrease in the relative number of nodes searched. This pruning more than compensates for the computational cost of the optimization, and again yields nearly exponential savings in time with the increase in search depth.

In summary, information-based discretization, when compared to random discretization yields substantially better decisions but at greater computational cost. Information-based discretization, when compared to uniform discretization, yields similar quality of decisions but with significantly lesser computational cost. This is consistent with the previous empirical study of [5].

We also experimented with varying Δt. Results showed that control with lookahead significantly outperforms greedy control. The policy leads to one of two symmetric equilibria in the upper quadrants where the pursuer's maximal turn affects no change in relative position.

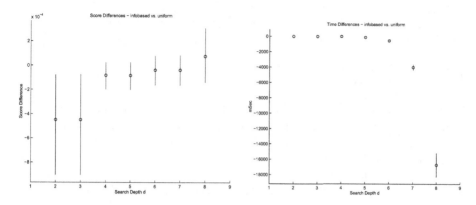

Fig. 5. Score and time difference confidence intervals for information-based versus uniform discretization with varying search depth

9   Discussion

As this is but one empirical study, it is worth taking some time to help the reader understand what to expect for significantly different games. Even without empirical study, we can sketch the gross effects on computational complexity.

Varying number of players: As we increase the number of players while holding the number of turns per player fixed, we linearly increase search depth, which *exponentially* increases search time.

Varying time horizon: As we increase the time horizon while holding the frequency of actions constant, we also linearly increase search depth, which *exponentially* increases search time.

Varying system dynamics: Our homicidal chauffeur example has continuous dynamics, but we could just as well have hybrid dynamics. However, different dynamics results in different computational complexity for simulation. Simulation run-time has a *proportional* effect on search run-time.

Varying system dimensionality: The dimensionality of a hybrid state has no bearing on the complexity of search except through its effect on the computational complexity of simulation.

Varying control input dimensionality: If we increase the number of control inputs, then to keep the sampling density constant, the number of samples would need to increase exponentially. Thus the breadth b and run-time of search would grow *exponentially*.

One common misunderstanding of advanced search techniques is the skill required to use them. There is an important distinction between search algorithms and search problems. Indeed, none of the search algorithm code of [5] needed modification. Rather, we simply redefined those elements corresponding to our DASAT hybrid system game definition. This has an important ramification: A change in the game definition results in change in the behavior recommended by search. Thus, to the extent that search is fast and efficient, search enables *model-*

based control where control is based on an internal model of system behavior and adapts control policy as the model changes.

10   Conclusions

The classical formalism for game-tree search assumes that the game is a discrete system. In order to apply such techniques to continuous or hybrid systems, the user must first approximate system dynamics by performing both action and action timing discretizations a priori.

We have extended the game formalism to allow both (1) dynamic sampling from closed, contiguous sets of allowable actions (i.e. control vectors) during search, and (2) general hybrid system dynamics. We have also introduced a new algorithm called Information-Based Alpha-Beta Search that works with a subclass of these games. This empirical study and that of [5, ch. 4] show that for two such games, Information-Based Alpha-Beta Search recommends control actions similar to that of uniform discretization, but at considerable savings in computational time.

Acknowledgements

We wish to thank Claire Tomlin for the problem suggestion, and Kim and Clif Presser for simplification of formulæ for our parabolic variant.

References

1. Michael S. Branicky. *Studies in Hybrid Systems: modeling, analysis, and control.* PhD thesis, Massachusetts Institute of Technology, Cambridge, MA, USA, 1995.
2. Rufus Isaacs. *Differential Games, 2nd ed.* Kruger Publishing Company, Huntington, NY, USA, 1975. First edition: Wiley, NY, 1965.
3. A. W. Merz. *The Homicidal Chauffeur – a differential game.* PhD thesis, Stanford University, Palo Alto, California, 1971. Report No. 94305, Department of Aeronautics and Astronautics.
4. Todd W. Neller. Information-based optimization approaches to dynamical system safety verification. In Thomas A. Henzinger and Shankar Sastry, editors, *LNCS 1386: Hybrid Systems: computation and control, First International Workshop, HSCC'98, Proceedings*, pages 346–359. Springer, Berlin, 1998.
5. Todd W. Neller. *Simulation-Based Search for Hybrid System Control and Analysis.* PhD thesis, Stanford University, Palo Alto, California, USA, June 2000. available as Stanford Knowledge Systems Laboratory technical report KSL-00-15 at www.ksl.stanford.edu.

Synthesis of Robust Control Systems under Resource Constraints

Luigi Palopoli[2]*, Claudio Pinello[2], Alberto Sangiovanni Vincentelli[2],
Laurent Elghaoui[2], and Antonio Bicchi[3]

[1] ReTiS Lab, Scuola Superiore S. Anna, Pisa, Italy,
palopoli@sssup.it
[2] Dept. of EECS, University of Berkeley California
pinello@eecs.berkeley.edu, alberto@eecs.berkeley.edu,
elghaoui@eecs.berkeley.edu
[3] Centro Piaggio, Facoltà di Ingegneria, Università di Pisa, Italy
bicchi@ing.unipi.it

Abstract. We address the problem of synthesizing real-time embedded
controllers taking into account constraints deriving form the implementation platform. Specifically, we address the problem of controlling a set
of independent systems by using a shared single CPU processor board.
Assuming a time-triggered model of computation for control processes
and a real-time preemptive scheduling policy, the problem of optimizing
robustness of the controlled systems is formulated. Decision variables of
the optimization problem are the processes' activation periods and the
feedback gains. The analytical formulation of the problem enables an
efficient numerical solution based on a Branch and Bound scheme. The
resulting design is directly implementable without performance degrada-
tions due to scheduling and execution delays.

1 Introduction and Related Work

The production of quality embedded software from the specification of control
algorithms is still a bottleneck in many industrial applications [1]. The most
evident problem is the difficulty in establishing a clear flow of information among
the activities of control designers and system engineers. The obvious results
are design cycles that are longer than needed; implementations are often over-
designed and serious difficulties arise in validating the overall design.

A possible solution is to mix algorithm design and implementation choice.
However, this is hardly possible when considering the complexity of the designs
that confront us in safety-critical applications such as transportation and industrial plant control. It seems that we are then in a quandary: on one side,
we need more separation to cope with design correctness and time-to-market,
on the other, we need to capture aspects of the design that couple all layers of
abstraction.

---

* The research presented in this paper was developed while the author was hosted as
a visiting scholar at the Department of EECS, University of California, Berkeley

C.J. Tomlin and M.R. Greenstreet (Eds.): HSCC 2002, LNCS 2289, pp. 337–350, 2002.
© Springer-Verlag Berlin Heidelberg 2002

To solve this problem, we advocate a design process that maintains clear separation of concerns but exposes to the algorithm expert the most critical parameters of the underlying hardware and software architectures. This goal can be achieved by identifying a set of abstraction levels that mark the progress from specification to implementation. Each abstraction layer has to be related to the next in the sequence by a "behavior containment" that should guarantee that whatever has been proven correct at one layer will stay correct in the next layer. The set of abstraction layers (also called platforms), the parameters that characterize the implementation layers, the constraints that are mapped down from the specification layers and of the tools that are used to map one layer into another constitute the so-called *platform-based design paradigms* [11].

In this paper, we apply this generic idea to the design of embedded controllers. In particular, we expose the scheduling policy parameters to the control layer so that an overall optimization problem can be formulated where control concerns such as stability and robustness are considered together with scheduling issues.

Other ideas have been proposed that can be cast in this overall framework. Generally speaking, a feedback controller is an agent exchanging a flow of information with the environment. From this standpoint, an implementation platform introduces limitations on the amount of information that can be circulated. An intriguing formulation of this concept can be found in a seminal paper by Roger Brockett [4]. Bandwidth and bit-rate constraints in communication links have been studied in [18] with respect to the stabilization of linear systems [18] and of state estimation [17, 13]. The application of LQG techniques to control synthesis with communication constraints is illustrated in [16]. A related area of research is the effect of quantization [19], where an optimization procedure is applied to the number of bits allocated to each signal and to other communication variables to minimize variance of the noise introduced by quantization. A different thread [3, 7, 6] considers quantization as an intrinsic feature of certain control systems.

Concurrency may be another source of complexity. Obvious examples are multi-agent applications, where a complex goal is attained by coordinating simpler behaviors [9]. Even a single agent may be specified as a set of periodically activated parallel processes. Very often parallelism in the application is not matched by parallelism in the implementation platform and a scheduling mechanism must then be introduced. In this context, one of the most interesting approaches is the use of parameters governing flows of information across shared resources (e.g, the processes' scheduling priorities) to optimize the control performance. Remarkable attempts to combine control synthesis and scheduling of communication channels are in [14, 8]. In both papers, an integrated formulation encompassing control and communication is proposed. The scheme that is considered for scheduling is Time Division Multiplexing. Authors provide results to design the control parameters once the schedule for the shared resource has been fixed. However, different scheduling choices can be only compared with exhaustive search, which is not necessarily a viable solution in many applications.

Two aspects are deemed relevant when dealing with a concurrent platform during control synthesis: 1) the timing behavior, 2) the constraints to the design parameters (e.g. sampling periods) deriving from limited resources. The two problems have strong dependencies. For example, in single processor scheduling, it is well known that preemptive algorithms[12, 5] ensure a better utilization of the processor resource. The price to be paid is the introduction of stochastic jitter in the emission of results which hinders the construction of realistic models for the delays.

In this paper, a more ambitious goal is pursued: devising a numerically efficient procedure to optimize the control performance operating at the same time on all the available design parameters. As a first step towards a general approach to embedded controller design and for the sake of simplicity, we consider only the problem of controlling *a set of scalar linear systems using a shared computational resource*. The underlying architecture is assumed to be based on a single CPU board shared among concurrent processes via a *preemptive scheduling scheme*. The concurrent model of computation adopted to model the timing behavior of processes is the Time-Triggered approach, proposed by Kopetz and adopted in important hardware platforms [10]. More recently, the Giotto programming language [15] adopted the same paradigm.

The performance metric used in our optimization approach is related to the robustness of the overall system. This metric is of particular relevance in all contexts where tight cost constraints are not only placed on the computation resources but also on the quality of sensors and actuators. The variables of the optimization problem are activation periods of different processes and the gains of the controllers. This is a mixed integer program since the activation periods can only assume integer values. We have devised a branch-and-bound approach where the relaxation of the problem to a continuous optimization problem yields tight and numerically affordable estimations for the lower and upper bound functions.

The paper is organized as follows. In Section 2, we review briefly the Time-Triggered approach and the results on Real-Time preemptive Scheduling. In Section 3, we formulate the optimization problem. In Section 4, we describe the optimization algorithm and offer some computational results. In Section 5, we give conclusions and present our plan for extending this approach to a larger class of systems.

2   Background

2.1   The Time-Triggered MoC

The time triggered model of computation assumes a set of periodic tasks τ_i. Every p_1 time units process τ_i becomes active and reads its inputs; then it computes the output values. Outputs are released right at the beginning of the next activation period and their values are sustained between two subsequent writings (according to a ZoH model).

In the sequel the term *job* will indicate each periodic activation of a process. It is worth observing that the timing behavior resembles the one of a Moore sequential circuit, where the delay between inputs and outputs is equal to the activation period p. The fixed delay virtually nulls jitter in the release time of the outputs, greatly simplifying the control law design.

2.2   Real-Time Schedulability of Periodic Processes

A scheduling policy is said to guarantee *schedulability* of a set of processes if all real-time constraints are respected. A necessary condition for achieving schedulability on a single CPU is:

$$\sum_{i=1}^{m} \frac{e_i}{p_i} \leq 1, \tag{1}$$

where e_i and p_i are integer numbers, counting the clock cycles required to compute process τ_i in the worst case and between successive activations of process τ_i, respectively. Moreover sufficient conditions can be derived for different scheduling algorithms. Popular examples are Rate Monotonic (RM) and Earliest Deadline First (EDF) for which a sufficient schedulability condition was derived in a seminal work by Liu and Layland [12]:

$$\sum_{i=1}^{m} \frac{e_i}{p_i} \leq U, \tag{2}$$

where $U = 1$ for EDF and $U = m(2^{\frac{1}{m}} - 1)(> 0.69)$ for RM. Other scheduling algorithms, called *Pfair* [2], guarantee schedulability under condition 2 with $U = 1$ on a single processor architecture and scale well also to multiprocessor architectures, by setting U equal to the available number of processors. It is worth pointing out that in schedulability analysis e_i are the *worst-case* execution times for processes and that conservative choices on U allow to achieve robustness with respect to unmodeled delays or to reserve space for other processes, as required.

2.3   Platform Definition

Given the choice of the time triggered MoC and of a class of real time schedulers, the implementation platform can be parameterized by:

$$U, e_1, \ldots, e_m, \tag{3}$$

to be used in (2). A m-tuple of activation periods $\mathbf{p} \in \mathbb{N}^m$ satisfying (2) is guaranteed to yield a design adhering to the MoC. It is worth noting that the set of parameters (3) may represent a family of implementation platforms, all meeting or exceeding those requirements. As a matter of fact information on the HW/SW architecture condensed in the proposed platform are: 1) it must ensure worst case execution time of e_i, 2) it has to be endowed with a preemptive RTOS, 3) the scheduling algorithm has to guarantee schedulability with total utilization U. As shown next, the proposed characterization for the platform leads to a compact analytical formulation of the control design problem.

3   Problem Formulation

Consider the following collection of scalar systems $\mathcal{S}_i, i = 1, \ldots, m$ each described by:

$$x_i(k + 1) = a_i x_i(k) + b_i u_i(k). \tag{4}$$

Assume $b_i \neq 0 \ \forall i = 1, \ldots, m$, i.e. all systems are completely controllable. Each system is controlled in feedback by a process τ_i. Such processes are implemented according to the time-triggered model of computation. The processing activity consists of deriving the x_i values from sensor data and computing the control values using a static feedback gain γ_i. The worst case execution time of each (*job* of) τ_i is denoted by e_i. Sensor processing activities may have very different execution times, depending on the type of sensors used on each sub-system[1], hence e_i may differ.

The control law applied to each system can be written as follows:

$$u_i(k) = \begin{cases} \gamma_i x_i(k - p_i) & k = hp_i, \\ u_i(k - 1) & hp_i < k < (h + 1)p_i, \end{cases} \tag{5}$$

where $h \in \mathbb{N}$. The resulting (time varying) closed loop dynamics is:

$$x_i(k + 1) = a_i x_i(k) + b_i \gamma_i x_i(k - p_i - k \bmod p_i). \tag{6}$$

3.1   Closed Loop Stability Analysis

In order to derive a time invariant representation, each $\mathcal{S}_i$ system is re-sampled taking one out of every p_i samples: $\hat{x}_i(h) = x_i(hp_i)$. The resulting dynamics can be written as: $\hat{x}_i(h + 1) = a_i^{p_i} \hat{x}(h) + \sum_{j=0}^{p_i-1} a_i^j b_i \gamma_i \hat{x}_i(h - 1)$. An equivalent form is given by:

$$\hat{\mathbf{x}}_i(h + 1) = \begin{bmatrix} 0 & 1 \\ \beta_i \hat{\gamma}_i & a_i^{p_i} \end{bmatrix} \hat{\mathbf{x}}_i(h), \tag{7}$$

where $\beta_i = \sum_{j=0}^{p_i-1} a_i^j$, $\hat{\gamma}_i = b_i \gamma_i$, and $\hat{\mathbf{x}}_i(h) = [\hat{x}_i(h - 1) \ \hat{x}_i(h)]^T$. The closed loop dynamics (6) of $\mathcal{S}_i$ can be related to the one of the considered subsequence thanks to the following:

Lemma 1. *System* (6) *is globally asymptotically stable if and only if system* (7) *is.*

System (7) is in standard companion form and its characteristic polynomial is given by

$$z^2 - a_i^{p_i} z - \beta_i \hat{\gamma}_i.$$

Applying Jury's criterion, system (7) is globally asymptotically stable if and only if, the following hold:

$$\beta_i \hat{\gamma}_i > -1 \tag{8}$$
$$\beta_i \hat{\gamma}_i < 1 + a_i^{p_i} \tag{9}$$
$$\beta_i \hat{\gamma}_i < 1 - a_i^{p_i}, \tag{10}$$

---

[1] In example, the position of a pendulum could be measured using a position encoder or processing the video feed from a camera.

where:

$$\beta_i = \begin{cases} p_i & a_i = 1 \\ \frac{1-a_i^{p_i}}{1-a_i} & a_i \neq 1. \end{cases}$$

The analysis of the system's stability turns out to be particularly easy for positive systems, i.e. $a_i > 0$. This assumption will be used throughout the rest of this paper and is valid whenever (4) is the result of sampling a scalar continuous LTI system. Hence, inequality (9) is implied by (10), and the following Proposition holds.

Proposition 1 *Consider system (6), then the following statements are true:*

1. *if $a_i = 1$ the closed loop system is asymptotically stable for all $\hat\gamma_i$ such that $-\frac{1}{p_i} < \hat\gamma_i < 0$;*
2. *if $a_i \neq 1$ the set of stabilizing solutions for $\hat\gamma_i$ is given by: $-\frac{1-a_i}{1-a_i^{p_i}} < \hat\gamma_i < (1-a_i)$. If the open loop system $\mathcal{S}_i$ is asymptotically stable $(0 < a_i < 1)$ then this set is non empty (a trivial stabilizing solution is $\hat\gamma_i = 0$). If $\mathcal{S}_i$ is unstable $(a_i > 1)$ then the set of stabilizing solutions for $\hat\gamma_i$ is non empty if and only if $p_i < \frac{\log 2}{\log a_i}$.*

3.2   Robustness Metric

In order to characterize the robustness of the closed loop system we introduce the following definition:

Definition 1. *Consider the discrete time linear system*

$$\mathbf{x}(k+1) = A(\gamma)\mathbf{x}(k), \tag{11}$$

where $\mathbf{x} \in \mathcal{R}^n$, $\gamma \in \mathcal{R}^m$. Let $\Gamma \subseteq \mathcal{R}^m$ be such that the system is globally asymptotically stable if and only if $\gamma \in \Gamma$. Let $||.||$ denote some norm in $\mathcal{R}^m$. We define stability radius μ *the radius of the largest norm ball (induced by $||.||$) contained in Γ; we define* stability center *the center of the corresponding norm ball.*

Using feedback law (5) for each $\mathcal{S}_i$, the corresponding stability radius $\mu_{\mathcal{S}_i}$ is a measure of the largest perturbation of the gain γ_i that can be tolerated without jeopardizing stability of the closed loop system.

Let $\mathcal{S}$ denote the collection of systems $\mathcal{S}_i$ with $i = 1, \dots, m$. A natural extension of Definition 1 for the collection is: $\mu_{\mathcal{S}} = \min_{i=1,\dots,m} \mu_{\mathcal{S}_i}$. A direct consequence of Proposition 1 is the following

Corollary 1. *The stability radius of system (6) with respect to variations of $\hat\gamma_i$ and to the $||.||_\infty$ norm is given by*

$$\mu_{\mathcal{S}_i} = \begin{cases} \frac{1-a_i}{2(1-a_i^{p_i})}(2-a_i^{p_i}) & a_i \neq 1 \\ \frac{1}{2p_i} & a_i = 1 \end{cases} \tag{12}$$

Moreover, the stability center is given by:

$$\hat\gamma_i = \begin{cases} -a_i^{p_i} \frac{1-a_i}{2(1-a_i^{p_i})} & a_i \neq 1 \\ -\frac{1}{2p_i} & a_i = 1 \end{cases} \tag{13}$$

Remark 1. Definition 1 could be extended by considering a weigthing matrix $W \succ 0$ and by defining μ as the radius of the largest weighted norm ball. This extension could be useful in practical applications without significantly changing the results presented below. However, to keep the notation as simple as possible, we will still refer to the stability radius as defined above.

Remark 2. The stability radius $\mu_{\mathcal{S}_i}$ is a monotone decreasing function of p_i. Moreover, if the system $\mathcal{S}_i$ is open loop asymptotically stable (i.e. $0 < a_i < 1$) then it is obviously stabilized with any choice of the sampling period and a lower bound for the stability radius (obtained with $p_i \to \infty$) is given by $1 - a_i$.

3.3   Optimization Problem

We are now in the condition to state the following problem:

Problem 1. Consider the collection $\mathcal{S}$ controlled by a set of time triggered periodic processes. Each τ_i, $i = 1, \ldots, m$ has a computation load e_i. Let U be the maximum utilization factor which guarantees schedulability for the assumed scheduling algorithm. Find the set of activation periods p_i and of feedback gains $\hat{\gamma}_i$ with $i = 1, \ldots, m$ such that: 1) the schedulability condition is respected, 2) the stability radius is maximized, 3) gains are at the stability center. e_i and p_i are integer numbers referred to the computer clock cycle, and $\hat{\gamma}_i \in \mathbb{R}$.

In essence the above problem consists of optimizing the system performance (stability radius) under real-time schedulability constraints.

Remark 3. Since in this paper we deal with scalar systems and the $|.|_\infty$ norm, the stability center and the stability radius can be computed in closed form from the activation periods p_i. Thanks to these assumptions, the mixed-integer Problem 1 can be reduced to the integer problem yielding the periods, the stability center being derived in a second step.

A related question is deciding whether for a given vector of computation requirements $e_1, e_2, \ldots, e_m$, a desired stability radius $\bar{\theta}$ can be achieved on a single CPU architecture. A solution to these problems will be presented next.

4   Optimization Algorithm

Problem 1 can be formalized as:

$$
\begin{cases}
\max_{\mathbf{p}} \mu_{\mathcal{S}} \\
\sum_i \frac{e_i}{p_i} \leq U \\
p_i < \frac{\log 2}{\log a_i}, & \text{if } a_i > 1 \\
\mu_{\mathcal{S}} \geq \bar{\mu} \\
p_i \in \mathbb{N} \backslash \{0\},
\end{cases}
\tag{14}
$$

where the decision variables $\mathbf{p} = [p_1, p_2, \ldots, p_m]^T$ are the activation periods of the processes τ_i, which are integer positive numbers, and $\bar{\mu}$ is the minimum stability radius acceptable for the problem. It is worth noting that if the problem encompasses open loop asymptotically stable systems, i.e. $a_i < 1$ for some i, then it is convenient to require, without loss of generality, $\bar{\mu} > 1 - a_i$. In fact if the optimal solution achieves an objective lower than $1 - a_i$, one could run control process τ_i at arbitrarily long periods p_i without effecting the cost function. Process τ_i would not actually improve robustness of the controlled system, the only real effect of including τ_i in the control problem would then be to make the admissible solution space infinite. Similarly systems with $a_i = 1$ may need a $\bar{\mu} > 0$ to ensure finiteness of the solutions space and to obtain a well-posed problem. For well posed problems the number of feasible solutions is finite. However, complete enumeration approaches may not be viable for large scale systems. A more effective approach is based on the use of a branch and bound scheme.

4.1   Branch and Bound Algorithm

In order to illustrate the proposed branch and bound algorithm it is useful to introduce some notation. $\mathcal{P} \subseteq \mathbb{N}^m$ will denote the set of period m-tuples $\mathbf{p}$ respecting the constraint inequalities; $\mu_l(\bar{\mathcal{P}})$, $\mu_u(\bar{\mathcal{P}})$ will denote respectively a lower bound and an upper bound of the objective function $\mu_S(\mathbf{p})$ on the region $\bar{\mathcal{P}}$. $\mathcal{L}$ will denote a list of the disjoint subregions of the solution space which are currently candidate for the solution. The μ_l function is assumed to be derived from an admissible solution. The μ_u function is required to have the property that, when applied to a set containing a single element, it returns the value of the cost function computed for that element. The branch and bound algorithm can be formulated as follows.

Algorithm 1
Insert $\mathcal{P}$ *into* $\mathcal{L}$
set variable μ^* *to* $\mu_l(\mathcal{P})$
choose $\mathbf{p} \in \mathcal{P}$ *s.t.* $\mu_l(\mathcal{P}) = \mu_S(\mathbf{p})$
set variable $\mathbf{p}^* = \mathbf{p}$
repeat
    choose a region $\mathcal{H}$ *from* $\mathcal{L}$ *and remove it from* $\mathcal{L}$
    partition $\mathcal{H}$ *into non-empty disjoint subregions* $\mathcal{H}_1, \ldots, \mathcal{H}_h$
    for each $\mathcal{H}_i$
        if $\mu_u(\mathcal{H}_i) \leq \mu^*$
            discard $\mathcal{H}_i$
        else
            insert $\mathcal{H}_i$ *into* $\mathcal{L}$
            if $\mu_l(\mathcal{H}_i) > \mu^*$
                set $\mu^* = \mu_l(\mathcal{H}_i)$
                set $\mathbf{p}^* = \mathbf{p} \in \mathcal{H}_i$ *s.t.* $\mu_S(\mathbf{p}) = \mu_l(\mathcal{H}_i)$
            endif
        endif
    end for each
until $\mathcal{L}$ *is empty*

For the problem under analysis the $\mathcal{H}_i$ subregions can be obtained by fixing some of the elements of the $\mathbf{p}$ vector. Let $\mathcal{I}(\mathcal{H}) \subseteq \{1, \ldots, m\}$ be the index set of periods that are fixed to yield $\mathcal{H}$, then a finer partition $\mathcal{H}_1, \ldots, \mathcal{H}_h$ can be obtained selecting one index z not in $\mathcal{I}(\mathcal{H})$ and fixing p_z to its h different admissible values[2]. The selection of the μ_u, μ_l functions is a particularly important issue. In fact, if the bounds are not tight, the algorithm does not "discard" a good number of regions resulting into a nearly exhaustive search. On the other hand accurate bounds may not be viable if overly expensive computation is required to derive them. In order to ensure correctness of the algorithm, the lower bound $\mu_l(\mathcal{H}_i)$ is assumed to be always constructed using some feasible solution $\mathbf{p}^* \in \mathcal{H}_i$ such that $\mu_S(\mathbf{p}^*) = \mu_l(\mathcal{H}_i)$.

One possible upper bound $\mu_u(\mathcal{H}_i)$ can be derived using $\min_{j \in \mathcal{I}(\mathcal{H}_i)} \mu_{S_j}(p_j)$, i.e. $\mu_u(\mathcal{H}_i) = \min\{\mu_u(\mathcal{H}), \min_{j \in \mathcal{I}(\mathcal{H}_i) \setminus \mathcal{I}(\mathcal{H})} \mu_{S_j}(p_j)\}$. This upper bound may be quite optimistic and becomes tighter as the number of fixed periods increases. When all periods are fixed, i.e. $\mathcal{H}_i = \{\mathbf{p}\}$, it becomes $\mu_u(\mathcal{H}_i) = \mu_S(\mathbf{p})$. Its computation cost is very low especially when periods are fixed incrementally. Different derivations for μ_u and for μ_l can be obtained considering the continuous relaxation of the problem, which is well posed for the positive systems $(a_i > 0)$ considered in this paper.

4.2   The Continuous Relaxation

The integrity constraint on the periods is dropped, i.e. $p_i \in [1, +\infty)$. In order to express the schedulability constraint in linear form it is convenient to make the change of variable $f_i = \frac{1}{p_i}$. The resulting problem is given by:

$$
\begin{cases}
\max_{\mathbf{f}} \mu_S \\
\sum_i e_i f_i \leq U \\
f_i > \frac{\log a_i}{\log 2} \quad (if \ a_i > 1) \\
\mu_S \geq \bar{\mu} \\
0 < f_i \leq 1,
\end{cases}
\tag{15}
$$

where $\mathbf{f}$ is the vector of decision variables f_i. Considering integer e_i and a uniprocessor platform $(U \leq 1)$, constraint $f_i \leq 1$ is implied by $\sum_i e_i f_i \leq U$ and will be henceforth dropped. Moreover, the following assumption will implicitly be used: $\bar{\mu} \geq \max_j (1 - a_j), \forall a_j < 1$. Introduce the following function:

$$
H(\mu) = \sum_i e_i \omega_i(\mu) - U,
\tag{16}
$$

where:

$$
\omega_i(\mu) = \begin{cases}
\frac{\log a_i}{\log 2 \frac{a_i - 1 + \mu}{a_i - 1 + 2\mu}} & a_i \neq 1 \\
2\mu & a_i = 1.
\end{cases}
\tag{17}
$$

---

[2] This set is finite because it is a projection of some subset of $\mathcal{P}$ which is finite. The number h varies with z.

The solution to Problem 15 can be found as shown in the following:

Proposition 2 *Problem 15 has a solution if and only if*

$$H(\bar{\mu}) \leq 0. \tag{18}$$

If condition 18 holds, then $H(\mu)$ has only one zero in the set $\mu \geq \bar{\mu}$ which is the optimal solution of Problem 15.

Proof. As a first remark observe that problem 15 can be written in the following form:

$$\begin{cases} \max_{\mathbf{f}} \mu \\ \mu_{S_i} \geq \mu \\ \sum_i e_i f_i \leq U \\ f_i > \frac{\log a_i}{\log 2} \quad (if \ a_i > 1) \\ \mu \geq \bar{\mu} \\ f_i > 0, \end{cases} \tag{19}$$

which, through simple computations, is equivalent to:

$$\begin{cases} \max_{\mathbf{f}} \mu \\ f_i \geq w_i(\mu) \\ \sum_i e_i f_i \leq U \\ \mu \geq \bar{\mu}. \end{cases} \tag{20}$$

Constraints $f_i > 0$ and $f_i > \frac{\log a_i}{\log 2}$ (for $a_i > 1$) have been removed since they are implied by $f_i \geq w_i(\mu)$. For a fixed μ, feasible solutions exist if and only if $H(\mu) \leq 0$. Since each w_i is strictly increasing in $\mu \geq \bar{\mu}$ also $H(\mu)$ is and this consideration leads to the proof.

Remark 4. If $\mu^{(c)}$ denotes the optimal solution, then decision variables associated to the optimal solution are given by $f_i^{(c)} = w_i(\mu^{(c)})$.

Remark 5. Condition 18 is interesting in itself since it addresses the problem of whether a platform is powerful enough to provide a specified level of performance $\bar{\mu}$.

Finding the zero $H(\cdot)$ can be very costly for large scale systems. Hence, it is convenient to find a lower and an upper estimation for the solution so as to bound the search. To this end, observe that nonlinearity in function H is due to the terms relative to $a_i \neq 1$. Considering the case $a_i < 1$ and restricting to $\mu \geq 1 - a_i$, we can observe that $w_i(\mu) = \frac{\log a_i}{\log 2 \frac{a_i - 1 + \mu}{a_i - 1 + 2\mu}}$, is concave and strictly increasing. Hence it is very easy to show the following inequality:

$$\overline{w}_i(\mu) \geq w_i \geq \underline{w}_i(\mu)$$

$$\overline{w}_i(\mu) = (\tfrac{3}{2} + 2\mu\tfrac{1}{a_i - 1}) \log a_i \tag{21}$$

$$\underline{w}_i(\mu) = (2 + 2\mu\tfrac{1}{a_i - 1}) \log a_i > 0.$$

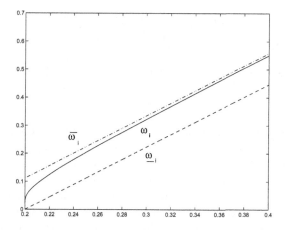

Fig. 1. Figure showing the upper and lower bound for ω_i for $a_i = 0.8$.

The meaning of the linear bounding functions appear clearly in Figure 1, where the case $a_i = 0.8$ is considered. A similar result can be found for $a_i > 1$ and $\mu \geq 0$:

$$\overline{\omega_i}(\mu) \geq \omega_i \geq \underline{\omega_i}(\mu)$$

$$\overline{\omega_i}(\mu) = (\tfrac{3}{2} + 2\mu\tfrac{1}{a_i-1}) \log a_i \tag{22}$$

$$\underline{\omega_i}(\mu) = (\tfrac{1}{\log 2} + 2\mu\tfrac{1}{a_i-1}) \log a_i > 0.$$

The use of linear approximations allows for a very fast computation of an upper and a lower bound of the optimal value for μ_S in Problem 15, thus limiting the search for the zero of $H(\cdot)$ to a small region. It can be interesting to take a glance at the form of the approximate solution in a simple case. Suppose, for instance, that all systems are open loop unstable ($a_i > 1, \forall i$). Denote by $\overline{\mu}^{(c)}$ the linear upper bound for the optimum, by $\overline{f}_i^c$ the decision variables for which it is attained, and introduce the variables:

$$w_i = \frac{\log a_i}{a_i - 1} \; ; \; \bar{U} = U - \sum_i e_i \frac{\log a_i}{\log 2}.$$

It is very easy to find:

$$\overline{\mu}^{(c)} = \frac{\bar{U}}{2\sum_j e_j w_j} \; ; \; \overline{f}_i^{(c)} = \frac{\log a_i}{\log 2} + w_i \frac{\bar{U}}{2\sum_j e_j w_j}.$$

For each decision variable $\overline{f}_i^{(c)}$ we can distinguish a term $\frac{\log a_i}{\log 2}$ necessary to achieve stability, which is summed to a weighted fraction of the scaled utilization $\bar{U}$. In this computation both factors relative to the systems dynamics (w_i) and to the execution time of the processes (e_j) are accounted for.

	System 1	System 2	System 3
a_i	0.992	1.0512	1.005
b_i	1	1	1

Table 1. Dynamical parameters of the controlled systems

The analysis of the continuous relaxation of Problem 14 is useful for it provides a pair of very interesting upper bound functions μ_l for the branch and bound algorithm. A low cost choice is the the optimal value of the restricted problem obtained using the lower linear approximation $\underline{w}_i$ of functions w_i (which correspond to looser constraints). A better upper bound is given by the exact resolution of the continuous relaxation. It requires solving the non-linear equation $H(\mu) = 0$. It is worth noting that fixing some of the decision variables f_i (as requested by the invocation $\mu_l(\mathcal{H}_i)$ in Algorithm 1) does not change substantially the way Problem 15 and its linear approximations are solved.

Lower bound $\mu_l(\mathcal{H}_i)$ are less easy to find. In this case the continuous relaxation provides good heuristics. A good lower bound can in most cases be obtained by solving Problem 15 (or its upper linear approximation) and and then by changing the non-integer periods to their ceiling (which is a conservative approximation with respect to the schedulability constraint).

4.3   Numerical Evaluation

We illustrate a possible design flow based on the results presented in the previous section on a simple example. We consider a set of three scalar systems, whose dynamics are described by the a_i, b_i parameters in table 1.

The results of the solution of the optimization problem related to different execution times for control processes are reported in table 2. The first three rows show different choices of computation times for control tasks. The second part of the table (from the third row) is devoted to the outcome of the Branch and Bound algorithm (optimal cost functions and periods for which it is attained). Finally the last rows show results of the continuous relaxation. In the first experiment, the task used to control the system $\mathcal{S}_1$ is assumed to be very demanding (100 time units for each execution).

This may be the result of a choice of a low quality sensor (requiring a heavy post-processing of the acquired data). As might be expected, the achieved stability radius is quite low (if compared with the other experiments). Moreover, the system requiring more "attention" (i.e. lower sampling period) is the most unstable one ($\mathcal{S}_2$). In the second experiment c_1 is lowered from 100 to 10 thus relieving the CPU of a remarkable workload. As a result, more aggressive policies on the choices of the activation periods may be selected improving the stability radius. In the third experiment the effects of increasing the computational load required by the task controlling system $\mathcal{S}_2$ are shown. It is possible to observe a remarkable performance degradation with respect to the second experiment.

	Exp. 1	Exp. 2	Exp. 3
e_1	100	10	10
e_2	1	1	5
e_3	10	10	10
μ_S	0.0095	0.0226	0.0136
p_1	159	29	65
p_2	10	8	10
p_3	37	19	29
$\mu_S^{(c)}$	0.0096	0.0232	0.0138
$p_1^{(c)}$	155.6	29.07	65.65
$p_2^{(c)}$	10.93	8.43	10.02
$p_3^{(c)}$	37.6	18.6	28.66

Table 2. Results of the optimization

Interestingly enough, the optimization process tends to penalize systems which are closer to stability while keeping unvaried, as much as possible, the activation period of the process controlling S_2. As a final remark, the continuous relaxation provides good estimation for both the objective function and the activation periods. For almost all cases periods corresponding to the optimal solution are lower or upper round up of the continuous relaxation. This is not true for in the first experiment for p_1, whose optimal value is 155.6 for the continuous relaxation and 159 for the discrete problem.

5   Conclusions and Future Work

In this paper, an integrated design procedure has been presented for determining optimal scheduling and control parameters for a set of controllers operating on scalar linear systems. The choice of a performance metric related to systems' robustness and of a preemptive scheduling model allows for a compact analytical formulation of the system design, amenable to an efficient numerical solution based on a branch and bound scheme. This is a first step towards more general results concerning mixed scheduling/control synthesis. The most natural continuation of this work is the extension of the approach to the control of multi-dimensional systems thus leading to potentially relevant industrial applications. Other important issues to investigate are alternative formulations for the platform constraints, with two distinct purposes: 1) alleviating, if possible, pessimism inherent to the choice of the time triggered approach, 2) extending the analysis to architectures with a higher degree of parallelism, such as multiprocessors and distributed architectures.

References

[1] In Springer-Verlag, editor, *EMSOFT 2001: First Workshop on Embedded Software, Lecture Notes in Computer Science*, 2001.

[2] S.K. Baruah, N.K. Cohen, C.G. Plaxton, and D.A. Varvel. Proportionate progress: A notion of fairness in resource allocation. *Algorithmica*, 6, 1996.

[3] A. Bicchi, A. Marigo, and B. Piccoli. Quantized control systems and discrete nonholonomy. *IEEE Trans. on Automatic Control*, 2001.

[4] Roger Brockett. Minimum attention control, 1997.

[5] G. Buttazzo. *Hard Real-Time Computing Systems: Predictable Scheduling Algorithms and Applications*. Kluwer Academic Publishers, Boston, 1997.

[6] David F. Delchamps. Extracting state information from a quantized output record. *Systems and Control Letters*, 1989.

[7] N. Elia and S. Mitter. Stabiliztion of linear systems with limited information. *IEEE Trans. on Automatic Control*, 2001.

[8] Dimitris Hristu and Kristi Moransen. Limited communication control. *System and Control Letters*, 37(4):193–205, July 1999.

[9] T. J. Koo, J. Liebman, C. Ma, and S. Sastry. Hierarchical approach for design of multi-vehicle multi-modal embedded software. In Springer-Verlag, editor, *EMSOFT 2001: First Workshop on Embedded Software, Lecture Notes in Computer Science*, 2001.

[10] H. Kopetz and G. Grnsteidl. Ttp-a protocol for fault-tolerant real-time systems. *IEEE Computer*, January 1994.

[11] K. Kuetzer, S. Malik, R. Newton, J.M. Rabaey, and A. Sangiovanni-Vincentelli. System-level design: Orthogonalization of concerns and platform-based design. *IEEE Transaction on coputer-aided design of integrated circuits and systems*, 21(27), 2000.

[12] C.L. Liu and J.W. Layland. Scheduling algorithms for multiprogramming in a hard-real-time environment. *Journal of the Association for Computing Machinery*, 20(1), 1973.

[13] G. N. Nair and R. J. Evans. State estimation under bit rate constraints. In *Proc. of the 37th IEEE Conference on Decision and Control*, Tampa, Florida, December 1998.

[14] H. Rehbinder and M. Sanfridson. Scheduling of a limited communication channel for optimal control. In *Proc. of the 39th IEEE Conference on Decision and Control*, Sidney, Australia, December 2000.

[15] C.M. Kirsch T. Henzinger, B. Horowitzm. Embedded control systems development with giotto. In *Proc. of ACM SIGPLAN 2001 Workshop on Languages, Compilers, and Tools for Embedded Systems (LCTES'2001)*, June 2001.

[16] S. Tatikonda, A. Sahaim, and S. Mitter. Control of lqg systems under communication constraints. In *Proc. of the 37th IEEE Conference on Decision and Control*, Tampa, Florida, December 1998.

[17] W.S. Wong and R. Brockett. Systems with finite bandwidth constraints - part i: State estimation problems. *IEEE Trans. on Automatic Control*, 42(9), 1997.

[18] W.S. Wong and R. Brockett. Systems with finite bandwidth constraints - part ii: Stabilization with limited infromation feedback. *IEEE Trans. on Automatic Control*, 44(5), 1999.

[19] L. Xiao, M. Johansson, H. Hindi, S. Boyd, and A. Goldsmith. Joint optimization of communication rates and linear systems. *submitted to IEEE Trans. on Automatic Control*.

Optimal Control of Quantized Input Systems[*]

Stefania Pancanti, Laura Leonardi, Lucia Pallottino, and Antonio Bicchi

Centro Interdipartimentale di Ricerca "Enrico Piaggio"
Università di Pisa, 56100 Pisa, Italy.
www.piaggio.ccii.unipi.it

Abstract. In this paper we consider the problem of optimal control (specifically, minimum-time steering) for systems with quantized inputs. In particular, we propose a new approach to the solution of the optimal control problem for an important class of nonlinear systems, i.e. chained–form systems. By exploiting results on the structure of the reachability set of these systems under quantized control, the optimal solution is determined solving an integer linear programming problem. Our algorithm represents an improvement with respect to classical approaches in terms of exactness, as it does not resort to any a priori state-space discretization. Although the computational complexity of the problem in our formulation is still formally exponential, it lends itself to application of Branch and Bound techniques, which substantially cuts down computations in many cases, as it has been experimentally observed.

1 Introduction

In this paper we consider the problem of optimally steering discrete-time dynamic systems of the form

$$x^+ = g(u, x), \ x \in \mathbb{R}^n, \ u \in \mathcal{U} \subset \mathbb{R}^m \tag{1}$$

where the input set, U, is quantized, i.e. finite or with values on regular lattices in $\mathbb{R}^m$.

Quantized control systems (QCS) arise in a number of applications because of several different physical phenomena or technological constraints. Although quantization is usually regarded as an approximation-induced disturbance to be rejected ([1, 2]), a different viewpoint has been taken more recently ([3, 4, 5, 6]) that quantization is a deterministic, memoryless nonlinear phenomenon that may affect inherent properties of the system in very specific ways, and that its study can, and should be performed directly. This approach is particularly meaningful when quantization is coarse, or when it is introduced on purpose in order to reduce the technological complexity of the control systems, as e.g. in mass-produced embedded systems or in distributed control systems.

---

[*] Work partially supported by CNR-Agenzia 2000 contract CNRC00E714-001, "Optimal Control Algorithms for Embedded Systems: Interplay between Continuous and Discrete Dynamics".

C.J. Tomlin and M.R. Greenstreet (Eds.): HSCC 2002, LNCS 2289, pp. 351–363, 2002.

Besides the fact that many system are quantized in nature, this paper also makes the point that introducing input quantization on purpose might be expedient in attacking notoriously difficult problems, such as the optimal steering problem considered here. In this paper, we will argue that this is the case at least for an important, albeit particular class of nonlinear systems, i.e. nonholonomic systems in chained form ([7]).

The problem of optimal control for chained-form systems in an unconstrained state space is considered in this paper in discrete-time with quantized inputs. Quantization effects may result in practice from the use of digital actuators (such as e.g. stepper motors) or sensors (encoders). On the other hand, quantization might also be introduced on purpose to provide algorithms to solve optimal control problems. Indeed, in this paper we will make the point that quantizing the input (even when this is available in continuous form) can be a good alternative to approaches using discretization of the whole state space (such as, e.g., in dynamic programming).

Our approach to the steering problem is based on the theory of quantized control systems, and exploits results reported in [8] (for a more detailed account, please see also [9]) about the lattice structure of the reachable set for this class of systems. In particular, conditions have been obtained under which the reachability set is a lattice, and for such lattice a complete description can be obtained by a finitely computable algorithm. The algorithm described in [8] offers a polynomial time, computationally very effective steering method for the system based on standard integer programming techniques.

To solve the optimal control steering problem, which turns out to be an integer linear programming problem, tools from graph theory are adopted. Although standard techniques cannot be applied directly, we propose a solution algorithm to solve the optimal steering problem for quantized chained form systems, which is shown to converge to the optimum.

The paper is organized as follows. We begin by introducing some basic definitions and ideas that will be necessary in the work. In Section 2 some properties of discrete chained-form systems related to reachability are explained. These properties are applied to develop the optimal control steering problem formulation (section 3) and the solution algorithm (section 4). As an application, in Section 5 we solve the steering problem for an n-trailers system, using previous results. Finally, in the last section, we present some conclusions and discuss future directions of research.

2   Problem Formulation and Related Results

We are interested in studying a particular class of nonlinear systems, and specifically two-input driftless[1] nonholonomic systems, which can be written (upon coordinate changes and state feedback) in a so–called chained–form. Such form is described by the ordinary differential equation

---
[1] a system is said to be driftless if all configurations are equilibrium under zero control.

$$\dot{x}_1 = u_1$$
$$\dot{x}_2 = u_2$$
$$\dot{x}_3 = x_2 u_1$$
$$\vdots = \vdots \qquad\qquad\qquad (2)$$
$$\dot{x}_n = x_{n-1} u_1$$

The chained-form has been introduced by [7] as a canonical form for some continous-time, driftless nonholonomic systems and has been since then used extensively in the automatic control literature for modelling and controlling systems that range from wheeled vehicles with an arbitrary number of trailers, to satellites ([10, 11, 12, 13, 14, 15, 16]). While many steering methods for chained form systems have been provided in the literature, optimal control for these systems is still a completely open problem.

Consider the case where inputs to the system, rather than being allowed to change continuously in time, are bound to switch among a finite set of different levels at given switching times, which are multiples of a given time interval. Assuming such sampling interval to be of unit length, a discrete time model of chained-form systems can be easily obtained from (2) by integration as

$$x_1^+ = x_1 + u_1$$
$$x_2^+ = x_2 + u_2$$
$$x_3^+ = x_3 + x_2 u_1 + \tfrac{1}{2} u_1 u_2$$
$$\vdots = \vdots \qquad\qquad\qquad (3)$$
$$x_n^+ = x_n + \sum_{j=1}^{n-2} x_{n-j} \frac{u^j}{j!} + u_1^{n-2} u_2 \frac{1}{(n-1)!}$$

We will assume that inputs $u = (u_1, u_2)$ can take values within a state-independent set of input symbols U, which is symmetric (i.e., if $u \in U$, then also $\bar{u} = -u \in U$). The set Ω of admissible control words (i.e. strings of admissible input symbols) is endowed with a composition law given by concatenation of strings. Because of the symmetry of U, every element $\omega \in \Omega$ has an inverse $\omega^{-1} \in \Omega$, simply defined as $(u_1 u_2 \cdots u_m)^{-1} = -u_m \cdots -u_2 -u_1, \pm u_i \in U, \forall i$. Let us denote by $\mathcal{A} : \Omega \times \mathcal{X} \to \mathcal{X}$ the state transition map, i.e. the map that associates to every initial state and every admissible input word, the corresponding end point reached by the state. In general one can write, $\forall \omega \in \Omega$

$$\mathcal{A}(\omega, x) = x + \Delta(\omega) + A(\omega, x), \qquad\qquad (4)$$

where, by some simple, if tedious, calculations it can be shown (see [9]) that

1. the mixed term $A(\omega, x)$ is linear in the sum of the first and the second components of the state;
2. the $\Delta(\omega)$ term is such that $\Delta(\omega^{-1}\omega) = 0$.

Hence, $\mathcal{A}(\omega^{-1}, \mathcal{A}(\omega, x)) = x$, i.e. system (3) is invertible.

In the state manifold of chained-form systems(2, 3) it is customary to distinguish a *base* subsystem, consisting of the first two state variables (x_1, x_2), and a *fiber* susbsytem with coordinates $(x_3, \ldots, x_n)$. Observe that the restriction of chained-form systems to the base variables is linear, and indeed trivial to control. On the other hand, the difficulty in controlling fiber variables increases with the dimension of the state space. A typical example of such situation is in parking maneuvers of tractor-trailer systems, where base variables are associated with the steering tractor, and fiber variables correspond to the configurations of the trailers (see section 5).

Accordingly, the reachability problem for discrete-time chained form systems can be decoupled in the analysis of reachability of the base space, and of the fiber space $\mathbb{R}^{n-2}$ associated with a reachable base point $(\overline{x}_1, \overline{x}_2)$. On the base space system (3) has the simple form

$$x^+ = x + u, \ x \in \mathbb{R}^2, u \in U. \tag{5}$$

For such linear driftless systems, the analysis of the reachable set has been characterized as follows ([8]):

Theorem 1. *A necessary condition for the reachable set from the origin R_0 to be dense is that U contains $n + 1$ controls of which n are linearly indipendent. If $u_1, \ldots, u_n \in U$ are linearly indipendent and there exists n irrational negative numbers $\alpha_1, \ldots, \alpha_n$ such that $v_i = \alpha_i u_i \in U$ for every $i = 1, \ldots, n$ then R_0 is dense. If there exists $m \leq n$ vectors v_i such that $\forall u \in U$, there exists m integers $a_i, \ldots, a_m$ such that $u = a_i v_i$, then R_0 is discrete. In particular, it is a lattice.*

Observe that the reachable set R_x from a generic point x is obtained by translation of R_0. Therefore, if the control set U is quantized, symmetric and rational (as it almost always is in cases of interest, and as we assume in the rest of this paper), the reachable set is a lattice.

Fixed a base point $(\overline{x}_1, \overline{x}_2)$, consider the subgroup $\tilde{\Omega} \subset \Omega$ of control words that take the base variables back to their initial configuration. In particular, these are sequences of inputs such that the sum of the first and the second components are zero, so that the quantity $A(\omega, x)$ and the first and the second components of $\Delta(\omega)$ are zero. The effect of such subgroup on the fiber subsystem can be described by

$$z^+ = z + v, z = (x_3, x_4, \cdots, x_n) \in \mathbb{R}^{n-2}, v \in \tilde{U} \tag{6}$$

where $\tilde{U} = \{\Delta(\omega), \omega \in \tilde{\Omega}\}$ and where $\Delta(\omega)$ denotes the $(n-2)$-dimensional projection of Δ on the fiber space. Clearly, $\tilde{U}$ is itself symmetric: indeed if $\omega \in \tilde{\Omega}$ then also $\omega^{-1} \in \tilde{\Omega}$ and $\Delta(\omega^{-1}) = -\Delta(\omega)$. The action of the subgroup $\tilde{\Omega}$ on the fiber is additive (namely, $\mathcal{A}(\tilde{\omega}_1, \mathcal{A}(\tilde{\omega}_2, x)) = A(\tilde{\omega}_1, x) + \mathcal{A}(\tilde{\omega}_2, x), \forall \tilde{\omega}_1, \tilde{\omega}_2 \in \tilde{\Omega})$, and the structure of the reachable set in the fiber is the same over every (reachable) base point.

For the set $\tilde{U}$ of all control inputs that can be applied to the fiber dynamics (6), corresponding to the set of input words $\tilde{\Omega}$ that drive base variables back to their initial values, the following result holds ([8]):

Theorem 2. *Let the control set U be quantized, symmetric and rational. Then, all elements $\Delta(\tilde{\omega}) \in \tilde{U}$ can be written as integer combinations of a finite set of generators Δ_i, uniquely determined from U. Each generator is a rational vector in $\mathbf{Q}^{n-2}$, corresponding to a control word $\tilde{\omega}_i \in \tilde{\Omega}$ in the original alphabet U.*

As a consequence, with reference to system (5), we can conclude that if the controls set U is rational and quantized, the reachability structure of a chained form discrete-time system is completely described by a lattice in the state space (the cartesian product of the base and fiber lattices). Such lattice structure, which plays a central role in our approach to solving the optimal steering problem, can be described completely by a finite number of generators, whose evaluation can be done in polynomial time with respect to the state space dimension and the number of control symbols in U ([9]).

3   Steering on Lattices: The Optimal Control Problem

Consider the system (3) with a quantized, rational and symmetric control set U. Let $H \in \mathbf{Q}^{n-2 \times m}$ denote the matrix whose columnns are the m generators $\Delta(\tilde{\omega}_i), i = 1, \cdots, m$. Without loss of generality, up to rescaling the fiber state space, we may take H to be an integer matrix. The *steering problem* on the fiber, i.e. the problem of finding a control sequence that takes the system (3) from an initial z_{start} to a desired z_{goal}, consists hence in solving a linear system of the form:

$$Hx = (z_{goal} - z_{start}). \tag{7}$$

Integer solutions $x \in \mathbf{Z}^m$ of this equation exist if an only if the initial and goal points differ by a vector belonging to the fiber lattice, which we will assume henceforth (in other cases, integer truncations of a real solution x will provide approximated steering to the goal, within a tolerance dictated by the lattice mesh).

Any solution $x = (x_1, \cdots, x_m) \in \mathbf{Z}^m$ of system (7) gives a sequence of cyclic control inputs that includes x_i instances of the words $\tilde{\omega}_i$. There are of course infinitely many possible solutions x, each corresponding to a combinatoric number of different possible sequences of control words $\tilde{\omega}_i$.

Optimal steering strategies among solutions of (7) will be considered introducing a cost p_i associated to the control symbol $u_i \in U$. The corresponding cost for a word $\omega = (u_1, u_2, \cdots, u_N), u_i \in U$ is defined as $C(\omega) = \|Px\|$, where x_i stands for the number of appearances of the symbol u_i in ω (with negative sign if $-u_i$ appears), and $P = \mathrm{diag}(p_i)$.

A constrained minimization problem can be considered at this point, i.e.

$$\min_x \|Px\|$$
$$\text{s. t.} \quad \begin{cases} Hx = x_{goal} - x_{start} \\ x \in \mathbf{Z}^m \end{cases} \tag{8}$$

leading to a linear integer program if a one-norm is considered, while using a two-norm would result in an integer quadratic program. Efficient algorithms do exist for both these problems: however, unfortunately, such formulation does not reflect the reality of our optimal control problem.

Indeed, in combining control words by concatenation cancellations of symbols may occur. To obtain the sum of two control actions $\Delta\tilde{\omega}_i, \Delta\tilde{\omega}_j$ on the fiber, corresponding to control words $\tilde{\omega}_i, \tilde{\omega}_j$ whose costs are $C(\tilde{\omega}_i)$ and $C(\tilde{\omega}_j)$, respectively, the sum $C(\tilde{\omega}_i) + C(\tilde{\omega}_j)$ is only an upper bound to the actual cost of the corresponding control. Indeed, cancellations of one or more trailing symbols in $\tilde{\omega}_i$ with an equal number of symbols leading in $\tilde{\omega}_j$ is possible. We will denote by $\hat{C}(\tilde{\omega}_i, \tilde{\omega}_j)$ the actual cost of the word pair $(\tilde{\omega}_i, \tilde{\omega}_j)$.

For example, if $\tilde{\omega}_i = u_1 u_2 u_3 u_4$ and $\tilde{\omega}_j = -u_4 u_5 - u_2 - u_1$, one has (in a minimum time problem) $C(\tilde{\omega}_i) = 4$ and $C(\tilde{\omega}_j) = 4$. However, the concatenation of $\tilde{\omega}_i$ with $\tilde{\omega}_j$ leads, by cancellations, to the control word $u_1 u_2 u_3 u_5 - u_2 - u_1$, so that $\hat{C}(\tilde{\omega}_i, \tilde{\omega}_j) = 6 < 8$. Obviously, cancellations are crucial in minimizing unnecessary maneuvers in the steering problem, and motivate the following reformulation of the optimal control problem.

Consider an oriented graph $G_0 = (N_0, A_0)$ with a set N_0 of $m + 2$ nodes, m of which are associated with generators $\Delta(\tilde{\omega}_i)$, and where a start node S and a goal node F are additionally considered. In the arc set A_0 of G_0, all arcs connecting the start and goal nodes S, F with all other nodes are included, i.e. $(S, i) \in A_0, i = 1, \ldots, m$ and $(i, F) \in A_0, i = 1, \ldots, m$. An arc (i, j) is included in A_0 only if $\tilde{\omega}_i$ and $\tilde{\omega}_j$ are not the inverse of each other. In particular, for every node $i \neq S, F$, the arc (i, i) is included in A_0.

To the arc $(i, j) \in A_0$ we associate the cost $\hat{C}_{i,j} \geq 0$ of the control sequence $(\tilde{\omega}_i, \tilde{\omega}_j)$, taking into account all possible cancellations. Notice that in general $\hat{C}_{i,j}$ is not equal to $\hat{C}_{j,i}$ (in the example above, for instance, $\hat{C}_{ji} = 4$).

A refinement step is necessary to finalize the graph construction for pairs $(\tilde{\omega}_i, \tilde{\omega}_j)$ where the number of cancellations is larger than the half-length of the shortest of the two words. Indeed, in this case it may happen that the cost of a triplet $(\tilde{\omega}_i, \tilde{\omega}_j, \tilde{\omega}_k)$ is underestimated by $\hat{C}_{ij} + \hat{C}_{jk}$. To avoid this problem, we remove in the graph the arc (i, j) corresponding to such pairs, and add a new node associated to $\Delta(\tilde{\omega}_i) + \Delta(\tilde{\omega}_j)$ with cost $\hat{C}_{ij}$. These new nodes are connected to all other nodes by arcs whose cost is evaluated as usual, with the exception of arcs corresponding again to cancellations of more than the half-length of either words, which are not considered in the new graph.

On the graph G_0, all possible combinations of the generating control words $\tilde{\omega}_i$ are represented by connected paths from S to F. The optimal control problem on the fiber space can hence be formulated as follows:

Given the oriented graph G_0, determine the minimum-cost path from S to F with the constraint that the sum of all Δ_i of visited nodes equals the desired fiber displacement $z_{goal} - z_{start}$.

Thus, the optimal control problem can be regarded as a minimum-cost path search on a graph, with a constraint on the sum of "tokens" collected at each visited node. Notice that G_0 contains cyclic arcs of type (i, i), allowing to collect an arbitrary integer number of the corresponding token $\Delta(\tilde{\omega}_i)$. The search problem is an $\mathcal{NP}$-complete linear integer programming problem ([17][18]), and differs substantially from standard shortest path searches on a graph because of the constraint and of the presence of cycles (cyclic paths are obviously never considered in unconstrained path searches). The following section proposes a correct and complete algorithm to solve this optimal control problem.

4   A Solution Algorithm

The non-standard nature of the optimization problem described above is such that even rather general solution techniques, as e.g. branch and bound, and commercial software tools for integer programming, cannot be used directly to solve the problem. We propose a procedure for the solution of this problem which basically consists of solving a sequence of problems of increasing complexity.

Consider first that an upper limit U on the optimal control cost can be easily obtained by evaluating the cost U_0 of *any* solution of the integer linear system (7) – for instance, a solution to problem (8).

At the first stage of the proposed algorithm, a new graph $G_1 = (N_1, A_1)$ is built by setting $N_1 = N_0$ and by removing all cyclic arcs from A_0, namely $A_1 = A_0 \setminus \{(i, i), \forall i\}$. A branch-and-bound algorithm is applied to search minimum cost, token-constrained paths on G_1. Within such branch-and-bound subprocedure, the token constraint is relaxed, hence a number of classical minimum cost path search problems are obtained, which are solved by the Dijkstra algorithm [19]. If an optimal solution is found with cost $U_1 < U$, the upper bound on the optimal cost is updated, $U \leftarrow U_1$.

At the $i + 1$–th step of the algorithm, a graph $G_{i+1} = (N_{i+1}, A_{i+1})$ is built that has $N_{i+1} = N_i + N_0 \setminus \{S, F\}$, and where A_{i+1} contains all connecting arcs between different nodes in N_{i+1} (without cyclic arcs). A branch-and-bound algorithm is used to find the constrained minimum cost U_{i+1}, and the upper bound is updated if $U_{i+1} < U$.

A stopping condition for the procedure can be provided as follows. A lower bound on the optimal control cost solution L is initially set equal to the cheapest cost L_0 of arcs of type (S, i) in the G_1. At each step, the lower bound is updated as $L = L_{i+1} = L_i + \hat{C}_c$, where $\hat{C}_c$ denotes the minimum cost of a closed cycle in the graph G_1. The value of $\hat{C}_c$ is determined once and for all at the beginning of the procedure, by solving a standard (unconstrained) minimum-cost path problem on G_1.

The overall procedure is stopped whenever $L \geq U$.

Theorem 3. *The solution algorithm is correct and complete.*

Proof. Because initial and goal configurations are assumed to belong to the lattice, the optimum exists. Also, because the action on the fiber of the whole group $\tilde{\Omega}$ of control inputs that correspond to the desired final value of the base variables, is generated by the finite set of generators $\Delta(\tilde{\omega}_i)$, $i = 1, \dots, m$, and this set is (implicitly, but completely) searched by the branch-and-bound algorithm at successive stages of the algorithm, the algorithm is correct. On the other hand, the two sequences $\{L_i\}_{i \geq 0}$ and $\{U_i\}_{i \geq 0}$ are strictly uniformly increasing and non-increasing, respectively, and at any stage it holds $L_i \leq U_i$. Hence the algorithm stops in a finite number of stages, all of which consist of an implicit search on a finite graph, i.e. of a finite number of operations.

The proposed algorithm has exponentially increasing complexity with the number of generators, as it uses a number of instances of a branch and bound procedure: this is hardly a surprise, as we are after all dealing with a nontrivial optimal control problem. However, performance can be improved by providing good initial estimates of the upper bound U_0. Some preprocessing of generators to facilitate the algorithm convergence can also help, and work is currently on-going in this direction. The next section will provide some numerical examples of application of the proposed algorithm.

5   Application to n-trailer Steering

As mentioned in the introduction, among the nonlinear systems which can be converted in chained form (2), wheeled vehicles represent a particularly interesting class.

The kinematic model of a tractor with n trailers is given by

$$
\begin{aligned}
\dot{x} &= \cos\theta_n v_n \\
\dot{y} &= \sin\theta_n v_n \\
\dot{\theta}_n &= \tfrac{1}{d_n} \sin(\theta_{n-1} - \theta_n) v_{n-1} \\
&\vdots \\
\dot{\theta}_i &= \tfrac{1}{d_i} \sin(\theta_{i-1} - \theta_i) v_{i-1} \quad i = 1, \ldots, n \\
&\vdots \\
\dot{\theta}_1 &= \tfrac{1}{d_1} \sin(\theta_0 - \theta_1) v_0 \\
\dot{\theta}_0 &= \omega
\end{aligned}
\tag{9}
$$

where (x, y) is the absolute position of the center of the axle between the two wheels of the rear-most trailer; θ_i is the orientation angle of trailer i with respect to the x-axis, with $i \in \{1, \ldots, n\}$; θ_0 is the orientation angle of the tractor axle with respect to the x-axis; d_i is the distance from the center of trailer i to the center of trailer $i - 1$, $i \in \{2, \ldots, n\}$; d_1 is the the distance from the wheels of trailer 1 to the wheels of the tractor; v_0 is the tangential velocity of the car, an input to the system, and ω is the angular velocity of the tractor, the second input to the system. The tangential velocity of a trailer i, v_i, is given by

$$
v_i = \cos(\theta_{i-1} - \theta_i) v_{i-1} = \prod_{j=1}^{i} \cos(\theta_{j-1} - \theta_j) v_0,
$$

where $i \in \{1, \ldots, n\}$. Incidentally, this model is identical to the model of a four-wheeled car pulling $n - 1$ trailers, provided $\theta_0 - \theta_1$ denotes the angle of the front wheels relative to the orientation θ_1 of the rear axle of the four-wheeled car.

Sørdalen in [10] has shown, by a constructive method, that system (9) can be converted in chained form. We consider here the application of our proposed optimal quantized control algorithm to the approximate determination of an optimal continuous control for system (9). This implies introducing time and control quantizations, and applying the computed solutions as piece-wise constant inputs to system (9). The quantized control set we consider is comprised of three inputs,

$$U = \left\{ \pm \begin{pmatrix} 1 \\ 0 \end{pmatrix}, \pm \begin{pmatrix} 0 \\ 1 \end{pmatrix}, \pm \begin{pmatrix} 1 \\ 1 \end{pmatrix} \right\},$$

corresponding respectively to straight motions, rotations about the axle center, and arcs of a circumference by the tractor.

We report the results of optimization runs for a tractor with 1 and 2 trailers. Minimum time controls are determined in each case, and a non-optimal trajectory is reported for comparison.

For the 1-trailer problem, the graph G_0 has 24 nodes. We have considered the problem with initial and goal configurations given by

$$x_{ic} = \begin{pmatrix} 0 \\ 0 \\ 0 \\ 0 \end{pmatrix} \quad x_{fc} = \begin{pmatrix} 0 \\ 0 \\ 0 \\ 1 \end{pmatrix}$$

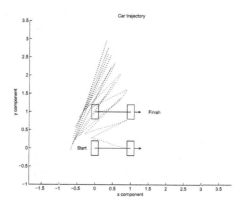

Fig. 1. Non optimal trajectory for the 1-trailer. The minimal time cost is 36.

For the 2-trailer problem, the graph G_0 has 36 nodes. We have solved the problem with initial and goal configurations given by

$$x_{ic} = \begin{pmatrix} 0 \\ 0 \\ 0 \\ 0 \\ 0 \end{pmatrix} \quad x_{fc} = \begin{pmatrix} 0 \\ 0 \\ 0 \\ 0 \\ 1 \end{pmatrix}$$

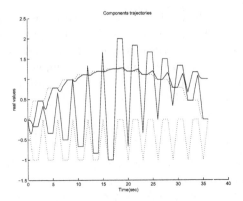

Fig. 2. The trajectories of the base variables (dashed) and fiber variables (continuos) fro the non-optimal 1-trailer solution.

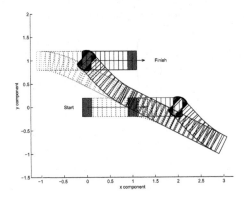

Fig. 3. Optimal trajectory for the 1-trailer problem. The minimal time cost is 8.

These example show that the proposed solution is applicable to problems in dimension up to 5. Larger dimensions of the state space are computationally expensive at this stage, although we expect that refinements on the choice of the generators could lead to an increase of the tractable dimension by one or two.

6   Conclusions

In this paper we have studied the optimal steering problem for chained-form systems by quantized control inputs. The reachable set for these systems class under quantized rational inputs is a lattice and this structure can be used to solve the optimal steering problem.

We have formalized the steering problem on lattices as an integer linear programming problem that cannot be solved directly by standard integer programming techniques. We have introduced a solution algorithm which is complete and correct.

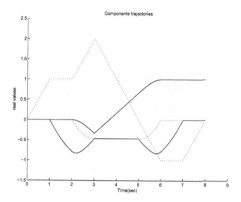

Fig. 4. The trajectories of the base variables (dashed) and fiber variables (continuos) for the optimal 1-trailer solution

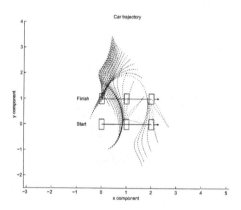

Fig. 5. Non optimal trajectory for the 2-trailer. The minimal time cost is 108.

We have proposed to apply this optimal control on lattices to solve the steering problem for continuos systems that can be converted in chained form: in particular, discretizing the time, we consider a quantized control, and solve the steering task on the lattice. The optimal control strategy obtained is then applied to determine piecewise-constant sub-optimal controls in continuos time. Applications give rather satisfactory results.

References

[1] J. E. Bertram, "The effect of quantization in sampled feedback systems," *Trans. AIEE Appl. Ind.*, vol. 77, pp. 177–181, Sept. 1958.

[2] J. B. Slaughter, "Quantization errors in digital control systems," *IEEE Trans. Autom. Control*, vol. 9, pp. 70–74, Sept. 1964.

[3] D. F. Delchamps, "Extracting state information from a quantized output record," *Systems and Control Letters*, vol. 13, pp. 365–371, 1989.

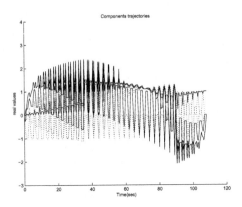

Fig. 6. The trajectories of the base variables (dashed) and fiber variables (continuos) for the nonoptimal 2-trailer solution.

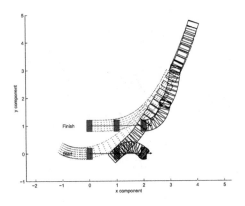

Fig. 7. Optimal trajectory for the 2-trailer. The minimal time cost is 12.

[4] D. F. Delchamps, "Stabilizing a linear system with quantized state feedback," *IEEE Trans. Autom. Control*, vol. 35, no. 8, pp. 916–926, 1990.

[5] R.W. Brockett, "Asymptotic stability and feedback stabilization," in *Differential Geometric Control Theory*, Millmann Brockett and Sussmann, Eds., pp. 181–191. Birkhauser, Boston, U.S., 1983.

[6] N. Elia and S. K. Mitter, "Quantization of linear systems," in *Proc. 38th Conf. Decision & Control*. IEEE, 1999, pp. 3428–3433.

[7] S. S. Sastry R. M. Murray, "Nonholonomic motion planning: Steering using sinusoids," *IEEE Trans. on Automatic Control*, vol. 38, pp. 700–716, 1993.

[8] A. Marigo, B. Piccoli, and A. Bicchi, "Reachability analysis for a class of quantized control systems," in *Proc. IEEE Int. Conf. on Decision and Control*, 2000, pp. 3963–3968.

[9] A. Bicchi, A. Marigo, and B. Piccoli, "On the recahability of quantized control systems," Tech. Rep. 44/2000/M, S.I.S.S.A./I.S.A.S., 2000, (in press on IEEE Trans. Autom. Control).

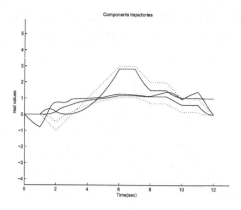

Fig. 8. The trajectories of the base variables (dashed) and fiber variables (continuos) for the optimal 2-trailer solution.

[10] O.J. Sordalen, "Conversion of the kinematics of a car with n trailers into a chained form," in *Proc. IEEE Int. Conf. on Robotics and Automation*, 1993, pp. 382–387.

[11] O.J. Sordalen and O. Egeland, "Exponential stabilization of nonholonomic chained systems," *IEEE Trans. on Automatic Control*, vol. 40, no. 1, pp. 35–49, 1994.

[12] R.M. Murray, "Nilpotent bases for a class of non-integrable distributions with applications to trajectory generation for nonholonomic systems," *Math. Control Signals Systems*, vol. 7, pp. 58–75, 1994.

[13] E. Sontag, "Control of systems without drift via generic loops," *IEEE Trans. on Automatic Control*, vol. 40, no. 7, pp. 1210–1219, 1995.

[14] C. Samson, "Control of chained systems, application to path following and time varying point stabilization of mobile robots," *IEEE Trans. on Automatic Control*, vol. 40, no. 1, pp. 64–67, 1995.

[15] I. Kolmanovsky and N.H. McClamroch, "Developments in nonholonomic control problems," *IEEE Control Systems*, pp. 20–36, December 1995.

[16] S. Sekhavat and J. P. Laumond, "Topological properties for collision free nonholonomic motion planning: the case of sinusoidal inputs for chained form systems," *IEEE Transactions on Robotics and Automation*, vol. 14, no. 5, pp. 671–680, October 1998.

[17] A. Schrijver, *Theory of Linear and Integer Programming*, Wiley Interscience Publ., 1986.

[18] L. A. Wolsey, *Integer Programming*, Wiley Interscience Publ., 1998.

[19] Eric V. Denardo, *Dynamic Programming: Models and Applications*, Prentice-Hall, Inc., Englewood Cliffs, New Jersey,, 1982.

Reconfiguration in Hierarchical Control
of Piecewise-Affine Systems

Tal Pasternak

Institute for Software Integrated Systems,
Department of Electrical Engineering and Computer Science
Vanderbilt University, P.O. Box 36, Peabody, Nashville, TN 37203
Tel: 1-615- 343-7472; Fax: 1-615- 343-7440
Tal.Pasternak@vanderbilt.edu

Abstract. The In this paper the problem of reconfiguration in hierarchical control of piecewise-affine systems in discrete time is considered as the choice of input constraints applied to the low-level control. It is shown how such reconfiguration can provide fault-tolerance to actuator faults while reducing the computational complexity of low-level control. The approach is based on partitioning the state space while taking into account multiple possibilities for the inputs available to low-level control. A so-called "reconfiguration database" is computed at design-time which determines the input constraints that provide for reachability between regions of a state-space partition. This database is used as a basis for reconfiguration decisions at runtime.

1 Introduction

The problem of control reconfiguration in fault-tolerant control is concerned with changing the input-output relation between a plant and its controller in such a way that ensures the achievement of a control objective [1]. Consider for example, the three-tank system in Figure 1. Valves and pumps are used by a controller in order to achieve a set-point of fluid levels. The choice of which valves and pumps are to be used by the controller is a reconfiguration decision. The system in this example is can be approximated as a piecewise-affine system in discrete-time.

Piecewise-affine systems have been receiving increasing attention by the control community because they provide a useful modeling framework for hybrid systems. Discrete-time piecewise-affine systems are equivalent to interconnections of linear systems and finite automata [2] and to a number of other hybrid models [3]. In particular, model predictive control can be applied to piecewise-affine systems by converting them to the equivalent mixed-logic dynamic form [4]. Another approach to control of piecewise affine systems, which is adopted in this paper, is hierarchical control.

Hierarchical control [5] includes low-level control, which may be implemented by model-predictive control, for example, and supervisory control, which operates on a discrete-event abstraction of the hybrid system. The discrete-event abstraction of the closed-loop system, which includes the low-level control and the plant, is obtained by

C.J. Tomlin and M.R. Greenstreet (Eds.): HSCC 2002, LNCS 2289, pp. 364–377, 2002.

reachability calculations that take into account the available plant inputs, which the low-level control manipulates.

In this paper, the reconfiguration problem in hierarchical control of hybrid systems, modeled as piecewise-affine systems in discrete time, is formulated as the problem of selecting input constraints that guarantee reachability. The main contribution of this paper is the reduction of complexity for low-level control, which is achieved by selecting from configurations which each use a limited number of actuators.

In relation to the problem of control reconfiguration, hierarchical control can provide fault tolerance at both the supervisory control level and at the low level. Consider again the three-tank system in Figure 1. The objective of the control system is to regulate the fluid level in tank 3. If a leak occurs in Tank 1, the supervisory controller supervises a phased process by which tank 1 is emptied and tank 2 is filled until a configuration is achieved which mirrors the original configuration. In such a multi-phased process the supervisory controller determines set points to be achieved by the low-level control while low-level control achieves these set-points using the pumps and valves. In case of a leak in tank 1, fault-tolerance is achieved by the supervisory controller at a high level by commanding the shut-down of tank 1 and its replacement by tank 2. The low-level control reconfiguration provides fault-tolerance by choosing which pumps and valves to use at each phase in such a way that set-points are reached. For example, if valve V_2 is faulty, low level control will be implemented using valve V_{23}.

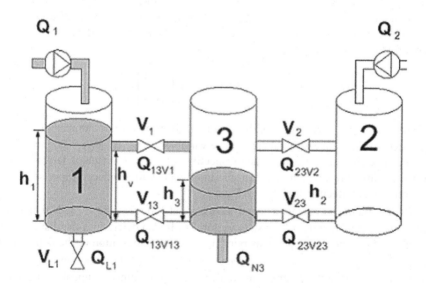

Fig. 1. Three Tank System with Tank 2 Empty

In this paper hierarchical control of piecewise-affine systems is proposed, based on partitioning the state and input space. The significance of considering the inputs when generating the discrete abstraction of the hybrid system is twofold: it is important both for reconfiguration and for limiting the complexity of the low-level control. With respect to fault-tolerant control reconfiguration, the input constraints can be interpreted as control configurations (i.e. which actuators may be used and in what range) as well as fault conditions (i.e. which actuators are fixed in position or limited in range due to fault). With respect to the implementation of the low-level control, the constraints imposed on the inputs affect the complexity of the problem by determining the number of control variables that can be manipulated by the low-level controller [6]. For example, in the three-tank system there are four valves and two pumps, but as will be shown in the next section, only two of these six actuators need to be used at any given time. By not having to consider the operation of the other four "stand-by" actuators, the complexity of the low-level control is reduced.

The next section outlines the proposed architecture. Section 3, shows the application of the method to the problem of control reconfiguration of the three-tank system shown in Figure 1. Section 4 explains the reconfiguration process and section 5 describes the design of the supervisory controller. Finally, section 6 concludes with a discussion and survey of related work.

2   Architecture Overview

The plant is modeled as a piecewise-affine system with continuous states $X \subseteq R^n$, a finite set of discrete states Q, and inputs $U \subseteq R^m$ operating in a hybrid state space $Q \times X$. An additive state disturbance is assumed, taking values in a polyhedral region $D \subseteq R^l$. The system is described by a set of $|Q|$ affine state-space difference equations of the form (1),

$$x(t+1)= A^q x(t)+ B^q u(t)+f^q +d(t) \quad \text{if} \begin{bmatrix} x(t) \\ u(t) \end{bmatrix} \in \chi_q. \tag{1}$$

where $\chi_q \subseteq X \times U$ are convex polyhedra (i.e. given by a finite number of linear inequalities) in the state and input space. The variables $x(t) \in X$, $u(t) \in U$, and $d(t) \in D$ denote state, in put and disturbance respectively at time t. Actuator faults are manifested as limitations which constrain the input values to a reduced input set $U_f \in U$. The control architecture is shown in Figure 2.

The fault and state detector identifies the plant state as a set $X_e \subseteq X$ which determines the possible values of the state vector $x(t)$. It also determines the disturbance set D and the fault-induced input constraints U_f. The implementation of the fault and state detector is beyond the scope of this paper. The sets X_e, D, U_f are assumed to be available correct conservative approximations, which are continually updated at each time step. All the sets are assumed to be convex polyhedra.

The system is designed with respect to some global control objective, as will be detailed in section 5. Based on the global control objective, the supervisory controller determines a control objective for the lower level control and the configuration manager.

Definition 1 (Control Objective). For a system operating in state space X at time t_0, a control objective (T, Ω, t) with T, $\Omega \subseteq$ X, is to reach a state $x(t_0+k) \in$ T, with $x(t_0+j) \in \Omega$, $\forall\ 1 \leq j \leq k-1$, for some $1 \leq k \leq t$.

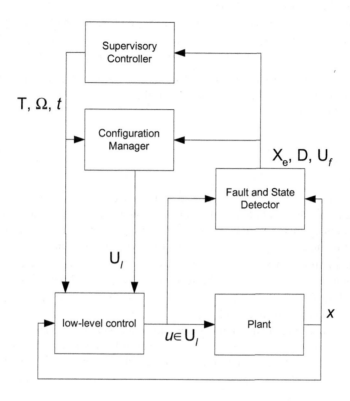

Fig. 2. Architecture

The supervisory controller specifies a set of alternate control objectives. The problem of achieving one of the control objectives is broken down into two levels.

Problem 1 (Reconfiguration). Given system (1), a set of control objectives O, a state and fault detection X_e, D, U_f, and a set of possible input constraints, $\bar{U} \subseteq 2^U$ determine input constraints $U_1 \in \bar{U}$ and a control objective (T, Ω, t) $\in$ O, such that system (1) with constraints $u \in U_1$ and disturbance set D can be driven to target set T, within k time steps, with $1 \leq k \leq t$ while staying in Ω for the first k-1 time steps and that $u \in U_1 \Rightarrow u \in U_f$.

Problem 2 (Low-Level Control). Determine inputs $u(t) \in$ U$_1$ needed to reach T within k time steps, with $1 \leq k \leq t$ while staying in Ω for the first k-1 time steps.

The low-level control problem is solved continuously by the low-level control module. When a control objective is achieved, the supervisory controller sets a new set of control objectives. Reconfiguration occurs when either of the following happens:

- The set of control objectives specified by the supervisory controller is changed, and no longer includes the current objective.
- The fault-induced input constraints become more restrictive and violate the current configuration. (i.e. $U_1 \bullet U_f$.)
- The disturbance set becomes larger and violates the current configuration.

When reconfiguration occurs, the configuration selects one of the control objectives from the set specified by the supervisory controller, and selects input constraints $u \in U_1$ for reconfiguration.

3   Example

In the three-tank system shown in Figure 1 the objective is to regulate the level of fluid in tank 3. The nonlinear continuous-time hybrid model is detailed in [7]. An approximation of this hybrid system as a mixed-logical dynamic system is given in [8]. In the nominal case, Tank 1 serves as a buffer tank, and tank 3 is regulated by controlling the flow between tanks 1 and 3 using valve V_1. One of the possible faults in the system is a leak in Tank 1. The scenario for control and reconfiguration of this system is shown in Figure 3. The control objectives (Ω, T, t) and input constraints U_1 for this scenario are shown in Table 1.

The results in Figure 3 and Figure 4 were obtained using the model in [7]. The low-level control was a implemented using PI controllers on the pumps, hysteresis switches on the valves, and additional simple switching elements. The scenario comprises of four phases:

1. The system starts with all tanks empty. Tank 1 and tank 3 are filled to their nominal levels.
2. The system is regulated at the nominal levels around $h_1=0.5$, $h_2=0$, $h_3=0.1$.
3. Following the detection of a leak in tank 1, the supervisory controller sets the control objective to filling tank 2, while regulating tank 3 and emptying tank 1.
4. The system is regulated around the set-point $h_1=0$, $h_2=0.5$, $h_3=0.1$, which mirrors the regulation of phase 2.

For the valves, a value of 1 is interpreted as the valve open, and a value of 0 as closed. Note that V_{23} is never opened in the configurations detailed in Table 1. This means that the configurations are tolerant to faults which cause V_{23} to be permanently closed. Note also that only two actuators are used in each phase.

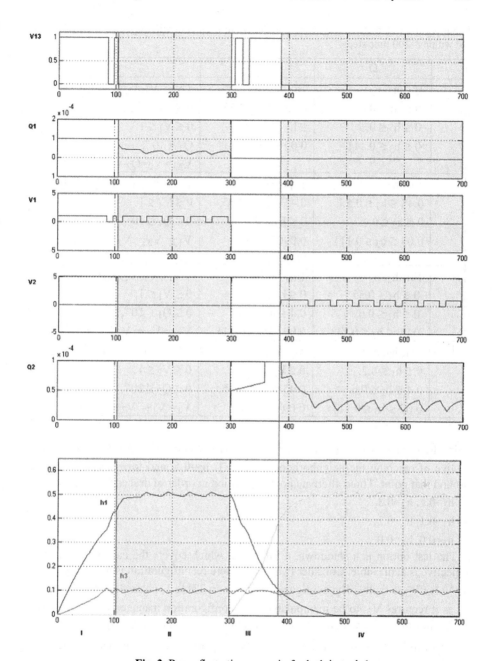

Fig. 3. Reconfiguration scenario for leak in tank 1

Table 1. Control Objectives and Configurations. For each phase the target set T must be acheived within t=200 time steps.

	Ω	T	U_l
1	{h_1, h_2, h_3 | $0 \le h_1 \le 0.6$, $0 \le h_2 \le 0$, $0 \le h_3 \le 0.11$}	{h_1, h_2, h_3 | $0.45 \le h_1 \le 0.55$, $0 \le h_2 \le 0$, $0.09 \le h_3 \le 0.11$}	{ V_{13}, V_1, V_2, V_{23}, Q_1, Q_2 | $0 \le V_{13} \le 1$, $0 \le V_1 \le 1$, $Q_1 = 10^{-4}$, $V_{23}= V_2=Q_2=0$}
2	{h_1, h_2, h_3 | $0.45 \le h_1 \le 0.55$, $0 \le h_2 \le 0$, $0.09 \le h_3 \le 0.11$}	{h_1, h_2, h_3 | $0.45 \le h_1 \le 0.55$, $0 \le h_2 \le 0$, $0.0905 \le h_3 \le 0.105$}	{ V_{13}, V_1, V_2, V_{23}, Q_1, Q_2 | $0 \le V_1 \le 1$, $0 \le Q_1 \le 10^{-4}$, $V_{13}= V_{23}= V_2=Q_2=0$}
3	{h_1, h_2, h_3 | $0 \le h_1 \le 0.55$, $0 \le h_2 \le 0.6$, $0.09 \le h_3 \le 0.11$}	{h_1, h_2, h_3 | $0 \le h_1 \le 0.2$, $0.4 \le h_2 \le 0.6$, $0.09 \le h_3 \le 0.11$}	{ V_{13}, V_1, V_2, V_{23}, Q_1, Q_2 | $0 \le V_1 \le 1$, $0 \le Q_1 \le 10^{-4}$, $V_{13}= V_{23}= V_2=Q_2=0$}
4	{h_1, h_2, h_3 | $0 \le h_1 \le 0.2$, $0.4 \le h_2 \le 0.6$, $0.09 \le h_3 \le 0.11$}	{h_1, h_2, h_3 | $0 \le h_1 \le 0$, $0.45 \le h_2 \le 0.55$, $0.09 \le h_3 \le 0.11$ }	{ V_{13}, V_1, V_2, V_{23}, Q_1, Q_2 | $0 \le V_2 \le 1$, $0 \le Q_2 \le 10^{-4}$, $V_1= V_{13}= V_{23}=Q_1=0$}

In phase three, shown in Table 1, the supervisory controller specifies a control objective of reaching the neighborhood of h_3=0.1, h_2=0.5, and for phase 4, regulation around that point. Three alternate points specified in order of descending priority are

- h_3=0.1, h_2=0.3,
- h_3=0.1, h_2=0.2,
- h_3=0.0, h_2=0.0.

The last option is a shutdown, a safe state, which covers the case where no other objective is achievable. Consider two cases where reconfiguration is necessary:

1. Valve V_2 is faulty. The configuration shown in Table 1, phase 4, is no longer valid as it requires V_2 to be manipulable. The configuration manager selects a configuration which uses V_{23} instead of V_2 to achieve the setpoint of h_3=0.1, h_2=0.3

2. From time t=380 sec onwards valve V_{23} is permanently open. The configuration shown in Table 1, phase 4, is no longer valid as it requires V_{23} to be permanently closed. In this case the same target set can be achieved, with different input constraints. Figure 4 shows this scenario. The system can still be controlled using pump Q_2 alone. The difference is that when using Q_2 alone, the disturbance that can be tolerated is smaller.

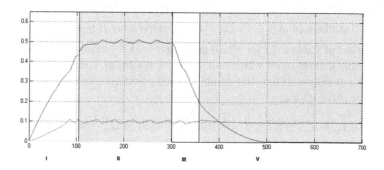

Fig. 4. Alternative ending to the leak scenario

4 Reconfiguration

The purpose of imposing constraints on the inputs is to reduce the number of manipulable input variables for the low-level control. If the low-level control is implemented by model-predictive control (MPC) – which is possible for piecewise-affine systems – the manipulable input variables are decision variables for the MPC optimization problem and reducing their number reduces the computational complexity [6]. Clearly, the reconfiguration task is required to have less computational cost than what is saved by not allowing all input variables to be manipulable by the low-level control. For this reason, the approach taken here is to perform the reachability calculations required for reconfiguration at design-time.

The configuration manager's task is to select input constraints which will guarantee reachability from the current state $x(t)$ to a target state set $T \subseteq X$ in t time steps without leaving $\Omega \subseteq X$ for the first t-1 time-steps. In this paper this process is called *reconfiguration*. It is proposed to perform the necessary reachability calculations at design time and store the results of these calculations in a reconfiguration database. A necessary condition for reachability is that a sequence of input vectors which satisfies the input constraints and the control objective exist. The following definitions will be instrumental in constructing the reconfiguration database.

Definition 2 (Robust One-Step Set). [9, section 2.3] For the system (1), with inputs $u(t) \subseteq U_l$ and disturbances $d(t) \in D$, the *robust one-step set* $Q(\Omega)$ is the set of states in X for which an admissible control input exists which will drive the system to Ω in one step, for any disturbance $d(t) \in D$ i.e

$$Q(\Omega) = \{\, x \in X \mid \exists u \in U \, \exists q \in Q : (x, u) \in \chi_q, \, \forall \, d \in D \quad A_q \, x + B_q u + f_q + d) \in \Omega \,\}.$$

Definition 3 (Robust Controllable [i,j]-step Set). For the system (1), with inputs u(t) $\in U_I$ and disturbances $d(t) \in D$, the *robust controllable [i,j]-step set* $K_i^j(\Omega, T)$ is the largest set of states in Ω for which an integer $i \le k \le j$ exists for which there exists an admissible control input which will drive the system to T in exactly k steps, while keeping the evolution of the state inside Ω for the first k-1 steps, for any time-varying disturbance $d(t) \in D$, i.e.

$$K_i^j(\Omega, T) = \left\{ x_0 \in R^n \mid \exists i \le k \le j \quad \exists \{u(t) \in U_{j_0}^{k-1} : \{x(t) \in \Omega_{j_0}^{k-1}, x(k) \in T, \forall \{d(t) \in D_{j_0}^{k-1}\} \right\}$$

Theorem 1. The robust controllable [i,j]-step set can be computed by the following recursive formula:

$$K_i^{j+1}(\Omega, T) = \begin{cases} T & i = j = 0 \\ Q(K_j^j(\Omega, T)) \cap \Omega & 0 < i = j \\ Q(K_j^j(\Omega, T)) \cap \Omega \cup K_i^j(\Omega, T) & i < j \end{cases} \qquad (2)$$

Proof. For i=j, the algorithm and proof is shown in [9, section 2.6]. For i < j, by definition $K_i^{j+1}(\Omega, T) = K_i^j(\Omega, T) \cup K_{i+1}^{j+1}(\Omega, T)$. Also, $\Omega = \bigcup_i \Omega_i \Rightarrow Q(\Omega) = \bigcup_i Q(\Omega_i)$ and $K_i^j(\Omega, T) = \bigcup_{i \le k \le j} K_k^k(\Omega, T)$, therefore,

$$K_{i+1}^{j+1}(\Omega, T) = \bigcup_{i+1 \le k \le j+1} K_k^k(\Omega, T) = \bigcup_{i \le k \le j} Q(K_k^k(\Omega, T)) \cap \Omega = Q(K_i^j(\Omega, T)) \cap \Omega$$

The robust controllable set for LTI systems can be computed using the invariant set toolbox [11]. The robust controllable set for PWA systems can be computed in an iterative way based on the one-step robust controllable set for each mode of the system. One such method is for computing robust controllable sets for piecewise affine systems is described in [9, section 4.5].

Reconfiguration provides fault tolerance by choosing input constraints, which are compatible with fault conditions. For example, if valve V_1 in the three tank system is fixed in position $V_1=0$, then any configuration constraint which is satisfied by $V_1=0$ is compatible with this fault.

The reconfiguration database consists of six-tuples $(\tilde{X}, \tilde{D}, \tilde{U}, \tilde{T}, \tilde{\Omega}, \tilde{t})$ for which it has been determined that $\tilde{X}$ is a robust controllable [1,t]-step set $K_1^{t}(\tilde{\Omega}, \tilde{T})$ for the system with disturbance $\tilde{D}$ and input constraints $\tilde{U}$. At runtime, the configuration manager's task is to find a six-tuple from the database, for which $X_e \subseteq \tilde{X}, D \subseteq \tilde{D}, \tilde{U} \subseteq U_f$, $\tilde{T} \subseteq T, t \le \tilde{t}, \tilde{\Omega} \subseteq \Omega$, based on X_e, D, U_f supplied by the fault and state detector and Ω, T, t supplied by the supervisory controller. The sets are all assumed to be convex polyhedral sets, so the computation of the set inclusions amount to the solution of linear programs. In general the robust controllable set for a piecewise affine system is not convex; however it is sufficient for the purpose of reconfiguration to use an inner approximation of the robust controllable set, which is convex, for the value of $\tilde{X}$ in the database.

By removing all reconfiguration options, which do not satisfy the necessary conditions for reachability, the search space for the low-level control is reduced, while ensuring the existence of appropriate control inputs to satisfy a control objective. The problem of designing the low-level control to select the optimal control inputs is beyond the scope of this paper. One possibility is to apply model-predictive control for which necessary and sufficient conditions for robust feasibility are known [10].

The reconfiguration database lists six-tuples $(\tilde{X}, \tilde{D}, \tilde{U}, \tilde{T}, \tilde{\Omega}, \tilde{t})$ for possible combinations of state and fault identification and control objectives given by the state and fault detector and the supervisory controller, respectively. The task of partitioning the state and input sets to determine these sets is the subject of the next section.

5 Supervisory Control

The supervisory control of a hybrid system can be approached as a discrete-event control problem, by abstracting the plant into a discrete event system preserving all properties of interest. In hierarchical control, this is done by forming a partition of the state space, for which it can be guaranteed that the system can be forced to reach a desired region by choosing appropriate controls. In this section the subject of partitioning the continuous state space will be considered. The control specification that forms the primary partition is given by the following definition.

Definition 4. (Global Control Objective) Given a set $Bad \subseteq X$ and a finite collection of sets $A_k \subseteq X$, $k \in K$, that includes an initial set $A_0 \subseteq X$, with $A_k \cap Bad = \varnothing$, a set valued map *next*: $K \rightarrow 2^K$ and a function time *time*: $K \times K \rightarrow Z^+$ the global control objective is that for the system with initial conditions $x \in A_0$ the continuous state will remain in any set A_k for at most *time*(k,k') time steps and then cross into $A_{k'}$ for some $k' \in$ next(k).

Remark 1. Definition 4 applies for the nominal case. In case of a fault, which necessitates reconfiguration, a degraded performance is assumed to be acceptable in which time constraints do not apply. In this case the global control objective requires an event sequence specified by the *next* relation, while the constraints specified by the function *time* do not apply.

Assume a given disturbance set D_k for each region A_k. Let $U_L \subseteq 2^U$ be the set of admissible input sets. The choice of input constraints is based on two considerations: fault-tolerance and reducing the number of manipulated variables. A configuration $U_l \in U$ will be tolerant to a fault if the configuration admits only input vectors which are not precluded by the fault. The additive state disturbance can also be used to model certain input faults (e.g. a leak in the tank).

Let $\Psi = \{\Omega_k\}$ be a collection of sets, which appear as invariant sets Ω in the reconfiguration database, and let $\Omega_0 = A_0$; $\Omega_k \subseteq A_k \; \forall k \in K$. It is required that at any trajectory starting in Ω_0 can be driven to follow the global control objective. This can be assured if

$$\forall x \in \Omega_k, \exists l \in \text{next}(k), \exists u \in U_L : x \in K_1^{\text{time}(k,l)}(\Omega_k, \Omega_l). \tag{3}$$

In the nominal case reconfiguration occurs when the system crosses into a target set from which reachability to the next target set is assured within the required time. When a fault occurs, the time constraint is not necessarily satisfied; however, the condition of Equation 3 ensures that the next state is reachable when reconfiguration occurs at any point along the trajectory. The collection Ψ can be calculated recursively by Algorithm 1.

Algorithm 1. (Compute Collection of Invariant Sets Ψ)

INPUT:
– partition π defining regions A_k, $k \in K$
– input constraints U_L
– disturbance set D_k for each A_k
BEGIN
  FOR each $k \in K$
    $\Omega'_k = A_k$.
  REPEAT
    FOR each $k \in K$,
      $\Omega_k = \Omega'_k$
    FOR each $k \in K$,
      $$\Omega'_k = \bigcup_{U_l \in U_L} \bigcup_{l \in \text{next}(k)} K_1^{\text{time}(k,l)}(\Omega_k, \Omega_l);$$
  UNTIL $\Omega_k = \Omega'_k, \forall k \in K$
END
OUTPUT
– Collection $\Psi = \{\Omega_k\}_{k \in K}$ of invariant sets.

The algorithm succeeds if it terminates and $\Omega_0 = A_0$. If the algorithm terminates successfully Equation 3 is satisfied. What remains is to partition the sets $\{\Omega_k\}_{k \in K}$ into regions such that from each region, it can be determined which next target set can be reached and by what configuration. This is performed by Algorithm 2.

Algorithm 2. (Partition sets Ψ, with configurations U_L).

INPUT:
– State space X
– Global control objective: K, $\{A_k\}$, *time, next*
– input constraints U_L

– disturbance set D_k for each A_k

BEGIN

$$\pi_f := (X \setminus \bigcup_{k \in K} A_k , A_0, \Omega_1, A_1 \setminus \Omega_1, \Omega_2, A_2 \setminus \Omega_2, ...)$$

FOR each $k \in K$, $U_l \in U_L$, $l \in$ *next*(k),

      compute partition: $\pi = (X \cap K_1^{\text{time}(k,l)}(\Omega_k, \Omega_l) , X \setminus K_1^{\text{time}(k,l)}(\Omega_k, \Omega_l))$

      Refine: $\pi_f := \pi_f \cdot \pi$

  END

END

OUTPUT:

– Refined partition π_f.

After finding the final partition, the supervisory controller and the state detector can be designed to specify their outputs in terms of the refined partition. When the system is in region A_k, the supervisory controller sets the control objective for the configuration manager and low level control as all the 3-tuples (Ω, T, t) with $\Omega = \Omega_k$, $T = \Omega_l$, $l \in$ *next*(k), $t = \text{time}(k,l)$. The state detector must detect partition crossing in the final partition so that when the system crosses into Ω_l, it can be determined in which region of the final partition the current state is, so that reconfiguration can proceed. The re-configuration database is also constructed based on the final partition and the possible control objectives. Throughout this section the disturbance set D_k was assumed to be given for each region A_k of the global control objective. The disturbance set provides another design parameter, which can be relaxed or tightened to enable the global control objective to be achieved or to increase robustness.

6   Conclusions and Related Work

In this paper, the subject of control reconfiguration in hierarchical control of piece-wise affine systems was considered as the problem of choosing input constraints for the low-level control to satisfy reachability requirements given by the supervisory controller. This approach provides fault-tolerance to actuator faults, while allowing the supervisory controller to handle major component faults. The computational complexity of low-level control is reduced by limiting the number of available inputs. The additional run-time computational cost due to reconfiguration is kept low by performing reachability analysis at design-time, and limiting run-time calculations to set inclusions.

The problem of reconfiguration in the control of piecewise affine systems as a choice of manipulated inputs, and the need to reduce the number candidate inputs in the process was considered in [6]. A number of methods were proposed in for reducing the number of candidate inputs, using the mixed-logic dynamic representation of the system. This paper adds to the work in [6] by considering the model-predictive control of a piecewise-affine system in the context of hierarchical control. In the context of hierarchical control, the option of changing set-points is considered simultaneously with the option of changing the set of manipulated actuators. As is shown in the example in section 3, when hierarchical control is used, reconfiguration can be handled at the supervisory control level to handle component faults (e.g. emptying the leaking tank and filling the redundant tank) while providing additional fault tolerance by low-level control reconfiguration (e.g. using the lower valve, if the upper valve is faulty). An approach to reconfiguration based on model-predictive control alone is less suitable than one based on hierarchical control when the prediction horizon which is needed for reconfiguration is much larger than the prediction needed for nominal control, because the complexity of the optimization problem solved by the model-predictive control algorithm grows with the prediction horizon.

In [5], hierarchical control of piecewise-linear systems (piecewise affine systems with an offset vector of zero) was investigated. This paper extends the approach of [5] by considering the possibility of selecting the input constraints at runtime. The introduction of faults which require reconfiguration, adds an additional requirement for partitioning the state space that when the system moves from an initial set to a target, the target set must be reachable, even if the input constraints changes before the target set is reached and after the initial set is left. In this case, the target set can be reached in a finite time providing a degraded - but safe - performance in the event of faults.

In [12, section 12.4] a hybrid control strategy is shown for the three-tank system, in which the system is reconfigured in steps when faults occur, while employing low-level control to manipulate the actuators and supervisory control triggered by crossing partitions in the state-space to coordinate the low-level control. This paper provides the foundation for verifying such a control strategy.

In [12, section 12.3] reconfiguration is performed based on a qualitative mode obtained by quantizing the system with a rectangular state space partition. The approach is applied to the three-tank benchmark problem. The approach presented in this paper differs in that it is hierarchical, and includes a low-level control component, which has a continuous range of values for the input variables available to it. This results better quality of control, while not sacrificing the robustness, which is provided by the supervisory controller that operates on a discrete level. In addition, the partition of the state space for supervisory control, as presented in this paper is based on the specification of a global control objective, and the ability of the low-level control to achieve intermediate objectives. Also note that the reconfiguration database proposed in this paper requires enumeration of configurations, but it does not require enumeration of faults.

The theory of invariant sets, the computation of invariant sets for piecewise affine systems, and the applicability of invariant sets to the feasibility of model-predictive control and are studied in [9] and recent results are published in [10]. These results are applicable to the computation of the robust controllable sets in the reconfiguration database.

Current work includes computation of convex approximations of robust controllable sets for piecewise affine systems and using it to generate the partition refinement and the reconfiguration database described in section 4 and section 5 of this paper.

An open problem in the method presented in this paper is how to partition the state space in such a way that time constraints of the global control objectives can be satisfied in the event of faults.

Acknowledgements. The work is supported by DARPA under F33615-99-C-3611 as part of the Software Enabled Control program, and by a Vanderbilt University Graduate Fellowship. The author wishes to thank anonymous reviewers for their constructive comments.

References

1. M. Blanke, C. Frei, F. Kraus, R.J. Patton, and Staroswiecki M "What is Fault-tolerant Control.", Plenary address, In *Proceedings of the IFAC Symposium SAFEPROCESS*, Budapest, pages 40-51, 2000
2. E.D. Sontag. Interconnected automata and linear systems: A theoretical framework in discrete time. In *Hybrid Systems III – Verification and Control*, R. Alur, T.A. Henzinger and E.D. Sontag eds. Lecture Notes in Computer Science, Vol. 1066. Springer-Verlag, Pittsburgh, USA, (1996), 436-448
3. W.P.M.H. Heemels, B. De Schutter and A. Bemporad. Equivalence of Hybrid Dynamical Models, *Automatica* 37(7), July 2001
4. A. Bemporad and M. Morari. Control of systems integrating logic, dynamics, and constraints, *Automatica,* 35(3), March 1999
5. X.D. Koutsoukos and P.J. Antsaklis. Hierarchical Control of Piecewise Linear Hybrid Dynamical Systems Based on Discrete Abstractions, *Interdisciplinary Studies of Intelligent Systems, Notre Dam University, Technical Report ISIS-2001-001*, February 2001
6. K. Tsuda, D. Mignone, G. Ferrari-Trecate and M. Morari. Reconfiguration Strategies for Hybrid Systems. In *Proceedings of the American Control Conference*, Arlington Virginia, 2001
7. J. Lunze. Laboratory Three Tanks System Benchmark for the Reconfiguration Problem. Technical report, Tech. Univ.of Hamburg-Harburg, Inst. of Control. Eng., Germany, 1998.
8. D. Mignone., *Moving Horizon Estimation and Fault Detection of Mixed Logic Dynamical Systems*, Postdiploma Thesis, Automatic Control Laboratory, Swiss Federal Institute of Technology, Zurich, Switzerland, August 1999
9. E.C. Kerrigan. *Robust Constraint Satisfaction: Invariant Sets and Predictive Control*. PhD thesis, University of Cambridge, UK, November 2000.
10. E.C. Kerrigan and J.M. Maciejowski. Robust Feasibility in Model Predictive Control: Necessary and Sufficient Conditions. In *Proceedings of the 40th Conference on Decision and Control*, Orlando, Florida, USA, December 2001
11. E.C. Kerrigan, MATLAB Invariant Set Toolbox downloadable from http://www-control.eng.cam.ac.uk/eck21/.
12. J. Lunze, J. Askari-Maranani, A. Cela, P.M. Frank, A.L. Gehin, B. Heiming, M. Lemos, T. Marcu, L. Rato, M. Starosweicki. Three Tank Control Reconfiguration. In *Control of Complex Systems*. K. Åstrom et al (eds.) Springer, London, pp 241-283, 2001.

Hybrid Kernels and Capture Basins for Impulse Constrained Systems

Patrick Saint-Pierre

Centre of Recherche Viabilité, Jeux, Contrôle
Université Paris IX - Dauphine
`saint-pierre@viab.dauphine.fr`

Abstract. We investigate, for constrained controlled systems with impulse, the subset of initial positions contained in a set K from which starts at least one run viable in K - the hybrid viability kernel - eventually until it reaches a given closed target in finite time - the hybrid capture basin. We define a constructive algorithm which approximates this set. The knowledge of this set is essential for control problem since it provides viable hybrid feed-backs and viable runs. We apply this method for approximating the Minimal Time-to-reach Function in the presence of both constraints and impulses. Two examples are presented, the first deals with a dynamical system revealing the complexity of the structure of hybrid kernels, the second deals with a Minimal Time problem with impulses.

1 Introduction

We consider a dynamical impulse system describing the evolution of a state variable $x \in X = \mathbb{R}^n$ which, in response to some events, may switch between a continuous evolution and an impulse evolution. Switches are triggered when the state reaches a closed set C. During some periods the state is governed by a continuous evolution until it reaches some state $x \in C$ where a reset to a new position $x^+ \in \Phi(x)$ occurs. We will distinguish between *solution* which, when reaching C, either may be reset or keep going the continuous evolution, and *strict solution* which, when reaching C, is necessarily reset.

Research efforts are devoted to the study of such systems mainly in extending the mathematical tools of the Control Theory (see [22, Zabczyk], [5, Bensoussan & Lions] and in developing methods for analysis, verification or control design for non linear hybrid systems (see for instance [20, Sastry], [19, Shaft & Schumacher], [21, Vaandrager & Van Schuppen], [2, Aubin]).

On the other hand the study of controlled system with state constraints has been widely developed this last decade using the main concepts of Set-Valued Analysis (see [3, Aubin & Cellina], [4, Aubin & Frankowska]) and Numerical Set-Valued Analysis (see [16, Saint-Pierre]) which can be regarded as a "Tool Box" for viability theory and numerical viability (viability, equilibria, stability, reachability, controllability, (see [1, Aubin], [14, Quincampoix], [17, Saint-Pierre]), optimal control (minimal time-to-reach problem, crisis time function, infinite

C.J. Tomlin and M.R. Greenstreet (Eds.): HSCC 2002, LNCS 2289, pp. 378–392, 2002.
© Springer-Verlag Berlin Heidelberg 2002

horizon optimal control (see [7, Cardaliaguet, Quincampoix & Saint-Pierre], [11, Doyen & Saint-Pierre]), differential games (discriminating and leadership kernels, conditional and guaranteed strategies, minimal hitting time function, robustness, qualitative analysis (see [13, Leitmann], [18, Seube], [8, Cardaliaguet, Quincampoix & Saint-Pierre], [10, Dordan]) and their applications to mathematical economics, finance, demography or biology as well as to enginery and automatics when taking into account constraints is unescapable.

The scope of this paper is to bridge these two fields in order to take into account explicit or hidden constraints that may occur when studying hybrid systems and to explore how numerical schemes can be implemented. Let us recall that the Viability Kernel Algorithm originally designed for computing viability kernels has been widen to approximate the smallest lower semicontinuous subsolution of the Hamilton-Jacobi-Belmann equation (see [12, Frankowska], [7, Cardaliaguet, Quincampoix & Saint-Pierre]). We prove that viability techniques can be extended with minor restrictions to hybrid systems first for computing the Hybrid Kernel which broadens the concept of Viability Kernel, second for computing the Minimal Time-to-reach function as example of Value Function.

2   Hybrid Viability Kernels

2.1   Definitions: Run, Hybrid, Strict Hybrid Solutions

1. Let us consider a set-valued map $F : X \rightsquigarrow X$ that we assume to be Marchaud[1]. The continuous evolution is described by the differential inclusion

$$x'(t) \in F(x(t)), \text{ for almost all } t \in \mathbb{R}^+ \tag{1}$$

We denote by $\mathcal{S}_F^c(x_0)$ the set of all absolutely continuous solutions of (1) starting from x_0 at time $t_0 = 0$. We denote by $\theta^C(x(\cdot))$ the first time $t \geq 0$ when the solution $x(\cdot)$ reaches C.

2. Let us consider a set-valued map Φ defined on a closed set $C = Dom(\Phi)$ with compact values and closed graph. The impulse evolution is described by the recursive inclusion

$$x^{n+1} \in \Phi(x^n) \tag{2}$$

3. We denote by $\mathcal{S}_\Phi^d(x^0)$ the set of all discrete solutions $\{x^0, x^1, ..., x^k\}$ of (2) starting from $x^0 \in C$. If finite, k is the first index such that $x^k \notin C$.

Definition 2.1 *We call* <u>run</u> *of an impulse system* (F, Φ) *a sequence of elements* $\overrightarrow{x}(\cdot) := \{(\tau_i, x_i, x_i(\cdot))\}_{i \in I} \in (\mathbb{R}^+ \times X \times \mathcal{C}(0, \infty; X))^{\mathbb{N}}$, *where* τ_i *is the* i^{th} <u>cadence</u>, x_i *is the* i^{th} <u>reinitialization</u>, *with* $x_0 = x^0$, *and* $x_i(\cdot) \in \mathcal{S}_F^c(x_i)$ *is the* i^{th} <u>motive</u> *which is an almost continuous solution to (1) starting from* x_i *at time 0 until time* τ_i.

---

[1] Upper semicontinuous with non empty convex compact values and linear growth.

We denote by $S_{(F,\Phi)}(x_0)$ the set of runs starting from x_0. The set of indexes $I = \{0, 1, ..., n\} \subset \mathbb{N}$ can be finite $(n < +\infty)$ or infinite $(n = +\infty)$, satisfying

$$\forall i < n, \ \exists x_i(\cdot) \in \mathcal{S}_F^c(x_i) \text{ such that } x_i(\tau_i) \in C, \ x_{i+1} \in \Phi(x_i(\tau_i))$$

If $\tau_i = 0$, $x_{i+1} \in \Phi(x_i)$ and then $x_i(\cdot)$ is defined on an interval of length 0.

We set $T = \sum_{i=0}^n \tau_i$. Let us introduce a virtual lapse of time $\delta > 0$, sequences $(t_i)_{i \in I}$ and $(\vartheta_i)_{i \in I}$ given by $t_0 = \vartheta_0 = 0$, $t_{i+1} = t_i + \tau_i$ and $\vartheta_{i+1} = \vartheta_i + \tau_i + \delta$. We have $\vartheta_{i+1} = t_i + i\delta$. With any $t \in [0, T]$ we associate i_t satisfying $t_{i_t} \leq t < t_{i_t+1}$ and with any $\vartheta \in \mathbb{R}$ we associate i_ϑ satisfying $\vartheta_{i_\vartheta} \leq \vartheta < \vartheta_{i_\vartheta+1}$.

Definition 2.2 *With a run $\overrightarrow{x}(\cdot)$ we associate the* <u>expanded hybrid solution</u> *as the map $\vartheta \to x^e(\vartheta)$ defined by*

$$x^e(\vartheta) = x_0 + \sum_{i=0}^{i_\vartheta} \left(\int_0^{\tau_i^\star} x_i'(\tau)d\tau + \alpha_i^\star(x_{i+1} - x_i(\tau_i)) \right)$$

where the motive $x_i(\tau)$ is a solution to (1) starting from x_i at time 0 until time τ_i, $\tau_i^\star = \min(\tau_i, \vartheta - \vartheta_i)$ and $\alpha_i^\star = \max(0, \min(1, \vartheta - \vartheta_i - \tau_i))$. We call <u>hybrid solution</u> *associated with a run $\overrightarrow{x}(\cdot)$ the map $t \to x(t)$ given by $x(t) = x^e(t + i_t\delta)$.*

The expanded hybrid and the hybrid solutions are two parametrized representations of the same run. However, under slight assumption, there exists a one-to-one correspondence between expanded hybrid solutions and runs which fails when considering plain hybrid solutions.

For studying impulse systems, that we call *strict*, when the solution is necessarily reset every times the trajectory reaches C to some position x^* belonging to $\Phi(x^*)$, we need to introduce the following

Definition 2.3 *We call* <u>strict hybrid solution</u> *any hybrid solution such that*
$$\forall i \in I, \ x_i(\tau_i) \in C \text{ and } \forall \tau \in [0, \tau_i[, \ x_i(\tau) \notin C.$$

We note $S_{(F,\Phi)}^e(x_0)$ (resp. $\widetilde{S}_{(F,\Phi)}^e(x_0)$)) the set of extended (resp. strict) hybrid solutions starting from x_0.

Let K be a closed set. We search the largest domain of initial positions from which starts at least one run remaining forever in K. We can assume without loss of generality that $C = K \cap \Phi^{-1}(K)$ and we denote by $S_{(F,\Phi,K)}(x_0)$ the set of runs $\overrightarrow{x}(\cdot)$ starting from x_0 and viable in K. An impulse constrained system is characterized by the triple (F, Φ, K).

The notion of hybrid kernel has been introduced in [2, Aubin]. It is characterized in terms of capture basin when $K \backslash C$ is a repeller[2].

---

[2] We recall that a set D is a repeller if all solutions leave D in a finite time. The capture basin of a set C under constraint K for the dynamic F, denoted $Capt_F(C, K)$, is the set of initial position x^0 from which there exists a solution $x(\cdot) \in \mathcal{S}_F^c(x^0)$ remaining in K until it reaches C in finite time.

Definition 2.4 *The* hybrid (resp. strict hybrid) kernel *of K for the impulse system (F, Φ, K) is the largest closed subset of initial states belonging to K from which starts at least one (resp. strict) hybrid viable solution. We denote this set $Hyb_{(F,\Phi)}(K)$ (resp. $\widetilde{Hyb}_{(F,\Phi)}(K)$).*

We have $\widetilde{Hyb}_{(F,\Phi)}(K) \subset Hyb_{(F,\Phi)}(K)$. We are going to prove that the hybrid kernel is closed and that hybrid and strict hybrid kernels can be approximated by a sequence of discrete viability kernels associated with suitable discrete systems.

Assumptions and Approximated Impulse Systems

We assume that
- C is compact and $\Phi : C \rightsquigarrow X$ is upper semi-continuous with compact values:

$$0 < \delta_{inf} \leq \inf_{x \in C} \inf_{y \in \Phi(x)} d(x, y) \leq \sup_{x \in C} \sup_{y \in \Phi(x)} d(x, y) \leq \delta_{sup} \tag{3}$$

so that Φ has no fix point and its graph is closed. We set $\forall x \notin C, \Phi(x) = \emptyset$.
- K is a compact set and F is a Marchaud map satisfying $\sup_{x \in K} \sup_{y \in F(x)} \|y\| \leq M$.

This assumption implies that F is closed. As usual in the context of set-valued numerical analysis we need to consider "good" approximations F_ρ of F in the sense that $Graph(F_\rho)$ remains in a not too large neighborhood of F

$$\begin{aligned}
i) \quad & Graph(F_\rho) \subset Graph(F) + \phi(\rho)\mathcal{B}_{X \times X} \\
ii) \quad & \bigcup_{x' \in \mathcal{B}(x, \rho M)} F(x') \subset F_\rho(x)
\end{aligned} \tag{4}$$

where $\mathcal{B}_{X \times X}$ denotes the unit ball of $X \times X$ and ϕ goes to zero when ρ.

Let be $h > 0$ and set $C_h := C + h\mathcal{B}$. With the set-valued map Φ we associate

$$\Phi_h(x) := \bigcup_{\tilde{x} \in \mathcal{B}(x, h) \cap C} \Phi(\tilde{x})$$

Proposition 2.5 *If Φ is closed (its graph is closed) on $C \times X$, then Φ_h is closed.*

Proof —— Let $(x^n, y^n) \in Graph(\Phi_h)$ be a sequence converging to (x^*, y^*). From the definition of Φ_h, $\forall n$, $\exists \tilde{x}^n \in \mathcal{B}(x^n, h) \cap C$ such that $y^n \in \Phi(\tilde{x}^n)$. Since $\tilde{x}^n$ belongs to a compact subset and since C is closed, there exists a subsequence $\tilde{x}^n$ converging to $\tilde{x} \in \mathcal{B}(x^*, h) \cap C$. Since Φ is closed on C, we have $y^* \in \Phi(\tilde{x}) \subset \Phi_h(x^*)$ and consequently $(x^*, y^*) \in Graph(\Phi_h)$. ∎

Consistency of numerical schemes subordinates h to ρ in such a way that any element of $x + \rho F_\rho(x)$ sufficiently close to C belongs to C_h. We can choose[3]

$$h = \rho(M + \phi(\rho)). \tag{5}$$

---

[3] For computing viability kernels we refer to [16, Saint-Pierre].

2.2   The Viability Kernel Algorithm

The *discrete viability kernel* of K for G denoted $\overrightarrow{Viab}_G(K)$ is the largest closed subset of K of initial position from which there exists at least one sequence solution to the discrete dynamical system remaining in K:

$$x^{n+1} \in G(x^n), \quad \forall n \in \mathbb{N} \tag{6}$$

The *viability kernel algorithm* consists in the construction of a decreasing sequence of subsets K^n recursively defined by

$$K^0 = K, \text{ and } K^{n+1} = K^n \cap \{x \mid G(x) \cap K^n \neq \emptyset\} = K^n \cap G^{-1}(K^n) \tag{7}$$

which converges to $\overrightarrow{Viab}_G(K)$ (cf. [16, Saint-Pierre]):

Proposition 2.6 *Let $G : X \rightsquigarrow X$ be an upper semi-continuous and compact set valued map and K a compact set. Then $Lim_{n\to\infty} K^n = \overrightarrow{Viab}_G(K)$. Let F_ρ satisfying (4) and set $G_\rho = Id + \rho F_\rho$, then $Lim_{\rho\to 0} \overrightarrow{Viab}_{G_\rho}(K) = Viab_F(K)$*

2.3   Approximation Schemes for Impulse Systems

Let us fix a time step ρ and $h = \rho(M + \phi(\rho))$. We replace the derivative $x'(t)$ of x at time t by the difference $\frac{x^{n+1}-x^n}{\rho}$ where x^n stands for $x(n\rho)$ with $x^0 = x(0)$. We consider the set $\{x^{n+1} = x^n + \rho\varphi^n \mid \varphi^n \in F_\rho(x^n)\}$ of successors of x^n. We set

$$S_\rho(y) = \begin{cases} y & \text{if } y \notin C_h \\ y \cup \Phi_h(y) & \text{if } y \in C_h \end{cases} \text{ and } \tilde{S}_\rho(y) = \begin{cases} y & \text{if } y \notin C_h \\ y \cup \Phi_h(y) & \text{if } y \in \partial C_h \\ \Phi_h(y) & \text{if } y \in \text{Int}(C_h) \end{cases}$$

Since Φ_h is closed, the graphs of set-valued maps S_ρ and $\tilde{S}_\rho$ are also by construction closed. We consider the discrete dynamical systems

$$\begin{aligned} i) \quad & x^{n+1} \in G_\rho(x^n) = \{S_\rho(x^n + \rho\varphi) \mid \varphi \in F_\rho(x^n)\} \\ ii) \quad & x^{n+1} \in \tilde{G}_\rho(x^n) = \{\tilde{S}_\rho(x^n + \rho\varphi) \mid \varphi \in F_\rho(x^n)\} \end{aligned} \tag{8}$$

Proposition 2.7 *If F and Φ are closed and if F is compact valued, then for all $\rho > 0$, G_ρ and $\tilde{G}_\rho$ are closed.*

The proof is similar to the proof of Proposition 2.5. Let us choose ρ such that

$$2M\rho < \delta_{inf} \tag{9}$$

We add to the discrete dynamical systems (8) i) and ii) two variables which evaluate a discrete time t^n and the number of resets that took place until t^n:

$$t^{n+1} = t^n + \rho \text{ and } r^{n+1} = \begin{cases} r^n & \text{if } d(x^{n+1}, x^n) \leq \rho M \\ r^n + 1 & \text{if } d(x^{n+1}, x^n) \geq \delta_{inf} \end{cases}$$

Thanks to assumption (3), evaluation of the distance between two successive states allows to distinguish between continuous and impulse evolutions and consequently to know whenever x^n is or isn't in a neighborhood of C.

2.4   Impulse Viability Algorithm

Let be $\widetilde{K}_\rho^0 = K_\rho^0 = K$. We define sequences $\widetilde{K}_\rho^p$ and K_ρ^p by

$$\widetilde{K}_\rho^{p+1} = \{x \in \widetilde{K}_\rho^p \mid \widetilde{G}_\rho(x) \cap \widetilde{K}_\rho^p \neq \emptyset\}, \quad K_\rho^{p+1} = \{x \in K_\rho^p \mid G_\rho(x) \cap K_\rho^p \neq \emptyset\} \quad (10)$$

In other words, $x \in K_\rho^{p+1}$ if and only if $x \in K_\rho^p$ and $\exists \varphi \in F_\rho(x)$ such that $S_\rho(x + \rho\varphi) \cap K_\rho^p \neq \emptyset$ that is to say that $x + \rho\varphi \in S_\rho^{-1}(K_\rho^p)$ and (10) becomes:

$$\widetilde{K}_\rho^{p+1} := (Id + \rho F_\rho)^{-1}(\widetilde{S}_\rho^{-1}(\widetilde{K}_\rho^p)) \cap \widetilde{K}_\rho^p, \quad K_\rho^{p+1} := (Id + \rho F_\rho)^{-1}(S_\rho^{-1}(K_\rho^p)) \cap K_\rho^p$$

Since the graphs of $\widetilde{S}_\rho$, S_ρ and $Id + \rho F_\rho$ are closed and K is compact, $\widetilde{K}_\rho^p$ and K_ρ^p are compact. Decreasing sequences $\widetilde{K}_\rho^p$ and K_ρ^p converge in the sense of Painlevé-Kuratowski to limit sets $\widetilde{K}_\rho^* = \overrightarrow{\mathrm{Viab}}_{\widetilde{G}_\rho}(K)$ and $K_\rho^* = \overrightarrow{\mathrm{Viab}}_{G_\rho}(K)$ satisfying

$$\widetilde{K}_\rho^* = (1 + \rho F_\rho)^{-1}(\widetilde{S}_\rho^{-1}(\widetilde{K}_\rho^*)) \quad \text{and} \quad K_\rho^* = (1 + \rho F_\rho)^{-1}(S_\rho^{-1}(K_\rho^*)) \quad (11)$$

2.5   Approximation of the Hybrid Viability Kernels

We have to prove that the limit $\mathrm{Lim}_{\rho \to 0} K_\rho^*$ exists and is equal to $Hyb_{(F,\Phi)}(K)$ and that it remains true, under restrictive assumptions for strict impulse systems. This derives from the following properties which proofs are annexed.

Proposition 2.8 *Under assumptions (3) and (4), we have*

$$\mathrm{Limsup}_{\rho \to 0} K_\rho^* \subset Hyb_{(F,\Phi)}(K) \quad \text{and} \quad \mathrm{Limsup}_{\rho \to 0} \widetilde{K}_\rho^* \subset Hyb_{(F,\Phi)}(K) \quad (12)$$

and

Proposition 2.9 *Let us assume (3) and (4). Then* $Hyb_{(F,\Phi)}(K) \subset K_\rho^*$.
from which we deduce our main result

Theorem 2.10 (Hybrid Kernel) *Let us assume (3) and (4). Then* $Hyb_{(F,\Phi)}(K) = \mathrm{Lim}_{\rho \to 0} K_\rho^*$ *which is closed.*

Case of strict impulse system The difference between hybrid and strict hybrid solutions arises from that any strict solution cannot encounter C without being reset whereas hybrid solution may follow a continuous path even if it encounters C. The strict hybrid kernel is not necessarily closed as shown in the following example.

Exemple Let us consider the impulse dynamical system given by

$$\begin{cases} F(x,y) = (-1,0) \\ \Phi(x,y) = \{x+1\} \times \{x+y+1\} \\ C = \{(x,y) \text{ such that } \sup(|x|,|y|) = 1 \text{ and } ((x \leq 0) \text{ or } (y \geq 0))\} \\ K = [-2,2] \times [-2,2] \end{cases} \quad (13)$$

It is easy to check (see figure 1) that the strict hybrid kernel is not closed.

We aim to give a sufficient condition implying the convergence of discrete strict hybrid kernels $\widetilde{K}_\rho^*$ to the strict hybrid kernel

Let be $\partial C^r := \{x \in \partial C \text{ such that } \exists p_x, T_{\partial C}(x) = \{y \mid \ < p_x, y > = 0\}\}$, the regular part of the boundary of C.

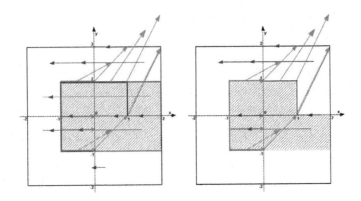

Fig. 1. Closed hybrid and non closed strict hybrid kernels.

Proposition 2.11 (Strict Hybrid Kernel) *Let us assume (3), (4), that F is Lipschitz on a neighborhood of C and that the two following properties hold true:*
(A0) $\forall x \in \partial C^r$, $F(x) \cap T_{\partial C}(x) = \emptyset$,
(A1) $\forall x \in \partial C \backslash \partial C^r$ *any solution of (1) starting from x leaves K in finite time without reaching C.*
   Then $\widetilde{Hyb}_{(F,\Phi)}(K) = \mathrm{Lim}_{\rho\to 0}\widetilde{K}_\rho^*$ *and* $\widetilde{Hyb}_{(F,\Phi)}(K)$ *is closed.*

Proof —— Let be $x_\rho^0 \in \widetilde{K}_\rho^*$ a sequence converging to some element x^0. From Proposition 2.8, $x_0 \in Hyb_{(F,\Phi)}(K)$ and so there exists a viable run $\overrightarrow{x} = \{(\tau_i, x_i, x_i(\cdot)\}_{i\in I}$ starting from x_0 solution of system (F, Φ, K) and there exist viable runs $\overrightarrow{x_\rho} = \{(\tau_{\rho i}, x_{\rho i}, x_{\rho i}(\cdot)\}_{i\in I}$ starting from x_ρ^0 such that the sequence of associated expanded strict solutions $x_\rho^e(\cdot)$ converge uniformly to $x^e(\cdot)$ when $\rho \to 0$.

   Assume that $x_0 \notin \widetilde{Hyb}_{(F,\Phi)}(K)$. Then, there exists $j \in I$ such that $x_j(0) = x_j$, $x_j(\tau_j) \in C$ if $\tau_j < \infty$ and $\exists \widehat{\tau}_j \in]0, \tau_j[$ such that $x_j(\widehat{\tau}_j) \in \partial C$.

   • If $x_j(\widehat{\tau}_j) \in \partial C^r$, from assumption **(A0)** there exist $\eta > 0$ and $\gamma > 0$ such that $< p_{x_j(\widehat{\tau}_j)}, x_j(\widehat{\tau}_j - \eta) - x_j(\widehat{\tau}_j) >< -\gamma$ and $< p_{x_j(\widehat{\tau}_j)}, x_j(\widehat{\tau}_j + \eta) - x_j(\widehat{\tau}_j) >> \gamma$. Using a continuity argument, since F is Lipschitz, $\exists \widehat{\rho}$ such that $\forall \rho \leq \widehat{\rho}$:

$$\exists \widehat{\tau}_{\rho j} \in [\widehat{\tau}_j - \eta, \widehat{\tau}_j + \eta] \subset]0, \tau_{\rho j}[, x_{\rho j}(\widehat{\tau}_{\rho j}) \in \partial C$$

which is impossible since $x_\rho(\cdot)$ is the hybrid solution associated with the run $\overrightarrow{x_\rho}$ is a strict hybrid solution.

   • If $x_j(\widehat{\tau}_j) \in \partial C \backslash \partial C^r$, then from assumption **(A1)** the hybrid solution $x(\cdot)$ associated with the viable run $\overrightarrow{x}$ would leave K in finite time which is impossible. ∎

   We can replace assumption **(A1)** by a global assumption of emptyness of the viability kernel of $K\backslash C$ under F (see [2, Aubin]).

Corollary 2.12 *Let us assume (3) and (4). If K is a repeller for F and if no solution starting from C and immediately leaving C reaches C then*

$$\widetilde{Hyb}_{(F,\Phi)}(K) = \mathrm{Lim}_{\rho\to 0}\widetilde{K}_\rho^*.$$

Proof —— Since no solution starting and immediately leaving from C reaches C and, since K is a repeller for F, all solutions leave K in a finite time. So that any hybrid viable solution which encounters C at some position x_* must necessarily be reset from x^* to a position belonging to $\Phi(x^*)$ for maintaining viability. ∎

2.6   Example of Numerical Computation of Hybrid Kernels

We consider the impulse dynamical system:

$$
\begin{aligned}
(x_1', x_2') &= F(x_1, x_2) = \left(+x_2 + \frac{\|X\| - a}{\|X\|} x_1, \, -x_1 + \frac{\|X\| - a}{\|X\|} x_2\right) \\
(x_1^{n+1}, x_2^{n+1}) &= \Phi(x_1, x_2) = (x_1^n - 1, \, x_2^n)
\end{aligned}
\tag{14}
$$

where the set of constrains is $K = \{(x_1, x_2) \in [-c, c]^2, \|(x_1, x_2)\| \geq \varepsilon\}, c > a > \varepsilon$.

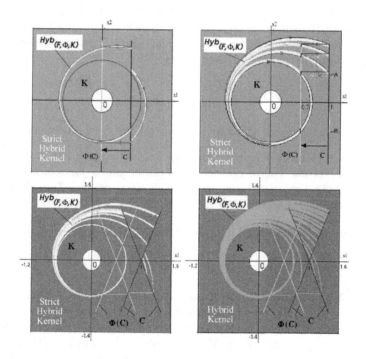

Fig. 2. Structure of the strict hybrid kernel whenever $C \cap Viab_F(K)$ is $\emptyset$ or not.

The continuous dynamic describes a process for which the circle $\mathcal{C}(0, a)$ centered at O and of radius a is the $Viab_F(K)$ which is an unstable limit circle: in the lack of impulse any solution starting out this circle leaves K in finite time.

On figure 2 up right, the reset set is a segment $C = \{X = (x_1, x_2) \mid x_1 = 1, \, x_2 \in [-1, 1]\}$ which does not encounter $Viab_F(K)$. The viability kernel $Viab_F(K)$ is contained in the hybrid kernel and periodic runs are contained in $Viab_F(K)$. On figure 2 up left, $C = \{X = (x_1, x_2) \mid x_1 = 0.5, \ x_2 \in [-1, 1]\}$ encounters $Viab_F(K)$. This changes the structure of the hybrid kernel: periodic runs are no more contained in $Viab_F(K)$ but they exist somewhere else.

On figure 2 down, the reset set is a pair of segments $C_\alpha = \{X = (x_1, x_2)$ such that $(x_1 + 0.4x_2 = 1$ or $x_1 - 0.4x_2 = 1)$ and $x_2 \in [-1, 1]\}$. The hybrid kernel is shown down right and the strict hybrid kernel is shown down left. We can see that the topological structure of hybrid kernels may become very complex.

3   Capture Basin and Minimal Time Function for Target Problem with Impulses

Let $\mathcal{T}$ be a closed target to be reached in finite time satisfying $\mathcal{T} \cap C = \emptyset$. The Capture Basin of $\mathcal{T}$ is the domain of the minimal time-to-reach function and the epigraph of this function is the viability kernel of an extended dynamic (see [7, Cardaliaguet, Quincampoix & Saint-Pierre]). This holds true in presence of impulses. In the same context, in [9] E. Crück has obtained similar results allowing the development of numerical schemes approximating the Minimal Time function for impulse dynamics. Let us define

$$F_{\mathcal{T}}(x) := \begin{cases} F(x) & \text{if } x \notin \mathcal{T} \\ co(F(x) \cup \{0\}) & \text{if } x \in \mathcal{T} \end{cases}$$

The set-valued map $F_{\mathcal{T}}$ is Marchaud and we deduce from Theorem 2.10:

Theorem 3.1 (Viable Capture Basin) *Let us assume (3) and (4). Then $Hyb_{(F_{\mathcal{T}}, \Phi)}(K)$ is the largest closed set of initial points for which there exists at least one hybrid solution viable in K which either reaches $\mathcal{T}$ in finite time or remains in the hybrid kernel for F of $K \backslash \mathcal{T}$: $Hyb_{(F, \Phi)}(K \backslash \mathcal{T})$.*

Let us introduce the extended impulse dynamic (Ψ, Ξ) with constraint $K \times \mathbb{R}^+$

$$(x', z') \in \Psi_{\mathcal{T}}(x, z) := F_{\mathcal{T}}(x) \times \{-1\} \text{ (or } F_{\mathcal{T}}(x) \times [0, 1] \text{ if } x \in \mathcal{T})$$
$$(x^{n+1}, z^{n+1}) \in \Xi(x^n, z^n) := (\Phi(x^n), z^n)$$

Theorem 3.2 (Minimal Time Function) *Let us assume (3) and (4). Then $Hyb_{(\Psi_{\mathcal{T}}, \Xi)}(K \times R^+)$ is the largest closed set of initial points (x_0, z_0) for which there exists at least one hybrid solution $x(t)$ viable in K until it reaches $\mathcal{T}$ in a finite time $\tau \leq z_0$. Moreover, $V(x_0) = \min\{z_0 \mid (x_0, z_0) \in Hyb_{(\Psi_{\mathcal{T}}, \Xi)}(K \times R^+)\}$ is the Minimal Time-to-reach function which is the smallest positive lower semicontinuous supersolution of the following HJB equation*

$$\forall\, x \in Dom(V) \backslash C, \ \max_{u \in U} < f(x, u), -\frac{d}{dx}V(x) > -1 = 0 \qquad (15)$$

The proof is also a consequence of Theorem 2.10 and is similar to the proof given in [7] for control problems. The domain of V is the K-Viable Capture Basin of C for (F, Φ).

Example - Consider the so-called Zermelo swimmer problem studied in [7]. We look for the minimal time function. Let us introduce an impulse dynamic allowing jumps from some points to other ones given by the following impulse dynamical system:

$$(x', y', z') = (b - ay + c_f u, c_f v, -1) \in F(X)$$
$$(x^{n+1}, y^{n+1}, z^{n+1}) = (x^n - 2 + c_r u, y^n + c_r v, z^n) \in \Phi(X)$$

(16)

where control $(u, v) \in B(0, 1)$, $K = [-6, 6] \times (-5, 5] \times R^+$ and $C = \{(i, j), i \in \{-6, -4, -2, 0, 2, 4\}, j \in \{-2, -1, 1, 2\}\}$

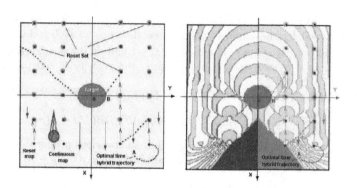

Fig. 3. The impulse dynamic and the level curves of the Minimal Time function.

Dynamical system and target are shown on figure 3 left. The continuous evolution corresponds to the down arrows pointing to a ball of radius c_f, the impulse evolution correspond to the up arrows pointing to a ball of radius c_r. The constraint set K is the square area. The reset set is the collection of dark points. The level curves of the minimal time function are represented on the right. The knowledge of this (approximated) function, solution to the HJB equation, allows to determine the optimal (approximated) synthesis: two (approximated) optimal viable trajectories are computed, the one starting from A and reaching the target in a minimal time is superimposed on the right.

Annex: Proofs of Propositions 2.8 and 2.9

Proof of Proposition 2.8 —— The usual way to prove inclusion (12) is to construct a suitable sequence of equicontinuous piecewise linear approximations and, thanks to Ascoli-Arzela and the Convergence Theorems, to check right properties of the limit. However, for impulse systems, the equicontinuity property of approximated solutions fails at reset times. For this reason, to bypass the lack of equicontinuity of the hybrid solution, we introduced the expanded hybrid solution.

Let ρ be fixed, $x^0 \in \widetilde{K}_\rho^*$ (resp. $x^0 \in K_\rho^*$) and let $x_\rho^d = (x^0, x^1, ..., x^n, ...)$ be a discrete solution to (8) i) (resp. (8) ii)) starting from x^0 and viable in K obtained by choosing $\varphi^n \in F_\rho(x^n)$ (we omit when it is not necessary - but do not forget - the dependency of all items with respect to ρ).

With x_ρ^d we associate the continuous piecewise linear function $\vartheta \to \overline{x}_\rho^e(\vartheta)$ given by

$$\overline{x}_\rho^e(\vartheta) = \begin{cases} x^n + (\vartheta - \vartheta^n)\varphi^n & \forall \vartheta \in [\vartheta^n, \vartheta^n + \rho[\\ x^n + \rho\varphi^n + \frac{1}{\delta}(\vartheta - (\vartheta^n + \rho))[x^{n+1} - (x^n + \rho\varphi^n)] & \forall \vartheta \in [\vartheta^n + \rho, \vartheta^{n+1}[\end{cases}$$

The second line in the definition of $\overline{x}_\rho^e(\vartheta)$ is effective only if $\vartheta^{n+1} = \vartheta^n + \rho + \delta$, that is when a reset occurs at step n. If not, $\vartheta^{n+1} = \vartheta^n + \rho$.

Thanks to such a transformation we build a continuous, piecewise linear and differentiable solution except when $\vartheta = \vartheta^n$ and $\vartheta = \vartheta^n + \rho$ where it admits only right derivative. For all n and for all $\vartheta \in]\vartheta^n, \vartheta^{n+1}[$ we have

$$\frac{d\overline{x}_\rho^e}{d\vartheta}(\vartheta) = \begin{cases} \varphi^n & \text{if } \vartheta \in]\vartheta^n, \vartheta^n + \rho[\\ \frac{1}{\delta}(x^{n+1} - (x^n + \rho\varphi^n)) & \text{if } \vartheta \in]\vartheta^n + \rho, \vartheta^{n+1}[\end{cases}$$

In order to distinguish the evolution governed by the continuous dynamic and the evolution governed by the impulse dynamic we choose $\delta = \frac{\delta_{inf}}{M+1}$. Also, on interval $]\vartheta^n, \vartheta^n + \rho[$, the velocity is upper bounded by $M + 1$ and, in the second case, if $x^{n+1} \neq (x^n + \rho\varphi^n)$, that is to say when a reset occurs, the velocity is constant and lower bounded by $M + 1$.

If $d(x^{n+1}, x^n) \leq \rho M$, that is if $r^{n+1} = r^n$, from (4) we have for all $\vartheta \in]\vartheta^n, \vartheta^{n+1}[$:

$$\frac{d\overline{x}_\rho^e}{d\vartheta}(\vartheta) \in F_\rho(x^n) \subset F(\overline{x}_\rho^e(\vartheta)) + \phi(\rho)\mathcal{B} \subset \mathcal{B}(0, M + \phi(\rho))$$

If $d(x^{n+1}, x^n) > \rho M$, that is if $r^{n+1} = r^n + 1$, the previous property holds true for all $\vartheta \in]\vartheta^n, \vartheta^n + \rho[$ and, from (3) we have for all $\vartheta \in]\vartheta^n + \rho, \vartheta^n + \rho + \delta[$:

$$\frac{d\overline{x}_\rho^e}{d\vartheta}(\vartheta) = y^n \in \Phi_h(x^n + \rho\varphi^n) - (x^n + \rho\varphi^n)$$

and so, on this interval, the derivative is constant and satisfies : $(M + 1) \leq \|\frac{d\overline{x}_\rho^e}{d\vartheta}(\vartheta)\| \leq (M + 1)\frac{\delta_{sup}}{\delta_{inf}}$. Thus we have

$$\sup_{\vartheta \geq 0} \|\frac{d\overline{x}_\rho^e}{d\vartheta}(\vartheta)\| \leq (M + 1)\frac{\delta_{sup}}{\delta_{inf}}$$

The family of functions $\vartheta \to \overline{x}_\rho^e(\vartheta)$ is equicontinuous. Since K is compact, the family is uniformly bounded and from Ascoli-Arzela theorem, it is relatively compact. There exists a subsequence denoted $(\rho_k)_k$ converging to 0 such that $\overline{x}_{\rho_k}^e(\cdot)$ converges uniformly to a function $\overline{x}^e(t)$ when $k \to \infty$:

$$\overline{x}_{\rho_k}^e(\vartheta) \to \overline{x}^e(\vartheta), \quad \text{uniformly } \forall \vartheta \geq 0 \tag{17}$$

Moreover, from Alaoglu theorem, the sequence of derivatives $\frac{d}{d\vartheta}\overline{x}_\rho^e(\cdot)$ is bounded in $L^\infty(O, \infty; X, e^{-b\vartheta}d\vartheta)$, it is included in a weakly compact subset of $L^1(O, \infty; X, e^{-b\vartheta}d\vartheta)$. There exists a subsequence still denoted $(\rho_k)_k$ such that $\overline{x}_{\rho_k}^e$ converges weakly to the derivative of $\overline{x}^e(\cdot)$ when $k \to \infty$:

$$\frac{d\overline{x}_{\rho_k}^e}{d\vartheta}(\vartheta) \rightharpoonup \frac{d\overline{x}^e}{d\vartheta}(\vartheta), \quad \text{weakly a.e. } \vartheta \geq 0 \tag{18}$$

Lemma 3.3 *For all ϑ_0, one of the two following properties holds true:*
i) $\exists \eta_0 > 0$ such that $\forall \vartheta \in]\vartheta_0, \vartheta_0 + \eta_0]$, $\|\frac{d\overline{x}^e}{d\vartheta}(\vartheta)\| \leq M$ and $\overline{x}^e(\vartheta) \in K$
ii) $\exists \overline{\vartheta} \in [\vartheta_0 - \delta, \vartheta_0], \exists \overline{y} \in \Phi(\overline{x}^e(\overline{\vartheta})) - \overline{x}^e(\overline{\vartheta})$ s.t. $\forall \vartheta \in]\overline{\vartheta}, \overline{\vartheta} + \delta[$, $\overline{x}^e(\vartheta) = \overline{x}^e(\overline{\vartheta}) + \frac{\vartheta - \overline{\vartheta}}{\delta}\overline{y}$.

In the first case $\overline{x}^e(\cdot)$ is a locally viable solution to differential inclusion $\frac{d\overline{x}^e}{d\vartheta} \in F(\overline{x}^e)$ defined on a right neighborhood of ϑ_0. In the second case $\frac{d\overline{x}^e}{d\vartheta}(\vartheta) = \frac{1}{\delta}\overline{y}$ on $]\overline{\vartheta}, \overline{\vartheta} + \delta[$.

Proof of Lemma —— Let ϑ_0 be strictly positive. Consider the following property
$(\mathbf{P_\vartheta})$ $\exists \eta_0 > 0, \exists k_0 \in \mathbb{N}, (\vartheta \in [\vartheta_0, \vartheta_0 + \eta_0]$ and $k \geq k_0 \Rightarrow \|\frac{d\overline{x}_{\rho_k}^e}{d\vartheta}(\vartheta)\| \leq M + \varphi(\rho_k))$
and the alternative: "$(\mathbf{P_\vartheta})$ is true or false":

a) If $(\mathbf{P_\vartheta})$ is true then, by construction $\frac{d\overline{x}_{\rho_k}^e}{d\vartheta}(\vartheta) \in F(\overline{x}_{\rho_k}^e(\vartheta)) + \varphi(\rho_k)\mathcal{B}$. Let ϑ be fixed and k going to infinity. Since F is upper semi continuous with convex compact values, Convergence Theorem ([1, Aubin] Thm. 2.2.4) implies that the weak limit $\frac{d\overline{x}^e}{d\vartheta}(\cdot)$ satisfies

$$\frac{d\overline{x}^e}{d\vartheta}(\vartheta) \in F(\overline{x}^e(\vartheta)) \text{ and } \|\frac{d\overline{x}^e}{d\vartheta}(\vartheta)\| \leq M \text{ for almost all } \vartheta \in [\vartheta_0, \vartheta_0 + \eta_0].$$

b) If $(\mathbf{P_\vartheta})$ is false, its contrapositive holds true and since the norm of the derivative $\|\frac{d\overline{x}_\rho^e}{d\vartheta}(\vartheta)\|$ is by construction either lower to $M + \varphi(\rho)$ or greater or equal to $M + 1$ we have: $\forall \eta > 0, \forall k, \exists \vartheta \in [\vartheta_0, \vartheta_0 + \eta], \exists k' \geq k$ s.t. $\|\frac{d\overline{x}_{\rho_{k'}}^e}{d\vartheta}(\vartheta)\| > M + 1$.

Then there exists a step $n_{k'}$ such that

$$i) \quad \vartheta^{n_{k'}} + \rho_{k'} \leq \vartheta < \vartheta^{n_{k'}} + \rho_{k'} + \delta$$
$$ii) \quad \overline{x}_{\rho_{k'}}^e(\vartheta^{n_{k'}}) = x^{n_{k'}}$$
$$iii) \quad \overline{x}_{\rho_{k'}}^e(\vartheta^{n_{k'}} + \rho_{k'}) = x^{n_{k'}} + \rho_{k'}\varphi^{n_{k'}} \in C_{h'}$$
$$iv) \quad \overline{x}_{\rho_{k'}}^e(\vartheta^{n_{k'}} + \rho_{k'} + \delta) = x^{n_{k'}+1} \in \Phi(\overline{x}_{\rho_{k'}}^e(\vartheta^{n_{k'}} + \rho_{k'}))$$

Consequently, if we set $\overline{y}_{\rho_{k'}} = \dfrac{x^{n_{k'}+1} - (x^{n_{k'}} + \rho_{k'}\varphi^{n_{k'}})}{\delta}$ we have

$$\frac{d\overline{x}_{\rho_{k'}}^e}{d\vartheta}(\vartheta) = \overline{y}_{\rho_{k'}} \in \frac{\Phi_h(x^{n_{k'}} + \rho_{k'}\varphi^{n_{k'}}) - (x^{n_{k'}} + \rho_{k'}\varphi^{n_{k'}})}{\delta}.$$

and $\overline{x}_{\rho_{k'}}^e(\vartheta) = x^{n_{k'}} + \rho_{k'}\varphi^{n_{k'}} + \dfrac{\vartheta - (\vartheta^{n_{k'}} + \rho_{k'})}{\delta}\overline{y}_{\rho_{k'}}$

Let $\eta \to 0$ and $k \to \infty$. Since $\vartheta \in [\vartheta_0, \vartheta_0 + \eta]$ we have from i)

$$\vartheta^{n_{k'}} + \rho_{k'} \leq \vartheta \leq \vartheta_0 + \eta \text{ and } \vartheta_0 \leq \vartheta < \vartheta^{n_{k'}} + \rho_{k'} + \delta$$

so that, since there exists a subsequence of $\vartheta^{n_{k'}}$ which converges to $\overline{\vartheta}$, since functions $\overline{x}_\rho^e(\cdot)$ converge uniformly and since Φ is closed, we have

$$i) \quad \overline{\vartheta} \leq \vartheta_0 \leq \vartheta \leq \overline{\vartheta} + \delta$$
$$ii) \quad \overline{x}^e(\overline{\vartheta}) \in C$$
$$iii) \quad \overline{x}^e(\overline{\vartheta} + \delta) \in \Phi(\overline{x}^e(\overline{\vartheta}))$$
$$iv) \quad \overline{x}^e(\vartheta) = \overline{x}^e(\overline{\vartheta}) + (\vartheta - \overline{\vartheta})\frac{\overline{x}^e(\overline{\vartheta}+\delta) - \overline{x}^e(\overline{\vartheta})}{\delta}.$$

So we have $\dfrac{d\overline{x}^e}{d\vartheta}(\vartheta) = \dfrac{1}{\delta}\overline{y} \in \dfrac{\Phi(\overline{x}^e(\overline{\vartheta})) - \overline{x}^e(\overline{\vartheta})}{\delta}$, $\forall \vartheta \in [\overline{\vartheta}, \overline{\vartheta} + \delta[$ Moreover, since the sequence $x^{n_{k'}}$ is contained in K, the limit solution $\overline{x}^e(\vartheta)$ is contained in K except the open segment joining any point in C to its reset position which membership to K is not required. ∎

Reconstruction of the hybrid solution. It remains to prove that the limit solution $\overline{x}^e(\vartheta)$ is an expanded hybrid solution associated with the initial impulse system (F, Φ, K).

We can assume that $x_0 \notin C$. If not we will start, if it exists, from the first reset position which does not belong to C. From the limit solution $\overline{x}^e(\cdot)$ we recover the hybrid solution by a change of variable. For this task, we consider the sequence ϑ_i defined from $\vartheta_0 = 0$ as follows:

$$\vartheta_1 = \inf\{\vartheta > \vartheta_0 \text{ such that } \overline{x}^e(\vartheta) \in C \text{ and } \|\frac{d\overline{x}^e}{d\vartheta_+}(\vartheta)\| \geq M+1\}$$

and $\vartheta_1 = +\infty$ if it does not exists a time $\vartheta > 0$ where $\overline{x}^e(\vartheta)$ belongs to C and is reset at $\Phi(\overline{x}^e(\vartheta))$. If not

$$\vartheta_i = \inf\{\vartheta \geq \vartheta_{i-1} + \delta \text{ such that } \overline{x}^e(\vartheta) \in C\} \text{ and } \|\frac{d\overline{x}^e}{d\vartheta_+}(\vartheta)\| \geq M+1\}$$

and $\vartheta_i = +\infty$ if there is no further time $\vartheta > \vartheta_{i-1} + \delta$ where $\overline{x}^e(\vartheta)$ belongs to C. With any $\vartheta > 0$ we associate the index $i(\vartheta) = \{i \mid \vartheta_i \leq \vartheta < \vartheta_{i+1}\}$, we set $t = \vartheta - i(\vartheta)\delta$ and, for all index i, $t_i = \vartheta_i - i\delta$.

Then the map $t \to x^*(t) := \overline{x}^e(t + i\delta)$, for all $t \in [t_i, t_{i+1}[$ satisfies $x^*(t_i) = \overline{x}^e(\vartheta_i)$ for all i. When ϑ spans $[0, +\infty)$, t spans some interval $[0, \overline{T})$. The upper bound $\overline{T}$ may be finite or infinite. It is finite when, after a finite number of switches between continuous and impulse evolutions, the solution becomes purely impulsive jumping from $C \cap K$ to $C \cap K$.

We have now to check that the solution $x^*(\cdot)$ is an hybrid solution associated with a run $\overline{x}^{\divideontimes}$ satisfying the definition 2.1. Indeed, for all $i > 0$, on each interval $]t_i, t_{i+1}[$, the general convergence theorem (see [1, Aubin], [16, Saint-Pierre]) implies that the solution $x^*(\cdot)$ remains in K and satisfies the differential inclusion

$$\frac{dx^*}{dt}(t) \in F(x^*(t)) \text{ for almost all } t \in]t_i, t_{i+1}[.$$

Let us set $\tau_i := t_{i+1} - t_i$, $x_i^* := x^*(t_i)$ and let us define the motive $x_i^*(\cdot)$ by $x_i^*(\tau) = x^*(t_i + \tau)$ on the interval $[0, \tau_i]$.

At any time $t_i < +\infty$ the solution is reset from the position $x^*(t_i) = x_i^*(\tau_i) \in C$ to the position $x_{i+1}^* \in \Phi(x^*(t_i))$. Then, from this position starts the solution $x^*(\cdot)$ which is viable in K forever or until it reaches anew C at position $x^*(t_{i+1})$ where it is reset at a position belonging to $\Phi(x^*(t_{i+1}))$. So that the corresponding run is precisely $\overline{x}^{\divideontimes} = \{(\tau_i, x_i^*, x_i^*(\cdot)\}$.

We have proved that, for any ρ and for any sequence of elements $x_\rho^0 \in \widetilde{K}_\rho^*$ or $x_\rho^0 \in K_\rho^*$, when $\rho \to 0$, there exists a subsequence converging to some element x^0 and a run $\overline{x}^{\divideontimes}$ starting from x^0 at time $t = 0$ which is a viable run associated with the impulse system (F, Φ, K). ∎

This ends the proof of Proposition 2.8.

Proof of Proposition 2.9 —— Let $x^0 \in Hyb_{(F,\Phi)}(K)$ be an arbitrary initial position. There exists at least one viable run $\overline{x} = \{(\tau_i, x_i, x_i(\cdot)\}$ with $x_0 = x^0$ solution to the impluse system (F, Φ, K). Let us denote $x(\cdot)$ an hybrid solution starting from x^0 and remaining in K.

Let $\rho > 0$ be a given time step satisfying condition (9). With any τ_i we associate $\nu_i = Integer(\frac{\tau_{i-1}}{\rho}) + 1$ and $n_i = \sum_{j=1}^{i} \nu_j$ with $\nu_0 = n_0 = 0$.

Let us define the sequence $(x_{\rho n})_n$ as follows: for all $n \in \mathbb{N}$ we set
- $i_n := \{i \in I \text{ such that } n_i \leq n < n_{i+1}\}$,
- $x_{\rho,n} = x_{i_n}(n - n_{i_n})$, with $x_{i_n}(0) = x_{i_n}$ and $r_{\rho,n} = i_n$

We shall prove that the sequence $(x_{\rho,n})_{n \in N}$ is a solution to the discrete system (8) and conclude that x^0 belongs to any K_ρ^*. Indeed we have

- either $\|x_{\rho,n+1} - x_{\rho,n}\| \leq \rho M$, then for all $t \in [n\rho, (n+1)\rho]$, $x'(t) \in F(x(t))$. Since $x_{\rho,n+1} \in x_{\rho,n} + \sum_0^\rho F(x(\rho n + \tau))d\tau$, we deduce from (4-ii)) that

$$x_{\rho,n+1} \in x_{\rho,n} + \rho F_\rho(x_{\rho,n}) \subset S_\rho(x_{\rho,n})$$

- or $\|x_{\rho,n+1} - x_{\rho,n}\| > \rho M$, then from (3), there exists $t^* \in [n\rho, (n+1)\rho[$ such that $x(t^*) \in C$ and a reset occurs at this time. This necessarily implies that $x_{\rho,n} \in C_h$ since, from (5), $h \geq M\rho$ and that $x_{\rho,n+1} \in \Phi_h(x_{\rho,n}) \subset S_\rho(x_{\rho,n})$.   ∎

References

[1] AUBIN J.-P. (1991) VIABILITY THEORY Birkhäuser, Boston, Basel, Berlin

[2] AUBIN J.-P. (1999) *Impulse Differential Inclusions and Hybrid Systems: A Viability Approach*, Lecture Notes, University of California at Berkeley

[3] AUBIN J.-P. & CELLINA A. (1984) DIFFERENTIAL INCLUSIONS, Springer-Velag, Grundlehren der math. Wiss. # 264

[4] AUBIN J.-P. & FRANKOWSKA H. (1990) SET-VALUED ANALYSIS,

[5] BENSOUSSAN A. & LIONS J.-L. (1984) IMPULSE CONTROL AND QUASI-VARIATIONAL INEQUALITIES, Gauthier-Villars

[6] BENSOUSSAN A. & MENALDI (1997) *Hybrid Control and Dynamic Programming*, Dynamics of Continuous, Discrete and Impulse Systems, 3, 395-442

[7] CARDALIAGUET P., QUINCAMPOIX M. & SAINT-PIERRE P. (1997) *Optimal times for constrained non-linear control problems without local controllability* Applied Mathematics & Optimization, 36:21-42

[8] CARDALIAGUET P., QUINCAMPOIX M. & SAINT-PIERRE P. (1999) SET-VALUED NUMERICAL METHODS FOR OPTIMAL CONTROL AND DIFFERENTIAL GAMES, In STOCHASTIC AND DIFFERENTIAL GAMES. THEORY AND NUMERICAL METHODS, Annals of the International Society of Dynamical Games, 177-247 Birkhäuser

[9] CRÜCK E. (2001) *Problèmes de cible sous contrainte d'état pour des systèmes non linéaires avec sauts d'état* , C.R. Acad. Sci. Paris, t. 333, Série I, p. 403-408.

[10] DORDAN O. (1995) ANALYSE QUALITATIVE, Masson

[11] DOYEN L. & SAINT-PIERRE P. (1997) *Scale of viability and minimal time of crisis*, Set-Valued Analysis, 5, 227-246

[12] FRANKOWSKA H. (1991) *Lower semicontinuous solutions to Hamilton-Jacobi-Bellman equations*, Proceedings of 30th CDC Conference, IEEE, Brighton.

[13] LEITMANN G., (1979) *Guaranteed Asymptotic Stability for a Class of Uncertain Linear Dynamical Systems.* Journ. of Optimization Theory and Applic., 27(1).

[14] QUINCAMPOIX M. (1992) *Differential inclusions and target problems*, SIAM J. Control and Optimization, 30, 324-335

[15] QUINCAMPOIX M. & VELIOV V. (1998) *Viability with a target: theory and applications*, in **Applications of math. in engineering**, 47-54, Heron Press

[16] SAINT-PIERRE P., (1994) *Approximation of the Viability Kernel*, Applied Mathematics & Optimization, **29** (1994), 187-209.

[17] SAINT-PIERRE P., (1996) *Equilibria and stability in setvalued analysis: a viabili-ty approach.* Topology in nonlin. Analysis, Banach Center Pub. 35,243-255 Warsaw

[18] SEUBE N. (1995) *Robust Stabilization of Uncertain Systems.* Journal of Math. Analysis and Applications, 452-466.

[19] SHAFT (van der) A. & SCHUMACHER H. (1999) *An introduction to hybrid dynamical systems*, Springer-Verlag, Lecture Notes in Control, 251

[20] SASTRY S., (1999) NON LINEAR SYSTEMS. ANALYSIS, STABILITY AND CONTROL, Springer-Verlag.

[21] VAANDRAGER F.W. & VAN SCHUPPEN J.H. (1999) HYBRYD SYSTEMS: COMPUTATION AND CONTROL Vol 1569 of LNCS. Springer-Verlag. Berlin.

[22] ZABCZYK J. (1973) *Optimal Control by means of switching* Studia Mathematica, 65,161-171

Ordered Upwind Methods for Hybrid Control

James A. Sethian[1] and Alexander Vladimirsky[2]

[1] Dept. of Mathematics, University of California, Berkeley, California 94720
sethian@math.berkeley.edu,
http://www.math.berkeley.edu/~sethian
[2] Dept. of Mathematics, Cornell University, Ithaca, New York
vlad@math.cornell.edu

Abstract. We introduce a family of highly efficient (non-iterative) numerical methods for a wide class of hybrid control systems. The application of Dijkstra's classical method to a discrete optimal trajectory problem on a network obtains the solution in $O(M \log M)$ operations. The key idea behind the method is a careful use of the direction of information propagation, stemming from the optimality principle. In a series of recent papers, we have introduced a number of Ordered Upwind Methods (OUMs) to efficiently solve the fully anisotropic continuous optimal control problems. These techniques rely on using a partial information on the characteristic directions of the Hamilton–Jacobi–Bellman PDE, stemming from the continuous variant of the optimality principle. The resulting non-iterative algorithms have the computational complexity of $O(M \log M)$, where M is the total number of grid points where the solution is computed, regardless of the dimension of the control/state variables. In this paper, we show how Ordered Upwind Methods may be extended to efficiently solve the hybrid (discrete/continuous) control problems. We illustrate our methods by solving a series of hybrid optimal trajectory problems with and without time-dependence of anisotropic speed functions.

1 Introduction

The dynamical programming approach to all (discrete, continuous, or hybrid) control problems relies on some version of the optimality principle [1]. The resulting equations for the value function are quite often non-linear and coupled (in the continuous case, we are referring to the system of difference equations which discretize the appropriate PDE). Solving a system of coupled non-linear equations using iterative numerical methods can be rather expensive. Our goal is to exploit the optimality principle to build fast numerical methods for equations arising in control theory. The basis for our techniques is the notion of *causality* (i.e., the direction of flow of information) corresponding to a particular class of the control problems.

In this paper, we introduce a family of highly efficient (non-iterative) "Ordered Upwind Methods" (OUMs) for a wide class of hybrid control problems. These methods combine the notion of discrete causality (the basis for Dijkstra's

C.J. Tomlin and M.R. Greenstreet (Eds.): HSCC 2002, LNCS 2289, pp. 393–406, 2002.

method [5]) with the causality of continuous anisotropic control problems (stemming from our recent work on Hamilton–Jacobi PDEs [12]). The resulting computational complexity is the order of $O(M \log M)$, where M is the total number of mesh points used to discretize the continuous state space of the system[1].

We apply these methods to a collection of representative problems from hybrid (discrete/continuous) optimal trajectory planning. A traveler wishes to find the minimum time necessary to reach some pre-defined destination in the domain Ω, where the speed may depend on the direction of motion; this might be applicable, for example, to walking in an area of hilly terrain. Here, we imagine the continuous problem in which motion in any direction is allowed. Furthermore, suppose that bus lines are also available from some fixed points to other given points; these represent discrete links/transitions superimposed on the continuous domain. The considered generalizations include dependence of continuous dynamics upon the discrete state (a traveler carries a pair of skates, which can be put on/taken off, thus changing the anisotropic speed function on different slopes) and time-dependent dynamics (a traveler becomes more tired - and slower - as time goes by, and buses follow their prescribed schedules instead of waiting for the traveler at the stop).

The outline of this paper is as follow. In Section 2, we review Dijkstra's method for discrete control, framed as a single-pass algorithm whose efficiency comes from exploiting the causality (i.e., the direction of flow of information). In Section 3, we show how to build Ordered Upwind Methods for continuous optimal control, again exploiting the (obtained and updated during the computation) knowledge of the flow of information. In Section 4, we show how to develop Ordered Upwind Methods for hybrid control systems and illustrate these algorithms by solving several test-problems.

2   Discrete Control: Dijkstra's Method

Consider a discrete optimal trajectory problem on a network. Here, given a network and a time-penalty associated with each node, the global optimal trajectory problem is to determine the quickest path from a starting node to some exit set in the network. Dijkstra's method [5] is a classic algorithm for solving this problem; it is used to compute the minimal time of exiting starting at any node of the network, and the solution is obtained in $O(M \log M)$ operations. We note that the time-penalty can depend not only on the particular node, but also on the particular link chosen in that node. Thus, Dijkstra's method applies to both *isotropic* and *anisotropic* control problems. The distinction is minor for discrete problems, but significant for continuous problems. Dijkstra's method is a "single-pass" algorithm; if r is the maximum incidence of the nodes in the network, each point on the network is "updated" at most r times to produce the

---

[1]   For the sake of notational clarity, we restrict our discussion to hybrid systems with continuous state component in R^2; all results can be restated for R^n and for meshes on manifolds.

solution. This efficiency comes from a careful use of the direction of information propagation and stems from the optimality principle.

We briefly summarize Dijkstra's method, since its overall structure will be important in explaining our Ordered Upwind Methods. For simplicity, imagine a rectangular grid of size h, where the time-penalty $C_{ij} > 0$ is given for passing through each grid point $\boldsymbol{x}_{ij} = (ih, jh)$. Given a starting point, the minimal total time U_{ij} of arriving at the node $\boldsymbol{x}_{ij}$ can be written in terms of the minimal total time of arriving at its neighbors:

$$U_{ij} = \min \left(U_{i-1,j}, U_{i+1,j}, U_{i,j-1}, U_{i,j+1}\right) + C_{ij}. \tag{1}$$

To find the minimal total time, Dijkstra's method works as follows. All the mesh points are divided into three classes: *Far* (no information about the correct value of U is known), *Accepted* (the correct value of U has been computed), and *Considered* (adjacent to *Accepted*).

1. Start with all mesh points in *Far* ($U_{ij} = \infty$).
2. Move the boundary mesh points ($\boldsymbol{x}_{ij} \in \partial\Omega$) to *Accepted* ($U_{ij} = q(\boldsymbol{x}_{ij})$).
3. Move all the mesh points $\boldsymbol{x}_{ij}$ adjacent to the boundary into *Considered* and evaluate the tentative value of U_{ij} using the values at the adjacent *Accepted* mesh points according to formula 1.
4. Find the mesh point $\boldsymbol{x}_r$ with the smallest value of U among all the *Considered*.
5. Move $\boldsymbol{x}_r$ to *Accepted*.
6. Move the *Far* mesh points adjacent to $\boldsymbol{x}_r$ into *Considered*.
7. Re-evaluate the value for all the *Considered* $\boldsymbol{x}_{ij}$ adjacent to $\boldsymbol{x}_r$. If the new computed value is less than the previous tentative value for $\boldsymbol{x}_{ij}$ then update U_{ij}.
8. If *Considered* is not empty then go to 4).

The described algorithm has the computational complexity of $O(M \log(M))$; the factor of $\log(M)$ reflects the necessity of maintaining a sorted list of the *Considered* values U_i to determine the next *Accepted* mesh point. An efficient implementation of the algorithm can be constructed using heap-sort data structures.

3   Continuous Control: Ordered Upwind Methods

Consider now the problem of continuous optimal control; here, the goal is to find the optimal path from a starting position to an exit set. It is well-known that Dijkstra's method does not converge to the continuous solution as the mesh is refined. This can be seen by considering the simple problem of a uniform Cartesian grid with a constant time-penalty $C > 0$ for passing through every node. The minimal time from a starting point to an end point is the Manhattan distance on this grid times C. Thus, Dijkstra's method produces the solution to the partial differential equation

$$\max(|u_x|, |u_y|) = h \cdot C,$$

where h is the grid size (see [10]). As h goes to zero, this does not converge to the solution of the continuous Eikonal problem given by

$$|u_x^2 + u_y^2|^{1/2} = C$$

Thus, Dijkstra's method cannot be used to obtain a solution to the continuous problem.

3.1   Dijkstra-like Solvers for Isotropic Continuous Control Problems

In the isotropic case, when the speed depends only on the position and not on the direction of motion, two recent algorithms, namely Tsitsiklis's Method [15],[16] and Sethian's Fast Marching Method [9] have been introduced to solve the problems with the same computational complexity as Dijkstra's method. Both methods exploit information about the flow of information to obtain this efficiency; the causality allows one to build the solution in increasing order, which yields the Dijkstra-like nature of the solutions.

Both algorithms result from a key feature of Eikonal equations, namely that their characteristic lines coincide with the gradient lines of the viscosity solution $u(\boldsymbol{x})$; this allows the construction of single-pass algorithms. Tsitsiklis' algorithm evolved from studying isotropic min-time optimal trajectory problems, and involves solving a minimization problem to update the solution. Sethian's Fast Marching Method evolved from studying isotropic front propagation problems, and involves an upwind finite difference formulation to update the solution. Each method starts with a particular (and different) coupled discretization and each shows that the resulting system can be decoupled through a causality property. We refer the reader to these papers for details on ordered upwind methods for Eikonal equations.

3.2   Ordered Upwind Methods for General Anisotropic Continuous Control Problems

Consider now the general continuous optimal trajectory problem, in which the speed function depends on both position and direction. In [12], Sethian and Vladimirsky built and developed single-pass "Ordered Upwind Methods" for the anisotropic continuous optimal control problems. They showed how to to produce the solution U_i by recalculating each U_i at most r times, where r depends only on the degree of anisotropy present in the PDE and on the mesh structure, but not upon the number of mesh points. The convergence to the viscosity solution was proven, and numerical schemes were developed for a wide range of applications.

Building efficient single-pass methods for general optimal control problems is considerably more challenging than it is for the Eikonal case, since the characteristics no longer coincide with the gradient lines of the viscosity solution. As a result, the characteristics and gradient lines may in fact lie in different simplexes. Therefore, the approximation U_i to the min-time function $u(\boldsymbol{x_i})$ may well depend upon the approximate min-time value U_j at some adjacent mesh point x_j even if U_i is smaller than U_j. This is precisely why both Sethian's Fast Marching Method and Tsitsiklis' Algorithm cannot be directly applied in the anisotropic (non-Eikonal) case: it is no longer possible to de-couple the system by computing/accepting the mesh points in the ascending order.

We now explain the idea behind Ordered Upwind Methods for general continuous optimal control. The key idea behind the Ordered Upwind Methods for the non-Eikonal optimal control (introduced in [12],[17]) is to use the measure of the local anisotropy of the speed function to limit the number of *Accepted* points that might contribute to the update of each *Considered* point. Consider the anisotropic min-time optimal trajectory problems, in which the speed of motion depends not only on position but also on direction. The value function u for such problems is the viscosity solution of the static Hamilton-Jacobi-Bellman equation

$$\max_{a \in S_1} \{(\nabla u(x) \cdot (-a))f(x, a)\} = 1, \, x \in \Omega,$$
$$u(x) = q(x), \qquad\qquad\qquad\qquad x \in \partial\Omega. \tag{2}$$

In this formulation, a is the unit vector determining the direction of motion, $f(x, a)$ is the speed of motion in the direction a starting from the point $x \in \Omega$, and $q(x)$ is the time-penalty for exiting the domain at the point $x \in \partial\Omega$. The maximizer a corresponds to the characteristic direction for the point x. If f does not depend on a, Eqn. 2 reduces to the Eikonal equation, see [1]. Furthermore, we assume that

$$0 < F_1 \le f(x, a) \le F_2 < \infty,$$

and define the anisotropy ratio $\Upsilon = F_2/F_1$.

Technical comment: This is sufficient to show that the value function is continuous in the interior of Ω (and is equal to the viscosity solution of Eqn. 2) even in the presence of continuous-state constraints: the above assumptions can be used to demonstrate both Soner's tangentiality along the boundary of the constraint set (as in [14]) and the local controllability near $\partial\Omega$ (as in [2], for example). For every point $x \in \Omega$, we define the *speed profile* $S_f(x) = \{af(x, a) \mid a \in S_1\}$, and note that, if all speed profiles are convex, then a min-time optimal trajectory exists for all points in Ω; for non-convex speed profiles the value function $u(x)$ is still well-defined even if no minimizing trajectory exists for that point (see [17],[13] for the detailed discussion).

In [12,17], the following two lemmas were proven:

- **Lemma 1.** Consider the characteristic passing through a point $\bar{x} \in \Omega$ and a level curve $u(x) = C$, where $q_{max} < C < u(\bar{x})$. The characteristic intersects that level set at some point $\tilde{x}$. If $\bar{x}$ is distance d away from the level set then

$$\|\tilde{x} - \bar{x}\| \le d\frac{F_2}{F_1}. \tag{3}$$

- **Lemma 2.** Consider an unstructured mesh X of diameter h on Ω. Consider a simple closed curve Γ lying inside Ω with the property that for any point x on Γ, there exists a mesh point y inside Γ such that $\|x - y\| < h$. Suppose the mesh point $\bar{x}_i$ has the smallest value $u(\bar{x}_i)$ of all of the mesh points inside the curve. If the characteristic passing through $\bar{\boldsymbol{x}}_i$ intersects that curve at some point $\hat{\boldsymbol{x}}_i$ then

$$\|\hat{\boldsymbol{x}}_i - \bar{\boldsymbol{x}}_i\| \leq h\frac{F_2}{F_1}. \tag{4}$$

This means that one may use the anisotropy ratio to exclude a large fraction of the *Accepted* points in computing the update of any *Considered* points.

Building on these results we construct the following single-pass method. As before, mesh points are divided into three classes (*Far*, *Considered*, and *Accepted*). The *AcceptedFront* is defined as a set of *Accepted* mesh points, which are adjacent to some not-yet-accepted mesh points. Define the set AF of the line segments $\boldsymbol{x}_j\boldsymbol{x}_k$, where $\boldsymbol{x}_j$ and $\boldsymbol{x}_k$ are adjacent mesh points on the *AcceptedFront*, such that there exists a *Considered* mesh point $\boldsymbol{x}_i$ adjacent to both $\boldsymbol{x}_j$ and $\boldsymbol{x}_k$. For each *Considered* mesh point $\boldsymbol{x}_i$ we define the part of AF "relevant to $\boldsymbol{x}_i$":

$$NF(\boldsymbol{x}_i) = \left\{ (\boldsymbol{x}_j, \boldsymbol{x}_k) \in AF \,|\, \exists \tilde{\boldsymbol{x}} \text{ on } (\boldsymbol{x}_j, \boldsymbol{x}_k) \text{ s.t. } \|\tilde{\boldsymbol{x}} - \boldsymbol{x}_i\| \leq h\frac{F_2}{F_1} \right\}.$$

We will further assume that some consistent upwinding update formula is available: if the characteristic for $\boldsymbol{x}_i$ lies in the simplex $\boldsymbol{x}_i\boldsymbol{x}_j\boldsymbol{x}_k$ then $U_i = K(U_j, U_k, \boldsymbol{x}_i, \boldsymbol{x}_j, \boldsymbol{x}_k)$. For the sake of notational simplicity we will refer to this value as $K_{j,k}$.

1. Start with all mesh points in *Far* ($U_i = \infty$).
2. Move the boundary mesh points ($\boldsymbol{x}_i \in \partial\Omega$) to *Accepted* ($U_i = q(\boldsymbol{x}_i)$).
3. Move all the mesh points $\boldsymbol{x}_i$ adjacent to the boundary into *Considered* and evaluate the tentative value of
   $U_i = \min_{(\boldsymbol{x}_j, \boldsymbol{x}_k)NF(\boldsymbol{x}_i)} K_{j,k}$.
4. Find the mesh point $\boldsymbol{x}_r$ with the smallest value of U among all the *Considered*.
5. Move $\boldsymbol{x}_r$ to *Accepted* and update the *AcceptedFront*.
6. Move the *Far* mesh points adjacent to $\boldsymbol{x}_r$ into *Considered*.
7. Recompute the value for all the *Considered* $\boldsymbol{x}_i$ within the distance $h\frac{F_2}{F_1}$ from $\boldsymbol{x}_r$. If the new computed value is less than the previous tentative value for $\boldsymbol{x}_i$ then update U_i.
8. If *Considered* is not empty then goto 4).

- **Efficiency:** This results in a "single-pass" method since the maximum number of times each mesh point can be re-evaluated is bounded by the number of mesh points in the $h\frac{F_2}{F_1}$ neighborhood of that point. Thus, this method formally has the computational complexity of $O((\frac{F_2}{F_1})^2 M \log(M))$. Moreover, since the *AcceptedFront* is approximating the level set of the viscosity solution u, as the mesh is refined, the complexity will behave as $O(\frac{F_2}{F_1} M \log(M))$. Here, the "efficiency" refers to the complexity of computing an approximate solution on a fixed grid; the above orders of complexity are proven for the implementation using heap-sort data structures [12,17].

- **Convergence:** In [12,17] we prove the convergence (assuming the continuity of f) of the numerical solution to the viscosity solution of the PDE for a particular update formula K_{ij}, related to the iterative schemes described in [7], [8], and [6]. The asymptotic order of convergence of the method generally depends upon the order of the upwinding update formula $U_i = K(U_j, U_k, \boldsymbol{x_i}, \boldsymbol{x_j}, \boldsymbol{x_k})$.
- In [12] we also use the above method with other the finite-difference upwinding update formulas, obtained as the anisotropic generalizations of the discretizations presented in [11]. The notable advantage of this approach is that it can be easily generalized for the higher-order upwinding finite difference approximations.

3.3   Numerical Results

The first example we consider corresponds to finding geodesic distances on a surface. Consider a pedestrian walking with the unit speed on a surface $z = g(x, y)$. The pedestrian is interested in finding the shortest path on the surface. As shown in [12], the problem can be solved in the $x - y$ plane by considering the dynamics of the pedestrian's shadow. The shadow will move from point A to point B in the plane, as the pedestrian walks from $(A, g(A))$ to $(B, g(B))$ on the manifold. The speed of the shadow in the direction $\boldsymbol{a} \in S_1$ is, therefore,

$$f(x, y, \boldsymbol{a}) = \left(1 + (\nabla g(x, y) \cdot \boldsymbol{a})^2\right)^{-\frac{1}{2}}.$$

Solving the equation 2 in the $x - y$ plane with the boundary condition $u(B) = 0$, we obtain the level sets of the min-time to exit function u. The characteristics of the PDE will correspond to the globally optimal trajectories for the pedestrian's shadow (and, hence, to the projections of the pedestrian's optimal walking paths). Figure 1 illustrates the solution of this PDE for the surface $g(x, y) = 45 \sin(\frac{\pi x}{50}) \sin(\frac{\pi y}{50})$ over the square $[0, 100] \times [0, 100]$.

 We now make the problem harder by accounting for the fact that the (sustained) speed of walking on the surface is generally dependent on the slope of the surface in that direction. Let θ be the angle between the direction of motion on the surface and the positive direction of z-axis:

$$\theta_{\boldsymbol{a}} = \frac{\pi}{2} - \arctan(\nabla g(x, y) \cdot \boldsymbol{a}).$$

If the pedestrian is moving on the surface with the positive speed $\phi(\theta_{\boldsymbol{a}})$, then the shadow moves in the direction $\boldsymbol{a} \in S_1$ with the speed

$$f(x, y, \boldsymbol{a}) = \phi(\theta_{\boldsymbol{a}}) \left(1 + (\nabla g(x, y) \cdot \boldsymbol{a})^2\right)^{-\frac{1}{2}}.$$

We use two different slope-dependencies $\phi_w(\theta) = \sin^6(\theta) + 0.1$ and $\phi_s(\theta) = 2 \sin^{40}(\theta) + 0.1$, generating the speed functions f_w and f_s. (In our simplistic model, we consider them as speeds for *walking* and *skating* on the surface, respectively.) The level sets of the corresponding min-time functions are shown in Figure 2.

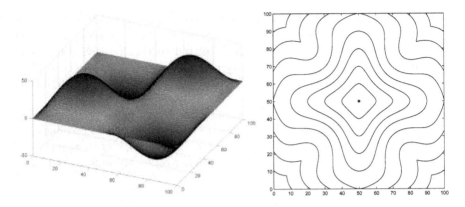

Fig. 1. The test surface and the level sets of the min-time function (for traveling to the origin with unit speed).

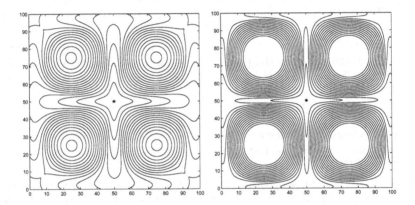

Fig. 2. The min-time function for walking (left) and skating (right) to the origin.

Our third example is the problem of finding an optimal continuous trajectory for traveling on the manifold if the traveler becomes "tired" (i.e., slows down) as time goes by:

$$f_{wt}(\boldsymbol{y}, \boldsymbol{a}, t) = f_w(\boldsymbol{y}, \boldsymbol{a})\psi(t),$$

where ψ is a positive, monotone decreasing function of t. This is a simple example in which the speed function depends on time in the controlled dynamics.

In general, the time-dependence of speed conflicts with the optimality principle: the optimal route from A to B might be irrelevant for computing the optimal route from C to B even if that optimal route passes through the point A. A simple way to deal with the situation is to add the time to the state variables, but the computational cost of such a solution is prohibitive. We use a different approach instead: reversing the direction of information propagation.

If the dynamics were time independent (i.e., $\boldsymbol{y}'(t) = f(\boldsymbol{y}(t), \boldsymbol{a}(t))\boldsymbol{a}(t)$), we would use $u(B) = 0$ as a boundary value for the HJB PDE:

$$\max_{\boldsymbol{a} \in S_1} \{(\nabla u(\boldsymbol{x}) \cdot (-\boldsymbol{a}))f(\boldsymbol{x}, \boldsymbol{a})\} = 1,\ \boldsymbol{x} \in \Omega. \tag{5}$$

The level sets $u(\boldsymbol{x}) = T$ would include all the points, **from** which one could (optimally) travel to B in time T. In principle, the value function u could be used to compute the optimal route to B **from** any point in the domain.

For the time dependent dynamics (i.e., $\boldsymbol{y}'(t) = f(\boldsymbol{y}(t), \boldsymbol{a}(t), t)\boldsymbol{a}(t)$), we are using the initial condition $u(A) = 0$ and solving the HJB PDE:

$$\max_{\boldsymbol{a} \in S_1} \{(\nabla u(\boldsymbol{x}) \cdot \boldsymbol{a})f(\boldsymbol{x}, \boldsymbol{a}, u(\boldsymbol{x}))\} = 1,\ \boldsymbol{x} \in \Omega. \tag{6}$$

The level sets of the viscosity solution ($u(\boldsymbol{x}) = T$) include all the points, **to** which one could (optimally) travel from A in time T. In principle, the value function u could be used to compute the optimal route from A **to** any point in the domain[2].

Figure 3 shows the level sets of the viscosity solution $u(x)$ for the speed function $f_{wt}(\boldsymbol{y}, \boldsymbol{a}, t) = f_w(\boldsymbol{y}, \boldsymbol{a})e^{-\lambda t}$.

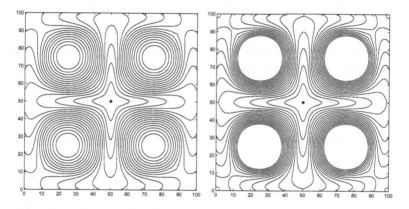

Fig. 3. The min-time function for walking **from** the origin with time-dependent speed: $\lambda = 0.001$ (left) and $\lambda = 0.005$ (right). The level sets are plotted at the same values as in Figure 2.

---

[2] It is easy to see that, if the speed f is not a continuous function of time, the value function u does not have to be a continuous function of $\boldsymbol{x}$. In such cases, the HJB equation 6 can still be interpreted if $u(\boldsymbol{x})$ is substituted by $\limsup_{\boldsymbol{y} \to \boldsymbol{x}} u(\boldsymbol{y})$.

We also note that a wide class of static convex Hamilton–Jacobi PDEs of the form $\|\nabla u\| F\left(\boldsymbol{x}, \frac{\nabla u}{\|\nabla u\|}, u\right) = 1$ can be interpreted as the HJB equation 6 and, therefore, can be solved by the OUMs; see [13] for details.

4   Ordered Upwind Methods for Hybrid Control Problems

The Fast Marching Method for the continuous isotropic Eikonal equation can be extended to hybrid control, as was done in [3],[4]; this can be applied in cases in which the speed of motion is isotropic (dependent only upon the current state of the system). We now extend the continuous control Ordered Upwind Methods to compute the value function for the hybrid systems with the general (anisotropic) continuous-state dynamics.

4.1   Formulation of Algorithm

Hybrid systems are often modeled as hybrid automata, represented by a directed graph with continuous dynamics at each node. The continuous state of the system evolves according to the chosen continuous control and the differential equations specified for the particular node; when certain conditions are satisfied, the transition to another node may occur, leading to a change in the dynamics of a continuous state of the system.

In order to find an optimal hybrid control numerically, we also need to discretize the continuous state space corresponding to each discrete state of the hybrid system. Let X_i be the discretization of the continuous state space corresponding to the hybrid automata node σ_i. The full computational mesh $X = \bigcup X_i$ will also include the directed links representing transitions between different modes of continuous dynamics. Let $\boldsymbol{x}_i \in X_i$ be a node for which the transition rules are satisfied. Define the sets

$$L_{from}(\boldsymbol{x}_i) = \{\boldsymbol{x}_j \in X_j \mid \text{there is a transition from } \boldsymbol{x}_i \text{ to } \boldsymbol{x}_j\}$$

and

$$L_{to}(\boldsymbol{x}_i) = \{\boldsymbol{x}_j \in X_j \mid \text{there is a transition from } \boldsymbol{x}_j \text{ to } \boldsymbol{x}_i\}$$

(*jump successors* and *jump predecessors* of $\boldsymbol{x}_i$ in the terminology of [4]). These transitions are represented in X by the directed links $(\boldsymbol{x}_i, \boldsymbol{x}_j)$ with the associated transition/link costs $C_{ij} \geq 0$.

As before, mesh points are divided into three classes (*Far, Considered, Accepted*). The *AcceptedFront* is defined as a set of *Accepted* mesh points, which are adjacent to some not-yet-accepted mesh points. Define the set AF of the line segments $\boldsymbol{x}_j\boldsymbol{x}_k$, where $\boldsymbol{x}_j$ and $\boldsymbol{x}_k$ are adjacent mesh points on the *AcceptedFront*, such that there exists a *Considered* mesh point $\boldsymbol{x}_i$ adjacent to both $\boldsymbol{x}_j$ and $\boldsymbol{x}_k$. For each *Considered* mesh point $\boldsymbol{x}_i$ we define the part of AF "relevant to $\boldsymbol{x}_i$":

$$NF(\boldsymbol{x}_i) = \left\{(\boldsymbol{x}_j, \boldsymbol{x}_k) \in AF \mid \exists \tilde{\boldsymbol{x}} \text{ on } (\boldsymbol{x}_j, \boldsymbol{x}_k) \text{ s.t. } \|\tilde{\boldsymbol{x}} - \boldsymbol{x}_i\| \leq h\frac{F_2}{F_1}\right\}.$$

We also define the set of *Accepted* "neighbors" accessible via discrete transition links $LA_{\text{from}}(\boldsymbol{x}_i) = L_{\text{from}}(\boldsymbol{x}_i) \bigcap Accepted$. We will further assume that some consistent upwinding update formula is available for each "mode" of continuous dynamics: if the characteristic for x_i lies in the simplex $x_i x_j x_k$ then $U_i = K(U_j, U_k, x_i, x_j, x_k)$. For the sake of notational simplicity we will refer to this value as $K_{j,k}$.

1. Start with all mesh points in Far ($U_i = \infty$).
2. Move the boundary mesh points ($x_i \in \partial \Omega$) to $Accepted$ ($U_i = q(x_i)$).
3. Move all the mesh points x_i adjacent to the boundary (and all the x_i s.t. $LA_{\text{from}}(x_i) \neq \emptyset$) into $Considered$ and evaluate the tentative value of
$$U_i = \min \left\{ \min_{(x_j, x_k) NF(x_i)} K_{j,k}, \ \min_{x_s \in LA_{\text{from}}(x_i)} \{U_s + C_{is}\} \right\}.$$
4. Find the mesh point x_r with the smallest value of U among all the $Considered$.
5. Move x_r to $Accepted$ and update the $Accepted Front$.
6. Move the Far mesh points adjacent to x_r into $Considered$.
7. Move the Far mesh points in $L_{\text{to}}(x_r)$ into $Considered$.
8. Recompute the value for all the $Considered$ x_i such that $\|x_r - x_i\| \leq h\frac{F_2}{F_1}$ or $x_i \in L_{\text{to}}(x_r)$. If the new computed value is less than the previous tentative value for x_i then update U_i:
$$U_i = \min \left\{ U_i, \ \min_{(x_r x_j) \in NF(x_i)} K_{r,j}, \ U_r + C_{ir} \right\}.$$
9. If $Considered$ is not empty then goto 4).

The efficiency of the resulting method is $O\left(\left(\frac{F_2}{F_1} + d \right) M log M \right)$, where M is the total number of mesh points in X and d is the maximum number of discrete transitions/links from a single mesh point.

4.2   Examples

As the first example, we consider the problem of finding an optimal trajectory on a surface; the continuous problem is augmented by assuming that there are discrete transitions between a finite number of pre-defined points on the mesh. A realistic analogue is the time-optimal path planning for traveling on a varied landscape if there are shuttle buses waiting for travelers at pre-defined locations x_i and carrying them (for a fee - or time penalty - $C_{ij} \geq 0$) to the pre-defined locations x_j. Thus, even if the traveler is trying to get from A to B, it might save him time to diverge from the geodesic path to the point C if the shuttle going from C to D is fast and if D is not far from the final destination.

This example is not the most general possible hybrid system, since the directed discrete links (i.e., the transitions) change only the position in the continuous state space but not the underlying dynamics. Thus, we are able to compute the value function using a single discretization X of the continuous state space and superimposing on it the "shuttle lines" (Figure 4). This example can also be interpreted for the buses (unlike shuttles, buses are not waiting for the traveler); if C_{ij} is the average time for traveling on bus from x_i to x_j, including the average waiting time at the bus stop. In this case, the computed value function is interpreted as the expected value of the time taken by the optimal route.

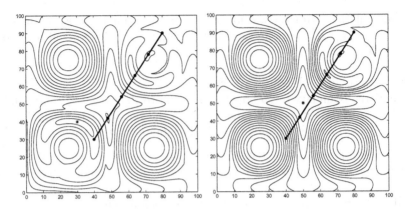

Fig. 4. The min-time function for traveling **to** the point B in the presence of shuttles (left), and the min-time function for traveling **from** the point A in the presence of the buses running on schedule (right).

Our second test problem involves the buses going exactly on schedule[3]. This is an example of the discrete dynamics depending on time: the time-penalty associated with the bus-route transition is assumed to be infinite at all times other than the scheduled departures. As in the fully continuous case, this endangers the optimality principle: the optimal route from A to B might be irrelevant for computing the optimal route from C to B even if that optimal route passes through the point A. (The optimal route from A to B could include catching a bus, which might be gone by the time we get from C to A.)

As before, we deal with this difficulty by setting the boundary condition to be zero at the "source" A rather than the "target" B. As shown in Figure 4, the level sets of the viscosity solution ($u(x) = T$) include all the points, **to** which one could (optimally) travel from A in time T.

For a more complete and realistic example, we now demonstrate the application of OUMs to "real" hybrid control problems - i.e., the problems, in which taking the discrete transition forces a change in the dynamics (rather than just a position of) the continuous state. In most cases, such problems require using multiple discretizations X_i of the continuous state space, corresponding to multiple nodes σ_i of the hybrid automata. Consider a person walking on a varied landscape, but also carrying a pair of inline roller skates. This *walker* has an option of paying the time-penalty (spending time to put on the skates) to become a *skater* and to modify his speed function as a result. Correspondingly, the *skater* can pay a different time-penalty to take of the skates and return to *walking*. We compute the value function u for this problem using two copies (X_s and X_w) of the discretized continuous state space[4]. Figure 5 shows the level sets of $u(x)$

---

[3] Depending on where you live, this may be extremely unrealistic.

[4] Of course, if the time-penalties are zero, the optimal strategy will correspond to the value function obtained by using the speed $f = \max\{f_w, f_s\}$. In this simple case,

computed under the assumption that putting on the skates requires 10 seconds and taking them off - only 5.

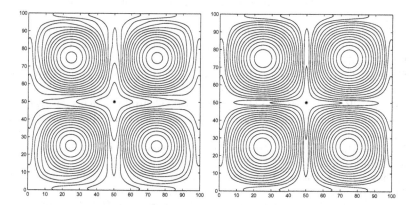

Fig. 5. The min-time function for traveling to the origin using the hybrid (walking/skating) dynamics: for those, who start out walking (left), or skating (right). The level sets are plotted at the same values as in Figure 2.

5   Conclusions

We have demonstrated that single-pass Ordered Upwind Methods can be built for a variety of anisotropic hybrid control problems. The obvious generalizations of the considered optimal hybrid trajectory problems (simultaneously taking into account multiple modes of continuous dynamics, time dependence of the continuous and discrete controls, etc) can be treated similarly. The continuous state constraints can be handled by representing only the constraint set in the meshes X_i; the numerical evidence confirms the convergence to the viscosity solution even for piecewise continuous anisotropic speed functions [12].

We are currently investigating applicability of OUMs to other classes of PDEs, and to other application domains. Work in progress includes devising Ordered Upwind Methods for differential games and extending the capabilities to more complex systems [13].

References

1. Bellman, R.: Introduction to the Mathematical Theory of Control Processes. (1967) Academic Press, New York.

---

the calculation can be performed using a single discretization X of the continuous state space.

On the other hand, if the speeds f_w and f_s were fully isotropic, this problem would reduce to the second example considered in [4].

2. Bardi, M. & Falcone, M.: An Approximation Scheme for the Minimum Time Function. (1990) SIAM J. Control Optim., 28, 950-965.
3. Branicky, M.S. & Hebbar, R.: Fast marching for hybrid control. (1999) Proceedings, IEEE Intl. Symp. Computer Aided Control System Design, Kohala-Kona, HI, August 22-27.
4. Branicky, M.S., Hebbar, R., Zhang G.: A fast marching algorithm for hybrid systems. (1999) Proceedings, IEEE Conf. on Decision and Control, Phoenix, AZ, December 7-10.
5. Dijkstra, E.W.: A Note on Two Problems in Connection with Graphs. (1959) Numerische Mathematik, 1, 269-271.
6. Gonzales, R. & Rofman, E.: On Deterministic Control Problems: an Approximate Procedure for the Optimal Cost, I, the Stationary Problem. (1985) SIAM J. Control Optim., 23, 2, 242-266.
7. Kushner, H.J.: Probability Methods for Approximations in Stochastic Control and for Elliptic Equations. (1977) Springer-Verlag, New York.
8. Kushner, H.J. & Dupuis, P.G.: *Numerical Methods for Stochastic Control Problems in Continuous Time. (1992) Academic Press, New York.*
9. *Sethian, J.A.: A Fast Marching Level Set Method for Monotonically Advancing Fronts. (1996) Proc. Nat. Acad. Sci., 93, 4, 1591-1595.*
10. *Sethian, J.A.: Level Set Methods and Fast Marching Methods: Evolving Interfaces in Computational Geometry, Fluid Mechanics, Computer Vision and Materials Sciences. (1999) Cambridge University Press).*
11. *Sethian, J.A. & Vladimirsky, A.: Fast Methods for the Eikonal and Related Hamilton–Jacobi Equations on Unstructured Meshes. (2000) Related Hamilton–Jacobi Equations on Unstructured Meshes,* Proc. Nat. Acad. Sci., 97, 11, 5699-5703.
12. Sethian, J.A. & Vladimirsky, A.: Ordered Upwind Methods for Static Hamilton-Jacobi Equations: Theory and Algorithms. (2001) Center for Pure and Applied Mathematics Technical Report PAM-792 (University of California, Berkeley).
13. Sethian, J.A. & Vladimirsky, A.: Ordered Upwind Methods for a Variety of Control Problems. Generalizations and Optimizations, in progress. (2001).
14. Soner, M.H.: Optimal control problems with state-space constraints. (1986) SIAM J. Control Optim., 24, 552-562 and 1110-1122.
15. Tsitsiklis, J.N.: Efficient algorithms for globally optimal trajectories. (1994) Proceedings, IEEE 33rd Conference on Decision and Control, Lake Buena Vista, Florida, December (1994), 1368-1373.
16. Tsitsiklis, J.N.: Efficient algorithms for globally optimal trajectories. (1995) IEEE Tran. Automatic Control, 40, 1528-1538.
17. Vladimirsky, A. : Fast Methods for Static Hamilton-Jacobi Partial Differential Equations. (2001) Ph.D. Dissertation, Dept. of Mathematics, Univ. of California, Berkeley.

Discrete-Time Refinement of Hybrid Automata*

Thomas Stauner

BMW Car IT, Petuelring 116, D-80809 München, Germany
stauner@in.tum.de, Phone: +49 89 3101987

Abstract. Notations like hybrid automata are highly useful in the development process of hybrid systems to document requirements in early design steps. When it comes to implementation a part of the requirements will be realized in software in a discrete-time manner. We therefore study sufficient conditions which ensure that an automaton operating in discrete-time *refines* a hybrid automaton with its underlying continuous time model. Our notion of refinement provides that vital properties which have been established for the hybrid automaton also hold for its refinement. Furthermore, we outline a method how to derive a discrete-time refinement from a hybrid automaton.

1 Introduction

In our view notations which allow a joint specification of discrete and continuous behavior, such as hybrid automata [1], are highly useful for eliciating, elaborating, discussing and documenting requirements of hybrid systems. Furthermore, such formal notations are the basis for computer-aided validation methods like simulation and model checking. In later design steps the elaborated abstract, mixed discrete and continuous model can then be refined towards implementation. [11] and [12] propose such processes.

Moving from an abstract model based on a continuous time scale to implementation amounts to changing to a discrete-time execution scheme for those components in the model which are implemented on (or in) digital hardware. Due to the cost structure and flexibility of software-based solutions, such discrete-time execution usually is desired for large parts of a hybrid system. In order to ensure that vital properties of the abstract model are satisfied in the implementation oriented discrete-time model, the change of the execution scheme must be performed in a controlled way. This is an essential prerequisite for the utility of development processes of hybrid systems which build upon hybrid notations and an early validation of the obtained hybrid models, before implementation related decisions are made. Such decisions e.g. include the partitioning of a model into submodels with different time scales.

Therefore, this paper identifies conditions under which the transition from continuous-time to discrete-time is a refinement step which preserves vital system

---

* This work originated at the Institut für Informatik, TU München, and was supported with funds of the DFG under reference number Br 887/9 within the priority program *Design and design methodology of embedded systems*.

C.J. Tomlin and M.R. Greenstreet (Eds.): HSCC 2002, LNCS 2289, pp. 407–420, 2002.
© Springer-Verlag Berlin Heidelberg 2002

properties. The paper considers discrete-time refinement of hybrid automata. It is derived from [12] where a similar, more extensive theory is developed for the HyChart notation [4]. The work presented in the paper only regards isolated automata without event based communication. Automata with input and events are considered in [12].

Related Work. A refinement notion similar to ours is also used in [2]. In [7] the authors give proof rules which allow them to deduce the validity of duration calculus formulas in discrete-time from the validity of the formulas in continuous-time. In our view this can be regarded as refining the contiuous time formulas. The refinement method we develop is based on a hybrid automata dialect which allows some imprecision in the taking of transitions and the values of variables. Other variants of hybrid automata with uncertainties are introduced in [5, 3]. In particular, [3] is closed to our approach.

Overview. This paper is organized as follows. First, we explain effects of a discrete-time execution of components of a hybrid system and their implications on hybrid automata in Section 2. Section 3 defines hybrid automata, refinement and so-called discrete-time hybrid automata, which satisfy some restrictions that allow their direct implementation in discrete-time. With this basis, Section 4 presents a refinement technique for the transition from (general) hybrid automata to discrete-time hybrid automata. Finally, we draw some conclusions in Section 5. The online version of the paper, available under http://www4.in.tum. de/~stauner/papers/, additionaly contains an appendix with an example. The paper assumes some familiarity with hybrid automata [1].

2   Implementation Effects

In our view hybrid automata-like notations can beneficially be used for requirements capture and the early design steps of hybrid embedded systems. In these phases designers usually want to express that some discrete actions (or *transitions*) are taken when certain conditions are satisfied. They are not so much interested in the detailed timing, i.e. in possible small delays between the (first) satisfaction of conditions and the execution of the corresponding actions. They are, however, aware that such delays exists when the model is implemented digitally. One primary reason for such delays is that the digital components can only sense the status of their environment within the discrete time grid given by their clock. In our view sampling rates and timing uncertainties are implementation related effects. Therefore we think it is not adequate to already consider them in detail in early design phases. Nevertheless abstract models occurring in early design phases must be designed in a way that tolerates small delays without violating vital system properties. For instance, in control theory it is known that delays, such as those caused by sampling, can lead to instability. Otherwise, if the model's correctness relies on the absence of any delays, it cannot be implemented later on.

Besides timing uncertainties, there is a further kind of deviations from the ideal model. When an action which is triggered by the boundary crossing of a continuosly evolving quantity x, i.e. triggerd by a condition like $x \geq c$, is taken by a digital component, the boundary c will usually already be exceeded. In other words, in case of actions which depend on the value of variables that evolve continuously, the timing uncertainty corresponds to an uncertainty in the actual value of the variable for which the action is executed. For given analog dynamics, one kind of uncertainty can be derived from the other.

Fig. 1 visualizes the effect of sampling on the detection of a boundary crossing for boundary value c. For trajectory x and sampling period T, the boundary crossing of x is detected with delay. The crossing of trajectory y is not detected with sampling period T, because it happens between two consecutive sampling instants. Trajectory y thus indicates that the boundary crossing cannot be detected with arbitrary precision with sampling. For hybrid automata employing such boundary crossing events as guards of

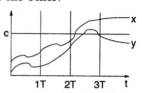

Fig. 1: Delayed or failing detection of boundary crossing events caused by sampling.

transitions, this means that transitions can usually not be taken immediately when enabled, but with some delay or, under awkward circumstances, not at all. Considering the value of the trajectory when such a transition is taken, we see that in the depicted example x is already greater than c at $3T$. Obviously, the delayed execution of transitions may violate invariants which are required to hold for the system or may lead to instability, because of too late reaction.

Implementation effects on analog dynamics. Let us now regard the analog dynamics of a hybrid component. The analog dynamics on the one hand affects the discrete dynamics (the state transitions) and on the other hand it can affect external components. We assume the dynamics are given by some differential equation $\dot{x} = f(x)$. In this case we distinguish two kinds of effects resulting from an implementation of the analog dynamics in discrete time. At sampling instants the discretized analog dynamics in general only yields an approximation of the exact dynamics. As an analogy, think of a numerical algorithm (the discretized analog dynamics) that computes the solution to $\dot{x} = f(x)$ for given initial value x_0. At each interpolation point kT of the algorithm, it will provide an approximation of the exact value of the solution $x(kT)$. Like in numerics, we call the deviation between the exact value and the approximating value at sampling instants the *discretization error*. It affects the discrete part as well as external components that depend on x. A further error results between sampling instants, where the discretized analog dynamics does not produce new output. In this paper, we choose to extend the (discretized) analog dynamics' output at a sampling point over the interval until the next sampling instant by holding it constant. In control systems terminology, this correponds to a so-called *zero-order hold*.[1] The effect of this strategy is that there is a further deviation of the output w.r.t. the exact dynamics between sampling instants. At the sampling

---

[1] Other extension strategies besides the zero-order hold would be feasible as well, but, as Ogata [10] mentions, more complicated construction schemes for continuous-time signals from discrete-time signals are usually not used in control applications.

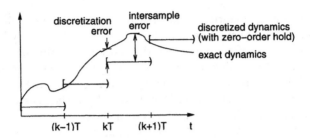

Fig. 2. Discretization error and intersample error.

points this deviation however vanishes. We therefore call it the *intersample error*. Both kinds or errors are visualized in Figure 2. We define the intersample error as the maximum deviation between the exact value and the time-extended output of the discetized analog dynamics during a sampling period. In hybrid automata, this error affects the discrete dynamics, because between sampling points the exact dynamics could enforce a transition, while no transition may be necessary for the discretized dynamics which simply remains constant during a sampling interval. Furthermore, the environment of a component is affected by this error.

Impact on verification. The effect of discrete time implementation also has to be considered when planning verification steps for a system. Namely, there is not much sense in formal, exhaustive verification of abstract models with tools like model checkers, if the properties established for the abstract model can not be transfered to the implementation, because the abstract model is unrealistically precise. In contrast, verification is helpful if the abstract model is liberal enough to comprise effects that result from its implementation, like time delays and deviations from the exact continuous dynamics. Model checking techniques which weaken the exactness with which analysis of hybrid models is performed have been proposed in [5, 6] and [3].

Methodology. As a result, the models of a system component specified in the requirements capture phase and the early design phase should allow for timing uncertainties and uncertainties in the analog dynamics. In hybrid automata, invariants which overlap with transition guards can be used to express uncertainty w.r.t. when exactly a transition is taken. In order to specify the uncertainty associated with the analog dynamics we introduce a relaxation constant into our dialect of hybrid automata (see below). To deal with the intersample error we introduce a further relaxation when we consider the traces produced by a hybrid automaton.

From an external point of view which only observes the generated traces, the uncertainties in the model leads to sets of traces. In further design steps the timing uncertainty and the permitted deviations from the analog dynamics can be used by the designers to select a sampling rate for the embedded hard- and software that guarantees (1) that transitions are taken within the delay permitted by the relaxed model and (2) that the discretized analog dynamics is sufficiently precise. The selection process can be guided by the modeling tool and may involve standard techniques from control theory, like Shannon's sampling theorem. This way a new model which only generates a subset of the traces of the original model is obtained. The new model is therefore called a *refinement* of the original one. Properties which were true for the original model can then be transferred to the new model: If every trace of the original model is guaranteed to satisfy a given property, then all traces of the new model will also satisfy the property, because every new trace also is in the trace set of the original model. A mode detailed study of properties is given in [12].

3   Preliminaries Concerning Hybrid Automata

Hybrid automata. For our purpose, we modify the standard definition of hybrid automata [1] in some aspects. First, we omit synchronization labels. In connection with external components, synchonization labels may enforce the immediate taking of a transition in a hybrid automaton. This is too precise to allow flexible refinement of the automaton. Second, we introduce a relaxation of the continuous activities in the automaton. This means that variables need not evolve exactly as specified by the activity, but some deviation from the specified exact evolution is permitted. As we will see below, this relaxation acts as an upper bound on the permitted discretization error in a discrete-time implementation. Third, the semantics of invariants is slightly different in our model. We only require that the invariant of a location holds, if time passes in that location. When a location is left or entered via a transition the invariant need not hold. This way transient locations, i.e. locations in which no time passes, can be specified. We use this in our discrete-time dialect of hybrid automata introduced below. Finally, we do not consider any input here in order to simplify the presentation. Discrete-time refinement which also regards external input is studied in [12].

In this paper a *hybrid automaton* A is a 7-tuple $(X, V, inv, init, Act, \varepsilon_{dis}, E)$ with the following meaning:

X is a finite ordered set $\{x_1, ..., x_n\}$ of variables over $\mathbb{R}$. A valuation s is a point in $\mathbb{R}^n$, the value of variable x_i in valuation s is the i-th component of s, s_i. Often we also use notation $s.x_i$ to denote the value of variable x_i, instead of writing s_i. $\mathbb{R}^n$ is also called the *data-state space* of the automaton. When Φ is a predicate over the variables in X, we write $[\![\Phi]\!]$ to denote the set of valuations s for which $\Phi[X := s]$ is true.

V is a finite set of locations. A state of automaton A is a tuple (v, s) consisting of a location $v \in V$ and a valuation s.

inv is a mapping from the set of locations V to predicates over the variables in X. $inv(v)$ is the *invariant* of location v. When time passes in v, only valuations $s \in [\![inv(v)]\!]$ are allowed.

$init$ is a mapping from the locations in V to predicates over X. $init(v)$ is called the initial condition of v. (v, s) is an initial state if $init(v)$ is true for s.

Act is a mapping from the locations in V to convex predicates over $X \cup \dot{X}$, where $\dot{X} = \{\dot{x}_1, ..., \dot{x}_n\}$ and $\dot{x}_i$ denotes the first time derivative of x_i, dx_i/dt. A predicate over variables in a set Y is called *convex* if it is a finite conjunction of inequalities $<, \leq, >, \geq$ between arithmetic terms over Y.[2] When control is in location v the variables evolve according to differentiable functions which approximatly satisfy the activity $Act(v)$.

ε_{dis} is a mapping from the locations in V to the nonnegative real numbers $\mathbb{R}_+$. For each location $\varepsilon_{dis}(v)$ specifies a permitted error by which the continuous evolution (according to *Act*) may be affected.

A finite set E of edges called transitions. A transition $(v, jp, v') \in E$ has source location v and target location v'. jp is called the transition's jump condition. It is a convex predicate over variables $X \cup X'$, where $X' = \{x_1', ..., x_n'\}$. x_i' stands for the value of variable x_i after the transition is taken, while x_i refers to the value before the transition is taken. Jump conditions are structured into a guard and a body. The guard is the precondition for the transition and if the transition is taken, the body determines the next value of the variables. The guard is a convex predicate over variables X and the body is a convex predicate over variables $X \cup X'$. If the guard is true the body is satisfiable.

All of the above mappings are total.

Semantics. The *transition-step relation* $\rightarrowtail$ is defined as $(v, s) \rightarrowtail (v', s')$ iff there is a $(v, jp, v') \in E$ such that the variables change according to the jump condition, i.e. $jp[X, X' = s, s']$ is true. Transition steps are discrete, no time passes while they are taken. Unlike standard hybrid automata we do not require that the location invariants hold in the source or destination location. For our purpose, this is more convenient for enforcing transitions.

The δ *time step relation* $\rightarrowtail_\tau^\delta$ is defined as $(v, s) \rightarrowtail_\tau^\delta (v, s')$ iff there are two differentiable functions $\rho, \tau \in [0, \delta] \rightarrow \mathbb{R}^n$, $\delta \geq 0$, with

- $\tau(0) = s$ and $\tau(\delta) = s'$
- the invariant of v is satisfied during $[0, \delta)$: $\tau(t) \in [\![inv(v)]\!]$ for $0 \leq t < \delta$
- τ is within $\varepsilon_{dis}(v)$ distance of ρ: $d(\tau(t), \rho(t)) \leq \varepsilon_{dis}(v)$ for $t \in [0, \delta]$, where $d(., .)$ is the Euclidean distance on $\mathbb{R}^n$.
- the activity $Act(v)$ is satisfied for ρ: $Act(v)[X, \dot{X} := \rho(t), \dot{\rho}(t)]$ is true for $t \in [0, \delta]$, where $\dot{\rho}(t) = (\dot{\rho}_1(t), ..., \dot{\rho}_n(t))$.

Note that the regarded location's invariant need not hold at the end point δ. A function τ for which there is a function ρ such that the last two items from above hold, is said to *satisfy Act(v) up to ε_{dis}*.

The *hybrid step relation* $\blacktriangleright$ is defined as $(v, s) \blacktriangleright_\tau^\delta (v', s')$ iff there is a $s'' \in \mathbb{R}^n$ such that $(v, s)(\rightarrowtail)^*(v', s'') \rightarrowtail_\tau^\delta (v', s')$, where R^* is the arbitrary but finite iteration of relation R (including the 0-fold iteration, i.e. the identity relation).

A *(continuous-time) execution* of a hybrid automaton is a finite sequence of hybrid steps $(v_0, s_0) \blacktriangleright_{\tau_0}^{\delta_0} (v_1, s_1) \blacktriangleright_{\tau_1}^{\delta_1} ... \blacktriangleright_{\tau_\ell}^{\delta_\ell} (v_{\ell+1}, s_{\ell+1})$, where $s_0 \in [\![init(v_0)]\!]$ and $\ell \in \mathbb{N}$. A *trace* is obtained from an execution by mapping the execution to a function over (a subset of) the time axis $\mathbb{R}_+$. For an execution $(v_0, s_0) \blacktriangleright_{\tau_0}^{\delta_0} (v_1, s_1)$ $\blacktriangleright_{\tau_1}^{\delta_1} ... \blacktriangleright_{\tau_\ell}^{\delta_\ell} (v_{\ell+1}, s_{\ell+1})$, the corresponding trace τ is defined by: $\tau(t) = \tau_i(t -$

---

[2] Equality can be defined as a macro.

$\Sigma_{k=0}^{i-1}\delta_k$) for $t \in [\Sigma_{k=0}^{i-1}\delta_k, \Sigma_{k=0}^i\delta_k)$, where $\Sigma_{k=0}^{-1}x$ is defined to be 0. τ is a piecewise differentiable function[3] if the execution is non-zeno, i.e. if it does not contain infinitely many transition steps within a finite time interval. Its domain is $[0, \Sigma_{k=0}^\ell \delta_i)$. We write $Tr(A)$ to denote the set of all traces of a hybrid automaton A.

The relaxation R_ε of a set of traces T is defined by $R_\varepsilon(T) = \{\sigma \in PD \mid \exists \tau \in T.\, dom(\tau) = dom(\sigma) \wedge \forall t \in dom(\tau).\, d(\tau(t), \sigma(t)) \leq \varepsilon\}$, where $dom(\tau)$ is the domain of function τ and PD is the set of piecewise differentiable functions from (subsets of) $\mathbb{R}_+$ to $\mathbb{R}^n$.

Refinement. We say that a hybrid automaton B is a *refinement* of hybrid automaton A iff the set of traces of B is contained in that of A, i.e. $Tr(B) \subseteq Tr(A)$. In order to consider a discrete-time execution scheme as a refinement of a hybrid automaton, some more freedom is necessary due to the intersample error. We therefore use relaxation R_ε: A hybrid automaton B is an ε *refinement* of a hybrid automaton A iff $Tr(B) \subseteq R_\varepsilon(Tr(A))$.

On an abstract level, we can regard universal properties, i.e. properties which have to be satisfied for all executions of a system, as sets of traces (cf. [9]).In this point of view a universal property P is satisfied by a hybrid automaton A iff $Tr(A) \subseteq P$. It is satisfied by the ε relaxation of A, respectively, iff $R_\varepsilon(Tr(A)) \subseteq P$. By the definition of refinement it is obvious that a refinement (ε refinement) of an automaton A is guaranteed to satisfy a universal property P if A (the ε relaxation of A) satisfies P. Note that a more comprehensive study of properties of hybrid systems is given in [12].

Discrete-time hybrid automata. In order to talk about discrete time systems we need a way to specify such systems first. As we want as much similarity to hybrid automata as possible, we do not introduce a new automata model but introduce syntactic restrictions on hybrid automata which ensure that an automaton satisfying these restrictions can in essence only produce traces which are step functions over an equidistant discrete time grid.

A hybrid automaton $A = (X, V, inv, init, Act, \varepsilon_{dis}, E)$ is called a *discrete-time hybrid automaton (DHA)* of time granularity $T > 0$ iff:

- $X = \{x_1, ..., x_n, c\}$ for $n \in \mathbb{N}$. X contains the special variable c called the *clock* of A.
- The invariant of every location is of the form $(c = 0 \wedge p) \vee c \neq T$, where p is a predicate over $X \setminus \{c\}$.
- The initial condition of every location is of the form $p \wedge c = 0$, where p is a predicate over $X \setminus \{c\}$.
- The activity of every location is $\dot{c} = 1 \wedge \bigwedge_{x \in X \setminus \{c\}} \dot{x} = 0$. Hence, only the clock changes in time steps.
- $\varepsilon_{dis} = 0$
- The set of transition E can be split into two disjoint sets E_l and E_u such that the following holds. The guard of every transition in E_l is a predicate of the form $c = 0 \wedge p$ where p is a convex predicate over $X \setminus \{c\}$. The body

---

[3] A function is piecewise differentiable iff every finite interval can be partitioned in finitely many subintervals such that the function is differentiable on each subinterval.

of every transition in E_l does not modify c. The guard of every transition in E_u is of the form $c = T \, \wedge \, p$ where p is a convex predicate over $X \setminus \{c\}$ and the body of every transition in E_u is of the form $q \, \wedge \, c' = 0$ where q is a convex predicate over $X' \setminus \{c'\}$. Furthermore, for transitions in E_u source location and destination location coincide.

Transitions in E_u reset the clock c. The rest q of their body is intended to perform some numerical computation and determine the value of the variables at the next discrete time instant $k \cdot T$, $k \in \mathbb{N}$. Thus q is intended to replace the continuous update of the variables which is performed by the activities in a hybrid automaton by a discrete update. Therefore, transitions in E_u are also called update transitions. While the activities are differential equations, q will usually result from a difference equation or a more complex numerical computation.

The guards of the transitions and the invariants are chosen in a way which ensures that time T after the last transition was taken, a transition in E_u must be taken (in order to update the variables' values according to an approximation of a differential equation) and then transitions in E_l can be taken or time can progress. Transitions in E_l can only be taken after a transition in E_u, because their guard requires that c is 0. Transitions in E_l are called logic transitions, since they are intended to model the logic-based switching between control modes. Furthermore, we point out that due to the form of the invariants and since activities only modify c, the following holds: If an invariant is true for a valuation s with $s.c = 0$ then a time step of duration T is possible.

Executions and traces of DHA. The executions of a DHA A result from the hybrid step relation as above. It is easy to see that the traces generated by a DHA A and projected on $X \setminus \{c\}$ are piecewise constant functions in which points of discontinuity can only occur at time instants $k \cdot T$, $k \in \mathbb{N}$. In order to simplify proofs in the following we now introduce further step relations which more directly correspond to the operational behavior of DHA.

The *logic-step relation* $\dashrightarrow_l$ is defined as $(v, s) \dashrightarrow_l (v', s')$ iff $(v, s) \dashrightarrow (v', s')$ by a transition in E_l. We define the update relation $\dashrightarrow_u$ as $(v, s) \dashrightarrow_u (v', s')$ iff $(v, s) \dashrightarrow (v', s')$ by a transition in E_u. Note that $v' = v$ holds due to the form of the transitions in E_u. The *control-step relation* $\rightsquigarrow$ is defined as $(v, s) \rightsquigarrow^\ell_{(\mu_i)} (v, s')$ iff (μ_i) is a sequence of functions and there are s_i for $i \in \{0, \dots, \ell - 1\}$, $\ell \geq 1$, and s_ℓ such that $(v, s_i)(\leadsto^T_{\mu_i}; \dashrightarrow_u)(v, s_{i+1})$, where ; denotes the sequential composition of relations, $s_0 = s$, $s_\ell = s'$ and every function $\mu_i \in [0, T] \rightarrow \mathbb{R}^{n+1}$, $i \in \{0, \dots, \ell - 1\}$, in the sequence (μ_i) is defined by $\mu.c(t) = t$ and $\mu.x(t) = s''_x$ for $x \in X \setminus \{c\}$. Informally, a control step $\rightsquigarrow^\ell_{(\mu_i)}$ spans ℓ sampling intervals without being interrupted by logic steps. It may be regarded as the execution of a discrete-time control law. The *discrete-time hybrid step relation* $\rhd^\ell_{(\mu_i)}$ is defined as $(v, s) \rhd^\ell_{(\mu_i)} (v', s')$ iff there is a $s'' \in \mathbb{R}^{n+1}$ such that $(v, s)(\dashrightarrow)^*(v', s'') \rightsquigarrow^\ell_{(\mu_i)} (v', s')$. We remark that the invariant of v' must be true for s'', because no control step is possible otherwise.

Every finite trace τ of a DHA A can be extended to a trace τ' which is defined on $[0, k \cdot T)$ where k is the smallest natural number such that $dom(\tau) \subseteq dom(\tau')$. In other words, τ can be extended to a trace which ends at a sampling step. The reason is that invariants do not become false for values of c in $(0, T)$. Therefore, we now restrict our attention to traces which end at sampling steps.

A *discrete-time execution* of a DHA is a finite sequence of discrete-time hybrid steps $(v_0, s_0) \triangleright \, _{(\mu_{i,0})}^{\ell_0} (v_1, s_1) \triangleright \, _{(\mu_{i,1})}^{\ell_1} \cdots \triangleright \, _{(\mu_{i,m})}^{\ell_m} (v_{m+1}, s_{m+1})$, where $s_0 \in [\![init(v_0)]\!]$. Corresponding to the traces of continuous-time executions, the trace τ of such a discrete-time execution is defined by: $\tau(t) = \mu_{i,j}(t - t')$ for $t \in [t', t' + T)$ and $t' = (\Sigma_{k=0}^{j-1} \ell_k + i) \cdot T$. If we restrict our attention to traces which end at sampling instants, the set of traces generated for a DHA by discrete-time hybrid steps and by continuous-time hybrid steps coincide. The proof is simple and omitted here. The similar property does not hold on the level of executions, since the hybrid step relation includes idle steps and time steps of duration less than T while a single discrete-time hybrid step lasts at least time T.

4   Refinement to Discrete Time

We start with a theorem that establishes a sufficient condition for a DHA B to be an ε refinement of a hybrid automaton A. Then, a systematic way to construct such a DHA B from a specific type of hybrid automata is introduced.

4.1   Refinement Theorem

The way we formulate the theorem below is motivated by the desire to be able to consider invariants (and transitions) in separation from activities when refinement is regarded. Therefore, we do not explicitly relate control steps of a DHA to time steps of a hybrid automaton, but consider the satisfaction of invariants (item 3 below) and activities (item 4 below) separately. This requires to abstract the set of functions (or evolutions) permitted by the activities of a hybrid automaton by a set of evolution constraints. Typically, such an abstraction can be the set of all Lipschitz continuous functions with Lipschitz constant less or equal to a given constant.[4] In the following we write S for the set of functions which abstracts the activities and call it the set of evolution constraints. We write S_t for the set of all functions in S whose domain is a superset of $[0, t)$.

Theorem 1. *Let $A = (X, V, inv_A, init_A, Act_A, \varepsilon_{dis}, E_A)$ be a hybrid automaton and let $B = (X \cup \{c\}, V, inv_B, init_B, Act_B, 0, E_B)$ be a DHA of time granularity T. B is an ε refinement of A if there is a set of evolution constraints S for A such that the following holds.*

1. the initial conditions in B result from those of A by adding conjunct $c = 0$ (clock initialization) to them: $\forall v \in V. \, init_B(v) \equiv init_A(v) \, \wedge \, c = 0$

---

[4] A function τ is Lipschitz continuous iff there is a constant $L \geq 0$ such that $\forall x, y \in dom(\tau). \, d'(\tau(x), \tau(y)) \leq L \cdot d(x, y)$ where d and d' are metrics on domain and rage, respectively, of function τ.

2. *if a logic step is possible in B, a similar step is possible in automaton A:*
   $\forall u, v. u \oplus_l v \Rightarrow \pi_X(u) \rightarrow \pi_X(v)$, *where* $\oplus_l$ *is the logic step relation of B and*
   $\rightarrow$ *is the transition step relation of A.* π_X *denotes projection of valuations of*
   B to valuations of A, i.e. the projection eliminates the valuation of variable
   c. Note that c must be 0 by definition of logic steps, which means that logic
   steps can only occur at sampling instants.

3. *the invariant of a location v of A is guaranteed to remain true during a*
   sampling period, if the invariant of v in B is true at a sampling instant,
   i.e. for c = 0. In other words, for a start state (v, s) no activity of A can
   violate the invariant of v during time T, if the invariant of v in B for
   valuation s' with $\pi_X(s') = s$ *and* $s'.c = 0$ *is true:*
   $$\forall v \in V, s' \in \mathbb{R}^{n+1}. s'.c = 0 \wedge s' \in [\![inv_B(v)]\!] \Rightarrow (\forall \tau \in S_T. \tau(0) = \pi_X(s') \Rightarrow$$
   $$\forall t \in [0, T). \tau(t) \in [\![inv_A(v)]\!])$$

4. *for every control step* $(v, s) \triangleright^{\ell}_{(\mu_i)} (v', s')$ *of B, (1) there is a function* $\tau \in$
   $[0, \ell \cdot T] \rightarrow \mathbb{R}^n$ *which is in the* ε_{dis} *neighborhood of a function* ρ *that satisfies*
   $Act_A(v)$ *and (2)* τ *and the respective* μ_i *agree at sampling instants and (3)*
   between sampling instants they agree up to ε*. Formally:*
   $(v, s) \triangleright^{\ell}_{(\mu_i)} (v', s') \Rightarrow \exists \tau, \rho \in [0, \ell \cdot T] \rightarrow \mathbb{R}^n$.

   $(\forall t \in [0, \ell \cdot T]. Act(v)[X, \dot{X} := \rho(t), \dot{\rho}(t)] \wedge d(\tau(t), \rho(t)) \leq \varepsilon_{dis}) \wedge$
   $\forall i \in \{0, \ldots, \ell - 1\}. \pi_X(\mu(iT)) = \tau(iT) \wedge$ (sampling instants OK)
   $\forall t \in [0, \ell \cdot T). d(\pi_X(\mu(t)), \tau(t)) \leq \varepsilon \wedge$ (intersample response OK)
   $\pi_X(s') = \tau(\ell \cdot T)$ (last value OK)
   where function $\mu \in [0, \ell \cdot T] \rightarrow \mathbb{R}^{n+1}$ *is defined by* $\mu(t) = \mu_i(t - i \cdot T)$ *for*
   $i \in \{0, \ldots, \ell - 1\}$ *and* $t \in [iT, (i+1)T)$.

5. *set S of evolution constraints indeed is an abstraction of the trajectories*
   produced by the activities of A. In other words, every function τ *which*
   satisfies $Act_A(v)$ *up to* ε_{dis} *for a* $v \in V$ *is in S. Formally:* $\forall \tau. (\exists \rho. \forall t \in$
   $dom(\tau). Act(v)[X, \dot{X} := \rho(t), \dot{\rho}(t)] \wedge d(\tau(t), \rho(t)) \leq \varepsilon_{dis}) \Rightarrow \tau \in S$

B is also called a discrete-time ε refinement *of A.*

The proof of the theorem proceeds by induction over the discrete-time hybrid step relation. (Remember that the traces of B, which – without loss of generality – end at sampling instants, can be constructed from iterating the discrete-time hybrid step relation starting from a state that satisfies the initial condition of B.) Assumption 1 of the theorem assures that every initial state of B is an initial state of A (disregarding variable c). Assumption 2 assures that for every logic step of B there is a corresponding transition step of A. Assumptions 3 to 5 guarantee that for every control step of B there is a corresponding time step of A which produces a trace that is similar to that of B up to ε. Technically, assumption 4 assures that for a control step of B there is a corresponding function τ satisfying the respective activity of A. Assumption 3 then ensures that the invariant of the location in which the control step takes places is not violated by any activity, i.e. that a time step is indeed possible. In the formal proof, assumption 3 must be applied inductively ℓ times for a control step spanning ℓ sampling intervals. A detailed proof of a similar, more complex theorem in the context of *HyCharts* is given in [12].

4.2   Constructing Discrete-Time Refinements

In the following we introduce a method how to derive a DHA B and a time granularity $T > 0$ from a hybrid automaton A such that B satisfies assumptions 1 to 4 of Theorem 1. The method requires that A has a certain form described below.

First, note that Theorem 1 already determines that B must have the same locations as A, the same variables plus clock c and $\varepsilon_{dis} = 0$ for B. Furthermore, assumption 1 of the theorem derives the initial conditions in B from those in A by adding a clock initialization. The activities of B are fixed by the definition of DHA. Thus, what is left, is to derive the invariants, the sets of transitions E_l and E_u and the time granularity T for DHA B from automaton A.

4.2.1 Invariants and Logic Transitions   We start with the invariants and logic transitions E_l and derive constrains on T.

Ideal and relaxed invariants. For our method, we require that the invariants of A are constructed from the transitions by negating the transition guards and introducing a relaxation of these "ideal" invariants. In more detail, we require that the invariant $inv_A(v)$ of a location v in A is constructed in the following way. First, the ideal invariant of v is defined as the conjunction of the negated guards of all transitions with source location v. As all guards are convex predicates over X, the ideal invariant ϕ can schematically be rewritten as $\bigwedge_{i=1}^{g}(\bigvee_{j=1}^{h_i} at_{i,j})$ where each $at_{i,j}$ is a negated comparison of arithmetic expressions over X. The relaxed invariant ψ results from relaxing the negated atoms. In detail, each negated comparison $at_{i,j}$ is rewritten in the form $a_{i,j}\#0$, where $a_{i,j}$ is an arithmetic expression and $\# \in \{<, \leq\}$. Then this predicate is replaced by atom $at'_{i,j} \equiv a\#\varepsilon_{i,j}$, where $\varepsilon_{i,j} > 0$ is a constant. Thus, ψ is given by $\bigwedge_{i=1}^{g}(\bigvee_{j=1}^{h_i} at'_{i,j})$. The constants $\varepsilon_{i,j}$ provide that the relaxed invariant remains true for some trespassing of threshold 0 in the expressions $a_{i,j}\#0$. This means that the relaxed invariant does not become false at once when a transition guard becomes true, but it remains true for some more time, until the threshold is trespassed by amount $\varepsilon_{i,j}$. On essential idea in time-discretization is to choose the time granularity T in a way which ensures that a clock tick lies within every time interval in which the value of such expressions $a_{i,j}$ rises from 0 to $\varepsilon_{i,j}$.

Definition of B's invariants and logic transitions. With these preliminaries we define the invariants and logic transitions of B as follows. For every location v with relaxed invariant ψ in automaton A, we define $inv_B(v) \equiv (c = 0 \wedge \phi) \vee c \neq T$, where ϕ is the ideal invariant corresponding to ψ (resulting from the negation of transition guards in A, as explained above). Furthermore, the set of logic transitions E_l of B is defined by adapting the transitions of A by adding $c = 0$ to all transition guards and adding $c' = c$ to the bodies such that c remains constant: $E_l = \{(v, g \wedge c = 0 \wedge b \wedge c' = c, v') \mid (v, g \wedge b, v') \in E_A\}$. With these guards and invariants, a logic transition in B must be taken, if at a sampling instant, i.e. for $c = 0$, the current location's ideal invariant ϕ is false.

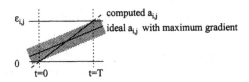

Fig. 3. Worst case in the evolution of $a_{i,j}$: Due to ε_{dis}, the evolution of $a_{i,j}$ is affected by an error $\delta_{i,j}$ (in grey in the figure). The computed value of $a_{i,j}$ therefore crosses the interval $[0, \varepsilon_{i,j}]$ faster than it could in the ideal case.

Constraints on T. We now assume that all invariants in A are relaxed invariants as explained above. Furthermore, we assume that maximal gradients $l_{i,j}$ limiting the evolution of the arithmetic expressions $a_{i,j}$ during any period of continuous evolution are given. We require that the $l_{i,j}$ are derived from a set S of evolution constraints which limits the continuous evolution of the variables of A (cf. assumption 5 in Theorem 1). In order to provide that a sampling tick lies in every interval in which a transition in automaton A must be taken, we synthesize constraints on T from the (relaxed) invariants of A and the maximal gradients. Let ψ be a relaxed invariant of A and let $at'_{i,j} \equiv a_{i,j} \# \varepsilon_{i,j}$ be its (relaxed) atoms, as above. From each such atom we derive the constraint $T \le \frac{\varepsilon_{i,j} - 2 \cdot \delta_{i,j}}{l_{i,j}}$, where $\delta_{i,j}$ is the error by which the computation of $a_{i,j}$ is affected (cf. Fig. 3). It results from the error ε_{dis} with which the continuous evolution of the variables is affected. For instance, the computation of expression $x + y$ is affected by the error in x plus that in y.

Correctness. Assumption 2 and 3 of Theorem 1 are satisfied, if B is derived as described, the constraints on T are satisfied and S is the set of evolution constraints used in Theorem 1. For assumption 3 we have to show that the invariant of A cannot be violated in a time step of duration T, if the invariant of the corresponding location of B is true before the step. In other words, no transition of A is enforced between two sampling instants where B can react. We prove this as follows. Let $v \in V$ and $s' \in \mathbb{R}^{n+1}$ with $s'.c = 0$ and $inv_B(v)$ is true for s'. By construction of the invariants of B this means that the ideal invariant ϕ of v must be true for $\pi_X(s')$. Let τ be an evolution of the variables which (1) satisfies the assumptions S on maximal gradients used for the computation of the $l_{i,j}$, which (2) starts with $\pi_X(s')$ and which (3) last for at least time T. We show that no atom $at'_{i,j}$ of the (relaxed) invariant ϕ of v in A becomes false for evolution τ on the interval $[0, T)$, if the corresponding ideal atom $at_{i,j}$ is true for $\pi_X(s')$. At time $t = 0$, $\tau(0) = \pi_X(s')$ and $at_{i,j}$ therefore holds by assumption, i.e. $a_{i,j} \# 0$, $\# \in \{<, \le\}$. The worst case is that τ rises with its maximum gradient and that the errors in its computation ε_{dis} sum up. During time T, $a_{i,j}$ can only increase by $l_{i,j} \cdot T$ due to the assumptions on the maximal gradients. Thus, allowing for the worst case effect of $a_{i,j}$ being already above 0 by the worst case error $\delta_{i,j}$ at time 0 and being $\delta_{i,j}$ below the computed value at time T, we get that at time T the computed value of $a_{i,j}$ can at most be $\delta_{i,j} + l_{i,j} \cdot T + \delta_{i,j}$ (see Fig. 3). Provided the constraints on time granularity T are satisfied, this is still less or equal to $\varepsilon_{i,j}$ for $t = T$ and strictly less than $\varepsilon_{i,j}$ for $0 < t < T$. Thus, $at'_{i,j}$ is true during the interval $[0, T)$. Applying this argument to all atoms that are true at $t = 0$, the relaxed invariant is guaranteed to remain true during that interval. (Remember that the relaxed invariant is a conjunction of disjunctions of atoms. Thus, one atom must have been true for $t = 0$ in every disjunction, if the relaxed invariant was true at that time.)

4.2.2 Update Transitions   For the construction of the set E_u of update transitions, we suggest to use techniques from numerical mathematics or control theory. Numerical techniques for the solution of initial value problems can be used to approximate the variable evolution according to the activities in hybrid automaton A. In order to use such techniques in our context, we require that the respective numerical algorithm can be written as the iterated application of a jump condition at time steps kT, $k \in \mathbb{N}$. Thus, the values of the variables at time $(k + 1)T$ must be computed from their values at time kT and this computation must be specifiable as a convex predicate p over variables $X \cup X'$, where $X' = \{x_1', ..., x_n'\}$, the x_i refer to the variable values at the last sampling step kT, $k \in \mathbb{N}$, and the x_i' refer to the values at the next step $(k + 1)T$. For simple algorithms, like the Euler backward method or the trapezoidal method this is possible [8, 10]. Depending on the problem, more complex methods may also be applicable if Theorem 1 is modified by allowing extensions of the state space of B (see [12] for a more detailed discussion).

Definition of B's update transitions.   Given a convex predicate p whose iterated application at time steps kT computes an approximation to the activity of location v in A, a corresponding update transition in B is defined by $(v, c = T \wedge p \wedge c' = 0, v)$. Set E_u of B consists of one such transition for each location v.

Constraints on T and applicable algorithms.   In order to satisfy assumption 4 of Theorem 1 the algorithm used to define the update transition of a location v must satisfy some restrictions on its accuracy. First, the approximating values at time instants kT and the exact value according to the activity of v in A must agree up to ε_{dis}. In terms of numerical mathematics this means that T must be chosen small enough to guarantee that the so-called *global discretization error* is less or equal to ε_{dis}. In the context of control theory methods, Shannon's sampling theorem may also be applicable to obtain a further constraint on T. Second, the computed approximating value for time kT must be within $\varepsilon + \varepsilon_{dis}$ of the exact values throughout the following sampling interval $[kT, (k+1)T)$, where ε is the constant with which the traces of A are relaxed in Theorem 1. Provided a variable x evolves at most with gradient l, this means that $\varepsilon + \varepsilon_{dis} \leq l \cdot T$ must hold. Thus, the sampling rate T is constrained further due to the intersample error.

Note that if the activities of A merely specify a linear evolution of the variables in X, then simple numerical integration methods like Euler backward are exact. No discretization error occurs. This is utilized in the example in the appendix of the online version of this paper.

5   Conclusion

The paper summarized some of the results in [12]: It identified sufficient conditions under which an abstract specification of a hybrid system given by a hybrid automaton can be refined to execution in discrete-time. A method was described that allows us to derive the discrete time model from the hybrid model provided some restrictions are satisfied. In the development process of hybrid systems such a method can be applied to move from early abstract models of the system towards implementation.

For application is practice we suggest to build specializations of the general method in [12], which also regards input signals and events. Furthermore, we remark that automata which require a high precision w.r.t. the time when transitions are taken and w.r.t. their continuous activities can seriously hamper discrete-time refinement and hence implementation. From a methodological point of view, this suggests to avoid such precise models in early development steps.

Acknowledgment. We thank Jianjun Deng for his valuable feedback on a draft version of this paper.

References

[1] R. Alur, C. Courcoubetis, N. Halbwachs, T.A. Henzinger, P.-H. Ho, X. Nicollin, A. Olivero, J. Sifakis, and S. Yovine. The algorithmic analysis of hybrid systems. *Theoretical Computer Science*, 138:3–34, 1995.

[2] R. Alur, R. Grosu, I. Lee, and O. Sokolsky. Compositional refinement of hierarchical hybrid systems. In *Proc. of HSCC'01*, LNCS 2034. Springer-Verlag, 2001.

[3] M. Fränzle. Analysis of hybrid systems: An ounce of realism can save an infinity of states. In *Proc. of Computer Science Logic (CSL'99)*, LNCS 1683. Springer, 1999.

[4] R. Grosu, T. Stauner, and M. Broy. A modular visual model for hybrid systems. In *Proc. of FTRTFT'98*, LNCS 1486. Springer-Verlag, 1998.

[5] V. Gupta, T.A. Henzinger, and R. Jagadeesan. Robust timed automata. In *Proc. of HART 97*, LNCS 1201. Springer-Verlag, 1997.

[6] T.A. Henzinger and J.-F. Raskin. Robust undecidability of timed and hybrid systems. In *Proc. of HSCC'00*, LNCS 1790. Springer-Verlag, 2000.

[7] D. V. Hung and P. H. Giang. Sampling semantics of duration calculus. In *Proceedings of FTRTFT '96*, LNCS 1135. Springer-Verlag, 1996.

[8] M. K. Jain. *Numerical Solution of Differential Equations*. Wiley Eastern Ltd., New Delhi, 1979.

[9] Z. Manna and A. Pnueli. *The Temporal Logic of Reactive and Concurrent Systems*. Springer-Verlag, 1992.

[10] K. Ogata. *Discrete-Time Control Systems*. Prentice-Hall, 1987.

[11] D. Sinclair. Using an object-oriented methodology to bring a hybrid system from initial concept to formal definition. In *Proc. Int. Workshop on Hybrid and Real-Time Systems (HART'97)*, LNCS 1201. Springer-Verlag, 1997.

[12] T. Stauner. *Systematic Development of Hybrid Systems*. PhD thesis, Technische Universität München, 2001.

Control of Switched Hybrid Systems Based on Disjunctive Formulations

Olaf Stursberg[1,2] and Sebastian Panek[2]

[1] currently with: Dept. Electr. and Comp. Eng., Carnegie Mellon University,
5000 Forbes Ave, Pittsburgh PA 15213, USA;
olaf@ece.cmu.edu
[2] Process Control Lab (CT-AST), University of Dortmund,
44221 Dortmund, Germany;
s.panek@ct.uni-dortmund.de

Abstract. This contribution addresses the task of computing optimal control trajectories for hybrid systems with switching dynamics. Starting from a continuous-time formulation of the control task we derive an optimization problem in which the system behavior is modelled by a hybrid automaton with linear discrete-time dynamics and discrete as well as continuous inputs. In order to transform the discrete dynamics into an equation-based form we present and compare two different approaches: one uses the 'traditional' M-formulation and one is based on disjunctive formulations. The control problem is then solved by mixed integer programming using a moving horizon setting. As illustrated for an example, the disjunctive formulation can lead to a considerable reduction of the computational effort.
Keywords. Disjunctive Programming, Hybrid Automata, Mixed Integer Programming, Optimal Control, Switched Dynamics.

1 Introduction

In recent years, the research on optimal control of hybrid systems has brought up various approaches (see, e.g., [1, 2, 3, 4, 5, 6, 7]) which differ with respect to the considered class of models, the posed optimization problem, and the notion of time (continuous or discrete). We are adopting the discrete-time fashion in this paper in order to design a completely algorithmic procedure which does not require user intervention once the modeling is completed. However, our approach starts from a hybrid automaton with continuous-time dynamics since this seems to be the more natural way of specification. For the latter, we use a class of systems that is hybrid in the sense that switching between different dynamics is possible either because of autonomous events or by triggering inputs. This type of dynamics has been found suitable to model, e. g., certain procedures in process control [8, 9]. The continuous-time model is then approximated by a hybrid automaton with linear discrete-time dynamics and the control task is formulated as an optimization problem which can be solved by mixed integer programming.

C.J. Tomlin and M.R. Greenstreet (Eds.): HSCC 2002, LNCS 2289, pp. 421–435, 2002.
© Springer-Verlag Berlin Heidelberg 2002

The crucial step, which is not described explicitly in many publications on this subject, is to transform the transition structure of the automaton into constraints of the optimization problem. We specifically present two formulations for this purpose: One is based on so-called *M-formulations* which are well known in the mixed integer programming community as a means to include logical decisions into programming problems [10]. A drawback of the M-approach is the large number of binary variables that these formulations require, and usually they lead to relatively poor relaxations when the problem is solved by Branch-and-Bound techniques.

To improve the solution performance, techniques originating from the fields of *Constraint Programming* [11] or particularly *Disjunctive Programming* [12] seem to be good alternatives. It is known from literature [13] that disjunctive programs can require considerably less binary variables and that they can lead to tighter relaxations during the solution than programs based on the M-approach. We therefore propose a scheme to specify the optimal control task for hybrid systems as a programming problem based on *disjunctive formulations*. The M-approach and the disjunctive formulation are compared, and we illustrate the whole controller design procedure by applying it to a processing system example.

2   The Optimal Control Problem for Switched Hybrid Systems

2.1   The Continuous Time Formulation

We investigate the problem of computing those continuous and discrete input trajectories which drive a system with switching dynamics from a given initial state into a target state or region. This transition should be optimal with respect to a suitable objective function, as described by the following continuous time optimization problem:

$$\min_{\boldsymbol{u}(t), \boldsymbol{v}(t)} \Omega(t, \boldsymbol{x}(t), \boldsymbol{u}(t), \boldsymbol{v}(t)), \tag{1}$$

$$\Omega = \int_{t_0}^{t_f} (\alpha(t, \boldsymbol{x}) + \beta(t, \boldsymbol{u}) + \gamma(t, \boldsymbol{v}) + \delta(t)) dt,$$

s.t. $\boldsymbol{x}(t) \in \boldsymbol{X}, \boldsymbol{u}(t) \in \boldsymbol{U}, \boldsymbol{v}(t) \in \boldsymbol{V} \quad \forall t \in [t_0, t_f]; \quad \boldsymbol{x}_0 \in \boldsymbol{X}, \quad \boldsymbol{x}(t_f) \in R_T,$

$$\boldsymbol{x}(t) = \boldsymbol{x}(t_k^s) + \int_{t_k^s}^{t} \boldsymbol{f}_z(\boldsymbol{x}(t), \boldsymbol{u}(t), \boldsymbol{v}(t_k^s)) dt, t \in]t_k^s, t_{k+1}^s]. \tag{2}$$

Within these equations, $\boldsymbol{x}(t)$ denotes the continuous state trajectory defined on the state space $\boldsymbol{X}$, and $\boldsymbol{u}(t) \in \boldsymbol{U} = [u_1^-, u_1^+] \times \ldots \times [u_{m_u}^-, u_{m_u}^+]$ with $u_j^-, u_j^+ \in \mathbb{R}$ is the continuous input trajectory. The discrete input $\boldsymbol{v}(t) \in \boldsymbol{V} = \{\boldsymbol{v}_1, \ldots, \boldsymbol{v}_{n_v}\}$ switches at time points $t_k^s \in [t_0, t_f]$ between finitely many options and only finitely often in the interval $[t_0, t_f]$, i. e., it is constant for $t \in [t_k^s, t_{k+1}^s[$. While

$x_0 = x(t_0)$ denotes the starting point of the optimization, the target region is given by $R_T = [x_{T,1}^-, x_{T,1}^+] \times \ldots \times [x_{T,n}^-, x_{T,n}^+] \subset X$ with $x_{T,j}^-, x_{T,j}^+ \in \mathbb{R}$ (and, of course, $x_0 \notin R_T$).

The system dynamics according to (2) has been formally introduced as a hybrid automaton in [9], and we sketch the behavior here only briefly: The finite set $T^s = \{t_1^s, \ldots, t_{n_T}^s\}$ with $t_k^s \in [t_0, t_f]$ contains all points of time at which either the input $v(t)$ changes or the system autonomously switches its continuous dynamics. The latter is described by a set of ODEs $\dot{x} = f_z(x, u, v)$. The identifier z denotes the discrete state that changes according to a transition function $\phi : Z \times X \times X \times R \to Z$, in which Z is the finite set of discrete states and R a finite set of polyhedral regions. The latter result from a set $E = \{e_1, \ldots, e_{n_E}\}$ of hyperplanes that partition X into convex and disjunct regions. One state $z \in Z$ is assigned to each $r_i \in R$. A transition between two states $z_1, z_2 \in Z$ is taken if the trajectory $x(t)$ crosses a hyperplane $e_j \in E$ at the time t_k^s. It is assumed that $x(t)$ is continuous for all $t \in [t_0, t_f]$. Hence, the new continuous state follows from (2) by integrating the ODE that is valid for the current discrete state and the discrete input $v(t)$.

Considering this behavior, the objective function Ω in (1) seems to be appropriate to cover a large range of potential costs. It contains the following terms:

- $\alpha(t, x) = \mu_1(t) \cdot \|w_1 \cdot (x(t) - R_T)\|_{p_1}$ describes the distance between the current state and (the nearest boundary) of the target region (weighted over the state component by w_1) with a suitable norm $\| \bullet \|_{p_1}$;
- $\beta(t, u) = \mu_2(t) \cdot \|w_2 \cdot (u(t) - u_S)\|_{p_2}$ contains the deviation of $u(t)$ from a reference vector u_s (with weights w_2 and a suitable norm $\| \bullet \|_{p_2}$);
- $\gamma(t, v) = \mu_3(t) \cdot \begin{cases} w_3 : & \text{if } v(t^-) \neq v(t) \\ 0 : & \text{else} \end{cases}$ adds the amount w_3 to the costs if the input $v(t)$ switches ($v(t^-)$ is the left-side limit of $v(t)$);
- $\delta(t) = \begin{cases} \mu_4(t) : & \text{if } x(t) \neq R_T \\ 0 : & \text{else} \end{cases}$ is the weighted sum of the time required to reach R_T.

The factors $\mu_1(t), \ldots, \mu_4(t)$ are appropriate weights for the contributions of these four terms.

The determination of the optimal trajectories $u^*(t)$, $v^*(t)$ for the problem given in (1,2) is difficult for the following reasons:

(a) The inputs can be changed arbitrarily without any restrictions with respect to the sequence of their values, the number of switching events of $v(t)$ (as far as finite), and the points of time at which changes occur.
(b) The continuous dynamics is given by possibly nonlinear ODEs.
(c) The switching between different dynamics as well as the terms α, γ, and δ introduce further nonlinearities into the optimization problem.

2.2   The Discrete Time Case

In order to make the solution easier with respect to the first two points, we approximate the problem by a discrete-time formulation of switched linear dynamics. The following type of automaton (taken from [9]) is suitable for this approximation:

Definition 1. *Hybrid Automaton $A_{L,D}$*
A hybrid automaton with switched linear discrete time dynamics is defined by:

$$A_{L,D} = \{\boldsymbol{X}, \boldsymbol{U}, V, E, Z, f^D, \phi^D\} \tag{3}$$

in which $\boldsymbol{X}$ denotes the convex continuous state space $\boldsymbol{X} := \{\boldsymbol{x} \in \boldsymbol{X} \mid \boldsymbol{C} \cdot \boldsymbol{x} \leq \boldsymbol{d}, \boldsymbol{C} \in \mathbb{R}^{q \times n}, \boldsymbol{d} \in \mathbb{R}^{q \times 1}, q \in \mathbb{N}\}$. The continuous inputs $\boldsymbol{u}(t)$ are defined on the space $\boldsymbol{U} = [u_1^-, u_1^+] \times \ldots \times [u_{m_u}^-, u_{m_u}^+]$ with $u_j^-, u_j^+ \in \mathbb{R}$, and the discrete inputs $v(t)$ on $V = \{\boldsymbol{v}_1, \ldots, \boldsymbol{v}_{n_v}\}$, $\boldsymbol{v}_j \in \mathbb{R}^{m_u \times 1}$. The trajectories $\boldsymbol{x}(t)$, $\boldsymbol{u}(t)$, and $\boldsymbol{v}(t)$ are now based on a discrete time domain $t_k \in \{t_0, t_1, \ldots, t_f\}$, i. e., they are constant on each interval $[t_k, t_{k+1}[$.

The set $E = \{e_1, \ldots, e_{n_E}\}$ of hyperplanes $e_j := \{\boldsymbol{x} \in \boldsymbol{X} \mid \boldsymbol{c}_j \cdot \boldsymbol{x} = d_j, \boldsymbol{c}_j \in \mathbb{R}^{1 \times n}, d_j \in \mathbb{R}\}$ partitions $\boldsymbol{X}$ into a set of convex and disjunct polyhedral regions $R = \{r_1, \ldots, r_{n_R}\}$. Such a region is given by $r_i := \{\boldsymbol{x} \in \boldsymbol{X}, e_i \in E \mid J = \{1, 2, \ldots, n_E\}, H_i \subseteq J, \forall h \in H_i : \boldsymbol{c}_h \cdot \boldsymbol{x} \sim_h d_h, \sim_h \in \{<, \leq\}\}$, and $\bigcup_{i=1}^{n_R} r_i = \boldsymbol{X}$. A state z from the discrete state set $Z = \{z_1, \ldots, z_{n_z}\}$ is assigned to each region $r_i \in R$ by $\sigma : R \to Z$.

The current continuous state follows from the transfer function $\boldsymbol{f}^D : \boldsymbol{X} \times \boldsymbol{U} \times V \times Z \to \mathbb{R}^n$ according to $\boldsymbol{x}_k := \boldsymbol{x}(t_k) = \boldsymbol{A}_{z,\boldsymbol{v}_{k-1}} \cdot \boldsymbol{x}_{k-1} + \boldsymbol{B}_{z,\boldsymbol{v}_{k-1}} \cdot \boldsymbol{u}_{k-1} + \boldsymbol{L}_{z,\boldsymbol{v}_{k-1}}$ with matrices $\boldsymbol{A}_{z,\boldsymbol{v}_{k-1}} \in \mathbb{R}^{n \times n}$, $\boldsymbol{B}_{z,\boldsymbol{v}_{k-1}} \in \mathbb{R}^{n \times m_u}$, and $\boldsymbol{L}_{z,\boldsymbol{v}_{k-1}} \in \mathbb{R}^{n \times 1}$ depending on the discrete state $z_{k-1} = z(t_{k-1}) \in Z$ and the discrete input $\boldsymbol{v}_{k-1} = \boldsymbol{v}(t_{k-1})$.

The discrete transition function $\phi^D : Z \times \boldsymbol{X} \times \boldsymbol{X} \times R \to Z$ computes the current discrete state z_k according to the following rule: A transition $z_1 \to z_2$ between two states $z_1, z_2 \in Z$ occurs in t_k if $\boldsymbol{x}_{k-1} \in r_1$, $\sigma(r_1) = z_1$ and $\boldsymbol{x}_k \in r_2$, $\sigma(r_2) = z_2$, $\boldsymbol{x}_k \notin r_1$. If r_1 is left across e_j the transition guard is: $(\boldsymbol{c}_j \cdot \boldsymbol{x}_k \leq d_j) \wedge (\boldsymbol{c}_j \cdot \boldsymbol{x}_{k+1} > d_j)$ if e_j is assigned to r_1, or $(\boldsymbol{c}_j \cdot \boldsymbol{x}_k < d_j) \wedge (\boldsymbol{c}_j \cdot \boldsymbol{x}_{k+1} \geq d_j)$ if e_j is a part of r_2.

Transitions and changes in $\boldsymbol{v}(t)$ and $\boldsymbol{u}(t)$ are only possible at those points of time which are contained in T. A mapping $\rho : T \to \boldsymbol{X} \times Z$ defines a run of $A_{L,D}$ as the sequence $\rho(t_0), \rho(t_1), \ldots, \rho(t_f)$ of hybrid states $\rho_k := \rho(t_k) = (\boldsymbol{x}_k, z_k)$, such that:

(a) Initialization: $\rho_0 = (\boldsymbol{x}_0, z_0)$ with $\boldsymbol{x}_0 \in r^* \in R$, $\sigma(r^*) = z_0$, $z_0 \in Z$.
(b) Progress: $\rho_k = (\boldsymbol{x}_k, z_k)$ for $t_k \in T \setminus \{t_0\}$ results from:
*   1. continuous evolution:*
        $$\boldsymbol{x}_k = \boldsymbol{f}^D(\boldsymbol{x}_{k-1}, \boldsymbol{u}_{k-1}, \boldsymbol{v}_{k-1}, z_{k-1});$$
*   2. discrete transitions:*
        $$z_k = \phi(z_{k-1}, \boldsymbol{x}_{k-1}, \boldsymbol{x}_k, r_i).$$

◇

In order to translate the original continuous time behavior into the one of $A_{L,D}$, the three following steps are carried out:

(I) The time domain $t \in [t_0, t_f]$ is transformed into $t \in T$. For simplicity, we here use a constant time step $t_k = k \cdot \Delta t$, $k \in K = \{0, 1, 2 \ldots, k_f\}$ and approximate $\dot{x}$ by $x_k = x_{k-1} + \Delta t \cdot f_z$. The extension to better approximations of the differential quotient and to variable time steps is straightforward [9].

(II) If the optimization is carried out over the complete horizon K in a single run, the ODEs in (2) are linearized at the center point of each region and for suitable values of u. For strongly nonlinear dynamics it might be necessary to split each r_i into a set of subregions with separate points of linearization. For the moving horizon strategy described in the next section, the ODEs are linearized at the initial point of each single optimization.

(III) The objective function Ω is reformulated for the discrete time setting such that the optimization problem becomes:

$$\min_{u_k, v_k} \left(\sum_{k \in K} \mu_{1,k} \cdot \|w_1 \cdot (x_k - R_T)\|_1 + \mu_{2,k} \cdot \|w_2 \cdot (u_k - u_S)\|_1 \right. \tag{4}$$

$$+ \sum_{k \in K \setminus \{0\}} \mu_{3,k} \cdot \begin{cases} w_3 : & \text{if } v_k \neq v_{k-1} \\ 0 : & \text{else} \end{cases} + \left. \sum_{k \in K} \mu_{4,k} \cdot \begin{cases} 1 : & \text{if } x_k \neq R_T \\ 0 : & \text{else} \end{cases} \right)$$

$$\text{s.t. } x_k \in X, x_0 \in X, x_{k_f} \in R_T, u_k \in U, v_k \in V$$

$$x_k = x_{k-1} + \Delta t \cdot (A_{z, v_{k-1}} \cdot x_{k-1} + B_{z, v_{k-1}} \cdot u_{k-1} + L_{z, v_{k-1}}) \tag{5}$$

and subject to the transition dynamics of $A_{L,D}$.

3   The Mixed-Integer Formulation of the Control Problem

To solve this problem, the logical decisions in (4) and the transition structure of $A_{L,D}$ are expressed by relations between binary variables, and the solution is then determined by mixed integer programming (MIP).

3.1   A Formulation Based on the M-approach

One possibility to map the logic part of the problem into inequalities that act as optimization constraints is the formulation usually referred to as *M-Approach*. It has been published some decades ago in [14, 10] and extensions are described in [15]. The approach provides a set of expressions to formulate logical statements on continuous variables in an equation-based form. It has been adopted for the control of Mixed Logical Dynamical (MLD) Systems in [4], and in [8] to formulate optimization problems for hybrid automata. We here present a set of M-formulations (MF) which transfer (4,5) in a program completely written in equation-based form and which require less binary variables than the approaches published before:

Table 1. M-Formulation of $c_j \cdot x_k \sim d_j \Leftrightarrow b_{k,j} = 1$.

$c_j \cdot x_k \leq d_j \quad \leftrightarrow \quad b_{k,j} = 1$	$c_j \cdot x_k < d_j \quad \leftrightarrow \quad b_{j,k} = 1$
$c_j \cdot x_k - d_j \leq M^+ \cdot (1 - b_{k,j})$	$c_j \cdot x_k - d_j < M^+ \cdot (1 - b_{j,k})$
$c_j \cdot x_k - d_j > b_{k,j} \cdot M^-$	$c_j \cdot x_k - d_j \geq b_{j,k} \cdot M^-$

Transformation 1: For a given hyperplane e_j with $c_j \cdot x_k \sim d_j$ ($c_j \in \mathbb{R}^{1 \times n}$, $x_k \in \mathbb{R}^{n \times 1}$, $\sim \in \{<, \leq\}$, $d_j \in \mathbb{R}$) it has to be decided to which half-space the current state belongs. Using a binary variable $b_{k,j} \in \{0,1\}$ to express the result, the formulations in Tab. 1 are equivalent. The parameters M^- and M^+ follow from: $M^- = \min_{x_k \in X} \{c_j \cdot x_k - d_j\}$, $M^+ = \max_{x_k \in X} \{c_j \cdot x_k - d_j\}$. If a region r_i results from the conjunction $\bigwedge_{h \in H_i} c_h \cdot x_k \sim d_h$ ($H_i \subseteq J$), the product $b_{k,i} := \prod_{h \in H_i} b_{k,h}$ of the corresponding binary variables $b_{k,h}$ must equal one iff $x_k \in r_i$. With $|H_i|$ as the cardinality of H_i, this can be expressed by the following linear inequalities:

$$\forall h \in H_i: \quad b_{k,i} \leq b_{k,h}; \quad \sum_{h \in H_i} b_{k,h} - |H_i| + 1 \leq b_{k,i}. \tag{6}$$

Obviously, $\sum_{i=1}^{n_R} b_{k,i} = 1$ applies for all $k \in K$. It is important to note that $b_{k,i}$ can alternatively be defined as continuous variable $b_{k,i} \in [0,1]$ without changing the constraints. This reduces the number of binary variables by $n_R \cdot |K|$.

Transformation 2: The dynamics being valid in t_k is determined by the current region and the current discrete input. We introduce $n_v \cdot n_R \cdot |K|$ new variables $b_{k,i,l} \in \{0,1\}$, each of which equals 1 iff the specific combination of v_k (the lth element of V) and $x_k \in r_i$ is given, and zero otherwise. This assignment is ensured by (6) and the following equations:

$$b_{k,i,l} \leq b_{k,i} \; \forall \, l \in \{1, \ldots, n_v\}, \quad \sum_{l=1}^{n_v} b_{k,i,l} = 1. \tag{7}$$

As shown in Sec. 3.2, the large number of binary variables $b_{k,i,l}$ can be replaced by continuous variables if a slightly different set of equations is used. To select the model which corresponds to $b_{k,i,l}$, we write for all $k \in K \setminus \{0\}$:

$$x_k = x_{k-1} + \Delta t \cdot \sum_{i=1}^{n_R} \sum_{l=1}^{n_v} b_{k,i,l} \cdot (A_{z,v_{k-1}} x_{k-1} + B_{z,v_{k-1}} u_{k-1} + L_{z,v_{k-1}}). \tag{8}$$

Since we want to obtain a linear optimization problem, the products of variables need to be linearized. The following M-formulations linearize the product $\xi_{k,i,l,j} := x_{k,j} \cdot b_{k,i,l}$ with $j \in \{1, \ldots, n\}$:

$$\xi_{k,i,l,j} \leq M_j^+ \cdot b_{k,i,l}, \quad \xi_{k,i,l,j} \leq x_{k,j} - M_j^- \cdot (1 - b_{k,i,l}),$$
$$\xi_{k,i,l,j} \geq M_j^- \cdot b_{k,i,l}, \quad \xi_{k,i,l,j} \geq x_{k,j} - M_j^+ \cdot (1 - b_{k,i,l}) \tag{9}$$

with the constants $M_j^- = \min_{\boldsymbol{x} \in \boldsymbol{X}}\{x_j\}$, $M_j^+ = \max_{\boldsymbol{x} \in \boldsymbol{X}}\{x_j\}$. The product $\pi_{k,i,l,j} :=$
$u_{k,j} \cdot b_{k,i,l}$ $(j \in \{1, \ldots, m_u\})$ is linearized in the same manner.

Transformation 3: Finally, the evaluation of the objective function involves
some logical decisions: The contribution of the first term in (4) depends on the
value of $\boldsymbol{x}_k$ relative to R_T, i. e., it has to be checked if $x_{k,j} < x_{T,j}^-$ or $x_{k,j} > x_{T,j}^+$.
These tests can be formulated similar to the inequalities in Tab. 1, e. g. for the
lower bounds of R_T by: $x_{k,j} - x_{T,j}^- < M_j^{+\downarrow} \cdot (1 - b_{j,k}^\downarrow)$, $x_{k,j} - x_{T,j}^- \geq M_j^{+\downarrow} \cdot b_{j,k}^\downarrow$
with appropriate lower and upper bounds $M_j^{-\downarrow}$, $M_j^{+\downarrow}$ of $x_{k,j} - x_{T,j}^-$, and binary
variables $b_{j,k}^\downarrow$ that assume the value one iff $x_{k,j} < x_{T,j}^-$. If the latter is true, the
distance $(x_{k,j} - x_{T,j}^-)$ is added to the objective function, for which the product
$b_{j,k}^\downarrow \cdot (x_{k,j} - x_{T,j}^-)$ has to be linearized according to (9). The same binary variables
can be used to rewrite the fourth term of (4). To evaluate the third term, the test
$\boldsymbol{v}_k \neq \boldsymbol{v}_{k-1}$ is based on the variables $b_{k,i,l}$ and additional binary variables $y_{k,l} \in$
$\{0, 1\}$: Expressions similar to those in Tab. 1 allow to specify the implication
$\sum_{i=1}^{n_R} b_{k,i,l} + b_{k-1,i,l} > 1 \leftrightarrow y_{k,l} = 1$. If then $\sum_{l=1}^{n_v} y_{k,l} \leq 0$ applies, the contribution
of the term is set to $\mu_{3,k} \cdot w_3$, and to zero otherwise.

3.2   The Disjunctive Formulation of the Control Problem

The MF converts the optimization problem into a completely linear representation in equation-based form in which the transition structure and logical decisions are mapped into binary variables. However, the number of binary variables,
as an important criterion for the complexity, is large – even if the $b_{k,i}$ are defined
as continuous variables. We therefore propose an alternative formulation which
is motivated by the notion of *Disjunctive Programming*. It has been introduced
by E. Balas (see e. g. [12]) and extended by I. E. Grossmann et al. [13, 16] in
the context of process synthesis. The idea is to express those constraints, that
are valid only if certain logical propositions are satisfied, in a disjunctive form.
For example, if a binary variable b_j denotes that a set of convex and bounded
constraints $\boldsymbol{g}_j(\boldsymbol{x}) \leq \boldsymbol{0}$ for $\boldsymbol{x} \geq \boldsymbol{0}$ is exclusively valid for $b_j = 1$, this can be
formulated by the disjunction:

$$\bigvee_{j \in J} \begin{bmatrix} b_j \\ \boldsymbol{g}_j(\boldsymbol{x}) \leq \boldsymbol{0} \end{bmatrix} \tag{10}$$

The convex hull over all disjunctive terms in (10) can be written by [13]:

$$\boldsymbol{x} = \sum_{j \in J} \boldsymbol{w}_j, \quad 0 \leq \boldsymbol{w}_j \leq \lambda_j \cdot \boldsymbol{x}^+$$

$$\lambda_j \cdot \boldsymbol{g}_j(\boldsymbol{w}_j/\lambda_j) \leq \boldsymbol{0}, \quad \sum_{j \in J} \lambda_j = 1, \quad 0 \leq \lambda_j \leq 1. \tag{11}$$

The vectors $\boldsymbol{w}_j$ contain continuous auxiliary variables, $\boldsymbol{x}^+$ is the vector of upper bounds of $\boldsymbol{x}$, and the scalars λ_j determine the weight of the constraints $\boldsymbol{g}_j$. If $\lambda_j = 1$ applies, the corresponding disjunctive term evaluates to be true, and $b_j = 1$. It is shown in [13] that the convex hull formulation in (11) leads to tighter LP-relaxations than the corresponding MF, when standard Branch-and-Bound algorithms are used to solve the problem as an MILP. We here propose a disjunctive formulation (DF) of the control problem which takes advantage of this effect. Writing (4/5) in disjunctive form is straightforward since the determination of the region and the choice of $\boldsymbol{v}_k$ are clearly disjunct options ($\forall k \in K \setminus \{0\}$):

$$
\bigvee_{i=1}^{n_R} \bigvee_{l=1}^{n_V} \left[\begin{array}{c} b_{k,i,l} \\ \boldsymbol{C}_i \cdot \boldsymbol{x}_k \sim d_i, \quad \boldsymbol{v}_l \in V \\ \boldsymbol{x}_k = \boldsymbol{x}_{k-1} + \triangle t \cdot (\boldsymbol{A}_{z,\boldsymbol{v}_{k-1}} \cdot \boldsymbol{x}_{k-1} + \boldsymbol{B}_{z,\boldsymbol{v}_{k-1}} \cdot \boldsymbol{u}_{k-1} + \boldsymbol{L}_{z,\boldsymbol{v}_{k-1}}) \end{array} \right] \tag{12}
$$

We use the expressions in (11) to transform this disjunctions in equation-based form. Since only one of the variables $b_{k,i,l}$ can be equal to 1 in each point of time, the λ_j have to assume 0 or 1 as well. To achieve this, the λ_j can either be declared as binary variables or be defined on the interval $[0, 1]$ with additional restrictions to ensure that they assume only 0 or 1. We first choose the first option and introduce the following rules in order to transform the disjunctions in (12) into inequalities:

Rule 1: *The equivalence* $(\boldsymbol{C}_i \cdot \boldsymbol{x}_k \le d_i) \leftrightarrow b_{k,i}$ *with* $0 \le \boldsymbol{x}_k \le \boldsymbol{x}^+$ *is replaced by:*

$$
\boldsymbol{C}_i \cdot \boldsymbol{w}_{k,i} \le b_{k,i} \cdot d_i, \quad \boldsymbol{0} \le \boldsymbol{w}_{k,i} \le b_{k,i} \cdot \boldsymbol{x}^+, \quad \sum_{i=1}^{n_R} \boldsymbol{w}_{k,i} = \boldsymbol{x}_k, \quad \sum_{i=1}^{n_R} b_{k,i} = 1,
\tag{13}
$$

where $b_{k,i} \in \{0, 1\}$. (The equations are slightly different for $\sim = <$.)

Rule 2: *If a continuous variable* x_k *is multiplied by a sum of binary variables* $b_{k,i}$ *(one of which is 1), then the products* $\xi_{k,i} := x_k \cdot b_{k,i}$ *are replaced by:*

$$
\sum_{i=1}^{n_R} \xi_{k,i} = x_k, \quad \sum_{i=1}^{n_R} b_{k,i} = 1, \quad 0 \le \xi_{k,i} \le b_{k,i} \cdot x^+ \quad \forall\, i \in \{1, \ldots, n_R\}. \tag{14}
$$

While these formulations require $x_k \ge 0$ (or $u_k \ge 0$ for the product $\pi_{k,i,l} := u_k \cdot b_{k,i}$ respectively), the application to systems with negative continuous variables x_k, u_k is straightforward by simply shifting their origin. The first term of the objective function in (4) can be linearized by (14) as well.

The two rules allow to rewrite the optimization constraints in (5) in the following form ($\forall \ k \in K \setminus \{0\}$, $i \in \{1, \dots, n_R\}$, $l \in \{1, \dots, n_V\}$):

$$x_k = x_{k-1} + \Delta t \cdot \sum_{i=1}^{n_R} \sum_{l=1}^{n_V} A_{z,v_{k-1}} \cdot \xi_{k-1,i,l} + B_{z,v_{k-1}} \cdot \pi_{k-1,i,l} + b_{k-1,i,l} \cdot L_{z,v_{k-1}}$$

$$\sum_{i=1}^{n_R} \sum_{l=1}^{n_V} \xi_{k-1,i,l} = x_{k-1}, \quad 0 \le \xi_{k-1,i,l} \le b_{k-1,i,l} \cdot x^+, \quad \sum_{i=1}^{n_R} \sum_{l=1}^{n_V} b_{k-1,i,l} = 1$$

$$\sum_{i=1}^{n_R} \sum_{l=1}^{n_V} \pi_{k-1,i,l} = u_{k-1}, \quad 0 \le \pi_{k-1,i,l} \le b_{k-1,i,l} \cdot u^+$$

$$c_i \cdot w_{k,i} \le b_{k,i} \cdot d_i, \quad w_{k,i} = \sum_{l=1}^{n_V} \xi_{k,i,l}, \quad b_{k,i} = \sum_{l=1}^{n_V} b_{k,i,l}, \quad \sum_{i=1}^{n_R} b_{k,i} = 1. \quad (15)$$

Whereas the variables $b_{k,i}$ are defined on $[0,1]$, the variables $b_{k,i,l}$ must be binary in (15) to ensure that only one model is valid in t_k. To reduce the number of binary variables again, it is a reasonable modification to define $b_{k,i,l}$ continuously on $[0,1]$ and to add the constraints:

$$b_{k,l} = \sum_{i=1}^{n_R} b_{k,i,l}, \quad \sum_{l=1}^{n_V} b_{k,l} = 1. \quad (16)$$

with new continuous variables $b_{k,l} \in [0,1]$. To enforce that these variables do not assume fractional values, a set of binary variables $d_{k,q}$, $q \in Q = \{1, \dots, \lceil log_2(n_V) \rceil\}$ is introduced. The values 0 or 1 are assigned to $b_{k,l}$ by formulating linear equations of the type: $b_{k,l} \sim c + \sum_{q \in Q'} \pm d_{k,q}$, with $c \in \mathbb{Z}$, $\sim \in \{\le, \ge\}$, and $Q' \subseteq Q$. The variables $b_{k,i}$ are constrained in a similar way using additional $\lceil log_2(n_R) \rceil$ binary variables[1].

3.3 A Moving Horizon Strategy

The modeling schemes presented in Sec. 3.1/3.2 lead both to linear mixed-integer programming (MILP) problems which can be solved, e. g., by Branch-and-Bound algorithms. Even though the schemes aim at obtaining small number of binary variables, the number grows linearly with $|K|$, i. e., the number of discrete options increases exponentially with the time horizon. The optimization is hence inherently limited to 'short' horizons. As a remedy, we use a moving horizon strategy as it is known from model predictive control: For each $k \in K \setminus \{k_f\}$, an MILP (considering the dynamics of $A_{L,D}$) is solved for a horizon $P = \{1, 2 \dots, k_P\}$ with usually $k_P << |K|$. The first control vectors u_1 and v_1 of the solution are applied to the original nonlinear automaton, and the latter is simulated for the time-period Δt which produces the new hybrid state (x_{k+1}, z_{k+1}). In the

---

[1] For the example of $n_V = 3$ and $Q = \{1,2\}$, the following equations force $b_{k,l}$ to 0 or 1: $b_{k,1} \ge 1 - d_{k,1} - d_{k,2}$, $b_{k,1} \le 1 - d_{k,1}$, $b_{k,1} \le 1 - d_{k,2}$, $b_{k,2} \ge d_{k,1} - d_{k,2}$, $b_{k,2} \le d_{k,1}$, $b_{k,2} \le 1 - d_{k,2}$, $b_{k,3} \ge -d_{k,1} + d_{k,2}$, $b_{k,3} \le 1 - d_{k,1}$, $b_{k,3} \le d_{k,2}$.

next step, the horizon P is shifted one time-step ahead, and the MILP is solved starting from the new state. The alternating use of the linear and nonlinear automaton corrects the differences between the behavior of both models in each step. This procedure is repeated until R_T is reached or $t_k = t_f$ applies.

The complexity grows obviously only linearly with $|K|$ in this case. A drawback is, however, that the obtained control trajectories $(u_1, u_2, \ldots, u_{|K|-1})$, $(v_1, v_2, \ldots, v_{|K|-1})$ are only suboptimal due to the limited look-ahead horizon. The modification with variable time-steps described in [9] allows larger look-ahead horizons even for small values of $|P|$.

4   Optimization of a Processing System Example

The approach is illustrated by considering the start-up procedure of a chemical reactor in which two dissolved substances A and B react exothermically to form a product D. A and B are fed into the reactor by two streams F_1 and F_2 with temperatures T_1 and T_2, and the outlet stream (for which a high concentration of D is desirable) is denoted by F_{out}. The reactor is equipped with a device to heat the content up to a required reaction temperature, and a cooling jacket allows to remove heat from the system once the reaction has started to produce an excess of heat. The streams F_1 and F_2 as well as the heater ($s_H \in \{0, 1\}$) can each be switched between two modes, i. e., $v = (F_1, F_2, s_H)$ can assume 8 different values. The stream F_{out} and the flow of cooling liquid F_C can be continuously controlled within given intervals, i. e., they form the continuous input $u = (F_{out}, F_C)$. The state vector $x = (V, T_R, c_A, c_B)$ contains the volume V, the temperature T_R, and the concentrations c_A and c_B of the reactor content. The reactor dynamics $\dot{x} = f(x, u, v)$ is specified by:

$$
V \in [0.1, 0.8]: \quad f^I =
\begin{pmatrix}
F_1 + F_2 - F_{out} \\
(F_1 \cdot (T_1 - T_R) + F_2 \cdot (T_2 - T_R))/V \\
\quad + F_C \cdot k_1 \cdot (T_C - T_R) \cdot (k_2/V + k_3) - k_4 \cdot r \\
(F_1 \cdot c_{A,1} - c_A \cdot (F_1 + F_2))/V + k_9 \cdot r \\
(F_2 \cdot c_{B,2} - c_B \cdot (F_1 + F_2))/V + k_{10} \cdot r
\end{pmatrix}
$$

(17)

$$
V \in \,]0.8, 2.2]: \quad f^{II} = \left(f_1^I, \; f_2^I + s_H \cdot k_6 \cdot (T_H - T_R) \cdot (k_7 - \frac{k_8}{V}), \; f_3^I, \; f_4^I \right)^{\mathrm{T}}
$$

with $r = c_A \cdot c_B^2 \cdot \exp(-k_5/T_R)$. The valid set of equations depends on V in order to model that the heater is effective only above a certain liquid level. The temperature behavior switches if this level is crossed. Since f^I and f^{II} are strongly nonlinear, we further partition the state space into two temperature intervals (at $T_R = 320$ K) such that four different regions exist overall. During the moving horizon procedure, the linearization is performed for the starting point of each optimization. However, if the optimization reaches a new region within the horizon P that model is used which is linearized at the center-point of this region.

The control objective for this system is to determine trajectories $(u_1, u_2, \ldots,$ $u_{|K|-1})$ and $(v_1, v_2, \ldots, v_{|K|-1})$ that drive the reactor from an initial state $x_1 = (0.1, 300, 0, 0)$ into the target region $R_T = [1.49, 1.51] \times [343, 347] \times [0.13, 0.17] \times [0.28, 0.32]$. This region corresponds to a mode of stable production, in which the reactor is filled up to a desired level, a required reaction temperature is reached and the product concentration is sufficiently high. Throughout the operation the safety constraints $T_R \leq 360$ and $V \leq 1.55$ have to be satisfied.

For simplicity, we consider only the first term of the objective function (the distance to R_T in (4)). The optimization was carried out with $|P| = 3$ and $\triangle t = 20$ using the Branch-and Bound solver CPLEX [17]. The optimization model for this horizon contains overall 3550 equations for the MF and 1335 equations for the DF. (Since most of these equations are indexed over several sets, the modeling effort is much smaller than one might expect from these numbers.)

The optimization results obtained for the disjunctive model are shown in Fig. 1: Thecontrol trajectories $u(t)$, $v(t)$ were computed by using the moving horizon setting, and the corresponding state trajectory $x(t)$ reaches R_T in 60 steps. The trajectories for the model based on the MF are the same – however, the computation times differ considerably: The MF with binary variables $b_{k,i}$ and $b_{k,i,l}$ took about 25 hours of CPU-time on a SPARC 2 workstation, the MF with binary variables $b_{k,i}$ but continuous $b_{k,i,l}$ terminated after 7 hours and 44 minutes, and the MF with continuous $b_{k,i}$ and $b_{k,i,l}$ required almost the same time. In comparison, the optimization of the disjunctive model was completed in only 13 minutes.

5   Comparison and Conclusions

It has to be discussed whether the drastic reduction of the computation time is a general property of the proposed disjunctive formulation. The complexity of the solution of an MILP problem is mainly determined by the number of binary and continuous variables, by the number of inequalities defining the constraints, by the structure of these constraints, and by the type of relaxation used within the chosen solution technique. With respect to the number of binary variables, the following equation hold for the three alternatives with continuous $b_{k,i,l}$:

$$n_b = (n_{b,OF} + n_{b,Reg} + n_{b,Inp}) \cdot |K| \quad \text{with: } n_{b,Inp} = \lceil \log_2(n_v) \rceil \qquad (18)$$

$$n_{b,OF} = \begin{cases} 2n & \text{for MF} \\ 3n & \text{for DF} \end{cases}, \quad n_{b,Reg} = \begin{cases} n_E + n_R & \text{for MF with } b_{k,i} \in \{0,1\} \\ n_E & \text{for MF with } b_{k,i} \in [0,1] \\ \lceil \log_2(n_R) \rceil & \text{for DF} \end{cases}$$

The terms $n_{b,OF}$, $n_{b,Reg}$, and $n_{b,Inp}$ denote the number of binary variables to specify the logic decisions within the first term of the objective function, the

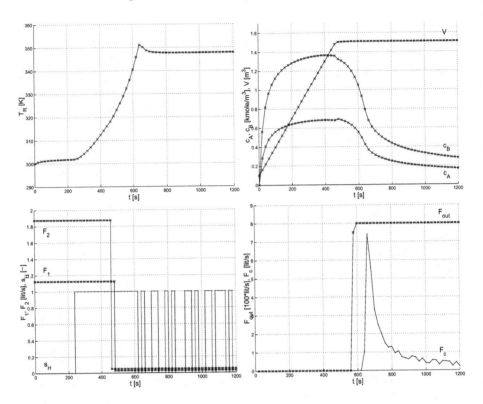

Fig. 1. Optimized state trajectories $x(t) = (V, T_R, c_A, c_B)$ and control trajectories $v(t) = (F_1, F_2, s_H)$, $u(t) = (F_{out}, F_C)$ of the nonlinear hybrid model.

region membership of x_k, and the decision about the discrete input. The latter equals the number of binary variables required to encode the set of discrete inputs and is identical for all formulations. The number $n_{b,OF}$ is smaller for MF since only 2 binary variables per dimension can specify whether x_k is above or below the lower and upper bound of the target region while the DF requires three variables to express that x_k is below, inside of, or above the bounds of R_T. The MF seems to be advantageous in this respect. Usually more important is the number $n_{b,Reg}$, and the MF with continuous variables $b_{k,i}$ is clearly preferable over binary $b_{k,i}$. (And, of course, the variables $b_{k,i,l}$ should be defined as continuous and not as binary variables, otherwise: $n_{b,Reg} + n_{b,Inp} = n_R \cdot (n_V + 1) + n_E$). For DF, $n_{b,Reg}$ equals the number of binary variables required to enumerate the regions. In order to see when DF is preferable over MF (with $b_{k,i} \in [0, 1]$), the relation $n_E > 1 + \log_2(n_R) > \lceil \log_2(n_R) \rceil$ is evaluated. Using a *granularity* parameter $g = n_E/n_R$ to denote the ratio of hyperplanes to regions, it follows that DF leads to a smaller number of binary variables for $g > n_E/2^{n_E-1} = g^*$. The possible values of g can be over-approximated (for arbitrary n) by[2]: $g^- = n_E/2^{n_E} \leq g \leq g^+ = n_E/(n_E + 1)$. Figure 2 shows that DF is preferable with respect to $n_{b,Reg}$ for large parts of the g/n_E-space[3].

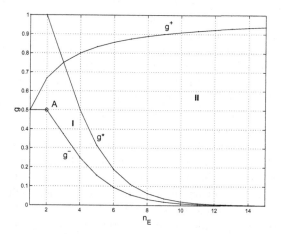

Fig. 2. Comparison for MF (with continuous $b_{k,i}$) and DF: $n_{b,Reg}$ is smaller for DF in area II (above g^*) and equal for MF and DF in area I (both bounded by g^-, g^+).

However, the number of binary variables is apparently not the only deciding effect: While it certainly contributes to the good results for the DF in comparison to the original MF (with discrete $b_{i,k}$), it cannot explain the advantage of DF over the MF with continuous $b_{i,k}$ for the example, since $n_{b,Reg}$ is the same for both formulations in this case ($n_E = 2$, $g = 0.5$; see point 'A' in Fig. 2). The number of continuous variables is slightly larger for DF and can hence neither serve as a reason. But an important factor is the relaxation obtained during the Branch-and-Bound solution of the MILP. As proven in [12], most relaxations of the disjunctive form are significantly tighter than the corresponding relaxations of the MF. This can considerably reduce the search space for the MILP and with that the computational effort. Another important factor is usually the number of constraints involved into the formulation: The considerable reduction of constraints observed for the example results from the fact that especially the linearizations according to (9) and (14) require much less equations for the DF:

---

[2] The upper bound follows from the consideration that each new hyperplane partitions only one of the regions obtained from the previously introduced hyperplanes. For the lower bound it is assumed that a new hyperplane partitions all previously existing regions – this is of course a conservative assumption.

[3] And DF is never worse w.r.t. $n_{b,Reg}$: Assume that $n_E < \lceil \log_2(n_R) \rceil$. For a given n_E, it follows for the largest possible n_R (the lower bound of g) that $n_E < \lceil n_E \rceil$. This inequality is false $\forall\, n_E \in \mathbb{N}$, hence the assumption does not hold.

While the MF leads to 4 equations for each product of a $b_{k,i,l}$-variable with each component of the continuous variables x_k and u_k, the DF contains only one equation for each linearization.

In summary, we have presented different formulations of an optimal control problem for hybrid systems in order to be able to use mixed-integer programming for the solution. The formulations chosen to transfer the transition dynamics into optimization constraints appear to have a significant impact on the efficiency with which the solution can be obtained. While the same optimal control trajectories result from all formulations, the disjunctive model seems to be strongly preferable with respect to the number of binary variables (for most configurations), the number of constraints, and the relaxations obtained during the Branch-and-Bound solution.

Since the optimization model is derived by linearization and time discretization, and since the optimization is performed on a limited moving horizon, it is in general not guaranteed that the generated control trajectories are the optimal ones for the original nonlinear automaton. From an engineering point of view, however, these solutions are certainly better than those obtained from an optimization that does not consider the discrete options as a degree of freedom at all. A thorough investigation of the difference between the solution for the nonlinear automaton and the solution obtained from our approach is a matter of current research. In addition, our current research is focussed on the use of *disjunctive programming* [13] rather than standard branch-and-bound techniques for solution. The intention is to develop an algorithm that exploits specific properties of the convex hull relaxation (11) of the DF.

Acknowledgements

We thank I.E. Grossmann for directing our interest to disjunctive programming and S. Engell for useful comments on details of this work. Financial support by the German Research Council (DFG) is gratefully acknowledged.

References

[1] Branicky, M.S., Borkar, V.S., Mitter, S.K.: A unified framework for hybrid control: Model and optimal control theory. IEEE Trans. Automatic Contr. **43** (1998) 31–45

[2] Sussmann, H.: A maximum principle for hybrid optimal conrol problems. In: Proc. 38th IEEE Conf. Decision and Control. (1999) 425–430

[3] Broucke, M., Di Benedetto, M., Di Gennaro, S., Sangiovanni-Vincentelli, A.: Theory of optimal control using bisimulations. In: Proc. 3rd Int. Workshop of Hybrid Systems: Comp. and Control. Volume 1790 of LNCS., Springer (2000) 89–102

[4] Bemporad, A., Morari, M.: Control of systems integrating logic, dynamics, and constraints. Automatica **35** (1999) 407–427

[5] Hedlund, S., Rantzer, A.: Optimal control of hybrid systems. In: Proc. 38th Conf. Decision and Control (Phoenix). (1999)

[6] Xu, X., Antsaklis, P.: An approach for solving general switched linear quadratic optimal control problems. In: Proc. 40th IEEE Conf. Decision and Control. (2001) 2478–2483

[7] Zhang, P., Cassandras, C.: An improved forward algorithm for optimal control of a class of hybrid systems. In: Proc. 40th IEEE Conf. Decision and Control. (2001) 1235–1236

[8] Stursberg, O., Engell, S.: Optimized startup-procedures of processing systems. In: Proc. 6th IFAC Symp. Dynamics and Control of Process Sys. (2001) 231–236

[9] Stursberg, O., Engell, S.: Optimal control of switched continuous systems using mixed-integer programming. In: Proc. 15th IFAC World Congress on Automatic Control (to appear). (July 2002)

[10] Williams, H.P.: Model Building in Mathematical Programming. 1st edn. J. Wiley P. (1978)

[11] Jaffar, J., Maher, M.: Constraint logic programming: A survey. Journal of Logic Programming **19/20** (1994) 503–581

[12] Balas, E.: Disjunctive programming and a hierarchy of relaxations for discrete optimization problems. SIAM Journal Alg. Disc. Meth. **6** (1985) 466–486

[13] Lee, S., Grossmann, I.: New algorithms for nonlinear generalized disjunctive programming. Comp. and Chemical. Eng. **4** (2000) 2125–2141

[14] Glover, F.: Improved linear integer programming formulations of nonlinear integer problems. Managem. Science **22** (1975) 455–460

[15] Cavalier, T., Pardalos, P., Soyster, A.: Modeling and integer programming techniques applied to propositional calculus. Comp. and Oper. Res. **17** (1990) 561–570

[16] Vecchietti, A., Grossmann, I.: Logmip: A disjunctive 0-1 nonlinear optimizer for process system models. Comp. and Chemical. Eng. **23** (1999) 555–565

[17] Brooke, A., Kendrick, D., Meeraus, A., Raman, R.: GAMS/CPLEX – A User's Guide. GAMS Development Corporation (1998)

Composing Abstractions of Hybrid Systems

Paulo Tabuada[1], George J. Pappas[1], and Pedro Lima[2]

[1] Department of Electrical Engineering, University of Pennsylvania
Philadelphia, PA 19104,
{tabuadap,pappasg}@seas.upenn.edu
[2] Instituto de Sistemas e Robótica, Instituto Superior Técnico
1049-001 Lisboa - Portugal,
pal@isr.ist.utl.pt

Abstract. The analysis and design of hybrid systems must exploit their hierarchical and compositional nature of in order to tackle complexity. In previous work, we presented a hierarchical abstraction framework for hybrid control systems based on the notions of simulation and bisimulation. In this paper, we build upon our previous work and investigate the compositionality of our abstraction framework. We present a composition operator that allows synchronization on inputs and states of hybrid systems. We then show that the composition operator is compatible with our abstraction framework in the sense that abstracting subsystems will the result in an abstraction of the overall system.

1 Introduction

The complexity of hybrid systems analysis and design motivate the development of methods and tools that scale well with dimension and exploit system structure. Hierarchical decompositions model hybrid systems using a hierarchy of models at different layers of abstraction. Analysis tasks are then performed on simpler, abstracted models that are equivalent with respect to the relevant properties. Design also benefits from this approach since the design starts at the top of the hierarchy on a simple model and is then successively refined by incorporating the modeling detail of each layer.

In addition, as systems are usually compositions of subsystems, one must take advantage of the compositional structure of hybrid systems. We seek, therefore, to take advantage of this compositional structure of hybrid systems to simplify the computation of abstractions. This simplification comes from the fact that it is much simpler to abstract subsystems individually and then interconnect them in order to obtain an abstraction, rather than to extract an abstraction of the system as a whole. In order to accomplish this, compositional operators need to be compatible with abstraction operators.

The notions of composition and abstraction are mature in theoretical computer science, and, in particular, in the areas of concurrency theory [10], [19], and computer aided verification [9]. Notions of abstraction such as language inclusion, simulation relations, and bisimulation relations have been considered in

C.J. Tomlin and M.R. Greenstreet (Eds.): HSCC 2002, LNCS 2289, pp. 436–450, 2002.

the context of hybrid systems. A formal model for hybrid systems allowing composition was proposed in [8], compositional refinements in a hierarchical setting are discussed in [2], and assume guarantee proof rules are presented in [4].

For purely continuous systems, the notions of simulation, and bisimulation had not received much attention [18]. Recently, similar notions were introduced in [11, 12] which has resulted in constructions of abstractions for linear control systems [11], and nonlinear control systems [12] while characterizing abstracting maps that preserve properties of interest such as controllability. Based on these results, in [16], we took the first steps towards constructing abstractions of hybrid systems while preserving timed languages. This allowed us to introduce in [17] an abstract notion of control systems comprising discrete, continuous and hybrid systems. This abstract framework was the natural setting to understand abstractions of hybrid control systems.

In this paper, we extend the hierarchical approach described in [17] towards compositionality. Following the approach described in [19], we introduce a general composition operator modeling the interconnection of subsystems and relate compositionality with abstractions. We prove that simulations and bisimulations of hybrid systems are compositional, and we also give necessary and sufficient conditions for bisimulations to be compositional.

This paper is structured as follows. In Section 2 we review the abstract control systems framework introduced in [17] and introduce the notions of simulation and bisimulation. In Section 3 we introduce a composition operator based on [19], modeling the interconnection of subsystems and relate compositionality with abstractions. We prove the main results of the paper showing that abstractions are compositional. We conclude at Section 4 by providing some topics for future research. In Appendix A we collect some mathematical facts and notational issues, and Appendix B contains the proofs of all the results.

2   Abstract Control Systems

In [17], we presented an abstract control systems framework which allows the treatment of discrete, continuous, and hybrid control systems in a unified way. This approach differs from other attempts of unification [7, 14] by regarding systems as *control* systems. We start by looking at discrete and continuous systems to gain some motivation for the general case.

Discrete Control Systems: Let (Q, Σ, δ) be a discrete labeled transition system, where Q is a finite set of states, Σ is a finite set of input symbols, and $\delta : Q \times \Sigma \longrightarrow Q$ is the next-state function. For simplicity, we restrict to deterministic transition systems, and note that δ is in general a partial function. Let us denote by Σ^* the set of all finite strings obtained by concatenating elements in Σ. In particular the empty string ε also belongs to Σ^*. Regarding concatenation of strings as a map from $\Sigma^* \times \Sigma^*$ to Σ^* we can give Σ^* the structure of a monoid. Furthermore, it is well known from automata theory [5], that the transition function δ defines a *unique* partial map from $Q \times \Sigma^*$ to Q satisfying the following properties:

$$\delta^*(q, \varepsilon) = q \tag{1}$$
$$\delta^*(q, \sigma_1 \sigma_2) = \delta^*(\delta^*(q, \sigma_1), \sigma_2) \tag{2}$$

A similar description of control system can also be given.

Continuous Control Systems: Let U be the space of admissible control inputs. Define the set U^t as:

$$U^t = \{u : [0, t[\rightarrow U \quad | \quad [0, t[\subseteq \mathbb{R}_0^+ \} \tag{3}$$

An element of U^t is denoted by u^t, and represents a map from $[0, t[$ to U. Consider now the set U^* which is the disjoint union of all U^t for $t \in \mathbb{R}_0^+$:

$$U^* = \coprod_{t \in \mathbb{R}_0^+} U^t \tag{4}$$

The set U^* can be regarded as a monoid under the operation of concatenation, that is, if $u^{t_1} \in U^{t_1} \subset U^*$ and $u^{t_2} \in U^{t_2} \subset U^*$ then $u^{t_1} u^{t_2} = u^{t_1 + t_2} \in U^{t_1 + t_2} \subset U^*$ with concatenation given by:

$$u^{t_1} u^{t_2}(t) = \begin{cases} u^{t_1}(t) & \text{if } 0 \le t < t_1 \\ u^{t_2}(t - t_1) & \text{if } t_1 \le t < t_1 + t_2 \end{cases} \tag{5}$$

The identity element is given by the empty input, that is $\varepsilon = u^0$. Let $\dot{x} = f(x, u)$ be a smooth control system, where $x \in M$, a smooth manifold and $u \in U$, the set of admissible inputs. Choosing an admissible input trajectory u^t, $f(x, u^t)$ is a well defined vector field and as such it induces a flow which we denote by $\gamma_x : [0, t[\rightarrow M$, such that $\gamma_x(0) = x$. We thus see that a smooth control system defines a partial map:

$$\Phi : M \times U^* \rightarrow M$$
$$(x, u^t) \mapsto \gamma_x(t) \tag{6}$$

satisfying:

$$\Phi(x, \varepsilon) = \Phi(x, u^0) = \gamma_x(0) = x \tag{7}$$
$$\Phi(x, u^{t_1} u^{t_2}) = \gamma_x(t_1 + t_2) = \gamma_{\gamma_x(t_1)}(t_2) = \Phi(\Phi(x, u^{t_1}), u^{t_2}) \tag{8}$$

We think of the monoid as the set of control actions available to influence the evolution of the system. In many cases, however, these available actions change from state to state. This dependence of the available actions on the states forces us to work with generalized monoids, see Appendix A for the correct definition.

Definition 1 (Abstract Control System). *Let S be a set and $\mathcal{M}$ a generalized monoid over S. An abstract control system over S is a map $\Phi : \mathcal{M} \rightarrow S$ respecting the monoid structure, that is:*

1. **Identity:** $\Phi(s, \varepsilon) = s$
2. **Semi-group:** $\Phi(s, a_1 a_2) = \Phi(\Phi(s, a_1), a_2)$

We now show how this definition is general enough to cover also hybrid control systems.

Hybrid Control Systems: The state space of an hybrid control system is a set of smooth manifolds X_q parameterized by the discrete states $q \in Q$, denoted by $X = \{X_q\}_{q \in Q}$. A point in X is represented by the pair (q, x). The set of available actions at each point is described by a subset of the following monoid:

$$\mathcal{M} = \coprod_{n \in \mathbb{N}_0} (U^* \cup \Sigma^*)^n \tag{9}$$

assuming that $U^* \cap \Sigma^* = \{\varepsilon\}$ and regarding U^* and Σ^* simply as sets. Let us elaborate on the product operation on $\mathcal{M}$. This operation is defined as the usual concatenation and therefore it requires finite length strings. To accommodate this requirement and still be able to have an infinite number of concatenations of elements in U^* we proceed as follows. Suppose that we want to show that $\sigma_1 u^{t_1} u^{t_2} \ldots u^{t_k} \ldots \sigma_2$ belongs to $\mathcal{M}$, where t_k is a convergent series. Instead of regarding each element in the string as an element in $\mathcal{M}$ (which would not allow us to define the last concatenation since it would happen after ∞) we regard σ_1 and σ_2 as elements of $\mathcal{M}$ and $u^{t_1} u^{t_2} \ldots u^{t_k} \ldots = u^{t'}$ as an element of U^* and consequently as an element of $\mathcal{M}$, where $t' = \lim_{k \to \infty} t_k$. This string is then regarded as the map $m : \{1, 2, 3\} \longrightarrow \mathcal{M}$ defined by $m(1) = \sigma_1$, $m(2) = u^{t'}$ and $m(3) = \sigma_3$. The product in $\mathcal{M}$ is then the usual concatenation on reduced strings, that is, strings where all consequent sequences of elements of U^* or Σ^* have been replaced by their product in U^* or Σ^*, respectively. Hybrid control systems are now cast into the abstract control systems framework as:

Definition 2 (Hybrid Control System). *An hybrid control system $H = (X, \mathcal{M}_X, \Phi_X)$ consists of:*

- *The state space $X = \{X_q\}_{q \in Q}$.*
- *A generalized monoid $\mathcal{M}_X$ over X.*
- *A map $\Phi_X : \mathcal{M}_X \longrightarrow X$ respecting the monoid structure and such that for all $q \in Q$, there is a set $Inv(q) \subseteq X_q$ and for all $x \in Inv(q)$, $\mathcal{M}_X(q, x) \cap U^* \neq \{\varepsilon\}$ and $\Phi((q, x), u^{t'}) \in Inv(q)$ for every prefix $u^{t'}$ of every $u^t \in \mathcal{M}_X(q, x)$.*

The semantics associated with the evolution from (q, x) governed by Φ and controlled by $a \in \mathcal{M}_{(q,x)}$ is the standard transition semantics of hybrid automata [3]. Suppose that $a = u^{t_1} \sigma_1 \sigma_2 u^{t_2}$, then $\Phi((q, x), a) = (q', x')$ means that the system starting at (q, x) evolves during t_1 units of time under continuous input u^{t_1}, jumps under input σ_1 and them jumps again under input σ_2. After the two consecutive jumps, the system evolves under the continuous control input u^{t_2} reaching (q', x'), t_2 units of time after the last jump.

2.1 Control System Abstractions

We now review the notions of simulation and bisimulation in the context of abstract control systems while referring the reader to Appendix A for the relevant notation.

Definition 3 (Simulations of Abstract Control Systems). *Let Φ_X and Φ_Y be two abstract control systems over X and Y with generalized monoids $\mathcal{M}_X$ and $\mathcal{M}_Y$, respectively and $F \subseteq \mathcal{M}_X \times \mathcal{M}_Y$ a generalized monoid respecting relation. Then Φ_Y is a simulation of Φ_X with respect to F or a F-simulation iff for any $x \in X$:*

$$y \in F_B(x) \implies \forall_{(x,a_x) \in dom(F)} \exists_{(y,a_y) \in F(x,a_x)} \quad \Phi_Y(y,a_y) \in F_B(\Phi_X(x,a_x))$$

The above definition slightly generalizes the usual notions of morphisms between transition systems in [19], since the inputs in $\mathcal{M}_Y$, if obtained from F, depend on the inputs on $\mathcal{M}_X$ as well as the state. It is straightforward to see that abstract control systems and relations satisfying the above condition form a category, that we call the *abstract control systems category*. The notion of bisimulation is defined as a symmetric simulation:

Definition 4. *Let Φ_X and Φ_Y be abstract control systems over X and Y with generalized monoids $\mathcal{M}_X$ and $\mathcal{M}_Y$ respectively. If $F \subseteq \mathcal{M}_X \times \mathcal{M}_Y$ is a generalized monoid respecting relation we say that Φ_X is F-bisimilar to Φ_Y iff Φ_Y is a F-simulation of Φ_X and Φ_X is a F^{-1}-simulation of Φ_Y.*

Although we used relations to define simulations and bisimulations we will assume through the remaining paper that F is the relation induced by a map $f : \mathcal{M}_X \longrightarrow \mathcal{M}_Y$. The approach taken to define bisimulation is similar in spirit to the one in [10], however instead of preserving inputs between bisimulations, we relate them through the map f. If one chooses a map f which is the identity on inputs we recover the notion of bisimulation in [10]. Several other approaches to bisimulation are reported in the literature and we point the reader to the comparative study in [13] and the references therein.

The notion of simulation allows to define several different types of abstraction since when $f : \mathcal{M}_X \longrightarrow \mathcal{M}_Y$ defines a simulation from Φ_X to Φ_Y, the map f_B takes state trajectories of Φ_X to state trajectories of Φ_Y [15]. This shows, in particular, that $f(\mathcal{L}(\Phi_X)) \subseteq \mathcal{L}(\Phi_Y)$, where $\mathcal{L}(\Phi)$ denotes the language generated by abstract control system Φ. When f is simply the inclusion of $\mathcal{M}_X$ into $\mathcal{M}_Y$, that is $f(x,a) = (x,a) \in \mathcal{M}_Y$ for every $(x,a) \in \mathcal{M}_X$ we recover the popular notion of abstraction based on language inclusion since $\mathcal{L}(\Phi_X) = f(\mathcal{L}(\Phi_X)) \subseteq \mathcal{L}(\Phi_Y)$. Under certain conditions on the relation F the computation of a simulation can be done algorithmically as described in [17].

3   Compositional Abstractions

In this section, we follow the categorical description of composition of transition systems as described in [19]. A variety of composition operations can be modeled as the product operation followed by a restriction operation.

3.1   Parallel Composition with Synchronization

The first step of composition combines two abstract control systems into a single one by forming their product. Given two abstract control systems $\Phi_X : \mathcal{M}_X$

$\rightarrow X$ and $\Phi_Y : \mathcal{M}_Y \rightarrow Y$ we define their product to be the abstract control system $\Phi_X \times \Phi_Y : (\mathcal{M}_X \times \mathcal{M}_Y) \rightarrow (X \times Y)$, $\Phi_X \times \Phi_Y((x, y), (a_x, a_y)) = (\Phi_X(x, a_x), \Phi_Y(y, a_y))$, where the actions available at each $(x, y) \in X \times Y$ are subsets of the direct product monoid $\mathcal{M}_X \otimes \mathcal{M}_Y$. The trajectories of the product control system consist of all possible combinations of the initial control systems trajectories. The product can also be defined in a categorical manner.

Definition 5 (Product of abstract control systems). *Let $\Phi_X : \mathcal{M}_X \rightarrow X$ and $\Phi_Y : \mathcal{M}_Y \rightarrow Y$ be two abstract control systems. The product of these abstract control systems is a triple $(\Phi_X \times \Phi_Y, \pi_X, \pi_Y)$ where $\Phi_X \times \Phi_Y$ is an abstract control system and $\pi_X \subseteq (X \times Y) \times X$ and $\pi_Y \subseteq (X \times Y) \times Y$ are projection relations such that Φ_X is a π_X-simulation of $\Phi_X \times \Phi_Y$, Φ_Y is a π_Y-simulation of $\Phi_X \times \Phi_Y$, and for any other triple (Φ_Z, p_X, p_Y) of this type there is one and only one relation $\zeta \subseteq Z \times (X \times Y)$ such that $\Phi_X \times \Phi_Y$ is a ζ-simulation of Φ_Z, and the following diagram commutes:*

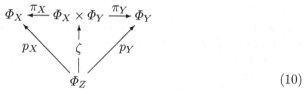

$$\text{(10)}$$

The relations π_X and π_Y are in fact those induced by the canonical projection maps $\pi_X : X \times Y \rightarrow X$, $\pi_Y : X \times Y \rightarrow Y$ and the relation ζ is easily seen to be given by $\zeta = (p_X, p_Y)$. This definition of product may seem unnecessarily abstract and complicated at the first contact, it will, however, render the proof of the main result on the compatibility of parallel composition with respect to simulations a much simpler task.

Example 1. Consider the transition systems inspired from [19] and displayed on the left of Figure 1 where the ε evolutions are not represented. The product of these transitions systems will consist of all possible evolutions of both systems as displayed on the right of Figure 1.

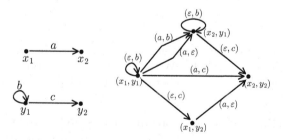

Fig. 1. Two transition systems on the left and the corresponding product transition system on the right.

In the product abstract control system, the behavior of one system does not influence the behavior of the other system. Since in general the behavior of a system composed of several subsystems depends strongly on the interaction between the subsystems, one tries to capture this interaction by removing undesired evolutions from the product system $\Phi_X \times \Phi_Y$ through the operation of restriction. Given a generalized submonoid $\mathcal{M}_L \subseteq \mathcal{M}_W$ we define the restriction of control system $\Phi_W : \mathcal{M}_W \to W$ to $\mathcal{M}_L$ as a new control system $\Phi_W|_{\mathcal{M}_L} : \overline{\mathcal{M}_L} \to L$ which is given by $\Phi_W|_{\mathcal{M}_L}(x, a) = \Phi_W(x, a)$ iff $(x, a) \in \mathcal{M}_L$ and $\Phi_W(x, a')$ belongs to L for any prefix a' of a. In general the domain of $\Phi_W|_{\mathcal{M}_L}$, $\overline{\mathcal{M}_L}$, may be strictly contained in $\mathcal{M}_L$ since restricting the base space implies also restricting the available inputs to those that do not force the abstract control system to leave the restricted base. If the generalized submonoid $\mathcal{M}_L$ has the same state space as $\mathcal{M}_W$ but "less" control inputs available at each state, then restriction is modeling synchronization of both systems on the control inputs. If on the other hand the available control inputs are equal but the state space of $\mathcal{M}_L$ is "smaller" then the state space of $\mathcal{M}_W$ then both systems are being synchronized on the state space. Synchronization on inputs and states is also captured by the operation of restriction by choosing a generalized submonoid with "less" available inputs and "smaller" state space. This operation also admits a categorical characterization.

Definition 6 (Restriction of abstract control systems). *Let $\Phi_W : \mathcal{M}_W \to W$ be an abstract control system, $\mathcal{M}_L$ a generalized submonoid of $\mathcal{M}_W$ and g and h two simulation relations such that $\mathcal{M}_L = \{(w, a_w) \in \mathcal{M}_W \mid g(w, a_w) = h(w, a_w)\}$. The restriction of Φ_W to $\mathcal{M}_L$ is a pair $(\Phi_W|_{\mathcal{M}_L}, i_{\mathcal{M}_L})$ where $\Phi_W|_{\mathcal{M}_L}$ is an abstract control system and $i_{\mathcal{M}_L} \subseteq \mathcal{M}_L \times \mathcal{M}_W$ is an inclusion relation such that Φ_W is a $i_{\mathcal{M}_L}$-simulation of $\Phi_W|_{\mathcal{M}_L}$ satisfying $g \circ i_{\mathcal{M}_L} = h \circ i_{\mathcal{M}_L}$ and for any other pair $(\Phi_Z, i_{\mathcal{M}_Z})$ of this type there is one and only one relation η such that $\Phi_W|_{\mathcal{M}_L}$ is a η-simulation of Φ_Z, and the following diagram commutes:*

$$\begin{array}{ccc} \Phi_W|_{\mathcal{M}_L} \xrightarrow{\;i_{\mathcal{M}_L}\;} \Phi_W \underset{h}{\overset{g}{\rightrightarrows}} \Phi_V \\ \eta \Big\uparrow \quad \nearrow{i_{\mathcal{M}_Z}} \\ \Phi_Z \end{array}$$

(11)

It is not difficult to see that the relation $i_{\mathcal{M}_L}$ is simply the inclusion $i_{\mathcal{M}_L}(a_l) = a_l \in \mathcal{M}_W$ for every $a_l \in \overline{\mathcal{M}_L}$. With the notions of product and restriction at hand, we can now define a general operation of parallel composition with synchronization.

Definition 7 (Parallel Composition with synchronization). *Let $\Phi_X : \mathcal{M}_X \to X$ and $\Phi_Y : \mathcal{M}_Y \to Y$ be two abstract control systems and consider a generalized submonoid $\mathcal{M}_L \subseteq \mathcal{M}_X \times \mathcal{M}_Y$. The parallel composition of Φ_X and Φ_Y with synchronization over $\mathcal{M}_L$ is the abstract control system defined as:*

$$\Phi_X \,\|_{\mathcal{M}_L}\, \Phi_Y = (\Phi_X \times \Phi_Y)|_{\mathcal{M}_L}$$

(12)

Example 2. Consider the transition systems displayed on the left of Figure 1. By specifying the generalized submonoid:

$$\mathcal{M}_L = \{((x_1, y_1), (a, b)), ((x_1, y_1), (\varepsilon, c))((x_1, y_1), (\varepsilon, \varepsilon)), ((x_2, y_1), (\varepsilon, c)),$$
$$((x_2, y_1), (\varepsilon, \varepsilon)), ((x_2, y_2), (\varepsilon, \varepsilon)), ((x_1, y_2), (\varepsilon, \varepsilon))\} \qquad (13)$$

it is possible to synchronize the event a with the event b on the parallel composition of these systems, while the remaining evolutions not controlled by a neither by b remain unchanged. The resulting transition system is displayed in Figure 2.

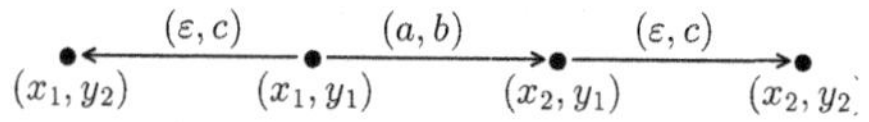

Fig. 2. Parallel composition with synchronization of the transition systems displayed on the left of Figure 1.

3.2   Compositionality of Simulations

We now determine if composition of subsystems is compatible with abstraction. A positive answer to this question is given by the next theorem which describes how the process of computing abstractions can be rendered more efficient by exploring the interconnection structure of hybrid systems.

Theorem 1 (Compositionality of Simulations). *Given abstract control systems Φ_X, Φ_Z (which is a F-simulation of Φ_X), Φ_Y, Φ_W (which is a G-simulation of Φ_Y) and the generalized submonoid $\mathcal{M}_L \subseteq \mathcal{M}_X \times \mathcal{M}_Y$, the parallel composition of the simulations Φ_Z and Φ_W with synchronization over $(F \times G)(\mathcal{M}_L)$ is a $(F \times G)|_{\overline{\mathcal{M}_L}}$-simulation of the parallel composition of Φ_X with Φ_Y with synchronization over $\mathcal{M}_L$.*

The above result was stated for parallel composition of two abstract control systems but it can be easily extended to any finite number of abstract control systems. The relevance of the result lies in the fact that, in general, it is much easier to abstract each individual subsystem and by parallel composition obtain an abstraction of the overall system.

Example 3. To illustrate the use of Theorem 1 we shall make use of the celebrated water tank system from [1]. Consider two water tanks that can be filled by water coming from a pipe as displayed on the left of Figure 3. The water level at tank A is measured by x_1 while the water level at tank B is measured by x_2. Each tank has also an outflow that causes a decrease in the water level. The outflow rate at tank A is v_1 while at tank B is v_2. This outflow can be compensated by a water inflow coming from the pipe on top of the tanks. This pipe has

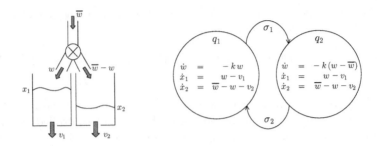

Fig. 3. Water tank system: Physical setup on the left and hybrid model on the right.

an inflow rate of $\overline{w}$ which can be directed to tank A or to tank B by means of a valve located in the pipe. Contrary to [1], we explicitly incorporate a first order model of the valve in the hybrid automaton describing this hybrid control system, displayed on the right of Figure 3. We now seek to abstract away the valve dynamics to obtain the usual model that considers the switching of the inflow from one tank to the other instantaneous[1]. Instead of computing an abstraction directly from this hybrid automaton we start by realizing that this automaton can be obtained by parallel composition of hybrid control systems H_X and H_Y modeling the pipe and the tanks, respectively, as shown in Figure 4. This compo-

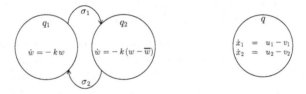

Fig. 4. Hybrid model of the pipe and water tanks on the left and right, respectively.

sition is synchronized on the generalized submonoid $\mathcal{M}_L \subseteq \mathcal{M}_X \times \mathcal{M}_Y$ defined by the equalities $u_1 = w$ and $u_2 = \overline{w} - w$. We now abstract the pipe model by aggregating all the continuous states in discrete state q_1 to 0 and all the continuous states in discrete state q_2 to $\overline{w}$. Theorem 1 ensures that composing H_Y with this abstraction will result in an abstraction of hybrid control system $H_X \|_{\mathcal{M}_L} H_Y$. The new synchronizing generalized monoid is obtained from $\mathcal{M}_L$ by replacing w by 0 on the continuous inputs in state q_1 and replacing w by $\overline{w}$ in the continuous inputs at discrete state q_2. This is also be described by the

---
[1] We remark that considering the water switching instantaneous leads to zeno trajectories [6], however this problem falls beyond the scope of the current paper.

equalities $u_1 = 0$, $u_2 = \overline{w}$ and $u_1 = \overline{w}$, $u_2 = 0$ valid at discrete states q_1 and q_2, respectively. The resulting hybrid control system is displayed in Figure 5. This example illustrates the clear advantage of exploring compositionality in

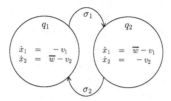

Fig. 5. Abstracted hybrid model of the water tank system.

computing hybrid abstractions. We have only computed continuous abstractions of one-dimensional control systems (for the pipe automaton), whereas if one would have proceeded directly from hybrid control system $H_X \parallel_{\mathcal{M}_L} H_Y$ without exploring the compositional structure, one would have computed continuous abstractions of the three-dimensional continuous control systems at each discrete location.

3.3   Compositionality of Bisimulations

In this section we extend the previous compatibility results from simulations to bisimulations. Although the product respects bisimulations the same does not happen with the operation of restriction so we need additional assumptions to ensure that bisimulations are respected by composition as stated in the next result.

Theorem 2 (Compositionality of Bisimulations). *Given abstract control systems Φ_X, Φ_Z (a F-bisimulation of Φ_X), Φ_Y, Φ_W (a G-bisimulation of Φ_Y) and a generalized submonoid $\mathcal{M}_L \subseteq \mathcal{M}_X \times \mathcal{M}_Y$ we have that the parallel composition of the bisimulations Φ_Z and Φ_W with synchronization over $(F \times G)(\mathcal{M}_L)$ is a $(F \times G)|_{\overline{\mathcal{M}_L}}$-bisimulation of the parallel composition of Φ_X with Φ_Y with synchronization over $\mathcal{M}_L$ iff $(F \times G)^{-1}|_{\overline{(F \times G)(\mathcal{M}_L)}} = (F \times G)|_{\overline{\mathcal{M}_L}}^{-1}$ where $\overline{(F \times G)(\mathcal{M}_L)}$ is the domain of $\Phi_Z \parallel_{(F \times G)(\mathcal{M}_L)} \Phi_W$.*

From the previous result we conclude that if we have a means of computing bisimulations and if we choose the synchronization generalized submonoid carefully we can compute bisimulations by exploring the interconnection structure of large-scale systems.

4   Conclusions

In this paper, we addressed the interplay between abstractions and compositionality of hybrid systems. Based on previous work on abstractions of hybrid control systems, we introduced a composition operator, and showed that this composition operator is compatible with abstractions based on simulations. Furthermore, we presented necessary and sufficient conditions for this operator to be also compatible with bisimulations. Current research is focusing on classes of hybrid systems and composition operators for which the abstraction process can be fully automated. Another important topic for future research is to understand which conditions guarantee that hybrid systems relevant properties are preserved by abstractions, and specially by composition operators.

Acknowledgments: The authors would like to thank Esfandiar Haghverdi for extremely stimulating discussions on category theory, and its use for hybrid systems. The first author was supported by Fundação para a Ciência e Tecnologia under grant PRAXIS XXI/BD/18149/98 while the second author was partially supported by DARPA ITO MoBIES Grant F33615-00-C-1707.

References

[1] R. Alur and T.A. Henzinger. Modularity for timed and hybrid systems. In *Proceedings of the 9th International Conference on Concurrency Theory*, volume 1243 of *Lecture Notes in Computer Science*, pages 74–88. Springer-Verlag, 1997.

[2] Rajeev Alur, Radu Grosu, Insup Lee, and Oleg Sokolsky. Compositional refinements for hierarchical hybrid systems. In *Hybrid Systems : Computation and Control*, volume 2034 of *Lecture Notes in Computer Science*, pages 33–48. Springer Verlag, 2001.

[3] T.A. Henzinger. The theory of hybrid automata. In *Proceedings of the 11th Annual IEEE Symposium on Logic in Computer Science*, pages 278–292. IEEE Computer Society Press, 1996.

[4] Thomas A. Henzinger, Marius Minea, and Vinayak Prabhu. Assume-guarantee reasoning for hierarchical hybrid systems. In *Hybrid Systems : Computation and Control*, volume 2034 of *Lecture Notes in Computer Science*, pages 275–290. Springer Verlag, 2001.

[5] John E. Hopcroft and Jeffery D. Ullman. *Introduction to Automata Theory, Languages and Computation*. Addison-Wesley Publishing Company, USA, 1979.

[6] Karl Henrik Johansson, Magnus Egersted, John Lygeros, and S. Sastry. On the regularization of hybrid automata. *Systems and Control Letters*, 38:141–150, 1999.

[7] E.A. Lee and A. Sangiovanni-Vincentelli. A framework for comparing models of computation. *IEEE Transactions on Computer Aided Design*, 17(12), December 1998.

[8] Nancy Lynch, Roberto Segala, and Frits Vaandrager. Hybrid I/O automata revisited. In *Hybrid Systems : Computation and Control*, volume 2034 of *Lecture Notes in Computer Science*, pages 403–417. Springer Verlag, 2001.

[9] Z. Manna and A. Pnueli. *Temporal Verification of Reactive Systems: Safety*. Springer Verlag, New York, 1995.

[10] R. Milner. *Communication and Concurrency*. Prentice Hall, 1989.

[11] George J. Pappas, Gerardo Lafferriere, and Shankar Sastry. Hierarchically consistent control systems. *IEEE Transactions on Automatic Control*, 45(6):1144–1160, June 2000.

[12] George J. Pappas and Slobodan Simic. Consistent hierarchies of affine nonlinear systems. *IEEE Transactions on Automatic Control*, 2001. To appear.

[13] Markus Roggenbach and Mila Majster-Cederbaum. Towards a unified view of bisimulation: a comparative study. *Theoretical Computer Science*, (238):81–130, 2000.

[14] J.J.M.M. Rutten. Universal coalgebra: a theory of systems. *Theoretical Computer Science*, 249(1):3–80, 2000.

[15] Paulo Tabuada. *Hierarchies and Compositional Abstractions of Hybrid Systems*. PhD thesis, Instituto Superior Técnico, Lisbon, Portugal, January 2002.

[16] Paulo Tabuada and George J. Pappas. Hybrid abstractions that preserve timed languages. In *Hybrid Systems : Computation and Control*, volume 2034 of *Lecture Notes in Computer Science*, pages 501–514. Springer Verlag, 2001.

[17] Paulo Tabuada, George J. Pappas, and Pedro Lima. Compositional abstractions of hybrid control systems. In *Proceedings of the 40th IEEE Conference on Decision and Control*, December 2001.

[18] A. J. van der Schaft and J. M. Schumacher. Compositionality issues in discrete, continuous, and hybrid systems. *International Journal of Robust and Nonlinear Control*, 11(5):417–434, April 2001.

[19] Glynn Winskel and Mogens Nielsen. Models for concurrency. In Abramsky, Gabbay, and Maibaum, editors, *Handbook of Logic and Foundations of Theoretical Computer Science*, volume 4. Oxford University Press, London, 1994.

A Notation and Mathematical Facts

A relation is a generalization of a function in the sense that it assigns to each element in its domain a *set* of elements in its codomain. Mathematically a relation F between the sets S_1 and S_2 is simply a subset of their Cartesian product, that is $F \subseteq S_1 \times S_2$. Given two relations $F \subseteq S_1 \times S_2$ and $G \subseteq S_2 \times S_3$ we can define their composition to be the relation $G \circ F \subseteq S_1 \times S_3$ defined by $G \circ F = \{(s_1, s_3) \in S_1 \times S_3 \; : \; \exists s_2 \in S_2 \;\; (s_1, s_2) \in F \wedge (s_2, s_3) \in G\}$. Given a relation $F \subseteq S_1 \times S_2$ we call $F^{-1} \subseteq S_2 \times S_1$ given by $F^{-1} = \{(s_2, s_1) \in S_2 \times S_1 \; : \; (s_1, s_2) \in F\}$ the inverse relation. An object that we will use frequently is the set valued map $F : S_1 \rightarrow 2^{S_2}$ induced by a relation F and defined by $F(s_1) = \{s_2 \in S_2 \; : \; (s_1, s_2) \in F\}$.

We also introduce some notation for later use. Given relations $F \subseteq S_1 \times S_2$, $G \subseteq S_3 \times S_4$ and a subset $L \subseteq S_1 \times S_3$ we define the new relations $F \times G$ and $(F \times G)|_L$ as $F \times G = \{((s_1, s_3), (s_2, s_4)) \in (S_1 \times S_3) \times (S_2 \times S_4) \; : \; (s_1, s_2) \in F \wedge (s_3, s_4) \in G\}$ and $(F \times G)|_L = \{((s_1, s_3), (s_2, s_4)) \in F \times G \; : \; (s_1, s_3) \in L\}$.

As explained in Section 2 we will need to work with generalized monoids. We start by recalling the notion of monoid. A monoid is a triple $(\mathcal{M}, \cdot, \varepsilon)$ where $\mathcal{M}$ is a set closed under the associative operation $\cdot : \mathcal{M} \times \mathcal{M} \rightarrow \mathcal{M}$ and ε is a special element of $\mathcal{M}$ called identity. This element satisfies $\varepsilon \cdot m = m \cdot \varepsilon = m$ for any $m \in \mathcal{M}$. We will usually denote $m_1 \cdot m_2$ simply by $m_1 m_2$ and refer to the monoid simply as $\mathcal{M}$. Given two elements m_1 and m_2 from $\mathcal{M}$ we say that

m_1 is a prefix of m_2 iff there exists another $m \in \mathcal{M}$ such that $m_1m = m_2$. We will be specially interested in generalized monoids obtained as follows. Let X be a set and $\mathcal{M}$ a monoid. Then we can regard $X \times \mathcal{M}$ as a set valued function $F : X \longrightarrow 2^{\mathcal{M}}$ which assigns to each $x \in X$ the monoid $F(x) = \mathcal{M}$. However, in general, not all the elements of $\mathcal{M}$ will be available at each point in X so that we need[2] a map $G : X \longrightarrow 2^{\mathcal{M}}$ such that $G(x)$ may be a strict subset of $\mathcal{M}$ with the property that $G(x)$ is prefix closed for every $x \in X$. Such a map will be called a generalized monoid over the set X and we shall denote it by $\mathcal{M}_X$. We will, interchangeably, regard a generalized monoid as a map from X to $2^{\mathcal{M}}$ or as the subset of $X \times \mathcal{M}$ defined by $(x, m) \in \mathcal{M}_X$ iff $m \in \mathcal{M}_X(x)$. A subset $\mathcal{M}_L$ of $\mathcal{M}_X$ which is also a generalized monoid will be called a generalized submonoid.

We now relate generalized monoids through relations. Let $F \subseteq \mathcal{M}_X \times \mathcal{M}_Y$ be a relation between generalized monoids. Then F induces a relation $F_B \subseteq X \times Y$ by $y \in F_B(x)$ iff $(y, m) \in F(x, m')$ for any $(y, m) \in \mathcal{M}_Y$ and $(x, m') \in \mathcal{M}_X$. We then say that the relation F is generalized monoid respecting iff satisfies:

- **Identity:** $y \in F_B(x) \Rightarrow (y, \varepsilon) \in F(x, \varepsilon)$
- **Semi-group:** $(y_1, m_1') \in F(x_1, m_1), (y_2, m_2') \in F(x_2, m_2)$
  and $(x_1, m_1m_1') \in \mathcal{M}_X \Rightarrow (y_1, m_1'm_2') \in F(x_1, m_1m_2)$.

B Proofs

Proof (of Theorem 1). Consider the product system $(\varPhi_Z \times \varPhi_W, \pi_Z, \pi_W)$ and the triple $(\varPhi_X \times \varPhi_Y, F \circ \pi_X, G \circ \pi_Y)$. By definition of product we know that there is one and only one relation ζ such that:

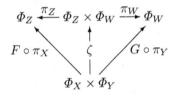

commutes and this relation is given by $\zeta = (F, G) = F \times G$, meaning that $\varPhi_Z \times \varPhi_W$ is a $F \times G$-simulation of $\varPhi_X \times \varPhi_Y$. Consider now the following diagram:

$$(\varPhi_X \times \varPhi_Y)|_{\mathcal{M}_L} \xrightarrow{\zeta \circ i_{\mathcal{M}_L}} \varPhi_Z \times \varPhi_W \underset{h}{\overset{g}{\rightrightarrows}} \varPhi_V$$

where g and h are equal only on the generalized submonoid $\zeta(\mathcal{M}_L)$. It is clear that $g \circ \zeta \circ i_{\mathcal{M}_L} = h \circ \zeta \circ i_{\mathcal{M}_L}$ since $\overline{\mathcal{M}_L} \subseteq \mathcal{M}_L$ implies $\zeta \circ i_{\mathcal{M}_L}(\overline{\mathcal{M}_L}) = \zeta(\overline{\mathcal{M}_L}) \subseteq \zeta(\mathcal{M}_L)$. Therefore, by definition of restriction there exists one and only one simulation relation η from $\varPhi_X \parallel_{\mathcal{M}_L} \varPhi_Y$ to $\varPhi_Z \parallel_{\zeta(\mathcal{M}_L)} \varPhi_W$ which is given by $\eta = \zeta \circ i_{\mathcal{M}_L} = (F \times G) \circ i_{\mathcal{M}_L} = (F \times G)|_{\overline{\mathcal{M}_L}}$. $\square$

---

[2] In general, a generalized monoid over a set X can be seen as a small category with elements of X as objects.

Proof (of Theorem 2). We now prove Theorem 2 through a series of results. We start by showing that product respects bisimulations:

Lemma 1. *Given abstract control systems Φ_X, Φ_Z (a F-bisimulation of Φ_X), Φ_Y and Φ_W (a G-bisimulation of Φ_Y) the product abstract control system $\Phi_Z \times \Phi_W$ is a $F \times G$-bisimulation of $\Phi_X \times \Phi_Y$.*

Proof. Consider the following commutative diagrams:

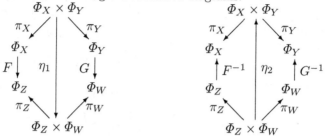

By definition of product there exists one and only one relation η_1 and one and only one relation η_2 such that the diagrams commute. In fact, η_1 is the relation $\eta_1 = (F \circ \pi_X, G \circ \pi_Y) = F \times G$ and $\eta_2 = (F^{-1} \circ \pi_Z, G^{-1} \circ \pi_W) = (F \times G)^{-1}$ meaning that $\Phi_X \times \Phi_Y$ is $F \times G$-bisimilar to $\Phi_Z \times \Phi_W$. $\square$

Under the proper assumptions the operation of restriction is also compatible with bisimulations:

Proposition 1. *Let Φ_X be an abstract control system, Φ_Y a F-bisimulation of Φ_X and $\mathcal{M}_L$ a generalized submonoid of $\mathcal{M}_X$ such that $F^{-1}|_{\overline{F(\mathcal{M}_L)}} = (F|_{\overline{\mathcal{M}_L}})^{-1}$. The restriction $\Phi_X|_{\mathcal{M}_L}$ is a $F|_{\mathcal{M}_L}$-bisimulation of $\Phi_Y|_{F(\mathcal{M}_L)}$.*

Proof. A similar argument to the proof of Proposition 1 shows that Φ_Y is a $F|_{\overline{\mathcal{M}_L}}$-simulation of Φ_X so that we will only show that Φ_X is a $F|_{\overline{\mathcal{M}_L}}^{-1}$-simulation of Φ_Y. Consider the following diagram:

$$
\begin{array}{c}
\Phi_Y|_{F(\mathcal{M}_L)} \\
\qquad \searrow {\scriptstyle F^{-1} \circ i_{F(\mathcal{M}_L)}} \\
\Phi_X|_{\mathcal{M}_L} \xrightarrow[i_{\mathcal{M}_L}]{} \Phi_X \underset{h}{\overset{g}{\rightrightarrows}} \Phi_V
\end{array}
\qquad (14)
$$

where g and h are equal only on the generalized submonoid $\mathcal{M}_L$. We will show that (14) commutes by proving the only nontrivial equality, $g \circ F^{-1} \circ i_{F(\mathcal{M}_L)} = h \circ F^{-1} \circ i_{F(\mathcal{M}_L)}$. Recall that the equality $F^{-1}|_{\overline{F(\mathcal{M}_L)}} = F|_{\overline{\mathcal{M}_L}}^{-1}$ implies that the domains of the relations are the same, that is $\overline{F(\mathcal{M}_L)} = F(\overline{\mathcal{M}_L})$. This allows to conclude that:

$$
\begin{aligned}
F^{-1} \circ i_{F(\mathcal{M}_L)}(\overline{F(\mathcal{M}_L)}) &= F^{-1}|_{\overline{F(\mathcal{M}_L)}} \circ F(\overline{\mathcal{M}_L}) \\
&= F|_{\overline{\mathcal{M}_L}}^{-1} \circ F|_{\overline{\mathcal{M}_L}}(\mathcal{M}_L) = \overline{\mathcal{M}_L} \subseteq \mathcal{M}_L
\end{aligned}
$$

Since (14) commutes we can invoke the definition of restriction to ensure the existence of a unique simulation relation from $\Phi_Y|_{F(\mathcal{M}_L)}$ to $\Phi_X|_{\mathcal{M}_L}$ which is given by $\eta = F^{-1} \circ i_{F(\mathcal{M}_L)} = F^{-1}|_{\overline{F(\mathcal{M}_L)}} = F|_{\overline{\mathcal{M}_L}}^{-1}$ thereby showing bisimilarity. □

The condition of the previous result is in fact also a necessary one as we now show:

Proposition 2. *Let Φ_X be an abstract control system, Φ_Y a F-bisimulation of Φ_X and $\mathcal{M}_L$ a generalized submonoid of $\mathcal{M}_X$. If the restriction $\Phi_X|_{\mathcal{M}_L}$ is a $F|_{\mathcal{M}_L}$-bisimulation of $\Phi_Y|_{F(\mathcal{M}_L)}$ then $F^{-1}|_{\overline{F(\mathcal{M}_L)}} = (F|_{\overline{\mathcal{M}_L}})^{-1}$.*

Proof. The following commutative diagram is a consequence of bisimilarity:

$$
\begin{array}{ccc}
\Phi_Y|_{F(\mathcal{M}_L)} & \xrightarrow{\ i_{F(\mathcal{M}_L)}\ } & \Phi_Y \\
{\scriptstyle F|_{\mathcal{M}_L}^{-1}}\downarrow & & \downarrow{\scriptstyle F^{-1}} \\
\Phi_X|_{\mathcal{M}_L} & \xrightarrow{\ i_{\mathcal{M}_L}\ } & \Phi_X
\end{array}
\tag{15}
$$

from which we get the following equality:

$$
i_{\mathcal{M}_L} \circ F|_{\mathcal{M}_L}^{-1} = F^{-1} \circ i_{F(\mathcal{M}_L)}
\tag{16}
$$

from which follows the desired equality $F|_{\mathcal{M}_L}^{-1} = F^{-1}|_{\overline{F(\mathcal{M}_L)}}$. □

Theorem 2 is just a restatement of Lemma 1 and Propositions 1 and 2 and is therefore proved. □

Optimal Control of Hysteresis in Smart Actuators: A Viscosity Solutions Approach

Xiaobo Tan and John S. Baras

Department of Electrical and Computer Engineering and
Institute for Systems Research
University of Maryland, College Park, MD 20742
{xbtan, baras}@isr.umd.edu

Abstract. Hysteresis in smart materials hinders their wider applicability in actuators. The low dimensional hysteresis models for these materials are hybrid systems with both controlled switching and autonomous switching. In particular, they belong to the class of Duhem hysteresis models and can be formulated as systems with both continuous and switching controls. In this paper, we study the control methodology for smart actuators through the example of controlling a commercially available magnetostrictive actuator. For illustrative purposes, an infinite horizon optimal control problem is considered. We show that the value function satisfies a Hamilton-Jacobi-Bellman equation (HJB) of a hybrid form in the viscosity sense. We further prove uniqueness of the viscosity solution to the (HJB), and provide a numerical scheme to approximate the solution together with a sub-optimal controller synthesis method. Numerical and experimental results based on this approach are presented.

1   Introduction

Materials with the intrinsic characteristics of built-in sensors, actuators, and control mechanism in their microstructures, are called *smart materials*. Smart materials and smart structures have been receiving tremendous interest in the past decade, due to their broad applications in areas of aerospace, manufacturing, defense, and civil infrastructure systems, to name a few. Hysteresis in smart materials, e.g., magnetostrictives, piezoceramics, and shape memory alloys (SMAs), hinders the wider applicability of such materials in actuators. Hysteresis models can be classified into phenomenological models and physics-based models. The most popular phenomenological hysteresis model used in control of smart actuators has been the Preisach model, see e.g., [1, 2, 3]. An example of physics-based model is the Jiles-Atherton model for ferromagnetic hysteresis [4], where hysteresis is considered to arise from pinning of domain walls on defect sites.

This paper is aimed at exploring the control methodology for smart actuators exhibiting hysteresis. We illustrate the ideas through the example of controlling a commercially available magnetostrictive actuator. Magnetostriction is

C.J. Tomlin and M.R. Greenstreet (Eds.): HSCC 2002, LNCS 2289, pp. 451–464, 2002.

the phenomenon of strong coupling between magnetic properties and mechanical properties of some ferromagnetic materials (e.g., Terfenol-D): strains are generated in response to an applied magnetic field, while conversely, mechanical stresses in the materials produce measurable changes in magnetization. This phenomenon can be used for actuation and sensing. Magnetostrictive actuators have applications in micro-positioning, robotics, ultrasonics and vibration control. Figure 1 shows a sectional view of a Terfenol-D actuator manufactured by Etrema Products, Inc. By varying the current in the coil, we vary the magnetic field in the Terfenol-D rod and thus control the motion of the rod head (or the force if the motion is blocked). Figure 2 displays the hysteresis observed in the magnetostrictive actuator.

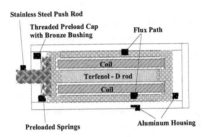

Fig. 1. A Terfenol-D actuator [5](Original source: Etrema Products Inc.)

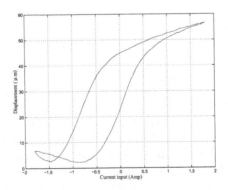

Fig. 2. Hysteresis in the magnetostrictive actuator

When the frequency of the current input I is low, the magnetostriction can be related to the bulk magnetization M along the rod direction through a square law, thus control of the rod head boils down to control of M. We will employ a low dimensional model [6] to represent the ferromagnetic hysteresis between M and the applied magnetic field H, where H is proportional to I in the low frequency case. The model is a hybrid system with both controlled switching and autonomous switching. It belongs to the class of Duhem hysteresis models and can be rewritten as a system involving both continuous control and switching control. Note that a low dimensional model for ferroelectric hysteresis has been proposed by Smith and Hom [7]. Their model has the same structure as that of the ferromagnetic hysteresis model we use in this paper. Therefore the approach we present in this paper will be fully applicable to control of smart actuators made of ferroelectric materials, e.g., piezoelectrics and electrostrictives.

Witsenhausen formulated a class of hybrid-state continuous-time dynamical systems and studied an optimal control problem back in 1966 [8]. The Pontryagin Maximum Principle or its variant was used in optimal control for hybrid systems in [9, 10]. By solving the Bellman inequality, a lower bound on the value function and an approximation to the optimal control law were obtained in [11, 12]. Yong studied the optimal control problem for a system with continuous, switching and impulse controls in [13]. With a unified model for hybrid control, Branicky, Borkar and Mitter proposed a generalized quasi-variational inequalities (GQVI) satisfied by the value function [14]. In this paper, we study optimal control of smart actuators using a viscosity solutions approach.

Dynamic programming is one of the most important approaches in optimal control. When the value function of the control problem is smooth, we can derive the Hamilton-Jacobi-Bellman equation (HJB) from the Dynamic Programming Principle (DPP), and in many cases, solving the (HJB) amounts to solving the optimal control problem. The value function however, in general, is not smooth even for smooth systems, not to mention for a hybrid system, like that in our model. Crandall and Lions [15] introduced the notion of viscosity solutions to Hamilton-Jacobi equations. This turned out to be a very useful concept for optimal control since value functions of many optimal control problems do satisfy the (HJB) in the viscosity sense; and under mild assumptions, uniqueness results for viscosity solutions hold [16]. We will explore this approach for control of smart actuators. This paper provides some flavors of this methodology by considering an infinite horizon control problem.

The paper is organized as follows. In Sect. 2, we present the hysteresis model and examine its properties. In Sect. 3, we formulate an optimal control problem based on the hysteresis model, and show that the value function satisfies a hybrid Hamilton-Jacobi-Bellman equation (HJB) in the viscosity sense. In Sect. 4, We prove that the (HJB) admits a unique solution in the class of functions to which the value function belongs. We describe the numerical scheme to solve the (HJB) in Sect. 5. This establishes the existence of a solution to the (HJB) as well as provides a method for synthesizing a sub-optimal controller. Numerical and experimental results are also reported in Sect. 5. Finally, conclusions and discussions are provided in Sect. 6.

Only key proofs are provided in this paper due to the space limitation. Other proofs can be found in [17].

2   The Bulk Ferromagnetic Hysteresis Model

Jiles and Atherton proposed a low dimensional model for ferromagnetic hysteresis, based upon the quantification of energy losses due to domain wall intersections with inclusions or pinning sites within the material [4]. A modification to the Jiles-Atherton model was made by Venkataraman and Krishnaprasad with rigorous use of the energy balancing principle [6]. The resulting model, named the *bulk ferromagnetic hysteresis model,* has a slightly different form from the Jiles-Atherton model. Also based on the energy balancing principle, they derived a bulk magnetostrictive hysteresis model [18], where high frequency effects are considered. At low frequencies, the magnetostriction can be related to the bulk magnetization through a square law [5], thus control of the bulk magnetization amounts to control of the magnetostriction. In this paper, we will restrict ourselves to the low frequency case to highlight the methodology of hysteresis control. Extension to the high frequency case is straightforward. We now briefly outline the bulk ferromagnetic hysteresis model.

For an external magnetic field H and a bulk magnetization M, we define $H_e = H + \alpha M$ to be the effective field, where α is a mean field parameter representing inter-domain coupling. Through thermodynamic considerations, the *anhysteretic magnetization* M_{an} can be expressed as

$$M_{an}(H_e) = M_s(\coth(\frac{H_e}{a}) - \frac{a}{H_e}) = M_s\mathcal{L}(z) \ , \tag{1}$$

where $\mathcal{L}(\cdot)$ is the Langevin function, $\mathcal{L}(z) = \coth(z) - \frac{1}{z}$, with $z = \frac{H_e}{a}$, M_s is the saturation magnetization of the material and a is a parameter characterizing the shape of M_{an} curve.

Define

$$f_1(H, M) = c\frac{M_s\frac{\partial \mathcal{L}(z)}{\partial z}}{a - \alpha c M_s\frac{\partial \mathcal{L}(z)}{\partial z}} \ ,$$

$$f_2(H, M) = \frac{ckM_s\frac{\partial \mathcal{L}(z)}{\partial z} - \mu_0 a(M_{an}(H_e) - M)}{k(a - \alpha c M_s\frac{\partial \mathcal{L}(z)}{\partial z}) + \mu_0 \alpha a(M_{an}(H_e) - M)} \ ,$$

$$f_3(H, M) = \frac{ckM_s\frac{\partial \mathcal{L}(z)}{\partial z} + \mu_0 a(M_{an}(H_e) - M)}{k(a - \alpha c M_s\frac{\partial \mathcal{L}(z)}{\partial z}) - \mu_0 \alpha a(M_{an}(H_e) - M)} \ ,$$

where c is the reversibility constant, μ_0 is the permeability of vacuum, k is a measure for the average energy required to break a pinning site. Note each f_i is smooth in H and M.

The bulk ferromagnetic hysteresis model is as follows [6]:

$$\frac{dM}{dH} = f_i(H, M), \text{ where } i = \begin{cases} 1, dH < 0, \ M < M_{an}(H_e) \text{ or} \\ \quad dH \geq 0, \ M \geq M_{an}(H_e) \\ 2, dH < 0, \ M \geq M_{an}(H_e) \\ 3, dH \geq 0, \ M < M_{an}(H_e) \end{cases} .$$

If we define a control $u = \dot{H}$, the model is rewritten as

$$\begin{pmatrix} \dot{H} \\ \dot{M} \end{pmatrix} = \begin{pmatrix} 1 \\ f_i(H, M) \end{pmatrix} u, \quad \text{where } i = \begin{cases} 1, \ u < 0, \ M < M_{\text{an}}(H_\text{e}) \text{ or} \\ \quad u \geq 0, \ M \geq M_{\text{an}}(H_\text{e}) \\ 2, \ u < 0, \ M \geq M_{\text{an}}(H_\text{e}) \\ 3, \ u \geq 0, \ M < M_{\text{an}}(H_\text{e}) \end{cases} \qquad (2)$$

Remarks:

- Note that the control u defined above is different from the physical current I we apply to the actuator. The current I is related to the state component H by a constant c_0 (the *coil factor*): $H = c_0 I$. Therefore from the control u, the current we will apply is $I(t) = I(0) + \frac{1}{c_0} \int_0^t u(s)ds$.
- The switching depends on both (the sign of) the continuous control u and the state (H, M), therefore the model (2) is a hybrid system with both controlled switching and autonomous switching [14, 19].

We can represent model (2) in a more compact way. Letting

$$\Omega_1 = \{(H, M) : M < M_{\text{an}}(H_\text{e})\}, \quad \Omega_2 = \{(H, M) : M \geq M_{\text{an}}(H_\text{e})\},$$

and $x = (H, M)$, we define

$$f_+(x) = \begin{cases} \begin{pmatrix} 1 \\ f_1(x) \end{pmatrix} & \text{if } x \in \Omega_2 \\ \begin{pmatrix} 1 \\ f_3(x) \end{pmatrix} & \text{if } x \in \Omega_1 \end{cases}, \quad \text{and } f_-(x) = \begin{cases} \begin{pmatrix} 1 \\ f_1(x) \end{pmatrix} & \text{if } x \in \Omega_1 \\ \begin{pmatrix} 1 \\ f_2(x) \end{pmatrix} & \text{if } x \in \Omega_2 \end{cases}.$$

Since $f_i, 1 \leq i \leq 3$, coincide on $\{(H, M) : M = M_{\text{an}}(H_\text{e})\}$, f_+ and f_- are continuous. We define two continuous control sets

$$U_+ = \{u : u_\text{c} \geq u \geq 0\}, \quad U_- = \{u : -u_\text{c} \leq u \leq 0\},$$

where $u_\text{c} > 0$ represents the operating bandwidth constraint of the actuator (recall $u = c_0 \dot{I}$). To ease the presentation, we make the dependence of switching on u explicit by introducing a discrete control set $D = \{1, 2\}$.

Now the model (2) can be represented as a system with both a continuous control u and a discrete mode (switching) control d:

$$\dot{x} = f(x, u, d) \triangleq \begin{cases} f_+(x)u, & u \in U_+, \ \text{if} \ \ d = 1 \\ f_-(x)u, & u \in U_-, \ \text{if} \ \ d = 2 \end{cases}. \qquad (3)$$

The (state-dependent) autonomous switching has now been incorporated into the definitions of f_+, f_-, thanks to the nice structure of the physical model. Note the model (3) belongs to the category of *Duhem* hysteresis model [20].

We can prove that the model enjoys the following properties:

Proposition 1 (Boundedness of f_i). *If the parameters satisfy:*

$$T_1 \stackrel{\triangle}{=} a - \frac{\alpha c M_{\mathrm{s}}}{3} > 0 \ , \tag{4}$$

$$T_2 \stackrel{\triangle}{=} k(a - \frac{\alpha c M_{\mathrm{s}}}{3}) - 2\mu_0 \alpha a M_{\mathrm{s}} > 0 \ , \tag{5}$$

then $0 < f_i \le C_{\mathrm{f}}, i = 1, 2, 3,$ *for some constant* $C_{\mathrm{f}} > 0.$

Proof. See [17]. □

Remark : Conditions (4) and (5) are satisfied for typical parameters. For example, taking the parameters identified in [5], $\alpha = 1.9 \times 10^{-4}$, $a = 190$, $k = 48$ Gauss, $c = 0.3$, $M_s = 9.89 \times 10^3$ Gauss and $\mu_0 = 1$, we calculate $T_1 = 189.8$, $T_2 = 8.40 \times 10^3$.

Proposition 2 (Lipshitz Continuity). *Functions $f_+(x)$ and $f_-(x)$ are Lipshitz continuous with some Lipshitz constant L, and $f(x, u, d)$ is Lipshitz continuous with respect to x with Lipshitz constant $L_0 = Lu_c$.*

Proof. See [17]. □

3   Optimal Control: The (HJB) and Viscosity Solutions

We first formulate an infinite horizon optimal control problem for the system (3). Define the cost functional with an initial condition x and a control pair $\alpha(\cdot) = \{d(\cdot), u(\cdot)\}$ as

$$J(x, \alpha(\cdot)) = \int_0^\infty l(x(t), u(t)) e^{-\lambda t} dt \ , \tag{6}$$

where the *discount factor* $\lambda \ge 0$. Note the *running cost* $l(\cdot, \cdot)$ is defined to be independent of the switching control d, since this makes sense in the context of smart actuator control. We require $u(\cdot)$ to be measurable. This together with Proposition 2 guarantees that (3) has a unique solution $x(\cdot)$(the dependence of $x(\cdot)$ on x and $\alpha(\cdot)$ is suppressed when no confusion arises).

The optimal control problem is to find the value function

$$V(x) = \inf_{\alpha(\cdot)} J(x, \alpha(\cdot)) \ ,$$

and if $V(x)$ is achievable, find the optimal control $\alpha^*(\cdot)$.

We make the following assumptions about $l(\cdot, \cdot)$:

- (A_1): $l(x, u)$ continuous in x and u, $l(x, u) \ge 0$, $\forall x, u$;
- (A_2): $|l(x_1, u) - l(x_2, u)| \le C_1(1 + |x_1| + |x_2|)|x_1 - x_2|$, $\forall u$, for some $C_1 > 0$.

Note (A_2) includes the case of quadratic cost.

We can show the value function is locally bounded and locally Lipshitz continuous.

Proposition 3 (Local Boundedness). *Under assumptions (A_1) and (A_2), $\forall \lambda > 0$, $V(x)$ is locally bounded, i.e., $\forall R \geq 0, \exists\, C_R \geq 0$, such that $|V(x)| \leq C_R$, $\forall x \in \overline{B}(0, R) \triangleq \{x : |x| \leq R\}$.*

Proof. See [17]. □

Proposition 4 (Local Lipshitz Continuity). *Under assumptions (A_1) and (A_2), $\forall \lambda > 2L_0$ with L_0 as defined in Proposition 2, $V(x)$ is locally Lipshitz, i.e., $\forall R \geq 0, \exists\, L_R \geq 0$, such that $|V(x_1) - V(x_2)| \leq L_R |x_1 - x_2|$, $\forall x_1, x_2 \in \overline{B}(0, R)$. In addition, L_R can be chosen to be $C(1 + R)$ for some $C > 0$.*

Proof. See [17]. □

Remarks: The proof of Proposition 4 uses the bounds for $|x_1(t) - x_2(t)|$ and $|x_1(t)|$, where $x_1(\cdot), x_2(\cdot)$ are two trajectories starting from x_1 and x_2. The bounds are obtained using Proposition 2 and the Gronwall inequality. One can get a sharper estimate for $|x_1(t)|$ (linear growth) by exploiting Proposition 1. This can be used to weaken the condition $\lambda > 2L_0$ to $\lambda > L_0$ in Proposition 4 and anywhere else it appears.

The value function satisfies the Dynamic Programming Principle (DPP) :

Proposition 5 (DPP). *Assume (A_1) and (A_2), $\lambda > 0$. We have*

$$V(x) = \inf_{\alpha(\cdot)} \{ \int_0^t e^{-\lambda s} l(x(s), u(s)) ds + e^{-\lambda t} V(x(t)) \}, \ \forall t \geq 0, \ \forall x \ . \tag{7}$$

Proof. The argument is standard, see [17]. □

Based on the (DPP), we can show that the value function $V(\cdot)$ satisfies a Hamilton-Jacobi-Bellman equation (HJB) of a hybrid type in the viscosity sense. Viscosity solutions to Hamilton-Jacobi equations were first introduced by Crandall and Lions [15]. Here we use one of the three equivalent definitions [21]:

Definition 1 (Viscosity Solution). *Let W be a continuous function from an open set $O \in \mathbb{R}^n$ into $\mathbb{R}$ and let DW denote the gradient of W (when W is differentiable). We call W a viscosity solution to a nonlinear first order partial differential equation $F(x, W(x), DW(x)) = 0$, provided it is both a viscosity subsolution and viscosity supersolution; and by viscosity sub(super)solution, we mean: $\forall \phi \in C^1(O)$, if $W - \phi$ attains a local maximum (minimum) at $x_0 \in O$, then $F(x_0, W(x_0), D\phi(x_0)) \leq (\geq) 0$.*

Theorem 1 (HJB). *Assume (A_1) and (A_2), $\lambda > 2L_0$. $V(x)$ is a viscosity solution of:*

$$\lambda W(x) + \max\{ \ \max_{u \in U_+}\{-u f_+(x) \cdot DW(x) - l(x, u)\},$$

$$\max_{u \in U_-}\{-u f_-(x) \cdot DW(x) - l(x, u)\}\} = 0 \ . \tag{8}$$

Proof. See [17]. □

4 Uniqueness of the Solution to the (HJB)

We would like to characterize the value function V as a unique solution to the (HJB). The uniqueness result basically follows from Theorem 1.5 in [22]. In [22], the author gave only a sketch of proof. For completeness, we will provide the full proof here.

Before stating the theorem, we first identify structural properties of the (HJB). We rewrite (8) as:

$$\lambda W(x) + H(x, DW(x)) = 0 \ , \qquad (9)$$

where

$$H(x, p) = \max\{\max_{u \in U_+}\{-uf_+(x) \cdot p - l(x, u)\}, \max_{u \in U_-}\{-uf_-(x) \cdot p - l(x, u)\}\} \ .$$

Proposition 6. *Assume (A_2). $H(x, p)$ satisfies the following:*

$$|H(x_1, p) - H(x_2, p)| \le C_R(1 + |p|)|x_1 - x_2|, \ \forall x_1, x_2 \in \overline{B}(0, R), \ \forall p \ , \quad (10)$$
$$|H(x, p_1) - H(x, p_2)| \le C_0|p_1 - p_2|, \forall x, \ \forall p_1, p_2 \ , \qquad (11)$$

for some $C_R > 0, C_0 > 0$, with C_R dependent on R.

Proof. We will only prove (10), since proof of (11) is analogous.

Without loss of generality, suppose $u_1 \in U_-$ attains the maximum in $H(x_1, p)$. Since $H(x_2, p) \ge -u_1 f_-(x_2) \cdot p - l(x_2, u_1)$,

$$\begin{aligned}
H(x_1, p) - H(x_2, p) &\le -u_1 f_-(x_1) \cdot p - l(x_1, u_1) + u_1 f_-(x_2) \cdot p + l(x_2, u_1) \\
&\le |p|L_0|x_1 - x_2| + C_1(1 + |x_1| + |x_2|)|x_1 - x_2| \\
&\le C_R(1 + |p|)|x_1 - x_2| \ ,
\end{aligned}$$

where C_R is a constant dependent on R. By symmetry, we conclude. $\qquad\square$

Remarks: As we have seen above, despite the hybrid structure of our physical model, $H(x, p)$ enjoys nice structural properties, which enables us to prove the uniqueness result.

From Proposition 4, we know that the value function $V(\cdot)$ belongs to the class

$$\mathcal{P}(\mathbb{R}^2) = \{W(\cdot): \ |W(x_1) - W(x_2)| \le C(1 + R)|x_1 - x_2|, \forall x_1, x_2 \in \overline{B}(0, R),$$
$$\text{for some } C > 0\}.$$

The following theorem is adapted from Theorem 1.5 in [22].

Theorem 2. *If (9) has a viscosity solution in $\mathcal{P}(\mathbb{R}^2)$, it is unique.*

Proof. Without loss of generality, we take $\lambda = 1$. Let $W(\cdot), V(\cdot) \in \mathcal{P}(\mathbb{R}^2)$ be viscosity solutions to (9). For $\epsilon > 0, \alpha > 0, m > 2$, define

$$\Phi(x,y) = W(x) - V(y) - \frac{|x - y|^2}{\epsilon} - \alpha(<x>^m + <y>^m) \; ,$$

with $<x> \overset{\triangle}{=} \sqrt{1 + |x|^2}$. Since $W(\cdot), V(\cdot) \in \mathcal{P}(\mathbb{R}^2)$, $\lim_{|x|+|y|\to\infty} \Phi(x,y) = -\infty$. By continuity of $\Phi(\cdot,\cdot)$, there exists (x_0, y_0) where Φ attains the global maximum. First we want to obtain bounds for $|x_0|, |y_0|$ and $|x_0 - y_0|$.

From $\Phi(0,0) \leq \Phi(x_0, y_0)$, and $W(\cdot), V(\cdot) \in \mathcal{P}(\mathbb{R}^2)$, we can get

$$<x_0>^m + <y_0>^m \leq C_\alpha(1 + <x_0>^2 + <y_0>^2) \; ,$$

where C_α is a constant independent of ϵ (but dependent on α). Since $m > 2$, there exists $R_\alpha > 0$ (independent of ϵ), such that $|x_0| \leq R_\alpha, |y_0| \leq R_\alpha$.

From $\Phi(x_0, x_0) + \Phi(y_0, y_0) \leq 2\,\Phi(x_0, y_0)$, we can derive

$$|x_0 - y_0| \leq \epsilon C'_\alpha \; , \tag{12}$$

with C'_α depending on α only.

Define

$$\phi(x) = V(y_0) + \frac{1}{\epsilon}|x - y_0|^2 + \alpha(<x>^m + <y_0>^m) \; ,$$

$$\psi(y) = W(x_0) - \frac{1}{\epsilon}|x_0 - y|^2 - \alpha(<x_0>^m + <y>^m) \; .$$

Since $W - \phi$ achieves maximum at x_0, and $V - \psi$ achieves minimum at y_0,

$$W(x_0) + H(x_0, D\phi(x_0)) \leq 0 \; , \tag{13}$$

$$V(y_0) + H(y_0, D\psi(y_0)) \geq 0 \; . \tag{14}$$

Subtracting (14) from (13) and using Proposition 6, we have

$$W(x_0) - V(y_0) \leq C_{R_\alpha}(1 + \frac{2}{\epsilon}|x_0 - y_0|)|x_0 - y_0|$$

$$+ \alpha C_0 m(<x_0>^{m-1} + <y_0>^{m-1}) \; .$$

Now fix α, construct a sequence $\{\epsilon_k\}$ with $\lim_{k\to\infty} \epsilon_k = 0$. We denote the corresponding maximizers of Φ as (x_{0k}, y_{0k}). Since $\forall k, (x_{0k}, y_{0k}) \in \overline{B}(0, R_\alpha)$, by extracting a subsequence if necessary, we get

$$\lim_{k\to\infty}(x_{0k}, y_{0k}) \to (x_\alpha, y_\alpha) \in \overline{B}(0, R_\alpha) \; . \tag{15}$$

From (12), we have $x_\alpha = y_\alpha$. For each ϵ_k, from $\Phi(x,x) \leq \Phi(x_{0k}, y_{0k})$, we can get

$$W(x) - V(x) - 2\alpha <x>^m \leq C_{R_\alpha}(1 + \frac{2}{\epsilon_k}|x_{0k} - y_{0k}|)|x_{0k} - y_{0k}|$$

$$+ \alpha C_0 m(<x_{0k}>^{m-1} + <y_{0k}>^{m-1}) - \alpha(<x_{0k}>^m + <y_{0k}>^m) \; ,$$

and letting $k \to \infty$,

$$W(x) - V(x) \le 2\alpha(C_0 m < x_\alpha >^{m-1} - < x_\alpha >^m) + 2\alpha < x >^m \quad.$$

Since $C_0 m < x_\alpha >^{m-1} - < x_\alpha >^m \le C''$ for some $C'' > 0$,

$$W(x) - V(x) \le 2\alpha(C'' + < x >^m) \quad.$$

Letting $\alpha \to 0$, we get $W(x) - V(x) \le 0$, $\forall x$. We conclude by noting W and V are symmetric. $\qquad \square$

From Theorem 2, if we can solve for a solution to (9) in $\mathcal{P}(\mathbb{R}^2)$, it must be the value function. One way to solve it is by discrete-time approximation.

5   The Discrete Approximation Scheme

The approximation will be accomplished in two steps. First we approximate the continuous time optimal control problem by a discrete time problem, derive the hybrid discrete Bellman equation (DBE), and show the value function of the discrete time problem converges to that of the continuous time problem locally uniformly. Following [16], we call this step "semi-discrete" approximation. Then we indicate how to further discretize (DBE) in the spatial variable, which is called "fully-discrete" approximation. The approaches we take here follow closely those in [16](Chapter VI and Appendix A).

Consider a discrete time problem obtained by discretizing the original continuous time one with time step $h \in (0, \frac{1}{\lambda})$. The dynamics is given by

$$x[n] = x[n-1] + hf(x[n-1], u[n-1], d[n-1]), \ x[0] = x \ , \tag{16}$$

and the cost is given by

$$J_h(x, \alpha[\cdot]) = \sum_{n=0}^{\infty} hl(x[n], u[n])(1 - \lambda h)^n \ , \tag{17}$$

where $\alpha[\cdot] = \{d[\cdot], u[\cdot]\}$ is the control. The value function is defined to be

$$V_h(x) = \inf_{\alpha[\cdot]} J_h(x, \alpha[\cdot]) \ . \tag{18}$$

It's not hard to show:

Proposition 7. *Assume A_1 and A_2, $\lambda > 2L_0$. Then $V_h(\cdot) \in \mathcal{P}(\mathbb{R}^2)$, and the coefficient C in defining $\mathcal{P}(\mathbb{R}^2)$ can be made independent of h.*

Following standard arguments, one can show:

Proposition 8 (DBE). *$V_h(\cdot)$ satisfies:*

$$V_h(x) = \min\{\min_{u \in U_+} \{(1 - \lambda h)V_h(x + huf_+(x)) + hl(x, u)\},$$
$$\min_{u \in U_-} \{(1 - \lambda h)V_h(x + huf_-(x)) + hl(x, u)\}\} \ . \tag{19}$$

It's of interest to know whether (19) characterizes the value function $V_h(x)$. Unlike in [16](Chapter VI), where a bounded value function was considered, we have V_h unbounded. But it turns out that with a little bit additional assumption, (19) has a unique solution.

Proposition 9. *There exists a unique solution in $\mathcal{P}(\mathbb{R}^2)$ to (19), if*

$$\frac{(1 - \lambda h)(\sqrt{C_0^2 + 4} + C_0)}{\sqrt{C_0^2 + 4} - C_0} < 1 \ , \tag{20}$$

where $C_0 = h u_c \left| \dfrac{1}{C_f} \right|$ and C_f is as defined in Proposition 1.

Proof. Let $\widetilde{V}_h(x) = V_h(x) < x >^{-m}, m > 2$, where $< x >\overset{\triangle}{=} \sqrt{1 + |x|^2}$. Since $V_h \in \mathcal{P}(\mathbb{R}^2)$, $\widetilde{V}_h$ is bounded. In terms of $\widetilde{V}_h$, (19) is rewritten as

$$\widetilde{V}_h(x) = (\mathcal{G}(\widetilde{V}_h))(x) \overset{\triangle}{=} \min\{ \tag{21}$$

$$\min_{u \in U_+} \{(1 - \lambda h)\widetilde{V}_h(x + h u f_+(x)) \frac{< x + h u f_+(x) >^m}{< x >^m} + h l(x, u) < x >^{-m}\},$$

$$\min_{u \in U_-} \{(1 - \lambda h))\widetilde{V}_h(x + h u f_-(x)) \frac{< x + h u f_-(x) >^m}{< x >^m} + h l(x, u) < x >^{-m}\}\} \ .$$

It suffices to show (21) has a unique solution. It's clear that the operator $\mathcal{G}(\cdot)$ maps any $\widetilde{W} \in BC(\mathbb{R}^2)$ into $BC(\mathbb{R}^2)$, where $BC(\mathbb{R}^2)$ denotes the set of bounded continuous functions. When (20) is satisfied, one can show that $\mathcal{G}(\cdot)$ is a contraction mapping. Hence we conclude using the Contraction Mapping Principle. □

The following theorem asserts that $V_h(\cdot)$ converges to $V(\cdot)$ as $h \to 0$. The proof can be found in [16](Chapter VI)(with minor modification).

Theorem 3. *Assume A_1 and A_2, $\lambda > 2L_0$, and (20). Then*

$$\sup_{x \in \mathcal{K}} |V_h(x) - V(x)| \to 0 \ as \ h \to 0, \tag{22}$$

for every compact $\mathcal{K} \subset \mathbb{R}^2$.

It was also shown in [16] that one can obtain a sub-optimal control for the continuous time problem when solving the (DBE). Theoretically the solution to (19) can be obtained by successive approximation. A practical approximation scheme for solving the (DBE) is described in [16](Appendix A, by Falcone), which we have followed in the numerical simulation. It was shown there that when space discretization gets finer and finer, the solution obtained via solving a finite system of equations converges to $V_h(\cdot)$.

Computation can only be done in a bounded domain. The domain we used in simulation is of the form $\overline{\Omega} = \{(H, M) : H_{\min} \le H \le H_{\max}, |M| \le M_s\}$. The constraint $|M| \le M_s$ arises from the physics, while the constraint on H is due to limitation on the range of current input. The value function of an optimal control problem with state-space constraints is a *constrained* viscosity solution to the (HJB) in $\overline{\Omega}$ [23], namely, a solution in the interior of $\overline{\Omega}$ and a supersolution in $\overline{\Omega}$. Theoretical results for the constrained state-space case are omitted in this paper.

The values we used for the model parameters are as those in the remarks following Proposition 1. The running cost was defined as $l(H, M, u) = 100(H - H_0)^2 + 0.1M^2 + 0.01u^2$, where H_0 corresponds to some desired steady current input. Other parameters: $H_{\min} = 19.8$, $H_{\max} = 407.8$, $H_0 = 213.8$, $\lambda = 1.58 \times 10^3$, $h = 5 \times 10^{-4}$, $u_c = 1.22 \times 10^3$. Each of U_+ and U_- is discretized into 20 levels, while each dimension of the state space is discretized into 40 levels.

Figure 3 shows the value function and the optimal feedback control map. Optimal trajectories obtained through simulation and experiments from three different initial conditions (A, B, C) are shown in Fig. 4, where the arrows indicate directions of evolution as well as stationary points of the closed-loop systems. Figure 5 shows the experimental setup.

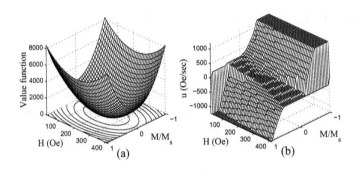

Fig. 3. (a) Value function and its level curves   (b) Optimal feedback control map

6   Conclusions and Discussions

In this paper, we have studied the viscosity solutions approach for optimal control of a smart actuator based on the low dimensional hysteresis model. We took the infinite horizon optimal control problem as an example and characterized the value function as the (unique) solution of a Hamilton-Jacobi-Bellman equation of a hybrid form. We pointed out how to solve the (HJB) and obtain a sub-optimal control by discrete time approximation.

Future work includes extension of this approach to other control problems of practical interest, including the finite horizon control problem, the time-optimal control problem and the H_∞ control problem. Also the stability issues associated with the closed-loop systems need to be investigated.

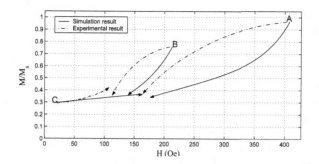

Fig. 4. Optimal trajectories

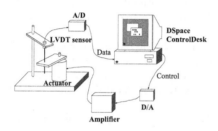

Fig. 5. Experimental setup

7 Acknowledgement

The authors wish to thank the reviewers for their valuable comments. The work in this paper was supported in part by the Army Research Office under the ODDR&E MURI97 Program Grant No. DAAG55-97-1-0114 to the Center for Dynamics and Control of Smart Structures (through Harvard University).

References

[1] Gorbet, R.B., Wang, D.W.L., Morris, K.A.: Preisach model identification of a two-wire SMA actuator. In: Proceedings of IEEE International Conference on Robotics and Automation. (1998) 2161–2167
[2] Hughes, D., Wen, J.T.: Preisach modeling and compensation for smart material hysteresis. In: Active Materials and Smart Structures. Volume 2427 of SPIE. (1994) 50–64
[3] Tan, X., Venkataraman, R., Krishnaprasad, P.S.: Control of hysteresis: theory and experimental results. In: Smart Structures and Materials 2001, Modeling, Signal Processing, and Control in Smart Structures. Volume 4326 of SPIE. (2001) 101–112
[4] Jiles, D.C., Atherton, D.L.: Theory of ferromagnetic hysteresis. Journal of Magnetism and Magnetic Materials **61** (1986) 48–60

[5] Venkataraman, R.: Modeling and Adaptive Control of Magnetostrictive Actuators. PhD thesis, University of Maryland, College Park (1999)

[6] Venkataraman, R., Krishnaprasad, P.S.: Qualitative analysis of a bulk ferromagnetic hysteresis model. In: Proceedings of the 37th IEEE Conference on Decision and Control, Tampa, Florida. (1998) 2443–2448

[7] Smith, R.C., Hom, C.L.: A domain wall theory for ferroelectric hysteresis. Technical Report CRSC-TR99-01, CRSC, North Carolina State University (1999)

[8] Witsenhausen, H.S.: A class of hybrid-state continuous-time dynamic systems. IEEE Transactions on Automatic Control 11 (1966) 161–167

[9] Piccoli, B.: Hybrid systems and optimal control. In: Proceedings of the 37th IEEE Conference on Decision and Control, Tampa, Florida (1998) 13–18

[10] Riedinger, P., Kratz, F., Iung, C., Zanne, C.: Linear quadratic optimization for hybrid systems. In: Proceedings of the 38th IEEE Conference on Decision and Control, Phoenix, Arizona (1999) 3059–3064

[11] Hedlund, S., Rantzer, A.: Optimal control of hybrid systems. In: Proceedings of the 38th IEEE Conference on Decision and Control, Phoenix, Arizona (1999) 3972–3977

[12] Rantzer, A., Johansson, M.: Piecewise linear quadratic optimal control. IEEE Transactions on Automatic Control 45 (2000) 629–637

[13] Yong, J.: Systems governed by ordinary differential equations with continuous, switching and impulse controls. Applied Mathematics and Optimization 20 (1989) 223–235

[14] Branicky, M.S., Borkar, V.S., Mitter, S.K.: A unified framework for hybrid control: model and optimal control theory. IEEE Transactions on Automatic Control 43 (1998) 31–45

[15] Crandall, M.G., Lions, P.L.: Viscosity solutions of Hamilton-Jacobi equations. Transactions of the American Mathematical Society 277 (1983) 1–42

[16] Bardi, M., Capuzzo-Dolcetta, I.: Optimal Control and Viscosity Solutions of Hamilton-Jacobi-Bellman Equations. Birkhäuser, Boston (1997)

[17] Tan, X., Baras, J.S.: Control of smart actuators: A viscosity solutions approach. Technical Report TR 2001-39, Institute for Systems Research, University of Maryland, College Park (2001) Available at http://www.isr.umd.edu/TechReports/ISR/2001/TR_2001-39/TR_2001-39.phtml.

[18] Venkataraman, R., Krishnaprasad, P.S.: A model for a thin magnetostrictive actuator. In: Proceedings of the 32nd Conference on Information Sciences and Systems, Princeton, NJ, Princeton (1998)

[19] Branicky, M.S.: Studies in hybrid systems: modeling, analysis, and control. PhD thesis, MIT, Cambridge (1995)

[20] Visintin, A.: Differential Models of Hysteresis. Springer (1994)

[21] Crandall, M.G., Evans, L.C., Lions, P.L.: Some properties of viscosity solutions of Hamilton-Jacobi equations. Transactions of the American Mathematical Society 282 (1984) 487–502

[22] Ishii, H.: Uniqueness of unbounded viscosity solution of Hamilton-Jacobi equations. Indiana University Mathematics Journal 33 (1984) 721–748

[23] Soner, H.M.: Optimal control with state-space constraint. SIAM Journal on Control and Optimization 24 (1986) 552–561

Series of Abstractions for Hybrid Automata*

Ashish Tiwari[1] and Gaurav Khanna[2]

[1] SRI International,
333 Ravenswood Ave,
Menlo Park, CA, U.S.A
Tel:+1.650.859.4774
Fax:+1.650.859.2844
tiwari@csl.sri.com
[2] Theoretical and Computational Studies Group
Long Island University, Southampton
Southampton NY 11968
gkhanna@liu.edu

Abstract. We present a technique based on the use of the quantifier elimination decision procedure for real closed fields and simple theorem proving to construct a series of successively finer qualitative abstractions of hybrid automata. The resulting abstractions are always discrete transition systems which can then be used by any traditional analysis tool. The constructed abstractions are conservative and can be used to establish safety properties of the original system. Our technique works on linear and non-linear polynomial hybrid systems, that is, the guards on discrete transitions and the continuous flows in all modes can be specified using arbitrary polynomial expressions over the continuous variables. We have a prototype tool in the SAL environment [13] which is built over the theorem prover PVS [19]. The technique promises to scale well to large and complex hybrid systems.

1 Introduction

Hybrid systems describe a wide class of systems that exhibit discrete and continuous behaviors, such as a digital system embedded in an analog environment. Since hybrid systems operate in safety-critical domains, for example, inside automobiles, aircrafts, and chemical plants, analysis techniques are needed to support the design process of embedded software while maintaining safety guarantees.

The development of tools and analysis techniques for hybrid systems is faced with two challenges. It has been shown that checking reachability for very simple class of hybrid systems is undecidable [11]. Several decidable classes have been identified, see [3] for a survey, but all of these classes are too weak to represent

---

* The first author was supported in part by DARPA under the MoBIES program administered by AFRL under contract F33615-00-C-1700 and NASA Langley Research Center contract NAS1-00108 to Rannoch Corporation. The second author acknowledges research support from Long Island University, Southhampton.

C.J. Tomlin and M.R. Greenstreet (Eds.): HSCC 2002, LNCS 2289, pp. 465–478, 2002.
© Springer-Verlag Berlin Heidelberg 2002

hybrid system models that arise in practical applications. In fact, the models of physical environment in real world scenarios are usually too large and complicated even for analysis tools built on semi-decision procedures and available technologies.

Abstraction is a technique to reduce the complexity of a system design, while preserving some of its relevant behavior, so that the simplified system is more accessible to analysis tools and is still sufficient to establish certain safety properties. Two powerful abstraction techniques, called predicate abstraction and data abstraction respectively, have been used quite successfully in analyzing discrete transition systems. In this paper, we present a very simple, yet quite effective, technique based on data abstraction, to construct a series of successively finer abstractions of a given hybrid system.

Hybrid automata [1, 17] are mathematical models for representing hybrid systems. In contrast to discrete transition systems, hybrid automata can make *both* discrete and continuous transitions and hence, its semantics are given in terms of the states, which are uncountably many, reached over a continuous real time interval. However, the theory of hybrid automata can be given in terms of infinite-state transition systems [11, 9] that contain uncountably many states, but are interpreted over discrete time steps. In this paper, we map the uncountable state space into a finite state space by an abstraction function. More specifically, the n-dimensional real space $\mathbb{R}^n$ is partitioned into zones which are sign-invariant for all polynomials in some finite set. Increasing the number of polynomials in this set results in finer abstractions. This basic idea, although in a much simplified form, is also at the core of qualitative reasoning techniques developed in the Artificial Intelligence community [20, 14, 21].

Our work extends conventional qualitative techniques in at least two ways. We keep track of the evolution of arbitrary polynomials (over the state variables), and not just the state variables, while constructing an abstraction. Second, whereas qualitative reasoning usually uses sign of only the first derivative, we deduce based on the signs of first n-th derivatives. The use of these two nontrivial extensions makes the technique substantially more powerful. Similar extensions, but without any theorem proving support, have been used for behavior prediction after a fault diagnosis in a dynamic physical system [16].

One other useful feature of our approach is that it can be used to construct a series of finer abstractions. This gives an iterative methodology to prove a safety property. Starting with a crude abstraction, we check whether the property of interest holds for this abstract system. If not, we create a finer abstraction and check the property again. We can repeat this until the property is either established or no further refinements of the system can be constructed. Since the resulting abstractions are discrete transition systems, techniques such as model checking can be used. Furthermore, unlike a lot of other works on analysis of hybrid systems [15, 5], we do not use any numerical methods and techniques.

The process of construction of the abstract system requires logical reasoning in the theory of reals. The first-order theory of real closed fields is known to be decidable [23] and the first practical algorithm, based on cylindrical algebraic decomposition, was given in [6]. We use the first-order theory of reals to represent sets of continuous states and use reasoning over this theory for creating abstract transition systems.

Preliminaries

The *signature* of the first-order theory of reals consists of function symbols $\{+, -, \cdot\}$, constants $\mathbb{R}$, and predicate symbols $\{=, >, \geq, <, \leq\}$. In this theory, the set of terms over a set X of variables corresponds to the set of polynomials $\mathbb{R}[X]$. The set $ATM(X)$, defined as $\{p \sim 0 : p \in \mathbb{R}[X] \, and \sim \in \{=, <, \leq, >, \geq\}\}$, is the set of all *atomic* formulas. The set $WFF(X)$ of first-order formulas (over X) is defined as the smallest set containing $ATM(X)$ and closed under the boolean operations (conjunction $\wedge$, disjunction $\vee$, implication $\Rightarrow$, and negation $\neg$) and quantification (existential $\exists$ and universal $\forall$). The *first-order theory* of *reals*, also denoted by $\mathbb{R}$, is defined as the set of all first-order formulas over the above signature (and a countable set of variables) that are true over the real numbers. We use the notation $\mathbb{R} \models \phi$ to denote the fact that the (first-order) formula ϕ is true in the theory of reals. The first-order theory of the real closed fields is a complete theory, that is every sentence in $WFF(X)$ is either true or its negation is true in this theory, and is known to be decidable [23, 6].

We denote formulas in $WFF(X)$ by ϕ, ψ, possibly with subscripts and use p to denote polynomials in the set $\mathbb{R}[X]$. We say a polynomial p occurs in a formula ϕ if there is an atomic formula $p \sim 0$ in ϕ. The rest of the notation follows the standard practice in hybrid systems literature.

2 Continuous Dynamical Systems

For simplicity, in this section we consider hybrid systems with no discrete components, that is, hybrid systems with exactly one mode of operation. A continuous dynamical system CS is a tuple $(X, Init, Inv, f)$ where X is a finite set of variables interpreted over the reals $\mathbb{R}$, $\mathbf{X} = \mathbb{R}^X$ is the set of all valuations of the variables X, $Init \subseteq \mathbf{X}$ is the set of initial states, $Inv \subseteq \mathbf{X}$ is the invariant set of states, and $f : \mathbf{X} \mapsto T\mathbf{X}$ is a vector field that specifies the continuous dynamics. Here $T\mathbf{X}$ denotes the tangent space of $\mathbf{X}$. We assume that f satisfies the standard assumptions for existence and uniqueness of solutions to ordinary differential equations. Note that the continuous dynamical systems we consider here are autonomous, that is, they have no inputs.

The semantics, $[\![CS]\!]$, of a continuous dynamical system $CS = (X, Init, Inv, f)$ over an interval $I = [\tau_a, \tau_z] \subseteq \mathbb{R}$ is a collection of mappings $\sigma : I \mapsto \mathbf{X}$ satisfying

(a) initial condition: $\sigma(\tau_a) \in Init$,
(b) continuous evolution: for all $\tau \in (\tau_a, \tau_z)$, $\dot{\sigma}(\tau) = f(\sigma(\tau))$, and
(c) invariant: for all $\tau \in [\tau_a, \tau_z]$, $\sigma(\tau) \in Inv$.

In case the interval I is left unspecified, it is assumed to be the interval $[0, \infty)$.

We assume that the flow derivative, f, is specified using polynomial expressions over the state variables X, that is $f \in (\mathbb{R}[X])^{|X|}$, where $\mathbb{R}[X]$ denotes the set of polynomials over the indeterminates X and coefficients in $\mathbb{R}$, and $|X|$ denotes the cardinality of X. These polynomials can be nonlinear in general.

Example 1. The actuator module in a simple electronic throttle control system is driven by a pulse-width modulated signal and can be described as a hybrid system with two modes: when the input signal is high, the system is in the "on" mode and is described by

$$\dot{V} = \tfrac{2000}{9}(24 - 2V - I) \qquad \dot{I} = \tfrac{1000}{15}(120 - 22I)$$

and when the input is low, the system is in "off" mode and is described by

$$\dot{V} = \tfrac{-2000}{3}I \qquad \dot{I} = \tfrac{2000}{15}(5V - 16I).$$

In each mode, therefore, the actuator behaves as a continuous dynamical system with two continuous variables V and I.

3   Discrete Transition Systems

A discrete state transition system DS is a tuple $(Q, Init, t)$ where Q is a finite set of variables interpreted over countable domains, $\mathbf{Q}$ denotes the (countable) set of all valuations of the variables Q over the respective domains, $Init \subseteq \mathbf{Q}$ is a set of initial states, and $t \subseteq \mathbf{Q} \times \mathbf{Q}$ is a set of transitions. The semantics, $[\![DS]\!]$, of a discrete state transition system $DS = (Q, Init, t)$ is the collection of all mappings $\theta : \mathbb{N} \mapsto \mathbf{Q}$ satisfying

(a) initial condition: $\theta(0) \in Init$, and
(b) discrete evolution: for all $i \in \mathbb{N}$, $(\theta(i), \theta(i+1)) \in t$.

In order to define a notion of *abstraction* precisely, we need to establish a correspondence between discrete evolutions $\theta : \mathbb{N} \mapsto \mathbf{Q}$ and continuous evolutions $\sigma : [0, \infty) \mapsto \mathbf{Q}$. This is done using discrete sampling.

Definition 1. *A discrete evolution $\theta : \mathbb{N} \mapsto \mathbf{Q}$ is a sufficiently complete discretization of a continuous evolution $\sigma : [0, \infty) \mapsto \mathbf{Q}$ if there exists a strictly increasing sequence $\langle \tau_0, \tau_1, \tau_2, \ldots \rangle$ of reals in the interval $[0, \infty)$ such that*
(i) $\tau_0 = 0$,
(ii) the function σ does not change on the domain (τ_i, τ_{i+1}), that is, $\sigma(\tau) = \sigma(\tau')$ for all $\tau, \tau' \in (\tau, \tau_{i+1})$, and
(iii) for all i, $\theta(2i) = \sigma(\tau_i)$ and $\theta(2i+1) = \sigma(\tau)$, where $\tau_i < \tau < \tau_{i+1}$.

Intuitively, a sufficiently complete discretization captures all the "different" (abstract) states in the given continuous evolution.

Definition 2. *Let $CS = (X, InitX, Inv, f)$ be a continuous dynamical system and $DS = (Q, InitQ, t)$ be a discrete transition system. We say DS is an abstraction for CS if there exists a mapping $abs : \mathbf{X} \mapsto \mathbf{Q}$ such that*

(a) abs(InitX) ⊆ InitQ,[1] *and*

(b) for every σ ∈ [[CS]], if σ′ is a sufficiently complete discretization of abs(σ), then σ′ ∈ [[DS]].

This definition of abstraction corresponds to the usual sense of abstraction, but applied to the infinite state transition system associated with a continuous (hybrid) system. We consider the problem of constructing discrete transition system abstractions for continuous dynamical systems in the sense of Definition 2. The definition and the procedure for constructing an abstraction naturally extends to hybrid systems, see Section 5.

4   Abstracting Continuous Dynamical Systems

Data abstraction refers to the idea of using a partition of the domain of interpretation as the new domain of interpretation for the state variables or expressions over the state variables. The focus in this paper is on performing data abstraction on continuous and hybrid systems. We use abstract variables that represent *polynomials* over the original continuous variables X and interpret them over a three valued abstract domain $\{neg, pos, zero\}$.

Given a continuous dynamical system $CS = (X, InitX, Inv, f)$, we construct the abstract discrete state transition system $DS = (Q, InitQ, t)$ in two steps. The first phase creates a finite set $P \subseteq \mathbb{R}[X]$ of polynomials over the continuous variables X which are used as the discrete variables Q. In the second phase, the initial states $InitQ$ and the transition relation t are computed.

Phase I: Obtaining a Set of Polynomials

Fixing the set P of polynomials for abstraction involves starting with a small set P_0 of polynomials of interest and adding to this set the time derivatives of polynomials in P_0. The initial set P_0 could contain, for example, the polynomials that appear in the statement of the property of interest that we want to establish for the given continuous system, or the polynomials that occur in the guards of mode change transitions for exiting this mode, etc. The phase I saturation process involves application of the following inference rule: *if $p \in P$, then add $\dot{p}$, the derivative (with respect to time) of p, to the set P unless $\dot{p}$ is a constant or a constant factor multiple of some existing polynomial in P.*

Since we assume that $f \in (\mathbb{R}[X])^{|X|}$, it follows that $\dot{p} \in \mathbb{R}[X]$ is a polynomial. However, note that for general flow derivatives f, specified using arbitrary polynomial expressions, the saturation process might not terminate. But there are special cases where this process is guaranteed to terminate.

---

[1] We shall use *abs* to also denote liftings of the function *abs* to sets and functions. Thus, $abs(InitX) = \{abs(\mathbf{x}) : \mathbf{x} \in InitX\}$. Similarly, if $\sigma : [0, \infty) \mapsto \mathbf{X}$, then $(abs(\sigma))(\tau) = abs(\sigma(\tau))$.

Nilpotent Systems. Consider the class of linear time invariant systems specified using a nilpotent matrix A. If we also use X to denote the column vector of state variables X, then the flow rate $f = AX$ and hence, $\dot{X} = AX$. A polynomial $p = \sum_i a_i x_i$ can be written, in matrix notation, as $\boldsymbol{a}^T X$, where $\boldsymbol{a}^T$ denotes the transpose of $\boldsymbol{a}$. Thus, $\dot{p} = \boldsymbol{a}^T \dot{X} = \boldsymbol{a}^T AX$ and $\ddot{p} = \boldsymbol{a}^T A^2 X$. Hence, if $A^n = 0$, then the n-th derivative of the polynomial p is $\boldsymbol{a}^T A^n \boldsymbol{x} = 0$. Thus, the saturation process is guaranteed to terminate for such systems.

Systems Such That $A^n = rA^m$. If the matrix A used to specify the flow of the continuous dynamical system CS is such that $A^n = rA^m$ for some constant $r \in \mathbb{R}$ and $n, m \in \mathbb{N}$, then again the saturation process can be shown to terminate. In particular, if $p = \boldsymbol{a}^T X$ is an arbitrary polynomial, then $\frac{d^n p}{d\tau^n} = \boldsymbol{a}^T A^n X = \boldsymbol{a}^T rA^m X = r\frac{d^m p}{d\tau^m}$. Since the n-th derivative of p is a constant multiple of the m-th derivative of p, it does not get added to the set P of polynomials in the saturation process.

We remark here that the termination of the saturation process is determined by *both* the initial set P_0 of polynomials *and* the flow derivative f.

General Case. Our abstraction technique works for general (possibly non-linear) time invariant systems whose flow is specified using polynomials. The termination of the saturation phase is not necessary for creating an abstraction. We can stop at any point and pass on the current set P to the second phase. A larger set P yields a finer abstraction as it results in a larger state space in the final abstract system.

Example 2. Consider the "off" mode of the actuator in Example 1. If we start with the set $P_0 = \{V, I\}$ of polynomials, the phase I saturation procedure first adds the polynomial $\dot{I} = 2000/15(5V - 16I)$ and then the derivative of this polynomial $\ddot{I} = 2000^2/15(-16V/3 + 77I/5)$. Since the derivative $\dot{V}$ is a constant multiple of the polynomial $I \in P$, it is not added. Note that we need not add the exact derivatives, but only a polynomial upto some constant factor. Although we can continue the process of adding derivatives, we stop the phase I here with the final set $P = \{V, I, 5V - 16I, -80V + 231I\}$.

Phase II: Constructing the Abstract Transitions

Let $CS = (X, InitX, Inv, f)$ be a continuous system and $P \subseteq \mathbb{R}[X]$ be a finite set of polynomials over the set X of variables produced by the first phase. The state variables Q in the corresponding abstract discrete system $DS = (Q, InitQ, t)$ contains exactly one new variable for each polynomial $p \in P$. Thus, $Q = \{q_p : p \in P\}$. These new variables are interpreted over the domain $\{pos, neg, zero\}$ and consequently the set $\mathbf{Q}$ of all discrete states is the set $\{pos, neg, zero\}^Q$ of all valuations of the variables Q over this domain. We shall represent any such valuation by the corresponding conjunction of atomic formulas. For example, the valuation $\langle q_{p_1} \mapsto pos, q_{p_2} \mapsto neg, q_{p_3} \mapsto zero \rangle$ will be thought of as the formula

$p_1 > 0 \ \wedge \ p_2 < 0 \ \wedge \ p_3 = 0$. We shall use such conjunctions and valuations interchangeably. The set of all conjunctions representing such valuations will also be denoted by $\mathbf{Q}$. Note that these conjunctions are in the set $WFF(X)$ of formulas over free variables X.

If $\psi \in \mathbf{Q}$ is a state in the abstract system DS, say represented as $\wedge_{i \in J_1} p_i > 0 \ \wedge \ \wedge_{i \in J_2} p_i < 0 \ \wedge \ \wedge_{i \in J_3} p_i = 0$, then the concretization function, γ, maps abstract states to sets of concrete states and is defined by[2],

$$\gamma(\psi) = \{x \in \mathbf{X} : \mathbb{R} \models p_i(x) > 0 \ \forall i \in J_1 \text{ and } \mathbb{R} \models p_i(x) < 0 \ \forall i \in J_2 \text{ and}$$
$$\mathbb{R} \models p_i(x) = 0 \forall i \in J_3\}$$

Conversely, if $x \in \mathbf{X}$ is a concrete state of the system CS, then the abstraction function, abs, maps a concrete state to an abstract state and is defined by,

$$abs(x) = \bigwedge_{i \in J_1} p_i > 0 \ \wedge \ \bigwedge_{i \in J_2} p_i = 0 \ \wedge \ \bigwedge_{i \in J_3} p_i < 0,$$

where $J_1 \cup J_2 \cup J_3$ is a partition of the set $\{1, 2, \ldots, |P|\}$ such that $i \in J_1$ iff $\mathbb{R} \models p_i(x) > 0$, $i \in J_2$ iff $\mathbb{R} \models p_i(x) = 0$, and $i \in J_3$ iff $\mathbb{R} \models p_i(x) < 0$.

The Initial States. Assume that the initial set of states $InitX$ for the continuous system is specified using a first-order formula ϕ_X over X. The initial set of states $InitQ$ consists of all valuations ψ of the abstract variables such that the formulas ψ and ϕ_X are simultaneously satisfiable. Specifically,

$$InitQ = \bigvee \{\psi \in \mathbf{Q} : \mathbb{R} \models \exists X : \psi \wedge \phi_X\}.$$

Lemma 1. *Let $CS = (X, InitX, Inv, f)$ be a continuous system with the initial states $InitX$ specified by the first-order formula ϕ_X. If DS, $InitQ$, and abs are as defined as above, then, $abs(InitX) \subseteq InitQ$.[3]*

The Transition Relation. We add an abstract transition $(\psi_1, \psi_2) \in t$ if all of the following conditions hold (for all polynomials $p \in P$):
(a) if $p < 0$ is a conjunct in ψ_1, then (a1) if $\mathbb{R} \models \psi_1 \Rightarrow \dot{p} < 0$, then $p < 0$ is a conjunct in ψ_2; (a2) if $\mathbb{R} \models \psi_1 \Rightarrow \dot{p} = 0$, then $p < 0$ is a conjunct in ψ_2; (a3) if $\mathbb{R} \models \psi_1 \Rightarrow \dot{p} > 0$, then either $p < 0$ or $p = 0$ is a conjunct in ψ_2; and (a4) if the valuation of $\dot{p}$ cannot be deduced from ψ_1, then either $p > 0$ or $p = 0$ is a conjunct in ψ_2;
(b) if $p = 0$ is a conjunct in ψ_1, then (b1) if $\mathbb{R} \models \psi_1 \Rightarrow \dot{p} < 0$, then $p < 0$ is a conjunct in ψ_2; (b2) if $\mathbb{R} \models \psi_1 \Rightarrow \dot{p} = 0$, then $p = 0$ is a conjunct in ψ_2; (b3) if

---

[2] Here, the notation $\mathbb{R} \models p(x) > 0$ means that the polynomial p evaluates to a positive number on the point $x \in \mathbb{R}^{|X|}$.

[3] We use a formula and the set of valuations it represents interchangeably as the context disambiguates the intended meaning.

$\mathbb{R} \models \psi_1 \Rightarrow \dot{p} > 0$, then $p > 0$ is a conjunct in ψ_2; and (b4) if the valuation of $\dot{p}$ cannot be deduced from ψ_1, then either $p > 0$, $p = 0$, or $p < 0$ is a conjunct in ψ_2;
(c) if $p > 0$ is a conjunct in ψ_1, then (c1) if $\mathbb{R} \models \psi_1 \Rightarrow \dot{p} < 0$, then either $p > 0$ or $p = 0$ is a conjunct in ψ_2; (c2) if $\mathbb{R} \models \psi_1 \Rightarrow \dot{p} = 0$, then $p > 0$ is a conjunct in ψ_2; (c3) if $\mathbb{R} \models \psi_1 \Rightarrow \dot{p} > 0$, then $p > 0$ is a conjunct in ψ_2; and (c4) if the valuation of $\dot{p}$ cannot be deduced from ψ_1, then either $p < 0$ or $p = 0$ is a conjunct in ψ_2.

This completes the phase of adding transitions to the abstract system. Note that the sign of $\dot{p}$ can be directly read off from ψ_1 if $\dot{p}$ was added to P in phase I. If not, then we add non-deterministic transitions from ψ_1 assuming all possibilities for the sign of $\dot{p}$. In the final step, we refine this abstract system to eliminate unreachable states and transitions.

Refining the Abstraction. We note that certain abstract states (and transition to/from those states) can be deleted because either they are infeasible or are explicitly disallowed by the given invariant set Inv of the concrete system. In particular, if the invariant set Inv is specified using a first-order formula ϕ_{Inv}, then we can delete all abstract states ψ such that $\mathbb{R} \not\models \exists X : \psi(X) \wedge \phi_{Inv}(X)$. We can also remove all transitions to/from these eliminated abstract states. Note that this process implicitly removes infeasible abstract states, that is, states $\psi(X)$ such that $\mathbb{R} \not\models \exists X : \psi(X)$.

This completes the construction of the abstract system $DS = (Q, InitQ, t)$ for the continuous dynamical system $CS = (X, InitX, Inv, f)$.

Theorem 1. *Let $CS = (X, InitX, Inv, f)$ be a continuous system and $DS = (Q, InitQ, t)$, be the discrete abstraction as defined above. Then, DS is an abstraction (Definition 2) for CS.*

Note that even though the abstract transition system is a finite-state system, we need not explicitly represent the states and transitions. We can obtain the abstract system implicitly with the states and transitions specified using predicate formulas.

Example 3. Following up on Example 2, we can construct the abstract transition system on the set $P = \{V, I, 5V - 16I, -80V + 231I\}$ of polynomials. Assume that the initial abstract state[4] is $I > 0 \wedge V > 0 \wedge 5V - 16I < 0 \wedge -80V + 231I > 0$. Out of the $3^4 = 81$ abstract states, only 17 are feasible and the infeasible states can be identified using a theorem prover. For example, the state $I = 0 \wedge V > 0 \wedge 5V - 16I < 0 \wedge -80V + 231I > 0$ is infeasible and a decision procedure for reals can be used to deduce that this formula is unsatisfiable.

The outgoing transitions from the initial state $I > 0 \wedge V > 0 \wedge 5V - 16I < 0 \wedge -80V + 231I > 0$ are obtained as follows: (a) since $I > 0$ and $\dot{I} < 0$ (as $5V - 16I < 0$), in the successor state either $I > 0$ or $I = 0$, (b) since $V > 0$

---

[4] The initial abstract state is obtained from the stable states in the abstract transition system for the "on" mode of the actuator.

and $\dot{V} < 0$ (as $-I < 0$), in the successor state either $V > 0$ or $V = 0$, (c) since $5V - 16I < 0$ and $5\dot{V} - 16\dot{I} > 0$ (as $-80V + 231I > 0$), in the successor state either $5V - 16I < 0$ or $5V - 16I = 0$, and (d) since $-80V + 231I > 0$ and $-80\dot{V} + 231\dot{I}$ is unknown, in the successor state either $-80V + 231I > 0$ or $-80V + 231I = 0$. Out of the 16 potential successors, only 4 are feasible:

$$q_1 : I > 0 \ \wedge \ V > 0 \ \wedge \ 5V - 16I < 0 \ \wedge \ -80V + 231I > 0$$
$$q_2 : I > 0 \ \wedge \ V = 0 \ \wedge \ 5V - 16I < 0 \ \wedge \ -80V + 231I > 0$$
$$q_3 : I > 0 \ \wedge \ V > 0 \ \wedge \ 5V - 16I < 0 \ \wedge \ -80V + 231I = 0$$
$$q_4 : I = 0 \ \wedge \ V = 0 \ \wedge \ 5V - 16I = 0 \ \wedge \ -80V + 231I = 0.$$

Continuing this way, we can construct the complete abstract system containing 10 reachable abstract states. We also note that among these states, only the state q_4 is stable.

5   Hybrid Automata

The technique for constructing finite state abstractions of continuous systems extends naturally to hybrid systems. We skip the definitions and details here and refer to the full version of the paper. To summarize these results, the abstract system corresponding to the hybrid system $HS = (Q, X, Init, Inv, t, f)$ and a finite set P of polynomials (over X) is a discrete state transition system $DS = (Q^A, Init^A, t^A)$, where $Q^A = Q \cup (Q_P = \{q_p : p \in P\})$ is the set of discrete variables, $Init^A \subseteq \mathbf{Q^A}$ is the initial states, and $t^A \subseteq \mathbf{Q^A} \times \mathbf{Q^A}$ is the set of transitions. The new discrete variables Q_P are interpreted over the domain $\{pos, neg, zero\}$ as before. Thus, the set of states in the abstract system $\mathbf{Q^A}$ is $\mathbf{Q} \times \{pos, neg, zero\}^{Q_P}$.

Let $q^a = (q, \phi) \in \mathbf{Q^A}$ be a state in the abstract system, where $q \in \mathbf{Q}$ is a discrete state of the hybrid automaton HS and ϕ is a valuation of the variables in Q_P over $\{pos, neg, zero\}$. We think of ϕ as a formula in $WFF(X)$ as before. The transitions in the abstract system DS from the state q^a are obtained as a union of two kinds of transitions:

1. *Abstractions of the discrete transitions:* If $(q, Cond, q') \in t$ is a discrete transition of the hybrid automata HS, where $q, q' \in \mathbf{Q}$ are discrete states and $Cond \subset \mathbf{X}$ is a set of continuous states (or the guard) represented by, say, the predicate formula ψ over the variables X, then there is an abstract transition $((q, \phi), (q', \phi)) \in t^a$ if $\mathbb{R} \models \exists X : (\phi(X) \wedge \psi(X))$.
2. *Abstractions of the continuous transitions:* The rule for constructing new abstract transitions from the continuous flows is the same as before. We note that the first component of the state is left unchanged, that is, we add a new abstract transition $((q, \phi), (q, \psi))$ in t^a if ψ can be obtained from ϕ using the rules given before in Section 4 (applied to the flow corresponding to the discrete state q).

Note that we can handle cases where the set $\mathbf{Q}$ of discrete states in HS is infinite as long as the number of distinct "modes" (each of which can be specified as a formula over Q) are finite.

Theorem 2. *Let $HS = (Q, X, Init, Inv, t, f)$ be a hybrid automata and $P \subseteq \mathbb{R}[X]$ be a finite set of polynomials over the set X of real variables. If $DS = (Q^A = Q \cup Q_P, Init^A, t^A)$ is the discrete transition system constructed by the above method, then DS is an abstraction for HS.*

We illustrate the abstraction technique on a simple hybrid system example.

Example 4. Consider a thermostat that controls the heating of a room. Assume that the thermostat turns the heater on when the temperature x is between 68 and 70 and it turns the heater off when the temperature is between 80 and 82. Suppose the continuous dynamics in the on and off modes is specified respectively by the equations

$$\dot{x} = -x + 100 \quad and \quad \dot{x} = -x.$$

If we assume that the heater is initially off and the room temperature is between 70 and 80, the hybrid automaton is given by $HS = (Q, X, Init, Inv, t, f)$, where $Q = \{q_1\}$ is the set of discrete variables, $\mathbf{Q} = \{on, off\}$ is the set of discrete states (thus, $q_1 \in \{on, off\}$), $X = \{x_1\}$ is the set of continuous variables, $\mathbf{X} = \mathbb{R}$ is the set of continuous states, $Init = \{(off, x) : 70 < x < 80\}$ is the initial condition, $Inv = \{(on, x) : x < 82\} \cup \{(off, x) : x > 68\}$ is the invariant set, $t = \{(on, x, off) : x \geq 80\} \cup \{(off, x, on) : x \leq 70\}$ is the set of discrete transitions, and $f(on) = -x + 100$ and $f(off) = -x$ specifies the continuous flow rates.

Now, the set of polynomials that appear in the guards are $\{x - 70, x - 80\}$, and polynomials in the invariant specification are $\{x - 68, x - 82\}$. The derivative of each of these four polynomials is $\dot{x}$. In the mode when the heater is on, this evaluates to $-x + 100$ and in the mode when the heater is off, this is $-x$. Hence, we have two more polynomials, $\{x, x - 100\}$, in the set P. Note that further saturation of the set P of these six polynomials under time derivative yields no new polynomials.

Using the saturated set P of six polynomials, we can construct an abstraction for the thermostat hybrid model and we show the final result Figure 1. In the figure, transitions arising from the continuous and discrete evolutions of H are drawn in different colors. Furthermore, the representation of abstract states has been simplified. For example, the expression $70 < x < 80$ denotes the conjunction $70 < x \wedge x < 80 \wedge 68 < x \wedge x < 82 \wedge -x + 100 > 0 \wedge x > 0$. This conjunction is logically equivalent to $70 < x \wedge x < 80$.

6   Implementation and Related Work

The SAL tool set provides interfaces that can be used to construct discrete abstractions of hybrid systems as described in this paper [13]. The quantifier

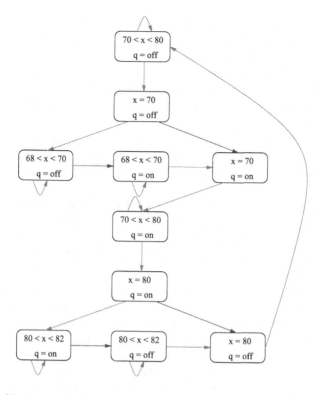

Fig. 1. Abstract transition system for the thermostat hybrid automata

elimination decision procedure for the real closed fields is implicitly used to decide the implications over the real numbers. The tool QEPCAD [12], which is built over the symbolic algebra library SACLIB [4], is integrated to the theorem prover PVS [19] for this purpose. We are working on adding more explicit interfaces into SAL to directly construct such abstractions for hybrid systems.

The discrete abstractions we construct do not store information about the duration of a continuous run. However, our technique extends, quite easily, to time variant systems by simply explicitly considering time as another continuous variable. Note that we can get some timing information in the abstractions if we include polynomials containing this variable for time in the set P.

Qualitative reasoning has been used by researchers in the AI community for modeling and analyzing physical systems in the face of incomplete knowledge of the system dynamics [20]. The idea is to interpret a continuous variable, say x, over an abstract domain of the form $\{(-\infty, c_0), c_0, (c_0, c_1), c_1, (c_1, c_2), c_2, \ldots, c_n, (c_n, \infty)\}$, where $c_0, c_1, \ldots, c_n \in \mathbb{R}$ are constants. Model construction involves keeping track of the sign of the derivative of x. In [20], the authors give a method for proving temporal properties about systems specified (incompletely) using *qualitative* differential equations. In [14] and [21], the authors assume a (more) completely specified input model (using differential equations, for example) and construct an abstraction either incrementally [14] or directly [21]. The latter approach has been implemented in CHARON [2]. Our paper substantially extends the idea of qualitative reasoning by allowing for arbitrary *polynomials*, and not just state *variables*, for defining the qualitative state space. Additionally, we also use the signs of higher order derivatives in the procedure. As a result, the abstractions we obtain have more information and are more useful from an analysis point of view.

There has been a lot of work on constructing abstractions for hybrid systems. These works can be categorized based on the semantics of the hybrid system considered, the class of formulas preserved, the class of hybrid systems considered, the class of abstract systems generated, and whether the abstractions are conservative or accurate. Accurate abstractions, or bisimulations, lead to decidability results [3]. In [18], the interest is in abstracting certain restricted classes of linear hybrid systems into another simpler class of hybrid systems called *timed* automata. The paper [10] abstracts a nonlinear hybrid by a linear hybrid automata.

One can naturally associate an infinite state transition system, with uncountably many states, with a continuous dynamical system or a hybrid system. However, different abstractions preserve different behaviors of this infinite transition system. In [11], certain discrete transitions of the hybrid system are marked *observables*, and the abstraction preserves the observable behavior. In other cases [8], the discrete states in a run of the system are observed and the abstraction preserves this sequence of discrete states. In [5], the constructed abstraction captures all the discrete transition made by the system. In our work, the overall behavior of the hybrid system is abstracted with respect to a finite set of polynomials and the original discrete states. In particular, the behavior inside a continuous evolution is captured too. However, our method for computing the abstract transitions is more approximate (and consequently much simpler computationally) than some of these other methods as we only use information contained in the signs of the n-th derivatives (for fixed n) of some expressions. It should, however, be noted that as in [5], our abstractions do not retain any timing information apart from the temporal ordering of abstract states. However, timing information can be introduced either by treating t as another state variable with $\dot{t} = 1$, or by incorporating quantitative timing information in the process of constructing an abstraction as in [22].

In the future we plan to further mechanize our technique and investigate its use for doing test vector generation for hybrid systems that would cover all regions of the state space, where a region is defined as the subspace which is sign-invariant for a set of polynomials. We also plan to explore further the integration with methods that employ additional quantitative information to create an abstraction.

Acknowledgements. We would like to thank Dr. J. Rushby, Dr. N. Shankar, and the anonymous reviewers for their helpful comments.

References

[1] R. Alur, C. Courcoubetis, T. A. Henzinger, and P.-H. Ho. Hybrid automata: an algorithmic approach to the specification and verification of hybrid systems. In *Hybrid Systems* [7], pages 209–229.

[2] R. Alur, R. Grosu, Y. Hur, V. Kumar, and I. Lee. Modular specifications of hybrid systems in CHARON. In *Proc of 3rd Intl Workshop on Hybrid Systems: Computation and Control*, volume 1790 of *LNCS*, pages 6–19, 2000.

[3] R. Alur, T. A Henzinger, G. Lafferriere, and G. J. Pappas. Discrete abstractions of hybrid systems. *Proceedings of the IEEE*, 88(2):971–984, July 2000.

[4] B. Buchberger, G. E. Collins, M. J. Encarnacion, H. Hong, J. R. Johnson, W. Krandick, R. Loos, A. M. Mandache, A. Neubacher, and H. Vielhaber. SACLIB 1.1 user's guide. In *RISC-Linz Report Series, Tech Report No 93-19*. Kurt Gödel Institute, 1993. www.eecis.udel.edu/~saclib/.

[5] A. Chutinam and B. H. Krogh. Verification of polyhedral-invariant hybrid automata using polygonal flow pipe approximations. In *Hybrid Systems: Computation and Control*, volume 1569 of *LNCS*, pages 76–90. Springer-Verlag, 1999.

[6] G. E. Collins. Quantifier elimination for the elementary theory of real closed fields by cylindrical algebraic decomposition. In *Proc. Second GI Conf. Automata Theory and Formal Languages*, volume 33 of *LNCS*, pages 134–183, 1975.

[7] R. L. Grossman, A. Nerode, A. P. Ravn, and H. Rischel (eds.). *Hybrid Systems*, volume 736 of *LNCS*. Springer-Verlag, Berlin, 1993.

[8] M. R. Henzinger, T. A. Henzinger, and P. W. Kopke. Computing simulations on finite and infinite graphs. In *Proceedings of the 36th Annual IEEE Symposium on Foundations of Computer Science FOCS*, pages 453–462, 1995.

[9] T. A. Henzinger. Hybrid automata with finite bisimulations. In *Proc. 22nd ICALP*, volume 944 of *LNCS*, pages 324–335. Springer-Verlag, 1995.

[10] T. A. Henzinger, P-H. Ho, and H. Wong-Toi. Algorithmic analysis of nonlinear hybrid systems. *IEEE Transactions on Automatic Control*, 43:540–554, 1998.

[11] T. A. Henzinger, P. W. Kopke, A. Puri, and P. Varaiya. What's decidable about hybrid automata? *Journal of Computer and System Sciences*, 57:94–124, 1998.

[12] H. Hong. Quantifier elimination in elementary algebra and geometry by partial cylindrical algebraic decomposition version 13. In *The world wide web*, 1995. www.eecis.udel.edu/~saclib/.

[13] Computer Science Laboratory. SAL: Symbolic analysis laboratory. http://www.csl.sri.com/projects/sal/.

[14] T. Loeser, Y. Iwasaki, and R. Fikes. Safety verification proofs for physical systems. In *Proc. of the 12th Intl. Workshop on Qualitative Reasoning*, pages 88–95. AAAI Press, 1998.

[15] I. Mitchell, A. Bayen, and C. Tomlin. Validating a hamilton-jacobi approximation to hybrid system reachable sets. In M. D. Benedetto and A. L. Sangiovanni-Vincentelli, editors, *HSCC 4th Intl. Workshop*, volume 2034 of *LNCS*, 2001.

[16] P. J. Mosterman and G. Biswas. Monitoring, prediction, and fault isolation in dynamic physical systems. *AAAI-97*, pages 100–105, 1997.

[17] X. Nicollin, A. Olivero, J. Sifakis, and S. Yovine. An approach to the description and analysis of hybrid systems. In *Hybrid Systems* [7], pages 149–178.

[18] A. Olivero, J. Sifakis, and S. Yovine. Using abstractions for the verification of linear hybrid systems. In *Proc. of the 6th Computer-Aided Verification CAV*, volume 818 of *LNCS*, pages 81–94, 1994.

[19] N. Shankar, S. Owre, and J. M. Rushby. *The PVS Proof Checker: A Reference Manual*. Computer Science Lab, SRI International, 1993.

[20] B. Shults and B. J. Kuipers. Proving properties of continuous systems: qualitative simulation and temporal logic. *AI Journal*, 92:91–129, 1997.

[21] O. Sokolsky and H. S. Hong. Qualitative modeling of hybrid systems. In *Proc. of the Montreal Workshop*, 2001. Available from
http://www.cis.upenn.edu/~rtg/rtg_papers.htm.

[22] O. Stursberg, S. Kowalewski, I. Hoffmann, and Preußig. Comparing timed and hybrid automata as approximations of continuous systems. In P. Antsaklis, W. Kohn, A. Nerode, and S. Sastry, editors, *Hybrid Systems IV*, volume 1273 of *LNCS*, pages 361–377. Springer-Verlag, 1997.

[23] A. Tarski. *A Decision Method for Elementary Algebra and Geometry*. University of California Press, 1948. Second edition.

Author Index

Lecture Notes in Computer Science

For information about Vols. 1–2201
please contact your bookseller or Springer-Verlag